Cleared for Takeoff: Memoirs of an Air Traffic Controller
Copyright © 2020 by John R. Potter

All rights reserved. No part of this publication may be reproduced, stored in a retrieval system, or transmitted in any form or by any means electronic, mechanical, photocopying, recording, or otherwise without the prior written permission of the publisher and copyright owner.

Published by John R. Potter

ISBN 978-1-7356942-0-7

CLEARED FOR TAKEOFF
MEMOIRS OF AN AIR TRAFFIC CONTROLLER

JOHN R. "RUSTY" POTTER

To the memory of Bobby Price, my colleague and friend of many years, who could have told this story far better than I.

Acknowledgements

Although I have received encouragement from many people, there are four without whose interest and support I might not ever have undertaken this project, much less completed it:

My wife Gail, who spent endless hours listening, cajoling, and helping me refine the final draft.

Larry Wilson, a fellow controller and friend, who offered enthusiasm and prodding all along the way ("Hey, you left me with a Cherokee in the ditch. You have to keep writing and get him out!")

My copy editor, Richard Westlund, who spent long hours saving me from my own verbiage and showing me the way to final publication.

Janice, the talented graphic artist who designed the book and its explanatory diagrams.

About the Author

John R. "Rusty" Potter was born in New Hampshire, and enjoyed boating at an early age. He joined the Navy and became a naval aviation officer—a prelude to a long career as an air traffic controller, instructor and trainer. During the course of 35+ years with the Federal Aviation Administration (FAA), he guided more than 500,000 aircraft from propeller-driven trainers to jumbo jets that flew to destinations around the world. He also trained hundreds of controllers, as well as college and even high school students in the intricacies of managing traffic in one of the nation's most congested aviation settings. Recognized throughout his career for his conscientious approach to the demanding responsibilities of air traffic control, Potter also made significant contributions to air safety on a national level.

Table of Contents

1. Beginnings 3
2. Anchors Aweigh 5
3. Becoming a Controller 50
4. On the Job Training 68
5. Serious Stuff on Ground Control 90
6. Training on Local Control 110
7. Mastering Radar Control 154
8. Taking Control 203
9. Interactions 255
10. Becoming an Instructor...272
11. PATCO Takes Action 310
12. A Change in My Status 343
13. Entering a New World 362
14. Out of Tamiami 418
15. Returning to Miami 445
16. Winding Up My Air Traffic Career 482
17. Teaching the Next Generation..496
A Few Postscripts 526
Glossary 529

Introduction

Everyone has a story to tell. In "Memoirs of an Air Traffic Controller," I describe my career in a profession that is something of a black box to most readers. Pilots and controllers will find much of the material interesting and engaging, while the uninitiated can gain a better understanding of the world of flying and air traffic control (ATC). Air traffic control is largely an exercise in hard work and common sense, and my hope is that readers will see parallels to their own experiences and learn something about mine.

Despite my attempts to keep the narrative basic enough for the average reader, there are places where some will struggle. Nevertheless, there is something here for everyone—accidents and incidents, sharp exchanges between pilots and air traffic controllers, some hair raising "saves" by both, some flashes of real humor, and a few (mostly gentle) digs at the FAA bureaucracy. Anyone who has worked hard to master a technical skill and rise in an organization will easily relate to the passages describing initial training and the subsequent opportunities described here.

Has air traffic control changed a great deal in the 50-plus years since I began my career? Yes and no. Automation capabilities have increased steadily, providing controllers with ever more sophisticated capabilities.

But no one has yet invented a software program that can duplicate the mix of multi-tasking, innovation, and sixth-sense intuition that are staples of successful performance in the job. In this sense my reflections on the ATC profession remain relevant today. Therefore, if you are considering a career in air traffic control, reading about the challenges and opportunities you are likely to face in the years ahead may serve as a source of inspiration or a cautionary tale.

The descriptions of events in these memoirs are as accurate as imperfect memory can make them. With a few exceptions, flight numbers, call signs and names of individuals are modifications of or outright substitutions for their true identities. Eastern 401, Valujet 592, and TWA 514 are the actual identifications of the aircraft involved in their respective accidents; Delta 229, Delta 836, Braniff 343, and Eastern 855 are likewise correctly identified in recounting the incidents they experienced. Several of the side numbers used in passages about general aviation are from aircraft I have flown, but most were not involved in the events described. The exceptions are Cessna 8767 Golf and Skylane 89 Uniform whose call signs are correctly represented.

Dave Carmichael, Martin Hansen, Joel Cole, Jim Buckles, Bob Ulanch, Stan Psczolkowski, Andrew Haines, Bill Cassada, David Larson, David Hinson, Jane Garvey, Cecil Hall, and Ron Liszt are the real names of individuals who contributed positively either in their professional roles or in supporting me, or both. All other names are first or last names only, or pseudonyms, no doubt providing only the thinnest cloak of anonymity to those who served at Miami Tower during my years there. To this ever diminishing group I say with complete candor that any errors of fact or chronology are strictly mine.

1. Beginnings

I was four years old, sitting in my dad's lap in the driver's seat of his 1939 Packard. He was working the accelerator, brake and clutch, while I wrestled with the steering wheel. As long as we were going straight I managed to keep the car on the road, but any significant turn required his greater strength. Every time we were in the car together, I badgered him with entreaties to "let me drive."

Eight years later, I was driving my mother's 1948 Buick convertible up and down the length of our 100-foot driveway without a parent in the passenger seat. I had gotten pretty good at managing the standard shift transmission, and the four years until I would reach the age to get a driver's license seemed an impossibly long period.

Two years later, a friend and I were picked up by the police for joyriding on public roads in vehicles "appropriated" from clueless neighbors who never imagined that "those nice boys" would do such a thing. Fortunately I was still a juvenile, so this record essentially disappeared when I turned 16.

At age 17, I was able to "captain" an 85-foot motor yacht. It was a converted Army air-sea rescue vessel built in 1945 and never put into service. My dad had purchased it as military surplus at an unbelievably low cost. Since age 11, I had watched him make intricate docking maneuvers using the different reverse-forward combinations of the twin screws that powered the boat. Now, he asked me to take the boat from City Island, New York, to Newport, Rhode Island, with an overnight stop in Essex, Connecticut. My "crew" was my younger brother and his friend, plus my mother, who had no practical knowledge of boating. At Essex there was a large crowd on the dock observing my approach and landing, and I was nervous, hoping things would go well. Fortunately, they did—but how in the world did my dad trust me with this responsibility?

A year later I graduated from Phillips Exeter Academy, a high-powered New England prep school. It had been a long grind. Through endless hours of study, including numerous violations of the "lights out" hours, I managed to acquit myself pretty well. I seemed to be good at foreign languages, and had won some prizes in competitive examinations. I thought about becoming a translator at United Nations, or an analyst for the Central Intelligence Agency (CIA) or the National Security Agency (NSA). But I already knew that the average "desk job" was not for me. I wanted something with a clear purpose, where achievement and results would be plainly visible. Boat captain? Pilot? Something else?

My college years at Princeton University didn't yield any telling inspirations about future direction. I majored in English, believing that a good command of language would be a valuable asset no matter where I ended up. Could I be a writer? Maybe, but what would I write about? And did I really have the skills? I still remember a comment by one of my professors on a course paper I had written: "You say the obvious well." Hmm, thank you—(I think). Between freshman and sophomore years, I served as a tutor in French and Spanish for high school students. This was fun, and immensely rewarding to see my students catching on. At that point, I started thinking about becoming a teacher.

At age 21, I was just beginning my senior year and getting ready to walk out of Princeton with my bachelor's diploma. I spent many hours wrestling with my career decision, when Uncle Sam stepped into the picture.

2. Anchors Aweigh

"Congratulations John, you're in the Navy." With those words, the recruiter who had just sworn me in set me on a course that would lead me to eventual certification as an air traffic controller.

It was 1963 and I was still in my senior year at Princeton. It was just a year and a half after the Berlin wall went up, and the first rumblings of U.S. involvement in the war in Vietnam were beginning to be felt. Many of my classmates had opted for graduate school, which temporarily shielded them from the draft via the educational deferment. But because I had no definite career goals, this path held little appeal for me. However, I knew that I didn't want to be drafted.

Back in the fall of 1962, only a month after the Cuban missile crisis, recruiters from all the armed services had come to the Princeton campus to troll the waters for likely officer candidates. My father had been a Navy man in World War II, and service on a ship seemed vastly preferable to the possibility of huddling in a muddy foxhole as an Army infantryman. The Navy recruiting booth was staffed by "black shoes" (surface ship officers) and "brown shoes" (pilot and aircrew officers also known as "Airedales"). The advantages of service with the "Airedales" became apparent to me in short order.

Many of the Navy's airborne squadrons were land-based, including anti-submarine units and hurricane hunters, some were in the U. S., while others were overseas in places like Puerto Rico and Rota, Spain. The "brown shoes" also passed out glossy brochures describing the life of a cadet at the U. S. Naval School of Pre-Flight in Pensacola, Florida, showing tanned, fit men in their Navy whites golfing and riding in a red convertible with attractive girls as passengers. (There were no women cadets in those days.) This was the sheerest propaganda, as I was later to discover, but in the moment it was pretty persuasive.

I took a battery of tests, which showed that I was preliminarily qualified to be a naval aviation observer (NAO). That specialty was later re-christened to naval flight officer (NFO). There were several designations within the NAO classification: navigator, radar intercept officer (RIO), and electronic countermeasures (ECM) specialist, to name three. After passing a physical examination and a background check, I was duly sworn in as an NAO. I was told to report for training in the fall after graduation, provided I had completed my degree and not run afoul of the law in any way that would constitute grounds for disqualification.

A Brand New World

On October 2, 1963, I arrived at the Naval Air Station in Pensacola and walked into the brand new world of Pre-Flight's "Indoc" battalion. Any pre-conceptions I may have entertained of a friendly, collegial atmosphere (not to mention girls and red convertibles) were quickly dispelled. As anyone who has undergone boot camp or any kind of primary military training can attest, that first chapter is designed to shock you to your core. The cadet officer who escorted me and several others into the building welcomed us in the only civil tones we were likely to hear for quite some time, saying, "Gentlemen, this is a damn fine program."

Immediately thereafter we were back in the hallway, where another cadet officer, standing in front of one of my hapless companions, faces separated by three inches, screamed at the top of his lungs, "Passageway, you maggots!" From this point onward, any reference to a place or object that had a shipboard counterpart was to be made using naval terminology. The hallway was a passageway, the walls were bulkheads, the floors were decks, and the bathroom was the head. There would be no walking in the passageways. Double-time was the only mode of locomotion that would be countenanced, interrupted only by the requirement to "brace" the bulkhead (stand at attention, back pressed to the wa—er, bulkhead) any time a cadet officer or one of the marine drill instructors passed. While braced, one had to greet these superiors in a commanding (i.e., loud) voice: "Good evening, sir!" In most instances the salutation resulted in a close face-to-face encounter with the individual so greeted, and a deafening response such as, "I can't hear you, you pansy!" After three or four repetitions of the greeting, the "bracee" would be instructed to "carry on," and would resume double-timing down the passageway.

"Indoc" lasted an interminable ten days, without a moment's respite from punishing runs at 5:00 a.m. to endless inspections of rooms and uniforms, all punctuated by random time-outs for "recitation." We were expected to have committed to memory the entire chain of command from the president all the way down to our platoon leader. It wasn't difficult if you were asked to name the president or the secretary of the Navy, but it was easy to trip up if you were buttonholed about the admiral serving with the Joint Chiefs of Staff or the commanding officer of the Pensacola Naval Air Station. Even after "Indoc" this was one of the prime offenses for being put on report and spending Saturday afternoon marching off demerits, after being cited for "UR"—unprepared for recitation.

Developing Teamwork

Despite the unrelenting harassment in the Indoctrination Battalion (or because of the pressure, as the Navy would have it), our class began to develop a sense of unity and solidarity. We learned to spot discrepancies in each other's uniforms, the occasional "Irish pennant" (a wayward sheet corner projecting below the springs of our bunk beds), smudged brass on a belt buckle, or a scuffed shoe toe ("What did you shine those shoes with mister, a Hershey bar?") There were even moments of surreptitiously shared humor, all the more delightful for the need to keep them invisible to the cadet officers and drill instructors. Pity the unlucky cadet caught smiling or laughing at anything! During one of the many marching exercises that were a staple of Indoc training, the drill instructor (DI) was demonstrating the correct way to perform an about-face. This of course necessitated turning his back to the platoon, creating a brief moment for us to wipe a sweaty brow, scratch an itch, or relax from the position of attention. A wave of not-quite-stifled laughter rippled through the ranks as the DI, facing away from us, shouted, "Now when I have my back turned, I don't want to see a lot of moving around!"

"Indoc" eventually ended. We traded in our shapeless "poopy suits (fatigues)" for uniforms that essentially mirrored those of the officers who instructed us. Then the real business of pre-flight got under way, serving up a mix of academics, PT (physical training) and military training. The academics were essentially free of the pressures and harassment of the initial phase, and introduced us to a host of new and interesting subjects—aerodynamics, navigation and flight physiology among them. PT, for the most part, emphasized the team. On a long run, the slowest man would be put at the head of the formation and everyone would adjust to that pace. Other portions required a strictly individual effort, like the "O" (obstacle) course, and swimming. On more than one occasion I thanked my lucky stars that I was a decent swimmer, as I watched the instructors wielding bamboo poles rapping the fingers of the panic-stricken poor swimmers trying to clutch the side of the pool.

Military training was the one area where some of the elements of "Indoc" remained in place. There were many inspections, marching and rifle-bearing drills, and the possibility at each morning formation that a necktie would be insufficiently blocked, or the end of a belt would not exactly meet the 3-inch requirement. A deficiency in any of these areas had consequences, none of them good from the cadet's perspective. A failed academics test could put one back a class, meaning a minimum of one extra week of Pre-Flight. The inability to run the "O" course in the specified time or to complete one of the swim exercises meant two days of "practice" during the precious two hours that we had to ourselves each day, and then an "opportunity" to pass that phase on a third day.

Class cohesion increased as the weeks went by, and we began exchanging ideas and opinions about the Navy and about aviation. It soon became apparent that the pilot candidates, who outnumbered us NAOs by about four to one, looked at the Navy as a golden opportunity to receive free flight training that would be eminently marketable to the airlines when their military tour was up. This was perfectly captured years later in a scene from the 1982 movie, "An Officer and a Gentleman," in which Lou Gossett, in the role of a marine drill instructor, informs the new recruits "Before you start flying for United Airlines, you got to get through me!" Many of my fellow cadets were well informed about the perks of an airline pilot career—high pay (about $40,000 a year for a captain in the mid-1960s), liberal time off, and a chance to see the world on the company's dime.

By contrast, a qualified naval aviator holding the rank of lieutenant could expect to earn about $10,000 per year, with no guarantees of time off, and face the distinct possibility of being shot at while "seeing the world." No piloting career opportunities existed, post-military service, for NAOs, and I began to wonder if I had made the right decision in choosing this option with its shorter active duty commitment. This was the point where I began to think of a post-Navy career direction. Would there be any way to qualify as an airline pilot without the Navy training? It turned out later that it might be possible. But before that point, I had several moments of doubt about this whole flying business, as will become clear.

Two additional dates from Pre-Flight training remain crystal clear in my memory. One was November 22, 1963, as we were forming up for the regularly scheduled Friday inspection and parade. Our marine sergeant drill instructor was in full cadet harassment mode, picking out minor uniform discrepancies, incorrectly placed hats (I mean, "covers"), and generally informing us that we were the sorriest looking bunch of mothers he had ever laid eyes on. Then, a cadet officer ran up to him and interrupted his tirade, saying that President Kennedy had been shot in Dallas. As it happened, our platoon was near enough to hear the exchange, and an audible gasp went up from the ranks. The sergeant was dumbstruck for an instant, before informing the cadet officer to carry on. He paused for a moment, then in tones that we had never heard from him before said, "You gentlemen should know that the president was shot in the head. Right face! Forward march!" The parade and inspection went forward normally, but the change in atmosphere was palpable throughout the base. We still double-timed, all scheduled activities remained in place, but there would be no more gung-ho sounding off at every instant until further advised. Flags were at half-mast, and even the DIs and cadet officers were more subdued. That weekend Lyndon Johnson was sworn in as president, and we no longer imitated Kennedy's Boston accent in reciting the chain of command.

The other date was one we had longed for, and at times felt would never arrive. It was February 14, 1964, the day we graduated. For us

AOCs (aviation officer candidates with college degrees), it meant being commissioned as an ensign. A strong cold front had passed through the Pensacola area the day before, and we were standing at attention on an open field in 30-degree weather with about 25 knots of wind blowing across the parade ground. In addition, a number of covers were unceremoniously swept from heads onto which they had been insufficiently jammed. These were duly retrieved by the DIs and returned to their owners with a stare icier than anything the weather could provide. After the ceremony, in the time-honored naval tradition, our non-commissioned drill sergeants were the first to salute us, and we in turn favored them with a dollar bill. Chapter one in our training was now complete.

Brown Shoes

With Pre-Flight behind us, the pilot candidates and NAOs were sent to their respective next phases of training. For the pilots, it was off to Saufley Field, where they would receive primary flight instruction in the Beechcraft T-34. For the NAOs, it was simply a matter of reporting to a different building to attend Basic NAO School. We could now live off base if we chose—no more room inspections, forced marching, or physical training. We were issued flight gear consisting of an orange flight suit, specialized boots and gloves, and a fighter jock's helmet equipped with headphones. The course lasted eight weeks with a renewed emphasis on all the specialties among which an NAO might choose or be assigned. For the first time we actually rode in an airplane for training hops designed to test and reinforce the concepts taught in class. The first such flight was in the Beechcraft C-45, known as the Twin Beech or, more colloquially, the "bugsmasher." Six of us sat in bucket seats lined up behind the two pilots, with a very limited view of the outside world. The order of the day was that each of us would keep a navigational log, recording times and

C-45

altitudes at various points, estimates to the next point, fuel remaining, estimated heading corrections for the reported wind in order to make good a specified course, true airspeed versus indicated airspeed, etc. The cabin was cramped, the engine noise deafening, and the air filled with hydraulic fluid fumes. As we juggled our logs on our knees, we all turned various shades of green fighting off airsickness. When the hop was over, I found my enthusiastic anticipation of life as an NAO considerably dampened.

There were several flights in the NAO syllabus conducted in the Grumman S2-F, a twin-engine carrier-based anti-submarine aircraft. This was a step up from the smaller "bugsmasher," but we were still confined as a group to the back of the airplane, with little outside visibility, balancing logs and our E6-B "computers" (glorified slide rules for computing wind drift, true airspeed, density altitude and other flight information) on our knees. These exercises were rather to be endured than appreciated.

But at about the midway point, there was a flight scheduled in the North American T-28, a tandem-seat, low-wing trainer with a sliding canopy. The pilot sat in front, while the trainee rode in back. This one hop changed everything for me, as I took in a 360-degree panorama of the world below, and studied the instrument panel that duplicated everything on the pilot's display. The growl of the big R-1820 radial engine was loud, but with a full view of the horizon, I experienced none of the queasiness of the earlier flights, and began to understand the relationship between the instrument readings and what the airplane was actually doing. This seemed to me the ultimate in flying—until my first ride in a jet aircraft.

T-28

To be eligible for this next phase of training, each of us had to undergo sessions in the altitude chamber and the ejection seat simulator. The altitude chamber brought home in no uncertain terms the reality of the classroom training on flight physiology. In groups of four or five at a time we entered the chamber, donned oxygen masks, and waited till the air pressure was reduced to a level equaling the environment at flight level 330 (33,000 feet). We each in turn removed our oxygen masks and proceeded to perform a simple task, such as playing a solitaire hand. As I watched the men ahead of me in the exercise spill the cards on the floor, their lips turning blue, and their expressions changing from focused concentration to glassy-eyed passivity, I promised myself that no such thing would happen to me. When it was my turn, I started off well enough, but very quickly saw my own hands making jerky, spastic movements, scattering the cards. The next thing I knew, my oxygen mask was being held in place over my mouth and nose by one of the instructors. It was a sobering lesson in the effects of high altitude hypoxia.

The ejection seat familiarization consisted of a thorough briefing, followed by an abrupt ride up the rails of the simulator. The main point of the briefing was the importance of being correctly positioned in the seat if it became necessary to eject from the airplane. Elbows, knees, feet, and the spine were all at risk, given the terrific forces of an ejection sequence and the narrow confines of a jet fighter cockpit. The simulator used an explosive charge only half as powerful as those installed in the airplanes, but there was more than one black and blue butt among our numbers when the exercise was complete.

Taking to the Air

With the altitude chamber and the ejection seat training entered into our logbooks, we could now be scheduled for our first experience in a Navy jet trainer, the North American T-2 Buckeye. This was a modestly powered (by jet standards) tandem seat aircraft with a low wing and a bubble canopy. As with the T-28, the student occupied the rear seat with the pilot up front, and once again the full view of the world below and the instrument panel array were thrilling. There was hardly any discernible engine noise; only the hiss of a 400-knot slipstream over the airframe. Turbulence at jet altitudes was minimal, and the speed with which distances were covered, by contrast with the slower propeller-driven aircraft, was astounding. Part of the flight was dedicated to very high frequency (VHF) omni-directional range (VOR) orientation—determining position by the indications of these primary navigational aids. At first I was at a total loss to interpret the meaning of the omni-range bearing selector (OBS) as related to aircraft heading, the TO/FROM window (meaning whether the course set on the OBS would lead the aircraft toward or away from the station) and the left/right positioning of the CDI (course deviation indicator) needle indicating which side of the radial (the bearing to or from the station) the aircraft was on. I eventually determined that it was simpler than it seemed, and once the position was determined, the pilot could initiate appropriate action.

An integral element of these training flights, while not emphasized in the NAO syllabus, was the role of air traffic control. When the weather was favorable, the low altitude hops in the propeller aircraft could be conducted under visual flight rules (VFR). This meant that there was no FAA requirement to file a flight plan, although Navy policy mandated that a VFR flight plan be filed for flights that would proceed beyond certain limits from the airport. It also meant that maintaining separation from other aircraft was the pilot's responsibility, a procedure known as "see and be seen." On VFR flights, the NAO students were counseled emphatically to keep our heads on a swivel in order to assist the pilot in locating potential traffic conflicts.

Several of the low altitude hops were conducted in weather that would not permit VFR operations (by regulation, any time the visibility was less than three miles or the ceiling was below 1,000 feet), and no flights above flight level 180 (18,000 feet) were permitted to operate under VFR regardless of weather conditions. In these cases, the pilot had to file an instrument flight rules (IFR) flight plan. I did not fully understand IFR operations until several years later after receiving my instrument ticket as a commercial pilot, and even our Navy pilot instructors were often heard discussing and debating various aspects of IFR. Both in the ready room and during IFR flights, the pilots were visibly more serious, more focused, and very much on guard against "screwing the pooch," as they put it, while under ATC control. It was understood that any serious infraction of the FAA's IFR regulations could result in having their wings pulled, effectively grounding them. The fundamental differences between VFR and IFR operations were that under VFR, the pilot was required only to contact ground control for taxi and the tower for takeoff or landing clearance. IFR operations required adherence to all instructions issued by ATC (heading, altitude, speed, navigation). The main advantage was that flight was permitted through clouds, or in weather conditions below VFR minimums, using the aircraft instrumentation instead of outside visual references.

During the IFR training hops, the NAOs wore headsets, and heard everything the pilots heard, but without understanding much of the exchanges. We all agreed that "those controllers talk a mile a minute, and I can't make heads or tails of what they're saying." I was already beginning to pick up on the cooperative/adversarial nature of the controller/pilot relationship, and, being at this point more in the pilot camp, I shared their predominant view that controllers were like cops waiting to issue a ticket for any procedural violation. I also came to share the pilot view that ATC seemed to have eyes in the cockpit, and that even the most minor digressions from assigned heading, altitude, or airway to be flown would be instantly detected, eliciting a sharp rebuke. Only much later did I learn that the controller had to work with minimal information, especially regarding rate of climb/descent or turn, and the pilot's flight intention.

Final Training

Basic NAO School ended in late April, leaving a final phase of training before permanent assignment to a squadron. This was to take place at the Naval Air Station in Glynco, Georgia, would last another eight weeks, and would determine the specialties within which we would be designated. We learned that certain designations inevitably meant carrier duty, while others were most likely to place us in shore-based organizations. Our instructors had their own take on the pros and cons of each option, and were pretty candid in their assessments. Being a radar intercept officer (RIO) meant riding in the back of an F-4 fighter locating and targeting enemy aircraft. But as the officers with RIO experience pointed out, this was not the most dangerous aspect of the job. Far riskier, according to them and the pilots who flew these combat operations, were carrier operations themselves, especially night carrier landings. All had seen, and some had lived through, night ops gone bad, ranging from an undershoot and a fiery collision with the carrier's fantail, to a series of "bolters" (missing the arresting wire with the tail hook). In the latter situation, either fuel exhaustion would require the crew to eject (and hope for the best as the carrier receded into the darkness at 25 or 30 knots), or the late application of go-around power would result in a crash into the sea with the ship overrunning the airplane in a matter of seconds. Added to these stark possibilities was the fact that the RIO had no control over the airplane, being totally dependent on the judgment and skill of the pilot.

Electronic counter-measures (ECM), navigation, and the anti-submarine warfare specialties were more likely to lead to an assignment with a transport wing, the hurricane hunters, shore-based anti-submarine units, or the advanced early warning (AEW) command. All of these flew large multi-engine aircraft that could not operate from a carrier. Although "needs of the service" would always pre-empt individual preferences, we would be permitted to express our choices at the end of the training. The billets would be awarded in order of class ranking, so that there was a high premium on getting the highest grades possible.

Several of the training flights were conducted aboard the EC-121, the Navy version of the Lockheed Super Constellation, whose primary mission was AEW patrol. This aircraft was large enough to accommodate the entire class during missions that could last up to six hours, and afforded us the opportunity to learn the practical aspects of navigation and electronic countermeasures. Another part of the syllabus consisted of simulated RIO missions in the North American Sabreliner, or T-39 as it was designated by the Navy. These had an immediacy that appealed to the more adventurous among us, as we identified the "enemy" aircraft (without the threat of return fire), computed its speed and course, and issued instructions to our pilot establishing an optimum intercept angle and firing range. No doubt the few among our number who chose the RIO option were influenced by these hops.

EC-121

By the end of the eight weeks, I had narrowed my preferences to either an AEW squadron or the hurricane hunters. When I learned that the principal base for east coast AEW patrols was Argentia, Newfoundland, and that the hurricane hunters were based in Puerto Rico, I chose the hurricane hunters as my first preference. Although the prospect of flying into a hurricane was somewhat daunting, I was encouraged by the fact that the squadron had never lost an airplane. I later saw sobering evidence of the risks associated with these operations, but, as events unfolded, not as a member of the squadron. On the day we received our assignments, I was informed that I would be based in Puerto Rico as a member of VU-8, or Utility Squadron 8, rather than the hurricane hunters. Even our instructors were not entirely sure what a utility squadron did, or how we would receive our designations as ECM operators. They thought the mission had something to do with providing training for ships and airborne combat units. In any case, it would be shore duty with only a remote possibility of engaging in combat operations, and I left Glynco for a 30-day leave before my reporting date at the U. S. Naval Station, Roosevelt Roads Puerto Rico.

Joining the Squadron

Life as an NAO in VU-8 was a far cry in every respect from the customs and rigors of the training command. Even as recently minted ensigns, we were welcomed into a highly egalitarian fraternity of fellow officers, where everyone below the rank of commander (which was everyone except the commanding officer (CO) and the executive officer (XO) were on a first-name basis. We normally addressed the CO informally as "Skipper," and all interactions between officers were friendly and collegial, much as might be expected in a civilian setting. I soon learned that my reporting date (September 1964) had fallen into a slack period for the squadron. Our mission of providing training services tended to be concentrated in the winter months, when the ships and air groups preferred to deploy from their cold weather bases. Although training flights were scheduled every day, the overall pace of operations left ample time for settling into life at "Roosy." Our orientation included a tour of the naval station, including the hangars and flight lines of the other units at the airfield. One of these units was VW-4, the hurricane hunter squadron to which I had requested assignment back at NAS Glynco. On the flight line there was a C-121 (the Navy Super Constellation) that had been severely damaged during a hurricane penetration. The entire airframe was visibly twisted. There were dozens of holes where rivets had popped out of place, and several panels hung loosely under the wings. The flight crew had been lucky to make it back from the mission and, it seemed to me, I had been lucky to be assigned to VU-8.

Every officer in our squadron had a "desk job" supporting the administrative operation of the organization. I was to be the officer in charge of the electronics division, whose functions were doubly important because of the remote-controlled target drones we operated. This was my first experience of actually supervising enlisted personnel, and the sharp divide between the commissioned and enlisted ranks was immediately apparent. The dynamic went something like this: Any question of equipment readiness or the performance of assigned tasks was always answered in highly positive terms. Any attempt to verify these assurances evoked clear (if unexpressed) resentment. Any actual finding that what was reported was not entirely true resulted in strongly expressed regret, pledging that the reason for the incorrect report would be ferreted out, and that the person responsible would be held accountable. It was a fine line to tread, both for me and the chief petty officer in charge of the division. I knew essentially nothing about electronics, and relied heavily on the chief. Of course, he wanted the division to appear in the best possible light, but could not afford to be seen as covering up even minor discrepancies.

Over time, it became clear that most officers looked at our administrative responsibilities as a nuisance, interfering with our squadron's "real" purpose, which was flying. All of us preferred to be in the air, rather than on the ground dealing with personnel issues, supply line glitches, and the endless stream of teletype communications, many of which seemed designed to burden our lives without in any way supporting our mission. There were three categories of teletype messages, each with its own clipboard and stack of accumulated messages, labeled logically and imaginatively as "Routine" (the thickest stack), "Priority" (the thinnest), and "YGBSM" ("You Gotta Be Shitting Me", nearly as thick as the Routine category).

For me and my fellow NAOs, the airborne mission was to operate telemetry relay equipment installed in the squadron's six Lockheed P2-V Neptune aircraft. The P-2V had been in service since 1945 as a submarine hunter, and was still used by many active anti-submarine warfare (ASW)

P-2V

F-9. © Meunierd Dreamstime.com

groups. Our aircraft were the older models, retired from their original mission, with all the ASW gear removed, and configured to carry the wing-mounted Firebee target drone and the telemetry relay equipment. All the exercises that VU-8 supported were carried out in a huge area of the ocean north of Puerto Rico designated for weapons training by ships and air groups. The area was the Atlantic Fleet Weapons Range (AFWR or "aff-warr" as we referred to it verbally). Because many of these operations occurred "over the horizon," the data transmitted by the target drones could not have been captured without the airborne platform of the P2-V, flying in circles at 10,000-12,000 feet, relaying the transmissions to AFWR headquarters at Roosy. The missions were long, the aircraft was unpressurized and uninsulated, and the equipment we operated was located in a section with only two side-mounted portholes. Although any day in the air was preferable to a day spent as a "ground-pounder," these flights didn't provide much in the way of increased knowledge or information about flying.

In addition to the P2-V, the squadron operated five other aircraft types, among them the T-28 two-seat trainer I had first flown in during Basic NAO School. The role of the T-28 was to fly wing on the F-9 Cougars, unpiloted aircraft that had been converted to remote controlled drones, and to set them up on the so-called "hot leg" as targets for training the crews of ships and air groups with a combat mission. But these exercises occurred only a few times a year, and the majority of the T-28 flights were for pilot proficiency. As I made friends with the pilots, I told them of my interest in flying and became a frequent rear seat occupant on these proficiency flights. Although it was not strictly legal, they allowed me to take the controls on a number of occasions, and even to fly "under the hood"—a canvas hood pulled into place over the rear cockpit, eliminating any view of the outside world and requiring the airplane to be flown solely on instruments.

Pilot Dreams

Before long I was hooked on being a pilot, and joined the Navy flying club—a group of civilian and Navy pilots who supported a fleet of three Cessna 150s, two Cessna 172s, and a Cessna 182 through club dues. The Navy did not directly fund this activity, but some of the club members were certified aircraft mechanics, while others were certified (civilian) flight instructors. The Navy also provided fuel at cost. Taken together, these factors resulted in the unbelievably low rate of $6 per flight hour, including fuel, for a Cessna 150. I began my flight instruction with one of my squadron mates, including landing practice at Humacao, a nearby uncontrolled airport. The two-seat 150 was a far cry from the T-28, requiring a feather-light touch on the controls, and a healthy recognition of the limited climb performance provided by the 100-horsepower engine in hot weather. I eventually got the hang of it, and one day, after a few trips around the traffic pattern, my instructor said, "Well, I don't think you need me in here anymore." We landed, he stepped out of the airplane, and I was released for my first solo.

C-150

As I taxied back to the runway, I was smiling broadly—but when I lined up in position and began advancing the throttle, a little voice in my head said, "what if you screw up? There's nobody here to help you." The airplane gathered speed, and I lifted off, much more quickly, without the extra weight of the instructor. The climb performance, too, was much better, and soon I was at pattern altitude, transmitting my position on the Unicom frequency (an intra-pilot frequency used at uncontrolled fields), and judging my turn to base leg. As I approached the runway, it looked as though I was descending a little too rapidly, but a small power

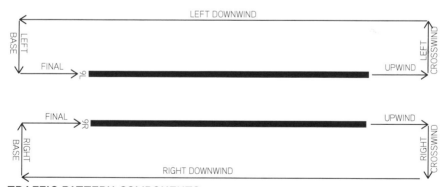

TRAFFIC PATTERN COMPONENTS

The components of a traffic pattern are designated as "legs" (upwind, crosswind, downwind, base, and final). The upwind is flown immediately after takeoff. In the left-hand pattern, crosswind is a 90-degree turn to the left, followed by another 90-degree left turn downwind. The turns to base leg and final are also to the left, lacing the aircraft in alignment with the runway in use. In a right-hand pattern all turns are made to the right.

C-172

increase quickly corrected the descent, again thanks to the lighter weight of the aircraft. Two touch and go's and a full stop, and then the instructor climbed back aboard and we headed back to Roosy. There were several club members at the clubhouse when we taxied in, including a group of four men getting ready to fly into San Juan in one of the 172s. They all offered their congratulations on my first solo, and in time-honored tradition, they cut out the back of my shirt and posted it on the clubhouse wall bearing the notation that I had soloed on this date, February 15, 1966. It was one of the most thrilling and satisfying days of my life.

But the next day at the squadron, I was greeted by a group of subdued individuals with long faces. One officer came up to me and said, "Hey, did you hear? Four guys were killed in a 172 last night on their way back from San Juan. We think they flew into a thunderstorm and crashed." This was one of those moments reminding me that for all the fun of flying, a routine flight could turn disastrous in an instant. I have no doubt that my conservative attitude toward flying, especially with respect to weather, originated in part from that accident the day after I soloed.

At that point in my Navy career, I had logged about 20 hours of flight instruction. The minimum required for a private pilot certificate was 40 hours combined instructed and solo time, including a solo cross-country flight of at least 150 nautical miles. Puerto Rico was only about 100 miles long, and I could have accomplished the cross-country requirement by hugging the coastal perimeter. But this did not seem the best way for me to hone my flight planning and navigational skills. As luck would have it, I was scheduled for a trip back to the States on the P-2V to Homestead Air Force Base about 25 miles south of Miami. We had two free days before the return to Roosy, during which time I met the solo cross-country requirement in a way I will always remember as one of the most fun flying days ever.

A Challenging Flight

At the time, my brother was undergoing flight training at Opa-locka Airport, about seven miles north of Miami International Airport, and we came up with the idea of renting a couple of 150s and making a "formation" flight together. Neither of us had the skill to operate in a true formation, so we agreed to remain a comfortable distance apart but within visual contact of one another. I underwent the requisite checkout with the fixed based operator (FBO) at Opa-locka supplying the airplanes, and soon we were airborne, headed for the west coast of Florida. We communicated on 122.9, the unofficial pilot-to-pilot common frequency, and hammed it up big time, referring to each other as "Red Dog Leader" and "Red Dog One." When one of us would spot traffic, we would alert the other by transmitting "Bogey at 12 o'clock high, closing." Our first stop was Marco Island, which was just beginning to be developed as a major resort, and landed on a small paved strip a few yards from the beach. We were hot and sweaty from the hour plus of low altitude operations under an August sun. After pulling the airplanes clear of the runway, we stripped to our shorts and dove into the clear waters of the Gulf of Mexico. Later, liberally coated with sand and salt, we discovered a pipe and spigot protruding through the sparse grass where the airplanes were parked. Someone had left a discarded hydraulic fluid can nearby, and we took turns filling it and pouring fresh water over ourselves. Thus refreshed, we took off again and headed north to Page Field in Fort Myers, where I had my logbook endorsed by a ramp attendant, substantiating that portion of the cross-country flight.

The last leg of the trip was to be a return to Opa-locka, which would take no more than an hour and a half. The fuel gauges in both airplanes indicated a reserve of about half the nominal four- hour, 30-minute flying time that a full fuel load would provide. But after we took off, it became obvious that the prevailing winds from the east would significantly slow us down in comparison to the tail-wind assisted groundspeed we had made good on the way over. Moreover, the skies to the east were darkening ominously as the usual pattern of summertime thunderstorms settled over the Florida peninsula. We put aside the pseudo-fighter-jock banter and discussed the situation, ultimately making the conservative call, which was to land and refuel before setting out over the Everglades. Fortunately, Immokalee Airport, a remote strip about 30 miles east of Fort Myers, was directly ahead with a generously long 5,000-foot runway, and we set up for our respective approaches. We unfortunately did not have a current Airport Directory, the FAA publication that listed the services and facilities at every public-use airport, and were chastened to discover that there was no civilization of any kind at the field. Naples Airport was about the same distance from Immokalee as Fort Myers and would afford a slightly shorter flight back to home base, so we elected to reverse course, land at Naples, and depart once more, with any concerns about sufficient fuel put to rest.

This alteration of our flight plan cost us about 45 minutes in total, and as we progressed toward the east, we could see a towering black wall of cloud buildup, no doubt containing the kind of violent meteorological conditions that figured in many an accident report. I had never encountered anything similar in Puerto Rico, and with my 38 hours of student pilot experience I was not feeling supremely confident about my ability negotiate these conditions safely. The FBO that had rented us the airplanes wanted the one my brother was flying to be returned to Tamiami Airport, about 18 miles south of Opa-locka, and so as the east coast of Florida hove into view, he broke off to the south and we parted ways. This left me with about 15 miles to go on my own, as the sun disappeared behind the clouds, and a blast of distinctly cooler air from the gust front filled the cabin through the wide-open air vent.

The good news was that the airport was still VFR, and I had it in sight. Then I tuned in to the automatic terminal information service (ATIS) a recorded broadcast that includes current information, like the runways in use, winds, altimeter, ceiling, and visibility. I was encouraged by all the information transmitted with the exception of the wind direction and velocity. As is typical when the outflow from a thunderstorm is dueling with the prevailing wind, both the direction and the velocity were varying widely from moment to moment. I knew that the sooner I got on the ground the better off I would be. Taking a few seconds to rehearse my call to the tower, I keyed up my mic: "Opa-locka tower, Cessna 8767 Golf, student pilot, ten miles west with information Charlie for landing." The tower replied, "Cessna 8767 George, Opa-locka tower, make straight-in approach Runway 9 Left, report a mile west of the expressway." I acknowledged the instructions and lined up with the designated runway, wondering if the tower would offer a further update on the wind, or whether I would have to request it. I didn't have to wait long. Within less than a minute the controller transmitted, "67 George, wind now 360 at 25, gusting to 35. Would you like to use Runway 36?" I certainly wasn't about to try a landing on 9 Left with a 90-degree, 35-knot crosswind, and quickly replied, "67 Golf, affirmative." He replied, "67 George roger, enter left downwind for 36 Right, report turning downwind." (I could tell by the controller's use of "George" that he was older and experienced, having grown up in the business before the more phonetically friendly words of "Alpha," "Bravo," "Golf" and others replaced "Able," "Baker," "George," etc.)

As I entered the pattern, the wind pushed my groundspeed at least 50 per cent higher than usual, and I turned late, and was pushed farther from the field. Rolling out on my final approach, I set power at the usual level but realized that wasn't enough against 25 or 30 knots of headwind. An increase in power remedied the situation. As I reached the last mile to touchdown and about 300 feet of altitude, turbulence from the ground began to kick the airplane around wildly. The stall warning horn blared intermittently as I passed over the threshold, and at last, with an ungainly "galumph," the airplane landed safely, stopping less than 100 feed from the point of touchdown—the shortest roll-out I ever experienced. I stopped to catch my breath, and the controller waited a few moments before transmitting a solicitous, "67 George, how are you doing?" I replied, "OK now," and began a slow, cautious taxi to the ramp, the wings rocking continuously from the increasingly strong wind gusts.

Gaining Flight Experience

Back at the naval station in Puerto Rico, I took advantage of every possible opportunity to get flight experience, from "stick time" in the T-28 with my squadron mates to solo flights and continued instructional hops in the flying club 150s. My instructor worked with me to prepare for the next goal, which was passing the examination for a private pilot certificate. There were several steps required to become a private pilot: the minimum number of logged flight hours; a recommendation from my flight instructor; successful completion of a written exam; an oral exam; and finally a check ride during which a specified set of maneuvers had to be satisfactorily demonstrated. In due course I met the flight hour requirement, passed the written exam, and received my instructor's recommendation, leaving only the oral and the check ride to go. I located an FAA designated examiner based at a nearby airfield, and encountered one of the many colorful individuals I would meet in the aviation world.

On the day of my check ride I flew into Arecibo, an uncontrolled field located west of San Juan, to meet the designee who would administer the (hopefully) last two steps of my quest to become a private pilot. I taxied up to a small ramshackle hangar, where there was a twin-engine Beechcraft Baron, engine cowlings removed, being worked on by several people. One was a white-haired older man with a prominent belly, covered by a filthy tee-shirt bearing a liberal patina of engine oil and fried chicken grease from the half-consumed box on the port wing. I wondered if I had somehow mistaken the agreed upon meeting place for my check ride, but when I inquired where I might find Mr. Miller, the man in the tee shirt replied, "You're lookin' at him." I identified myself, and he proceeded to multi-task, holding a drumstick in one hand, a wrench in the other, and peppering me with questions like: "What's the stalling speed of this airplane (the 150)? What's the procedure if you lose your radio at a controlled airport? What's variation? How often does this airplane have to be inspected? What's the difference between true and indicated airspeed?" I managed to answer them all correctly, and in due course he gave a few instructions to his fellow workers in Spanish, then informed me that it was time for the check ride.

As Miller climbed into the right seat of the 150, it exhibited a visible list to starboard. I performed a quick mental calculation based on my estimate of his probable weight and the maximum gross weight of the airplane. It seemed possible that we might be over max gross, and I wondered if this was the first part of the test, to see if I would question him. I decided that discretion was the better part of valor— presumably, we were equally invested in the ability of the airplane to get off the ground. And how likely would an examiner be to pass an applicant who in effect had called him too fat? As we started to fasten our seat belts, it was immediately apparent that his was too short to connect around his considerable girth, and he cast it aside, saying, "Let's go." I knew that it was an FAR (Federal Air Regulation) that each occupant of an aircraft was required to wear a seat belt during takeoff and landing, and I could not let this pass. I said, in as light a tone as I could manage, "You know, we have to use seatbelts for takeoff and landing, are you trying to catch me on headwork?" "Oh, hell no," he replied, "these things are always too short for me, we'll be all right."

We taxied to the active runway, while I attempted to muster my best professional-pilot baritone in announcing our intentions on Unicom, and took off. Our climb rate was a meager 200-300 feet per minute (vs. a normal 800-1000 fpm rate during solo flights), but we eventually reached a suitable altitude for the maneuvers I was required to demonstrate—stalls and stall recovery, slow flight and others, all while remaining within specified altitude parameters. Miller took the controls once or twice to show me a technique, and even I, novice that I was, quickly recognized that despite his appearance and manner, he was a skilled pilot. He had a fine touch and the airplane responded smoothly to his commands. In due course we returned to the field, executed a couple of approaches and landings, and taxied back to the hangar (and the fried chicken).

As he was filling out the requisite paperwork and endorsing my log book (never saying explicitly that I had passed the check ride), Miller happened to mention that he was employed as a corporate pilot for RonRico, the major Puerto Rican rum distillery. And I then noticed the registration number on the Baron's fuselage, N1RR. During the rest of my time at Roosy, flying as often as I could, I several times heard Miller's voice on various ATC frequencies, calling in and acknowledging air traffic control transmissions with, "Roger, one double R." I left Arecibo with my temporary private pilot certificate in hand, happier about flying than on any day since my solo, and certain that I was now a "real" pilot. On that day my logbook showed a total of 65 hours combined instructed and solo time. Although I could now legally carry passengers, I had basically earned the right to keep learning (or, as my squadron mates assured me, the right to be dangerous). Later events would highlight both of these themes in no uncertain terms.

This Could Be Dangerous

One of the perks of being a certificated private pilot was that flying club rules now permitted me to check out in the four-place airplanes, the Cessna 172 and the 182. The 172 was one of the most common models

C-182

in the general aviation fleet, and was referred to as "the Chevy-6 of general aviation." Its handling characteristics were very similar to those of the 150. But the Cessna 182 was another matter, with its 230-horsepower engine, cowl flaps, and constant speed prop. In due course I developed an understanding of the relationship between manifold pressure and engine RPM, and an appreciation of the significantly improved capabilities of the "Skylane" in contrast to those of the 172 and 150. I became qualified for night flying, which added another full layer of cognitive demands. As the pilots at the squadron (never short on dark humor) put it, "Flying at night is exactly the same as flying in the daytime except you can't see anything."

From this point forward, I was on a single-minded mission—to accumulate as many flight hours as possible, and earn my commercial and instrument ratings. The member-friendly flying club rates made it possible for me to fly often, as did the questionably legal practice of flying "St. Thomas Specials." These were trips to St. Thomas in the U. S. Virgin Islands, some 40 miles east of Puerto Rico, carrying people who wished to spend a day of duty-free shopping and sight-seeing on the island. The flight rules permitted private pilots to carry passengers on what were termed "bona fide equally shared expense" trips. In no way was it legal to carry persons or cargo for hire, or under the provisions governing charter operations. While the private pilots who flew these hops did not put money in their own pockets, the club charged a premium above the actual cost of the flights, and we who flew them added two hours of free flight time to our log books for each round trip.

Most of my dozen or more "St. Thomas Specials" as the pilot unfolded routinely, but one trip flown by another club member resulted in a hair-raising incident that should have put an end to these operations. The pilot had three women passengers in the 172, and was preparing for the return trip from St. Thomas to Roosy. The battery power was too low to actuate the starter motor, and so he elected to start the engine by "propping" the airplane, that is, by spinning the propeller by hand. He instructed his front seat passenger to hold the brakes (which is done by applying foot pressure to the top of the rudder pedals) while he spun the propeller. The engine sprang to life with the throttle positioned at an abnormally high power setting, and as the airplane moved forward, the passenger pushed hard on the brakes, causing the stops in the seat tracks to fail. The seat toppled backwards, leaving the front seat passenger sprawled in the laps of those in the back, and with pressure on the brake pedals removed, the airplane accelerated rapidly with no one at the controls.

The pilot fortunately scrambled out of the way in time to avoid being struck by the propeller, then gave chase as the Cessna exited the ramp and began a slow turn to the west, heading for the seawall at the approach end of Runway 9, and a drop off into deep water. For a time he managed to hold on to the left wing strut, but as speed increased, he eventually had to let go. In a stroke of incredible good fortune, the airplane continued its slow turn until it ran up a shallow embankment and into a chain link fence where the propeller became entangled and the engine abruptly stopped. There was considerable damage to the aircraft, but the passengers emerged unhurt, although badly shaken. There was never an official investigation into the incident, likely because there were no injuries and the airplane damage was not severe enough to meet the FAA definition of "substantial."

The St. Thomas Special operations continued, and one day I had my own experience of a near accident. I had flown a family of three adults to St. Thomas on the morning of that day, and was preparing for the return flight late in the afternoon. The adults were all obese, pushing the limits of both gross weight and weight and balance. To my consternation, as the group approached the airplane I saw that they had with them a child about eight years of age, and well on his way to the same corpulence as his parents. They said they would "just hold the boy on our laps." I pointed out that the airplane was designed to carry a maximum of four people, and that each was required to have a seat belt. I told them that I would have to make two trips, and that the second trip would have to be the next day because VFR flight at night was prohibited outside the confines of Puerto Rican airspace. The mother began crying, while the father became visibly angry, saying they could not afford a hotel room and the extra cost of the additional flight. He said if I did not carry them all, he would "talk to somebody" when they got back to the naval station.

Here was an incipient case of "get-home-itis," a condition figuring in many accident reports, where poor weather, mechanical problems, or (in this instance) airplane performance, were (mis) judged by the pilot as being subordinate to the need to make the flight. I knew that gross weight and weight and balance computations included a "fudge" factor, and I had heard from my squadron mates who had civilian experience in the 172 that it could "haul a load." Ignoring my better judgment, I agreed to make the flight with all four of them as passengers.

The St. Thomas airport had a single east-west runway, designated as 9-27, 5,000 feet long. The prevailing winds were from the east, nominally favoring Runway 9, but there was a set of hills immediately beyond the departure end. Even with a moderate tail wind, Runway 27 was often assigned or requested, because it ended at the water's edge with no obstructions to contend with. As we taxied out for a Runway 27 departure, I was experiencing considerable uneasiness. There would be a tail wind, which would increase our takeoff roll (bad news), but obstructions would not be a factor (good news); the heaviest passenger was in the front (good news), but there were two hefty adults and a fat kid in the back (bad news).

As I applied power for takeoff, acceleration was slow, and I knew enough to keep the airplane on the ground to allow speed to increase as much as possible. As the available runway disappeared behind us, the end came up fast, and I pulled back gently on the yoke. To my relief, we became airborne, but were not climbing. I realized that we were in ground effect, a condition related to the aircraft wing span that reduced drag and permitted flight near the ground with less power than would be needed even a few feet higher. What would happen as we flew past the runway end? Would we sink into the water, or would we sink only until the positive forces of ground effect again occurred? We were on a knife-edge of minimum performance, but ever so slowly, once the friction of tires on the pavement was eliminated, our speed began to increase, and we were able to climb, at a rate lower than any I had ever experienced, or ever would again. It took 25 minutes, and more than half the total mileage of the flight, to reach our cruising altitude of 2,500 feet. I vowed never again to push the limits of aircraft performance, and on future flights took care to brief my passengers fully, admonishing them to keep the total weight of their personal belongings and duty-free purchases below an absolute maximum.

More 'Learning Experiences'

Two other incidents occurred on later flights during my time in Puerto Rico, one involving the insidious accumulation of small factors, and the other in an unexpected, "quick and dirty" development. In the first instance, I had flown the 182 into San Juan International Airport to pick up two friends scheduled to arrive from the States that afternoon. When I reached the Eastern Airlines counter, I saw that the flight I was to meet was marked "delayed." Over the course of several hours, and a number of revised estimates by Eastern ground agents, it became clear that the delay would be substantial, ultimately resulting in an arrival time just before 9:00 pm. I greeted my friends, helped them collect their baggage, and eventually loaded up the 182 for the return flight to Roosy. As we began to taxi, I turned the rheostatic control knob that governed instrument panel illumination, only to find that the instrument panel remained completely dark. Next I tried the map light, which had only a single brightness setting, and was not ideally placed to illuminate the instrument panel, although it did produce enough ambient light for me to discern the readings. As we proceeded along the taxiway, the ground controller issued us this transmission: "Skylane 89 Uniform, be advised, it appears your aft position light is inoperative." "89 Uniform, roger," I replied, wondering if the tower personnel would write up the infraction, and whether I would be hearing from Flight Standards, the FAA branch that enforced regulations. I also wondered if the discrepancy would be noted by the Navy controllers back at the naval station—the military could be very strict about seemingly minor matters.

We departed on Runway 8, in the direction toward Roosy, for what should have been a routine 25-minute hop. I was already reviewing my preparations for this flight, and realized that I should have checked the lighting systems of the aircraft before I ever left for San Juan. Of course, I had not anticipated a night operation since the whole trip had been expected to take place during daylight hours. Still, I had read enough accident reports and FAA enforcement actions to know that a great many of them contained the finding: "The pilot failed to ensure that the aircraft's mechanical condition was adequate for the proposed flight." Once the lights of San Juan were behind us, I noticed that the visibility was unaccountably poor. It was as though were flying into a light, but increasingly dense haze, although no such condition had existed back at the airport. Two clues pretty quickly revealed the cause of, if not a solution to, the problem: The view out the side window was completely clear, and a faint image of the cabin interior was being reflected back from the interior of the windscreen. Something was coating the outside surface, and its effects were becoming more pronounced by the minute. As a subsequent examination confirmed, the oil reservoir in the propeller hub, an integral component of the constant-speed propeller system, was leaking, and the slipstream was depositing the oil on all the forward surfaces of the airframe. The effect was subtle enough to be undetectable in daylight, but against a dark night sky, with the unusually bright illumination of the cabin by the map light, forward visibility was almost completely obscured.

    We had at least 15 more minutes flying time to the naval station airfield, an uncomfortably long period to mull some important questions: Would the windscreen become completely opaque, or would there be enough transparency to permit an approach and landing? Could I complete the flight portion safely with the map light turned off, improving outside visibility but losing the ability to read the instrument panel? What would happen to the propeller if the oil supply were completely exhausted? Would it remain at the last selected pitch setting, go to extreme coarse or fine pitch, or gyrate between the two extremes with each revolution, possibly resulting in catastrophic failure? Since the only thing I had immediate control of was the map light, I turned it off, and with the interior reflection eliminated I could just make out the horizon. Once every 30 seconds or so I turned the light back on for a brief look at the instrument panel, quickly extinguishing it after ensuring that our altitude was steady and the engine readings were all normal.

As the flight progressed, forward visibility became increasingly fuzzy, and from my position in the left seat, I was forced to direct my view further and further to the left, where the oil coating on the windscreen was less advanced. As we approached Roosy, I was thankful for the left-hand traffic pattern that flying club aircraft were routinely assigned—from my position in the left seat, it would have been extremely difficult to execute a right-hand pattern, since I would have had to look through the most heavily coated part of the windscreen during the critical turns to base leg and final. Fortunately, there was no other traffic to follow, and the control tower issued landing clearance as we approached mid-field on downwind. With my right hand on the throttle and my left hand on the control yoke, I could no longer operate the map light, which I elected to leave off in order to maximize the limited visibility available. This meant that I would not be able to monitor airspeed and altitude readings, but would have to rely solely on (greatly compromised) external visual cues, and "seat of the pants" feel for aircraft performance. I reduced power and began a turn to base leg, adding what I believed to be the right amount of nose-up trim for the correct approach speed.

So far, things were looking good, and instead of turning final at the usual point, I initiated the turn a tad early, rolling out on a heading about 20 degrees right of direct alignment with the runway so that I could keep the threshold in sight as long as possible. With the runway beneath us, there was no choice but to roll left and line up. We were high, but with a runway length of 10,000 feet, I was not concerned about a long landing. The runway was also generously wide, and with forward visibility essentially non-existent, the runway lights on the left side were my only means of maintaining alignment. I throttled back a few more RPMs, then flared and pulled the power back to idle, soon regretting these too-early actions. We slammed onto the runway surface with a bone-jarring thump, the hardest landing I had ever experienced in any airplane, immediately thereafter suffering a severe bump over the arresting cable always in place in case a jet returned with a hydraulic failure.

Night landings can offer a variety of subtle miscues under the best of conditions, and with the severely reduced outside visibility and no instrument references available, I had misjudged our altitude initiating the flare and the final power reduction, resulting in a much higher rate of descent than normal in the few seconds before contact with the runway.

I crossed my fingers that we had not blown a tire or otherwise damaged the airplane, and as it turned out, we had not. My passengers were pretty quiet as we taxied to the flying club ramp.

The second incident occurred about a year and a half later, after I had earned both my commercial pilot and flight instructor ratings. The first of these I received from the memorable Mr. Miller after a far more exacting check ride than the one he had administered for my private ticket. The flight instructor designation could not be granted by a designee like Miller, but required a successful oral exam and check ride by an FAA examiner. My examiner was Mr. McGregor from the San Juan Flight Standards District Office (FSDO) He was different from Miller in every respect—slim, soft-spoken, conservatively dressed, personable, but all business. I had been told by other flight instructors that the toughest part of earning the credential was the oral examination. According to them, if you "aced" the oral, the examiner would go easy on you during the flight check. My experience seemed to support this theory, as I found the flying portion easier than the commercial check ride, and after I passed McGregor was highly complimentary of my performance on the oral. At this point I had about six months left on my tour of duty at Roosevelt Roads, and I resolved to make the most of it by providing flight instruction. That meant the students paid the cost of the airplane, and I could charge for my time. I took on every student I could, flying almost every day.

Pilot Personalities

Instructed flights posed their own set of challenges. I learned that there were two personality types that warranted extra vigilance on the instructor's part: the brash, over-confident student who wanted no part of ground school instruction, and the timid student who always wanted to be told what to do rather than applying the knowledge in the air. It didn't take me long to recognize the importance of including in every pre-flight briefing the following clear statement: "When I say "I've got it," that means you are to take your hands and feet off the controls immediately and I will fly the airplane."

Predictably, some students were naturals. Within the first hour of instruction they would demonstrate a fine touch on the controls, and an instinctively correct response when the airplane was buffeted by turbulence. Other students never seemed completely comfortable, exhibiting "white-knuckle" tendencies (that is, grasping the control yoke so tightly as to cut off circulation to the fingers) on every flight. These individuals were usually competent in their general knowledge and ability to operate the airplane within correct parameters, but they were "rough" rather than "smooth" pilots. The white-knuckle types would make abrupt control inputs, as for example, turning to a new heading when reaching a bend in an airway instead of anticipating the turn and rolling into and out of the turn smoothly. It was also unusual for these individuals to touch down gently during landing. Instead of flaring gradually, they would tend to pull back sharply on the yoke, either early, resulting in giving up airspeed and lift too soon (as I had done on my night landing in the 182), or late, failing to arrest the descent and bleed off airspeed. In both cases the airplane would touch down with a jolt, and in the second case would often bounce back into the air.

I did not experience any truly "hairy" incidents until the day I flew with Cayco, a Filipino mess steward assigned to the Bachelor Officers Quarters (BOQ). Mess stewards were rated at the lower echelons of the enlisted ranks, and I was surprised that he had the money to spend on flight instruction. When I mentioned this at the squadron, the senior officers told me that typically most of these guys never spent a dime of their income. They never went off base, always ate in the chow hall, and lived in the barracks. Those with wives and families sent most of their money home. Cayco did not have a family, but saved almost all his income, and wanted to learn to fly. He had had about seven hours of instructed time when he came to me, and so I expected him to have at least some of the rudiments down pretty well. He was outgoing, friendly, and about my height. He also had a heavy accent, which perhaps should have rung the first warning bell. During the pre-flight briefing he was alert and attentive, a broad smile on his face, nodding vigorously, and enthusiastically repeating, "Yes, Mr. Potter!" at regular intervals.

During the flight, Cayco's attitude was the same, except that in most cases when I gave him instructions, he would nod vigorously and reply, "Yes, Mr. Potter!" without actually performing the required action until I repeated myself several times.. I tried slowing down my speech rate and enunciating very clearly, but with little effect. The whole flight had consisted of air work, so that the only landing would occur at the end of the lesson. When it came time to return to the field, we had a moderate left crosswind on our approach to Runway 6. We had been operating in an area southwest of the airport, and had been instructed by the tower to make a straight-in approach. With the runway in sight, Cayco lined up directly with the centerline. Rate of descent was looking good, clearance to land was issued when we were about three miles out, but because of the crosswind we had drifted right and were now lined up approximately with the runway edge. We still had about two miles to go, and I said without urgency, "OK, now you can see that we are drifting right. Correct back to the left." "Yes, Mr. Potter!" Cayco responded with a big smile. He took no action to correct our course. We were below 500 feet with the runway sliding further to the left. In the time it took me to repeat my instructions several times and him to acknowledge them and then fail to comply, we had descended another hundred feet or so. If we did not take corrective action immediately, it would be impossible to complete the landing.

"OK, I've got it", I declared emphatically, reaching for the yoke and the throttle and placing my feet on the rudder pedals. I stepped on the left pedal and applied light pressure to the left side of the yoke. The airplane felt as though the gust locks were still in place, and I could not move either control. Cayco's hand, was tightly clutching the throttle. "Ok, I've got it!" I yelled, and once more, his beatific smile in place, Cayco replied, "Yes Mr. Potter!" The controls were still frozen in place, with the grass area on the right side of the runway coming up fast. "Cayco! Let go of the controls!" I shouted. Legs locked against the rudder pedals and white knuckles grasping the yoke and throttle, he made no move to comply. We would be in the grass in about 10 seconds if I didn't do something. I let go of the throttle, or more accurately, of Cayco's right hand, and gave him two hard judo chops, one to each arm. This seemed to get the message across, as he immediately dropped both hands into his lap. I still had no rudder control, but I immediately applied power, regained altitude to about 150 feet, and made a gentle turn back to the runway centerline. I reached over and tapped Cayco on the knees, which he fortunately understood and got his feet off the rudder pedals. Instead of landing in the first 1500 feet of the runway as was usual, we were past the 5,000 foot point when we touched down. Once again, I was grateful for the 10,000 feet of concrete we had available, and I struggled to reduce my breathing rate and regain control of myself as we taxied to our position. "Yes, Mr. Potter" my ass!

Tense Moments in the Squadron

Our VU-8 squadron experienced several accidents and incidents during my time at Roosy, including one resulting in serious injury. Several were close calls that could have ended very differently. I was among the crew aboard the P-2V in two instances where the circumstances of a routine flight turned potentially ominous. Both of these occurred on cross-country hops, the first in the first few minutes after departure, and the second on final approach after a six-hour flight to Norfolk, Virginia. All crew members were required to wear headsets during takeoff and landing, so that we could talk to each other via the onboard intercom system, and could monitor pilot communications with air traffic control.

In the first case, we were about 20 minutes out of Roosy, over the water, under the control of San Juan Center Radar Approach Control (CERAP), a combined en-route and terminal control facility. Suddenly there were two sharp reports, each accompanied by a bump that could be felt throughout the aircraft. From my position in the back of the airplane I could see into the cockpit, as the pilot and co-pilot turned towards each other with unmistakable looks of "What just happened?" on their faces. The two bumps were immediately followed by a severe vibration, and the two pilots went into action, hands flying around the cockpit, feathering the port wing reciprocating engine, shutting down the fuel flow, and firing up the auxiliary jet engines mounted on each wing. The vibration decreased, and the reassuring whine of the jets was audible to all on board.

Through my headset I heard the following exchange: "San Juan, Navy Golf Foxtrot Zero One, we just lost an engine, request vectors back to Roosevelt Roads." The controller asked, "Are you declaring an emergency?" The pilot said, "Negative, but we'd like expeditious handling to the extent feasible." We made it back to the field without further incident. Later examination revealed that the big radial engine on the port wing had "swallowed a jug," meaning that a valve stem had broken off and was creating havoc within the affected cylinder, potentially resulting in an in-flight fire. We were also lucky that the problem occurred when it did. If we had been hundreds of miles from land, we would have had to rely on the starboard reciprocating engine alone. Jet engine fuel consumption was off the charts. In routine operations, the jets were used only for takeoff and the last 30 minutes of flight before landing.

The second incident could have been far more serious. It was winter time, and we were on a ground controlled approach (GCA) to Norfolk, a procedure where the controller "talks down" the pilot. The weather was IFR, close to instrument approach minimums. As I listened to the unbroken litany of instructions from the GCA operator, it seemed that the approach was progressing normally: "On course, on glide path, five miles from touchdown, altitude should be 1,500. On course, slightly below glide path, correcting. Slightly left of course, turn right heading 283. On glide path." At a point where I estimated we were at about 1,000 feet and two minutes from touchdown, the controller's voice was interrupted by the plane commander saying to the co-pilot, who was flying the airplane, "You're awfully fast." The co-pilot replied, "I feel like I'm about to fall out of the sky." No more was said on the intercom, and we made what felt like a normal landing. Later, in the debriefing on the ground, the pilots were visibly sober, revealing that when we had broken out of the overcast, the nose attitude indicated that far from being fast, we were way slow, basically on the edge of a stall.

During a post-flight inspection, the mechanics determined that the airspeed pitot tube, a device measuring air pressure generated by the airplane's forward motion, had been partially obstructed by ice. This accounted for the erroneously high airspeed indication. An additional factor was that pitot heat, which had been selected, was not functioning, likely because in the warm weather of Puerto Rico it had not been used in a number of years. A few months later, a detailed account of our experience appeared in the Navy periodical, "Approach" that published accounts of accidents and serious incidents.

Flying Two Planes at Once

The other serious incidents experienced by VC-8 (now "Fleet Composite Squadron 8," a new designation replacing "Utility Squadron 8") all involved the two fighter jet types operated by the squadron, the Vought F-8 Crusader and the Grumman F-9 Cougar. The mission of the F-8 was to fly wing on the F-9 drone, and control it en route to the area of AFWR dedicated to fleet weapons exercises. This was a demanding operation, requiring the pilots of the single-seat F-8 to in effect fly two airplanes at once. Practice hops were scheduled daily in order to keep pilot proficiency at peak levels.

Each officer in the squadron rotated through the position of operations duty officer (ODO), whose duties were to man the desk in the officers' ready room. The ODO was responsible for radio communications with all aircraft on local hops, to update the status board regarding the maintenance status of each airplane, and generally to accept and respond to routine daily communications to the squadron. With about 40 officers available, "the duty" came around once every five or six weeks. One day when it was my turn, everything had been progressing routinely until there came the terse words, "ODO, line, Saltspray 7 just went in, the pilot's in the chute," over the "squawk box," the intercom between the maintenance crew on the flight line and the ODO desk, "Saltspray" was the call sign for all our aircraft on routine operational flights, and the numbers seven through twelve were assigned to the F-8s. The windows in the ready room provided a clear view of the departure end of Runway 6, and every man in the room could see what appeared to be a normally deployed parachute descending over the water just beyond the runway end.

Nevertheless, there was cause for concern. Lieutenant Snow was a big man, and the confines of the F-8 cockpit were decidedly narrow. Remembering my experience in the ejection seat simulator, I recognized that Lt. Snow could possibly have been injured during the ejection sequence. Moreover, a safe landing in the water was no sure thing, given the encumbrance of the pilot's flight gear and the possibility of becoming entangled in the parachute. After a moment of stunned disbelief, someone shouted, "Launch the helo!" and the helicopter pilots ran for the flight line. The parachute disappeared from view, and after several agonizingly long minutes, the helicopter lifted off. Once at the crash site, the helo pilots transmitted these reassuring words: "The pilot appears to be OK. He's in a boat. We're moving in to pick him up now." We all breathed a collective sigh of relief, believing that the rescue was complete. Lt. Snow was immediately transported to the base hospital for a full medical checkup, and it was several days before he returned to the squadron.

Only then did we learn the rest of the story. He had been fortunate to land right beside a small Puerto Rican fishing vessel, whose occupants pulled him aboard within a minute or two of his landing in the water. The boat was equipped with a sail, and Lt. Snow had not removed his parachute harness. When the helicopter approached, two things happened: the rotor wash, generating a wind force in excess of 60 knots, filled the mainsail, nearly capsizing the boat, and re-inflated the parachute, dragging Lt. Snow back into, and under, the water. As he described it, he was fighting for his life as he struggled to open the harness fasteners. Being a laid-back, good humored individual, he described the whole experience with a smile on his face, saying his only complaint was a sore butt. In the aftermath of the accident, a training film was shown to the whole squadron, emphasizing the critical importance of the principle that "when the fire goes out, you go out." Lt. Snow had experienced a flame-out at about 1500 feet, and without power the F-8 sank like a rock. He only had seconds to recognize the situation, get positioned, and pull the ejector. When the film showed a fighter jet instrument panel with the fuel flow and EPR gauges falling to zero following a flame-out, Lt. Snow got a good laugh when he called out, "Yep, that's what it looks like."

Another incident involving the F-8 occurred during a routine training flight by our new commanding officer, Commander Geer. As he prepared for landing, he experienced a major mechanical malfunction. The F-8 was equipped with a pivoting wing whose leading edge could be raised seven degrees above its normal position, generating more lift without an unacceptably high nose attitude during landing. The wing also had hydraulically controlled slats, or "droops," on the leading edge. When Commander Geer raised the wing and deployed the slats, the droop actuators failed. The slipstream pressure folded the slats back under the wing, breaking them off, and causing them to slice into the fuselage and the main fuel tank. Commander Geer immediately added power, and the airplane became stable. But the higher power setting, in conjunction with the fuel loss, meant that there was very little time before he would need to decide to land or eject.

After Commander Geer reported his situation, several other F-8 pilots gathered around the ready room radio, and discussed the options. Some felt that ejection was the safest course; others believed that a safe landing could be made. After a brief discussion, Commander Geer elected to attempt a landing even though there was considerable risk. The slowest airspeed at which the aircraft remained controllable was about 230 knots, 70 or 80 knots above the F-8's normal landing speed. It would have to be an arrested landing, and there was some doubt as to whether the tail hook would hold at such a landing speed. Additionally, it was all but certain that the tires would blow, and if the tail hook did fail, the pilot would have essentially no braking capability. The crash crew stationed themselves alongside the runway, and we all watched the approach from the flight line. Even those of us who were not F-8 pilots could see that this was going to be an extremely "hot" landing.

As the airplane touched down, we saw two puffs of smoke from the blown tires of the main landing gear. We held our collective breath as the tail hook hit the wire, and to our relief the aircraft immediately slowed to a stop. The crash crew went into action, spraying fire suppressant foam on the wheel rims so that the leaking fuel would not start a fire. The airplane was extensively damaged, requiring several months of repair and maintenance, but Commander Geer emerged uninjured.

Two accidents in our squadron involving the F-9 Cougar were related to malfunctions of the remotely controlled autopilot system. The first occurred on short final while the airplane was being controlled by the ground-based "Fox" cart, a mobile platform positioned to the right side of the runway about 1500 feet from the approach end. The aircraft had completed a series of "hot legs," pre-determined courses during which control of the drone was conducted from a powerful hilltop radio station. After each run, an F-8 would fly up to the drone to assess any damage done by shipboard anti-aircraft artillery. If there was only slight damage, or none at all, and the airplane remained controllable, it would be brought back to base at the end of the exercise. The approaches were always made to Runway 24, over the water, as the approach to Runway 6 was over populated areas of the naval station. On the day in question, there was a group of field tents occupied by a marine battalion adjacent to a crossing runway, along with a flight line of several F-4 Phantom fighter jets. The marines were in the middle of an extended exercise simulating deployment to an area with a temporary runway and no other facilities. When the crew of the "Fox" cart sighted the undamaged drone about five miles out, they took over control and began the approach procedure. As the airplane reached the runway threshold, the autopilot link failed. The nose pitched up, precipitating a stall and a rapid roll to the left. In the space of about three seconds the operation turned from routine to catastrophic, resulting in a fiery crash into the marine flight line, and taking out two of the F-4s. Bits of debris flew into the tent area, but fortunately the marines were elsewhere on maneuvers.

It was the only time during my tour of duty that an F-9 drone on an operational run was lost other than to weapons damage from a ship or combat air group. While an accident like this was always bad news, this one occurred at a particularly inopportune time because the exercise was being monitored by the San Juan admiral whose command included VC-8. The admiral was a "black shoe"—a surface ship officer not well versed in aviation operations. Although we had conducted many exercises with the F-9 that ended routinely, the admiral was unimpressed, declaring unsmilingly, "It looks like this operation needs some work." He also did not appreciate the fact that the "Fox" cart crew, observing that they had lost control of the airplane, had run for their lives in case the aircraft rolled right instead of left. It was at least six months before we conducted another F-9 exercise.

The other incident involving the Cougar was a freak accident that occurred on the ground, and nearly cost a young lieutenant his life. The airplane was positioned on an unoccupied portion of the ramp with the nose oriented at right angles to the runway. The pilot's seat had been replaced with a tank containing the fluid used to generate smoke during drone exercises. The tank was configured in the approximate shape of a pilot seat, but had no cushioning or seat belts, since the only reason a pilot needed to be in the airplane was when it was stationary, undergoing checks of the autopilot system, as was the case on the day in question. The young officer was seated on the smoke tank wearing no helmet or other flight gear, with the cockpit canopy open, the engine running, and the brakes applied.

As he was checking the various functions of the autopilot, the brakes suddenly released and the throttle advanced to full power. As the airplane accelerated across the ramp, the pilot attempted to throttle back both manually and using the autopilot controls, but the autopilot had locked the throttle and brakes in place, and the lieutenant didn't have time to activate the master disconnect switch. Within a few seconds the aircraft crossed the taxiway and the active runway, crashing through the underbrush on the far side. With the cockpit located in the extreme nose, and the full weight of the engine directly behind it, the F-9 offered little pilot protection in a head-on collision with anything solid. In addition, there was a strong likelihood of fire if the fuel tank were ruptured. The control tower sent an alert and the crash crew raced to the accident site. The airplane had come to a stop and had not broken up, but heat from the jet blast had ignited a substantial fire in the dry vegetation bordering the runway, and the engine was still operating at full power. The crash crew reported that the pilot was not in the aircraft. There were some tense moments until the crash crew did locate the pilot, injured and unconscious, some distance behind the aircraft. He was immediately transported to the base hospital, and remained there for about two weeks.

In the aftermath of the accident, and with the pilot unavailable for comment, there was considerable speculation about why the malfunction occurred. Why had not the master disconnect function or the fuel cut-off capability been utilized? Was the decision to leave the aircraft correct, given that the airplane had held together? Ultimately, the pilot was absolved of any negligence or misjudgment, given the suddenness of the occurrence and the short period of time available in which to take action. Later examination of the wreckage indicated that the airplane had come to an abrupt stop, meaning that if he had stayed in the cockpit unsecured by a seat belt and shoulder harness, he might have been severely injured or killed. When he returned to the squadron, his head heavily bandaged, he recounted his actions as the incident was developing: "I saw 60 knots and accelerating on the airspeed indicator, and I dived over the side. The next thing I knew I woke up in the hospital." It was a near thing, but most of us believed we could not have made a better decision if we had been in his place.

Airline Stars in My Eyes

As my tour of duty at U. S. Naval Station Roosevelt Roads drew to a close, I began feeling out the prospects of becoming an airline pilot. I applied to all the major U. S. carriers, and to a few smaller companies that provided air taxi or commuter service. In this initial round, the form letters I received all contained versions of the following statements:

"Dear Mr. Potter, Thank you for your interest in [XYZ] Airlines. At the present time the minimum requirements for pilot applicants include certification as a commercial pilot with instrument rating and 1,000 hours pilot in command experience in large multi-engine aircraft. Please keep us informed of your status so that we may contact you in the future in the event our requirements should change."

It was pretty clear that my 350 hours of flight time in single-engine Cessnas did not impress anyone in the airline personnel departments. Nevertheless, I believed that the quest was not hopeless, based in part on the experience of my brother Hop ("Red Dog Leader") who, by this time, had been hired by Eastern. On the date he was hired, his logbook showed 280 hours of single-engine time and endorsements as an instrument-rated commercial pilot. But he had had a most fortunate "golden" first interview with Eastern, conducted by an individual not much older than himself, with a similar educational and social background. They had hit it off, setting the stage for the next phase—an interview with Eastern's chief pilot. As he walked into the chief pilot's office, my brother encountered an entirely different atmosphere. The man behind the desk was grey-haired, in his late 50s, and gave every appearance of being overworked and under pressure. There was a stack of pilot applications in front of him and an ashtray overflowing with cigarette butts. His greeting was, "280 hours, huh? I can't believe what they're sending me. You think you can fly a transport airplane?" The "interview" was basically a monologue lamenting the poverty of experience in the pilot applicant pool. My brother felt that he had reached the end of the line, but incredibly, the session ended with a big sigh from the chief pilot and instructions to report for the physical exam. Despite his minimal experience, Hop went on to a full career with Eastern, eventually becoming a 727 captain before Eastern folded its wings in 1991.

The lesson for me was that if you could get your foot in the door, and get the right kind of support within the company, you could be offered a job without meeting the officially required qualifications. Still, there was one more piece of the puzzle that I realized I had to put in place—the instrument rating. In Puerto Rico there were few if any opportunities to train for the instrument check ride. Moreover, the Navy flying club airplanes did not meet the FAR requirements relating to inspection and calibration of the instruments utilized in IFR operations. Since an applicant needed a minimum of 40 hours instructed instrument time, including an IFR cross country flight of at least 250 miles, I did not see any way of qualifying for the rating while on full-time duty at the squadron.

By good fortune, I had accumulated enough earned leave that I was able to travel back to the States for two weeks of training with Burnside-Ott, a large, well staffed, and well equipped flight school based at Opa-locka, the site of my first brush with severe weather. Burnside-Ott had a fleet of Cessna 150s and 172s numbering more than 60 aircraft. The whole operation was professionally run, from scheduling to billing, ground school, simulator instruction, and actual IFR flying. From day one and on each day thereafter I spent a minimum of one hour in class, one hour in the simulator, and four hours in the airplane divided between one hop in the morning and one in the afternoon. These days were long and exhausting, but I had the bit in my teeth, and I hung in there. Toward the end of the second week I had logged the requisite hours, received the needed endorsements from my instructor, and passed the written examination. The final two steps, as in the private, commercial, and instructor pilot certifications, were an oral exam and the check ride itself.

Despite the long hours and hard work, my experience with the Burnside-Ott people had been uniformly positive. My instructor had been supportive throughout, assuring me that I would have no problem with either the oral exam or the flight check. But when I walked into the office of the examiner, I sensed a distinct change in the atmosphere. The man had a dour expression on his face, and without a greeting or preamble of any kind ordered me to sit down. I had scarcely settled into place when he began peppering me with questions, covering definitions of IFR terminology, regulations, and aircraft and pilot requirements for instrument flying. I felt that I had given the correct answer to each question, but at one point he threw up his hands in apparent exasperation, saying, "Well, that's about enough of this. You need to go back to the books." He had never told me where I had made errors in my responses, and I was at a complete loss as to how to respond. I assumed that this was the end of the process for now, but surprisingly he said we would go out to the flight line, "If you think you can pass a check ride." My confidence at this point was understandably not at its highest, but I had only a few more days available, and I calculated that if I did pass the check ride that would leave only the oral exam, which I could perhaps retake back in Puerto Rico.

We took off, and soon I was under the hood with the examiner playing the role of air traffic control, issuing instructions and communicating with ATC for the several instrument approach procedures we were to fly. At one point during the air work portion, he suddenly grabbed the yoke and shouted, "I've got it!" I immediately released the controls and the examiner pushed the nose over sharply as negative g's lifted charts and pencils towards the cabin roof. I raised my head just enough to look through a small portion of the windscreen and saw a huge white and blue form flash by in an instant, seemingly not more than twenty feet above us. At the same time there was a short but audible roar that I recognized as being the sound of multiple large radial engines, and a sharp bump of turbulence. The whole encounter lasted only about five seconds, and the examiner, without comment, leveled off and told me to take the controls. After a few more maneuvers, we landed at Opa-locka and taxied back to the ramp. As we taxied in we passed a row of Lockheed Super Constellations, recently retired from service with Eastern Airlines, awaiting sale to the highest bidder—likely countries in Central and South America. The blue and white color scheme was the one I had seen on the aircraft with which we had experienced a near miss during the check ride.

The examiner still had the same expression on his face that I had seen when I first entered his office. He took my logbook and began writing in it without saying a word. When he handed it back, it bore the notation that I had successfully passed the instrument flight check. With that I was done for the day, but without any understanding of what it meant to have passed the flight portion but not the oral for the instrument rating. I quickly found my instructor, and gave him a synopsis of my experience with the examiner, including the near miss with the Eastern Connie. My instructor's take regarding the oral was, "Yeah, he's like that. Don't worry, I'll get you a retake with a different examiner." Then he added, "I'm sure you did fine on the check ride, but that guy is famous for busting people. The close call with the other airplane may have helped you out since he probably didn't want you reporting the event to anybody."

I wasn't sure how soon I would be able to re-take the oral, but on the next day I was introduced to another examiner, younger than the first, who exhibited the upbeat, positive approach I had come to expect from the Burnside-Ott personnel. My instructor had slipped me the information that "Mike" was much more focused on IFR procedures than certification and inspection standards, and that there was a specific airway segment of the local low altitude airways chart that he liked to use in questioning an applicant. I looked the chart over carefully beforehand (and reviewed everything I had studied for the first go around, "just in case," finding nothing indicating that my earlier answers had been incorrect). Sure enough, after a pleasant greeting, Mike went immediately to the designated portion of the chart, and I sailed through his questions easily. At the conclusion, he said, "I don't see what the problem was. You know this stuff cold."

End of the Tour

Back at Roosy for my final two months of active duty service, I went into high gear updating my applications to the airlines, showing more total flight time and my recent certification as an instrument-rated pilot. In due course, the responses started coming in: "Dear Mr. Potter, Thank you for your interest in (XYZ) Airlines. At the present time the minimum qualifications for pilot applicants are…" etc., etc. It was becoming increasingly apparent that there would be no seamless transition from active duty naval officer to civilian airline pilot, and it was high time to consider a "Plan B." I learned that the FAA, after a five-year freeze on hiring air traffic controllers, was now on an aggressive recruitment campaign, even advertising the profession through television commercials. It occurred to me that air traffic control experience might be a useful credential to include in my airline applications, and I resolved to look into this opportunity as soon as I was transferred back stateside. In the meantime, I continued to work through my second-tier preferences, sending out resume updates, and continuing to receive the same monotonous form letters.

About a month before my tour of duty with VC-8 was due to end, my commanding officer called me into his office to make the obligatory pitch that I should stay in the Navy. The naval mission would be seriously compromised without my services, and the satisfactions and benefits of a military career far exceeded any realistic expectations in civilian life, he assured me. I had certainly enjoyed my time with the squadron, and I recognized the benefits of being in a shore-based organization that did not have a combat mission. I told my CO as much, saying that if I could spend the next 20 years at Roosevelt Roads, I would seriously consider remaining on active duty. As a gung-ho careerist, he informed me in serious tones that that would not be possible, and that my next assignment would be sea duty, a prerequisite to career advancement.

Any doubts I may have harbored about returning to civilian life had been swept away about a year earlier by my one exposure to sea duty. I had spent four days aboard a destroyer escort (DE) as a liaison officer while the ship was conducting exercises with VC-8's F-9 drone targets. The black shoe Navy was a far cry from the relaxed, egalitarian society enjoyed by us brown shoes. At every turn, the CO and XO of the ship were gigging the men about their shoe shine, brass polish, haircut, or the "Irish pennant" of an insufficiently tucked in shirt tail.

At one point, I came indirectly into the skipper's line of fire. My squadron mates who were flying the F-8s and remote controlling the drones were on a tactical frequency that was piped through speakers all over the ship, and they made some good-humored, derisive remarks about "a sorry looking j.g. with brown shoes looking kind of seasick." After the second or third such transmission, the destroyer captain announced in a loud voice, "I better not hear any of my people talking that kind of crap on the radio." There was no air conditioning on the old DE (this was August in the Caribbean), the desalination gear was offline so that there was no fresh water for showers, and the temperature below decks in the sleeping quarters was above 110 degrees. I had only brought one extra uniform aboard, and after the second day both of mine were wrinkled and filthy. I wondered if the ship's captain would target me for my unsquared-away appearance. Compounding all of these negatives was the food. Nothing fresh was served. Milk, eggs, potatoes and other staples were reconstituted from dried form, and even the drinking water had a flat, tinny taste. When I left the ship at the conclusion of the exercise, I was exhausted, queasy, and dehydrated. When I returned to my air-conditioned quarters and regular food prepared in a kitchen, I made a silent promise that I would never, ever again complain about duty at Roosy.

Convinced that I did not intend to make a career of the Navy, my CO, who was a fair minded individual, shook my hand and wished me well in my future endeavors, clearing the way for the many preparations incidental to a permanent transfer and release to the inactive reserves. At some point during this period, I noticed a sensation of blockage in my right ear. Ear blocks, which can result when pressure in the Eustachian tubes does not equalize with ambient air pressure after a descent from altitude, were not all that uncommon among pilots and aircrew, and generally resolved themselves in a day or two. But after more than a week I was still experiencing the same sensation, and made a trip to the flight surgeon for an examination that revealed very little. He told me that it did not appear to be a routine ear block, and that I should consult a specialist when I returned stateside. The condition was not severe, and I shrugged it off for now, having no inkling that this was the beginning of a problem I would deal with for the rest of my life.

Mustering Out

In the first week of January 1968, I boarded a Pan American Boeing 707 from San Juan to Miami, and transferred to an air taxi for the short hop to Key West. I was assigned to the Key West Naval Air Station for administrative processing prior to my release from active duty. This process would normally have taken only a few days, but as it was unfolding, questions about the ear block surfaced. Since it had occurred while I was on active duty, there was a chance it could be classified as a service-connected disability, meaning that the Navy would have to foot the bill for whatever corrective action was needed. I was sent to Homestead Air Force Base in Miami, where there was a fully equipped hospital, for testing, and where a determination was made that surgery was probably indicated. The flight surgeon at Homestead said that I would be eligible for treatment at the VA hospital, but he recommended seeing an established otolaryngologist in a civilian hospital.

As I was mulling over these choices, several weeks went by, during which time two events occurred that threatened to delay my out-processing, perhaps even returning me to an active duty squadron. The first of these was the capture of the USS Pueblo by North Korean naval forces in an area that the Koreans considered territorial waters. The Pueblo was a surveillance ship, passively collecting electronic transmissions from radio and radar sources. The United States claimed that the seizure of the ship occurred outside the territorial limit as defined by international law, saying that the Koreans had committed an act of war. U.S. military alert levels were increased, and we who were about to be discharged were left wondering whether our active duty tours would be extended.

By the end of the month, it appeared that we would be released on schedule, but on January 30, the North Vietnamese attacked Saigon, bringing the battle to the very gates of the American embassy. The Tet offensive, as the attack came to be known, threw into serious question the entire American military and political strategy in Vietnam, and those of us waiting to be transferred to "the First CivDiv" (First Civilian Division) feared again that we might be looking at a longer military career.

It took several more weeks of administrative action to clear the way for my discharge, but on February 13, one day shy of the four-year anniversary of my graduation from Pre-Flight, I left the base for the last time, wearing civilian clothes and holding the documents assigning me to the inactive reserve. Despite the fact that I had looked forward eagerly to this day, it was a little unsettling to realize that I was no longer part of any organization, and that I had no income nor any job prospects. Fortunately for me, my father, who had been discharged from the Navy after World War II under circumstances not unlike my own, was living in Miami and agreed to give me temporary lodging. While this hospitality was more than welcome, I didn't sleep too well that first night as I considered my uncertain future.

3. Becoming a Controller

The next day I awoke early, charged up and ready to make some aggressive moves toward charting a future course. I still had my stack of airline applications, and through my brother I had learned the name of the individual in Eastern's corporate offices who was the key initial contact for a pilot applicant. The airline's headquarters were located adjacent to Miami International Airport, so that it would be easy to meet with him if he agreed. He took my telephone call, and we had a pleasant conversation that basically went nowhere, concluding with the same advice contained in the rejection letters, that I should keep my resume updated in the event Eastern's hiring criteria should change.

I hung up the phone, picked up the telephone directory, and searched under U.S. Government for listings under the Federal Aviation Administration. There were listings for FAA headquarters (Washington D.C.) and FAA Southern Region (Atlanta, Georgia), with a sub-listing entitled "Miami Area Office" with a local number and address at the southeast corner of Miami International, less than a mile from Eastern's ramp and hangars. I dialed the number and explained to the lady who answered that I was interested in learning about a career in air traffic control.

As I learned through later experience with the government bureaucracy, the immediate and informative response I got was a happy exception to the norm. In tones upbeat and personable she told me, "Yes sir, we can help you with that. The person you need to talk to is Mr. Carmichael. If you will wait just a moment, I will connect you with him." After a few moments I was talking to Dave Carmichael, a personnel specialist who had begun his FAA career as a controller at Miami Air Route Traffic Control Center (ARTCC). He told me that his schedule was open, and we agreed to meet the next day. Suddenly, the future was looking a lot brighter.

When I met with Dave the next day, he was solicitous, interested, and entirely attentive to my summation of experience as a pilot and military officer, interjecting comments like, "That's great background" and "That will really help you in the ATC field." He then proceeded to walk me through the different air traffic controller options and the required steps leading to selection for training in the field. He explained that there were three different branches (options) of air traffic control: flight service, en route, and tower/ terminal. I was at least minimally aware of the difference between these functions, having interacted with each of them at different times on both training and solo flights, as well as having monitored communications during my 800 hours of air crew time on military missions.

Flight Service was basically a clearinghouse for flight plans, weather reports and forecasts, Notices to Airmen (NOTAMS), and other information relating to airports and navigational facilities. The one function provided by Flight Service that actually directed pilot navigation was direction-finding guidance. From a pilot's radio transmissions, a Flight Service operator could determine the bearing of the aircraft and direct it to the airport. This kept many pilots who were lost or low on fuel from coming to grief. It worked well in sparsely populated areas, but because it provided only a straight line from point A to point B, it could cause a pilot to fly through a prohibited area or the airport traffic area of a different airport at locations near large population centers. There were also cases where Flight Service provided airport advisory service at fields that were either uncontrolled or where the control tower did not operate 24 hours a day. In these circumstances, Flight Service would simply relay general traffic information to pilots who were approaching or departing from the airport.

The en route function was carried out in the continental United States by 20 air route traffic control centers, each responsible for large geographical areas at all navigational altitudes. To qualify at a center, a trainee had to master a great deal of information relating to airway structure, navaid service volumes (the range at which a navaid could provide reliable reception and guidance), letter of agreement provisions with adjacent centers or with tower/ approach control facilities within the applicable area, and even airport information at locations where transfer of control occurred directly between the en route facility and a control tower. The centers were divided into areas, and typically the controllers became qualified in only one or two areas rather than being required to learn the information for the entire facility. Some low-altitude sectors demanded a dynamic tactical form of control, but once an aircraft reached typical en route altitudes (generally above 10,000 or 12,000 feet), the operation was much more strategic. A typical center sector would be staffed by three specialists: an "A" man, whose duty it was to keep flight data (speeds, altitudes, routings) up to date; a "D" man, whose function was to identify and resolve potential conflicts based on the flight data (sometimes with a lead time of an hour or more); and a radar controller to monitor the operation and apply tactical resolutions as necessary.

The third option, terminal control, came in two flavors. The most basic was a VFR tower, responsible for takeoffs, landings, and aircraft ground movements. The airport traffic area was defined as a five nautical mile circle around the airport from the surface to 3,000 feet. By FAR, a pilot was required to establish two-way communication with the tower before entering this area. With the exception of minimum runway separation between two arrivals, two departures, or a departure and an arrival there were no separation standards for which a VFR tower was responsible, the sequencing within the airport traffic area being wholly dependent on traffic information and the ability of the pilots to see and be seen. This meant that when the weather was below VFR minimums, tower operations were shut down except for IFR flights controlled by a center or an approach control (and limited special VFR operations, about which more later).

The other type of terminal facilities were approach controls, operated either as non-radar facilities or terminal radar approach controls (TRACONs). These were placed in small (by en route standards) areas delegated by the responsible centers for air traffic control services at airports with a volume of IFR operations too high to be handled efficiently using en route procedures. The maximum range of terminal radar equipment was 60 miles, setting an absolute limit on the square mileage and configuration of TRACON airspace. The radar update rate was three times faster than in the center, separation standards were tighter, and the area displayed on a terminal scope was small scale, providing greatly enhanced detail.

In most radar approach control areas there was full coverage, meaning that non-radar separation need not be applied. Since the longest a high-performance aircraft would be under terminal control between the airport and the center boundary was about seven or eight minutes, the operation was almost exclusively tactical. While the amount of information a controller had to learn was usually less than what was required of a trainee in the center, at locations where a tower and approach control were co-located, each specialist was expected to check out through all tower and approach control positions. There were several levels of approach control facilities, as determined by the number of aircraft handled annually. The highest level (level 5) facilities were of course established at major airports near large cities.

We spent more than an hour in this discussion, before I asked Dave about the actual application process for an air traffic controller position, adding several questions about pay and benefits. He said the first step was to take a generic civil service test. These examinations were scheduled periodically in selected cities throughout the country. After passing the examination, an applicant would be subject to an FBI background check. Then there would be a face-to-face interview with FAA officials, and finally a medical and psychological profile exam. If the candidate met all of these requirements successfully, he would be placed on a list of eligibles based on his expressed preferences as to area of assignment. Dave pointed out that the more restrictive these preferences were, the longer it could take to be selected.

At this point I was thinking, "Well, first things first," and asked what I needed to do to take the civil service test. Dave handed me a simple three by five postcard that asked for some identification and contact information, based on which I would be notified by mail of the next scheduled exam in the Miami area. He also advised me to prepare for the exam by studying one of several publications available for that purpose. At the conclusion of the meeting, Dave had provided me with over two hours of his undivided attention, and a wealth of useful information.

Only later did I realize how fortunate I had been in this first encounter with the government bureaucracy. Most of my later interactions with other officials were exercises in frustration, incomplete information, and the fine art of bureaucratic blow off.

Getting the Ball Rolling

I left the Area Office, mailed the postcard, and headed for the nearest bookstore, where I bought a book with the title, "Preparing for the Civil Service Examination." It was dry, uninteresting reading, but did provide examples of the type questions one could expect to encounter on the test. Some were mathematical, others were verbal analogies or spatial perception exercises. I found myself referring to the material less and less frequently as the days passed, recognizing that the exam was fundamentally an aptitude test, similar in some ways to the SATs I had taken for college admission.

About three weeks later, in what I later recognized as lightning speed, I received notification of the date, time and place of the next civil service examination, to be given at the federal building in downtown Miami. When I arrived on the appointed day, I was ushered into a utilitarian room that had seen its better days, by a low-level civil service employee straight from central casting. His shirt was a white drip-dry, his clip-on tie, pants and shoes were black, his hair and complexion grey. No greeting or welcome of any kind, only the automaton-like repetition, as he handed each applicant a sign-in sheet, of "Find your name and sign beside it." We took our seats, and the proctor began a monotonous drone, informing us that the test would be given in timed segments. No questions would be allowed after the start of a segment, and there would be no opportunity to return to that section of the test once time had expired. Were there any questions? There was a ripple of laughter after we had opened our booklets to the first section and the proctor announced, "When I say start, start. Start."

At length we reached the final phase of the testing. I was feeling reasonably confident, having completed the prior segments within the allotted times, and having had plenty of experience with multiple choice questions on any number of tests in the Navy. It was clear that this last round was going to be different, as the proctor handed out a supplemental sheet with perhaps 15 or 20 numbered lines of letters, numbers and random symbols. Each line was 10 or 12 characters long. There were no questions printed on the sheet, but the explanation was soon forthcoming. In the same minimally inflected monotone, the proctor explained that this part of the exam was to test our ability to understand, process, and respond correctly to spoken information. Each instruction would be identified by the line number to which it referred, and would be given twice with a 10-second pause between readings. There would be a 15-second pause before the instructions for the next line were given. Our responses were to be recorded using our number two pencils on the same multiple choice answer sheet we had used on the earlier portions of the exam, and there was only one correct answer per line. Once again, there would be no questions permitted after the exercise began, nor any opportunity to review our answers after the last set of instructions. Were there any questions? As I looked around the room, I could see expressions of bafflement and consternation on many faces, and I was by no means sure of what to expect myself, but no questions were asked.

The proctor began, with each succeeding set of instructions more complex than the one preceding it:

"Line 1: If the fourth character in the sequence is a letter of the alphabet, mark A. If not, mark B."

"Line 2: If there are three consecutive numbers in the sequence, mark B. If not, mark A."

"Line 3: If the third and sixth characters are the same, mark C. If not, mark B."

"Line 4: If there are more letters than numbers in the sequence, mark B, unless the last character in the line is a triangle, in which case mark A."

"Line 5: If the sum of any two numbers bracketed by letters is ten or more, mark D. If the sum of any two numbers bracketed by letters is less than 10, mark B, unless the second of the two numbers is smaller than the first, in which case mark C."

There followed at least ten additional even more convoluted instructions, and beginning at about number four there began to be heard gasps of dismay throughout the room. Several people raised their hands, which of course the proctor ignored, sticking rigorously to the instruction timetable laid out in advance. I did my best to blank out the distractions, and to at least mark an answer for each lined item. At no time did I feel that I was reduced to a wild guess, but somewhere in my peripheral awareness

I realized that many of the applicants were doing just that, or had simply laid their pencils down, having totally given up on the exercise.

Somehow I had recognized that part of the key to these responses was eliminating extraneous information (for example, in line four there was no option for the case where there were more numbers than letters or an equal number of each, meaning that if the last character was a triangle, A was the answer. If not, B was the answer without having to count letters and numbers. In line 5, either every pair of numbers bracketed by letters had to total ten or more, or every pair had to total less than ten. In the first case, if any pair totaled more than ten, D was the answer. In the second case, you had to see if any of the pairs had a lower second number to choose between B and C.)

As our group exited the room, there was considerable complaining about the exam, especially the last section, which some people believed was not adequately explained in the pre-exercise briefing, or they believed that many of the per-line instructions did not give enough information to permit a valid answer. I heard an admittedly smug little voice in my head saying, "You missed the part about there being only one answer per line." For myself, I was feeling that I had certainly exceeded the minimum 70 percent passing score, and perhaps had done significantly better because I would get a five-point veterans preference bonus based on my military service.

When I received my results about two weeks later, I saw that my passing margin was not as comfortable as I had imagined. Furthermore, as the enclosed materials explained, the veterans' preference was only applicable after you achieved at least the minimum passing score, and could not be used to convert a grade from failing to passing. Nevertheless, with my combined score of 78 percent, I felt that the first hurdle had been cleared. As Dave Carmichael had explained to me, the FAA did not rank candidates based on the civil service exam. That came only after completion of the four-month training course at the FAA Academy in Oklahoma City, the last stop before assignment to a facility. Feeling buoyed by the successful accomplishment of this first step, I contacted Dave to find out what the next step would be and whether I needed to do anything to make it happen. As I had come to expect, Dave once again exceeded expectations by telling me I could either wait until the FAA and the FBI got their heads together and sent me the forms for the background check, or I could come to his office, complete the forms with his help, and he would see that they ended up in the right hands. No room for debate there, I figured, and by the end of the next day the forms were on their way.

Final Steps

Sometime in April I received notification that I had passed the background check. Next on the list was the FAA interview, which Dave assured me at this point would be a purely pro forma exercise. Nevertheless, I had never really been interviewed for a job, as the process of signing up with the Navy involved person-to-person contact at only three points—the recruiting booth, the physical exam, and the swearing-in ceremony. On the day of the interview, I tried to dress as I imagined an air traffic controller would: a short sleeved shirt and tie, dark trousers, matching socks and lace-up Thom McCann's (NOT wing-toe). I reminded myself of Dave's encouragement, and of the fact that compared to those of many applicants my credentials were pretty strong. (The minimum requirement at the time was "previous full-time employment in any job or occupation over a continuous two-year period", or something similar.) Many controllers had not completed high school, relying on their experience in military ATC facilities as a basis for consideration. Some had no pilot experience, and had formerly been school teachers, police officers, shoe salesmen, or been otherwise employed in fields unrelated to aviation.

As it turned out, my concerns were misplaced. The interview was conducted by a panel of supervisors and staff at Miami ARTCC, and they of course had in front of them the entirety of the documentation thus far generated in the process of evaluating my application. Within the first few minutes they asked several questions that amounted to, "Why does a guy with a four-year college degree want this job?" I of course was not about to reveal my master plan of collecting the ATC credential in the hope of parlaying it into an airline pilot position, but instead waxed rhapsodic about my love of flying and deep interest in anything and everything connected with aviation.

Through my pilot experience, I had come to have great respect for air traffic controllers and the incredible job they did. The panel did not seem to react, either positively or negatively, to this line of bull, I mean, heartfelt sincerity, but eventually moved on to other things. Could I think in three dimensions? Did I work well under pressure? Was I a team player? Why did I think I would make a good air traffic controller? There were no major curve balls, and I left under the impression that I had acquitted myself well enough. The one thing that bothered me was that none of the panel members had talked up the profession, or given any indication that they loved the job or were proud of what they did.

Within a few days I received a call from Dave, saying that I had passed the interview and that the next step was the physical exam and psychological profile. At this point I had a decision to make, as the ear block and attendant slight hearing loss had not changed. Should I mention this up front, or take my chances on the exam? My concern was that if this condition were reflected in my official record, it could be a show-stopper for a potential career in both flying and air traffic control. At length I decided to rely on Dave's judgment, laying out the facts, including the possibility of surgery, and asking him what he thought was the wisest course of action. He told me that the standards for air traffic controllers were similar to those of the second-class medical for pilots, meaning that there was some leeway for both hearing and vision. I already knew that for the airline transport rating, the certificate held by all airline pilots, the requirement was a first-class medical, where very little leeway existed. Dave suggested that I look into the surgical option, as it might eliminate any questions about medical qualification. He also pointed out that I would have to acknowledge this treatment, if I received it. So, I decided to go ahead and have the surgery, but it did not seem to appreciably change my condition.

The medical examination itself went without a hitch, and no issue was made of the surgery or of the results from the audiology portion, although a comparison of the graphs between my right and left ears showed a few decibels of loss on the right side. Next came the psych exam, called the 16-pf test (it purportedly measured 16 personality factors that had to fall within the limits defined by the test, and that supposedly indicated whether a person had the right kind of personality for the controller job). There was no way to prepare for the 16-pf, and while I was not worried about my ability to pass it, I did wonder what the theoretical ideal personality of an air traffic controller was. I decided that I would take the test honestly, that is, answering as truthfully as I could, and then if time permitted, go back and attempt to "psych out" what the examiners were trying to determine in each question. In most cases, it was an either/ or choice:

"Would you rather play a game of touch football with friends, or read a good book?" (Now let's see, is this about my willingness to be a team player, or my appreciation for the intellectual side of life? Or is it more general, trying to place me on the introvert/ extrovert scale? I'll go with the football game—manly, extroverted, just what is needed in a tough job.)

"When you are confronted with a problem, do you prefer to rely on your own knowledge and judgments, or to seek the advice of someone you trust?" (Do you have an outsized ego, or do you lack confidence in yourself? Hmm, you can't lack confidence in yourself either in the cockpit or the controller's chair—I'll go with the big ego.)

"Do you find it difficult to apologize to someone even when you have clearly been in the wrong?" (Are you too insecure to apologize, or are you "always right" regardless of facts or circumstances? I'll go with "no" on this one, I think it takes a strong person to own up to his mistakes.)

Later in my career, new applicants would ask me what kind of questions were on the 16-pf. I generally gave the following answer: "Oh, you know, the usual, like would you rather grab a six pack and hit the beach with your girlfriend or go to church with your grandmother." Most people laughed it off, but occasionally someone would ask me in all seriousness what the right answer was. In those cases I would say that there were no right or wrong answers on the test, but privately I believed that someone who needed to ask that question might not have the personality to be a controller.

What Have I Gotten Myself Into?

At this point, it was just a question of waiting to be selected from the list of eligible candidates. There had been no notice of having passed the 16-pf test, but I realized when Dave asked me for my preferences as to location that the last hurdle had been cleared. I had listed Florida as my first choice, picturing assignment to a facility in the Miami area, utterly failing to recognize that there were 500 miles between Key West and Tallahassee. This was brought home to me in fairly short order when I received a call from Dave about two weeks later. In his characteristically upbeat way, he informed me that I had been selected at Jacksonville ARTCC, with a reporting date less than a month away.

Once again, as I later came to understand, Dave saved me from possibly forfeiting my opportunity for a career in air traffic control, when I answered that I wanted to be in South Florida. (Jacksonville center was located north of the city, in a rural area, close to the Georgia state line). He told me that if an applicant refused an offer within his stated area of preference, the FAA might simply remove him from the candidate list, with no guarantee that he would be considered again even if he chose to repeat the application process. This was a moment that would define my entire future, as I tried to decide how to respond.

Before I could speak, Dave said, "I'll tell you what. I will just put this offer in the drawer, and if I am asked why you haven't responded, I will say that I have been temporarily unable to contact you. Let's give it a couple of weeks and see if any other opportunities open up." The likelihood of such individual and preferential treatment within the government bureaucracy was vanishingly small. Dave had done me the biggest favor of my life, and sure enough, within a few days I got another phone call in which he informed me that I had been selected at the Miami International Airport control tower, where I was to report for duty to the chief controller on August 26, 1968.

I felt a great sense of relief upon receiving this notification. Unfortunately, I had been reading author Arthur Hailey's bestseller "Airport," in which the main air traffic controller was depicted as a chain-smoking, hard-drinking individual, under immense pressure every day on the job, suffering from ulcers, and old beyond his years. I later discovered that the pressures of the job, while real, had been dramatically mischaracterized in the novel. But at that moment I wondered how tough it was going to be. And, although I had every intention of following through on this opportunity, there was one last long shot card in my pursuit of pilot employment.

For several months while the FAA application had been in the works, I had been working at Opa-locka airport as a line boy, pumping gas, towing airplanes to the hangar, meeting and greeting itinerant pilots, and performing other odd jobs at the behest of the boss. The pay was minimal, but many of us working the line held a far-out fantasy that one day a Learjet would taxi in and the pilot would emerge, asking "Hey, do you have your pilot ratings? I need a co-pilot for a trip up to New York and back." If I were the lucky one, I would immediately agree, and during the flight the captain would be impressed by my handling skills and knowledge of the ATC system. He would hand me an application form and go to bat for me with the aircraft owner. I would be hired and begin amassing the multi-engine jet hours needed to qualify for an airline position. The airlines would reduce their minimum hour requirement, and...as I said, it was a far-out fantasy.

As my reporting date at Miami Tower approached, I was experiencing all the emotions of any newly hired employee—excitement mixed with apprehension, as well as relief that I would once again be a member of an organization and have an income. I had little idea of what to expect, my only direct exposure to air traffic personnel having been the interview at Miami Center a couple of months earlier. Would it be rigidly formal, pseudo-military organization, or would it be more like the egalitarian culture of the Navy in VC-8?

I drove to the airport that morning dressed in a version of the same ensemble I had worn to the interview at the center, parked in the passenger parking lot (no parking garages yet in 1968) and entered the terminal. The tower was visible from the airport entrance, and seemed to be placed directly atop the airport hotel. I located a set of elevators (adjacent to another set) and pushed the button for the top floor. Upon emerging, I saw a door with a mechanical keypad, but no indication as to whether or not I was in the right place. I knocked several times, and eventually a pleasant individual, dressed in what I pictured as typical controller garb, answered the door. He said, "Oh, I think you got on the wrong elevator. Go back down to the lobby and take the one next to this one, that's the one that goes to the hotel."

Fortunately, I had brought the letter informing me of my reporting date, which I produced, saying that I was looking for the control tower. This seemed to leave the gentleman momentarily nonplussed. He studied the letter intently for several seconds, then called over his shoulder, "Hey Bob, one of the new guys is here. What should I do with him?" "Well, bring him in here, I guess," came the reply. "In here" was an office just off the hallway beyond the key padded door, and once inside, Bob introduced himself as the training officer, and the other man as a training specialist, whose name was Ron. They were immediately very cordial, asking me questions that seemed to indicate several things: they had had no advance warning of my arrival and no idea of my background and experience. It was also clear that no preparations for a "new guy" had been made. The conversation went something like this:

"So, where were you before here?"

"Well, I got out of the Navy six months ago."

"Oh, so you were a Navy controller?"

"No, I was an aircrew member."

"Well, where did you get your air traffic control experience?"

"I don't have any experience as an air traffic controller, only pilot ratings."

"Jesus, you mean they are sending you here as your first facility?"

"I guess so."

"Boy, I hope you make it here, it is going to a very long row to hoe. Well, let's see, I suppose they will start you out in the tower, is that right?"

"I haven't been briefed on the training process."

"Ok, you will probably start out on Flight Data and Clearance Delivery, so you will need to know the transponder codes and the frequencies to issue. Hey, Ron, what are those codes and frequencies for departures?"

"I think it's zero three hundred for the north bounds and a thousand for the south bounds. North departure is 128 point something, and I think south was just changed to something new"

(Then, turning to me): "Don't worry, they'll tell you all that stuff when you get up there. Let's get you a headset, and you can go into the radar room and monitor a position. Tomorrow we will figure out what kind of classroom training you will get."

This last statement was the only encouraging thing I had so far heard. I had a very unsettled feeling as I pictured myself walking up the tower steps knowing absolutely nothing, and depending on being briefed on the fly about "all that stuff." I was given a headset and escorted into the radar room, which was often called TRACON. Visions of the descriptions from Hailey's novel entered my head as I observed six men hunched over their radar displays talking in hushed tones. The room was dark, with panels of buttons for selecting frequencies, communication lines, and transponder codes located above each scope.

Ron introduced me to Jim, or "JW," his operating initials. Operating initials? What was that? After a few moments I saw that each time Jim selected a coordination line, he completed the verbal exchange by stating his operating initials, as did the controller who had answered the call. The

DAL9800	1473	MIA	MIA HEDLEY ORL CHESN BAXLY			
L/B757/E	P0720		DBN SINCA3 ATL			
393 ▮▮▮▮	370					

N793N 2	4624	MIA	+WINCO+			
PA28/A	P2240		MIA V97 PIE BKV			
486 ▮▮▮▮	80		O FRC			

EMJ753	4624	MIA	+WINCO+			
LR25/R	P2240		MIA V97 PIE BKV			
486 ▮▮▮▮	310					

GFT437	4755	MIA	+SKIPS+			
BE99/A	P2200		MIA VKS BR53V MYNN			
952 ▮▮▮▮	100					

FLIGHT PROGRESS STRIPS

This type of flight progress came into being with the advent of automation. In 1968 all the information was hand written and did not include the computer identification bar code (bottom figures in left hand block of each strip). In the first example, taking each block, top to bottom, left to right: DAL 9800 is the aircraft identification (Delta 9800); L/B757/E is the type aircraft and navigational equipment; 393 and the bar graph signify the computer identification; 1471 is the discrete transponder code; P0720 is the Greenwich mean time (Zulu time) proposed time of departure; 370 is the final altitude (37,000 feet); MIA is the departure airport; the next block is abbreviated nomenclature for the route of flight, Miami to Atlanta.

position was very busy, being located at the far end of the TRACON, and controlling southbound departures from Miami, arrivals and departures from Tamiami general aviation airport, and all traffic in and out of Homestead Air Force Base, 25 miles to the south.

At the time, during the height of the war in Vietnam, Homestead was the base for a number of fighter training squadrons as well as a fleet of

B-52 bombers belonging to the Strategic Air Command (SAC). Jim had a number of flight progress strips, narrow forms inserted into plastic holders, each representing an airplane, laid out in front of him. Each was covered with a mix of numbers and other arcane symbols, and often when Jim would make a transmission, he would add to the mix or scratch out some element of the previously entered information. He was talking rapidly, with many of the replies from the pilots "smeared" because two or more would transmit at once. When this happened, Jim had to re-issue his previous instruction. A few times, after such an occurrence, Jim would un-key his mic and let loose with a string of expletives. Two or three times I had to duck, as Jim picked up one of the flight progress strips and threw it the length of the room, calling out, "Give that to R-3!"

As I looked at the radar display, all I saw was a maze of lines and blips, and could not begin to relate Jim's control instructions to anything I was looking at. Jim was hyped up, intense, and I was getting the impression that he was an angry and mean individual. After probably 15 or 20 minutes, the activity slowed down, with only two or three aircraft on the frequency. At that point, Jim's demeanor completely changed, and he began talking to me in friendly tones. He was still speaking in the same deep, authoritative voice shared by many controllers that the rest of us referred to as "the voice of God." He did not attempt to explain the operation I had just witnessed, and at that point I couldn't think of anything to ask. In due course Ron returned to the radar room and escorted me back to the office. I was feeling pretty low, with a little voice in my head saying, "If I stay here a hundred years, I will never understand what I just saw."

New Trainees

When I reported for duty at the tower the next day, it was clear that the facility had begun gearing up for its new trainees. I met two other men who had arrived the previous day, and we were informed that for the next month or so we would be undergoing classroom training at Miami Center. Ron and Bob explained that for the previous five years the FAA had been under a hiring freeze. During that period retirements, resignations, medical disqualifications, and dismissals from the controller ranks had basically cut the controller corps in half, and the agency was now scrambling to bring the numbers back up.

Because of the long hiatus in hiring, the FAA academy, where controllers received four months of basic training and orientation, had been shut down, and was only now being brought back up to speed. Even at full capacity, the academy would have taken years to process the 8,000 or so new hires coming into the system, and so it had been determined that every facility would have to accept new employees and train them from scratch. This policy imposed an especially heavy burden on a facility like MIA, which in normal times would not accept new controllers without prior experience in less busy towers and TRACONs. So instead of a formal, four-month course of instruction, we would receive a highly accelerated one-month version conducted by training personnel at the center.

I learned very quickly that my fellow hirees had a substantial leg up on me in terms of experience. Randy Ward had been in the Air Force for 15 years, and worked at a number military towers and radar facilities, including Da Nang and Tan Son Nhut in Vietnam. In one year and perhaps more, Da Nang had racked up a traffic count higher than Chicago's O'Hare Airport, with shot-up combat aircraft flown by wounded pilots constituting a considerable portion of that count, and enemy mortars targeting the field. Timmy Timmons had had a single tour with the Navy, and had worked as a ground-control approach (GCA) operator. Randy was older, more mature and laid back, while Timmy was a high-energy, voluble hotshot. They both asked a ton of questions, exhibiting a high degree of familiarity with ATC, and using a vocabulary considerably beyond my ken.

When we reported to Miami Center the next day, we were introduced to Russ, a training specialist whose full controller career had been at the en-route center with no experience in tower or TRACON operations. It was clear that his assignment to instructing three "terminal pukes" for a month was not one that he relished, and his approach was basically to spoon feed us the information for the series of tests that we would take. I was initially concerned that Randy and Timmy would outshine me because they had received military training in ATC and had actually controlled air traffic.

As it turned out, my pilot ratings, and the subjects I had studied to earn them, put us all pretty much on an equal plane. The course covered weather, navigation, and some simple air traffic scenarios that required us to solve time-rate-distance problems and identify potential loss of

TRACON POSITIONS AT MIA IN 1968

In 1968 all the functions identified in the diagram existed and were performed on six small scopes aligned along a single wall. With the move in 1972 to a larger space most of the functions shown here were allocated to individual displays with a similar "back to back" placement of the positions. M1 M2 is a single scope for the two monitor positions utilized during the simultaneous parallel approach operation.

separation situations. Throughout the class periods, Russ would intersperse the lecture material with "observations" about the FAA in general and Miami Tower in particular. "I'll tell you guys," he once said, "You've got a bunch of bastards working over there." And, "If I won the Irish Sweepstakes, I wouldn't even bother to piss on the chief's desk, I'd hire somebody to do it for me." The comment about Miami Tower bothered me, as I pictured trying to become qualified in a busy terminal facility under the tutelage of "a bunch of bastards."

As I later discovered, what the comment really reflected was the substantial difference between en route and terminal operations. Each body of specialists believed that those who worked in their type facility were the "real" controllers, and that those in the other type were, at best, pretenders to the title of air traffic controller. There were multiple flows of air traffic between the center and the TRACON, with separation and routing requirements in place for each. As Russ put it, "We go round and round with that tower. They always fudge on the in-trail restrictions for the departures, but won't take the arrivals unless the separation is exact." Miami Tower personnel had the same complaint about the center operation.

I soon fell into a familiar pattern of stopping each day on the way to the center to buy a hoagie for lunch at a nearby delicatessen ($1.50 for a foot-long with the works). There was no cafeteria at the center at that time, and no opportunity to go out for lunch, despite the generously long lunch period. The actual class time probably occupied about 60 per cent of the day, the remaining hours being dedicated to Russ' digressions about the agency's ills and substantial break periods. Eventually the 30 days came to an end, and we took a final exam on all the material covered. I was somewhat buoyed when I scored higher than either Randy or Timmy, despite their prior experience. I was soon to learn that classroom training was one thing, and working live traffic quite another.

4. On-The-Job Training

My first day in the tower introduced me to the first two positions on which I would be trained, Flight Data (FD) and Clearance Delivery (CD). These two functions were carried out, in sequence, for each aircraft that had filed an IFR flight plan, which included the majority of departures from MIA. The main function of FD was to handle flight plans issued by Miami Center. These duties did not involve any actual control of traffic or communication with pilots.

After a pilot or an airline filed a flight plan, Miami Center would formulate a route as close as possible to the pilot's request. This would be communicated to Miami Tower via telephone and recorded on a flight progress strip by the Flight Data specialist. The next step would be for the Clearance Delivery controller to read the clearance to the pilot prior to taxi. Then the pilot would contact Ground Control for taxi clearance to the active runway.

Next came Local Control, the position that issued landing and takeoff clearances. After takeoff, the pilot would contact Departure Control, which guided the flight to one of the prescribed exit "gates" into Miami Center airspace using radar. The en route portion of the flight might pass

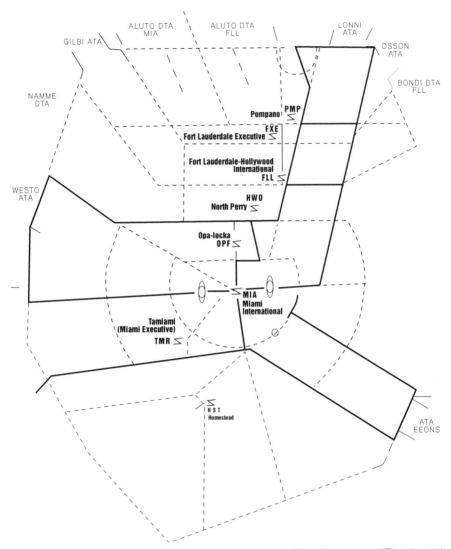

South Florida Airfields and Approach Transition Areas (ATAs) for MIA

through the airspace of several control centers and multiple sectors, finally being handed off to an approach controller at the destination airport. The approach controller would direct the aircraft to the active runway and instruct the pilot to contact the tower (Local Control). After landing and clearing the runway, the pilot would contact Ground Control for taxi instructions to the parking location. But all of these active control functions seemed pretty far down the road from where I stood on that first day.

My first instructor was an older man, Val Ripley, who had been a B-17 pilot during World War II. He rarely spoke of his wartime experiences, but when he did, everyone within earshot fell silent and paid rapt attention. He was soft spoken, with a slight touch of southern accent. At first he simply let me listen as he responded to and initiated calls. It went like this:

(On speaker) "Miami Tower, Miami Center, 47 line"

Val punched the button transferring the call to our headsets, then said, "Stand by, Center." He then punched a Hold button, and selected a third button connecting us to the TRACON flight data controller, saying, "TRACON, 47 line."

The response came, "TRACON's on."

Val selected the 47 line button again, and said, "Go ahead, center."

"OK, tower, got several for you:

"Eastern 10, DC-8, Kennedy airport as filed, Control 1150, flight level 230. Delta 491, DC-9, Chicago O'Hare as filed, J53, flight level 230. National 610, 727, full route clearance, cleared to the Philadelphia airport via control 1150 Wilmington, direct Salisbury, direct Woodstown direct, flight level 230," and continuing on similarly, at times reading a dozen clearances or more.

As the clearances were read, Val entered each piece of information into the appropriate box on the flight progress strip, using abbreviations for most of the elements: "EA" for Eastern, "DL" for Delta, "NA" for National, "JFK" for Kennedy, "ORD" for O'Hare, "PHL" for Philadelphia, "ILM" for Wilmington, "SBY" for Salisbury, "OOD" for Woodstown, while the identical entries were being made on the TRACON strips.

After the center controller read the last clearance, he would simply state his initials, "SE" (or sometimes more imaginatively, "Slow and Easy"). Val gave his initials, the TRACON specialist gave his initials, and all three controllers would punch off the 47 line, restoring it to speaker for the next call.

Handling the First Exchanges

All of this seemed simple enough, but as I learned at each position I trained on in the tower, it was really easy when you were standing in the back watching someone else work, and suddenly much harder when you were the one plugged into the frequency with your hand on

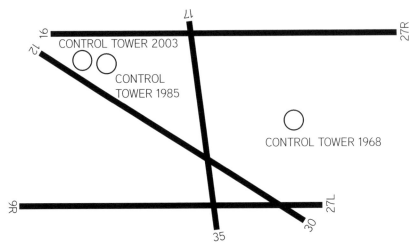

RUNWAY CONFIGURATION MIAMI INTERNATIONAL AIRPORT 1968

Runway numbering corresponds to the magnetic heading of an aircraft landing or taking off on that runway, calibrated to the nearest 10 degrees, with the initial and final zeroes omitted. An aircraft using Runway 12 would be on a magnetic heading of 120; for Runways 9 Left and 9 Right, 090; for the 27s, 270.

the transmitter key. I was also concerned that I did not know any of the abbreviations for airline company names, type identifiers, airports, VORs, or fixes. Val reassured me that these items would quickly become second nature to me, and that I should not worry about it. Nevertheless, I looked at the group of clearances just received, and began making notes on each abbreviation used, adding to my list each time Val entered a new abbreviation on a strip.

After a while, Val asked if I would like to try handling the next exchange with the center. I had my misgivings, but was determined to demonstrate a positive, go-getter attitude, and said I was ready. My first few attempts did not go well. In the first instance, CD had a request from a pilot, meaning that I would have to initiate the call. There had been no case where this had happened while I had been watching Val, but I jumped in:

"Hey data, I need a clearance for Learjet 144 Papa Alpha, going to Phoenix."

"Roger," I replied, then keying up the 47 line and suddenly realizing that I didn't know how to initiate the call. Even though I had said nothing, the center controller realized that the line was hot, and said, "Hey tower, you there, what you got?"

"Ah, ah, I need a clearance for a Learjet going to Phoenix."

"Ok, what's his number?"

"Ah, well, stand by one," looking at Val, who shrugged his shoulders. I froze, and Val stepped in, saying, "We'll call you back, center."

"Slow and Easy," and the line went dead.

Val put his hand on my shoulder, and said, in more patient tones than I often heard later in my training, "You know, as a controller, whenever you make a call or answer a call, you almost always need to write something either on a flight progress strip or a writing pad. Be sure you have both handy, no matter what position you are working." He then turned to CD, saying "What was that Learjet's number again?"

"144 Papa Alpha," came the reply, with a touch of annoyance.

"OK," Val said, then to me, "when CD gives you an aircraft number, before you do anything, write it down on a flight progress strip so you will be ready when you get the center on the line.

This was such an obvious point that I was kicking myself for my stupid oversight. At least I had the presence of mind to ask Val how to initiate the call before my next try. He told me, and I keyed up the line once again:

"Miami Center Miami Tower, clearance request."

"Miami Center's on."

"Request clearance on Learjet 144 Papa Alpha to Phoenix."

"Lear 144 Papa Alpha cleared to the Phoenix airport as filed, J43, flight level 230. Slow and Easy."

I had written "PH" for Phoenix, and "L" for Learjet, knowing that I could ask Val how to complete those elements after the call.

"RP," I replied giving my newly assigned operating initials for the first time, and feeling that I had basically handled the exchange correctly.

Val looked at me with what appeared to be an expression of disappointment, saying, "What did you forget?"

I thought for a second, then recognized my mistake. Damn! I had failed to get the TRACON data position on the line before copying the clearance. "So what do we do now?" I asked.

"Call the TRACON and read them the clearance."

I punched the button for the TRACON flight data position, saying, "TRACON, tower, I've got a clearance for you."

"OK, is the center on?"

"No, I didn't get you on the line when I copied it." Fortunately I had heard enough clearances read while Val was working the position that I was able to issue N144 Papa Alpha's correctly.

A few minutes later there came another call, triggering another exchange:

"Miami Tower Miami Center, 47 line."

I was determined not to screw up this time.

"Miami Tower's on, standby center." I hit the hold button, then the TRACON FD button, saying, "TRACON, 47 line."

I selected the 47 line again and said, "Go ahead, center."

The center controller reeled off three or four clearances, and I kept up reasonably well, substituting a letter or two for identification abbreviations I had not yet learned. We terminated the communication, giving our initials. Then, just as I was turning to Val hoping for a pat on the back, there came over the speaker from the TRACON, "Yeah tower, what you got?"

The TRACON controller had not immediately picked up the line, and had made the reasonable assumption that I would not give the center the go ahead until he announced himself. This was a lesson of major importance in all of ATC: you cannot consider a communication complete until you get an acknowledgement. Although I had made the call to the TRACON, I had not ensured that I received a response before going to the next step. With another layer of egg on my face, I repeated the clearances I had just received.

A Variety of Instructors

I continued training on Flight Data for several more weeks, with a number of different instructors. Some were patient and helpful, understanding my lack of prior experience. Others were immediately critical. For them, Flight Data was a mindless, do-it-in-your-sleep function, and a trainee who could not perform this simple task flawlessly was immediately suspect. I learned how to record an ATIS, how to acknowledge weather information received from the National Weather Service office located on the airport, and how to fill out a form when a pilot reported a condition requiring the emergency rescue equipment to standby at the runway during landing.

My note cards had become more numerous with each training session, and I was not sure whether it was permissible to use them, or whether my instructors expected me to have committed all the information to memory. In one instance I tucked them under some other papers, with just the corners sticking out. Apparently I involuntarily reached for them a few times, and my instructor for that day solved the problem, saying, "Don't stick your notes under all that other stuff. Put them out where you can see them. Then, when you realize you're not looking at them anymore, put them away." Sure enough, within a reasonable time I was working the position without a hitch, and without my notes. After a couple of months or so my supervisor approached me saying, "Congratulations, you are checked out on Flight Data." Although FD was a "nothing" position in the view of most of the fully certified controllers, it was tremendously satisfying to have cleared this first hurdle.

Moving to Clearance Delivery

Next, I began my training in Clearance Delivery. Like Flight Data, it did not involve any actual control of aircraft movements, but did require responding to clearance requests from pilots, either by reading a clearance or asking FD to get it from the center. At times, a clearance would not be immediately available, either because the pilot had not allowed sufficient time for processing between filing the flight plan and requesting the clearance, or because of some mistake in handling by the center or Flight Service, where many flight plans were filed, or by the airline companies that filed the flight plans for all their departures. These instances exposed me to my first experience of dealing with testy pilots, whose departure was being delayed because their flight plan could not be located. I picked up some useful strategies from my instructors for dealing with these cases, among them by querying the pilot as to when and where he had filed the flight plan. For general aviation aircraft, if the response was "Ten minutes ago with Flight Service," I could simply reply by saying some version of the following: "Citation 451 November Whiskey, be advised flight plan processing normally takes about 30 minutes. Expect clearance at 1455 Zulu, time now 1435." I learned early that when issuing an expected delay time, it was prudent to state a generously long period. That way, when the clearance became available sooner, ATC would earn a measure of good will for having reduced the actual delay below the estimate. The other circumstance causing a delay in receiving the clearance occurred when a pilot filed multiple legs in a flight plan that crossed time zones.

Since all times used in ATC operations were Greenwich Mean Time, or Zulu time, the correction factor for local time in different time zones depended on how far east or west of the prime meridian the time zone was located. If a pilot were to file a round robin flight plan from Houston to Miami and back, using the plus 6-hour conversion factor for determining Zulu time at Houston for both legs, the proposed departure time from Miami (plus 5-hour conversion factor) would be an hour later than the pilot intended, and flight plan processing would be delayed accordingly. For airline operations, CD could ask the pilot to check with the company dispatcher. In rare instances, when CD was not too busy, we could ask the pilot to read us his flight plan on the frequency, relay it to the center, and in that way expedite the request.

Reading clearances, was in principle, very simple. It consisted of using the flight progress strip prepared by FD, and repeating the verbiage the center had used. There were a few additional steps necessary to fully prepare the pilot, and the strip itself, for the next phase, which was taxi clearance from Ground Control. It went like this:

"Clearance Delivery, Eastern 10, IFR to Kennedy, ready to copy."

CD: "Eastern 10, Miami Clearance Delivery, cleared to the Kennedy airport via Control 1150 as filed. Maintain five thousand, expect flight level two three zero ten minutes after departure. Squawk zero three zero zero, departure frequency will be one two eight point zero."

Eastern 10: "Ok, Eastern 10, cleared to Kennedy as filed, Control 1150, five thousand, expect two three O ten minutes later, zero three hundred on the transponder and one two eight nothin' for departure control."

CD: "Eastern 10, readback correct. Say your gate number, advise you have received ATIS information Bravo."

Eastern 10: "Eastern 10 at Charlie 8, and we've got Bravo."

CD: (while talking, writing "C-8" and the letter "B" in the appropriate blocks of the flight progress strip, indicating the position from which the aircraft would be taxiing, that the clearance had been delivered, and that the pilot had the current ATIS information) "Eastern 10 roger, contact Ground Control one two one point eight for taxi."

Eastern 10: "Twenty-one eight for taxi, so long."

CD would then place the strip in the bay at Ground Control, which was the next position the pilot would contact.

Despite the fact that the aircraft receiving clearances were stationary, CD could get hairy during the "push" periods, when many flights filed for departure times that were the same or close together. Most of the major carriers all served the same northern cities, and there was tremendous competition to publish a slightly earlier departure time, to receive clearance ahead of the competing airline, and especially to get a taxi clearance before the others. This meant that there was not much discipline on the clearance delivery frequency, with several pilots transmitting at once, resulting in "smeared" transmissions, and preventing CD from responding to any of them. In my first few attempts to work the position during these busy periods, I totally lost control of the frequency. My instructors gave me some helpful hints:

If any item of information came through the squeal and static that occurred during these simultaneous pilot transmissions, CD could use that to single out and reply to one pilot, or sometimes more than one, and could keep his mic keyed to prevent further communication attempts until he had handled the ones he could identify. It went something like this:

Pilots: "Clearance Delivery, Delta (squeal, static, squeal)....parked at Charlie 4 (squeal, squeal)...IFR to Buenos Aires." It took me some time to pick up on these clues, but in addition to recognizing that each of those partial transmissions was made in a different pilot's voice, I eventually knew that only Eastern parked at the C-concourse gates, that neither Eastern nor Delta served Buenos Aires, and that since the last part of the call had been made in a distinctly American accent, it had probably come from Pan American. With these instantaneous flashes of recognition, CD could respond:

CD: "Aircraft at Charlie 4 and IFR to Buenos Aires standby, Delta flight calling for clearance, say again." A normal exchange with the Delta flight would occur, except that the last transmission from CD would be:

CD: "Delta 451, readback correct, contact ground one two seven point five, break, break, aircraft at Charlie 4, say your request." The exchange with Eastern would take place, concluding similarly, followed by a call to "aircraft IFR to Buenos Aires." The use of "break, break" indicated that CD was still using the frequency, and that other stations should not call.

'Do Whatever It Takes'

Another way for CD to stay ahead of the game, in the case where a partial pilot transmission included the destination, was to quickly scan the flight progress strips to identify any flights showing that destination. But sometimes even CD required a controller to "do whatever it takes," meaning that to prevent a situation from getting completely out of hand, actions that were not strictly by the rule book had to be taken. The most extreme example of this (at CD) that I ever observed occurred on the Monday after New Year's Day in 1969. Holiday traffic was at its peak, and the position was being worked by Jim Wheat, an older guy who had lost control of the situation. More and more pilots were trying to get a word in edgewise, and 30 or 40 flight progress strips were "cocked" in the Clearance Delivery bay, a standard indicator that the pilots had been told to standby. John Hall, a controller who had previously worked at Chicago O'Hare, relieved Jim, and took command, first keying his mic and transmitting three or four times, "All aircraft on Clearance Delivery frequency maintain radio silence until I call you."

At length the radio went quiet, and John transmitted, "All aircraft instructed to standby, be ready to copy, you are all cleared as filed to maintain five thousand, expect flight level two three zero ten minutes after departure. If your routing is northbound, squawk zero three zero zero, departure frequency one two eight point zero, if your routing is southbound, squawk one thousand, departure frequency one one eight point one. Information Yankee is current. If you are parked at concourses A through D or the north side of E, your ground control frequency is one two one point eight, if you are parked at concourses F through H or the south side of Echo your ground control frequency is one two seven point five. I will call each of you individually. Give me your gate number and acknowledge your clearance but do not read it back unless you have a question." In about five minutes, Clearance Delivery was back to normal, with each individual exchange taking no more than five seconds:

"Delta 1251, acknowledge"

"Delta 1251, got the clearance, Hotel 4."

"Eastern 635, acknowledge."

"Eastern 635, Charlie 6 with clearance."

Although pilots were not required to read back their entire clearance, it was an established normal practice intended to ensure that they and the

ATC system were on the same page from the moment the flight took off. John did what he thought was necessary to prevent massive delays from occurring, and no problems ensued.

How Things Work

By the end of October 1968, I was checked out on both Flight Data and Clearance Delivery. Even though I had not yet controlled any aircraft movements, I was now accepted as a member of the tower team. Ground control would be next, but for the time being I would work only the two positions on which I was qualified. There were a couple of instances that really brought home the team concept in working the tower operation. FD and CD, while not directly controlling airplanes, were expected to keep their eyes out the window, looking for situations that the other controllers might not have noticed. In one case, I was at CD and a fully certified colleague was at FD. The two positions were oriented in such a way that both controllers were looking directly at Runway 9 Left, the longest and most actively used runway on the airport. There was an aircraft on short final, having received landing clearance, when suddenly the man at FD, pointing at the airplane that was about to land, urgently shouted, "Send that guy around!"

Without hesitation, the controller at the Local Control position, which issued landing and takeoff clearances, transmitted, "Eastern 421, go around." The pilot applied power, the landing gear was retracted, and the pilot's voice came over the Local Control speaker, "What's the problem, tower?" FD was now standing, pointing with quick jabbing motions at the midfield point of the runway, where we all could now see a service van, painted in a light tan that blended perfectly with the color of the concrete, traveling at high speed toward the landing threshold of 9 Left. In calm, professional tones, the local controller responded, "Eastern 421, there was an unauthorized vehicle on the runway. The airport supervisor vehicle is chasing him down. Enter left downwind for 9 Left, we'll get you back in." What could have been a disastrous collision instead ended in a routine go-around, thanks to the heads-up alertness of the FD controller. Runway incursions of this type were not common, but they did happen from time to time because access to the airport was much less controlled before the events of 9-11-2001. Drivers with legitimate business on the field who were unfamiliar with the layout could easily end up on an active runway or taxiway.

In another case, Local Control had just issued takeoff clearance to a Boeing 707 operated by a South American carrier. As the aircraft began to roll, CD called out, "Tell that guy to abort." After a couple of repetitions (because of language problems), the pilot understood and the aircraft came to a stop. Through the binoculars, we could see that the metal shrouding on the number two engine had separated and been blown back several hundred feet by the jet blast. More ominously, a substantial stream of fuel was pouring from the damaged area, creating a dangerous fire hazard. At length the pilot was persuaded to shut down first the number two engine, then the other three, and to summon a company tug to tow the aircraft back to the ramp. In the meantime, the runway was closed for a considerable period as the crash crew and the sweeper cleaned up the fuel spill and cleared away the debris.

With each day on the job, I was becoming more attuned to the daily rhythms of the tower operation, and the overall culture of the (then) all-male work force. During slow periods, the experienced controllers seemed positively relaxed. As I gained experience, I came to realize that much of the constant awareness required of an air traffic controller was second nature to them, whereas for a "newbie" like me, I continually had to remind myself to focus, scan, and listen to what was going on around me. Even so, I was able to pick up on a number of things that were not directly related to operational matters. There was a considerable amount of joshing and exchanging good-natured insults among the troops. "He couldn't separate two flies with a screen door," was a common slur, since maintaining proper separation standards was the core mission of ATC. Most controllers were never at a loss for a snappy comeback. In one instance toward the end of an evening shift, someone announced, "When the shift is over, I think I'll go out and get drunk and get laid." A second man chimed in, "Yeah, I believe about half of that," and a third quickly adding, "Yeah, the getting drunk part!"

What About Sick Leave?

I tried to use these periods to learn more about how things really worked at the facility, questioning my co-workers in a way that I could not have done through official channels. Sick leave, one of the many benefits of federal employment, was officially defined as time off granted to an employee for a bona fide illness of his own or an immediate family member. But I had noticed that a controller could call in sick, take the day off, and reappear the next day in perfect health without being questioned. One day I asked about this, and while my inquiry did not elicit any truly useful information, it did open the door to a memorable round of repartee with two married controllers, Ed Blane, a tall, horse-faced individual with a receding hairline, and Earl Peavey, who was handsome and charming with a full head of nicely coiffed hair. The exchange went like this:

Me: "Hey, can you guys tell me what the deal is on sick leave? When can you actually use it without getting into trouble?"

Earl (in a crooning seductive voice): "Oh, that's when mama says, Oh, baby, don't go in to work today, come on over here and love me. THAT's when you take sick leave!"

Ed (with a completely serious expression): "If I heard that, I'd know I was in the wrong house."

There were also times for the discussion of more serious subjects, such as pay. Randy, Timmy, and I had been hired at the GS-6 level on the federal pay scale. In 1968, the base salary was about $6,100 a year, with additional amounts payable for Sundays (25%), evenings (6:00 pm to 6:00 am, 10%) and overtime (time and a half). Civil service rules at the time required a minimum year in grade before being eligible for promotion, but because the grade levels from GS-6 to GS-11 were considered training grades, and there was a critical need for fully certified air traffic personnel, these rules were relaxed. The FAA had been granted an exception via the so-called Whitten amendment, which provided that if a trainee had progressed to a certain level of competency, he could be promoted with only six months in the previous grade. It also provided that new hires with what was termed "suitable prior experience" could be hired at one of the intermediate pay grades.

This latter provision clearly fit Randy, with his 15 years of tower and TRACON experience. For Timmy, it was not so clear-cut, given his single tour of duty as a GCA operator. Nevertheless, the powers that be saw fit to reclassify them both at the GS-11 level, meaning that they skipped over the intermediate competency levels, and were waiting only to be fully checked out for promotion to the full performance grade of GS-12. Although I did not have the qualifications to be placed in the higher grades, the facility was scheduled to be upgraded to a GS-13 level in

December, and I would move to GS-7. Later on, I reached each successive tier of competency in time to be promoted after the six-month requirement (with a number of steep hills to climb in the interim).

In 1968, the Professional Air Traffic Controllers Organization (PATCO) won the right to be the exclusive bargaining unit representing all controllers. There were several other organizations to which government employees could belong, but PATCO was founded on the principle that air traffic controllers were a distinct breed, with concerns that could not be adequately addressed by a body representing the wider population of clerical and administrative employees. There was from the outset a more militant and confrontational posture on the part of the new bargaining unit, and an ongoing effort to achieve 100 per cent dues-paying membership by the people it represented. PATCO styled itself a union, although federal employees were by law denied the right to strike or to bargain directly for wages.

Nevertheless, at the national level the officers could lobby Congress for a higher pay scale, earlier retirement, second career training, and other benefits that did not currently exist. At the local level, a controller could have representation in the event he was subject to disciplinary proceedings, or in filing a grievance claiming some form of unfair treatment. I was handed a raft of materials touting the benefits of PATCO membership, among them a glossy magazine that stated some of the long-range goals of the organization, including a $25,000 a year salary, or pay comparability with airline captains. I asked some of the old hands how likely it was that these goals would be reached. Some said, "Don't believe any of that propaganda, there's no way in hell we'll ever make that kind of money." Others said, "Don't be too sure. I remember when everyone said there was no way in hell we would ever make ten grand a year, and look at us now." The average GS-12 controller salary was around $12,000 or $13,000 a year, with an increase of $2,000 a year or so right around the corner when the upgrade to GS-13 took effect.

One incident that occurred during the time I was qualified on only Flight Data and Clearance Delivery was a perfect illustration of how the agency bureaucracy worked. One of the watch supervisors came around one day asking each of us whether we would like to be called for overtime if additional staffing was needed. Many of the "FPLs" (full performance level) controllers wanted to be called, seeing the dollar signs of time and a half overtime pay. Others felt that their time off was sacrosanct, and did not wish to come to work on a day off for any amount of money. They could still be called, but only after all the people who wanted the extra work had been contacted. As the lowest-paid employee in the facility, I of course raised my hand immediately to volunteer.

Sam Parsons was from a military background, and very much about following the rules and asserting hierarchical authority over those below him. Quite brusquely, he informed me, "Not you. You have to be qualified on at least one operational position to work overtime." So much for that, I thought. On my next set of days off, a major front rolled through the area, creating the kind of conditions that made every position in the tower and TRACON a struggle, and triggering a number of sick leave calls to the facility. Although the callers claimed legitimate illnesses, everyone recognized the likelihood that they were suffering from "instrumentaitis," a reluctance to work under the difficult conditions of thunderstorms, rain, and reduced visibility (IFR, or "instrument" weather). When I answered a phone call at about 7:30 am, the tower supervisor asked me if I could come in and work overtime. I said, "Gee Joe, I'd really like to, and I could use the money, but Sam told me I was not authorized to work overtime because I am only checked out on FD and CD." "To hell with that," he replied, "get your ass in here, we need you!"

My first overtime shift was my first exposure to extended IFR weather, the usual South Florida pattern being a sudden rain shower that quickly dissipated, resulting in only a few minutes of below VFR weather conditions. Every position was running on high adrenaline, with none of the usual wisecracks and banter between controllers. The tower was equipped with a radar display, permitting the local controller to observe the aircraft on final approach, but the ground controller had no such advantage. Ground Control was difficult enough under the best of conditions, and without the ability to see the airport surface and taxiing aircraft, it was probably the most difficult control position in the entire facility. In addition, because of the number of sick leave absences, breaks were few and far between. It was one of those days, according to the veterans, when you really earned your money.

Toward the end of the shift, the weather lightened up a bit, and there was time for a limited amount of non-operational talk. In low tones I asked the man next to me how the facility could permit such wholesale absenteeism on a day when full staffing was most needed. He said, "Look, a supervisor can disapprove a sick leave request, but they never do. If a controller is required to work after claiming he is ill, and there was ever an accident or incident involving an airplane under his control, the FAA could be on the hook for millions. But the one thing you have to be careful of is pattern sick leave. Let's say your days off are Thursday and Friday, and you frequently take sick leave on Wednesday, stretching your break, they can nail you for pattern sick leave use."

Training on Ground

Later in December, I was working the 7 to 3 shift, assigned to Flight Data and Clearance Delivery combined. This was routine when the tempo of the operation was slow, and a second controller could be assigned as necessary when the positions needed to be split. I was now completely comfortable with the two positions, and enjoying being part of the controller fraternity. That morning, Gene Bukowski was assigned to the ground control position, and as he plugged in he turned to me, saying, "Say, neighbor, have you worked any ground control yet?" displaying his personable good humor. In quiet, deferential tones I replied, "No, Gene, only Data and Clearance Delivery," surmising that he might not want to be responsible for a green trainee during his first session on an active control position. "Well there's no time like the present, get your headset and plug in here with me," Gene said, instantly dispelling that notion.

My heart rate immediately went up about 30 per cent, as I recalled instances when even experienced controllers clearly had their hands full working a busy ground control session. I got relieved from CD/FD, and plugged in with Gene, knees locked, and with a death grip on my mic switch. Reflexively, I turned towards the window that I always looked out from the two positions on which I was qualified. Gene said, "Now, neighbor, don't just keep looking at 9 Left. You've got three runways out there, and the entire terminal ramp for the outbounds. Keep up a constant scan of the whole airport." I nodded nervously and began what I hoped was an acceptable scan. For the first 30 or 45 seconds, the frequency was entirely quiet, and I relaxed ever so slightly, just in time to receive the first call from a pilot who sounded distinctly sleepy:

"Miami ground, National 100, instruments to Washington, ready to taxi."

B-727

Gene didn't say anything, and I turned to him with what must have been a look of sheer panic, saying, "Gene! What do I say to him?"

"Well, neighbor, you just say to him, National 100 Miami ground, taxi to runway 9 Left," he replied, in a totally relaxed manner, with a big smile on his face.

"Wait, wait, say that again," I implored. Gene repeated the standard phraseology for issuing a taxi clearance, then waited expectantly. I keyed my mic and repeated Gene's words, pausing between phrases to be sure I had them all right.

"OK, 9 Left, National 100," the pilot transmitted in the same somnolent tones as his first transmission.

"Now when you issue taxi instructions, you should always be looking at the airplane you are talking to, or if he is not in sight, at the location where you expect him to enter the taxiway. Where is National 100," Gene asked.

I shook my head in bewilderment, as Gene reached into the Ground Control bay and picked out the flight progress strip for the aircraft. Of course! How many times had I written a gate number on a strip while working CD? I already knew the gate locations (odd numbers on the south and east side, even numbers on the north and west side of each concourse, labeled A through H). I turned toward concourse F where National Airlines parked, and sure enough, there was a Boeing 727 pulling away from the gate, about to join the diagonal taxiway that led to the 9 Left run up pad. The frequency went quiet again, and I was feeling pretty pleased with myself for having issued my first active control instruction.

Several more aircraft called, and I repeated the magic words of a taxi clearance, with Gene poking me in the ribs to remind to find the strip, and the airplane. The action was heating up, and at one point, after I issued taxi instructions to two aircraft, Gene said, "Who's going to follow who?" I had not yet learned the most basic rule in all of ATC, which was that if you were working more than one airplane, you had to make sure that any instruction you issued did not create a conflict with other traffic already moving. I had cleared a Northeast 727, exiting the ramp from the west side of concourse H, to taxi to 9 Left, and a Delta DC-9, coming from the east side, to do the same. There was going to be a tie at the end of the building as both pilots approached what was essentially a blind corner. "What do I do," I asked.

"Here, let me show you," Gene answered. "Delta 624, hold at the end of the concourse, look for a Northeast 727 ahead and to your right, follow him to 9 Left."

Pilot: "Delta 624 roger, hold, follow Northeast."

Gene: "Northeast 19, there will be a Delta DC-9 coming around the corner to your left, he will follow you."

Pilot: "Northeast 19, roger."

Gene turned the frequency over to me again, and in short order another situation developed similar to the one involving the Northeast and Delta flights. This time it was two Eastern 727s taxiing from opposite sides of concourse D. I was going to show Gene that I had learned from his example. After issuing taxi clearance to the second aircraft, I confidently transmitted:

"Eastern 314, follow a company 727 entering the taxiway from the north side of the concourse."

Pilot: "Eastern 314, roger, follow company."

As the other aircraft (Eastern 226) came around the corner, the pilot saw that Eastern 314 was slowly approaching from his left, and braked to a stop, transmitting, "Ah, ground control, do you want Eastern 226 to wait for this other fellow or go ahead?" In the meantime, Eastern 314, seeing that his traffic had stopped, also came to a stop in order to comply with the instruction to follow him. I quickly keyed my mic and transmitted, "Eastern 226, continue taxiing, company to your left will follow you."

Both aircraft began moving again. During the next quiet period, Gene took the opportunity to point out a couple of things to me, saying, "Now neighbor, remember those two Easterns a few minutes ago? You issued a taxi sequence, but you didn't tell the second guy what to expect, and they both stopped unnecessarily. Always give the pilots the picture so that they can help you make your plan work. Be short and concise. When it gets busier, Eastern can have five or six airplanes all taxiing at once, and they all want to be number one at the run up pad for departure." Clearly, there was much more to this ground control operation than endlessly repeating the canned phraseology for issuing a taxi clearance. And as I came to understand over time, more than any other control position in the facility, ground control required a controller to be fast on his feet verbally, and come up with clear innovative instructions that were nowhere published in the phraseology manual.

Funny Stuff on Ground Control

Over the next several months, I worked with a number of different instructors, and learned that I had been lucky to have Gene during my first day on the position. Others were not as patient or as good humored, and, while that put added pressure on me, I could see that there was pressure on them as well. The rule was that any error was the responsibility of the instructor, not the trainee, and every controller in the role of instructor had a legitimate concern that a trainee would do something with consequences so immediate that the mistake could not be corrected, or that a mistake would be missed in the heat of battle.

Nevertheless, even ground control had its lighter moments. One of the daily challenges at the position was the so-called ten o'clock rush every night on the evening shift. Before 1978, all airline fares were mandated by the Civil Aeronautics Association (CAA), and those fares were reduced for any flights after 10:00 pm. This meant that passenger loads on those flights were high, and that the major carriers, which all served the same major cities, were in fierce competition to be at the front of the departure queue, which could number 20 to 25 airplanes, all with a proposed departure time of ten o'clock. Predictably, first clearance delivery, then ground control, experienced a rash of undisciplined calls smearing each other and requiring numerous "say agains" in the lead-up to the witching hour. To compound the problem, especially at Eastern's gates, most of the aircraft were either 727s or DC-8s, painted identically, and using very similar call signs (e.g., EA 402, EA 404, EA 414). It was easy to make a mistake in grabbing a strip or issuing taxi clearance because of receiving only partial transmissions and because as the aircraft left the terminal area they rapidly disappeared into the darkness.

Eastern's flights made up nearly half of the ten o'clock departures, so that four or five 727s and a like number of DC-8s all taxied at once. There were two taxiways that converged at the 9 Left run-up pad, and pilots regularly exceeded the Dade County airport taxi speed limit of 15 miles per hour in an effort to beat out a competitor for a place in the single file line-up from which takeoff clearance would be issued. One evening the ground controller had an Eastern DC-8 on each of the converging taxiways with the two aircraft in a virtual tie at the run-up pad. Without realizing that he had the wrong flight progress strip for one of them, he initiated the following exchange:

GC: "Eastern 402, you're following a company DC-8 to your left, just passing the fire house."

EA 402: "I hope so, ground, we're still at the gate."

One day I was being instructed by Evan Gianetti, good controller but something of a hothead. It was during the early part of a day shift, when the activity level at the airport was fairly moderate. We were working the two ground control positions combined, and several other controllers were in the back of the tower awaiting a position assignment. At the time, the tower was equipped with battery-powered emergency transmitter/receiver devices called gonsets to be used in the event of a failure of the main radio system. Bill Clark, a tall skinny guy from New York and a known prankster within the facility, surreptitiously turned on the gonset that had the UHF frequency for ground control, and began quietly transmitting as though he were an airplane requesting taxi clearance. He used the call sign of an aircraft that was actually based at Miami, an Army C-47 (the military version of the venerable Douglas DC-3). He used enough of the call sign to be recognizable, but then allowed his voice to trail off as though the aircraft radio was malfunctioning. It went like this:

"Ground control, Army 9641....(trailing off):

Me: "Army aircraft calling ground, you are breaking up, say again."

"Ground, Army 964......"

Me: "Army aircraft, your radio is unreadable, try another transmitter"

After several more tries, Evan, who had been somewhat impatient and critical of me throughout the session, peremptorily snapped, "Don't talk to this asshole anymore. Let me have the frequency." Then, keying his mic, "Army aircraft calling Miami ground, your transmitter is unreadable. Get it fixed, use another radio, or stay off the air!"

"Miami ground, Army 9641…."

Evan: "Army aircraft, I say again, stay off the air, do not transmit again with that radio!"

"Miami ground, Army 9641…"

Evan: "Army aircraft, if you transmit again—" he paused, suddenly realizing that he had been tricked by Clark's use of the gonset, unkeyed his mic, and shouted, "I'll kill that f…ing Clark!"

At this, Clark and the rest of the controllers, who had realized from the start what Clark was doing, all erupted in guffaws of laughter. Evan was not amused. He yanked his headset out of the jack and told the supervisor to get him the hell out of the position and put someone else in. That was it for my training on that day.

In another instance, Timmy Timmons was being trained on ground control by an instructor who had spent most of his career at New York's John F. Kennedy tower and approach control, and was acknowledged to be one of the strongest controllers in the facility. Timmy received a radio call that was all too common on ground: a tug requesting clearance to tow an aircraft. The problem with tugs was threefold. The radios were uniformly of poor quality, being installed on a vehicle without protection from the elements; the noise of the tug engine fed into the operator's microphone, further degrading the communication; and most of the tug drivers were heavily accented, and not always as familiar with the airport and ground control procedures as they should be.

On the day in question, after numerous instructions to the tug driver to repeat his request, the instructor lost patience and violated one of the cardinal rules of ATC: DO NOT issue clearance or control instructions to anyone until you know both the location of the aircraft and where it wishes to go. He said to Timmy, "Ah, screw it, just clear him we'll figure out where is." Timmy then transmitted, "Tug calling ground control for tow clearance, proceed as requested." About ten minutes later, the tower supervisor took a phone call from the Dade County sheriff's department asking, "What the hell are you doing with this C-46 in the middle of LeJeune Road?" The aircraft had been located at the George T. Baker training facility, across the main thoroughfare that bordered the east boundary of the airport, and was being towed to a maintenance hangar on the field. Automobile traffic was blocked, and backed up at least a mile in both directions. It took over an hour to clear up the mess, and Timmy and his instructor received a solid round of ribbing over the incident.

5. Serious Stuff on Ground Control

Ground control was usually the first position that a new controller trained on, for the very good reason that the airplanes were moving slowly, could be stopped, and in any event were not likely to run into each other. It provided instructors and supervisors the opportunity to assess the decision-making skills of a trainee, his ability to control the frequency, and, perhaps most importantly, his ability to recognize his own limitations.

While there was always the pressure to "keep 'em moving," one of my early instructors told me, quote: "No one is going to thank you for taking more airplanes than you can handle." On ground control, this meant that clearance to taxi for departing aircraft could be modulated, generally by ordering the flight progress strips in the order of the aircraft calls, and informing each pilot, "Hold position, I have your taxi sequence, expect a five-minute delay," or something similar. Then, as the workload eased, taxi clearances could be issued in that same order. Arrival aircraft had priority, since their presence at a runway exit point or on a taxiway would remain a component of the ground control workload until they reached their gate or an uncontrolled ramp area. Of course, every rule had its exceptions, and there were times when an arriving aircraft could not get to its gate because the departure had been delayed at the gate to keep the operation manageable.

The one area where the ground controller had a serious safety responsibility was in issuing clearance to cross a runway. Recognizing and using runway crossing opportunities was one of the most important skills a trainee had to master. In principle, it was simple enough—you issued a crossing clearance when the runway was unavailable for either a landing or takeoff, meaning that as an arrival passed the intended crossing point, the airplane or vehicle could be cleared to cross behind the landing aircraft as it was rolling out.

Still, there were additional circumstances to consider. For example, would the crossing be complete before the arriving aircraft cleared the runway (some operators taxied slowly, and a towed aircraft could take much longer than that); if the arriving aircraft were smaller than an airliner, it was permissible for another small aircraft to land before the first cleared the runway; did the local controller have a departure in position on the runway, waiting only for the previous arrival to clear, or for sufficient space behind a previous departure; if so, would there be time to complete the crossing and launch the departure before the next arrival became a factor. Crossing behind a departure was also a possibility, but with all the same caveats, plus the additional constraint that in certain cases a succeeding departure could take off as soon as the preceding one became airborne, generally a shorter time than it took an arrival to clear the runway after landing.

Runway Crossings

Runway crossing situations were prime examples of the fact that no active control position operated in a vacuum, but depended on awareness between control functions and a strong sense of teamwork. While the ground controller was expected to use good judgment, the local controller, too, had a responsibility to ensure that the runway was clear before issuing landing or takeoff clearance. Although thousands of operations were conducted daily at MIA without incident, there were those persistent few that, for one reason or another, went wrong.

During my early years, first as a trainee and later a full controller, I came to realize that there were three things a controller needed to do to maintain a safe operation. In every accident or incident in which ATC actions were relevant, the controller did not fully perform one or more of them. I labeled these elements as F-E-M, or formulate, execute, and monitor. These were the primary elements of the multi-tasking environment in which every controller did his job, and they had to be constantly re-balanced as the traffic situation evolved.

Formulation, or planning, was always the starting point. You had to look ahead, extrapolating the movements of your airplanes, picturing where you wanted them to be one or two minutes from now, and deciding whether to issue instructions immediately, or at a later time within your planning window. Next came execution, actually the easiest of the three elements if the formulation function was done properly. Finally there was monitoring, that is, constantly reviewing the traffic situation in case (a) the plan you had in mind wasn't working out, (b) the execution was faulty (normally an error of timing), or (c) a pilot was not complying with the instructions.

Experienced controllers were generally very good at formulation and execution, meaning that the effort of the monitoring task was usually fairly low. But it also meant that the old hands were likely to minimize their attention to monitoring, relying instead on their experience and "sixth sense" to detect something that needed correcting. By contrast, a "newbie" like me devoted major attention to monitoring, which was necessary, but also detracted from the formulation and execution elements (which, in turn, created added demands for monitoring).

There were several incidents on ground control that highlighted the importance of each of the elements of the controller's job. Although it was not primarily a safety issue, there were two or three instances when a ground controller became eligible for the "golden tow bar award" when two taxiing aircraft ended up nose to nose on a taxiway without sufficient room to turn around. The only solution was to have a tug attach a tow bar and push one of them back far enough to turn on to an alternate taxiway. These were errors possibly of formulation, but definitely of monitoring, where the situation should have been recognized and corrected before it developed.

There were two cases of unauthorized runway crossings, both of which created a major collision hazard. The first involved an Avro-748, call sign Bahamasair 108, holding short of Runway 12, awaiting crossing clearance to taxi to the terminal. At the same time a Bahamasair tug, also

L-1011 © Allan Clegg Dreamstime.com

carrying the call sign 108, was holding short of Runway 9 Left, towing an aircraft to the maintenance hangar. The ground controller several times issued crossing clearance to the aircraft without receiving a response. After the third or fourth try, the pilot finally asked for confirmation of the instruction. The ground controller replied, "108, cross the runway." The tug driver took this instruction as being meant for him, and pulled onto 9 Left at the very moment the local controller issued takeoff clearance to a 727 holding in position on the runway.

Fortunately the local controller saw what was happening and immediately canceled the takeoff clearance just issued. The ground controller was possibly guilty of faulty planning, during which phase he should have recognized the potential problem of two identical call signs at different runways. But the real error was one of execution. He should have used the words "Bahamasair," omitting the word tug, and specified the identification of the runway to be crossed.

The most serious close call involving ground control occurred after clearance was issued to tow an L-1011 repositioning from the Eastern hangar on the north side of 9 Left to one of Eastern's gates at the terminal. Traffic was moderate, and there was no problem either with the formulation or execution—a routine clearance to tow to the departure (east) end of 9 Left and hold short of the runway. The tug operator acknowledged the instructions, but instead of complying with them, turned in the direction opposite to the route he should have followed to the departure end. Upon reaching a point directly across from Eastern's gate area, instead of holding short, he continued the tow onto the runway.

At that moment, a British Airways Boeing 707, heavily loaded for the eight-hour flight to London, was at about the midfield point accelerating for takeoff. The flight operated twice a week in those days, and routinely used every bit of the 10,500 feet available on 9 Left. The L-1011 was at about the 8,000-foot marker, and because of the speed of the 707, there was no possibility of aborting the takeoff and stopping in time. As the tower personnel recognized the situation, several of them reached for the alarm button to alert the crash crew, certain that a terrible collision was about to happen. The next few seconds were agonizing, but at the last second the pilot of the 707 "horsed it off," meaning that he pulled the nose of the aircraft up, as is the procedure during the takeoff sequence. The problem was that the proper airspeed for a safe takeoff had not yet been reached, and the possibility of a stall, or simply a failure to climb, would have meant that the collision could not be avoided.

By this time the towed aircraft was most of the way across the runway, but the 40-foot high tail of the 1011 was still in the path of the 707. In what can only be called an act of superb airmanship, the British pilot gently rolled the airplane left, elevating the right wing just enough to clear the tail of the other airplane, then quickly leveled the wings to regain the lift lost in the banking maneuver. Several roll oscillations were observed as the pilot struggled to stay airborne and accelerate to normal climb speed, but finally the aircraft stabilized, and a collective sigh of relief, punctuated by a number of well-chosen obscenities, was heard throughout the tower. The first radio transmission did not occur until "Speedbird," as the British Airways flights were designated, was more than five miles from the airport, then came the laconic, typically understated message from the flight crew:

"I say, tower, did you see that?"

Tower: "Yes sir, we sure did, we're looking into it now."

Pilot: "Well, I'm very sorry, but we are going to have to write that one up."

This incident, although mainly the fault of the tug driver, clearly implicated the ground controller, who failed to carry out the monitor function. It took several minutes from the time the tug turned the wrong way on the taxiway till the moment it entered the runway, ample time for the error to have been recognized and corrected. In a grim immediate postscript to the event, the tower supervisor called Eastern's maintenance number asking to speak to the person who supervised towing operations. He was informed that that supervisor was unavailable because he was out on the field towing an L-1011 to the gate.

By contrast, there were situations where a ground controller took an extra, proactive step to provide assistance to a taxiing aircraft. The terminal concourses, where airline parking gates were located, were laid out like the spokes of a wheel, meaning that the area between them was fairly confined where they connected to the terminal building, growing progressively wider as the "fingers" fanned out at their extreme ends. These sections of the ramp were termed non-movement areas, where pilots, tug drivers, and other equipment operators were responsible for the safety of their own movements, as distinct from the taxiways and runways that were controlled by local and ground.

Still, every taxi or tow operation from the gates began on a non-movement area, and it was almost routine in issuing taxi or tow instructions for the ground controller to add a phrase like "use caution for men and equipment on the ramp." When this was suggested to me as a good operating technique during my training, I asked how I was supposed to know whether there were men and equipment on the ramp. My bemused instructor replied, "There are ALWAYS men and equipment on the ramp."

One night on the evening shift, shortly after the 747 began service to MIA in the early 1970s, one of the big Boeings was parked at the end of Echo concourse. At the end of the adjacent Delta concourse, there was a DC-8 parked with its tail extending well into the ramp area, directly opposite the long wing of the 747. The ground controller was Ernest "Hercules (Herc)" Hunt, whose sobriquet derived from his muscular build. An experienced veteran, Herc had seen it all. An Air Jamaica 727 called for taxi and would have to pass between the tail of the DC-8 and the wing of the 747. Herc saw that the space was a little tight, triggering the following exchange:

Herc: "Air Jamaica 21, will you have room between the DC-8 and the 747?"

JM21: "Affirmative ground, we'll be all right."

Herc: "Air Jamaica 21, are you sure you don't want to hold there and get some wing walkers to walk you through?" (Wing walkers would walk along under the wing tips of the 727 to ensure clearance from the other airplanes.)

JM21: "Negative ground, we'll be okay."

The aircraft continued a slow taxi, then, as it came abreast of the 747 wing, abruptly stopped.

JM21: "Ground, Air Jamaica 21, I think we just hit something with our left wing."

The ramp supervisor was quickly on the scene, reporting in short order that there was visible damage to the wingtips of both the 727 and the 747. As always happened in situations like this, the ground control tapes were pulled, and instead of the Monday morning quarter backing that usually occurred, Herc received a well-deserved "attaboy" for his actions.

Freak Accidents

Some incidents on the ground were simply not preventable by the ground controller, as they fell in the category of a sudden freak event that could not have been anticipated, or actions by a pilot or other operator that defied understanding. In one case a BAC-111, a twin engine jet approximately the size and weight of a DC-9, under tow to a location on the north side of 9 Left, was holding short of the runway at the approach end. After an arrival aircraft crossed the threshold, the tow operator was issued a clearance to cross and began to move. All the runways were constructed with a crown, to facilitate water run-off, and the tug was clearly struggling to overcome the slight incline. As the aircraft reached the midpoint, its speed increased a little, but then unaccountably came to an abrupt halt, with the next arrival only a couple of miles out. The ground controller immediately began a series of exhortations to the tug driver to expedite the tow, warning of the impending landing, but without receiving a response or eliciting any movement.

The local controller sent the arrival aircraft around, and the ramp supervisor vehicle, designated "Ramp 20," was dispatched to assess the situation. What the ramp supervisor discovered was that as the airplane had picked up momentum on the downslope of the crown, the tow bar had broken at the point where it was connected to the tug. With the inertia of the BAC-111 behind it, the ragged end of the tow bar had been driven about twelve inches into the runway surface. The runway was closed for a considerable period until the airplane could be moved.

Two other cases involved actions by either a pilot or a mechanic taxiing an aircraft. One evening at about 9:00 pm, a Piper Cherokee exited runway 9 Left and requested taxi clearance to the general aviation parking area. The pilot stated that he was unfamiliar with the airport and needed progressive instructions, that is, detailed guidance during the taxi. In this instance it should have been a simple operation: taxi westbound on the parallel taxiway, look for two amber lights that marked the entrance to AirTech, an FBO (fixed base operator) serving general aviation. The lights were located at the end of a bridge that crossed a drainage ditch. As the airplane approached the bridge, the exchange went like this:

"Ground control, Cherokee 67 Papa, is this where I turn?"

Ground Control: "Cherokee 67 Papa, do you see the amber lights?"

Pilot: "67 Papa, affirmative."

Ground Control: "Cherokee 67 Papa, turn right there, AirTech will be ahead and to your right."

The pilot made a right turn about 20 feet short of the bridge, and the airplane went into the ditch. There was some discussion as to whether the term "right" in the ground controller's instruction could have been misconstrued as meaning "immediate" rather than indicating the direction of the turn, but most of us were left shaking our heads in disbelief.

On another day, early in the morning in mid-winter when it was still dark, a mechanic taxiing a BAC-111 requested clearance from the terminal to a hangar on the north side of 9 Left. The ground controller's instructions were short and simple:

"Ship one-eleven, proceed, cross Runway 9L."

There was no other traffic moving, no aircraft awaiting departure or inbound for landing, and the BAC-111 was exiting Concourse D, located in close proximity to 9 Left, and so there was no need to issue hold short instructions to await a crossing opportunity.

The heavily accented operator replied simply, "Rah-yer." A few minutes later, the aircraft came to a stop, clearly holding short of the runway. The ground controller watched for a minute or two, then issued, "Ship one-eleven, cross 9 Left," thinking that the mechanic had misunderstood the clearance to proceed all the way. Again came the one word reply, "Rah-yer," but the airplane did not move.

Several minutes later the following exchange took place:

BAC-111: "Ground control, you want me to cross right here?"

Ground Control: "Ship 111, affirmative, cross the runway straight ahead."

At length, the operator began a slow taxi, then, upon reaching the far side of the runway, applied a large, and audible, increase in power. The ground controller wondered a bit at this, but the airplane was observed taxiing at a normal rate of speed on the north side parallel taxiway, and the operation was soon concluded. Thirty minutes later, in the light of the early dawn, tower personnel observed three deep ruts in the grass area adjacent to the intersection the BAC-111 had been expected to use. Apparently, the mechanic at the controls took the instruction to "cross the runway straight ahead" literally, failing to make a slight turn to remain on the taxiway, and had instead powered through the grass area.

Odd Occurrences

Almost every day something occurred on the ground control position that either required an innovative action or provided a good laugh to the tower staff. One time a foreign operated C-46 cleared Runway 9 Right after landing and came to a stop, but could not be contacted on any of the tower frequencies. Even after repeated signals from the light gun, a backup procedure for directing aircraft without radio contact, the aircraft did not move. A few minutes later there came a phone call from the international flight service station saying that they had contact with the C-46 on HF, a radio band used for overseas flights that was not installed at MIA. The controller who answered the phone was able to issue taxi instructions on the telephone that were then repeated to the pilot, and the aircraft was able taxi.

There were several instances in which the ground controller had to direct the ramp supervisor vehicle to corral a loose dog on the runway or taxiway. In another, a United Airlines flight was approaching the run-up pad at 9 Right for departure when the following exchange took place:

Pilot: "Ah ground, United 210, there's a guy standing in the middle of the taxiway, and we can't get past him."

Ground Control: "United 210 roger, we'll get the ramp car out there to talk to him."

Ramp 20 was dispatched, but before he got to the location where the individual was blocking the taxiway, the United pilot transmitted again:

Pilot: "Ground, you're not going to believe this, but the guy is taking his clothes off."

In due course the ramp supervisor, accompanied by one of the Dade County sheriff department police cars based on the field, arrived on the scene. The individual was confronted in all his naked glory and whisked away. In a follow-up phone call with the ramp supervisor, we learned that the man's girlfriend was aboard the flight, and that he had described his actions as a protest over her leaving Miami.

On another day, one of the police cars called for clearance to proceed on the movement area, but had to repeat the request several times because of what sounded like barking interfering with the transmission. The vehicle was parked close to the tower and when clearance to proceed was finally issued, as the car pulled out onto the ramp, the bushy tail of a German shepherd was seen wagging in the rear window.

Back and Forth

Controllers were known for their ability to invent sharp, witty comebacks during their exchanges with pilots and other operators. The following examples involving taxi clearances issued to two Delta 747s in different instances illustrate the point:

Delta's gates were at the southeast corner of the terminal area, immediately adjacent to the Runway 27 Left run-up pad. But all 747s were required to use 27 Right because of its greater width and the 747s had to taxi more than a mile, compared to the few hundred feet to reach 27 Left. In the first case, the ground controller was Jack Kindler, a smooth, laid back individual who never got excited or raised his voice no matter how hectic the operation got. The exchange went like this:

"Ground, Delta 44 heavy ready to taxi with [ATIS information] Alpha."

Kindler: "Delta 44 heavy Miami ground, taxi to Runway 27 Right."

Pilot: "OK, Delta 44 heavy Runway 27 Left."

Kindler: "Delta 44 heavy negative, I say again, taxi to Runway 27 Right."

Pilot: "You mean we've got to taxi all the way over to the north side of the airport and get in that long line?"

Kindler: "Delta 44 heavy, affirmative, 747's are required to use 27 Right."

Pilot: "Well that's the most ridiculous thing I ever heard of. Do you know how much time we're going to lose and how much fuel we're going to burn on that long taxi? We're going all the way to San Francisco you know."

Kindler: "Delta 44 heavy, roger, 27 Right is closer to San Francisco."

In the second case, the exchange started out in much the same way. This time the ground controller was Tim Farris, a tall, pale-skinned man with piercing blue eyes and flaming red hair like a Viking warrior. Although he generally kept his cool when he had his mic keyed, he kept up a steady stream of profanity between transmissions, especially when things were not going to his liking. After an initial testy back-and-forth period, Tim convinced the 747 pilot to taxi to 27 Right. But the pilot wasn't finished. Throughout most of the taxi he made a number of gratuitous remarks:

Pilot: "This is a stupid way to operate." Or, "I don't know why you guys delay us like this." Finally he said, "This is just downright ridiculous. I could do a better job working ground control than this."

Tim had let the earlier comments go, but at this last one a telltale flush of red crept up from under the back of his shirt collar, and he shouted, "You son of a bitch!"

Then, keying his mic, transmitted in calm, professional tones, "I'll tell you what, captain, if you can stand the pay cut, we could use the help." It was an especially apt rejoinder, given that in those days a senior airline captain earned more than twice the salary of the highest paid controller.

Controllers got their licks in, but in one case a tug driver had the last laugh. At about 5:00 pm a tug requested clearance to tow a Boeing 707 from the north side of 9 Left to one of the terminal gates on the south side. This time period was routinely one during which the tower operation was very busy, and a slow moving tug that would need to cross the active runway and make its way through a steady stream of departures was a major nuisance. The ground controller, Tom Belt, instructed the tug to proceed eastbound on the parallel taxiway and hold short of 9 Left at midfield. Tom was not the most patient individual, and the demands of a tow operation with its attendant characteristics of slow movement, poor radio, and a heavily accented driver were a source of major irritation. The tug held for the better part of an hour, with an increasing number of transmissions from the driver complaining about the delay, and the sun setting in the west. One of the requirements for tow operations during hours of darkness was that the airplane display position lights. At length, the following exchange occurred:

Tug: (for at least the eighth or tenth time) "Ground, tug 144 request clearance to cross."

Belt: "Tug 144, continue holding, I'll get you across when I can, so stop calling me! And be advised, you are required to display position lights when towing after dark!"

Tug: "It was daytime when we requested clearance."

The most serious "off the wall" occurrence on ground control lasted for almost a week when the tower experienced the incident that we termed the phantom ground controller. Someone was using a VHF radio equipped with the ground control frequency, and was making random transmissions, including taxi clearances, runway crossing instructions, and many "wise guy" type comments that had nothing to do with the operation. While some of these comments amused us, it was hard to keep a sense of humor dealing with this unwarranted interference day after day. Some samples of exchanges that occurred while I was assigned to ground control:

Pilot: "Ground, Northwest 441, ready to taxi from Golf 17."

Me: "Northwest 441 ground, be advised we are experiencing unauthorized transmissions on ground control frequency. Taxi to Runway 9 Left."

Phantom: "Naw, don't you move, you stay right where you are."

Me: "Northwest 441, disregard that last transmission, taxi to Runway 9 Left."

Pilot: "OK, we got it, Northwest 441 cleared to 9 Left."

Phantom: "Cross the runway! Cross the runway!

The aircraft was nowhere near the runway, and in any event would not have had to cross it to carry out the taxi instructions, but I quickly looked to be sure there was no other vehicle or aircraft holding short that could have taken the instruction as legitimate.

Pilot: "Boy, this guy is a real pain. How long has this been going on?"

Phantom: "Who you calling a pain? I'll tell you who's a pain, you are!"

I chose not to respond, believing that the Northwest pilot had the picture, and not wishing in any fashion to egg the phantom on.

The individual clearly did not have controller experience, and the technical quality of the transmitter was audibly inferior to that of the tower equipment. Still, the possibility of a misunderstanding or an unauthorized movement could not be ignored, and each of us who worked ground during that period had to preface every one of our instructions with a caution to be alert for bogus transmissions, or immediately address each contact from the "phantom" by cautioning pilots and operators to ignore it. Finally, through the use of mobile vans with direction finding equipment, the individual was located in one of Eastern's maintenance spaces and taken into police custody.

Avoiding Gridlock

Most controllers considered ground control one of the least desirable position assignments. While any operator could be instructed to "stand by," a ground movement that was denied or delayed took up ramp or taxiway space that was always at a premium, and beyond a certain critical point, total gridlock could occur. This actually happened a few times, with the result that arriving aircraft had to be put in a holding pattern in order to relieve the pressure on the ground operation. For the most part, I enjoyed working ground control because so much of the job required innovative thinking and solutions, and because there was generally a lower risk factor than at other control positions where airplanes were moving at hundreds of miles per hour, and there was no stopping or back-up option.

One evening an incident occurred that distinctly fell into the category of not being enjoyable, resulting in the only time in my career that an aircraft for which I was responsible was damaged. I was monitoring a trainee who had come to MIA from the flight service option. He was determined to prove his worth at a big time terminal facility, despite having no prior experience controlling live traffic. Runway 9 Left was closed for construction, pending the installation of centerline lighting, which required an excavation several feet deep along its entire length. Most of the maintenance facilities, and all general aviation parking areas, were located on the north side of the runway, meaning that all arrivals intending to park at those locations landed on one of the other two runways and had to cross 9 Left at a point where the excavation had not yet occurred. These points were marked with lighted barricades, but the barrels and lights were regularly moved to accommodate the construction activities.

My trainee, "Mac" MacNamara, and I had been working the ground control position since about 8:00 pm, well after darkness had fallen, when a Piper Cherokee cleared Runway 12 and requested progressive taxi instructions to GAC. Mac immediately responded:

"Cherokee 71 Hotel, roger, turn northwestbound on the parallel taxiway, taxi to the end, then look for two rows of lighted barrels, taxi between them, then turn right on the north side taxiway and look for two amber lights, that is the entrance to AirTech."

A long pause followed, after which the pilot responded, "Cherokee 71 Hotel, say again?"

Mac spit out the same instructions, even more rapidly this time, and the pilot did not respond. I told Mac, "Look, you've got an inexperienced pilot, obviously unfamiliar with the airport, and he requested progressive instructions. Give it to him piece by piece."

Mac did as I suggested, and the airplane began to move, ever so slowly. As it approached the barricaded area, Mac told the pilot to taxi between the rows of lighted barrels. A moment later the airplane came to a stop, and the pilot transmitted, "Ground, 71 Hotel, I don't think I'm going the right way here." This was the moment where the incident could have been prevented, and I started to key my mic to instruct the pilot to hold his position, intending to summon Ramp 20 to provide assistance. But before I could act, Mac said, "71 Hotel, you're doing fine, just taxi straight ahead." The airplane moved forward, and suddenly the position light on the starboard wing was seen to drop precipitously. "Thanks a lot, ground, you just put me in the ditch," came the last transmission from the Cherokee. Later examination revealed that the propeller had been damaged, and the torque applied to the engine mounts as it struck the concrete had twisted the airframe, no doubt requiring a considerable outlay for the repairs.

Every fully qualified controller assigned to train a developmental knew that it only took an instant for the person in training to create a problem. On ground control, there was normally a longer period for either the instructor or the trainee to recognize a mistake and correct it, but in this case it was obvious that the nose wheel of the Cherokee had been almost in the ditch when the pilot stopped. It hadn't helped that the incident took place over a mile from the tower, in the dark, with the faint position lights of the aircraft barely discernible among the normal airport lighting and the construction barricades. Nevertheless, these were precisely the conditions that called for the assistance of the ramp supervisor, and as the controller "signed on" to the ground control position, I had been late in both the formulation and the execution of the proper action to keep the operation safe.

Non-Radar Training

In the fall of 1969, more than a year after I had reported to Miami Tower, and a few weeks after I checked out on Local Control, it was time to begin training in the TRACON. But before that could happen, there was an intermediate hurdle to clear in the form of a course in non-radar control. MIA had been a non-radar facility until 1963, at which time the first radar system was installed. There were still controllers in the facility who had been certified on and worked the non-radar operation, and were now instructors for trainees like me.

The purpose of non-radar training was to equip controller personnel with backstop procedures in the case of radar failure, which could, and did, happen with some regularity. In all phases of my training I found that one of the most difficult aspects of mastering the necessary skills was the absence of any experience or education in other walks of life that could serve as a template. Non-radar was no exception, and far more difficult than tower training or (later) radar training, principally because it was not dynamic. It was one thing to look out at moving airplanes on the runways and taxiways or to follow targets on a radar display, and quite another to peruse a stack of flight progress strips filled with numbers and arcane symbols in order to identify relative aircraft positions and traffic conflicts.

Non-radar was also a more reactive than proactive discipline. Every time a number was entered (a reported point, an estimate to a future point, or an assigned altitude) or crossed out (an altitude vacated) on a flight progress strip, a controller action was either required, permitted, ruled out, or none of the above. Discerning when and whether to act based on a static set of these hand written figures was the core skill of a proficient non-radar controller, and it was a skill that took years to develop.

Some of the non-radar separation standards did not seem, intuitively, to make good sense. For example, legal altitude separation was 1,000 feet, yet when one aircraft reported leaving a certain altitude, that altitude could be immediately assigned to another. So if the lower airplane descended slowly, and the one above descended rapidly, they could be separated by less than a thousand feet until the slow descending pilot reached the next level. On the other hand, aircraft in holding patterns 80 or 100 miles apart, if cleared to the same point without first establishing altitude separation, were considered in conflict the moment the second pilot received his clearance.

Fortunately non-radar training was all simulated, with the instructor playing the part of the pilots and adjacent ATC facilities, so the only real risk for me was the possibility of failing to complete the syllabus. It didn't take me too long to catch on to the approach control phase, as it was completely cut and dried. There were four altitudes available for arrivals in transitioning from the holding fixes, which were in center airspace and all separated from each other, and each arrival proceeded from its respective fix to another holding pattern over the outer marker, the final approach fix (FAF) for an ILS approach. The lowest aircraft was always number one in the approach sequence, even if it was not the first to reach the FAF. Once established in holding at the outer marker, the flights were "stepped down", meaning that as each airplane completed its approach, the ones above it could be descended in sequence. So a transcript of the non-radar approach operation might look like this:

1500Z

DL 294: "Miami Approach, Delta 294 entering holding at Chester, 10,000."

Controller: "Delta 294 Miami approach, cross Chester at 6,000, cleared over Chester direct Portland outer compass locator, hold as published, expect approach clearance at 1515 Zulu, time now 1500 Zulu."

DL 294: "Roger, Delta 294 out of ten for six, cross Chester at six, cleared over Chester direct Portland."

1502Z

EA 403: "Miami, Eastern 403 in holding at New River, level 10,000."

Controller: "Eastern 403 Miami approach, cross New River at 7,000, cleared over New River direct Portland outer compass locator, hold as published, expect approach clearance at 1525 Zulu, time now 1502 Zulu."

EA 403: "OK, that's cross New River at seven, cleared over New River direct Portland, and we're leaving ten for seven thousand."

These instructions required the pilots to descend to the assigned altitude within the confines of the protected holding pattern airspace. There could be variations if, for example, there was more than one airplane at a holding fix and no traffic at the other fixes awaiting clearance to the outer compass locator, or if several aircraft at one fix had been in holding longer than those at another.

Making Progress

With each instruction, the controller had to mark the appropriate flight progress strip, indicating the next point to which each aircraft was cleared, noting the requested altitude reports (90rl, 80rl, 70rl) arranged vertically, then crossing out these notations as the altitude reports were received. In the non-radar training syllabus, failure to cross out an altitude before re-assigning it to another aircraft was considered a separation error even if the pilot report had been received. I got caught on this more than once, with the instructor calmly telling me, "You've got two assigned nine thousand." "But I just received the report out of nine," I protested. "Separation is on the strips. If the strips don't show it, you don't have it," came the reply.

Once in the "stack" at the LOM (outer compass locator), the airplanes could be descended in sequence and cleared for the approach:

Here was a point at which it was easy to make a mistake as the approach controller. The rule was that after the first aircraft passed the outer marker, the next aircraft could be cleared for the approach with a restriction to cross the outer marker at a time at least two minutes later than the first. We relied on the old "drum" type clocks, where the hours, minutes and seconds were shown on a continuously rotating cylinder. When the tower reported an arrival past the outer marker, you had to look at the drum clock and note the time. We did not mark seconds on the flight progress strip, so that the notation might show, for example, "41." The trap was that if the time were actually 2141:45Z, and you then cleared the next airplane to cross the outer marker "at or later than 2143," the second pilot might reach the crossing point at 2143:10Z, resulting in only a one minute 25 second gap instead of the required two minutes. The technique was to always use a time three minutes later than the first report to insure that the two-minute minimum was met.

Controller: "Eastern 403, descend and maintain 1,500. Cross Portland at or later than 1519, time now 1516, cleared ILS 9 Left approach, report leaving 3,000."

EAL 403: "Eastern 403 out of three for fifteen hundred, cleared for the approach, understand cross Portland at or later than one-niner."

Controller: "Eastern 403 roger, contact tower 118.3, report Portland inbound."

As this lengthy representation shows, the time it took for two airplanes to arrive from the outer fixes and be cleared for an approach made the non-radar operation highly inefficient with any volume of traffic. Depending on its position in the center holding pattern, it could take five or six minutes for an aircraft to complete the pattern and proceed inbound after receiving clearance. Similarly, at the outer marker, even with a nominal two minute gap between arrivals, the interval was frequently much longer because of the need for the pilot to reach the final approach altitude and complete the circuit before commencing the approach.

As noted earlier, the approach phase of non-radar was "easier" than the departure phase. Non-radar departure control required an intimate knowledge of the airspace and airway structure through which and by which the aircraft were cleared. It also required the application of numerous rules, starting with a minimum ten minutes between aircraft outbound on the same route at the same altitude. But if a lead aircraft were slower, that ten minutes would not hold up for long. You had to understand airway separation, which calculated points at which separation between two routes was determined by the degree of divergence between them and distance from the navaid, as well as points on the departure routes that cleared the inbound flow of arrivals.

And at least in the non-radar training syllabus, it was not enough to simply keep the outbounds in their altitude stratum until reaching the point where you could issue a climb. You had to recognize whether there was actually any arrival traffic that was a factor. It was an automatic "gig" on the problem if you held a departure down unnecessarily. All of this you had to figure out from a stack of flight progress strips filled with numbers, crossed out numbers, future times (estimates to the next point), past times (points reported) and other "chicken scratch" entries filling the tiny scraps of paper.

When Radar Failed

I finally struggled through the non-radar class, and as it turned out, never had to work it for real after a radar failure. To my knowledge, there was never a problem or close call during the periods when the non-radar operation was being conducted, but at least one incident had the potential for serious consequences. It occurred one early morning when the weather was bad with ceiling and visibility values hovering around the minimums for an ILS approach. The radar had failed during the latter hours of the midnight shift, and the airport was on an east operation (landing and departing runways 9 Right and 9 Left). This was in 1969 or 1970, a time when there were only two full ILS systems installed at MIA, one serving 9 Left and the other serving 27 Left.

A Latin American carrier DC-6 arrived over Mango, then the arrival fix in the southeast quadrant of our airspace, and was cleared, as illustrated above, direct to the Portland outer compass locator. The pilot was cleared for the ILS 9 Left approach and reported the outer marker inbound. The weather had improved slightly, so that the controllers in the tower could just make out the landing threshold of 9 Left located at the northwest corner of the field. Each had a pair of binoculars focused on the point where they expected the airplane to break out of the overcast, expecting it to happen in about two minutes. Because the tower was situated between the two east-west runways, the 27 Left threshold, located at the southeast corner, was behind and to the left of the men with the binoculars.

At about the two-minute point, one of them caught something out of the corner of his eye, quickly turning to his left to observe the DC-6 rolling out on runway 27 Left. A playback of the approach control and tower tapes revealed that both controllers had used correct phraseology, naming Portland and referring to 9 Left in both the approach clearance and landing clearance. Nevertheless, the pilot had proceeded to Orange (so named for the Orange Bowl, over which it was located), the outer compass locator for 27 Left, and executed the ILS, landing on the wrong runway and opposite to the east operation flow. Had it not been for the early morning hour, there could well have been a departure taking off on 9 Right, nose to nose with the DC-6.

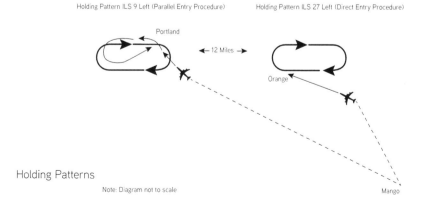

Holding Patterns

Once again, it appeared that the pilot's poor command of English had contributed to the incident. The approach plates to 9 Left and 27 Left appear quite similar, with the notation "LOM" printed on both, and it is probable that the words "left" and "outer compass locator" were the only ones that registered when the approach controller issued the clearance to Portland. The holding pattern for 27 Left was at least 12 miles closer to Mango than the corresponding pattern for 9 Left, and would have permitted a straight in entry as compared with the more time consuming parallel or teardrop entry required at Portland. If fuel remaining was also a concern, not unlikely in the case of an eight or ten hour flight from South America, a good case could be made for a likely set of circumstances leading to the flight crew's error (or perhaps deliberate decision).

6. Training on Local Control

At some point after certification on ground control, I began training on local control, the position that issued landing and takeoff clearances. Certain aspects of any control position were applicable to any other-- the principles of formulate, execute, and monitor were as relevant at the local control position as they had been on ground. But the demands and complexity on local put this operation in an entirely different category. Because of the prevailing winds in South Florida, the airport conducted an "east" operation over 90 per cent of the time, meaning that the lineup of departures for any of the three runways normally used (9 Left, 9 Right, and 12) was more than a mile away from the tower.

Although ground control did its best to place the flight progress strips in the local control bay in an order that matched the actual sequence of the aircraft awaiting departure, there were times when two or more strips were out of order. When this happened, the local controller ended up having to figure out who the number one airplane was. Under busy conditions, with closely spaced arrivals landing every two minutes or so, the time taken in correctly ordering the strips meant that the opportunity get a departure out between two arrivals would be lost.

Arrival traffic could be even more problematic, for a number of reasons. The IFR arrivals, principally the air carriers, were sequenced by approach control, and a list of their call signs was recorded on a writing pad in front of the local controller. Sometimes an error would be made in the order, and again, local would have to play "20 questions" with the pilot (actually, not more than two or three, relating to location, or requesting an "ident" where the pilot activated that feature on the aircraft transponder, and the target would momentarily "bloom" on the tower radar display). Nevertheless, with a tight sequence of jet aircraft barreling down the final at 150 knots or more, those few seconds could be critical with respect to launching a departure in an arrival gap.

Another problem that recurred with troublesome frequency was that the tower (local control) frequencies for MIA and Fort Lauderdale tower were similar—118.3 and 119.3 respectively. Either the approach controller would make an error in issuing the frequency change to the tower (rare), or the pilot would either incorrectly hear the frequency or make an error in dialing in the third digit on his radio (more common). The instruction to change to tower frequency normally occurred when the aircraft was about five miles from the runway, so that there was not more than two minutes to recognize and correct any error in the landing sequence or the frequency issued.

Besides the IFR arrivals, the local controller had to deal with VFR traffic. These aircraft were not sequenced by approach control, but had to be identified and fit into the approach control sequence by local control. Many pilots of VFR aircraft were not highly experienced, and would complicate the job of sequencing them by incorrectly reporting their position or distance from the airport. They would say they were east of the field when they were actually west; they would say they were five miles out when they were more like 20 miles; or even worse, report five miles west when they were right on top of the airport and in danger, as the old hands in the tower said, of becoming "a hood ornament on a DC-8." Often there was no opportunity to get them in because of the volume and tight sequencing of the approach control traffic. In these cases, they had to be instructed to hold outside the airport traffic area and issued an expected delay. Sometimes there would be as many as five or six VFRs holding, and it took forever to get them on the ground. (In later years, many of these difficulties were reduced or eliminated with the advent of VFR radar service programs, which required that all traffic be sequenced by approach control at high-density airports, and with the creation of Terminal Control/ Class B and Stage 3/ TRSA Areas, which restricted access to those airports).

Making Local Control Decisions

I had expected that after certification on flight data, clearance delivery, and ground control, local control would be somewhat easier. I could not have been more wrong. The aircraft worked at the earlier positions were either stationary or moving slowly, and they were all visible to the controller. On local, the departures were at a substantial distance from the tower, and the arrivals were either not visible until the last moments before landing, or not where they reported themselves to be. It was my first experience of having to make decisions and issue instructions based on incomplete and/ or incorrect information.

Predictably, the senior controllers were much better at this, and I made it a practice when I was not assigned a position, or activity was slow, to watch and listen to these men as often as possible. As noted earlier, it did not seem too difficult, observing the local control operation in "passive" mode, but it was entirely different when I had to take the reins myself. In a matter of seconds, under busy conditions, the controller had to make the following decisions and take the appropriate actions:

Were there any flow restrictions in place? At times either Miami Center or the TRACON would request increased spacing between departures traveling a certain route. If the first airplane in the departure queue was subject to such a restriction, that had to be taken into account in making the next determinations. If not, the controller could focus on the two types of separation he was required to provide: runway separation, which varied based on the type aircraft, and IFR separation (generally three miles) for two airplanes on instrument flight plans.

Dividing his attention between the tower radar displays (BRITE) and looking out the window, the controller had to determine if there was there a sufficient gap to launch a departure ahead of the next arrival. If so, the number one aircraft could be cleared for takeoff, or "immediate" takeoff, depending on the speed and distance from the airport of the arrival traffic.

If there was a previous landing, a quick determination had to be made as to whether it would clear the runway in time to use an otherwise sufficient "gap." If so, the next departure could be instructed to "taxi into position and hold," with takeoff clearance withheld until the landing aircraft cleared the runway.

Before issuing takeoff clearance, local control had to make a final judgment as to whether runway separation and IFR minimums would be met. And finally, it was "de riguer" to scan the runway immediately before pronouncing the magic words, "cleared for takeoff." More than a few times an alert local controller caught a situation where a slow tug or an errant vehicle had not yet cleared the runway.

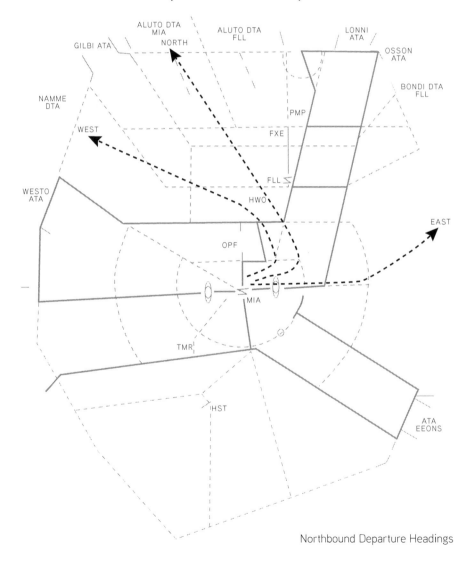

Northbound Departure Headings

There was also an entire second level of practical strategizing needed to expedite the departure flow and avoid overloading the three TRACON departure controllers after the aircraft entered the radar regime. On an east operation, there were three standard headings available for northbound IFR traffic: 090, 060, and 040 (See chart on prior page). For the southbound IFRs, there were also three standard headings: 120, 150, and 170. By alternating the departures between the north and south radar positions to the extent feasible, the local controller could provide extra separation between each pair. Varying the headings assigned to aircraft destined to the same departure controller could, to a lesser extent, achieve the same thing. Finally, it was expected that local would maintain an awareness of the departure routes the pilots had received at Clearance Delivery.

Departure Transition Areas

There were six departure transition areas (DTAs)—three north and three south. These were basically defined "gates" through which departing aircraft were delivered to Miami Center. In many instances, even if the next four or five airplanes awaiting takeoff were northbound, local could order the sequence to split them up among the available routings. Some of the "purists" added one more wrinkle, stated as "Don't give departure control any crossovers."

Since the three northbound DTAs were oriented roughly east, north, and northwest, it made sense, when practical, to assign eastbound aircraft 090, northbound 060, and northwest aircraft 040. In this way, the departure controller benefitted from a fanning effect such that none of the aircraft had to "cross over" another one to reach its assigned routing. The same techniques could be used for traffic routed to the south, where once again there were three standard headings north and three to the south. VFR aircraft were not assigned a heading and were simply instructed to make a left (or right) turn out of traffic.

This was all basic stuff. In addition to the traffic decisions and instructions, there were a number of advisories, some mandatory, others simply common sense, to keep the pilots informed. Local also had to override the TRACON radar position to advise the controller of each departure. So a playback of a local control exchange could go like this:

N6641U: "Miami tower, Mooney 6641 Uniform about 5 miles north for landing with (ATIS information) Papa."

Local: "Mooney 6641 Uniform Miami tower, report over Hialeah racetrack for left traffic runway 9 Left."

N6641U: "Tower, 41 Uniform, I'm not familiar with the race track."

NA 611: "Miami tower, National 611 with you about 6 [miles] out for 9 Left."

Local: "National 611 Miami tower, cleared to land runway 9 Left, wind 090 at 15."

NA 611: "OK, cleared to land, National 611."

Local: "Mooney 41 Uniform roger, report three miles north of the airport."

EA 327 (on 9 Left after landing): "Ah, tower, Eastern 327, be advised, the braking action on this runway is only fair."

Local: "Eastern 327 roger."

Local: "National 611, be advised braking action on 9 Left reported as fair by a landing 727."

NA 611: "National 611, roger."

Local: "United 414, runway 9 Left, taxi into position and hold, be ready for immediate [takeoff], traffic on a four mile final."

UA 414: "Position and hold, United 414, we'll be ready."

Local: "Eastern 327, turn right next intersection, contact ground [121] point 8."

EA 327: "OK, we'll make it, ground point 8, Eastern 327."

N6641U: "Tower, 41 Uniform, say again your last instructions?"

Local: "Mooney 41U, standby—"

Local (to ground control, crossing a tug behind EA 327): "Hey ground, tell that tug to kick it in the ass, I've got one in position."

N5030R: "Tower, Cessna 5030 Romeo ready at 9 Left."

Local: "United 414, fly heading 090, runway 9 Left, cleared for immediate takeoff."

UA 414: "090, cleared to go, United 414."

Local (overriding the radar position): "High departure, local, United 414 is off."

Radar controller: "OS [responds with operating initials]."

Local: "Cessna 5030 Romeo, hold short, landing traffic."

Local: "Mooney 41 Uniform, are you just entering left downwind at midfield?"

N6641U: "That's affirmative, 41 Uniform."

Local: "United 414, traffic is the Goodyear blimp three [miles] southeast, orbiting at 1000 feet."

UA 414: "United 414, got him in sight."

Local: "United 414 roger, contact departure control, good day."

UA 414: "Going to departure, United 414, so long y'all."

N7852Z: "Tower, Cessna 7852 Zulu, IFR to Palm Beach, ready at 9 Left."

Local: "Mooney 41 Uniform, your traffic is a National 727 on short final. Extend your downwind."

N6641U: "OK, extending downwind, 41 Uniform."

Local: "Cessna 7852 Zulu, hold short, landing traffic."

N7852Z: "52 Zulu, we'll hold."

Local: "National 611, turn right next intersection but before you go, how was the braking action?"

NA 611: "No problem for us, I'd call it good."

Local: "National 611 roger, contact ground point 8."

Local: "Mooney 41 Uniform, start your base, cleared to land Runway 9 Left, traffic is two Cessnas departing ahead of your arrival."

N6641U: "Cleared to land, Mooney 41 Uniform."

Local: "Cessna 30 Romeo Runway 9 Left, cleared for takeoff, left turn out approved."

N5030R: "Cleared for takeoff, Cessna 30 Romeo."

Local: Cessna 7852 Zulu, Runway 9 Left, taxi into position and hold, traffic a VFR Cessna 172 departing ahead of you will be northeastbound."

N7852Z: "52 Zulu, position and hold."

Local: "Cessna 52 Zulu, turn left heading 040, cleared for takeoff."

N7852Z: "52 Zulu, cleared for takeoff, heading 040."

Local (overriding departure control): North low, local, 7852 Zulu is off."

Radar controller: "IG."

Local: "Cessna 52 Zulu, contact departure control."

N7852Z: "52 Zulu, what was that departure frequency again?"

Local: "Cessna 52 Zulu, contact departure on 128.6."

N7852Z: "OK, 128.6, 52 Zulu."

These 55 transmissions (and sometimes more) could occur in a rapid-fire sequence lasting no more than three minutes. From the local controller's perspective, it was vitally important to be able to think and plan ahead while making real-time decisions and issuing real-time instructions.

However, this snapshot representation of a few minutes at the local control position, does not reflect the number of "smeared" radio calls and "say agains" that were routine during any busy session. Experienced controllers knew that if they could transmit as quickly as they could formulate their strategy, without having to wait for acknowledgements and without having to re-issue instructions because of "say agains," they would hardly ever be extremely busy. My take was that the radio link was both the lifeline and the bottleneck in the ATC system.

Taking Charge

Although I was finally certified on local control, it was a far steeper climb than the three previous tower positions. I had been in the facility for more than a year, but it took at least another year before I felt reasonably comfortable. I never really enjoyed working local, taking my turn when I was assigned, but not arriving early at shift change to get the position, as many other men did.

Unlike the radar positions, and even ground control, the options at local were comparatively limited. On radar, there were six individual maneuvers, and more if two or more were issued together, that a controller could instruct a pilot to perform: speed up, slow down, turn right, turn left, climb, or descend.

On ground, there were multiple taxiways, plus the ability to stop a taxiing aircraft or hold it at its parking position. On local, once an aircraft was established in sequence on the final, a speed increase would only make a tight gap more critical. Issuing S-turns could help slightly, but only if there was ample space behind the aircraft making them, because eventually the pilot would have to re-establish the aircraft on the final approach course, having reduced the interval between itself and the following traffic.

Altitude adjustments were out, because a fixed rate of descent was necessary in order to arrive at the correct touchdown point on the runway. This left only the option of requesting the pilot to reduce speed, but in a tight sequence, the aircraft were already at or close to their minimum approach speed, and even if a pilot could slow down by a few knots, there was not sufficient time in the five or six miles between initial contact with local and arrival over the threshold for those few knots to do much good. So it came down basically to repeating the same judgment call by the local controller, that is, estimating whether spacing between two arrivals was sufficient to launch a departure, without much opportunity for imaginative innovation.

If you guessed right, the departure got airborne with legal runway separation from the arrival. If not, the arrival had to be issued a go around, which could result in two large airplanes, both near their minimum control speeds, airborne in close proximity to one another. I always worked conservatively, meaning that I rarely had a go-around, but also being prodded at times by the tower supervisors to "keep 'em moving" because they thought I was not using every available arrival interval for the departure traffic. There was also a definite element of peer pressure, as everyone in the tower could see a lengthening queue of departures, an unused arrival gap, or a go-around.

Under Pressure

Even the controllers that liked working the position still had their share of "interesting moments." In one case, early in my training while I was assigned to ground control, Karl Schimmel, one of the three watch supervisors, decided to man local control one morning. This occasioned some surreptitious eye-rolling, because Karl, at age 50 plus, had never formally certified as a local controller. To make matters worse (i.e., more embarrassing for Karl) he was using a handheld microphone, with the pilot responses and TRACON coordination calls transmitted via speaker for all to hear. In addition, Karl wore his supervisory responsibilities very gravely, seldom exhibiting any sense of humor, and cutting us no slack when it came to an insufficiently blocked necktie, or a request to leave the facility even one or two minutes before the end of the shift.

At the time of the morning when Karl signed on to local, there were relatively few departures, but a moderate number of arrivals, chiefly because of Eastern's training flights. Eastern would launch four or five of these flights each morning, and they would make multiple approaches, providing a nice learning opportunity for anyone training on approach control. On the day in question, the radar display showed targets lined up for 9 Left and 9 Right, with roughly one mile between the final approach courses (the 9 Right traffic was to the right, or south, of the 9 Left traffic with the 9 Left traffic to the north).

So this is what we heard beginning a few minutes after Karl took the position:

TRACON: "Tower, approach, inbounds."

Karl: "Go ahead."

TRACON: "For 9 Left, Eastern 702, National 603, Lear 1025 Tango. For 9 Right, Delta 42, American 580, Continental 337. DM."

Karl wrote down the call signs, gave his initials, then began to receive calls.

EA 702: "Miami Tower Eastern 702 with you for 9 Left."

Karl: "Eastern 702 Miami Tower, cleared to land 9 Left."

EA 702: "Cleared to land, Eastern 702."

DL 42: "Delta 42's with you, tower, for the right side."

Karl: "Delta 42 Miami Tower, cleared to land 9 Right."

DL 42: "Cleared to land on the right, roger, Delta 42."

AA 580: "And tower, American 580, looks like we're out here behind Delta for 9 Right."

Karl: "American 580 Miami Tower, roger, number two for 9 Right, continue approach."

EAT 190: "Miami Tower, Eastern trainer 190 with you about six or seven out for 9 Left."

(Per the arrival sequence given earlier by the TRACON, the next call for 9 Left should have come from National 603).

Karl replied: "Eastern trainer calling Miami Tower, I've got nothing on you."

NA 603: "Hello Miami Tower, National 603 on final for 9 Left."

Karl: "National 603 Miami Tower, number two for 9 Left, continue."

NA 603: "National 603, roger."

EAT 190: "Tower, Eastern trainer 190 by the outer marker [about 5 miles from the runway]"

Karl: "Eastern trainer, I say again, I have no information on you."

CO 337: "Continental 337 checking in for 9 Right, tower."

Karl: "Continental 337, Miami Tower, number three for 9 Right."

N1025T: "Miami Tower, Lear 25 Tango inbound for 9 Left."

EAT 190: "Well how about it tower, is Eastern trainer 190 cleared to land or what?"

Karl: "Eastern trainer calling tower, I told you, I have no information on your flight!"

EAT 190: "Well then we're breaking it off to the south, Eastern trainer 190."

A few seconds later came an angry transmission:

AA 580: "Tower, American 580, we just had a near miss with a DC-9, couldn't have passed over us by more than 50 feet. We want a phone number to call the tower."

Karl quickly issued the telephone number, then yelled, "Somebody get me out of here!" Another controller took the position, and Karl stalked down the stairs, his customarily dour expression distinctly more pronounced than usual.

As soon as Karl disappeared from view, somebody said, "Jesus, do you believe that crap? I don't know why the hell he wants to work a control position anyway." There were a few other comments registering disbelief at what had just occurred, and since at that point I had little understanding of the local control operation, I asked one of the senior guys to explain it to me. His explanation was a real eye-opener:

"First of all, Karl had no business working the position. He has never trained or qualified on any tower or radar position in the facility. Secondly, it was obvious that the TRACON left that Eastern trainer out of the sequence when they called up the list of inbounds. All Karl had to do was override the TRACON controller and ask him who the trainer was following on the 9 Left final. Third, there were only three inbounds for 9 Left on the writing pad, but four targets shown on the BRITE display. He could have asked the trainer to ident, and observed that he was between Eastern 702 and National 603. Fourth, when Eastern said he was breaking off to the south, Karl should have immediately instructed him to break out to the north. Instead, he let him go south and run over that American inbound for 9 Right."

All transmissions on control frequencies and communication lines were recorded on large, multi-track spool recorders. These spools could be removed at any time to play back a specific time segment for any control position. On my next break I saw Karl in the playback room with a head set on advancing and rewinding the tape, making copious notes on a yellow legal pad. The expression on his face was hardly one of professional satisfaction.

SE-210 © Allan Clegg Dreamstime.com

Unusual Events

Like ground control, local afforded its own unusual events, ranging from the mildly amusing to the truly hairy to the catastrophic. Soon after my certification on local, I experienced a situation that started out looking as though it would qualify for the "truly hairy" category, but that in a flash turned into one of astonished relief on my part. There was an Air France Caravelle, designated the SE-210, inbound for 9 Right, about five miles out on final. The Caravelle, still flying in 1969, had been one of the first commercially viable airline jets to go into service, and was in regular service to MIA.

Controllers knew that, unlike all newer generation transports, the aircraft had no reverse thrust capability, meaning that the air crews had to rely on braking and aerodynamic drag to slow down after landing. The weather was marginal VFR, with reduced visibility and a low ceiling, the wind shifting from west to east and back again at short intervals. By the time I received the first call from Air France, the wind had shifted from 090 at 10 knots (meaning a head wind for a 9 Right landing) to 240 at 22 knots. The aircraft would have a quartering tailwind on the (then) 9,300-foot long runway. So the exchange with the French-accented pilot went like this:

AF 240: "Miami tower, this is Air France two four zero on approach to zero nine right."

Me: "Air France 240 Miami Tower, be advised the wind now 240 at 22. Would you prefer to break off the approach and land to the west?"

AF 240: "Negative, tower, we will land zero nine right, Air France two four zero."

Me: "Air France 240 roger, cleared to land 9 Right, wind 240 at 20, gusting to 25."

AF 240: "Roger, cleared to land runway zero nine right, Air France two four zero."

I still did not have the aircraft in sight during this exchange because of the low ceiling and the limited visibility in the light rain that had been falling for some minutes. I continued transmitting updates to the wind direction and velocity, also adding an advisory that the runway was wet, and then the Caravelle broke out of the overcast, high and fast. The pilot visibly steepened his approach, but it was obvious to the whole tower crew that this was going to be a long landing at high speed on a wet runway. Sure enough, the airplane was close to midfield when it touched down, and it was moving at a rapid clip. There was a possibility, because of the wet surface, that the tires could hydroplane, that is, not make contact with the runway, further degrading the pilot's braking capability.

Several of us reached for the alarm button to summon the crash crew, certain that the Caravelle was going to run off the end and crash into the piers holding the 27 Left approach lights. But as soon as the nose wheel touched down, the pilot deployed an 80-foot drag chute that billowed out tautly behind the aircraft, enabling the crew to reach taxi speed just in time to turn off at the 27 Left run-up pad, right at the end of 9 Right. There was a chorus of relieved laughter from all of us in the tower, none of whom knew the Caravelle was equipped with a drag chute. Although the military used them on many different aircraft types, to my knowledge no other commercial transport was similarly equipped, and I never saw another chute deployment during my time at MIA.

Four-Legged Visitors

On another occasion during a midnight shift in the tower, I was working ground control and local control combined, as was standard during the wee hours of the morning when there were at times as much as several minutes between transmissions on either frequency. A 727 made a landing on 9 Left, the first in perhaps 20 or 30 minutes. As the pilot exited the runway, he transmitted, "Tower, you've got a cow in the grass area just to our right here." I rogered the transmission, thinking you've got to be kidding me, it was probably just some shape in the darkness.

But I had experienced enough strange events at all the positions I worked that I immediately followed up by summoning Ramp 20 to investigate. Soon the station wagon with the rotating amber beacon was proceeding along the parallel taxiway to the intersection where the pilot had reported the cow. The ramp supervisor did not find the cow, but decided to inspect the entire length of the runway, after which he reported, "Ground, Ramp 20, there are cows all over this airport." This was potentially very serious, as any of the animals could be on the runway during a takeoff or landing, and there was insufficient lighting to determine if the runway was clear.

I informed the shift supervisor, which led to a discussion as to whether we should close the airport. We decided that Ramp 20 would stand by at the approach end of 9 Left and make a high speed run down its entire length just ahead of a landing or departure to clear the runway. The other runways would not be used in order to minimize the area that had to be patrolled. When daylight dawned, we saw at least 30 head of cattle placidly grazing from one end of the airport's 2,700 acres to the other. Sunrise fortunately occurred early enough that the daytime ramp agents were able to mount a roundup before the morning traffic volume grew too large.

Later investigation revealed that the gate to the quarantine pen—where animals imported from other countries were kept pending a veterinary examination—had come open, releasing the bovine visitors for their own self-guided tour of MIA. To some extent, the entire incident was an example of the dark humor truism, often expressed by controllers, as "I'd rather be lucky than good." There was no way of knowing when the escape from the quarantine pen had occurred, or how many landings and takeoffs had taken place before we realized what was going on.

My one genuine "save" as a local controller occurred several years after my certification on the position. It happened on one of the rare days when MIA had an extended period of solid IFR weather. Departures were backed up because of flow restrictions from both Miami Center and the TRACON radar controllers, and all arrivals were being vectored to the 27 Left ILS. At the time, the instrument approach to 27 Right did not have a glide slope, and in the heavy rain the weather minimums were too low for that approach. This meant that the spacing on the 27 Left final was tight. It was only many years later that ground radar was installed at the tower, and because of the near zero visibility, neither the ground controller nor the local controller could see the airplanes they were working.

There was a slightly larger gap between the next two arrivals, and I made the decision to launch my next departure, an Airlift International DC-8, between those landings. After the National 727 disappeared from the tower BRITE display, meaning that the aircraft should have landed, I waited about 20 seconds, before beginning the following exchange:

Me: "National 51, tower, verify that you are on the ground."

NA 51: "We're rolling out now tower, National 51."

Me: "Roger. Airlift 106 runway 27 Left, taxi into position and hold, traffic on a four-mile final."

RD 106: "Position and hold, Airlift 106."

Me: "National 51, report clear of the runway."

NA 51: "Okay, will advise, we should be able to make this next intersection."

NA 51 (about 20 seconds later, or enough time for the next arrival to have progressed one mile closer to the landing threshold): "Clear of the runway, National 51."

Me: "Airlift 106, cleared for immediate takeoff, traffic on a three-mile final."

RD 106: "Cleared for takeoff, Airlift 106."

As I stared into the blank wall of rain beating against the tower windows, I tried to visualize the heavily laden DC-8 accelerating to takeoff speed (Airlift was a cargo carrier, and they were always loaded to maximum gross weight), and it seemed that this "squeeze play" was going to work. But then my fortunately developed controller's sixth sense kicked in. Somehow I knew that something was not right:

Me: "Airlift 106, have you started your departure roll?"

RD 106: "Ah, negative tower, Airlift 106, we're just taking a look at our weather radar here to see where we want to go after we get airborne."

Despite two advisories about the position of the next landing for 27 Left and an acknowledged clearance for immediate takeoff, the pilot had held in position in order to check the cockpit weather display. Not for the first time in my career (or the last), I felt a jolt of adrenaline, observing on the BRITE that the next landing was about 20 seconds from touchdown. Priorities! Cancel Airlift's takeoff clearance, or send Delta around? Both had to be done. I split the difference:

Me: "Delta 642, be prepared for a go around, break, Airlift 106 cancel takeoff clearance, acknowledge."
RD 106: "Holding position, Airlift 106."
Me: "Delta 642, go around, traffic on the runway."
DL 642: "Going around, Delta 642."

All's well that ends well, but the Delta DC-9 could not have been higher than 200 feet when the pilot applied power for the go-around, and jet engines took a few seconds to spool up when the throttles were advanced. More than likely Delta overflew the DC-8 with only a couple of hundred feet to spare. We had had a number of go-arounds prior to this incident, as was common on days when the weather was down, and because of the hectic pace in the tower, no one else really knew what a close call it had been. The go-around was handled routinely, and the operation continued. The hairy minute or two I had just experienced on local exemplified one of the central facts about the job of air traffic controller, stated cynically, but with a solid kernel of truth, as "No one knows I am doing a good job until I don't do it."

Other Saves

MIA's local controllers performed many other "saves," far more than I knew about. One that I witnessed directly involved one of the South or Central American pilots with a very limited command of English who listened for key words, like "cleared to land" and "cleared for takeoff." The local controller was Randy Ward, the Air Force veteran who had reported for duty with Timmy Timmons and me. He had put a Northwest 727 in position on Runway 30 and the South American jet in position on 27 Right, intending to launch Northwest, headed to one of the northbound DTAs, first, delaying takeoff clearance to the southbound airplane until it could safely pass behind the 727. The departure ends of the two runways basically came together at the northwest corner of the airport, but once the Runway 30 departure was airborne, the 27 Right traffic could be safely launched with room to spare at the point where the flight paths crossed. Randy clearly enunciated the takeoff clearance to Northwest 185:

Randy: "Northwest 185, turn left heading 290, Runway 30 cleared for takeoff."
NW 185: "Cleared to go, heading 290, Northwest 185."

As he had been trained to do, as he was issuing the clearance, Randy scanned the length of the runway, observing that it was in fact clear. The Northwest pilot got airborne right at the moment that Randy observed the foreign aircraft in the air, creating a likely tie and collision at the crossing point. Thinking quickly, Randy saw three things: There was no opportunity to issue a turn to either aircraft, it was too late to have either of them land again and be able to stop before running out of runway, and the South American airplane was at a slightly higher altitude than Northwest 185. Within a second or two, he transmitted these four words:

Randy: "Northwest, keep it low."

Although the 727 was only one or two hundred feet in the air, the pilot leveled off, perhaps by now seeing the traffic approaching from his right, and slipped underneath the other airplane.

Randy then transmitted: "Sorry about that, Northwest, the other guy took off without a clearance."

The Northwest pilot acknowledged the information without comment, seeming to have seen that Randy's alertness had prevented a bad situation from becoming something far worse. Of course the tapes were played back to verify that in fact nothing had been said that the foreign pilot could have interpreted as a takeoff clearance, and the entire incident was eventually chalked up to another example of the language problem. The South American pilot had been instructed to taxi into position and hold, and was listening only for the next expected transmission, namely, cleared for takeoff. He had filtered out both the Northwest 185 call sign and the runway on which the takeoff was to be made, taking the words he had been waiting for as meant for him.

Another Close Call

Another close call occurred that did not involve a controller "save," was more than likely caused by the pilot's failure to understand English. MIA was again on a west operation, departing on 27 Right and 27 Left, landing on 27 Right and Runway 30. Local control was "split", meaning that operations on 27 Left and 30 were worked by South Local on a frequency separate from the one used by North Local controlling 27 Right. Constant coordination between the two local control positions was required because both controllers were launching aircraft into the same departure airspace, with the same separation standards applicable as if there were a single local controller.

Although Runway 30 was primarily used for arrivals, occasionally ground control would assign it to a northbound departure. The operational advantage was that as soon as the aircraft crossed the extended centerline of 27 Right after takeoff, it was no longer a factor to following traffic off 27 Right. On the day in question, a Lockheed Electra, designated the L-188, had been taxied to Runway 30 for a short hop to nearby Opa-locka airport, just six miles north of MIA. At the same time, there was an Air Mexico DC-8 about seven miles out for landing, seemingly slowed to a normal approach speed. So the sequence of communications went like this:

N271LB: "Tower, Lockheed 271 Lima Bravo ready at Runway 30."

South Local: "Lockheed 271 Lima Bravo roger, hold short." Then, overriding North Local: "Hey North Local, got an Electra to go off 30."

North Local: "OK, behind my Eastern 727 going into position" [on 27 Right].

South Local: "Lockheed 1 Lima Bravo, Runway 30 taxi into position and hold, traffic departing 27 Right."

N271LB: "Position and hold, Lima Bravo."

AM410 (heavily accented pilot): "Miami tower, this is Air Mexico four one zero, we approach Runway three zero."

South Local: "Air Mexico 410 Miami tower, cleared to land Runway 30, Electra traffic departing ahead of your arrival."

AM410: "Clear to land, Air Mexico four one zero."

For whatever reason, the 727's takeoff on 27 Right was delayed, but as soon as he had space, the south local controller cleared the Electra for takeoff. The pilot did not immediately apply power, and it was becoming obvious that it was going to be a tight squeeze between the L-188 and the DC-8. Finally the Electra began to roll, but too slowly to make the operation with Air Mexico work. Local issued go-around instructions, without receiving a response, repeating them several times with increasing urgency. The DC-8 crossed the threshold with the Electra still on the ground, not more than 1,500 feet down the runway, and with an overtake speed between the two airplanes in excess of 100 knots. There was no doubt in any of our minds that we were about to witness a disaster. But apparently the aviation gods were on our side that day, as the Electra, at what appeared to be an unbelievably slow speed, rose into the air. A number of profanities filled the tower as Air Mexico rolled out, passing under N271LB, ending up on the runway several hundred feet ahead of the slow-moving Electra. We speculated that because of the short distance to Opa-locka, the Electra pilot was carrying minimum fuel, with no passengers or cargo, thus enabling the short takeoff roll and slow liftoff speed.

Once again, it appeared that the DC-8 pilot had listened for the words he needed to hear ("cleared to land") and tuned out any and all further transmissions. Despite a seemingly unending stream of similar occurrences involving foreign carriers, we were all resigned to the fact that there would be no significant action taken against Air Mexico or the individual pilot. If such an egregious breech of FARs were committed by a domestic flight crew, both the FAA and the airline itself would take immediate action, but in the case of a foreign carrier, all reports of flight violations or incidents were routed through the U.S. Department of State. Any response, or lack of it, then became subject to larger diplomatic concerns, meaning that for all practical purposes, in most cases, no action was ever taken.

Coordination between control positions occurred regularly, sometimes because the traffic situation required it, other times at the controller's option either to respond to a pilot request or to expedite a particular operation. But coordination was something of a two-edged sword, in that it could benefit the controller initiating the action, but placed a new, and unexpected, demand on the controller receiving the call. The ability to judge correctly and consistently when to coordinate was one of the most important skills a controller had to master. There was a definite hierarchy of perceived proficiency throughout the controller corps, and one of the reasons an individual could be ranked lower by his peers is best described by some version of the following pronouncement: "That SOB calls you about every damn airplane he is working, but when you need something from him, he is always too busy to talk to you." There was a definite ethic in place that you managed your own traffic, in your area of responsibility, keeping your demands on other control positions to an absolute minimum.

One night during the evening shift there was an incident that could have ended very badly but for the timely coordination between Lanny Williams, the ground controller, and Don Harris, the local controller, under circumstances where another pair of specialists might not have made the effort. Traffic was relatively light, without a line-up of departures waiting. The next two arrivals for 9 Left were a Cessna 172 followed by an Eastern L-1011 with more than adequate spacing between them. The first available exit from the runway was 1,200 feet from the threshold, and was located directly opposite the principal general aviation parking area, nearly a mile from the control tower. Most single-engine GA aircraft could easily make this turnoff, and most did if they intended to park at the adjacent ramp. In practice, these aircraft sometimes did not contact ground control because by the time they changed radio frequencies, they had already crossed the north side parallel taxiway and had entered the non-movement area. Don cleared the Cessna to land, then, after observing the aircraft touch down, issued landing clearance to the L-1011, still about five miles out. Within the next minute or so, something prompted Don to initiate the following exchange:

Don: "Hey Lanny, did that Cessna ever call you?"

Lanny: "Negative. Where is he?"

Don: "I told him to call you, I guess he just exited at L-1 [the intersection opposite GAC] and went straight to the ramp."

Both Don and Lanny made several attempts to contact the Cessna, but received no response on either frequency.

Lanny: "Well, I don't have him, and I don't see any lights, so he must have reached his parking spot and shut down."

Don: "Yeah, I guess so."

By this time the Eastern 1011 was on short final, and would be on the ground in less than a minute. In much the same way that I had intuited a problem with Airlift 106, Don felt that something was not right, and took action:

Don: "Eastern 21, I hate to do this to you, but cancel landing clearance and go around, we can't find that Cessna that landed ahead of you."

The Eastern pilot acknowledged the instruction with a distinct lack of enthusiasm, then initiated the go-around, overflying the full length of the runway before being switched back to approach control for re-sequencing. In the meantime, Lanny had dispatched Ramp 20 to the GAC ramp to confirm that the Cessna had in fact taxied to the parking area, but shortly after the vehicle started its west bound progress from the terminal, the driver transmitted, "Ground, Ramp 20, the aircraft is on the runway, and two guys are pushing it." Guided by the position of the ramp vehicle, Don and Lanny each grabbed a set of binoculars and were able to see the 172 moving slowly down the runway, being propelled by two men pushing on the wing struts. The ramp supervisor assisted them in getting the aircraft clear of the runway and safely parked, then had the pilot call the tower. According to the pilot, at the moment the airplane touched down, it experienced a total failure of all systems. The engine stopped, and, probably because of low battery power, there were insufficient volts for the alternator to keep the radio and aircraft lights on line. The pilot said he knew the L-1011 was behind them. He and the passenger jumped out and began pushing, intending to save themselves, and the airplane, from being overrun from behind. The fact that they were still on the runway after Eastern went around meant that only Don's timely action had prevented a deadly collision.

Runway Incursions

Runway incursions (defined as any time an airplane or vehicle entered a runway without authorization, or when incorrectly authorized through controller error) were always of primary concern, particularly at high density airports. Statistically, a majority of these incidents occurred because a pilot or vehicle operator either did not understand the controller's instructions or became disoriented as to his location on the field. Over the years, a series of changes, both technological and procedural, were implemented to assist pilots/ operators and controllers in preventing these occurrences.

The worst runway incursion accident on record, in terms of loss of life, occurred in March 1977 in the Canary Islands when a KLM 747 initiated a takeoff without clearance while a Pan American 747 was taxiing on the runway in the opposite direction. Visibility was poor, and the aircraft collided, killing some 580 people. In the wake of the accident, FAA Order 7110.65, titled "Air Traffic Control," was revised to mandate that all runway crossings or other instances where ground control had traffic on an active runway required positive coordination with local control.

For those of us trained and certified under the old rules, this was a most unwelcome development. The last thing a busy local controller needed was the interruption and distraction of coordination calls from ground, possibly eliciting an erroneous approval for a runway crossing, or triggering a problem with some other aspect of his traffic. What happened to the principle that a good ground controller had to be able to pick his crossing opportunities, we wondered? In time, we got used to the new procedure, doing our best to live by the maxim, "You only ask for a runway crossing when the answer's yes." In other words, we were still picking our opportunities, but adding the step of coordination. Good local controllers would often observe that there was a pending crossing operation and volunteer, "Go ahead and cross that tug." Much later, there were automation capabilities installed that created flashing lights in the pavement to alert pilots that a runway was active, and displays in the tower that tracked ground traffic and issued verbal warnings when a runway was occupied.

One procedure always in effect at MIA involved the use of runways 9 Right and 12, which crossed at the southeast corner of the airport. There was about 8,000 feet available on both runways prior to the crossing point, so that in most cases a landing aircraft on either one was able to reach taxi speed and turn off well before the intersection. In the case of a 9 Right landing, the procedure was for local control to keep the aircraft on his frequency as it exited the runway and either clear the pilot to cross 12 to the terminal or instruct him to hold short. So the exchange following a 9 Right arrival could go like this:

Local: "Delta 483, turn left next intersection, hold short of Runway 12, remain this frequency."

DL 483: "Delta 483, roger, stay with you, hold short of 12."

Local (after the Runway 12 operation was complete): "Delta 483, cross Runway 12, contact ground control 127.5 after crossing."

DL 483: "OK, cross 12, and we'll call ground when we clear, Delta 483."

Although it was always a good practice to get a readback of critical instructions, during my early years it was not mandatory that a pilot transmit a readback in the case of "hold short." Later it became mandatory, requiring a controller to ask for a readback if it was not received from the pilot. Under busy conditions, this extra step added one more layer to an already heavy workload. Additionally, there was a clear FAR regulation that pilots were generally prohibited from crossing a runway without an explicit clearance, except in cases where they were instructed to taxi to a destination that required a runway crossing. In such cases, a good ground control technique was either not to use a destination after "taxi to" or phrase the taxi instructions differently, as in the following examples:

GC: "Delta 483, runway 9 Right taxi, hold short of runway 12." Or,

GC: "Delta 483, taxi eastbound on taxiway Tango, hold short of runway 12."

In the first case, the phraseology informed the pilot of the intended departure runway without implying a clearance to cross Runway 12 by the use of "taxi to". In the second case, no destination (the parking gate or designated ramp area) was specified until after the crossing clearance was issued. Another more general FAR stated that pilots were required to comply with all ATC instructions. In other words, a simple "Roger" or "Wilco" should have been a sufficient response from a pilot instructed to hold short. Nevertheless, the rule-making powers that be determined that a pilot who read back the instruction would be less likely to commit an infraction than one who had simply rogered it. The more cynical among us believed that the readback requirement was nothing more than a mechanism for pointing an accusing finger at a controller who failed to get it, as happened in a number of situations, including a particular instance in which I became a de facto "attorney for the defense" in making the case that the controller should not be blamed.

Early one morning at the start of a day shift, the local controller had put a US Airways 737 in position on Runway 12 while a Panamanian 727 was landing on 9 Right. The regulation that a departure could take off on one runway while a landing was in progress on another that crossed it had recently been changed, now requiring that the landing traffic either pass through the intersection, or hold short before takeoff clearance could be issued to the other airplane. So the exchange went like this:

Local: "Panther 790, turn left at Tango 5, remain this frequency, hold short of Runway 12 for departing traffic."

FAO 790: "Panther 790 roger."

Local: "US Air 235, turn left heading 090, runway 12 cleared for takeoff."

As US Air began its takeoff roll, accelerating to perhaps 60 or 80 knots, the Panther 727 crossed the hold line and entered the runway. Local immediately canceled the takeoff clearance, and the US Air pilot quickly throttled back, put the engines in reverse thrust, and braked hard. Later investigation revealed that the 737 had sustained some damage because of the emergency stop. As required, the local controller was relieved from the position pending a playback of the tapes and a determination as to exactly what had occurred. Also as required, a Flight Standards air carrier inspector was summoned to participate in a review of the incident. After the inspector had listened to the recording and was informed that the controller had been temporarily relieved of duty, he asked, "What are you going after your guy for? He didn't do anything wrong, the Panther pilot screwed up." Despite this eminently reasonable take on the whole business, the official determination at the regional level was, quote, "The primary cause of the runway incursion was the local controller's failure to obtain a readback of hold short instructions from the pilot of FAO 790.

This did not sit well with anyone. I wrote up the facility perspective on the event, which stated in part: "While we might speculate that a readback of the hold short instruction would have prevented the incident, its omission was not the cause. The unauthorized crossing occurred because the pilot violated an applicable FAR and an acknowledged ATC instruction." Unfortunately for the facility the determination by the Regional Office was not revised.

There was another case in which I was charged with exonerating the local and ground controllers from responsibility. A twin Cessna failed to follow ground control instructions, taxiing part way onto a runway in front of another aircraft that had been cleared for takeoff and was accelerating down the runway. The twin Cessna pilot slammed on the brakes, while the other pilot swerved left, and a collision was avoided. I faulted the actions of the Cessna pilot. In many cases of this kind, the tendency was to fault the controller for a "failure to observe" pilot non-compliance with instructions, but this time the determination turned out favorably for our guys.

As controllers, we were somewhat fatalistic when our actions were reviewed (or second-guessed, as we sometimes believed). We often asserted that judgments made from afar, and well after the fact, were suspect because "you had to be there." In this case, the incident was classified as a pilot deviation. In the perennial game of "you win some and lose some," the controllers won.

Pilot Misdeeds and Aircraft Malfunctions

There were other occurrences, some involving actions by pilots that were clearly violations of FARs or airport rules, others because of either unanticipated mechanical malfunctions or questionable pilot judgment.

In one case, a series of confounding errors occurred because of a pilot's inexperience and ineptitude. The incident took place in the middle 1970s after implementation of the Terminal Control Area (TCA) at MIA. The TCA was a newly created class of positive control airspace designed to limit traffic at and around high-density airports. Positive control meant that no aircraft could fly in the TCA without being radar identified and issued specific authorization to operate within the area. One of the restrictions was that any pilot operating to or from the airport had to hold at least a private pilot certificate. Student pilots could fly through the TCA, with appropriate clearance, but were prohibited from landing or taking off.

Procedures, in both the tower and the TRACON, had also changed since my early days as a trainee, largely because of a hugely significant upgrade to the radar system. Now, instead of every radar target appearing essentially identical, each aircraft worked within the ATC system had its own identification tag, generated by a computer and software complex known as the Automated Radar Tracking System (ARTS). Only a few short years later, we shook our heads in disbelief that the ARTS equipment had filled an entire room in order to provide the "astounding" capacity of some 250 KB.

In the tower, no longer did we have to receive a list of arrivals from the TRACON because we could simply read the aircraft identifications from the tower BRITE radar display. In addition, all traffic, including those pesky VFRs, was "tagged up" by approach control and sequenced with (mostly) proper separation—there were still times when the local controller had to get creative by applying visual separation or changing an airplane to a different runway to keep the operation safe and legal. The need to notify the departure controller of each aircraft was likewise eliminated because each aircraft would acquire its ARTS tag immediately after takeoff.

One evening after night had fallen, with clear weather and a moderate level of activity, the ground controller received an unexpected, and alarming, call from the pilot of a single-engine Cessna, triggering the following exchange:

Pilot: "Ground control, Cessna 578 Golf Hotel, taxiing in."
Ground: "Cessna 578 Golf Hotel Miami Ground, say your position."
Pilot: "I'm not sure. I just landed."

Ground: "Cessna 8 GH, which runway did you land on?"
Pilot: "I think it was 9 Right."
Ground (to the local controller): "Hey local, did you work a 578 GH into 9 Right?"
Local: "Negative. Where is he?"
Ground: "He says he's off 9 Right."
Local: "Well how in hell did he get there? He never called me."
Ground (to the pilot): "Cessna 8 GH, did you receive a landing clearance from the tower?"
Pilot: "Negative, I couldn't get anybody to answer me."

Soon the entire staff was looking at the exit points from 9 Right, finally seeing the small, dim position lights of the Cessna on the parallel taxiway.

The exchange resumed:

Ground: "Cessna 8 GH, what is your destination on the airport?"
Pilot: "I'm not sure, I'm supposed to pick somebody up coming in on Delta."
Ground: "Well, have you made arrangements with Delta to park at their gates?" (This was a requirement for any GA aircraft parking at the main terminal).
Pilot: "Negative. I didn't know I needed permission, I'm a student pilot."

So far, at least four procedural errors and FAR violations had occurred, with number five not far off:

1) A student pilot had entered the TCA without clearance.
2) A student pilot had landed at an airport within the TCA
3) The pilot had landed without two-way communications with the tower or a landing clearance
4) The pilot had failed to make arrangements with the airline to park at the gate, contrary to airport rules and the airline's policy
5) Student pilots are forbidden to carry passengers, and this pilot was about to pick one up

It had been a matter of dumb luck that the pilot had managed to position himself on the final to one of our main runways without being run over by the much faster air carrier jets that were lined up on the same final. To top it off, he had not used his landing lights, which would have at least increased the possibility that his presence could have been detected sooner. There was no explanation as to why he had failed to contact the local controller. More than likely he had selected an incorrect frequency.

At length, with the help of Ramp 20, the aircraft was escorted to Delta's gates, as the ground controller attempted to acquaint the young man with some basics about the TCA and the restrictions on student pilots. A short while later, the pilot called for taxi clearance, stating that his destination was Palm Beach. With difficulty, and after a further tedious exchange about the need for a departure clearance out of the TCA, he finally made it to Runway 12 from which he would take off. Local control put him in position, then used the standard language for issuing takeoff clearance: "Cessna 8 GH, Runway 12, turn left heading 060, cleared for takeoff." Everyone was watching closely, and a good thing it was that we were. Unbelievably, the pilot turned to 060, meaning that the airplane was on a heading 60 degrees left of direct alignment with the runway, and began to roll. Local shouted, "Cessna 8 GH STOP!" Fortunately, the Cessna did stop before going into the grass. Trying to control his adrenaline, Local transmitted, through tight lips, "Cessna 8 GH, the 060 heading is for after you are airborne. Follow the runway centerline during your takeoff."

N578 GH got airborne, and was worked by departure control until time for a handoff to Palm Beach. The TRACON had warned Palm Beach to be ready for this guy, suggesting that they get somebody from Flight Standards to meet him once he was one the ground. In subsequent exchanges we learned that the Palm Beach controllers had had their own set of issues with the hapless student.

Buzzing a Hotel

In another case, a National Airlines pilot was disciplined by the company for his repeated deliberate actions in "buzzing" a newly constructed hotel located just beyond the airport boundary and directly under the flight path of 9 Right departures and 27 Left arrivals. The hotel was a low, two-story structure that only just met the obstruction clearance requirements specified in Terminal Instrument Procedures (TERPS), the body of regulations that determined the maximum permissible height of a structure as a function of distance from the runway. There had been, and continued to be, a number of concerns and objections voiced by pilots and pilot groups before, during, and after construction of the hotel.

One of the more salient observations was based on a calculation showing that the extended landing gear of a 747 exactly on the glide slope of the 27 Left ILS approach, in the landing configuration, would pass over the roof of the building at a height of 41 feet. If the tolerances permitted in calibrating the instrument approach equipment and the aircraft instrumentation, plus the ability of the pilot to fly the glide slope without deviation, were to combine unfavorably, that margin of clearance could be appreciably reduced. And more than once, when the weather was down, we observed a pilot popping out of the overcast, low, and actually adding power to climb over the structure.

Periodically, members of the hotel staff would telephone the tower to say that an aircraft had passed overhead very low, creating noise and vibration that shook the building and alarmed the guests. These reports always occurred during an east operation, meaning that they resulted from an aircraft taking off with the engines set at or near maximum power. As a result of these calls, the tower began keeping a log of the complaints, eventually substantiating that in all cases they occurred immediately following the departure of a National Airlines 727 off 9 Right. The information was shared with National's chief pilot, and the "buzzing" incidents, where the pilot deliberately kept the aircraft as low as possible over the hotel, came to an end.

An ironic postscript to the whole affair occurred about a year later when one of our controllers attempted to board a National 727 for a jump-seat ride. The SF-160, or cockpit familiarization program, permitted controllers to occupy the jump seat during flight in order to observe air traffic control procedures from the pilot perspective. Nevertheless, it was totally up to the captain's discretion to allow or deny the jump seat privilege. On the day in question, Jim stepped up to the cockpit door and introduced himself. Initially, the greeting was cordial, as it almost always was in the many SF-160 rides I took. Then, as the conversation progressed, the tone changed dramatically:

Jim: "Morning, captain, Jim Muller, air traffic controller, I'd like to ride the jump seat with you if it's ok."

Captain: "Sure Jim, welcome aboard, go ahead and take a seat, I'm sure you know the drill."

Jim: "Thank you."

Captain: "So what facility do you work at Jim?"

Jim: "Right here at Miami Tower."
Captain (with a pronounced scowl): "You work at this tower?"
Jim: "That's right."
Captain: "Well, you're not riding with us, and you know why."
Jim: "Well, it's your call captain, but I don't know why."
Captain: "Don't try and bullshit me, you bastards turned me in."
Jim: "I'm sorry, I have no idea what you're talking about."
Captain: "It's about that god-damned hotel, and you know it!"
Jim (standing up and stepping out of the cockpit): "I still don't know what you mean."

A Dangerous Incident

The most serious, and dangerous, incident involving deliberate pilot actions occurred during a day shift soon after the "new new" tower was commissioned. For my first 17 years at MIA, the tower had been located atop the terminal building, giving us a birds eye view of the gates and terminal ramp area, but placing us at a distance of over a mile from the approach ends of our most actively used runways, 9 Left, 9 Right, and 12. The TRACON and administrative quarters were spaces leased from the Dade County airport authority, and because these areas were of prime importance to the county, there had been steadily growing pressure on the FAA to relocate the entire air traffic operation.

For several years we had watched the construction of a tower and TRACON building at the west field boundary, these facilities having been designed from the ground up for ATC purposes. There were a number of proposed dates for the move, and an equal number (minus one) of postponements, but finally the move across the field was accomplished in August 1985, one day short of my 17-year anniversary as a controller at MIA.

The new tower was in all respects a far cry from the 1957 version just vacated on the terminal side. It was 70 feet taller, topping out at some 200 feet above the airport surface. For the Local Control function, its position directly adjacent to the run-up pad between runways 9 Left and 12 was ideal when the airport was on an east operation, the type we ran about 90 per cent of the time. Inside the cab, many of the old "steam gauge" type dials had been replaced by digital readouts, and most lighting controls and the like were now activated by touch rather than by physical switches.

But it was not all good news. The terminal concourses were now more than a mile distant, seriously hampering Ground Control's ability to referee the traffic flows to and from the gates. And when we had to "go west," meaning landing and taking off on 27 Right and 27 Left, those operations occurred at a distance of almost two miles from the tower.

For me, those early days in the new tower were somewhat uncomfortable. It was like working at a different airport without the benefit of training and orientation. But within a couple of weeks I adapted, and the "new" operation became as routine as old one had been.

On the day in question, the local control position was being worked by Vincent Perrone, who had struggled during portions of his training. Suddenly, out of nowhere, a Cessna 172 appeared, approximately level with the tower cab, and headed straight for it. Vince was able to read the registration numbers on the fuselage, and began calling the pilot, at first without receiving any response. After several "strafing" runs at the tower, the pilot began a series of sharp turns and low altitude passes over the runways, and finally began transmitting on the local control frequency:

Pilot: "Whoo-ee! I've waited all my life to do this, so look out below!"

Vince: "Cessna 79 Romeo, be advised you are in violation of numerous FARs and you are creating a major safety hazard. Either depart the area or land on any runway."

79 Romeo: "No way tower, this is too much fun!"

For some 20 or 25 minutes, the pilot continued buzzing the tower, swooping low over a long queue of aircraft awaiting departures, and transmitting random celebratory calls on the radio. During this period, no aircraft were permitted to land or take off, because it was impossible to foresee where the rogue Cessna might be at any given moment. Although it was not clear what good it would do, the tower supervisor summoned the Coast Guard helicopter based at Opa-locka airport, and in due course, the following exchange took place:

Coast Guard: "Miami tower, Coast Guard Charlie Golf one three inbound your station."

Local: "Coast Guard Charlie Golf one three Miami tower, continue inbound, use caution the subject aircraft is all over the place, now at about 300 feet, headed northbound at mid field."

Coast Guard: "Coast Guard Charlie Golf 13 roger, we'll be watching for him. OK, we have him in sight, we're moving in now."

79 Romeo (in suddenly serious tones): "Tower, is the Coast Guard going to shoot me down?"

The helicopter had no offensive weapons on board, and in any case would not have shot the Cessna down within the field boundary. But one of the airline crews in the departure line-up, already delayed for many minutes, transmitted a single word: "Affirmative!" Whether the Cessna pilot believed the response came from the local controller or not, he immediately responded, saying, "I'm landing."

Within a minute or so, the Cessna landed on 9 Left, and was immediately surrounded by Ramp 20 and several county police cars. We later learned that the police had discovered an empty whiskey bottle in the aircraft, and that the pilot was definitely intoxicated. He was a flight instructor who had decided he had had enough of flying, and had chosen this method of exiting from the ranks of pilot certificate holders. Another hairy situation was concluded without any damage, injury, or loss of life.

Serious Accidents

There were other incidents and accidents during my years at MIA that did not turn out so well. One day a CL-44, a four-engine turboprop aircraft similar to the Lockheed Electra, took off on 9 Right. Lift-off appeared normal, but tower personnel observed that one of the wheels on the main landing gear had detached itself from the strut and was rolling down the runway at a speed nearly equal to the 120 knots plus of the airplane as it became airborne. The perimeter road ran parallel to the runway, separated from the airport property by a chain-link fence, and included a parking area where aviation aficionados could station their vehicles and watch the operation. There was a lone camper van in the parking area with several people on its roof, seated in lawn chairs. The tire veered to the right, appearing to be headed directly at the van, and crashing through the fence without slowing down at all. The people began a mad scramble off the roof, far too late to avoid any consequences should the tire have struck the vehicle, but the tire passed by harmlessly, ending up in a canal just beyond the road.

A few years later a Convair 880, a four-engine jet operated by a Nicaraguan company and hauling a load of cattle, came to grief during an attempted takeoff from 9 Left. For an undetermined reason, the aircraft left the runway at a high rate of speed and came to an abrupt stop in the canal bordering the north side parallel taxiway. There was no communication with the flight crew, either because they had been incapacitated or killed, or because the radios had been disabled. But it appeared that the cockpit area was intact, and there was no fire. Nevertheless, the situation was extremely critical because there was raw fuel all around the crash site and one of the engines was still operating at takeoff power. At length the engine was shut down by cutting off the fuel flow, but it took much longer to rescue the flight crew. The aircraft had come to rest nose down, and the cattle had been thrown against the cockpit door, preventing normal access. Rescuers had to use a diamond toothed saw to cut through the cockpit roof, a dicey operation at best because of the jet fuel contamination. When they reached the flight crew, they were unprepared for the condition in which they found them. Without ventilation, many of the cattle had died, releasing their bodily fluids, which had seeped through the cockpit door in copious amounts. The crew was soaked in a nauseating mix of blood, urine, and feces, but they had survived.

In another case, a DC-4 operated by a Central American carrier took off Runway 12 on a hot June day. It was a cargo flight, loaded to maximum gross weight, and possibly beyond. After struggling to get airborne, both the number one and number two engines failed, leaving the aircraft with serious asymmetrical thrust and insufficient power to climb. The pilot managed a brief transmission describing his condition, as the aircraft began a slow, uncorrectable left turn and a descent from an already critically low altitude. Local control issued, "Cleared to land any runway." The pilot attempted a 210-degree turn back to Runway 27 Right, but ran out of altitude about a quarter mile short of the threshold and crashed on NW 36th Street, a main thoroughfare that bordered the north boundary of the airport. The flight crew was killed, but there were no injuries on the ground because of one very fortunate happenstance. There was a freight train that had stopped automobile traffic at a railroad crossing on 36th Street east of the point where the DC-4 went down. If the crash had occurred even a few minutes earlier or later, there would have been numerous casualties apart from the flight crew.

Another fatal accident occurred in mid-1970 while I was still in training, and working a midnight shift with my crew. At the time, we were all following the plight of the Apollo 13 astronauts, whose spacecraft had suffered an in transit explosion on their way to a projected moon landing.

While the astronauts made it back safely, the crew of another DC-4 was not so fortunate. The airport was socked in with heavy ground fog, so dense that even from the modest height of 130 feet we were unable to see the ramp below.

In later years, the regulation prohibiting ATC from authorizing a takeoff or landing below certain visibility values was changed, putting the decision in the hands of the pilot rather than the air traffic controller, but at the time we were still bound by the old regulation. There was even prescribed phraseology: "Unable to issue departure clearance due to reduced visibility." There was no wind, and under such conditions during the midnight shift, because of noise abatement concerns, we usually ran the operation we informally called "easty-westy." Easty-westy meant that when traffic was light, takeoffs would be made to the west (27 Right and 27 Left) while landings would be made from the west (9 Left and 9 Right), thereby minimizing operations over the more densely populated areas of the city. A Guatemalan cargo flight had taxied to 27 Right, and had been holding for 15 or 20 minutes, waiting for the visibility to improve to the required minimum of one-quarter mile.

All tower controllers were required to pass an exam administered by the National Weather Service, after which they were required to take visibility observations. The ground fog remained stubbornly persistent, and at length the flight crew of the DC-4 advised the local controller that if they did not take off within the next five minutes, they would have to taxi back to the cargo apron to take on more fuel. We didn't think there was any problem with this, as the refueling operation might provide enough time for the visibility to improve. But the watch supervisor in the tower at the time took it upon himself to call the visibility "one-quarter mile in ground fog," and the DC-4 was cleared for takeoff.

As was the procedure at that time, local advised the departure controller that the DC-4 was rolling. But no radar target appeared, nor could either local or departure control raise the aircraft despite making numerous transmissions on both frequencies. Finally Ramp 20 was dispatched to check out the situation, and before long transmitted this urgent message: "Tower, get the crash crew out here ASAP! The airplane went through the fence at the end and he's on fire in the canal." The aircraft had used the entire 10,500-foot length of 27 Right without getting airborne, had gone through the chain link fence past the departure end, and crossed the perimeter road without striking any vehicles, likely because of the early hour.

We were all required to stay beyond the end of the shift until the administrative staff came in to take statements from each of us as to what position we had been working, what we had seen and heard, etc. By this time the sun had risen, burning off the ground fog, and enabling us to see the stark aftermath of the accident. At about the 6,000-foot point on 27 Right there appeared three ruts in the grass area to the right of the runway, indicating that the airplane had left the pavement without reaching takeoff speed. In addition, there was a trail of scattered cargo beginning at the same point and increasing in volume all the way to the edge of the canal.

One of the old hands asked if I would like to go down on the field and look at what had happened firsthand, and I of course agreed, thinking that we would not be allowed at the accident scene. But my veteran buddy convinced one of the ramp vehicles to take us out on the field. What had appeared from the tower as small lines in the grass were in fact deep trenches carved by the landing gear of the DC-4. There were still obvious pools of fuel, oil and hydraulic fluid in evidence, and I could not imagine what the area would have looked like if the airplane had been carrying passengers. The air was thick with the acrid smell of the fire, and I went home that morning with a renewed appreciation of the seriousness of my job.

Several questions presented themselves in the post-accident investigation, one of which could have meant big problems for the FAA. The old Douglas aircraft did not have a cockpit voice recorder or a black box from which operational information could be gleaned, but one possibility was that because of the long delay at the run-up pad at idle power, the spark plugs on one or more engines had become fouled. This could have resulted a loss of power or asymmetrical thrust, causing the aircraft to veer off the runway or fail to reach adequate takeoff speed. The question that did not get asked was whether the decision to call the visibility one-quarter mile had been justified.

Two other crashes of cargo flights occurred during my time at MIA. One was the so-called "Christmas tree" flight that occurred in December 1973 when a Lockheed Constellation attempted a takeoff from 9 Left carrying a load of evergreen trees to Central America. Once again, there was no cockpit voice recorder or black box to provide detailed information, but it appeared that the cargo had either been improperly loaded, had shifted aft during takeoff, or had simply exceeded the gross weight limit of the aircraft. The airplane could have stalled or been unable to climb. It had been a number of years since the captain had flown a Constellation, possibly contributing an additional critical element to the accident. In addition, the rules governing this type operation, where the operator chartered the aircraft from a third-party, were far less stringent than the Part 121 and 135 provisions of the FARs that applied to other commercial aviation ventures, and there were questions about the maintenance history of the old Lockheed.

The accident occurred during the early hours of the midnight shift, which began at 11:00 pm, a fairly active period during which there were a number of arrivals. Both the local controller and the departure controller were experienced veterans, whose comments on the override circuit were brief and to the point, without any panic on their part. A replay of the tapes surrounding the incident showed that the operation was completely normal until the last moment.

Pilot: "Tower, Lockheed 69 Charlie ready to go 9 Left."

Local: "Lockheed 69 Charlie runway 9 Left turn right heading 120, cleared for takeoff."

Pilot: "69 Charlie cleared to go, heading 120."

Local: "Lockheed 69 Charlie contact departure control."

Pilot: "69 Charlie."

A minute or two later there came a transmission from a pilot on final approach to 9 Left:

Pilot: Tower Braniff 907, you've got a big fire ball looks like right off the end of 9 Left."

The local controller whipped around, saw the fire and immediately hit the override to departure control:

Local: "Lockheed 69 Charlie just went in."

Departure controller: "Oh shit."

Mischief During Idle Times

There were a number of other events, great and small, that livened up life in the tower. Some of these were inadvertent, others deliberate, ranging from clever wisecracks to actions falling in the category of "the devil finds work for idle hands to do." Controllers are a restless, action-oriented bunch, and when there was not enough traffic to keep them busy, they often resorted to other avenues to keep themselves interested.

There were several instances where conversations in the tower were accidentally transmitted on a control frequency because of a stuck mic. This could happen for a couple of reasons, one of them being because the switch on a controller's headset literally became "stuck" in the transmit mode. In these cases, the situation was pretty easily recognized by the side tone, a feature enabling the controller to hear himself through the headset. He could then either un-stick the mic or get a replacement. The other reason, sometimes referred to as a hot mic, was that when a headset was incompletely "jacked in" to the radio port, the frequency could be live without providing feedback via the side tone. In these cases it could be several minutes, or even longer, before anyone noticed the condition.

A famous incident involving this latter condition occurred at Fort Lauderdale tower sometime in the 1970s. At the time, Fort Lauderdale-Hollywood International Airport (FLL) had only a single runway that could accommodate air carrier transport aircraft. The city was growing, air traffic was growing, but the airport capacity remained fixed, meaning that delays were increasing. Since delays cost the airlines revenue through increased fuel consumption and schedule disruption, not to mention passenger complaints, there was always pressure on the FAA to reduce delay times. The problem, when it came to airport capacity, was that the only solution was to provide more concrete by either lengthening an existing runway or building an additional one.

Building or expanding an airport is always a glacially slow process because of cost, environmental impact, and citizen opposition, and so delays remained persistent at FLL. So in quintessential bureaucratic fashion, the head of the air traffic division in the Southern Region paid a visit to FLL to observe the problem first hand. The visit was short, less than a full hour, and occurred during a time when traffic activity was light and no delays were occurring. Dan Fourer returned to Southern Region headquarters in Atlanta convinced that the delay problem was not all that serious, leaving the tower controllers scoffing. Two hours later, the line-ups of arrivals on final and departures on the taxiway were getting longer by the minute.

Identifying a workable gap in the arrival sequence, the local controller cleared a Martin 404, a twin-engine propeller aircraft, for takeoff on 9 Left. A few seconds after becoming airborne, with the landing gear in the process of being retracted, the Martin experienced simultaneous failure of both engines and settled back on the runway, creating a 50-foot rooster-tail of sparks, and shedding parts of its airframe as it slid to a stop. Later investigation revealed that the aircraft had been erroneously refueled with kerosene instead of aviation gas. There had been just enough gasoline for the airplane to taxi and take off, but when the jet fuel hit the carburetors, the engines seized up. When the tapes were played back, all the transmissions made with the mic keyed were standard and professional, but when the controller unkeyed, thinking he was off the air, the final statement on the recording was, "Where is that f...ing Fourer now?" Although it was embarrassing for the facility, for a long while the controllers retold the story with undiminished relish.

Another hot mic incident occurred at Miami tower, fortunately not involving anything of operational significance. During the midnight shift, Evan Gianetti, my ground control instructor duped by another controller pretending to be an airplane on the frequency, was holding forth on his favorite subject. He was known for his outspoken comments about sex and women, chiefly relating his own exploits, but occasionally simply throwing something out for effect. While one might assume that a subject near and dear to the hearts of the all-male workforce would be a welcome topic at any time, when Evan took the floor we basically all groaned in agreement—"not again!" But during one such instance, a tamer one by Evan's standards, someone else had the last word. It went like this:

Evan: "Hey, you know what I read in National Geographic? They said that there is a correlation in the average size of the male penis with the distance of the population from the equator."

Several voices: "Ah, come on Ev, give us a break."

Evan: "No, really. They said that the average penis size is largest near the equator, and smaller in populations further north."

Another voice: "Oh yeah, where are you from Ev?"

A third voice: "North Pole!"

On the night in question, Evan was recounting a romantic interlude with his latest girlfriend, sparing no details as to her physical endowments, the various stages of undress and foreplay, leading up to the final denouement. The tale had gone on for perhaps four or five minutes, when someone realized that Evan's frequency was hot, and gave the jack a push into the radio port. With normal reception restored, there came this anonymous comment from a pilot on the frequency: "Well, don't stop now, what happened next?"

One morning at about 3:00 am I was working the midnight shift in the tower with Johnny Renard and another of my teammates. Johnny was a hefty individual sporting a large belly and a butt to match. Traffic activity was essentially nil, and we were all in a relaxed state making idle conversation, with Johnny seated on the edge of the console where the headset jacks were mounted and other switches and indicators were located. Suddenly the ground control frequency came alive with an urgent transmission from the fire commander, the lead supervisor of the crash crew, as we observed a line of fire fighting vehicles emerging from the midfield fire station: "Ground control, fire commander, which runway is the emergency on?" Instantly we were all on high alert, rapidly scanning all the runways, but observing nothing. Eventually one of us transmitted, "Fire commander ground, we didn't call you out, and there is no emergency that we know of. Who notified you?"

"Well, the emergency alarm went off, that's all I can tell you," came the reply. After several more exchanges, and a determination that there was in fact no emergency, the vehicles returned to the fire station, leaving us to speculate that the alarm system had somehow malfunctioned. After perhaps 15 or 20 minutes, the fire trucks again came roaring out on to the field, and the fire commander was again asking where the emergency was located. Again we determined that there was no emergency, and the crash crew returned to their quarters amid a series of radio exchanges pledging to have the entire alarm system checked the next day.

So the crash crew had twice been unnecessarily awakened, and were understandably somewhat peeved, especially after the second incident. We basically chalked it up to a simple equipment failure. As we were reassuring ourselves that we were in no way at fault, Johnny stood up from his position on the console, and we observed a clipboard resting on the red button that activated fire station alarm. Johnny's king-sized rear end had partially covered the clipboard, exerting just enough pressure to activate the switch. In careful language the next day we informed the crash crew that we had discovered the problem with the alarm, and had taken corrective action.

Before we moved from the terminal building to "the west 40" as we described the new facility to which we moved in 1985, we used to get quite a few visitors to the tower. Often these impromptu tours were the result of our guys striking up a conversation with people (read, attractive young women) in the terminal, either passengers or individuals seeing off friends or family catching a flight. One evening Frank, a handsome and well-spoken young man, brought three such visitors to the tower, and was holding forth knowledgeably and engagingly about being a controller and what the ladies were observing. For the uninitiated, the whole ATC business is basically a fascinating mystery, with the dim lights on the control console, the airport lighting, the ballet of ground control movements, and the hushed, professional tones of the controllers issuing instructions. These visitors were no exception, hanging with rapt attention on every word Frank uttered. At one point, Frank said, "Well, that's about it for the tower. Would you like to see the radar room?" One of them answered, "Oh yes, we would love to see the radio room." As Frank began to lead them down the stairs, Joe, a known wiseass, said, as though it were the most normal, reasonable thing in the world, "Hey Frank, would you mind taking the trash down when you go?" The look of instant irritation on Frank's face, and uncertainty on the faces of the visitors, was priceless.

In another case involving tower visitors, and their cluelessness about ATC, the local controller was Roger Pomeroy, known to display his hilarious showmanship at every opportunity. He was a gifted mimic, spontaneously launching into entertaining routines as they occurred to him. He had us falling down with laughter as he provided imitations of Jimmy Stewart working local control, or John Wayne as the ground controller, or sending up fellow controllers or supervisors, especially those who were a little too serious and full of themselves. On the day in question, a group of four or five people was brought to the tower during a busy departure push. This is what they heard from Roger as the local controller:

"Eastern 740, turn right heading 290, runway 27 Right cleared for takeoff.

United 626, runway 27 Left, taxi into position and hold, traffic departing the right side.

Eastern 740, contact departure control. Yes sir, you have a good day too.

United 626, turn right heading 290, runway 27 Left cleared for takeoff

Delta 334, runway 27 Left taxi into position and hold.

United 626 contact departure control.

Delta 334, runway 27 Left, turn right heading 290, cleared for takeoff.

Delta 334, contact departure control. And look for a single story white house with a green roof as you pass over Miami Springs, and wave to my grandmother as you go by.

What the visitors had no way of knowing was that Roger had unkeyed his mic for the last transmission, so that it had not gone out over the air. They also probably did not realize that there was no way for a pilot to recognize a single building in a residential area, or to wave to someone on the ground. Nevertheless, one of them remarked, "Oh, isn't that sweet. He wants the pilot to wave to his grandmother." We had a hard time stifling our laughter until the visitors left.

Roger was involved in one of several incidents that were good for a laugh during a training day. At the time, the work force was divided into thirds, each group being assigned one of three sets of days off: Sunday-Monday, Wednesday-Thursday, or Friday-Saturday. This left Tuesday as the day when the entire complement of the facility was present. Each Tuesday, one of the groups would be assigned to eight hours of training, basically a period of briefings and information about airport construction, new procedures, and, as on the day in question, the inauguration of service into MIA by a new airline. The facility chief was always allotted a certain amount of time to address the troops, and on this day he was very happy to inform us that Miami Tower had received a nice compliment from a citizen who had overheard an exchange on ground control.

A nearby restaurant, the 94th Aero Squadron, located south of the perimeter road, with a full view of the airfield, had a radio tuned to ground control frequency and jacks for headsets at each table. The lady had been listening to ground control on the day when Frontier Airlines made its inaugural flight into Miami. According to the chief, she had called the facility and said she was greatly impressed by the professionalism and courtesy of the ground controller, who had made it a point to welcome the flight crew and provide extra attention to make sure the airplane got to the right concourse. At one point someone asked, "Okay, so who was the ground controller?" The chief, in yet another instance of shrinking credibility with the controllers, hemmed and hawed, ultimately admitting that he didn't know who the ground controller was, eliciting groans and frowns from everyone in the room.

After a brief pause, a quick exchange occurred between Roger and Billy Pierce, a long-time friend and one of the quickest wits in the facility:

Roger (puffing up proudly): "Hey, was that Frontier 104, about two weeks ago? I worked that guy in. Yeah, that was me!"

Billy, without missing a beat: "Damn, Pomeroy, is your mother still eating lunch every day over there at the Aero Squadron?"

On another training day, Billy got in an even sharper jab. The group that day included Paul Brume, a controller who had transferred from Chicago's O'Hare, then the busiest and toughest facility in the country. Paul never missed an opportunity to talk up O'Hare, and compare Miami unflatteringly as a small-time operation. The training agenda led off with a promotional film produced by United Airlines showing each phase of ATC handling for a flight from O'Hare to Dulles International in Washington, and included some candid shots of passengers in the terminal. In one brief sequence, a group of Navy enlisted men was shown walking along together, with just a few frames showing a men's room sign in the background.

It was at that moment that Paul spoke up, in typical fashion, saying, "All right you guys, take a look, that's Chicago O'Hare, a real man's facility."

Billy immediately chimed in, "Yeah, I figured that when I saw those sailors hanging around the bathroom."

PATCO vs. FAA

Another area giving rise to notable incidents was the constant friction between PATCO (Professional Air Traffic Controllers' Organization) and FAA management, especially when the contract between the agency and the union was being re-negotiated. One year in the 1970s the two parties had, once again, come to an apparent impasse over the same issues: controller compensation, working conditions, second-career training for specialists who became medically disqualified, annual leave provisions, and a host of other issues.

As a tactic to publicize PATCO's dispute with the agency, local union leaders engaged the services of a banner tow operation based at nearby North Perry airport, intending to allow the tow aircraft to overfly MIA with a banner reading, "FAA Unfair to Controllers." At the appointed time, the banner tow pilot contacted the approach controller, who acknowledged the call, and then advised the local controller. The aircraft used for these operations were of fairly ancient vintage and were not transponder equipped, meaning that in general they were prohibited from operating in the TCA as this particular flight was about to do.

As the aircraft approached the tower, two controllers engaged in a mock dispute over the meaning of one of the provisions of the 7110.65 manual, both demanding that the tower supervisor join them in reading the page containing the paragraph under discussion, and, not incidentally, distracting him from noticing the banner tow. There was only one comment recorded on the ground control frequency, made anonymously by the pilot of a taxiing aircraft: "Tower, I like your sign." But within a minute or two, Art James, the watch supervisor that day, came storming up the tower steps from the TRACON demanding, "All right you guys, where the hell is that banner tow?" A former supervisor, recently retired from MIA and now working as a charter pilot, had witnessed the operation from the general aviation ramp and telephoned the watch desk.

The entire tower staff feigned looks of injured innocence, saying that they hadn't seen any banner tow. As it happened, the airplane and banner were now far enough away that they could not readily be seen or the message read, and it appeared that the whole matter would be dropped. However, officials in the Southern Region had become aware of the incident and were demanding that the culprits responsible for it, and for embarrassing the FAA, be identified and disciplined. Tapes of both approach control and local control were played back, revealing the following:

Pilot: "Miami approach, PATCO One with you six miles south, heading northbound."

Approach: "PATCO One Miami Approach roger."

Approach (on coordination line to Local): "PATCO One six south."

Local: "Roger."

Pilot (on local frequency): "Tower PATCO One with you."

Local: "Copter One roger."

That was the full extent of the recorded transmissions. The regional office people were demanding that the facility punish the controllers for conducting an illegal operation, but there had been no clearance issued to the pilot to enter the TCA, and no aircraft side number had been used. Technically, the pilot, who was fully complicit in the whole affair, was in violation of FARs for entering restricted airspace, but there was no way of positively identifying either the aircraft or the individual. Both the approach controller and the local controller maintained that they were awaiting further information after initial contact, but that since none had occurred, no further action on the part of either of them was required.

While it is doubtful that the banner tow advanced the union's agenda in any way, it remained for years a subject much relished in the retelling as an example of how PATCO won that round. And when the local MIA chapter began to publish a newspaper of union, facility, and agency doings, it bore the title "The Banner," complete with a logo of a Piper Cub towing a banner, the legend deliberately made small and unreadable.

As mentioned earlier, when traffic was slow, controllers were seldom at a loss in creating an alternate activity to fill those periods. One day the "Sweathogs," as a particular controller team had christened themselves, were assigned to the tower, and a lull occurred. At the time, there were several plexiglass status boards reflecting equipment outages, ATIS information, and other items that were updated using a grease pencil. When a new entry was required, the Flight Data specialist would grab a handful of toilet paper to erase the board. Someone picked up the whole roll and began passing it around the tower, ad libbing some pseudo football commentary in the process. Soon another participant began unrolling the sheets, wrapping an ever-lengthening streamer around chairs, handrails, the ladder to the tower cab roof, even the typewriter on which the daily log was kept, until there was a veritable spider web of paper crisscrossing the operating spaces. Not to be outdone, somebody else whipped out a cigarette lighter and touched it to the paper, never anticipating what happened next. In an instant, the entire web was in flames, as people began jumping out of the way, slapping their clothes, and stamping on the charred embers as they hit the floor. It was all over in a few seconds, but the air was filled with a brown miasma of acrid smoke. There was only one small door to the catwalk that ran around the perimeter of the tower, which was immediately opened, but the ventilating effect was distinctly minimal.

In what was shaping up to be a fine example of mischief-makers brought to swift and sure justice, the watch supervisor chose that moment to make a visit to the tower. Will McCutcheon had come of age in a high-density northern facility, and was distinctly cast in the mold of the no-nonsense authoritarian boss. As he hit the top of the steps and took in the scene, he yelled, "What the hell HAPPENED up here?" Most of the people turned away, looking sheepish, and certainly not volunteering anything enlightening. But Pat Grillo, the recently promoted tower supervisor who had come to MIA from New York, and who was fast on his feet in dire circumstances, didn't miss a beat. "Well, I'll tell you Will, I am probably going to put in an award recommendation for Al here. Somebody threw a cigarette in the waste basket, and all of a sudden it flamed up, almost reaching the ceiling. Al grabbed the fire extinguisher and gave the basket a good blast, which put out the fire but blew flaming bits of paper all over the place. If he hadn't acted so quickly, things could have been a whole lot worse." Will considered this for a few moments, his countenance lightening up considerably, then said, "Good job, Al," and left the tower a few minutes later.

7. Mastering Radar Control

Miami Tower and Approach Control was in those days what was designated as Level 5, the highest classification available for a terminal facility. The classifications were based strictly on annual traffic count, so that any combined tower and radar operation with a count above 300,000 was so designated. By the mid-1970s, largely through the efforts of PATCO, the busier terminals and some of the centers had been upgraded in terms of pay, making the MIA controllers GS-14s. There was in some cases a perception of inequity, especially when at a neighboring facility, as in the case of Miami Center, the full performance controller grade remained at GS-13. Controllers at ZMA felt that they worked all the traffic that MIA did, both inbound and outbound, and were responsible for traffic at abutting facilities like Palm Beach in addition.

Nevertheless, there was some justification for the distinction. MIA routinely amassed a daily traffic count in excess of 2,000 operations, contained within an area roughly 60 miles north and south by 40 miles east and west. In the center, those 2,000 airplanes were divided up among ten different sectors (four arrival and six departure). Moreover, each of those sectors had hundreds of miles of airspace and altitudes from the surface to outer space to work with. At places like Atlanta or Chicago

O'Hare, where almost all the traffic operated from a single airport, radar procedures were comparatively simple.

But at MIA, there was a Level 3, soon to be Level 4, operation only 20 miles north, as Fort Lauderdale continued to experience traffic growth. Although the airspace delegations within the Miami TRACON were designed to permit the two airports to operate as independently from each other as possible, there was definitely increased complexity for a number reasons. Traffic off MIA for FLL, or vice versa, had to be separated and handed off within a very short time window; low-altitude traffic from MIA going north had to be worked by the FLL controller; southbound traffic from FLL had to be worked first by FLL Departure, then North High Departure, and later by South Departure at MIA.

But the basic concept at both Miami and Fort Lauderdale, was as follows: Arrivals would be routed via arrival transition areas (ATAs) located in the northeast and northwest quadrants of the terminal airspace (southeast and southwest quadrants also for MIA). Departures would be routed via departure transition areas (DTAs) between the arrival "corridors." Both airports were configured with parallel east-west runways, and were located more or less in the "middle" of the terminal area.

So to take the example of an east operation, an arrival would come in from the northeast at 8,000 feet and be assigned no lower while on the departure (east) side of the airport. It would be vectored to a downwind on a track perhaps six or eight miles north of the airport. Once on the arrival (west) side of the airport, the approach controller would issue descent and vectors to turn base and then an intercept heading to the final approach course for 9 Left. The departure controller would restrict his traffic to a maximum of 7,000 feet to pass under the 8,000-foot arrival, and only issue climb clearance when his airplane entered the next block of airspace that was clear of the arrival corridor. This was the operation on the "long" side of the airport, so designated because the arrival aircraft had to fly more miles, passing the airport on downwind and then turning 180 degrees back for an east landing. On the "short" side, that is arrivals from the northwest during an east operation, the approach controller could begin stepping down the aircraft on initial contact, in some cases issuing only one turn to final. The departure controller had airspace permitting him to cross the short side arrival flow either by "topping" it if the departure was capable of climbing above 9,000 prior to the arrival corridor, or by "tunneling" under it at perhaps 5,000 through a block where approach control could not go below 6,000 in the case of a slow climber or a filed altitude below 9,000.

Each position in both the tower and the TRACON was allotted a certain number of hours within which a trainee was expected to complete on the job training. Exceptions could be made extending those hours if the OJT instructors and the supervisor determined that, quote, "Progress is satisfactory and the employee is likely to certify within the extra hours assigned." There was also a grey area consisting of what was termed "familiarization," that is plugging in and watching a qualified controller work, or "bootleg training," where a controller providing familiarization allowed the trainee to work without logging the hours.

In my early years, there was a degree of informality and flexibility surrounding this practice that benefitted members of my generation. Later there were a few cases of complaints and formal grievances filed by individuals who averred that they had been treated unfairly because they had been given less familiarization time than someone else. The facility's predictable reaction was to specify an exact number of familiarization hours per position and to prohibit completely any OJT hours that were not logged. The complainants were invariably people who knew they were headed for a washout, and were grasping at straws in the hope of avoiding the inevitable. And so the climb to certification for the trainees who followed me became several degrees steeper without in any way helping the individuals lodging the complaints.

My familiarization sessions were conducted on the two main departure control positions and had taken place in the last month or two before I checked out on Local Control. The idea was that I would be a more proficient local controller if I understood what the departure controllers had to do with the airplanes after takeoff, and how my actions in the tower could help or hinder the departure control operation. As previously noted, watching an experienced controller work these positions and observing that he made it look like the proverbial piece of cake, I found myself wondering how hard it could be. Of course I was failing to take into account his total familiarity with the internal airspace divisions allocated among the seven radar positions, his knowledge of the airway structure, fixes, and navaids, and that vital "sixth sense" that enabled him to sniff out problems before they occurred and head them off.

The first order of business was to study this information in the classroom. Before too long I was able to identify the markings on a paper representation of the video map that overlay each radar display, but the real challenge was in understanding all the information that was not depicted. Airports, navaids, fixes and final approach courses were shown, but airways, VFR reporting points, and most significantly the blocks of airspace assigned to the radar positions were not. At most, a small angled tick mark might indicate the corner of a certain block, and from that you had to picture the entire area. In the beginning, one of the most difficult exercises was one that I used regularly when I became an instructor that I dubbed "name that airspace." The instructor would place a pointer at a random point on the map and ask the trainee to identify in the vertical dimension each position owning airspace and the range of altitudes for which it was responsible. The complexity was increased several fold because the blocks, and the altitudes, could differ depending, broadly, on the following variations:

- Miami east operation, Fort Lauderdale east operation; Miami west operation, Fort Lauderdale east operation. What had formerly been approach control airspace now became departure control airspace at Miami, and even the positions governing the Fort Lauderdale operation experienced minor airspace changes.
- Miami west operation, Fort Lauderdale west operation. Again, at Fort Lauderdale the former approach control area now belonged to departure control, and minor changes occurred for the Miami flow.
- The final variation occurred when Miami was east and Fort Lauderdale west, with each combination affecting to a greater or lesser degree the airspace of the positions controlling the other airport's traffic.

In 1970, the year I became fully certified, there were probably 50 or 60 different airspace configurations, a number that more than doubled to something over 140 distinct areas when the TRACON expanded from seven to 14 radar positions in 1972. Because that expansion coincided with the introduction of ARTS, the computer system that placed an identification tag on each airplane worked in the terminal ATC system, also furnishing "Mode C" altitude information, the emphasis on airspace knowledge decreased, not without some negative effects. Especially in those early years of automation, I felt fortunate to have qualified in the pre-ARTS era. As with any new system, ARTS could fail without warning, meaning that we had to rely on the skills of associating our flight progress strips with radar targets that had instantly become identical blips on the scope. The controllers who trained and certified post-ARTS we referred to as "ARTS babies" because when the system went down, they were at a serious disadvantage in keeping track of the identities of their airplanes.

My first radar position was R-3, or North High Departure Control. At that time North High was considered the easiest of the TRACON positions for several reasons. The aircraft controlled by R-3 were primarily air carrier jets, meaning that they had similar performance characteristics, were flown by professional pilots, and were all on instrument flight plans. As one of my instructors informed me early on, "North High is always a good operation as long as the tower doesn't hand you any weenies." (Uh-oh, had I handed the departure controllers any "weenies" from Local Control because I was not familiar with the radar operation?) The airplanes came off with at least minimum spacing (three miles), sometimes more, generally nicely lined up on the same tower assigned heading (090 east, 290 west), and assigned one of the three departure transition areas to the north. As a departure controller, there was a standard set of actions you had to take with each aircraft:

- Radar identify it within one nautical mile of the departure runway.
- Call the appropriate Miami Center sector with the departure time.
- Establish it on the airway or other route specified in the center letter of agreement.
- Issue climb to the filed altitude or the top of our airspace, whichever was lower (or coordinate for a different altitude if needed for separation).
- Make a handoff to the center controller before MIA's airspace boundary.
- Issue a frequency change to the appropriate Miami Center frequency after handoff.

So a transcript of the communications required for a single aircraft could go like this:

EA321: "Miami departure, Eastern 321 with you, leaving a thousand for five thousand."

Controller: "Eastern 321 Miami departure, radar contact, climb and maintain seven thousand, report leaving five thousand."

EA321: "OK, up to seven now, Eastern 321, we'll call you out of five."

Controller (on land line): "Hammock 49 line, Eastern 321 off at 46, RP."

ZMA controller: "Thank you, JW."

Controller: "Eastern 321, say altitude."

EA321: "Eastern 321 leaving three thousand."

Controller: "Eastern 321 roger, turn left heading 360."

EA321: "Coming left to 360, Eastern 321."

EA321: "And Eastern 321 is leaving five thousand."

Controller: "Eastern 321 roger, turn left heading 290, join J 43, climb and maintain flight level 230."

EA321: "OK, that's left to 290, join up on J 43, and we're leaving six for two three oh, Eastern 321."

Controller (on land line): "Hammock 49, handoff."

ZMA controller: "Go ahead, Hammock."

Controller: "Fifteen [miles] northwest of the Miami VOR, Eastern 321."

ZMA controller: "Radar contact, JW."

Controller: "RP."

Controller: "Eastern 321 contact Miami Center on one three two point four five, good day."

EA321: "Over to 132.45, so long y'all."

These 19 exchanges would occur over a period of perhaps eight or nine minutes, a representative amount of time between initial departure and handoff/ frequency change to the center. In some cases there could be a smaller number of communications if, for example, no interim altitude reports were solicited. But in those pre-automation days it seemed as if every other controller query was for altitude information because the departure airspace was structured in such a way that the outbound aircraft had to top a number of "shelves" or boundary lines where the lower altitudes belonged to another position. You had to be certain the climb rate was sufficient to keep your traffic in the altitude strata assigned to North High Departure. If arrival traffic was light, the tower could launch a high departure every minute and a half or two minutes, meaning that at times there could be as many as six or seven of these aircraft in R-3 airspace and on his frequency. This level of activity was generally pretty manageable, but there were additional sources of traffic that North High had to contend with.

Handling Different Traffic

The Miami North Low departure controller, who initially worked propeller-driven aircraft, would often hand off that traffic later to North High if a pilot had filed for a final altitude that would put it in the high departure airspace. Additionally, one of the departure transition areas (DTAs) was shared between the Miami and Fort Lauderdale controllers, so that, from the Miami perspective, a jet off Fort Lauderdale could "pop up" as a handoff in the middle of a nicely orchestrated flow from MIA. Under busy conditions, you could have eight or nine aircraft under your control, each requiring a minimum of 12 to 15 control instructions and coordination calls, all within the eight or nine minute period before the first airplane was handed off. And it was not just a matter of running through the standard litany of control and coordination phraseology. There was also a high degree of mental processing, planning and prioritizing the necessary actions, executing them, and then monitoring the entire picture so that all separation and letter of agreement requirements were met (remember FEM?).

Under very busy conditions, each radar position might be assigned an assistant controller, or handoff man, to handle the landline communications, but often this extra man would be "late to the party," either because there was not sufficient staffing, or the supervisor was late in recognizing the need. Still, the radar controller had the ultimate tactical weapon at his fingertips—the override button to the local controller to stop departures (departure control) or the line to the center to start putting arrivals in a holding pattern (approach control). At a radar position, in the final analysis, you had only yourself to blame if the operation got out of hand because of traffic volume. And in this regard, some controllers were often their own worst enemy, big ego types unwilling to stop or limit the traffic flow or to acknowledge that a little help from the handoff position would keep things under control. Others were more sanguine, perfectly willing to ask for help or accept it when offered, and not shy about voicing their pique if it were late in coming. The refrain of a recent popular song was more than once hummed, whistled, or sung when a handoff man showed up late: "Where were you when I needed you? Where were you when I wanted you?"

Learning the Basics

As compared with tower control, the radar operation required a more strategic posture on the part of the controller. On ground control, you could change the instructions to a taxiing aircraft just a few seconds before it reached the point where a turn to an alternate route was necessary. At the local control position, decisions were pretty much instantaneous, and usually not subject to revision. Cleared for takeoff, or hold short for the next landing? Cleared to land or go around? Approve a runway crossing or not?

At a radar position, there was a much stronger element of planning and anticipation. For one thing, a radar display is not a continuously moving real time depiction of aircraft tracks and positions. Rather, it is a series of "snapshots" being taken each time the radar sweep detects a target. Aircraft positions were updated once every four seconds, as terminal Approach Surveillance Radar (ASR) systems provided an antenna rotation rate of 15 times per minute.

Of greater significance, from my perspective as a new controller, was the additional time required for an aircraft to complete a turn to a newly assigned heading, based on the following factors: Controller issues a turn of 90 degrees, say from 090 to 360 (three seconds); pilot acknowledges the instruction (three seconds); pilot initiates the turn (two seconds); it will take at least two sweeps for the controller to observe the turn (eight seconds); depending on the speed of the aircraft, 30 seconds to one minute will be required to reach the new heading (the greater the speed, the slower the turn). So for a period of between 38 and 68 seconds, the aircraft will be flying an arc intended to result in a heading to the correct point, with a long eight seconds before the controller knows whether the aircraft is following his instruction.

Most air carrier jets accelerate as rapidly as possible after takeoff to the maximum 250 knots permitted below 10,000 feet, meaning that they fly a little more than a mile every 15 seconds. You had to lead the turn by a good margin in order for the aircraft to end up on the desired track, taking into account wind effects, and of course the ever-changing priorities at any control position. Predictably, I started out being extremely poor at judging the turns I issued, or as one of my instructors informed me, I hadn't yet learned "to see around corners."

There were other factors involved in radar control that were not always obvious. Radar transmissions are line of sight, so that, depending on the altitude of an aircraft and the elevation of the antenna itself, there is a minimum altitude for any given distance from the radar site at which an aircraft can be detected. Moreover, the radar signal propagates as a lobe, leaving a lower area close to the ground and an upper area close to the antenna without coverage. The lower area was generally not a problem, as minimum vectoring altitudes and FAR regulations insured that most aircraft operations would remain above it. The upper area was a different story. The greater the altitude of an aircraft close to the antenna, the wider the area became. We called it the "cone of silence" because when a pilot flew into it, the controller lost radar contact until the aircraft emerged on the other side.

There were conditions like blind speeds, where an aircraft could disappear from radar if its angular velocity matched up in a certain way to the speed and direction of the radar sweep, and so called "second time around," where an area of fixed clutter is detected by a second pulse of radar energy, but interpreted by the receiver as a reflection of the first pulse. The effect is to make it appear that the area is twice as close as its actual position. These latter two phenomena were essentially eliminated in later years with the advent of dual-channel radar systems.

By degrees, I got the hang of North High Departure, improving my ability to judge a turn correctly, and incorporating some board management tricks by keeping the flight progress strips for each aircraft oriented according to the DTA to which they were routed—for an east operation, slightly left (northwestern DTA), slightly right (eastern DTA), or centered (northern DTA). I also began to see techniques for orchestrating the flow.

For example, if spacing was a little tight on two air carriers on the same route, you could simply assign the following aircraft a maximum altitude of 9,000 feet so that the lead aircraft would leave 10,000 and accelerate while the 250-knot restriction remained in place for the one at 9,000. Once a satisfactory interval was established, the lower airplane could be issued climb clearance and would never close the gap on the traffic ahead ("never catch him with a catching stick" in the imaginative parlance that permeated the lexicon of the air traffic workforce).

You could also delay a turn for a few seconds to create additional spacing, issue a "zig-zag" off route vector and return to course, or possibly coordinate for a different route. These last three options added to the total workload because, as noted earlier, jet aircraft tended to turn slowly. A delayed turn could necessitate delaying a turn for a following aircraft, and an off-route vector could impose the need to do the same with following traffic, potentially snowballing into a major "fubar" (fouled up beyond all recognition, in polite terms). Coordination took valuable time and attention away from the task at hand, and, unless used judiciously, imposed penalties on other controllers.

It didn't take me long to see the several major pluses to the radar operation. Areas of jurisdiction were precisely defined, and generally limited to a fairly small portion of the 15-inch diameter representation of MIA's airspace on the video map. Unlike the tower, where you had to keep your head on a swivel and monitor 2,700 acres on the ground and 360 degrees around the airport in the air, radar required that you keep track of your airplanes in your airspace (with a weather eye to your boundaries in case of an errant penetration from a neighboring sector). This meant that the "picture" was always right there before you, and all you had to do was recognize what was happening and orchestrate your future actions accordingly.

To be sure, radar skills did not develop overnight, but I came to appreciate the relative orderliness of the radar operation. The one big problem at the radar positions was weather. Pilots did not want to fly into thunderstorms or even a fairly benign rain cloud. On a bad weather day, all the nicely defined airspace delimitations were out the window, with essentially every pilot picking his route through the storms, and requiring coordination at every turn. The reasons for routine epidemics of "instrumentaitis" and wholesale sick leave on such days became abundantly apparent to me.

The stresses of the radar operation during bad weather, for pilots and controllers alike, manifested themselves in different ways. The pilot in command of an aircraft had the final say as to what he was willing to do, notwithstanding the general FAR requirement that all air traffic control instructions had to be followed. If a pilot used his emergency authority, he was required to file a written report to the FAA, presumably subjecting himself to after-the-fact scrutiny about his decision by both the agency and, in the case of an air carrier, his chief pilot. For this reason, the emergency authority provision was rarely invoked. What often happened instead was a verbal, and often heated, tug of war on the control frequency as pilots requested routings that looked favorable but would put them in conflict with other traffic, while controllers issued alternate instructions that would assure traffic separation. There were several instances where pilot complaints about their handling in weather prompted the facility to analyze voice recordings of the exchanges. A couple of examples:

Controller: "Turn left heading 360."

Pilot: "We can't do that due to weather."

Controller: "Turn left immediately to any heading north of 030 and advise your new heading, you have traffic twelve o' clock six miles opposite direction at your altitude."

Pilot: "Well you do something with him because we're not moving!"

Another:

Controller: "Fly heading 200 for vectors to the ILS 9 Left approach."

Pilot: "Unable 200, we'll need about a 240 heading for weather."

Controller: "240 approved." (On override) "Hey departure, 10 south of Lonni deviating to 240."

Departure controller: "Point out approved."

Controller: "Descend and maintain 5,000."

Pilot: "Negative, we need to stay high for weather."

Controller: "Roger, maintain 8,000, advise when you can accept descent."

Controller: "Descend and maintain 3,000."

Pilot: "If we go lower we need to go all the way down to get below this stuff."

Controller: "Roger, descend and maintain 1,500." (On override): "Low departure, ten north of Miami descending to 1500."

Low Departure: "Point out approved."

Controller: "Turn right heading 270."

Pilot: "We can't take that heading. In fact we need about a 180 heading for weather."

Controller: "180 heading approved."

At this point the aircraft broke out of the bottom of the overcast about five miles north of the airport, but at right angles to 9 Left, the pilot exclaiming angrily:

"Oh, great! Look where you've got us now, we can't land from here!"

Controller: "Captain, you have refused every instruction I've issued and I've approved every deviation you requested. Where you are is where you got yourself, not where I got you."

Of course, the airplane still had to be put on the final, so there was much more to the exchange than the portion represented here, but the example serves to illustrate what it took to work just one airplane in bad weather, never mind the sharply increased complexity with six or eight aircraft on the frequency.

Good Guys, Bad Guys

I checked out on North High Departure in less time than it took for any of the tower positions, and despite the challenges of bad weather days, I found myself liking this radar business more and more. Because North High was my first position in the TRACON, I had no direct experience on any of the other positions, and it became apparent that to be really proficient a controller needed to understand the entirety of the radar operation. I picked up bits and pieces of this expanded knowledge both in the course of training and even after check out, learning along the way that much of what happened in adjacent sectors depended on the individuals working them.

Some of my instructors were brutally candid about their fellow journeymen, offering me observations like, "Now look, you got Ray over there working Fort Lauderdale departure. He doesn't give a hoot about your traffic, so he will put one of his airplanes directly under one of yours and then bug you for higher altitude." One time after I certified, "Ray over there" was again working Fort Lauderdale departure, and did exactly what my instructor had warned me about. When he coordinated for a higher altitude, my response was, "Approved subject the 0300 code at twelve o'clock one mile level at 7,000." This meant that Ray could either climb his airplane, with the same routing as mine, to 6,000, or vector it to get in trail separation, at which point I would be able to approve his request. Ray called me several more times, insisting more urgently each time that I approve an unrestricted climb for his traffic, with our two aircraft still in the same relative positions. I denied these requests, and eventually we each handed off our airplanes, still in close proximity, but with what I assuredly thought had to be altitude separation. A while later, I was summoned to the office of the Operations Officer, to listen to a tape.

The Operations Officer was Stan Hamlin, who was nearing the end of his career, and had been in management since before Miami became a radar facility, never having had radar experience of his own. He was basically a courtly southern gentleman type, not one to rant and rave, but more focused on smoothing out conflicts. As the tape progressed, I heard again all of Ray's coordination calls, my responses, and then, tellingly, this transmission from Ray to his airplane: "Delta 788 climb and maintain flight level 230." I couldn't believe my ears, as that climb clearance had immediately followed my final refusal to grant Ray a higher altitude. I looked at Stan questioningly, and he said, a touch ruefully, "You could have been more courteous."

Apparently either the pilot of Delta 788, or more likely the Miami Center controller to whom the flight had been handed off, had complained, triggering the playback to which we were now listening. Although no official determination was reached classifying the incident as an operational error, there was no reasonable conclusion other than that Ray had climbed his airplane into my airspace without approval and lost legal separation in the process. And yet, Stan seemed to be ascribing responsibility for the incident to my lack of "courtesy." Ray was a veteran controller with years of experience, and I was a new kid, which may have colored Stan's take, but I walked out of the office doing a slow burn. It was my first lesson in why there was so often conflict between working controllers and management.

Another incident on North High underlined the same management-controller dynamic, this time not involving an adjacent sector. I was being relieved from the position by a supervisor who had some strange quirks. At the time I was working only one airplane, the British Airways 707 on its way to London. I had already handed off the flight, but since it would still be in my airspace for another couple of minutes or so, I had not yet issued a frequency change. I briefed the supervisor, saying that I was planning on waiting a minute or two before switching Speedbird over to the center. Now, with only one airplane on frequency, a handoff already made, and no other traffic a factor, any other controller would have accepted the position, I would have been on my way, and my relief would have issued the new frequency. The supervisor remained silent, and I knew better than to unplug my headset before he acknowledged that the relief briefing was complete.

In due course I issued the frequency change, at which point "JK," John Kaplan, stated, "Okay, I've got it." As I stood up to leave, he said, "Just a minute. I know you are wondering why I didn't immediately take the position after you briefed me." I replied, "No, that's okay, John, no problem." I knew I didn't want to hear his explanation. But he pressed on, saying, "If Speedbird crashes at Heathrow tomorrow morning, they will play back the tapes from every position that worked him, and I don't want my voice on this tape." Unbelievable! Cue theme music from "The Twilight Zone."

Both of these incidents highlighted a fact that I took to heart early on. Some controllers set a high priority on doing things in a way that didn't leave any "hangers" for the people who would work the airplanes subsequently. Others were seemingly content to leave pending situations unresolved, leaving it to others to straighten things out later. There were several things wrong with the posture of this latter group, not the least of which was that unresolved potential problems usually became more critical as they developed. More generally, if every controller operated in that manner, the entire ATC system would rapidly become unworkable.

And so, as happens in most large organizations, there was a core of "good guys" who lived by the maxim, "Do everything necessary as early as possible." I was determined to be in this group, even though it required extra awareness and anticipation when working with "the other guys." Here are some examples of the difference between "getting it done early" and "I'll let the next guy figure it out" (but with a necessary explanatory preamble).

Later in my career, with the implementation of ARTS, the radar positions were assigned single letters. Every aircraft being worked by a position had the letter of that position superimposed over its transponder return. I was working the Fort Lauderdale Departure position, now referred to as "L." By this time the sectors south of FLL had been restructured, with the creation of a low altitude area assigned airspace from the surface to 4,000 feet ("Z" position by designation), and North High Departure (now known as "D") "owning" 5,000 to 7,000. There had also been a procedural change, so that low altitude traffic was no longer sent directly from the tower to the "low" man, but was first worked by D and then handed off to Z.

Traffic landing in Palm Beach Approach Control's airspace, directly adjacent to ours, was by letter of agreement between MIA and PBI assigned either 4,000 (propeller-driven aircraft) or 5,000 (jets). PBI traffic originating at MIA or points south had to transition the FLL Departure area through a portion of it where the maximum available altitude was 5,000. Although there was no procedural requirement, it was an accepted technique that "props" would be assigned 4,000 and jets 5,000 for handoff to the FLL controller. This worked well, leaving the props in Z's airspace, allowing D to "top" the props with jet traffic, and providing altitude separation for the L controller.

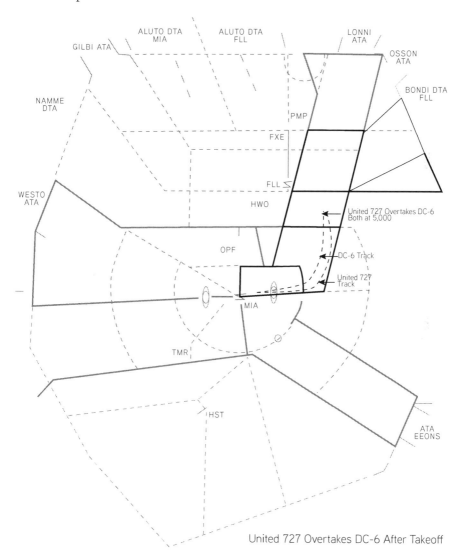

United 727 Overtakes DC-6 After Takeoff

On the day in question, the tower launched a Latin American DC-6 that had seen its better days. The transponder did not work, so there was no identifying ARTS tag, the radios were marginal, and the flight crew was heavily accented to the point of being impossible to understand. The tower advised the "D man" that one engine was trailing a thick plume of smoke, which fact the controller attempted to relay to the pilot without success. The radar target appeared as a tiny blip, no larger than a match head. The DC-6 was routed via Hammock, the northwestern DTA, with a final altitude of 8,000. On an east operation, as this was, the first 10 or 12 miles after takeoff kept airplanes going to PBI and to the northern and northwestern DTAs on the same routing. D cleared the old DC-6 to 5,000 and issued a turn to the north. Given the absence of a Mode C altitude indication and the virtual certainty of a slow climb rate, the airplane should have been pointed out to Z and remained D's responsibility since it would be in Z's airspace only temporarily and eventually reach the higher altitude stratum. Alternatively, D could have coordinated for an interim altitude of 4,000 and made a handoff to Z.

However, the D man shouted across the room, "Hey Z, I'm switching that primary target five northeast to you," passing the flight progress strip, with no altitude information entered. A minute or two later the tower launched a 727 with destination Palm Beach. D issued climb clearance to 5,000 and turned the airplane northbound, directly behind the DC-6. When the 727 was handed off to me at L, I issued traffic as "twelve o'clock one mile northbound, altitude unknown." At this point the Z man spoke urgently into my headset via the override, saying, "that primary target just ahead of United (the 727) is IFR at 5,000." I repeated the traffic call, adding the altitude information, and instructed the United pilot to descend immediately to 4,000. He replied, "That guy is right below us, no way we're descending." Fortunately, the small errors in altimeter calibration had put the two aircraft at slightly different levels, averting something much worse than the near miss that had just occurred. I reported the incident to the TRACON supervisor, telling him to expect a call from the pilot of the United 727, and shortly after the flight landed at PBI, that call came in.

The supervisor, Lester McNeil, managed to sweet talk the pilot out of filing an official report, but after hanging up the phone, he immediately had me and the other two controllers relieved from L, Z, and

D respectively. He escorted us into the tape playback room, and soon we were all listening to the radio and override exchanges preceding the near miss. The tape revealed that the D controller had not received an acknowledgement of the frequency change to Z, and that the pilot did not contact the Z controller until the moment the DC-6 reached 5,000, the point at which Z called me on the override. Lester was definitely "old school," and brooked no poor performance on the part of anyone. At the conclusion of the tape, he lit into the D controller: "What the hell did you mean climbing that DC-6 to one of your altitudes and then handing him off to Z? You didn't get an acknowledgement of the frequency change, never asked Z if the pilot had contacted him, and then proceeded to run over him with United. When you hand somebody off, you protect that airplane as long as it is in your airspace."

The D man began justifying himself saying that since the airplane was probably going to climb slowly, the Z man should work him, and that Z never said the pilot had failed to make the frequency change. The Z man said, with telling reason, "I thought you were keeping him on your frequency until you got him separated from United." What had actually been going on was D's unwillingness to work a primary target that was hard to track and difficult to control because of the poor communications. He put the burden on Z, who only by luck, and far too late, discovered the imminent traffic conflict.

Other Examples

Two other instances, actually each the flip side of the other, illustrate the difference between proactive control and letting others do the work. One of my co-workers was working the low altitude sector north of Fort Lauderdale ("G" position) while I was at "Z," responsible for low altitude traffic south of FLL. He accepted a handoff on a single-engine Cessna from Palm Beach at Miami's northern boundary, then immediately initiated a handoff to me via the ARTS automated function. This method caused the identification tag of the airplane to "flash" on and off, and the flashing would continue until I accepted the handoff. The pilot intended to land at Opa-locka, some 30 miles from the aircraft's present position, and only about six miles into my airspace. In other words, the aircraft would be in G's airspace for more than 20 miles, and, at a speed of about 90 knots, for more than 10 minutes. I observed the flashing ARTS tag, but did not take the handoff, as I couldn't believe the G controller would initiate the transfer of control so early. Maybe he just wanted to give me an early heads up, or maybe he "fat-fingered" the keyboard, inadvertently causing an unintentional action.

I was quickly disabused of these notions, when, not ten seconds after the flashing began, there came via the override in "Mike's" redneck accent, "Ain't you goin' to take 'at handoff?" I said, "Well, I thought I would wait until he was a little closer to my airspace." In even more irritable (and irritating) tones, Mike said, "Well now, I wouldn't be flashin' him to you if I didn't want you take him, would I?" Rather than spend any more time on this pointless interaction, I took the handoff, meaning that I now had to monitor all of my area plus most of Mike's. And it was a good thing I did keep an eye on the "G" traffic, because at least twice Mike threatened to run his other traffic over the Cessna I was now working, saying things like, "You see you got traffic four miles off your right at your altitude, don't you?" in an accusatory tone. I thought, but did not say, "No Mike, You've got traffic at twelve o'clock four miles that you have to protect since you have basically surrendered 20 miles of your airspace to me."

On another occasion, Mike and I were working the two adjacent low-altitude sectors. I had a slow single-engine aircraft whose routing would take it from my area to Mike's, and I initiated the automated handoff, as I always tried to do, at a point where the airplane was about two minutes from the boundary. Of course the distance in miles varied depending on the speed, so in the case of this 100-knot Cherokee, it was about four miles. For the next minute and a half or so the flight continued without the handoff being accepted, meaning that it was now about two miles from the boundary. Radar separation rules required that each controller keep his traffic one and a half miles from any boundary in order to preserve the minimum three miles from aircraft in the neighboring airspace. I had no choice but to hit the override and ask, "Can you take the handoff on Cherokee 86 Yankee?" Mike's reply allowed the flight to progress, but did nothing except increase my appreciation for the stark difference between "the good guys" and "the other guys." His response: "Yeah, yeah, I see him, Jesus Christ, keep your shirt on."

Working Satellite Fields

The next phase of my training was on the two other major departure control positions, Miami South Departure and Fort Lauderdale Departure. These two positions were similar to North High with respect to the scheduled air carriers. But there were other factors involved at each of them that complicated the operation. At South Departure, a majority of the Miami traffic consisted of foreign carriers, often operating older generation aircraft, and flown by pilots with limited English who were unfamiliar with American air traffic control procedures. A couple of real-life examples serve to illustrate the point:

An Air Mexico DC-8 pilot was instructed to change his transponder code via an instruction from a controller using textbook phraseology, "Air Mexico 408 squawk one three zero zero." The pilot heard the numbers and took them to mean an altitude, descending to 1300 feet at a distance nearly 100 miles from the airport. The aircraft flew through several sectors where the minimum safe altitude was considerably higher than 1300 feet before the error was discovered, only by sheer luck avoiding the obstructions that dictated a higher minimum altitude.

In another case, the pilot of a Guatemalan DC-4 was issued an altimeter setting of three zero zero six. The result was a turn to a heading of 360, and a premature entry into center airspace without a handoff. Fortunately both the center controller and the South Departure controller recognized the situation and resolved it without incident.

There was additional complexity at South Departure because the position was responsible for Tamiami Airport, a general aviation field that at that time boasted a traffic count second only to Miami's, the highest in Florida, as well as military traffic at Homestead Air Force Base. At the Miami departure control positions, traffic off Miami was released "automatically," meaning that the tower did not have to get permission to launch each airplane specifically and individually, but only had to communicate the "off time" of each. At the "satellite" fields, as all airports other than Miami were designated, there was a coordination loop that had to be completed before an aircraft was released, which could go like this:

TMB (Tamiami tower, on speaker): "Miami, Tamiami, release request."

MIA South Departure (after switching from speaker to headset): "Miami." (I was trained never to say "go ahead" in answering any call coordinating an aircraft movement because of the possibility that the controller making the request might "go ahead" and take the action before a firm handshake about what was intended had occurred).

TMB: "Request release on November 5030 Romeo, Cessna 172, Bradley [the northern DTA], 7,000, followed by Citation 551 Alpha Lima, Citation 500, Pineapple [the southeastern DTA], flight level 330, both off 9 Right."

MIA (first locating the flight progress strips-or not): "Can you give the Cessna a left turn to 290 and the Citation runway heading?"

TMB: "Affirmative, Miami."

MIA: "OK, they are both released, RP."

TMB: "LD."

When traffic was slow to moderate, these exchanges were not a problem, but under busy conditions the time spent on the landline meant that the basic functions of formulate, execute, and monitor were temporarily suspended, so that when the coordination was complete a period of "catch up" was usually required. Sometimes a flight progress strip had not been delivered to the departure position, meaning that the whole communication would have to be repeated later. In addition, in the above example, the Citation would have to be fit into the flow of Miami departures routed via the Pineapple DTA, and there was no way to anticipate, at the time the release was granted, what the traffic picture would be when the airplane actually got airborne.

Another factor, essentially absent from North High, were the calls from VFR traffic requesting service. Although service to VFR aircraft was always subordinate to the primary ATC function of separating airplanes on IFR flight plans, the sheer volume of these contacts at times made it difficult to control the frequency. Part of the problem was that a high percentage of VFR flights were conducted by low experience pilots—students, newly certificated private ticket holders, and even those with more advanced ratings who had not yet received instrument training. Radio discipline was often poor, as was the condition of the radios themselves. The aircraft operated by flight schools led hard lives, the radios and electrical systems alternately cooked by the Florida sun and steeped in high humidity. These factors aside, the VFR pilots in many cases did not have a good grasp of how to use the services available to them. They could request any or all of the following:

- VFR flight following. The aircraft would remain in radar contact until the pilot canceled the request or the controller terminated radar service.

If the pilot experienced any difficulty, help in the form of search and rescue could be immediately dispatched and the exact location of the airplane would be known.
- Radar advisories. Workload permitting, the controller would provide traffic information to assist the pilot in avoiding other aircraft via the see-and-be-seen method.
- Navigational assistance. A pilot unsure of his position could request vectors (assigned headings) to an airport or other location, or in later years, permission to enter positive control airspace around major airports.
- Weather information. Although terminal ASR systems were not designed primarily to detect weather, the heaviest and most dangerous cells would be displayed, and the controller could suggest routings clear of these areas.
- Practice approaches. Traffic permitting, the controller could vector the airplane to the final approach course of an instrument approach, providing an aspiring pilot the needed practice to pass an instrument rating check ride.

A Typical VFR Call for Service

So ideally, from the controller perspective, a call for VFR service would go like this:

Pilot (waiting for a break on the frequency): "Miami departure control, Skyhawk 61244."

MIA departure controller: "Skyhawk 61244 Miami departure."

Pilot: "Miami, Skyhawk 244, Cessna 172, just departed Tamiami VFR to Sarasota, request flight following and traffic advisories. We filed for 6,500 via Victor 97." In a single transmission the pilot had provided everything the controller needed to know, instead of requiring a time consuming round of "20 questions" to elicit the information.

MIA: "Cessna 244 roger, squawk one two zero zero and ident." Seeing the target "bloom," the controller would continue, "Cessna 244, radar contact six miles northwest of Tamiami. Say altitude and report reaching 6,500."

Pilot: "Ok, 244, we're leaving 3,000 and will advise reaching 6,500."

Except for subsequent traffic calls and possibly handing off the flight to another control position, the exchange was complete, having required perhaps no more than 30 to 45 seconds.

Unfortunately, with a less-experienced pilot in the cockpit, the communications loop was more likely to go something like this:

Pilot (interrupting a call already in progress): (Squeal, squeal, static) "…per 424 with you leaving a thousand."

Controller (knowing the next departure from Miami would be Clipper 424, and having the flight progress strip in front of him): "Clipper 424 Miami departure, did you just report leaving 1,000?"

PA 424: "Clipper 424 affirmative, we're (squeal, static)."

Controller: "Clipper 424 roger, radar contact, climb and maintain 7,000."

PA 424: "If that was for Clipper 424, you were blocked."

Controller: "Clipper 424, I say again, radar contact, climb and maintain 7,000."

Pilot: "Miami departure, 61244."

Controller: "November 61244 Miami departure."

Pilot: "Roger, Miami."

Controller: "November 61244, say your request."

Pilot: "I just wanted to let you know that I'm here."

The pilot provided no information that the controller could act on, and so there was a choice to be made. Depending on workload, and of course whether the controller was a proactive type or a path of least resistance type, the next transmission could end the exchange with something like, "N61244 roger, have a nice day." But unless you could justify such a response on the basis of workload, it was not advisable. Where was the aircraft? Was it in the middle of an airport's traffic area, or on the final approach course at Miami, about to become a hood ornament on a 727? And the pilot might erroneously believe that he was receiving some type of radar service.

In most cases, the exchange would continue:

Controller: "November 61244, say your position and aircraft type."

Pilot: "244, we're over the shoreline and we're a Cessna 172."

Of course, the shoreline ran the entire length of the Miami TRACON's airspace, some 60 miles—assuming the Cessna was even in Miami's airspace.

Controller: "Clipper 424, turn left heading 100, receiving Bimini proceed direct."

Pilot: "Miami, we're not going to Bimini."

Controller: "Cessna 244, that transmission was not for you, break break, Clipper 424, did you copy?"

PA 424: "Got it okay Miami, 100 degrees and direct Bimini."

Controller: "Cessna 244, where did you take off from, and how long ago?"

Pilot: "We took off at Tamiami about five minutes ago."

From this the controller could determine that the aircraft was pretty much due east of Tamiami at the coast. It could hardly be anywhere else, because it would take about five minutes to reach the coast from Tamiami.

Controller: "Cessna 244, say your intentions."

Pilot: "We just want to do a little sightseeing up and down the beach."

Controller: "Cessna 244, roger, maintain VFR, remain clear of the airport traffic areas at Miami and Fort Lauderdale, if you go that far north."

For most controllers, this was a reasonable conclusion to this particular event, given that the pilot clearly did not know what to ask for. He had been issued correct cautionary advice, given his likely position, and the whole incident had already taken three to four times as long as the interaction with the pilot who understood radar services to VFR aircraft. Although some controllers might have queried the pilot as to the specific service desired (e.g., "Are you requesting radar advisories?"), my takeaway from the training I received was never to do that. Without enough experience to ask for the service, it was almost certain that the pilot would not understand what he was accepting, or foregoing, in responding to such a direct question. Moreover green pilots almost always answered any direct question in the affirmative, only adding to the uncertainties about whether pilot and controller were on the same page. For example, a pilot might report that he was VFR inbound to Tamiami. The controller might attempt to determine the aircraft's location by asking the pilot if he was south of the airport, and the reply would be in the affirmative. After a few more questions, the controller might begin to suspect that in fact the airplane was inbound from the north, and if asked, the pilot would again reply in the affirmative.

Over-Reliance on Controllers

Another problem with low experience pilots was their tendency to rely on controllers to make decisions that were clearly a pilot's prerogative. In later years, after check out on South Departure, the following incident occurred when a VFR Cessna departed Tamiami on a mid-summers night while a number of thunderstorms still lingered in the area. The exchange went like this:

N7177F: "Miami departure Cessna 7177 Foxtrot."

Me: "Cessna 7177 Foxtrot Miami departure."

N7177F: "Roger sir, 77 Foxtrot just took off Tamiami headed over to Naples. Can you help me get around these storms?

Me: "Cessna 77 Foxtrot, squawk one two zero zero and ident, say your type Cessna."

After radar identifying the Cessna 172, I advised the pilot, "Cessna 77 Foxtrot, be advised my radar does not depict all the weather cells in the area. I can point out the heaviest of them, but I can't guarantee that you will be able to remain in VFR conditions."

The pilot replied, "77 Foxtrot, roger."

A few minutes later the exchange resumed:

N7177F: "Miami, 77 Foxtrot, my engine is running rough."

Me: "Cessna 77 Foxtrot roger, say your intentions."

N7177F: "Well I don't know, Miami, what do you think I should do?"

Me: "Cessna 77 Foxtrot, well sir, it's your decision, but if it was me I would not be heading out over the Everglades at night with thunderstorms in the area and a rough running engine. I would return to Tamiami and at least get the engine looked at."

N7177F: "Ok Miami, I'll head back to Tamiami, thanks a lot."

It made me wonder, afterwards, why the pilot had even asked what he should do, the obvious answer being the one I had given him. And what if I had demurred, simply saying that it was his decision? Would he have continued on, and how would the incident have been reconstructed if the pilot had come to grief? Based on other incidents involving ATC and VFR pilots, where a crash and death or injury occurred, court cases had tended to fix blame on controllers for failing to intercede in what were clearly pilot decisions. Most judges were not pilots, issuing rulings that said, in effect, "He was an inexperienced pilot, and you are an experienced controller. How could you let him continue his flight under the circumstances?" The fact that in most cases the controller had communicated all pertinent information to the pilot never seemed to alter the outcome in these cases.

Homestead Air Force Base Traffic

So at South Departure the controller was working a mix of high-performance air carriers and smaller general aviation aircraft off Miami. There was no low altitude sector south of the airport comparable to the airspace on the north side, and so no opportunity existed to offload these lower performance airplanes. In addition, as described above, there was a considerable amount of VFR satellite field traffic. On top of it all, there was Homestead Air Force Base, which at the time was running a traffic count of several hundred thousand operations a year. Military operations were conducted on an entirely different basis than normal civilian flying, the primary focus being on mission completion. Because most of the flights in and out of Homestead were training hops, there was a high priority placed on accomplishing everything mandated in the operational orders for a particular exercise. This meant that fuel capacity was always pushed to the limit as the commanders of these exercises attempted to squeeze in that "last run" before returning to base.

There were additional factors that made the Homestead operation difficult, ranging from communications to aircraft performance and the coordination demands of working with the Air Force GCA unit responsible for an area about 15 miles across with altitudes 3,000 and below surrounding the field. In the late 1960s, military aircraft were equipped almost exclusively with radios utilizing the ultra-high frequency (UHF) band as distinct from the very high frequency (VHF) band used by civilian operators. In addition, a training flight usually consisted of four aircraft which, when flying in formation, could be controlled as a single entity, but which usually wanted to "break up" when returning to base. Breaking up meant that the airplanes would peel off from the formation one at a time and would then have to be separated from each other as well as from any other traffic that was in the picture. A request to break up from the flight leader was often accompanied by the need to assign each pilot a discreet frequency. This all generally happened in the last 20 miles before handoff to GCA, so that the controller was very quickly faced with a hugely increased workload, consisting of the following:

He was now working four airplanes instead of "one" (the formation flight).

The airplanes were rapidly closing on the airport, all with minimum fuel.

Because of the discreet frequency assignments and the UHF radios, none of the military pilots could hear each other or any of the VHF transmissions from the civilian fleet, nor could any of the civilian pilots hear the military communications. This meant that, from the perspective of the controller, who was listening to and transmitting on five frequencies simultaneously, there was a barrage of smeared transmissions and "say agains" almost every time someone keyed a microphone. Compounding these disadvantages was the fact that the F-4s, as most of these training flights were, all had similar call signs—Gourd 41, Gourd 42, Gourd 43, Gourd 44, for example. Even when a controller transmission was not smeared, the wrong pilot would often respond, and sometimes make a maneuver intended for another aircraft. Finally, the controller would have to relinquish valuable frequency time to make handoffs to GCA, with the attendant temporary loss of the basic FEM functions.

Fighter aircraft were designed for extremely high performance. This meant that in most cases they could not be assigned speed restrictions, eliminating one of the most basic techniques a controller could use in orchestrating an arrival sequence. In the departure phase, the flight leaders always wanted an unrestricted climb, which amounted to an almost vertical, and rapid, ascent to flight levels. To accommodate this demand, the controller had to give Homestead a wide berth with his other traffic, thereby lengthening the time before a handoff could be made to the center.

There was one other "joker in the deck" at Homestead, that being the so-called "scramble" flights. The purpose of scrambles was to intercept unidentified aircraft penetrating the Air Defense Identification Zone (ADIZ). The ADIZ was a perimeter line around U.S. airspace designed as a boundary that no pilot approaching the United States was allowed to cross without positive identification of the aircraft by the military air defense command. Homestead (HST) had a single runway, designated as 5-23, and operated primarily on Runway 5 because of the prevailing east wind. Scrambles, however, always took off on 23 regardless of wind conditions, creating an instant problem with, for example a bunch of low fuel F-4s landing in the opposite direction. Scrambles had priority over all other operations with the exception of aircraft emergencies, meaning that there was little leeway to delay or otherwise plan for their departure. So, was the low fuel status of the F-4s an emergency? Not unless one of the pilots so declared. But if you broke one of them out to accommodate the scramble, you could be creating an emergency, in which case the scramble could be delayed. But by this time it could be barreling down Runway 23 in afterburner, possibly leaving the aircraft broken out with insufficient fuel to make it back to the airport. Even without conflicting opposite direction traffic, you still had to protect the flights already in the picture, and by their nature these high-priority operations were always of the "quick and dirty" variety. After a scramble operation, we used to joke that the pilots hadn't been the only ones "scrambling."

The North Side is Tougher than the South

Fort Lauderdale Departure served up many of the same challenges as did Miami South, but differed in some significant ways as well. While there were fewer foreign air carriers to contend with, there were four general aviation airports for which the position was responsible, all of which were home bases to flight schools. These training facilities enrolled a large number of foreign students, the majority from South and Central America, but many others hailing from places like Japan, Germany, France, and several Arabic-speaking nations. The combination of limited English, low pilot experience, and lack of familiarity with the U.S. air traffic control system made for some "interesting" times.

In addition, the coordination demands at the position were far more extensive than at Miami South. In Miami's south sector, there were only two satellite airports to deal with (Tamiami and Homestead), while the Fort Lauderdale controller was constantly on the landline to five different towers, as well as Palm Beach Approach Control for tower en route traffic and low altitude overflights. Finally, the Fort Lauderdale Departure airspace was much more complicated, requiring the controller to route his traffic around, under, or over the separate arrival flows to Miami and Fort Lauderdale, and to keep a close eye on Miami North High.

The traffic at Miami North imposed an extra workload on Fort Lauderdale Departure via handoffs of low-altitude aircraft headed north, and by the need, first, to position FLL jet departures routed to the DTA shared with North High in a strategically correct position to be afforded an unrestricted climb, then to coordinate for that climb. In later years, when the TRACON expanded from seven to 12 positions, and in recognition that one controller, even with a handoff man, could not provide effective service with so many disparate demands, the facility revised its procedures, creating separate low-altitude sectors north and south of Fort Lauderdale, and even later establishing totally independent departure routings for Miami and Fort Lauderdale traffic headed north.

In the meantime, though, I had to learn to handle the position with skills so far only partially developed, looking at double slash beacon codes (that is, all targets looking alike) and utilizing flight progress strips, in those days hand written at Flight Data and therefore at times almost indecipherable. (Truth to tell, I was as guilty as anyone of the illegible scrawl on the strips when I worked Flight Data, writing a mile a minute to keep up with the rapid verbiage coming over the landline. More than once, after delivering strips to a radar position, I received comments like, "Man, you must have been trained as a doctor, I can't read a damn one of these things.")

Another factor, present in all OJT situations, but weighing especially heavily on instructor and trainee alike at Fort Lauderdale Departure, was controller technique. Fundamentally, it came down to the perceived priorities in carrying out the formulation and execution elements of controller multi-tasking. One of the best features of radar control was the number of different ways of getting the job done, and it was essential that any controller develop his own tool box and bag of tricks. The problem, in training, was that the instructor had his methods, established over long years of doing the job, while the trainee was climbing the steep incline of the learning curve. It was actually easier, for the trainee, in the early stages, when he would just do what the instructor told him, then try to make a particular technique his own.

During the period of my OJT instruction, the facility did not assign one man to train me; rather, I would plug in with whichever controller was working the position I was training on that day. After I became fully certified, I recognized the value of this method, enabling me, as it had, to mix and match the ideas of the various individuals who had been my instructors. But before check out, and particularly in the final sessions leading up to that longed-for day, it could get pretty uncomfortable, as I tried to use my methods while the instructor pushed me to use his. After each training period there was a de-brief and a form filled out documenting the trainee's performance. A couple of contrasting de-briefs make the point, first after training with Pete, then after training with Joe:

Pete: "Okay, now remember when you had those four or five off Fort Lauderdale and Fort Lauderdale Executive, called you for release? You should have ignored the call, and when you answered Exec, the guy went into a long song and dance about who was next, when he would be ready to go and all that b.s. You should have cut him off and gotten back to your traffic, which flew extra miles at low altitude while you were tied up on the landline."

Me: "Well, I didn't realize that the exchange would take so long."

Pete: "See, that's the problem. It almost always takes longer than you expect. Traffic on the ground can't hurt you. Your priority is the ones in the air."

On another day:

Joe: "Okay now, remember when you had those four or five off Fort Lauderdale and Exec called you for a release? You ignored that call for several minutes. Exec had to call back a couple of times, and you delayed that Learjet that was ready to go. You could have released him in about ten seconds, and he would have been out in front of the Fort Lauderdale guys. As it was, the Lear took a penalty on the ground, and later in the air because he was stuck under the other traffic. Those airliners don't have any more priority than a GA airplane."

Me: "Well, I felt that my airborne traffic had priority."

Joe: "It has priority for separation, which you had, but not for service, which would not have been compromised by releasing the guy off Exec. Besides, those satellite towers are always bitching that we don't answer the line. You don't want to add any fuel to that fire."

As noted earlier, from the trainee's perspective, it often seemed like you couldn't win for losing.

A Non-Radar Facility

Another difference at the Fort Lauderdale position as compared with the Miami departure control operations was that during my training and for several years thereafter, Palm Beach was a non-radar facility. For traffic landing in Palm Beach's area, there were only three altitudes available:

2,000, 3,000, and 4,000. The area was small enough that the only holding pattern airspace was at the final approach fix for the runway in use at Palm Beach International. During the morning rush from both Miami and Fort Lauderdale, there was enough Palm Beach traffic that the three altitudes could all be in use at once, meaning that no additional traffic could cross the boundary until the "bottom" airplane vacated 2,000 and the ones above were stepped down. Once an aircraft was cleared into PBI's area at 4,000, it was imperative that the Fort Lauderdale Departure controller advise Fort Lauderdale tower to hold Palm Beach traffic on the ground, and to advise Miami North to tell our tower to check for release on these departures.

Once in a while, in the heat of battle, the Fort Lauderdale controller would take the action too late, or our local controller would let one of these aircraft get off. In that case, the airplane had to be held on our side of the boundary until Palm Beach could free up an altitude for it. This worked a major hardship on the Fort Lauderdale controller, because an air carrier making a gentle 360-degree turn covered a huge area, constraining the entire operation of the position.

The only "plus" to having a non-radar approach control adjacent to ours was that there was no need to make handoffs. Once an altitude became available, all we had to do was advise the Palm Beach controller of the identification and type of the next airplane, separate him from our traffic, and issue a frequency change. In fact, a handoff was by definition a radar function so that at times, when one of the many Miami Center radar sites was shut down, we had to transfer low altitude traffic to the center in the same manner as we did with Palm Beach.

Still, our mindset was very much based on the radar environment, and we were sometimes a little casual in our terminology, referring to these non-radar transfers of control as "handoffs." Among ourselves, as controllers, we let this slide, but we cut our supervisors no such slack. Art James, the oldest watch supervisor in the facility, during these periods when there was a scheduled outage of the center radar, would invariably advise us as follows:

Art: "Now you departure controllers, the center won't have radar coverage below 8,000 in the Hammock sector beginning at 1300 Zulu [8:00 am local time], so you're gonna have to make non-radar handoffs."

Anonymous voice from one of the departure positions: "Hey Art, what's a non-radar handoff?"

Art: "Well damn it, you know what I mean," and he would stalk up and down the floor between the rows of radar displays, continuing to mutter imprecations under his breath.

Coordination with Towers

So much of the structured orderliness of the Miami departure positions was nonexistent in the Fort Lauderdale sector. On a nice VFR day, the operation at the lower altitudes was a mish-mash of competing radio transmissions, with airplanes on random routings and at random locations, including at times the middle of an airport's traffic area or beyond our airspace boundaries. While any call could be ignored temporarily, if you did not respond pretty promptly, the pilot would transmit again, further compromising valuable frequency time. The same dynamic applied in responding to coordination calls from the towers. If you did not answer within 10 or 15 seconds, the call would be repeated, often in more insistent tones, resounding through the TRACON speaker for all to hear.

It was easy to forget, in dealing with the satellites, that the controller calling you was taking time away from his traffic as well, and could ill afford to remain on the landline for any appreciable period of time. A certain amount of push-pull between us and the satellites was inevitable, and the individuals on both ends of the landline struggled, with varying degrees of success, to control the frustration inherent in these exchanges. I did my best to answer promptly when called and to be patient when a tower did not immediately respond to my communications. Some of our people hated to work the Fort Lauderdale position, and took it out on the towers verbally every time there was a contact. I hated to be the one to relieve one of these guys, because, not surprisingly, the tower controllers, after an hour or more of abuse from Miami, were themselves thoroughly ticked off.

A representative sampling of how two different controllers might work the position during a typically hectic session, starting with Doug, short-fused and impatient, followed by Joel, calm, professional and not easily upset:

N6241J: "Miami approach, Cherokee 6241 Juliet."

Doug: "Lauderdale tower, 58 line, give me ten miles in trail on Bradley departures."

N41J: "Miami approach Cherokee 8241 Juliet."

Doug: "Eastern 625 contact Miami Center on 132.45"

(Squeal squeal, static): "…2.45" (squeal, static) "…41 Juliet."

Doug: "41 Juliet, quit calling me! I hear you, I'll answer you when I can!" (Unkeying his mic), "son of a bitch, damn zoomers!"

N41J: "Roger Miami, 41 Juliet, request a practice approach at Fort Lauderdale Executive."

Doug: "41 Juliet, I told you to stand by! Maintain radio silence until I call you."

FLL Tower: "Miami Lauderdale, 58 line, two to go." (Two minutes elapse, as Doug receives other calls).

FLL Tower: "Miami Lauderdale, 58, two to go."

Doug: "You don't have to keep calling me! I'll answer when I can! What have you got?"

FLL: "Two for Bradley, Eastern 291, flight level 230, Delta 620, flight level 230."

Doug: "Northeast 25, contact Miami Center on 134.1"

NE 25: "Ok, 134.1 for Northeast 25."

FLL: "Miami, are Eastern and Delta released?"

Doug: "Yes, damn it, they're released. What is your problem, you got a bad headset or something?" (Doug had not released them).

(Eastern 291 and Delta 620 take off at Fort Lauderdale with five miles between them).

Doug: "Lauderdale 58, I told you ten miles between Bradley's, what the hell is wrong with you people?"

FLL: "Sorry Miami, we didn't get the restriction." (Doug did not get an acknowledgement when he advised the tower of the restriction).

Contrast this sequence of communications with the same scenario worked by Joel:

N6241J: "Miami approach, Cherokee 6241 Juliet."

Joel (writing the call sign on a flight progress strip): "Cherokee 6241 Juliet, Miami, unable any VFR services for the next ten minutes. Stand by, and I will call you back."

N41J: "Roger, Miami."

Joel: "Eastern 625, contact Miami Center on 132.45, good day"

EA625: "132.45, Eastern 625, so long y'all."

FLL Tower: "Miami, Lauderdale, 58 line, two to go."

Joel: "Standby Lauderdale, call you back in two minutes." (Joel handles other calls, ending with): "Northeast 25, contact Miami Center on 134.1."

Joel: "Lauderdale, Miami, 58 line, what have you got?"

FLL: "Two Bradley's, Eastern 291, flight level 230 followed by Delta 620, flight level 230."

Joel: "OK, Lauderdale give me 10 miles in trail between Bradley departures until further notice, they are both released, JC."

FLL: "Thank you, RR."

Joel: "Did you get the 10 mile restriction?"

FLL: "Got it ok, Miami."

Joel: "Cherokee 6241 Juliet, Miami approach, say your request."

N41J: "Roger, 41 Juliet request a practice approach at Executive."

The Cherokee pilot called Doug four times, including the time smearing the frequency change issued to Eastern 625. Although the pilot was guilty of poor radio discipline, it was par for the course, and Doug never issued the magic words of "stand by" until the fourth call. Fort Lauderdale tower called twice, and even after his impatient response to the second call Doug never granted the release, triggering yet a third call from FLL. The Eastern and Delta flights routed over Bradley came off without proper in trail spacing because Doug never got an acknowledgement when he issued the 10-mile restriction earlier. And when N41J didn't receive any further communication, he would undoubtedly have called a fifth time.

Joel took a few extra seconds in responding to the Cherokee pilot's initial call, thereby eliminating the three subsequent calls experienced by Doug. He took two seconds to respond to Fort Lauderdale tower, eliminating a second call, and did not take the time to issue the in-trail restriction over Bradley until he actually had two flights to which it applied. He also ensured acknowledgement of his transmissions both on the frequency and on the landline and was polite and professional throughout, making it easier on everyone, not least of all himself. Many of us recognized that impatience and hostility got you nowhere, and in fact only intensified the difficult circumstances of a busy session. Others never seemed to learn.

Roadblock at Approach Control

By early 1970, I was closing in on check out at all the positions except the Miami approach sector. It seemed likely that with a few more hours of

OJT, I would be certified on both the Miami South and Fort Lauderdale departure positions. As had been the case during the earlier phases of my training, I began instruction on the next position before completely finishing up on the previous ones. I had certainly had my setbacks and plateau periods on those positions, but the Miami approach operation ended up bringing me within a whisker of washing out of the program. All the advantages and options available in the departure control functions were turned on their heads. Controlling departures meant that the flow originated at a single point, stretched out into larger volumes of airspace and multiple altitudes, with the lead aircraft accelerating away from those in trail.

At approach control, the flow originated at multiple points, fed into increasingly confined airspace, ending at a single altitude, with the lead aircraft continually slowing down. Compounding these factors was the fact that under busy conditions, there were two approach control positions whose traffic had to be interleaved to the two main east-west runways. Instead of the simple "1000 and three" rule (minimum altitude and mileage separation standards) that governed most IFR operations, there were a number of different requirements for spacing traffic sequenced to 9 Right and 9 Left, the final approach courses only one mile apart. With two approach control positions operating, the basic concept was that South Approach would take his traffic to 9 Right while North approach vectored to 9 Left.

But pilots always preferred to use the runway that was closest to their parking gates, and short taxis were definitely preferable to longer routes if you were a ground controller. This meant that there was a significant amount of "runway swapping" between the two approach controllers in order to provide the most expeditious service to the arrivals and to minimize the demands on ground control. If traffic was moderate, the two controllers had to coordinate with each other to determine the arrival sequence and to "borrow" the adjacent final for traffic parking on the opposite side of the airport.

Under busier conditions, a coordinator position between the two radar positions was staffed to orchestrate the total flow and coordinate runway use. That position was called "CI", a short acronym for "Coordinator IFR", whose function it was to act as a referee between the two approach controllers, determining runway assignments and the sequence of arrival traffic. The "CI" man could make or break the operation. Often one or the other of the controllers would disagree with a decision made by CI and would want to argue about it. CI had to be tough and assertive, but also able to temper those attributes with a little diplomacy and flexibility. A competent CI controller said very little, but sat in front of the strip bay between the controllers, ordering the flight progress strips early enough to allow the controllers to take appropriate action, via tactical vectoring and speed control, to sequence their traffic as the strips indicated. There was nothing worse than a CI who constantly re-shuffled the order until, at times, it became impossible to make the sequencing work.

Even with a strong performer at CI, during an arrival push there were a number of factors that an approach controller had to deal with. In those days there was no central flow control function to help keep the traffic volume within the capacity of the airport to accept it. Fuel was cheap, meaning that both the pilots and airline management wanted every flight to fly as fast as possible for as long as possible.

At MIA, the main push occurred between about 11:00 am and 12:30 pm, as all the morning departures from northern cities converged on us. It was routine during the "noon balloon," as we referred to this daily event, to go into extended holding at the arrival fixes. Each approach controller had a handoff man who would pull the aircraft out of the holding patterns in a way that kept the operation manageable, and who, like CI, could make or break the operation. Take too many airplanes, and you could "tube" (meaning overwhelm) the controller; take too few, and the final approach course could "dry up," under-utilizing runway availability and lengthening holding pattern delays. If you were in the controller chair, you were at the mercy of the guy working handoff.

Then there was the ever-present compression factor. The airplanes coming over the arrival fixes at 8,000 feet were all at 250 knots. By the time they were lined up on the final, they were generally all at 170 knots. And even aircraft assigned the same speed in most cases were not all moving at the same rate, because by FAR, pilots had the discretion to operate within plus or minus ten knots of the speed assigned. In addition, speed over the ground varies, for any given indicated airspeed (IAS), in relation to altitude. Under no wind conditions, an indicated airspeed at sea level is equal to ground speed, but ground speed increases by about two percent for every 1,000 feet of altitude.

In other words, an airplane at 2,000 feet indicating 200 knots is actually moving over the ground at 208 knots. At 10,000 feet and 200 knots the ground speed becomes 240 knots, meaning that the higher trailing airplane is closing the gap on the lower lead airplane by about one mile every two minutes. Just to make it even more interesting, wind speed and/or direction can differ markedly between one altitude and the next. For example, if the lead airplane encounters a head wind as it reaches final approach altitude, a nicely established interval with the following traffic begins to deteriorate as compression again rears its ugly head.

Working approach control, you had only the tools available at other radar positions—vectoring, speed control, and altitude—but each of these had limitations that did not apply to the same extent at departure control. Vector headings, especially those issued to turn an aircraft from downwind to base leg and from base to final, had to be extremely precise in terms of timing. Even a few seconds delay because of a smeared transmission or a non-response from a pilot could cause a gap on the final to be missed. In that case, there were five or six miles of unused capacity on final, and the airplane still had to be fit in later in the sequence. Speed control was critical in maintaining the customarily minimal separation between arrivals, but, as noted above, it was far from exact. Moreover, the longer the final became, the more time there was for small differences in ground speed to work against a consistent interval.

Altitude separation could be used to a limited extent, such as when a slower aircraft came over an arrival fix ahead of a faster one. In some cases you could keep the faster one at a higher altitude and pass up the slower one. But this became another element in the controller's workload. Was there enough time and distance, taking into account the speed differential, to make it work, or was it necessary to start slowing the faster one early so that it would not overtake the lead airplane? At times altitude separation was advisable (and in later years mandatory) when clearing an aircraft for a visual approach to one runway with other traffic on the adjacent final.

The ATIS typically included an advisory that approaches to both 9 Right and 9 Left were in use. Once a pilot reported receipt of the ATIS and had the airport in sight, he could be cleared for a visual approach with traffic right beside him lined up for the other runway. Still, it was possible that the aircraft might overshoot the final, and if it happened, altitude separation kept things safe and legal. So although vertical separation could be used on an interim basis, at the end of the day every airplane you were working had to end up at the same speed, the same altitude, and with minimal separation from other aircraft.

All of this meant that each of the controller multi-tasking elements became incrementally more critical at approach control. Even a "perfect" sequence had to be monitored intently to be sure that separation was being maintained, not only on "your" final approach course, but also with the "other guy's" traffic. There could be as many as six or eight pairs of airplanes that had to be scrutinized constantly. Not only that, but because of the runway swapping that commonly occurred, you had to be confident that the other controller was doing his job as well as you hoped you were doing yours. There was an additional dimension to the approach control operation that did not apply at the other positions. A string of departures would have widely varying distances between each pair because of the way the tower launched them and because of the flexibility in technique available to a departure controller. Others in the TRACON, especially before the advent of the ARTS automation that put an identification tag on each flight, could not tell whether a departure controller was doing an optimum job separating and expediting traffic.

But once you had a line up on final, every man in the room became an expert, critically judging whether you had a nice "tight" final, or if it looked sloppy, with inconsistent intervals plainly visible. On top of it all, more so than at any other position, approach control was an exercise in artistry. One of the veterans, who had come from Chicago O'Hare, was heard to remark, after a busy session resulting in a "string of pearls" sequence, "Look at that f....ing Rembrandt, will ya?"

This, then, was the environment into which I was thrust for training on approach control, and from the start it did not go well. Because the tolerances were so fine, with the ultimate goal being consistent spacing on final at or near the minimum, instructors were more keyed up and exacting. Although I had become reasonably proficient at judging turns at departure control, where every high performance airplane was at 250 knots or higher, I had to refine that skill when working approach. The arc of a turn varied greatly depending on ground speed, so that I had to estimate (in the beginning, guess) how much lead time to use for each vector heading I issued. And it was not only the critical turns from downwind to base and base leg to final.

If you did not offset the downwind leg quite precisely, it was nearly impossible to space correctly on the traffic ahead. For example, traffic on the final approach course at 9 Left followed a track of 90 degrees magnetic. Two such airplanes spaced eight miles apart left a gap that could be filled from the downwind, resulting, ideally, in two nice four-mile intervals. To make that happen, the downwind track had to be 270 degrees magnetic, offset from the final four miles to the north.

Basically, with airplanes at the same speed (normally 170 knots), the technique was to turn the aircraft on downwind to a base leg heading of 180 directly "at" the one he was to follow. Because of the time it took to make the turn, and the combined passing speed of 340 knots, all things being equal, it worked out pretty well. Of course, "all things" were rarely equal, ranging from wind conditions, to pilot technique, to blocked radio transmission, to language problems. It took a ton of experience to identify the subtle cues requiring adjustments on the approach controller's part. Had an aircraft descended low enough to be able to make the approach? There was limited time for altitude queries. How about ground speeds? Pilots knew only their indicated airspeed, and there was no direct indication of speed over the ground. In later years, with the advent of ARTS, the automation computed and displayed both an altitude and a ground speed for every airplane, a huge advantage to the controller.

Sequencing the Aircraft

One of the things I finally learned in training was the extent to which you could help yourself out by figuring out your sequence early and taking some immediate action. Should you let the number two aircraft on final keep its speed up and close the gap on traffic ahead, or slow him down to preserve the gap? If you preserved the gap, would there be an airplane on downwind in the right position to use it? If you did preserve the gap, should the airplane you intended to put in it be slowed, or allowed to keep its speed up? But the day when I could make these judgments with some reliability was a long way off.

As reflected in my training reports, I could hardly do anything right. A representative OJT session would go like this:

Eastern 325: "Miami approach, EA 325 with you, slowing at ten, cleared to 8,000."

Me: "EA 325 Miami approach, roger, maintain 8,000, fly heading 200."

Instructor (immediately taking the frequency): "EA 325, disregard that last transmission, proceed as previously cleared." To me: "Look, that guy is still in center airspace. You can't issue control instructions until he is on our side of the boundary. The center gave him a crossing restriction at Kingfish of 8,000, and you just canceled it. He doesn't want to be at 8,000, he wants to stay at ten so he doesn't have to reduce to 250 knots. Your instructions allowed him to descend without meeting the crossing restriction. He could have come into our airspace high and fast, and that would have put him in Fort Lauderdale departure's area. The heading you issued took him off the inbound airway, and the center might have been basing separation from other traffic on him flying that airway. The best way to acknowledge an initial call like that is to tell the pilot what runway and approach to expect, and to verify that he has the current ATIS—neither of which you have done, by the way, so do it now."

Me: "EA 325, expect ILS Runway 9 Left approach, verify you have received information Bravo."

EA 325: "OK, the ILS for 9 Left, and we've got Bravo, Eastern 325."

ME: "EA 325 turn right heading 270."

EA 325: "270, EA 325."

Instructor (to me): "You're early on that turn to downwind. He's going to be about eight miles north of the final. You have a nice gap on final behind National 421, but it will be hard to hit from such a wide downwind."

Me: "EA 325, turn left heading 250."

EA 325: "OK, 250 now for EA 325."

Instructor (to me a little later): "Turn him back to 270, you want your downwind offset by about four miles."

Me: "EA 325 turn right heading 270, descend and maintain 3,000."

EA 325: "Back to 270, EA 325, and we're leaving eight for three."

Instructor (to me): "See, he's still at 250 knots. You should have slowed him before issuing descent. It's almost impossible for a high performance aircraft to slow down and descend at the same time."

Me: "EA 325, reduce speed to 170."

EA 325: "EA 325, OK, 170, but we'll have to level off for a while to get slowed down."

Me: "EA 325, turn left heading 180."

EA 325: "Coming left to 180, EA 325."

Instructor (to me): "What's his altitude? He told you he would have to level off."

Me: "EA 325, say altitude."

EA 325: "We're just leaving five for three, EA 325."

Me: EA 325, turn left heading 120, cleared ILS 9 Left Approach."

Instructor (immediately taking the frequency): "EA 325, can you make the approach from there?"

EA 325: "We're a little high, but we'll manage."

Instructor: "EA 325 roger, you'll go through the localizer [the radio signal aligned with the runway], turn further left heading 060 to re-intercept. Six miles from Portland, cleared ILS 9 Left approach."

The pilot acknowledged the approach clearance, and the instructor issued instructions to contact the tower. The training session continued, with variations on the above sequence of events occurring in each of my contacts with subsequent arrivals. At length we were relieved from the position, and headed into the break room where my instructor began writing a lengthy and detailed training report. The training report form listed about 25 different items upon which a trainee's performance was to be judged. Some were procedural, such as whether the developmental knew his airspace, others were related to communications phraseology. But the most important items related to the elements that defined the "formulate, execute and monitor" functions. These had titles like judgment, awareness, and traffic management. Well into my allotted hours for certification on approach control, I continued to receive notations of either "Unsatisfactory" or "Needs Improvement." As an example, from the session above:

Procedural: "Mr. Potter issued control instructions to EA 325 while the aircraft was still in center airspace, contrary to the provisions of FAA Order 7110.65. He did not inform the pilot of the approach and runway to expect, nor did he verify that the pilot had the ATIS until prompted to do so."

Judgment: "Mr. Potter has difficulty vectoring to the downwind with the appropriate offset. This degrades his ability to judge the turns to base leg and final, resulting in either an overshoot or too much/ too little spacing on traffic ahead and following."

Awareness: "Mr. Potter attempted to issue a speed reduction to EA 325 while the aircraft was in descent, requiring the pilot to level off in order to comply. He did not ascertain the altitude of EA 325 before issuing the turn to base leg, resulting in a turn to final above the ILS glide slope, contrary to the provisions of FAA Order 7110.65."

Traffic Management: "Because of his continuing difficulties at the approach control positions, Mr. Potter is overly conservative in the number of aircraft he feels comfortable working, and frequently applies speed control earlier than appropriate or necessary, thereby degrading the efficient use of existing airport capacity."

At the earlier radar positions, although I had my struggles initially, in each case I began to get the hang of it within a reasonable time. No matter how smart or capable you might be, there was no substitute for confidence, and the growing conviction that you could do the job correctly. Unfortunately, at Miami approach, my experience seemed to be exactly the opposite of what was required. I began to dread going into work, actually trying to duck training opportunities by being assigned to the positions I was checked out on. But then there occurred an FAA-wide event that broke the cycle, at least temporarily.

A PATCO Sick-Out

On March 25, 1970, PATCO called for a nation-wide "sick-out" of all bargaining unit members, meaning basically the entire controller work force. The union's grievances were manifold, from dissatisfaction with inferior equipment, disagreement with the method of classifying facilities and pay grade, objections as to how overtime was paid, to the need for revising retirement eligibility and the absence of second career training after medical disqualification.

Federal law prohibited federal employees from engaging in strikes or other so called "concerted actions" designed to withhold their services from the government, and every controller had signed an employment agreement setting forth these prohibitions. Nevertheless, PATCO was confident that it had the FAA over a barrel because there were no ready replacements for certified air traffic control specialists. In the lead up to the sick-out there were a number of meetings of the Miami Tower PATCO chapter, and as a new member I of course attended. There was a considerable amount of adrenaline and testosterone flowing at these events, with the old hands aggressively asserting that "we will show the FAA we will not be subjected to these conditions."

The problem for me was that I was still in what was called a career-conditional status, basically a probationary period during which I was not eligible for the protections guaranteed in civil service law. If I participated in the proposed action, my employment could be terminated without so much as a fare-thee-well. At one of these meetings I voiced my concern to a small group of my veteran co-workers, and to my relief Evan Gianetti said, "No, this is not your fight. You will get fired if you go out. And you better not get sick for real while this is going on. Trust me, the FAA would not understand." The others in the group nodded their agreement, and I was spared what could have been a fateful decision.

In the event, only about 2,000 of 13,000 controllers nationwide participated in the sick out, but at some facilities, Miami Tower included, the percentage was substantially higher. The FAA was woefully unprepared, apparently having expected that the job action would never materialize. It fell to the individual facilities to keep the understaffed system manageable, and of course the busiest centers and approach controls, being the hardest hit, were the ones that imposed the most draconian restrictions. I spent most of the sick-out period in the tower, where I was checked out on all the positions. I remember those days as being the hardest ever at ground control, as we had to line up different groups of aircraft according to their destinations and release times. The available taxiway capacity for a group of airplanes subject to a static ground hold was limited, all the more so because traffic with shorter delay times, or none, as in the case of most of the South American carriers, had to have a clear route to the runways.

One day I was assigned to the TRACON, where I was qualified on only North High Departure, and it was frankly a relief not to have to spend my shift wrestling with ground control. North High was less busy than usual, as was Fort Lauderdale Departure, because of all the restrictions on anything headed to northern airports. Because of the short staffing, positions were "combined up" in a way that would never have been done under normal circumstances, and at one point, after I had been at North High for about an hour, it was combined with Miami South. Since I was still in training on Miami South, I of course assumed that I would be relieved. But Sam Parsons, the regulations-bound hardliner who had told me I could not work overtime when I was new in the tower, told me to take both functions at the North High scope. I said, "Sam, I am not checked out on South Departure." He gave me a hard look, then said, "Well, you've worked it haven't you? You go ahead and take it, it will only be for a little while." I shook my head in amazement, and keyed up the South Departure frequency, saying a silent prayer that nothing would go wrong.

Approach Control Training Redux

The sick-out continued for about ten days, with the controllers who had participated returning to work a few at a time, having "recovered" from their stated illnesses. All of these men were theoretically subject to dismissal from federal service for their illegal concerted action, but because of the financial penalties to the aviation industry during the sick-out, the courts ordered the FAA to take them back. That did not mean, however, that they could not be punished. Most were given suspensions without pay, one day for each day they had been out. Like many bureaucratic decisions, this one had some consequences that caused either laughter or frustration, depending on where one's sympathies lay.

In order to provide staffing during the suspensions, the facility had to schedule overtime. So from a financial standpoint, the government was saving a day's pay at the cost of an overtime day paid at time and a half. Moreover, a substantial number of those called for overtime were the very ones who either had served, or would serve, a suspension period, meaning that they were able to recoup a sizeable portion of the salary lost while suspended. One of the old hands told me, with a big smile on his face, "I'm happy as hell. I had seven days off while I was "sick," another seven days off while I was suspended, all without using one minute of annual leave, and with the overtime pay, I got back about half of the money I lost. So the way I look at it, I had a two-week vacation while getting a strong message across to the FAA."

For me, the sick-out period had provided a welcome relief from the discouragement of approach control training, and there was a very large element of team spirit and can-do attitude among those of us who had worked during those days of short staffing. My confidence level was back up to a reasonable level, and I resolved to act on a plan I had been considering for quite a while. I had come to realize that part of the problem at approach control was that I was still working with the same team with which I had begun training in the tower a year and a half earlier. To some extent, they still saw me as that zero-experience new kid who couldn't even work Flight Data without screwing up.

I made up my mind to ask for a team change, reasoning that my new team members would make their judgments about me with my current level of proficiency as their baseline. There was a downside, however. I had heard comments made in disapproving tones about trainees who "shopped" teams, hoping to end up with a Santa Claus supervisor who would slide them through training and check them out. I knew I would have to approach this carefully.

The first step was to convince my supervisor, then a fellow team member who had been temporarily promoted to the position, to support my request. Joe was one of the strongest controllers in the facility, having worked at JFK tower and approach control in the days before the radar functions of the New York airports were split off from the towers and combined in the "Common I" (common IFR room), later re-christened the New York TRACON. He had a no-nonsense approach to the job, and I was a little worried about how he would react—with good reason, as it turned out. He told me he didn't believe in team changes during training, and that if I couldn't make it with this team, I wouldn't be able to make it with any other. But he added that he would allow me to make my case to Stan Hamlin, the operations officer. This was not encouraging. In all likelihood, Stan would follow the recommendation of my first-line supervisor, and I would be back in training with, perhaps, an additional black mark against me for having tried to leave the team.

When I entered Stan's office, he and Joe were already there. The memory of my previous visit, when Stan had blamed me for "discourtesy" in not allowing Ray to climb an airplane through my traffic above, was still fresh. But he greeted me with a warm smile, which could portend good things, since it was obvious that Joe had briefed him about what I had in mind. I had rehearsed my pitch carefully, and I began, "Stan, I would like to request a team change. I really appreciate everything my team members have done to get me this far, and I think they could use a break too. As I'm sure you know, things haven't been going too well for me at approach control, and I'm hoping some fresh eyes might see something that could help me get off this plateau. I promise you, this is the only time I will request a team change. If I don't start progressing, you will not have to give me additional hours or wash me out. I will terminate training and hope for transfer to a lower-level facility."

Stan smiled, and said, in his cordial southern tones, "Well, we certainly want to give you every opportunity to qualify here. If you believe a team change would help you, we will certainly assign you to a new team." I said, "Thank you, Stan," feeling that the weight of the world had been lifted from my shoulders.

And so, with the sick-out over, the suspensions served, and things more or less back to normal, I began training with my new team. Individual controller teams had their own distinct personalities, and I immediately saw that this group had a different attitude. To put it simply, they had a lighter touch, with each other, with sister teams, and, most happily from my perspective, towards me as a trainee. They said things like, "We really lucked out with the trainees we got. You and Randy (Ward) and Timmy (Timmons), you couldn't ask for better." It was really a good feeling to know that they put me in the same category as the two guys who came to MIA with former ATC experience. From the start it was clear that they were coming from the position that I was going to check out, only needing enough training to get me there.

My first day back at approach control, which I had not worked in over a month because of the sick-out, I plugged in with Frank, a younger guy nearer my age than any of my former team mates. We hit it off immediately, over time becoming friends outside of work. Still, on that first day, the little voice in my head told me, "This better go well, or you will be right back where you were before the team change."

As the session began, I recalled past criticisms and comments on training forms, doing my best to at least make new mistakes rather than repeating old ones. My turns to downwind were better, but my instincts for speed control were still off, and the intervals on the final approach course still looked ragged. Frank had said almost nothing, which signified either that I was doing better, or he was saving up a full blown critique for the de-brief. As we sat down at the table in the break room, Frank said, "Yeah, that was all right. You still have a ways to go, but you obviously have what it takes. You just have to hang in there." On the training form, he wrote something like, "Spacing on final could have been a little tighter, but no serious problems." I could have kissed him on the top of his head! At the end of the shift I went home with a serious dose of newfound confidence, at last seeing the finish line in the grueling marathon of training.

As it worked out, I continued to progress towards check-out on Miami

South and Fort Lauderdale Departure, certifying on both positions within a few weeks. At approach control, I began to make real progress, training nearly every day. Ever so slowly, I began to get the hang of speed control, and as I did so, I saw how absolutely essential it was to a good approach control operation. In the early stages, speed control, for me, had been a major bugaboo. I had believed that if I could just vector airplanes and issue approach clearances, the job would be much easier. Wrong! I had come full circle, now wondering how I, or anyone, could do the job without the critical tool of speed control.

Once a year the facility realigned all the teams, in some cases preserving a core of original members and assigning a new supervisor, in others creating a new group of people who had not worked together on the same team. This would take place sometime in June or July, and I was not happy at the prospect. What if I ended up with a group similar to my first team? I hoped with all my might that I would check out on approach before the realignment, but it was not to be. Even if my new instructors were more like Frank and company, they would still want a few hours to make their own judgments, and I had yet to work a "perfect" session. Well, there was no help for it. With the new teams formed in late July, and a different supervisor assigned to ours, my OJT continued.

I guess fortune was really smiling down on me, because my first training session was basically "golden"—nice even spacing on final, no go-arounds, and easy interactions with the approach controller working alongside of me. I looked at the "string of pearls" I had created with justifiable satisfaction, later seeing Marv, my instructor, talking to Art James, our supervisor. Marv pointed at the scope where the line-up of arrivals was displayed, nodding his head affirmatively, with a slight smile on his face. I hoped this meant what I thought it did, and as it turned out, I was right.

As was required for any certification, the instructor and supervisor had to agree that I should be recommended for check-out on approach, and they made that recommendation. This left one more hurdle, the certification check ride, to be conducted by Lester McNeil, probably the toughest evaluator in the facility. Even with fully certified controllers, it was not uncommon for Lester to stand behind them making critical comments, even sometimes relieving them from the position if he thought they were not moving traffic the right way.

I had watched Lester give approach control check rides on more than one occasion, and had noticed that he often criticized what he considered "rote" performance on the part of the trainee. As noted earlier, the basic concept was to establish a downwind offset from the final by the same amount as the interval you were aiming for, then turning the downwind airplane directly at the traffic to be followed. For an arrival to 9 Left from the north, this meant a downwind track of 270, a base leg of 180, and a turn to final of 120 for a 30-degree intercept of the localizer. But in the real world of variable winds, different aircraft speeds, individual pilot technique, and a downwind that could be a mile or two different than the ideal four-mile offset, this template had to be fine-tuned. When a trainee constantly used 180 and 120 for the turns to base and final, Lester would say, for all in the TRACON to hear, "Don't you know any headings besides 180 and 120?"

Somewhere along the line I had picked up the insight that a small, but invaluable, amount of flexibility could be gained by measuring out incrementally the degrees of turn issued. For example, instead of waiting till the airplanes were abeam and using 180, you could issue the vector a tad early to a heading of perhaps 210 or 200. Then, as the turn developed, you could judge whether you were late, early, or exactly where you wanted to be. If you were late, before the pilot rolled out on 210, you would issue a heading further left to perhaps 160 or 150, and again observe how the turn was developing. Then you could issue the final heading to intercept the localizer sooner, to further close the gap, or later if necessary to establish exact spacing. If you were early, you could let the airplane ride on a 210 heading, then bring him to 180 or further left as needed. If you were exactly where you wanted to be, you just continued the turn to 180 and then issued the 120 intercept heading.

So on the day of my check ride, I used some of this technique. After about an hour, Lester said the check ride was over, telling Marv, Art, and me to come with him. Normally, if you passed, you would be informed immediately. If you didn't, a private consultation was likely to ensue. Although I didn't think I had screwed up in any major way, this four man departure from the TRACON did not inspire great confidence. When we reached the break room, Lester said, "Well, you are checked out on approach control. But you have to realize that you are still pretty green." Then, turning to Art, "You make damn sure you watch him, and don't

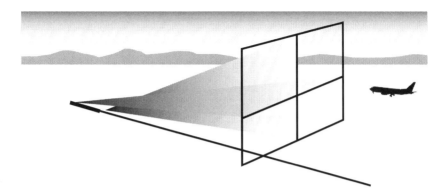

The horizontal plane represents the localizer signal, providing azimuth (left-right) guidance to correct alignment with the runway. The vertical plane represents the glide scope signal, providing vertical guidance to the runway surface.

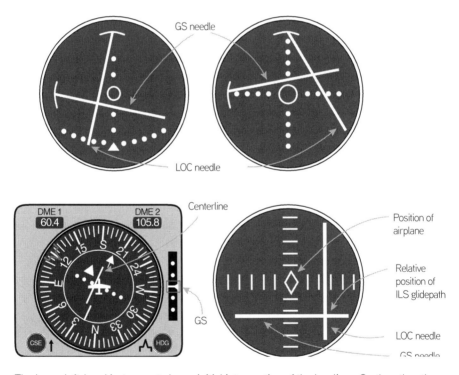

The lower left-hand instrument shows initial interception of the localizer. On the other three instruments the aircraft is represented by the circle or diamond in the center. The localizer is the vertical bar, the glide slope is the horizontal bar. At the upper left, the aircraft is right of course and must correct to the left, also is above the glide slope and must descend to re-acquire it. With the two bars intersecting at right angles over the airplane symbol, the aircraft is on course and on glide slope.

let him get in there during the busiest periods for a while." With that, on August 3, 1970, I became a fully certified controller at Miami Tower and approach control. August 3 was also date that would be of momentous consequence 11 years hence.

8. Taking Control

When Lester signed the certification form for approach control, I experienced the same dual reaction as I had had the day I first soloed an airplane back in Puerto Rico. On the one hand, I would no longer have to listen to the constant corrections of an instructor or bear the burden of worry as to whether I would check out or not. On the other, there was definitely a companion component of, "What if I screw up? There is no one here to bail me out." Of course there was the satisfaction of the congratulations I received on making it through the program. Many of the accolades were based on the fact that I had certified at MIA without prior air traffic control experience, and that I was the first and only trainee to have done so in the history of the facility. I got comments like, "You checked out in what, less than two years? You must be pretty damn good."

As it turned out, my record stood until 1981, the year of the PATCO strike. In the intervening years I saw a number of people from lower level facilities wash out of training, coming to the realization that a big part of being successful was simply having the grit and determination to keep on plugging. Some of the people who ended up going back to their former facilities did not actually wash out—they simply gave up, unwilling to make the seemingly endless effort that OJT demanded. I didn't see myself as being endowed with exceptional perseverance, but the fact remained that I had achieved something that better qualified people had not.

Still, I was not (at least not yet) by any means "pretty damn good." I remembered what my squadron mates back at VC-8 had told me after I got my private pilot rating, that I now had a license to be dangerous. But fortunately, in the weeks and months following my check out, I never had a serious problem, and by degrees it became obvious that I was getting experience that amounted to a kind of "OJT Phase 2." This was a period as critical as all my hours under instruction, a time of self-training where I learned more clearly my strengths and limitations, and refined the all-important sixth sense of intuiting problems in the making.

Although I was now fully certified, there was one last curve ball coming my way related to approach control. There were three additional positions staffed during busy sessions at approach control. One was CI, a coordinator function, and the other two were handoff positions. Handoff controllers accepted traffic from Miami Center, established holding of aircraft when necessary, then determined when additional arrivals could be taken from the holding patterns.

In later years, the qualification to work CI and the handoff positions depended on passing a certification check ride on each. But in 1970, once you checked out on the radar function, you were automatically signed off on CI and handoff. These were tough positions, far harder, it seemed to me, than working the airplanes. At handoff, there was constant pressure from the center to pull traffic out of the holding patterns, as there was an upper limit to the altitude at which the aircraft in the patterns could be safely separated from adjacent airspace.

As noted earlier, there were five arrival fixes, two of them south of the airport and three to the north, so that under busy conditions there were two handoff positions manned. You had to look at the other guy's traffic load as well as your own, and there was always some degree of tension between the handoff controllers in determining whose traffic had priority.

One of my early experiences at handoff, on a nasty weather day, brought home this lesson in spades. The man at CI was helping me and the other handoff controller mightily by telling us specifically when, and from which fix, to take airplanes. I was to take two from Kingfish, on the long side for that day's east operation, and one from Chester on the short side, while south side handoff was not to take any additional traffic for five minutes. As I saw "my" airplanes emerge from the holding pattern, I noticed that there were three or four inbound from the south. CI saw them too, and basically asked the south handoff man what the hell he was doing. The south guy got a little hostile, saying that his airplanes had been delayed too long, and that it was time to take them. This action completely torpedoed what had been, to that point, a nicely controlled operation. CI said, through gritted teeth, "Both of you guys tell the center it will be at least 15 minutes before we can take any more arrivals." This had ominous implications, because FARs mandated that pilots carry enough fuel to reach their destination with a pre-defined reserve, plus 45 minutes' worth in addition in case of holding. We were already experiencing holding times of 15 or 20 minutes, and if the pilots started declaring fuel emergencies, we would be in a world of hurt.

For my part, I wondered what the radar controllers were going to do with six or seven more airplanes when the plan had been to take only three, and I was frankly happy that I was not working radar. What ended up happening was something I had seen before, generally when we lost the use of one runway because of a disabled aircraft. Both approach controllers had to vector their traffic through a "double downwind", meaning flying a normal downwind, then reversing course to a point abeam the airport, and finally reversing course again. This was extremely work intensive, in confined airspace that was not designed for such an operation, but after long minutes things got pretty much back to normal.

One of the biggest challenges at handoff was the initial decision to begin holding. You had two bays full of flight progress strips showing ETA's at the arrival fixes, based on which to determine how many at the front end of the push you could accept before going into holding. The name of the game was to take as many as possible, and allow them to keep their speed up, thereby reducing the number that would have to hold, and also keeping delay in the pattern to a minimum. Of course the key element was in judging what constituted "as many as possible." How many was the other handoff man going to take? How closely spaced in time were that first five or six at the front end? The number varied at every session, depending on weather, runway availability, and even, although this was never expressed openly, the strength of the two men at the scopes.

After the facility made the decision to train on handoff and CI separately, I observed a new guy under instruction at handoff who clearly had a ways to go. His instructor was IG, an old hand who, like several others in the facility, sounded like "the voice of God" whenever he spoke on the frequency or landline. It was the middle of the noon balloon as Frank, the trainee, took handoffs from the center. Both controllers were pretty busy, and it was probably already beyond the time that holding should have been issued. But every time the center called, Frank took another handoff. After the seventh, IG pulled Frank's headset out of the jack and plugged it into the control frequency, saying in deadpan, sepulchral tones, "Now, work 'em." Frank sputtered and fidgeted, having learned a hard but necessary lesson.

CI was even tougher, especially for a new guy who had just checked out on approach. You had to keep the picture on twice as many airplanes as you did in the controller's chair. You had to figure out a sequence much earlier than you did as a controller. On top of that, if you were sitting between two seasoned veterans, it was not uncommon for them to question your judgments and decisions about the arrival order. In some cases, they would simply ignore you and talk to each other about how they were going to run things. In others, they would take you on directly, saying things like, "That's really a piss-poor call," and then you would have to decide whether to stand your ground or change the sequence—not only whether to change it, but also how to change it. Although I was certainly questioned at times when I was at CI, I never really experienced an ugly confrontation. But there was one incident involving a new boy in the position that I will never forget.

Walter, a physically small man who literally looked as though he belonged in junior high school, had just checked out on approach. Walter was on my team, and I knew him to be a sharp controller. He received a lot of ribbing about his youthful appearance, but he never let it get to him. In the culture of the facility at that time, you never, ever, wanted to give the appearance of having a thin skin. One day when he was assigned to CI, the two controllers got into it big time, first attacking Walter, then talking over him, calling each other every profane name in the book. At first Walter tried to calm them down, but they were not about to listen to a little punk fresh off certification. Finally the volume of the exchange reached a point where he turned to the supervisor and said with uncharacteristic vehemence, "Get me the hell out of here!" The supervisor had already seen what was going on, and put a new man in at CI. I talked to Walter later, assuring him that no one would blame him for the incident and that it would all soon be forgotten.

New TRACON, New Chief

I still remember the period from August 1968 to August 1970 as the longest two years of my life, a period of constant struggle to learn the skills of an air traffic controller accompanied by the unrelenting worry about failure. Not unexpectedly, as an FPL, I began to see the weeks, months, and even the years, start to slip by with surprising rapidity. The enduring paradox of the job was that it was always the same, and never the same—same procedures, same phraseology, even the same airplanes, day after day. And yet you never plugged in on any given day and encountered exactly what you had seen the day before. For one thing, as a wise veteran had informed me early on, "things never go like they're supposed to."

In ways great and small, this was the one axiom of the business you could absolutely count on. Did the departure aircraft use the correct frequency for departure control? If not, how long before someone realized it and took steps to correct the problem? Did the arrival aircraft call the right tower? More than once a pilot was talking to FLL tower while inbound to MIA or vice versa. Had a pilot taken a control instruction intended for another aircraft? How soon would you detect the error? How about equipment failures or pilot mistakes? The radar or communications frequencies could fail at any moment, and if a pilot misheard a frequency change, he could end up streaking away on the last assigned heading to parts unknown, out of communication with ATC. Then there were the bad weather days, when the logically laid out airspace divisions no long applied, as pilots and controllers alike struggled to find safe routes through the storms. I experienced all of these things during my "OJT Phase 2" period, and became better able to anticipate, detect, and correct them when they occurred.

As 1972 approached, Martin Hansen, the chief controller who had selected me, announced that he would soon retire. I did not learn until sometime after my full certification that he had basically stuck his neck out, bucking the higher-ups in the bureaucracy, to allow Randy, Timmy and me to remain at MIA. As noted earlier, because the FAA Academy had been closed for five years during the hiring freeze, the agency had been forced to place new hires in all facilities, including level 5 towers, for training. But the Southern Region, the next level down from Washington headquarters, had offered to move the trainees at level 5s to smaller towers. Martin had prevailed upon his bosses to allow us to stay at Miami, apparently convinced that we had the right stuff for a high-density terminal. This meant that as soon as we checked out, we were at the top of the pay scale, and presumably able to write our own tickets for any future moves we might choose to make. It could take years to get to a place like Miami via one or more intermediate steps at small airports, not to mention having to repeat training at each of them. The three of us had lucked out in a big way, thanks to Martin's support.

Martin had been one of the first controllers at Miami when the tower opened in 1941, and had chosen his retirement date in order to see through two major changes at the facility. The old TRACON, with its six small radar displays, would be replaced by a larger room containing nine larger consoles, three of which were configured to accommodate two functions. This meant that we would have the capacity for 12 distinct radar positions—great news, especially as related to the increasing number of low altitude VFR operations north and south of Fort Lauderdale. But of even greater significance would be the concurrent implementation of ARTS, the automation system that would permit any transponder-equipped airplane to display its identification, Mode C altitude, ground speed, and the position controlling it. There was a period during which the new TRACON was fully up and running, ARTS and all, but could not be used because the automation system needed one more round of testing before it could be used operationally. During this period, we were encouraged to spend time at the new scopes, practicing on the keyboards the entries to place identification tags on the airplanes, make handoffs, and add information such as destination airport or route of flight. This exercise was completely off line, so to speak, as actual control would remain in the old room until the switchover date.

Change always brings about some unforeseen consequences, and in the case of this interim period, a couple of them, amusing to the irreverent controller force, were downright embarrassing from management's perspective. Many of the airplanes were given realistic call signs with real-world destinations. But some guys just could not resist the opportunity to be creative, their imaginations often running to the x-rated, placing call signs like "Papa Uniform Five Five Yankee (PU55Y—letter and number resolution was somewhat hazy. A 5 could look suspiciously like an s)" or "Eastern Trainer Mike Echo (EAT ME)" on the targets. Other tags were even more explicitly vulgar or profane. For the most part, after a session of these fun and games, most controllers would delete all the tags, leaving a clean scope for the next individual. But at least twice, whether through design or neglect, the tags were left on the scope, the lettering at maximum size, easily readable from across the room. The chief twice brought groups of dignitaries into the room, and had to do a rapid about face when he saw what was on the displays.

Moving to the new TRACON

The move to the new TRACON was a welcome development, for many reasons. The space was larger and more open, with new carpeting, and better ventilation. The background noise level was greatly reduced compared with the old room, where the ancient tile floors picked up every foot scuff and every dropped flight progress strip, with our headsets faithfully capturing these sounds. It was not until the 1980s that smoking in the operating quarters was prohibited, and we had a lot of smokers in the facility. The improved ventilation made life easier on those of us who did not smoke, not to mention the impact on the physical surroundings.

A visit to the old TRACON, after we had moved out, with normal lighting restored, revealed a yellow tinge on every square inch of every surface, and even weeks later the stale odor of tobacco smoke lingered. But of course the biggest advantages were the increased number of control positions and the new automation capabilities. The latter of these included the ability to display computer generated targets for training purposes. When a particular display was put in training mode, all real world targets disappeared, leaving the scope clean for as many training targets as needed for a particular training exercise. This would later have major implications for Miami TRACON training in general, and me in particular.

There were several operational pluses:
- No more duplication in writing flight progress strips. Drop tubes, simple lengths of PCV pipe leading from the local control positions

to the two departure control scopes had been installed. So when a departing aircraft took off, the local controller had only to drop the strip holder down the appropriate tube. The need for the TRACON flight data position to make a copy of every strip in the tower had been eliminated.

- A larger display area per sector because the scopes themselves were larger. This made it easier to discern trend information, especially turn rate or an aircraft that veered off course. It was also important because, as helpful as the individual identification tags were, there were times when the tags overlapped, making them difficult to read, or even to see which tag went with which airplane. The larger sector areas minimized this difficulty.
- A "quick look" feature that displayed the traffic at neighboring positions. It was now easier to see traffic near your boundary, or to recognize an airplane that would be handed off to you later, greatly enhancing the formulation/ planning phase of your particular operation.
- Continual display of altitude and ground speed information. How many thousands of times had we had to ask a pilot to "say altitude?" Now you could just look at the mode C readout. If relative aircraft speeds were critical to maintaining separation, the ground speed of each was right there.
- Automated handoffs. No more calls on the override, distracting the other controller and taking time away from your own traffic. Enter the position symbol, slew and enter, and the tag would flash on the display of the intended recipient. When he took the handoff, via a similar easy slew and enter action, the tag would flash at your scope, signaling that you could now issue a frequency change.
- Best of all, no more constant effort of having to correlate the identical double slash beacon codes displayed with the appropriate flight progress strips in a bay full.

Not long after the move to the new TRACON, our new chief arrived on the scene. I was somewhat uneasy, knowing that Martin had looked out for me, and I expressed some of this to the old hands. I saw by their reactions that they were not worried. They said things like, "Look, if you stay here any length of time, you will see chiefs come and go. Martin was old school, but most of these guys nowadays don't have any real investment in the facility, and are only filling in another square on their resume in order to work their way up the ladder. Miami Tower is you and me and the rest of the guys."

As it turned out, this assessment was pretty accurate, although Cal Jarvits, transferring from O'Hare, clearly had a different approach than the former regime. He had been a controller, a team supervisor, and ultimately the operations officer in Chicago, so he was definitely familiar with life in the trenches. This manifested itself in a couple of different ways. He made it a point on most days to make at least a short appearance in both the tower and the TRACON, letting us know that he cared about the operation, and better informing himself so that he could make the right calls when it came to a procedural change or processing an operational error. At times he went a step further, plugging into local control or approach control and working the position without any classroom training or book review. There were mixed reactions from the controllers who backed him up, some impressed by his willingness to get his hands dirty, so to speak, others resentful of having their tickets put on the line by their boss.

The Flat Scopes

One of the first issues that Cal had to take on vis-a-vis the union was the so called "flat scopes" that had been installed in the new TRACON. These were the displays designed to accommodate two control positions. From the FAA's point of view, this "two for one" capability was a nice innovation, as the ARTS-capable new scopes each cost a pretty penny. An added advantage was the space saved in the TRACON if one display could do the job of two. But from the controller's perspective there were some sizeable disadvantages, summarized below:

At the "flats," one controller had a square-on view of the display, the near edge of it, or south portion of the airspace, being directly in front of him. This more or less corresponded to the controller view at the vertical scopes where south was at the bottom and north was at the top. But the other position had to be worked from a "wing," located to the right of the primary position, and giving the guy working it a skewed view, about 30 degrees removed from the square-on perspective. It complicated things mightily to have to make the mental adjustment of recognizing that a target heading directly toward you was tracking about 150 instead of 180, and to apply that correction to every vector you issued.

Another issue, affecting both positions, was the fact that the display was flat. To draw an analogy, it was like trying to read a newspaper lying flat on a table. With a newspaper, you could pick it up and angle it, so that you were looking at it in about the same way you would look at a vertical radar display. At the flat scopes, you could only lean forward so that you were looking down at your traffic, and when it got busy, both guys did that. So while they butted heads, each trying for a better view, their radio transmissions were constantly feeding through each other's headset.

There was a problem with overlapping tags. With traffic from two positions competing for display space, the overlap problem was greatly compounded.

What finally cemented the opposition of the controllers to the "flats" was the way the facility had installed the drop tubes at the north and south departure positions. The tubes terminated directly over the center of the displays, dropping the strip into a steel bicycle basket that had been modified by cutting out a portion of one side. The wire ends of the basket mesh had not been crimped or filed down after the metal shears had done their job, and there were a number of profane outcries as a controller reached for a strip and withdrew a bloody hand.

PATCO took up the cause of getting rid of the flats in a big way. It was a tailor-made issue for the union, as there was a clear "wrong" that had to be put "right." Controllers were being "injured" by the metal baskets; controllers were developing "severe back problems" because of having to lean over the displays to work their traffic; controllers were experiencing "eyestrain" because the automation tags at the far end of scope were so hard to read; controllers were filing Unsatisfactory Condition Reports (UCRs), because of the way the radio transmissions from the two positions interfered with each other.

Cal Jarvits was having none of it. He had dealt with union issues at O'Hare, and the TRACON there had used flats for several years without any of the problems alleged by Miami Tower PATCO, he said. He basically told us to man up, quit whining, and get the job done. It was clear that as long as Cal was our chief, we would be stuck with the flat scopes. I certainly agreed that working from the "wing," or any time there were two of us at one of the flats, the problems of radio interference and tag overlap were real. But I thought the business about eyestrain, back strain, and injury was a stretch. Fortunately, the supervisors were pretty much on our side, doing everything they could to combine positions up at the verticals in a way that didn't require two men at the flats.

Cal made another decision early on that I disagreed with and that was never reversed in all my remaining years at MIA. He walked into the TRACON one day and saw that there was a controller at the CI position, then asked the supervisor what "that guy" was doing. The supervisor explained the function, but Cal was unimpressed. He said, "Get him out of there. We never had a position like that at O'Hare, and we worked a lot more airplanes than you guys do. I want controllers talking to each other." From that day forward, the CI position was never again manned. While it was true that with mostly VFR weather and every airplane carrying an identification tag the approach control operation was now considerably easier, when the weather was IFR, we badly missed the services of CI.

Dade-Collier Airport

In 1968, the year I reported to Miami Tower, construction had begun on what was to be the largest airport ever built, located some 30 miles west of MIA deep in the heart of the Everglades. Because of population growth in South Florida, and a concomitant increase in air traffic, it had been decided that a reliever airport was needed. As the job progressed, environmental concerns loomed larger and larger, ultimately bringing the project to a halt, with only a single runway and no support facilities having been built.

Dade-Collier Airport, so named because it was located at the boundary line between the two counties, was re-purposed as a training field, where pilots training and transitioning to a new aircraft could practice without hampering commercial flights. The identifier for Dade-Collier became "TNT" (for training and transition?), and initially it was pretty busy. Eastern's pilot training flights constituted the bulk of the traffic, but other aircraft came from more distant locations. As time went on, the airlines increasingly relied on ever-improving flight simulators, and eventually the only regular users at TNT were general aviation operators. As traffic decreased, controller staffing at TNT was reduced, first from 24/7 coverage to 16 hours a day, then to even fewer manned hours. At one point the staffing became a single controller who would spend 24 hours at the tower, working two 8-hour shifts with the mandatory minimum 8-hour break period between them.

During the period of single controller staffing, there occurred a couple of noteworthy incidents, one of them causing the controller on duty to be put under a glaring spotlight, and the other implicating the Miami TRACON.

In the first case, an Eastern DC-9, carrying a group of pilot trainees, was making multiple approaches and landings. It was the only aircraft in the pattern, with the controller routinely issuing landing or low approach clearances. After several hours the man on duty needed a bathroom break, and transmitted to the DC-9 crew, "Eastern trainer 195, tower frequency will be unmanned for the next 10 minutes. You are cleared for multiple approaches and landings at your discretion." The pilot acknowledged the information, and the controller left the tower. When he returned a few minutes later, he did not see the aircraft, and transmitted several queries without receiving a reply. He was not unduly concerned, surmising that the training exercise had been concluded, and that the crew had headed back to MIA. In a short time there came a knock on the tower door. When he answered the knock, he saw a man in a dirty and torn Eastern uniform, who calmly asked, "Do you mind if I use your phone? We had a little problem."

The "little problem" was that Eastern trainer 195 had come in too low, landing short of the runway and mushing through a chain link fence and the surrounding vegetation. The controller had not noticed the aircraft at the far end of the 10,500-foot runway, partially obscured as it was by the Everglades greenery. Although the aircraft was badly damaged, none of the flight crew had suffered serious injury, and it was evident that air traffic control was not in any way at fault. At least, that was PATCO's position in defending the controller against the agency's intention to fire him for dereliction of duty. The FAA contended that there was no excuse for abandoning a control position with live traffic on the frequency. PATCO countered that the purpose of air traffic control was to separate airplanes from each other, that there had been no other traffic present, and that the flight crew had elected to continue the operation at their discretion. Moreover, union officials asserted, it was not realistic to expect one man to work for hours on end without a break, especially a bathroom break. If the FAA wanted the frequency continuously manned, they said, it should assign two controllers per shift at TNT. Eventually the controller was exonerated, traffic continued to decline, and finally TNT became an uncontrolled airport.

A Training Incident

But before that happened, during a period when the staffing hours changed depending on the day of the week, the Miami TRACON experienced an incident that sounded more serious than it actually was. Dade-Collier's airspace was a non-radar sector belonging to Miami Center. Only two altitudes were available, meaning that a maximum of two aircraft on IFR flight plans could operate in the area at the same time. Pilots understood that the only way to get meaningful training was to cancel IFR before leaving the Miami TRACON radar sector that abutted Dade-Collier. Still, initially Miami had to issue an IFR clearance to the aircraft departing for TNT, and that clearance had to be approved by the TNT controller. It was all completely routine. When a trainer took off the Miami South Departure controller would call TNT, saying something like, "Dade-Collier, Miami, got one headed your way." The controller would answer, and Miami South would say, "Eastern trainer 193, DC-9, two thousand." Initials would be given, and the coordination would be complete until the pilot canceled IFR and MIA would so inform TNT.

On the day in question, two trainers were outbound to the training airport. We at Miami didn't worry too much about the staffing hours at Dade-Collier, reasoning that if no one answered our call, the tower was closed. So the exchange went like this:

MIA: "Dade Collier, Miami, inbound."

TNT: "Hello?"

MIA: "Yeah, got one for you, Eastern trainer 191, DC-9, 2,000, MK"

TNT: "Ah, yeah, OK."

The handoff man assisting Miami South Departure, who had made the call, was waiting for the other controller's operating initials, but when they weren't forthcoming, he simply terminated the call. A few minutes later a second trainer departed:

MIA: "Dade-Collier, Miami, got another one for you. Eastern trainer 175, 727, 3,000, MK."

TNT (after a long pause): "Yeah, OK. Listen, do you need to keep calling me? I'm trying to get cleaned up out here."

MIA: "Well, we've got traffic for you."

TNT: "Well, OK."

Although there was certainly a lot of informality on the coordination lines, the handoff man was puzzled by these strange responses, and said as much to the radar controller. "Hello?" No initials given? Getting "cleaned up?" There were times that controllers referred to their actions at the end of a busy period as "getting cleaned up," but Dade-Collier was working no traffic when the coordination calls were made. What in the world was the man cleaning up? After several minutes, curiosity got the better of the guys at South Departure, and they asked the supervisor to call TNT on the telephone. A short while later, the supervisor informed them that Dade-Collier was closed, and that he had only been able to talk to a maintenance man who was cleaning the facility. "MK" and the radar man shook their heads in disbelief, saying, "Can you believe that crap? The guy's answering the phone and approving clearances, and he's a janitor!"

An L-1011 Goes Down

As 1972 came to a close, Miami experienced an event that brought major official and media scrutiny. It was my habit when arising early for a 7:00 am shift to tune in to one of the local radio stations that carried news. As I did so on the morning of December 30, I heard the announcer say that an Eastern Airlines L-1011, call sign Eastern 401, had crashed in the Everglades the previous evening. Much has been written about the accident, and a number of films produced, including dramatizations and documentaries. The crash occurred because the altitude-hold function of the aircraft's autopilot became disengaged and the flight crew did not notice that the airplane was descending.

However, the Miami approach controller was excoriated in the press. It became known that the ARTS system supplied a constant altitude readout for every tagged aircraft, and there were outraged demands to know why the controller had not observed the descent and alerted the pilots. The crash occurred in the early hours of the midnight shift, a typically busy period when all of the TRACON radar functions were performed at one or two scopes. The approach controller was working South Departure plus North and South Approach combined, with a traffic load of seven airplanes at the time of the crash. Seven airplanes is a lot, especially given the precision needed for spacing and sequencing on the finals.

Eastern 401 had been vectored to a location 17 miles west of the airport and assigned an altitude of 2000 feet while the flight crew attempted to remedy an unsafe landing gear indication. The flight was safely separated from the other traffic, and so the controller was simply waiting for the pilots to report that the problem had been resolved and the aircraft was ready to make its approach and landing. It was completely understandable that the controller would not constantly monitor the altitude of an airplane that was supposed to be in level flight and was no factor to any other traffic, but the media, and the public, did not see it that way.

One unfortunate circumstance adding to their focus on the controller was a single transmission to Eastern 401 that was later determined to have occurred during the descent. A replay of the tapes contained the following: "Eastern 401, everything okay out there?" Although the intent of the call was simply to get an update on how the landing gear problem was progressing, the press represented this communication as being the controller's response to seeing the Mode C altitude field on the ARTS tag unwinding downward. Why, they demanded to know, had the controller not specifically queried the flight crew about the fact that they were no longer at 2000 feet? CJ, the man in question, was hauled into court countless times over the next six years as survivors of the crash, or families of those who had died, brought a series of lawsuits against Eastern and the FAA.

That morning, I accelerated my routine, realizing that this was going to be a different and difficult day at the tower. It was, in fact, one of the most trying days I ever experienced in the tower, where I was assigned for the full eight hours. In addition to our normal traffic, there was a constant stream of helicopters and fixed-wing GA aircraft shuttling back and forth from the airport to the crash site as rescue efforts continued and local TV stations kept up a constant feed of the activities. We received numerous calls on all our frequencies asking about the accident, meaning that we were spending a lot of time inventing new ways to say that we could not discuss those details over the air.

A Heroic Effort

In the aftermath of the accident, there was good news and bad news. What didn't get reported in the media were the heroic efforts of the Miami controllers who worked all through the remainder of the midnight shift and into the next day to assist the rescue operations. The airplane had almost totally disintegrated on impact, but because there was no fire, 75 of the 176 passengers and crew survived. To assist the local medevac flights, helicopters operated by the military services were brought in. But these pilots were unfamiliar with the area and the location of hospitals. Gene Bukowski, my first instructor on ground control, used his knowledge of the area to guide these flights to their destinations, no doubt saving the lives of many seriously injured survivors. And, primarily as a result of the accident, the ARTS system was redesigned to include an altitude alert feature. Now, when a Mode C report indicated an altitude below the minimum calculated for a certain area, an aural alarm would sound, and a flashing red "LA" would appear in the data tag of the aircraft.

But for CJ, his trials did not end with Eastern 401. Six months later, again working the midnight shift, CJ was awaiting a call from a cargo carrying DC-7 shortly after takeoff on 27 Left. Radar detected and displayed a small weather return just off the departure end of the runway. The pilots never made radio contact, meaning that there was no opportunity to request, or be offered, vectors around the weather. The airplane never emerged on the far side of the small cell, and local police soon reported an impact crater and debris field just beyond the area where the cell had formed. Most of us worked our whole careers without ever having one of our airplanes go down or having to deal with accident fatalities, but CJ, in no way at fault in this case, had lived through the experience twice in less than a year.

Wake Turbulence

The 1970s was a period when, from the controller perspective, more and more of the responsibilities that should have remained in the hands of pilots were either partially or totally assigned to controllers. Following several accidents attributable to wake turbulence encounters, the FAA revised the rulebook, adding provisions requiring increased separation standards and mandatory phraseology when wake turbulence might become a factor. It had long been understood that any airplane, much like a boat in the water, generated a wake from the moment it became airborne till the moment it landed. The difference was that these wingtip vortices, caused when high pressure air under a wing traveled over the tip to the low pressure area on the top surface, (a) were not visible, and (b) could cause a roll moment to a trailing aircraft. In extreme cases, the roll so induced could exceed the capacity of a correction.

The new requirements primarily affected the approach control and the local control positions. At approach, the standard three-mile minimum now became four miles, five miles, or even six miles depending on the types of both the lead and following aircraft. Even in the case of a visual approach, where the pilot was responsible for establishing his own interval on the traffic ahead, it was still necessary to issue a cautionary advisory for wake turbulence. In the tower, again depending on aircraft types, there were several different applications of wake turbulence rules. If a small aircraft was departing from an intersection behind a large aircraft using the full length of the runway, the required delay was three minutes—unless the pilot at the intersection waived the wake turbulence requirement—unless the full-length aircraft was a "heavy" (300,000 pounds or greater gross weight), in which case he could not waive the three minutes. If both aircraft were using the full length, there was no wake turbulence delay for the smaller airplane behind a large, but there was a mandatory (i.e., not waivable) two minutes required behind a heavy.

Many pilots did not understand these distinctions, and the exchanges on the frequency could at times get testy and/or humorous. There were a number of charter operations at MIA, flown by experienced pilots in light twin-engine aircraft like the Piper Aztec and Twin Comanche models, who well understood wake turbulence, but not the rules we were required to go by. Some of our guys ran out of patience early when things got aggravating, but not so Sonny, who kept a light touch even when a pilot was fuming, as witness the following exchange:

Aztec N619JH: "Tower, Aztec 619 Juliet Hotel ready at the intersection 9 Left"

Sonny (at Local Control): "Aztec 619 JH Miami Tower, hold for wake turbulence."

N619JH: "I'll waive wake turbulence."

Sonny: "619 JH, unable, you are following a heavy DC-8 departing full length."

N619JH: "Well, what's the delay?"

Sonny: "9JH, expect a three-minute delay."

N619JH: "Tower, yesterday I was following a DC-8 and you told me it was only two minutes."

Sonny: "9JH, if you were using the full length, it would be two minutes."

N619JH: "Tower, I am never going to get into his wake turbulence, I will be airborne 5,000 feet before his liftoff, and I will make an immediate turn away from his flight path."

Sonny: "9JH, understand. Hold for wake turbulence."

N619JH: "Who the hell makes up these ridiculous rules anyway? Let me ask you something, are you a pilot?"

Sonny: "9JH, negative, are you an air traffic controller?"

Regardless of Sonny's telling rejoinder, the incident underlined the fact that pilots, at least the experienced ones, were more than capable of judging whether or not wake turbulence would affect their intended operation. In a perfect world, we believed, controllers would simply issue takeoff clearances and the pilots would request a delay if they considered it necessary for safety.

One day I had an opportunity at local control to observe the effects of wake turbulence directly. A Delta heavy DC-8 had departed on 9 Right, with a light twin, a Cessna 402, about a mile out on final for landing. The 402 pilot intended to park at the "H" (Hotel) concourse, located at the far end of the runway, and requested a long landing. This was to avoid the long taxi he would have to make if he landed at the normal point. There was no traffic behind him and none awaiting departure, so I approved the request, transmitting, "Twin Cessna 67 Foxtrot, wind 060 at 8. Caution wake turbulence departing heavy DC-8, runway 9 Right cleared to land, long landing approved."

Wingtip vortices move downward and outward from the point at which they are generated, rotating in the vertical plane, sinking at a rate of about 1,000 feet a minute, and traveling laterally at about five knots. On a calm day, the vortices created by the DC-8 would have moved off the runway before the twin Cessna landed. But the northeast wind prevented the vortex on the left side from moving beyond the concrete surface, and the 402 remained airborne as it passed beyond the lift-off point and under the flight path of the heavy jet. In an instant the aircraft snap rolled to the left, reaching a bank angle of at least 60 degrees, with the left wing almost touching the runway. Fortunately, perhaps because friction with the ground had degraded the intensity of the vortex, the pilot was able to recover and set the aircraft down normally. But it was a near thing.

Mandatory Radar Services

Another development during this period which, in my view, compromised the "purity" of the radar operation was the establishment of mandatory radar services to VFR aircraft. Before these new requirements were levied, the rules of the game were clear: the ATC system existed for the purpose of separating aircraft on instrument flight plans from one another. Advisories to VFR pilots fell strictly in the category of "additional services," meaning that a controller had total discretion, based on his IFR workload, as to whether or not to provide them. A pilot could then decide whether or not to continue his flight without radar services.

I myself experienced this pilot decision loop one day. I continued to keep up my flying skills during the whole time I was at Miami, and one day a friend and I had filed an international cross country flight plan from Tamiami to Bimini. We received advisories from the Miami departure controller and requested further flight following from Miami Center. But when we contacted the center controller, we received the standard curt denial of our request: "Cessna 61644, unable VFR flight following due to IFR traffic."

In most instances, a general aviation pilot would simply continue on his way without any further interaction. But by now I was an "insider" in the mysterious world of ATC. Our aircraft was a single-engine 172, and I answered the center as follows: "Miami Center, 644, we are not about to set out over 40 miles of open ocean in a single-engine airplane without radar following. How much delay do you estimate before you can provide it?" It seemed apparent that the controller had never received a response like this, answering, "Cessna 644, it will be at least 20 minutes," no doubt thinking that would get us out of his hair. I responded, "644 roger, we will hold ten miles east of the Biscayne VOR until the service is available. Please keep us advised." Although we did make several "donuts" in the air as we absorbed the delay, it was nowhere near 20 minutes, and soon we were on our way. This was how the system was supposed to work. A VFR pilot was denied service until the controller could provide it without compromising his primary responsibilities.

As noted earlier, a controller could also limit the number of airplanes in his sector by stopping departures or having the center issue holding to arrivals. Together these rules, at least in theory, gave the controller all the tools he needed to manage his traffic. But through a combination of political pressure and improved technology, the FAA was persuaded to grant increased access to ATC to the general aviation community. Various GA advocacy groups such as Aircraft Owners and Pilots Association (AOPA) had long complained that commercial operators, the airlines in particular with their 2,000 or so aircraft, got all the services, while general aviation, with its 100,000 airplanes, paid the bulk of the costs.

At MIA, our first exposure to mandatory VFR services came in the form of so-called Expanded Radar Service, or ERS. In the case of departures, instead of being able simply to issue takeoff clearance and a turn out of the traffic pattern, the tower now had to provide each pilot with a departure frequency and make sure the pilot received and acknowledged the frequency change. Because there were no set radar separation standards, the radar controller could receive a string of VFRs with the targets practically touching, creating a major spike in his workload and, as we saw it, a corresponding degradation of efficient service to our IFR traffic. All of this generated some thorny, and unresolved, operational questions: Once the GA pilot contacted departure control, was the flight back in the realm of additional services? If not, for how long and to what extent, did the mandate to provide ERS apply? If ERS remained an additional service, despite the fact that the pilot was required to contact the radar controller, the individuals on both ends of the exchange could be caught in a nonsensical communications loop, to wit:

Pilot: "Miami departure Mooney 6821 Yankee with you."

Controller (already working six or seven airplanes): "Mooney 6821 Yankee Miami departure, radar contact. Unable VFR advisories due to IFR traffic, radar service terminated one mile northeast of Miami, frequency change approved."

Clearly, in this scenario, no "service" was being provided. What usually happened was that the controller told the tower to stop departures until the workload again became manageable. And so both the airliners and the GA aircraft sat on the ground, taking delays they would not have incurred before the advent of ERS.

The problems with departures loomed even larger at approach control. A successful approach control operation depended on some very precise elements—downwind offset, speed control, timing and execution of vectors to base leg and final. Many VFR pilots were totally unfamiliar with radar operations, did not know about ERS, and continued to call the tower for landing instructions. Local controllers spent an annoying amount of time responding to these calls by advising the pilots to contact approach. At the approach positions, it seemed as though these calls always came at the exact moment you needed the frequency for a critical vector. Generally the pilots making these calls were already in close proximity to the airport, meaning that there was often no place to fit them into the existing sequence of arrivals. Moreover, there were no defined holding points for VFRs. It took a lot of effort, and frequency time, to get one of these flights into an area that was safe, but close enough to the final to use a gap when one became available. Sometimes a controller would slow down all the high performance aircraft and create a perfect slot, only to find that the GA pilot had no idea how to fly the necessary vector heading to fill it, or even worse, that he had simply left the frequency and departed for parts unknown.

Experienced pilots, our friends from the charter services, objected mightily to these procedures. In commercial operations, time is money, and they railed against the delays and increased fuel burns imposed by ERS. Somebody high up in the FAA hierarchy had forgotten the two-part basic principle that allowed the air traffic control system to function properly: Service is available only when it is requested, and when there is capacity to provide it.

A New Terminal Control Area (TCA)

The next iteration of mandatory VFR service occurred in April 1973 when the Terminal Control Area (TCA), was established at MIA. Historically, a majority of midair collisions had occurred in high-density terminal areas between a high performance airplane on an IFR flight plan and a smaller, slower GA airplane operating under visual flight rules. The idea of the TCA was to create an area of so-called "sterile" airspace around the major airports, an area specifically off limits to VFR flights unless the pilot requested, and the controller granted, clearance to enter it. Once within the TCA, these flights were afforded positive control separation via altitude assignments and vectoring. The AOPA and other groups complained that there had not been a sufficient opportunity, through public hearings, for the concerns of general aviation to be considered, and that to exclude categorically a particular class of operators was inequitable and discriminatory.

But from the controller perspective, the new procedures were a big improvement over ERS. To operate in the TCA, an aircraft had to be capable of communicating on the appropriate VHF frequencies, and to be equipped with a transponder so that it could display an ARTS tag and Mode C altitude information. In order to land at the primary airport (MIA), a pilot had to hold at least a private pilot certificate. Best of all, under busy conditions, a VFR arrival could be instructed to remain clear of the area until such time as the controller could work him safely. There were separation standards for VFRs, variable depending on aircraft types and wake turbulence requirements, that had the effect of giving radar controllers some breathing room, and benefitted the local controllers as well. All arrivals were now sequenced by approach control. At Local Control, we still had to monitor the final to be sure the gaps were holding up, but no longer did we have to play 20 questions to locate and fit into the sequence a slow GA airplane flown by a low-experience pilot.

To be sure, there were definitely some growing pains after the TCA was implemented. After the Arab oil embargo of 1973, oil prices spiked, and Venezuela, with its rich petroleum resources, was a major beneficiary. As a result of this newfound bounty, MIA saw an increasing number of high-end GA airplanes with Venezuelan registrations in our daily traffic flow. Many of these pilots had little experience, or a poor command of English, or little understanding of U.S. air traffic control, or a combination of all three. Not surprisingly, TCA violations occurred routinely among this group of operators. In an effort to stem the number of such occurrences, any time we observed a "bandit" as we called them within the TCA, we would place an ARTS tag on the aircraft identifying it as "TCA1," "TCA2," etc., in the hope that eventually the pilot would contact either our tower or one of the satellites. We could then have the pilot contact the facility by telephone and attempt, with varying degrees of success, to explain the facts of life to him.

Even the old-school airline pilots at times got tripped up by the new procedures. Many of them in their earlier careers had flown mostly under non-radar procedures. In the non-radar system, airplanes were pulled out of a holding pattern in a set way, that is, lowest airplane first. But with radar we would often first take an airplane that was best positioned in the pattern, not necessarily the lowest. More than once we received an indignant phone call asking why "the guy above me got in first." Because of the inefficiencies of non-radar, if the weather was good, the pilots would often cancel IFR as soon as they were told to expect holding, hoping to steal a march on the holding pattern stack and have the tower work them in VFR. Sometimes this worked to their advantage.

But the old hands at MIA remembered having eight or ten airliners on Local frequency, with a 20-mile final, and most of the aircraft out of sight. By degrees, as a new generation of pilots became accustomed to radar procedures, they came to recognize that they were better off sticking with the approach controller than trying to beat the system by canceling IFR. Still, we had a couple of instances post-TCA implementation where an airline crew would cancel their instrument flight, perhaps remembering prior instances where it had worked to their benefit. The difference was that now they were operating under visual flight rules and could be told to remain clear of the TCA, basically taking a back seat to the IFR flights. I remember a particular exchange that went like this:

Miami Center (on landline): Lonni, 50 line, Delta 1215 canceled IFR, coming to you, SE."

MIA Approach: "Roger, EJ."

DL1215: "Miami approach Delta 1215 with you descending out of 7500 VFR."

MIA Approach: "Delta 1215 Miami approach roger, remain clear of the Miami TCA, expect a one five minute delay."

DL1215: "You say a 15-minute delay? We canceled so that we could get right in without any delay."

MIA Approach: "Delta 1215, unable VFR service for the next one five minutes due to IFR traffic."

DL1215: "Well in that case, we'll take our IFR back."

MIA Approach: "Too late, it has already been canceled."

Over time the growing pains subsided as both pilots and controllers adapted to the new way of doing things.

Good Days, Bad Days

In August 1973 I celebrated the five-year anniversary of my reporting date to MIA. I now had three years of experience in "OJT Phase 2" and finally felt that I had my feet solidly on the ground. I saw where I ranked in the unspoken hierarchy of controller skills, as I observed at least four different groups classified roughly as follows:

The Hotshots: These were guys who always operated right at the edge, taking every airplane that came their way, never asking for help, and resentful when it was offered. Lester McNeil was a prime example of this type. He pushed us, saying things to the local controller like, "If you don't have to apologize to that departure man [for launching two airplanes too close] once in a while, you are not doing your job."

The Cool, Calm and Collected: This group never got excited, could work a bunch of airplanes, but knew where to draw the line to keep the operation manageable. They were the real pros in my book.

The Middle of the Road Conservatives: I included myself in this category because we were not flashy, did not move the traffic as fast as the Hotshots or the Cool Calm and Collecteds, but stayed out of trouble and minimized the instances where we had to impose on a fellow controller.

The In-Over-Their Heads: There was actually a range of abilities within this group. Many of them did fine under light or moderate traffic conditions, but began sinking fast when the tempo picked up. Some were always hyper and excitable, afraid that things might get out of hand at any moment, regardless of traffic volume. Others (and I wondered how some of them had even managed to certify) simply could not handle anything above the moderate level and would stop departures, initiate holding, or refuse to take handoffs. The supervisors knew who they were, and took pains to avoid putting them in positions during predictably busy periods.

Not too long after check-out I had occasion to work beside Jack Kindler at approach control. He was definitely a member of the Cool Calm and Collected group, but at least twice I had seen him coolly and calmly ask a supervisor to relieve him at approach if he was working next to one of the In-Over-Their- Heads, saying that he felt the other controller was not working safely. I was a little uneasy myself as I plugged in, but things seemed to go without a hitch until we were both relieved in the course of normal rotation. Afterwards, Jack came up to me, saying that I had done a good job and that he would work next to me any time. Acknowledgements like this were rare among controllers, and I basically felt that I had been awarded the best kind of gold star.

On another day I was assigned to the tower, working Local Control. Traffic was light to moderate, and there was the usual light-hearted banter among the tower crew. As far as I knew, I was working as I always did, not pushing "squeeze play" departures, but taking advantage of arrival gaps as they occurred. Lester McNeil was also in the tower, joining right in to the conversations. After I was relieved, Lester buttonholed me in the hallway, saying something like, "What the hell did you think you were doing at Local a while ago?" I did not reply, because I didn't understand what he was asking me. He said, "When you are plugged into Local, your job is to move traffic, not bullshit with your buddies and miss gaps for your traffic." Holding up his forefinger and thumb about one half inch apart he continued, "I came that close to pulling you off the position. I'll be watching the next time you're on Local." I was feeling considerable consternation, but fortunately that was the only time he took me on directly about some aspect of my performance.

Once again the annual team change shuffle took place sometime in the early fall. My new supervisor, recently promoted, was one of the guys who had trained me on my initial team. I was no longer the new kid, but I was still the junior man among five or six veterans. One day in December, there was a prolonged cold front passage during our day shift, causing hours of hard rainfall, shifting winds, and ceiling and visibility values hovering right at minimums. I was assigned to South Approach Control, vectoring to the single instrument approach available to me and to North Approach, serving runway 27 Left. Every pilot wanted to deviate around weather cells, and many would not take the critical turn to join the final, meaning that gaps were missed and the line-up of airplanes was getting longer and longer. Not unexpectedly, there were a fair number of go-arounds, and a corresponding increase in holding pattern delays. It was a typically nasty IFR weather day. But all in all we were getting the job done—until CC121, a DC-6, contacted me leaving the Mango holding pattern.

This one flight nearly "tubed" the whole operation, introducing just about every negative element possible into our already maximum effort to keep things under control: poor radios, so that many of my transmissions went unacknowledged, or required a series of "say agains;" poor, practically incomprehensible English; no transponder, causing the target to disappear for long seconds or minutes in the heavy weather returns on the radar display; and, most ominously, although not initially apparent, insufficient navigation capability. The pilot was not taking the headings I issued, instead making deviations on his own around the weather cells. The radar target, even when it was not obscured by weather, was a tiny pinprick primary return, moving so slowly that at times it was not distinguishable from the general clutter on the scope.

Although I had several times issued descent clearance, I had never received a clear response indicating that the pilot had understood and complied. With no mode C altitude reporting, I knew only that the aircraft was somewhere between 6,000, the altitude at handoff from the center, and 2,000, the altitude to which I had cleared it. After what seemed a very long period, I finally had CC121 in position to clear the pilot for the ILS approach to 27 Left. I got an unintelligible response, but it appeared that the approach clearance had been received. I switched the flight to tower frequency, and brought my attention back to my other traffic. In the next minute and a half or so, the exchanges on the frequency and the landline went like this:

CC121 (about 30 seconds after the frequency change to tower): "What heading you want me to fly?

Me: "CC121, I don't want you to fly a heading. I want you to fly the localizer for the 27 Left approach."

CC121 (more insistently): "What heading you want me to fly!!?"

Me: "CC121, you are cleared for the ILS 27 Left approach. Join the localizer, and contact Miami tower immediately on 118.3"

About that time the local controller called on the override, saying, "Hey, I am not working that Charlie Charlie, send him to me." I replied, "I've switched him twice, I'll try again." Before I could issue the frequency change for the third time, the local controller was again in my ear, saying, with adrenaline fueled urgency, "If you're still working him, send CC121 around now!" I immediately keyed my mic and transmitted, "CC121, go around, I say again go around." There was no response from the pilot, but about 20 seconds later, the whole building shook, and even in the TRACON we could hear the muffled roar of the DC-6's four engines.

In the attempt to reconstruct what had happened, we did not have much to go on. The ARTS system stored the tracks of transponder equipped aircraft, but as a primary target, CC121 had created no traceable record of its route. It seemed likely that the primary reason for the incident was the fact that many of the secondary South and Central American carriers did not have VHF navigation capability in their older airplanes. This meant that they could not fly VOR airways, or in this case, an ILS approach. In that period, most of the navaids south of the border were high-frequency non-directional beacon (NDB) facilities, operating on the same band as commercial radio stations. In other words, for domestic operations, it was not cost effective for the operators to install VHF navigation equipment. It was extremely rare for these operators to land anywhere in the U.S. other than Miami, where 98 percent of the time the weather VFR, and when cleared for an ILS approach, the pilots simply used the "Mark-8 Eyeball" to get to the runway. The crew of CC121 had never informed us that it could not fly the 27 Left localizer, attempting to fake it in extreme weather, and ending up about halfway between our two main runways.

Although the tower controllers never saw the airplane, the noise and vibration it caused as it overflew the 130-foot tower indicated that it was probably at 200 or 300 feet—that is, within a whisker of a catastrophic collision. The rest of the day was (relatively) uneventful, with two exceptions: after the go-around, I had to work CC121 again, but this time the flight crew landed safely. Then, just as the shift was ending, a Northwest Airlines 747 ran off the end of the runway, closing it for more than a week until proper equipment could be brought in to move the giant aircraft. When I left the facility, feeling pretty drained, I was looking forward to a quick trip home and a relaxing evening. But it was not to be. During the shift, the two rear wheels of my car had been removed by thieves, sticking me with a cab fare, the cost of new tires, and a busy next day.

On our next team training day, which occurred less than a week after my experience with CC121, we gathered in the training room for a typical series of briefings on matters ranging from need to know, nice to know, to YGBSM. Prime among the offerings in this latter category were things identified as "mandatory briefing items." The facility had run afoul of this requirement when an evaluation team, armed with a list of numbers designating orders, notices, advisory circulars and other publications as "mandatory," could not find in the facility records confirmation that these items had been briefed. Through research of various indexes listing the numbers and the titles of the documents in question, we believed we had unearthed an explanation for the missing briefings that would eliminate this particular "gig" from the final report.

A few examples of the subjects designated as mandatory: "En Route Standards in the Alaskan FIR (flight information region)," "Snow Removal Procedures at Newark Airport," "Altitude Separation Above

Flight Level 290." Our position was that none of these directives in any way applied at MIA, which was not an en route facility and was pretty far from Alaska, where we didn't get much snow, and where our top altitude was Flight Level 230. Nevertheless, the "gig" stuck, and thereafter, when something that clearly had no applicability to our operation came around, it would be placed in the read file with the notation, "Mandatory Briefing Item, No Impact at MIA," and the controllers would sign for it without reading it. You had to love bureaucracy.

I don't recall any of the briefing items for that particular day, but I remember the preamble to them, delivered by Bill, my new supervisor. He had been one of the toughest instructors on my original team, often taking over the frequency when he saw an omission or other misdeed on my part. He had not (yet) had occasion to criticize me in his supervisory capacity, but I became instantly alert when he opened the meeting with these words: "Before we get into the briefings, I want to talk about the other day, the nasty one, when our team was assigned to the approach control sector." I thought, "Uh oh, the whole operation involving CC121 was a near disaster, and he is about to point out some things that I should have done differently." Bill continued, "Everybody in this room busted their ass during that shift, and you all deserve a pat on the back. But one guy in particular did an outstanding job. I'm talking about Rust Potter, who kept everything from falling apart with that DC-6." Around the table, a round of smiles broke out, and everyone applauded. Another veteran chimed in, saying "Damn right! You kept that whole sector from going down the pipe." Bill added, "Considering where he started from, Rust is the most improved controller in the whole facility." My teammates nodded in agreement, and I basked in the glow.

Union Militancy

During the 1970s PATCO took an increasingly confrontational posture in its dealings with the FAA. There were now PATCO offices at both the regional level (Atlanta) and the national level (Washington D.C.), as well as facility representatives in every field facility. John Leyden became the national president, and had the respect of rank and file union members because of his efforts to convince Congress of the needs of the air traffic service. He lobbied for the bread and butter issues that most mattered, like better equipment, earlier retirement, and of course an improved pay scale. He laid out the case for these and other issues respectfully, but with solid evidence gleaned from having done his homework. But at the lower levels of the organization, especially it seemed to me in the individual facilities, it was a different story. Grievances and Unsafe Condition Reports were filed with increasing frequency, often over things that I felt were inconsequential. (One of the most ridiculous filings in the latter category was against some trees planted beside the walkway leading to the terminal entrance. The guy had scraped his head on an overhanging branch). I voiced my opinion to more than one local president of our chapter. I said I was all for the efforts at the national level, where real change might be accomplished, but that I couldn't see the point of antagonizing facility management over such penny ante items. Facility chiefs were limited in what they could do for us, but they could certainly make life less pleasant in small ways if they so chose. The union reps answered me with various versions of, "You always have to let them know you are there."

A case in point involved the counting of flight progress strips. Automation eventually took over this task, but in the early days it was done manually. Each hour all the strips were collected and sorted into separate categories: air carrier, air taxi, general aviation, and military. A number for each category was entered on a form laid out as a grid, and at the end of the day the 24 lines for each were added resulting in a final number on the bottom line. Then these four numbers were added to compute a grand total. It was a moderately tedious job, but took only a few minutes each hour and somewhat longer on the midnight shift when the final tally was reckoned.

PATCO had filed a grievance stating that strip counting was clerical work, and was therefore not one of the controller job elements as defined in the union contract. The FAA countered that it was an integral part of the Flight Data function. Eventually a determination was reached exempting strip counting as a controller responsibility. This meant that the function now fell to the supervisors, who did not always have time during the busy periods of the day to keep up with the tally hour by hour. More than once they had to stay beyond the end of their shift to catch up. I personally did not object to counting the strips, and could see that the supervisors were plenty busy with more important tasks. But even though I did the job willingly, if infrequently, some of my colleagues, and especially the union rep, took me on about it, telling me in so many words that I was undermining union credibility by "giving away something that was won at the bargaining table." I certainly didn't want to get into a permanently adversarial relationship with PATCO, so I tried to restrict my strip counting to the midnight shift when I could find a quiet corner to do it unobtrusively.

I found some of the posturing by the union more amusing than militant, and in one case I had a golden opportunity to defuse a deliberately created confrontation. Bill Klegg had recently been promoted to supervisor, instantly incurring the opprobrium (some real, some voiced only for effect) of his former colleagues. Before his promotion, Bill had participated in the hydroplane races conducted at the Miami Marine Stadium. Several other guys had acted as his pit crew, and Bill had had several wins in his boat, christened "Miss PATCO." One day John Hall, who had been an early union rep at O'Hare, saw a chance to stir the pot of union activism at Bill's expense. Bill and several of us were in the hallway as John stepped out of the TRACON and immediately got in Bill's face, saying "So now you're a management puke. I'll tell you one thing, you better get that Miss PATCO name off the side of your boat, you scumbag." In a moment of divine inspiration, I piped up in tones mimicking John's, saying "Yeah Bill, you better get rid of that name and call your boat "Mis(s) Management." Everybody had a good laugh, including John.

There was only one time in my career that I needed help from the union. I had been involved in a near miss between two air carriers that occurred while I was working North Approach Control. When minimum separation between two airplanes was lost, the incident was classified as a system error (later re-christened operational error). Although there was a certain amount of "benefit of the doubt" involved in identifying these occurrences (after all, who could tell the difference between a legal three miles and an illegal 2.9 miles?), in this case the error was glaring, and visible to the entire TRACON. A Delta 727 was approaching our airspace, having been handed off by the center. As was standard, the aircraft was still in center airspace when the sequence of calls and landline communications began:

Delta 229: "Miami approach, DL 229 with you, level 8,000, with information Charlie."

Me: "DL 229 Miami approach roger, expect a visual approach runway 12."

So far so good. I had not issued control instructions to an aircraft outside of my airspace, and there was no reason to believe that it would do anything other than follow the prescribed routing. But after only a minute or less, I saw that the target was heading more than 30 degrees right of the expected track, and directly into the Bradley departure transition area. The communications resumed:

Me: "DL 229, turn left immediately, proceed direct Biscayne."

DL 229: "Well we just need to get around this little buildup, then we'll get back on course."

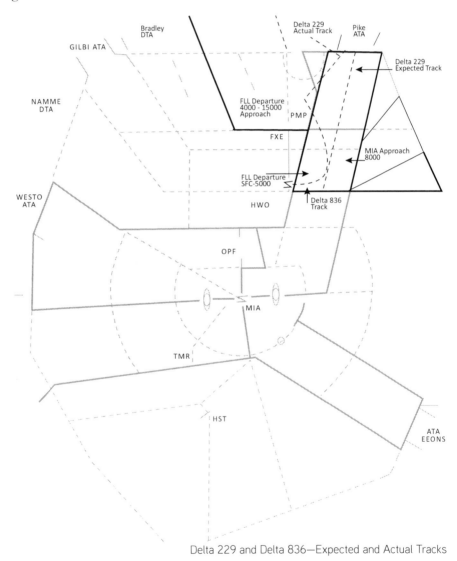

Delta 229 and Delta 836—Expected and Actual Tracks

About this time I saw that there was a Delta DC-8 departure off Fort Lauderdale climbing out of 5,000 and heading about 340. The ARTS data block showed that an electronic handoff had already been made to the Bradley sector.

Me: "DL 229, negative, turn left immediately heading 090 and intercept the Biscayne 018 radial."

DL 229: "Just give us another minute, we're almost clear of this thing."

Me (on the override to the Fort Lauderdale departure controller): "Are you still working Delta 836?"

FLL Departure: "Who?"

Me: "DL 836. Stop him at 7,000, he's got opposite direction traffic at 8,000."

FLL Departure: "Oh, shit. He's already switched to the center."

By this time DL 229 had begun to turn back to the south, but it was too late. In cases like this, the last-ditch maneuver was to call the traffic and hope that the pilot could avoid it visually, even if legal separation had been lost.

Me: "DL 229 you have traffic 12 o'clock three miles out of 7,000 climbing through your altitude."

DL 229: "Can't see him, we're in the soup."

A few seconds later there occurred the longest moment of my life as a radar controller. The targets of Delta 229 and Delta 836 came together in what was called a merged plot, both showing an altitude of 8,000 feet. Alarmed cries went up throughout the TRACON, and it seemed forever until the next radar sweep showed that the airplanes had passed. Neither flight crew ever knew how close they had come.

Every controller, somewhere in the back of his mind, nursed the nightmare of a collision between airplanes for which he was responsible. Right behind that was the worry about causing a system error. Regardless of the circumstances, you knew that if you had done something different, the separation loss would not have occurred. In the case of the two Deltas I wondered if I had screwed up trying to get DL 229 back on course, or leaving him at 8,000. As it worked out, if I had left him on the southwesterly heading or descended him, the two flights would have missed by a larger margin, or perhaps with legal separation, even though he was clearly outside approach control airspace. But this was hindsight. There had been no way to tell, in the moment, how soon Delta

229 would have started or completed the left turn issued in my second transmission, or how fast Delta 836 would have climbed through 8,000. Still, this was a bad error, and I had been working one of the airplanes.

In the aftermath, I experienced a series of days more miserable than any since my training on approach control five years earlier. I tried to put on a good face, remembering that others in the facility had had their own "deals" as we called these incidents, but apparently I wasn't very good at hiding my feelings. Even Sam Parsons, who was hardly the tuned in intuitive type, took me aside at one point and said, "You need to stop walking around here with that hangdog look on your face. You're not the first guy to have an error, and you won't be the last. You can't let this thing get to you, or you won't be able to do your job." I knew he was right, but I couldn't seem to shake the little voice in my head that kept repeating, "if only."

A System Error

When a system error occurred, the facility convened a review board, usually chaired by the operations officer, and consisting of a select group of controllers and supervisors. The board listened to all the recorded radio transmissions and landline communications, studied the playback of the aircraft radar tracks, and interviewed the people who had worked both airplanes. Most errors were cut and dried—a controller had allowed one of his aircraft to stray into another sector and get too close to another man's traffic; or he had issued climb clearance hoping to "top" conflicting traffic ahead and did not monitor the situation closely enough to see that the plan was not working. In these cases, the review process took only two or three days and resulted in a report that identified the primary and secondary (if any) cause(s) of the incident.

But in the case of the two Deltas, the problem had begun in center airspace when the flight crew of Delta 229 deviated from the standard routing. It was possible that the loss of separation could end up being classified as a pilot deviation, where the aircraft commander did not follow ATC instructions.

At all events, Miami Center personnel were asked to join the board and the investigation extended all the way back to their first contact with the aircraft, some hundreds of miles before the handoff to Miami approach. At one point the flight crew had advised the center controller that, "We may need to deviate around some of these buildups ahead." The center controller had replied, "Deviations approved, just advise me of what you need." For the next 10 to 20 minutes, the aircraft had remained on course without further comment, and had only begun the turn around the weather cell as the crew was in the process of contacting me.

Instead of the usual two or three days, the deliberations of the review board went on for several weeks. The review was behind closed doors, the various steps of its investigation and its development of findings confidential until the final report was complete. To me, the wait seemed interminable. When the final report was published, several things happened—I immediately understood why the process had taken so long, and I quickly traded in my "mea culpa" posture for a new found sense of indignation and a readiness to take up arms in my own defense.

The salient findings of the report were (1) that the primary cause of the error was the failure of "Controller A" (the Miami Center specialist) to advise Miami Approach that he had approved deviations for Delta 229 and (2) that a contributing cause was quote "the failure of Controller B (me) to issue positive control instructions." Now just a damn minute! "Proceed direct Biscayne" and "Turn left immediately heading 090 to intercept the Biscayne 018 radial"? How were these not positive control instructions? On the other hand, I could see why Miami Center was angry about being outvoted by the majority and being stuck with the primary cause finding. We knew that even if the center controller had advised us in advance of the approval for deviation, since the pilot never told anyone when he turned off course, the outcome would in no way have been different.

The final steps in processing a system error were (1) a review of the board's findings by the facility chief, resulting in either concurrence or non-concurrence in whole or in part; (2) a review at the regional office, providing a second opportunity to concur or not; (3) and finally a memo to the facility documenting the final disposition of the matter. Before the review by the chief, I had an opportunity to make my own comments about the report. I wrote a letter addressed to Cal Jarvits asking for an explanation as to why my two transmissions attempting to get Delta 229 back on course were not considered positive control. His reply was that it was not within his purview to respond to my question, but that he would append my letter to the package forwarded to the Southern Region. A day or two later I realized something about the report that I had not noted initially. There was a page with the title "Official Transcript of Miami North Approach Control communications from 1703Z to 1718Z." That was the period that Delta 229 had been on my frequency, but the entries seemed exceedingly sparse for a 15-minute time span. I distinctly remembered working traffic in addition to Delta 229, but none of these other contacts was reflected. More tellingly, my attempt to have the Fort Lauderdale departure controller stop Delta 836 at 7,000 was missing. I wrote a second letter to Cal asking that he include in his remarks the fact that the transcript was not complete in that it omitted contacts with other traffic and my coordination call regarding Delta 836.

After receipt of my second letter, but before replying to it in writing, Cal summoned me to his office. When I got there I found that my supervisor was also present. Together they adopted a contrapuntally paternal tone, saying things like, "You know, you really shouldn't be writing these letters. They won't do you any good in the region, and all you are doing is drawing attention to yourself. Some of those people have long memories, and if you ever have another deal, they won't remember you favorably. Your best bet is to let the process play out. Once it is over and done with, it will never be brought up again, nor will it reflect on your career or any aspect of your performance evaluations." I said something like, "You may be right, but I believe I have been unfairly named as a contributing cause of the error, and if I don't make my case now, I will never get the opportunity." They shook their heads disapprovingly, but my two letters were included in the review package.

I understood very well that in almost all cases the review of board findings by a chief and a regional office official resulted in predictable rubber-stamp complete concurrences, so I tried to resign myself to this unfortunate blemish on my record. Several months went by, and I was by degrees able to shake off the effects of the whole experience and get back to doing a creditable job. Finally one day Sam Parsons called me into his office to tell me we had received the results of the regional review. He said, "Well, it looks like you are off the hook. Take a look," handing me a thick stack of papers. On top of the facility review board documents, the chief's concurrence, and my letters was a two-page memo bearing the Southern Region letterhead. The memo showed a series of lines, each titled identically with the corresponding section of the original report. It began:

A. Primary Cause: "The primary cause of the error was the failure of Controller A to coordinate with Miami Approach Control his earlier approval for Delta 229 to deviate around weather." Concur.

B. Contributing Cause: "A contributing cause of the error was the failure of Controller B to issue positive control instructions." Non-concur. Because of the short time interval between initial contact by Delta 229 and the loss of separation, and the fact that the aircraft had begun a deviation prior to contact, and unknown to the controller, there was not sufficient time for any action that would have prevented the error."

I guess I was still harboring some tension, because the flood of relief that swept over me as I read those words was something I have never forgotten. But there were still a couple of chapters to play out before the whole thing was finally and forever behind me. I said to Sam, "Well, this is great news. I'd like a copy of the entire package." Sam wrinkled his brow and began shaking his head, saying, "Well I don't know about that. We really don't want these things getting out." I couldn't believe my ears, and said, "Sam, this is the equivalent of a Supreme Court decision overturning a lower court ruling finding me guilty. I think I am entitled to the document that absolves me." But Sam was adamant, and so for the first time as a PATCO member I went to the facility rep and pleaded my case. By the end of the day I had the package in my hand.

Fast forward to the next rating period which occurred perhaps seven or eight months later. My supervisor now was Val Riley, one of my first instructors on Flight Data and Clearance Delivery in the tower. He was not at all familiar with the events beginning with the error and ending with the final determination by the Southern Region, and this was the first time that he would rate my performance. He approached me with a sort of rueful smile, indicating that he was on my side, but in a bind. He said, "Rust, I had planned to give you an outstanding rating, but as I understand it, I can't do that because of that system error you had."

I felt a swell of anger, remembering the bland assurances of the chief and my former supervisor assuring me that the system error (of which I had been absolved!) would in no way reflect on my record or future performance evaluations. But I didn't want to respond the wrong way to Val, and I bit my tongue, then took a deep breath, and began, "Val, I know you don't know any of the background to this, so let me fill you in. First off, the review by the Southern Region determined that I did not contribute to the error. Secondly, both the chief and my previous supervisor assured me in no uncertain terms that the error would not be a factor in my future ratings. I appreciate that you believe I deserve an outstanding rating, and I hope you will give me one. But if it ends up being anything below outstanding, I will use my opportunity in the employee comments section to document the facts as I just told them to you."

Val was a mild-mannered gentlemanly type, and as a new supervisor had not yet conducted any performance evaluations. The last thing he wanted was a controversy involving a dissatisfied employee. A slight frown appeared on his face as he rubbed his chin thoughtfully, then said, "Well, let me talk to Lester, and I will get back to you." Lester McNeil was the acknowledged arbiter of matters like this, so I was hopeful, if unsure what his take might be. But in a day or two Val again approached me, a big smile on his face, saying, "I talked to Lester, and he said that system error was not your fault. So you will get an outstanding rating." I smiled all the way to my first assigned control position of the day.

Doing the Pilots' Job

During my years at MIA, the "controller Bible," as FAA Order 7110.65 was called informally (the formal title was simply Air Traffic Control) by degrees increased in volume and detail. The principal reason was that in the aftermath of almost every accident or incident, either through a court ruling or a recommendation of the National Transportation Safety Board (NTSB), the agency added requirements to the manual based on such rulings or recommendations.

For more experienced controllers, a category in which I now cautiously included myself, these additional layers did little to enhance safety. We believed that the purpose of most of them served only to provide some legal armor to the FAA, or to designate clearly someone to blame in the event of a future event similar to the one on which a particular revision to the order was based. Many of these changes were new phraseology requirements involving cautionary advisories or mandatory pilot read-backs. Examples mentioned earlier included:

- Pilot read-backs of hold short instructions, based on incidents where pilots crossed a runway even after acknowledging the instruction to hold short. (E. G., the runway incursion of the Panther 727, wherein the cause of the incursion was determined to be the controller's failure to obtain a read back from the pilot).

- Wake turbulence separation and advisories. If a pilot encountered wake turbulence in situations where he was responsible for the interval behind other traffic, the controller could be "gigged" for failing to issue a wake turbulence advisory even though he had advised the pilot of the type aircraft he was following and his distance behind it. (E.G., a visual approach or a VFR pilot with the lead aircraft in sight).
- Low altitude alerts based on the automated indication that an aircraft was too low. Even before the ARTS system was enhanced to provide the "LA" in a data block, there had been a push to require the controller to issue an alert to any aircraft that descended below a safe altitude. In a minor win for controllers, the handbook phrase requiring a controller to transmit these alerts was amended to include the words "if observed."

From our perspective, the point was that once an altitude was assigned, a pilot was responsible for complying, and in any event a combination of circumstances like those leading to the Eastern 401 crash was exceedingly rare. Moreover, the automated "LA" function had an additional feature related to rate of descent. In certain situations, aircraft descending rapidly, but safely, were projected to exceed the minimum safe altitude triggering the "LA" and aural warning even while the airplane was higher than that minimum. VFR aircraft, Mode C equipped but untagged by ARTS and not being worked by ATC, would also set off the warnings. This meant that the indications became constant and routine, to the point of losing their urgency. A coordination requirement was added to the mix in cases where both the TRACON and a tower received an alert and the TRACON controller was required to call the tower to be sure the alert had been noted and acted upon. All of these factors required endless transmissions of "low altitude alert, check your altitude" in the hope of catching a vanishingly small number of actual problem descents.

One of the biggest changes to approach clearance phraseology came about primarily as a response to an accident that occurred in 1974. A TWA 727 had been vectored for a VOR approach to Dulles Airport serving Washington. In general, the execution of a non-precision approach (that is one without glide slope) permitted the pilot to descend at his discretion after passing the final approach fix. TWA 514 was 44 miles from the airport when the flight crew received approach clearance. They descended to 1,800 feet, the specified altitude at the final approach fix (six miles from the airport), although a crossing restriction at an intermediate fix was shown on the approach plate as 3,400. Due to some turbulence-induced minor variations in altitude, the airplane hit the ground, which was at about 1,650 feet, killing everyone aboard.

Most controllers, and many pilots as well, believed that the flight crew had made a fatal error in leaving the last ATC assigned altitude (4,000) before establishing the aircraft on a published portion of the approach, where a different altitude was prescribed, notwithstanding the approach clearance. And in fact the cockpit voice recorder contained a comment by the captain pointing out the 3,400-foot restriction. But the NTSB findings awarded a generous share of the blame to the FAA based on the ambiguity as to whether the approach clearance kept the aircraft in the "radar regime," where the minimum vectoring altitude would still apply, or released the pilots to navigate on their own, including altitude selection.

The upshot of it all was that the phraseology for issuing the vast majority of approach clearances now included the addition of an altitude restriction, which could take several different forms, and used up valuable frequency time. A comparison of the old and the new phraseology:

Old: "Delta 125, four miles from Innes, turn left heading 120, cleared ILS 9 Right approach."

New: "Delta 125, four miles from Innes, turn left heading 120, maintain 1,500 until established on the localizer, cleared ILS 9 Right approach."

Or: "Delta 125, six miles from Gritt, cross Gritt at or above 3,000, cleared ILS 9 Right Approach."

Shown as stand-alone examples, the extra verbiage may not appear to amount to much. But those extra one or two seconds during busy periods really added up. Why, we wondered, could there not have been a simple amendment to FARs stating that when cleared for an instrument approach a pilot should maintain the last assigned altitude until it was superseded by information on an identifiable portion of the published procedure.

More Rule-Making

Sometime after the Miami TCA was established, a second round of rule-making created similar areas around a group of "next-busiest" airports, including Fort Lauderdale. Initially termed "Stage 3" service, the intent was to afford traffic utilizing these fields some of the safety and service benefits conferred by radar control. Participating aircraft could be assigned altitudes and vector headings, with positive separation standards in place. This time around, the VFR advocacy groups came prepared, and made a vehement case that the FAA was slowly but surely squeezing general aviation out of the NAS (national airspace system, including airports), saying that the proposed Stage 3 areas were nothing more than newly created TCAs by another name.

I would love to have been a fly on the wall during these hearings, watching (as I and others believed) sound operating principles being sacrificed to political pressure. The agency was finally able to sell the new airspace divisions as being no more restrictive than the long-established requirements of an airport traffic area. The rules for VFR pilots regarding the five-mile, surface to 3,000 foot area around an airport were that to enter such an area, whether for landing or to transition through it, a pilot need only establish two-way radio communication. At times this could be problematic, as shown in a hypothetical exchange:

Pilot: "Tamiami Tower, Cardinal 5166 Yankee."

TMB: "Cardinal 5166Y Tamiami Tower."

Without further communication the pilot could now legally fly through the airport traffic, without having furnished any information as to his position or intended route. The controller could not issue meaningful instructions or traffic advisories either to the Cardinal or any other traffic that might be in the picture.

Tower controllers receiving an initial call like this one learned to respond with more than the call sign alone, transmitting something like, "Cardinal 5166Y Tamiami Tower, remain clear of the Tamiami airport traffic area, say your intentions." Now the burden was on the pilot, who was required by FARs to comply with air traffic control instructions. But this was "ass-backwards," in the vernacular. If the purpose of an airport traffic area was to regulate and orchestrate the operations within its confines, it should be a pilot's responsibility to request entry, not a controller's duty to affirmatively deny entry until a pilot's intentions could be determined.

Nevertheless, in formulating the rules for Stage 3, the agency again relied on the two-way communication rule, again requiring controllers to instruct every pilot who did not provide position and route information to remain clear of the area until that information could be ascertained. In addition, unlike the regulations governing the TCA, there were no specific aircraft equipment or pilot certification requirements, so that a student pilot, flying an airplane with no transponder or Mode C altitude reporting, had as much right to operate in Stage 3 airspace as any other operator.

The rules went even further, stating that pilots who would enter the area would be "assumed to be requesting Stage 3 service." So now the airspace was open to operators who were receiving a service that they had not requested and did not understand, mixing with other traffic that was knowingly under Stage 3 control, and a third group of "bandits" who had established two-communication and entered the area without being radar identified. We were separating "participating" aircraft, including those that didn't know they were participating, from each other, and hopefully not missing traffic calls on the non-participants. A coordination burden was also added in cases where one of the two-way communication bandits was inbound for landing. The tower had to call the approach controller to request a "slot" in the radar established sequence.

There was one provision in the Stage 3 rules that provided a nominal benefit to the radar controller that experienced pilots like the charter operators understood and utilized regularly. A pilot requesting entry could advise the controller on initial contact that he did not want radar services by transmitting "Negative Stage 3." We could still assign a transponder code and put a tag on the aircraft, making it easier to work other traffic around it, and to create a slot for the tower in the landing sequence.

One incident involving two Stage 3 aircraft turned out okay, giving us all a good laugh in the aftermath, but once again reflected the difficulty of working with pilots who were not used to radar procedures, and in some cases did not even know they were under radar control. It happened at Fort Lauderdale one day when runway 9 Right was closed. In those days 9 Right at FLL was short, something under 5,000 feet, meaning that it was suitable only for smaller general aviation type aircraft. Procedures called for the low altitude controller south of FLL, the "Z" man, to work most of the GA airplanes to 9 Right while the Fort Lauderdale Approach controller ran the sequence to 9 Left. But on this day, all traffic would land on 9 Left. Perhaps because it was not a standard operation to have two controllers coordinating for use of the same runway at FLL, perhaps because of a smeared radio transmission, or perhaps because the two controllers changed their minds a couple of times, the event unfolded something like this: two GA airplanes were on opposite downwinds, N6168B, a Cessna 172 north of the field (left downwind), N889JW a Piper Cherokee, south of the field (right downwind). With similar performance characteristics, either aircraft could follow the other without a problem.

Z Man (coordinating with the "R" Man, the Fort Lauderdale Approach controller): "Hey, you want me to follow your Cessna with my Cherokee?"

R: "Affirmative, follow me."

R (to Z Man, a few seconds later): "I can't get my guy to answer me, go ahead and run that Cherokee."

Z: "Cherokee 9 JW, start your base."

R (to Z): "Disregard, the Cessna is turning inbound, put your guy behind me."

Z (to R): "You want me to follow you now?"

R (to Z): "Nah, never mind, I'll follow you." (Apparently Z didn't hear this).

Z: "9 JW your traffic is Cessna Skyhawk on left base, report him in sight."

N99JW: "Traffic in sight."

Z: "9JW, roger, follow the Cessna for 9 Left, contact Fort Lauderdale Tower 119.3."

R (almost simultaneously): "Cessna 68 B, your traffic is a Cherokee on right base, report him in sight." By this time the Cessna had already begun to turn final.

N6168B: "Traffic in sight."

R: "Cessna 68 B, follow the Cherokee, contact Fort Lauderdale Tower 119.3"

The Cessna pilot saw the Cherokee to his right, and broke out of the final to follow him. The Cherokee pilot, complying with instructions to follow the Cessna, continued in a right turn to get behind him. The two aircraft ended up in an ever tightening circle, prompting a call from Fort Lauderdale Tower:

FLL: "Miami Lauderdale on the 52 line, what's the story with these two guys? They each say they were told to follow the other guy."

Z: "Switch them back to me, I'll straighten it out."

With both aircraft now on his frequency, the Z man, assuming that N68B had been told he was number one for the airport, questioned the pilot, asking why he kept flying in circles. The pilot responded, "I'm trying to follow this guy, but he keeps trying to get on my tail." The old saw that truth is stranger than fiction certainly applied in the strange world of ATC.

Back in the Tower

Because MIA operated 24/7, each controller team in rotation was assigned the midnight shift, (or simply "Mids" as we referred to it). In my early years, the mids came around about every two months or so and lasted for one full work week, a five-day period. During this period the staffing consisted of a full team, seven or eight controllers, plus a team supervisor and a watch supervisor. Other facilities around the country had relaxed the dress code so that neckties were not required during these wee hours of the morning, but Miami had not yet done so. People bidding in from other places found this, and other things, backward or downright strange.

Karl Schimmel, one of the "watchies," never failed to notice, and demand correction of, a necktie not sufficiently blocked. He also sported a paper bag over his bald head, and a microphone apparatus that looked like something out of a World War II aircraft carrier communications center. The paper bag was protection from the overactive air conditioning system that chilled the operating quarters to uncomfortably low temperatures. The microphone was in the shape of a horn, angled up towards the speaker's mouth from a breastplate suspended from the shoulders, the whole assembly weighing at least six or eight pounds.

Despite these idiosyncracies, Karl was a company man through and through. One of the regulations applicable in all federal agencies was the prohibition against sleeping on duty, and Karl made it his business to patrol the facility vigilantly, making sure that no one, whether working a control position or not, succumbed to the temptation to put their head down "just for a moment." Predictably, some people were better at staying alert than others, and there were a couple of incidents that could be seen as validating Karl's anti-sleeping actions.

In one case my friend Frank was working Flight Data at about 3:00 am when the center called to issue a group of clearances. For whatever reason, the center controller paused in the middle of the call, advising Frank to "stand by." Frank was holding the handset to his ear, and as the seconds passed his grip on the device relaxed while his eyelids became heavier and heavier. At length the handset clattered to the top of the console, followed by Frank's head, which landed with a gentle thump. He had fallen sound asleep in the space of no more than 30 seconds, and neither the noise of the falling headset nor the rap to his cranium disturbed his slumbers.

Fortunately for Frank, Karl was not present in the tower, but on another occasion when Frank was on duty Karl thought he had nailed the sleeping culprit. Frank had put his head down, "just for a moment" when Karl appeared at the top of the tower stairs. Quietly he approached Frank, then leaned down so that their two faces were only inches apart. Without opening his eyes, Frank said, "Kiss me, and I'll turn you in." Karl stepped back abruptly amid the chuckles of the other controllers.

Another incident was potentially much more serious. Earl Peavey was working all the radar positions combined at a single display as a lone Eastern 727 departed at 2:00 am for Freeport in the Bahamas. After coordination with the center, Earl cleared the flight direct Freeport at 15,000 feet. About 12 or 14 minutes, with the airplane at least 60 miles into center airspace, he was jolted awake by the following transmission: "OK Miami, Eastern159 entering holding at Freeport, do you want us to call Miami Center?" Earl was a known cut-up, and if he had reflected for a moment he might have thought better of his reply, but his comedic instincts overruled his professional side. He keyed his mic and said, "I'm sorry, all them guys are gone to eat," pretending to be a janitor. The Eastern pilot quickly contacted the center on his own.

Eastern was not the only carrier operating these late flights to the Bahamas. Southeast Airlines, a company with only two or three airplanes, also ferried the "midnight gamblers" to and from the islands where casinos operated. The pilot corps was correspondingly small, and we came to realize that we were talking to the same pilots night after night. Their aircraft were usually the only ones on the frequency, and so a degree of informal chit chat often occurred.

One night in the tower we were cued by approach control, as the Southeast flight was inbound, that the pilot had advised us to, quote, "Check out the blonde in the white dress." These trips always terminated at Concourse E, where customs was located, with parking for the Fairchild F-27s that Southeast operated right at the base of the tower. After exiting the aircraft, the passengers and crew had to walk across a short section of the ramp to enter the terminal, and we had our binoculars trained on that area, observing a steady stream of individuals but no blonde in a white dress. Could we have missed her? As we were about to give up the search, two more people appeared—a blonde in a white dress, followed by one of the pilots. As the lady disappeared into the terminal building, the pilot hung back a few steps until she was out of sight. He then turned his face up towards the tower cab and began a series of cheerleader movements, as if to say, "How about that?"

Most people hated the mids, and did their best to trade that week with someone from another team assigned to either the day shift or evening shift. For the married men, it was understandable that being on a schedule totally at odds with the normal routine of their family members was a major hardship. But for me, and a very few others, the mids represented a break from the hustle and bustle of the busy traffic hours between 7:00 am and 11:00 pm. After the first "all-nighter," I had no trouble sleeping during the day or staying awake during the shifts on the following nights.

The early and late portions of the shift (11:00 to midnight and 6:00 to 7:00 am) could be somewhat active, but outside of those hours all the active functions could be handled at two positions—ground and local combined in the tower, all radar operations combined at a single scope. Particularly in the TRACON, it was really liberating to be able to ignore all the airspace delegations and simply use the entire 40 by 60 mile area, from the ground to FL 230 (later 16,000) to separate your traffic. You could work 10 or 12 airplanes under these conditions without once having to coordinate with anybody or even breaking a sweat.

We would even make some temporary agreements with the center, allowing them to route airplanes direct to the airport, at any altitude, and without speed restrictions. The pilots loved it, and the frictions and tensions of the other shifts were largely absent. At the time, Eastern had a number of 727s in their fleet designated as "QC" or quick-change aircraft. During the midnight hours all the seats could be removed and replaced with cargo pallets. Without passengers, the pilots of these flights could relive their fighter jock days, being cleared for an approach abeam the airport at 10,000 feet, and basically executing a wingover to descend for landing.

A Midnight Moment

Despite the generally relaxed pace, even the mids had their "moments." In one case a Brittan-Norman Islander, a small high-wing "prop" plane, was inbound from the Bahamas a couple of hours into the shift. The pilot reported that his fuel was a little low, and requested expeditious handling to the airport. The approach controller, himself a pilot, immediately informed the local controller of the situation and vectored the Islander for a visual approach to Runway 12, saving a couple of minutes of flying time as compared to an approach to 9 Left. The pilot reported the airport in sight, was cleared for the approach, and switched to tower frequency, without any indication that there was a problem.

After perhaps 10 or 15 minutes, the approach controller called local on the override, asking if the pilot had made it in safely, assuming that he had since there had been no communications to the contrary. Jim, the local controller, who had transferred from New York, replied in his thick "New Yawk" accent, "Nah, he ran out of fuel about two miles out and landed in the car lot." (At the time there was a huge train yard directly under the approach path to Runway 12 where auto shipments were off loaded awaiting transfer to the various dealerships). The conversation immediately became more urgent:

Approach: "Well Jesus, did you notify anybody?"

Jim: "Not really, the guy said he landed okay and he was not hurt and the airplane wasn't damaged."

Approach: "Call the operations desk at the Region and tell them what happened, and don't be too specific about how long ago it happened."

Jim: "Well there's really no problem, the guy was talking to me on his radio from the ground."

Any off-airport landing was to be reported immediately, and if it ever came to light that Miami Tower had let long minutes go by before making the report, there could have been major repercussions. But in due course the airplane was brought to the airport, the pilot wrote up a statement, and the affair ended without a black eye to the facility.

In later years, the watch supervisors were eliminated from the midnight staffing, leaving team supervisors in charge of the watch. They were much more forgiving about sleeping, as long as it was not done on an active control position, and in fact were not above catching forty winks themselves under the right circumstances. In one case, I had a prime opportunity to get the supervisor "on the record," that is on a recorded line. Although the recording was anonymous, and there was essentially a zero chance that it would ever be played back, the man in question received a fair amount of good natured ribbing and facetious promises to "visit him in Leavenworth" after the fact. He was a big guy, easily 300 pounds, and had draped himself over two or three chairs in the TRACON before falling asleep. Soon his snores filled the room, and I could not resist stretching my mic over towards his face and keying the "hot" line to the tower. The hot line fed into the speakers at every tower position, and after a few seconds someone in the tower keyed the TRACON hot line that fed more than a dozen speakers saying, "What was THAT?"

One of the favorite places to catch a few Zs was behind the radar indicators where cooling fans built into the units discharged a steady stream of warm air at floor level. In one hilarious case, when the day shift arrived, all the midnighters gathered up their things and didn't "let the door hit them in the ass" on the way out—all except one, that is. At about 11:00 am, four hours after the mid shift ended, an individual came stumbling out from behind the scopes sporting wrinkled clothes, tousled hair, and a large red spot on his forehead where it had rested on the floor. The catcalls and laughter followed him out the door and into the hallway as he made an embarrassed exit.

Employee Programs

In 1978 I celebrated my ten-year anniversary at Miami Tower. Unbelievably, at least in my own mind, I was now one of the veterans. Many of the people who had trained me had reached full retirement eligibility, or had gone out under the provisions of the Office of Workers Compensation (OWCP) by claiming a service-connected disability. The program had been designed for people like construction workers or law enforcement officers who had suffered physical injuries, the extent and permanence of which could be evaluated initially and periodically to determine the basis for the compensation awarded.

For controllers, these OWCP filings were largely submitted on the basis of psychological trauma. They would consist of documentation from an accredited psychologist or psychiatrist substantiating their claims that they had had a close call with two airplanes and were now having nightmares about running two together, and ending with a determination that the individual was no longer fit to control live traffic. Of course, compared with physical injury, the degree and severity of such mental afflictions was far harder to verify or evaluate, and in any case the FAA could not afford to allow someone with this kind of history on record to continue on the job.

So while some of the cases were legitimate, the program was ripe for abuse, with the FAA having "sweetened the pot" by creating second career training. If a controller lost his medical clearance, second career training provided that he would receive two years of full salary while undergoing approved training, paid for by the agency, to prepare him for a new occupation.

Some of the applications for the program were laughably transparent—golf pro for a dedicated golfer, bartender for a known party animal, or sex therapist for a practicing ladies' man. One case I remember with particular relish, as it involved a guy who gave every appearance of being a full-fledged "whacko." The dress code in place when I was hired had long since been bargained out of existence by the union, and Steve wore trousers and a matching top made of flour sack material. He had a full beard, a head of hair long enough to reach below his shoulders, and a perpetual expression of unspecified mania in his eyes. When he claimed psychological disability, most of us believed that if anyone had a bona fide case, he did.

Most people avoided Steve, but I felt that he needed a friend, and did my best to treat him as I would any other co-worker. For some reason he felt comfortable confiding in me during the time that his second career application was being processed, telling me that he been turned down for a couple of occupations—bag boy at Publix and sanitation worker come to mind. I responded sympathetically, and finally one day he approached me with a big smile on his face saying that his application had been approved. It went like this:

"Yo, Rusty, I've got my second career."

"Well alright! What's it going to be?"

"CIA, man!"

"CIA?" This immediately struck me as being the height of improbability. But then I thought, considering the spooky impenetrability of the spy agency, maybe Steve was just the sort of far out non-conformist that they could use in some fashion.

Steve continued, "Yeah man, Culinary Institute of America—chef's school."

Equal Opportunities

Before second career training, the agency, along with the rest of the federal government, had in place an anti-discrimination program known by the acronym EEO—Equal Employment Opportunity. Its purpose was to support the goal of creating a workforce reflecting the demographics of the population at large in place of the predominantly white men's club that the civil service had traditionally been. In the abstract, the principle was sound, given the cultural preferences (not to say prejudices) of the 1950s and the '60s in the pre-civil rights legislation era. Entry into the air traffic control profession, a small fraternity of men who believed they were endowed with a unique set of "balls and brains," was a tough nut to crack for women and minorities. Many senior managers were veterans of a military that excluded women from all but a small number of administrative functions and that had been racially segregated until 1948.

Nevertheless, by slow degrees the number of female and minority employees began to grow. Unfortunately, the EEO program, designed to correct past injustices, in many cases became the vehicle for specious claims of discrimination where none existed. If an employee was not selected for promotion, he or she could file an EEO claim, and a full investigation would ensue. If the findings did not produce a result to the employee's liking, the next step could be a lawsuit. In handling these incidents, the FAA became its own worst enemy, always seeking an accommodation that would persuade the employee to withdraw the claim instead of allowing the administrative and/ or legal process to play out. The predictable result was a proliferation of EEO claims by people who had nothing to lose, and almost certainly something to gain, simply by setting the wheels in motion.

There was a typically bureaucratic dimension to EEO as well, where one of the elements of every supervisor's job description required him to "support EEO initiatives." There was one potential and one actual "gig" in facility evaluations that left us shaking our heads in amused irritation. At one point we had four or five minority employees (out of a total complement of 100), and training department records showed that a minority employee had washed out and returned to his previous facility. During the same period, about five non-minority trainees had failed to check out. On the EEO portion of the evaluation checklist, this could be reported as, "20 percent of minority employees failed to complete training compared to only 5 percent of non-minorities." An earlier finding was that "the facility has hired no female supervisors." The fact that we still had no female controllers in the facility for an "in-house" bid, nor any bids from the outside on a supervisory position at MIA, cut no ice with the evaluation team.

In later years, after court rulings enshrined sexual harassment and hostile work environment principles into law, the agency made some of the same mistakes as it had with the EEO program. Before these rulings, any workplace could become a minefield for women in particular, with some male employees and even supervisors trying to leverage their position on the organizational chart to extort sexual favors.

But the new rules became a new form of the proverbial two-edged sword. If an employee made a claim, no matter how it was adjudicated, he or she would experience a degree of ostracism that made life at work difficult if not impossible. Once again, the agency bent over backwards to "settle" these claims (that is, convince the employees to withdraw them). One of the most egregiously obvious manipulations of the grievance procedure occurred when a sexual harassment claim was filed by a white male. In a sensitivity training workshop, the male participants were required to run a gauntlet of women who slapped or grabbed at them as they passed by. In the aftermath, the claimant stated that he had felt "demeaned and humiliated" by the experience. However, he said, he would get over these traumatic feelings promptly if the agency would pay him $75,000, and the FAA caved. For us "dinosaurs" of the previously all male fraternity, there was a newfound element of "walking on eggs" lest we inadvertently revert to an expression from the salty lexicon of yesteryear and give unintended offense.

Two incidents illustrate the "before and after" of this period. Kathy, a controller from a smaller facility, had bid on a position at MIA. She came to the facility to be interviewed by the new chief. Kathy was a no-nonsense young woman, who spoke her mind in the plainest language. The conversation included this exchange:

"Now, I want you to understand that you are bidding into a high-density facility, where the intensity of the operation and the pressures are likely to be very different than what you experienced at your present facility. You are going to be working with mostly male controllers, and their language can get pretty raw at times. I don't want you to come running to my office every other day because someone said a couple of four-letter words in the tower or TRACON. If you are not prepared for that, please don't take this job."

In later years, the chief would have lost his job for saying these things, but at the time it was a reasonable caution to a prospective employee. Presumably, if he had any concerns, they were firmly laid to rest by Kathy's reply:

"Hey, as long as it's not directed at me personally, I don't give a shit."

Bad Language in the TRACON

Years later, in July 2001, with the new rules in place and managers now accountable for instances of sexual harassment or hostile work environment claims, there occurred an incident tailor made for the very kind of conflict these rules were certain to precipitate. Lanny Williams, a fellow controller, was now an operations manager, the new designation for the position formerly called watch supervisor. It was a "second level" job, meaning one step above the operations supervisors who directly ran the operation.

During a slow period, one of the controllers in the TRACON became engaged in a loud and prolonged exchange with another man, using every obscene and profane expression in the book. Lanny asked the man's supervisor to tell him to tone it down. Thereafter the employee filed a grievance in which he complained that his right to free speech was being infringed upon. The union took up the cause and wrote an open letter to facility management saying that if supervisors were going to police the language used in the operating quarters, controllers had the right to know exactly which words were permitted and which were not. The letter proceeded to list a group of vulgarisms and profanities followed by a request that management reply by approving or disapproving each of them individually. All of this unleashed a firestorm of protest, including a significant component from the union members themselves. Someone faxed a copy of the letter to the wife of the union rep, pouring copious amounts of fuel on the fire.

Soon officials at the Southern Region became involved, leading to a conference call with Lanny, the facility manager, the union rep, and the region executives. The upshot of the conference was that the union would remove the letter if management agreed not to question the language used in the operating quarters. This decision seemed to fly in the face of established law related to sexual harassment and hostile work environment, and Lanny, in his role as a manager, decided to take his case beyond the FAA. I was by this time in a staff position where one of my duties was to draft communications for management's signature, so Lanny asked me to craft a description of the incident to be forwarded to Bob Graham, then U.S. senator from Florida. The gist of the letter was that the facility, and by extension the agency at large, inevitably risked grievances and lawsuits if managers were prohibited from taking actions to prevent illegal actions for which they were accountable, and asked that Congress weigh in on the matter. Before a reply could be received, the attacks of September 11 occurred, and this "minor" issue vanished in the wake of larger concerns.

9. Interactions

As noted earlier, from the time I reported to MIA in 1968 until the move to the "west 40" at the west boundary of the airport, the tower and TRACON were located atop the terminal building. In 1973 Dade County closed the employee parking lot adjacent to the terminal and created a remote parking area making it necessary to ride a shuttle bus. There was, not surprisingly, a certain amount of built-in "interaction" between the (still) all-male controller group and the female employees who worked as ticket agents, cashiers, and in many other capacities, even including police officers.

Next to the elevator bank on the airport lobby level there were three or four chairs, with the agreed upon designation as "the reviewing stand." During breaks we would occupy these seats and enjoy the seemingly endless parade of attractive women passing by. Or sometimes we would observe instances of harried passengers, usually family groups, dealing with the pressure and hectic pace of a crowded airport. Those of us who were young and single rolled our eyes as a husband dragging three or four heavy bags and a wife propelling a couple of screaming kids passed by, exchanging dagger looks or pointed verbal exchanges. But between the reviewing stand, the bus rides, and patronizing shops and restaurants, relationships blossomed.

One of our guys married the lady who worked at the Traveler's Insurance desk. Another married the clerk at one of the newsstands. Other liaisons were more temporary in nature, and I was not the only single man who benefitted from the cultural sea changes occurring in the 1970s. On two different occasions as I was riding the bus to the parking lot, a woman sat down beside me and all but asked me outright to take her home. There were also a couple of cases where we had to "encourage" one of our guys to recognize and act on an opportunity. In one instance Manny, a college student intern earning credits for work experience at the facility, was with us at the reviewing stand. Two young female security agents, the ones who inspected luggage on the way to the departure gates, walked past drawing appreciative glances, at least from us controllers. A few minutes later, one of them came back, addressing herself to Manny:

"Hi. Did you see me and my friend walk by here a little while ago?"

Manny, casting his eyes downward and shaking his head: "No I didn't, really."

"You didn't see us? She was the one with blonde hair."

"No, no, I really didn't."

"Well, she wants to meet you."

Shaking his head and scuffing his feet, "No, I don't think so."

At this point Al, who was standing beside Manny, shot him an elbow to the ribs, saying, "Man, you need to go with this girl and at least meet the other one."

Manny looked completely taken aback, but then agreed to go meet his admirer. We never learned anything about the outcome.

The 1970s was also a time before the courts made some critical landmark rulings regarding women's rights. The airlines hired young attractive women as stewardesses and provided uniforms consisting of hot pants and high heels, or other deliberately provocative attire. When they got "too old," they would be let go from their positions and new, younger women would be hired in their place. And it went beyond discriminatory employment termination and revealing uniforms. Both Continental and National Airlines used blatant sexism in their advertising, Continental running a TV spot for some months in which a flight attendant pledged that at Continental Airlines, "We really move our tail for you." Even our guys in the tower picked up on the slogan, instructing Continental pilots who were taxiing too slowly or blocking an alleyway between concourses to "Please move your tail and allow inbound traffic to pass you."

But National, in addition to creating television blurbs where a stewardess in uniform exhorted viewers to fly National, saying, "I'm Denise (or Mary, or Lisa, or Susie), fly me to New York," actually painted the names of the women in the ads on side of their airplanes. From our standpoint at ground control, this occasioned a lot of breaches of radio discipline. Some of them, truthfully, were ours, but the majority came from pilots of competing carriers. The exchange would go like this:

GC: "Eastern 612, taxi runway 9 Left, follow the National 727 ahead and to your right."

EA 612: "Oh, we will follow Denise (or Mary, or Lisa, or Susie) anywhere, anytime."

In time, both Continental and National pulled those ads, and in the case of National, repainted their aircraft. The instances of unruly male passengers making trouble for the cabin crew with endless comments about moving their tail, or wanting to "fly them" on the way to New York eventually exerted enough pressure to compel the change.

A Guided Tour

One day the TRACON received a call from Delta Airlines notifying us that they would be conducting some kind of public relations flight that afternoon. Apparently the flight crew members were not Miami based, and the caller asked if one of our personnel could accompany the flight crew in the cockpit and narrate the flight. The supervisor made a general announcement asking for volunteers. I was still pretty new, and I thought the opportunity should go to one of the older hands. But nobody raised a hand, so I did. I never did get clear what the exact purpose of the flight was, but it appeared that it was for people who had never flown before to demonstrate the safety and comfort of air travel and, not incidentally, to generate some potential new customers for Delta. I didn't get any specific guidance as to what I should say during the narration, so I simply pointed out landmarks, throwing in occasional information about our heading, altitude, and airspeed. I also managed a couple of indirect plugs for air traffic control, saying that we were being kept safe from other traffic by the radar controller, or had just received landing clearance from the tower. A couple of weeks later the facility got a letter from Delta expressing thanks for my participation, and shortly thereafter a woman I knew, who had been on the flight, asked if I had been the narrator.

A more comprehensive effort aimed at members of the public who were afraid to fly was led by a pilot who flew for Pan American. As I understood the program, it encompassed a number of aspects relating to air travel. The groups who signed up for it were taken through Pan Am's training facilities to receive lectures on the admirable safety record of American air carriers and even demonstrations of the cockpit simulators. They were briefed on aircraft maintenance, taking tours of the hangars where airplanes were being worked on, then came to the facility to observe air traffic controllers in action. The graduation exercise, for those whose apprehensions had been sufficiently allayed, was a short flight, the end goal being to create some converts from the "safe on the ground" group to potential airline customers.

We had perhaps two or three groups come to the facility each year, and, like most of the public, most of these individuals seemed impressed, if not enlightened, by the hushed tones and unfamiliar words heard in both the TRACON and the tower. One evening shift I was in the TRACON when the supervisor announced to us all that the "afraid to fly" tour would be coming through shortly. From our observations of earlier tours, we were well aware that some of the people who were afraid to fly were attractive women, so our interest definitely perked up as the group entered the room. Most of the radar displays were placed so that our backs were to the door when were on position, and several controllers turned around for a first-hand view. Those heads quickly swung back to the displays as one of the first visitors to enter exclaimed in alarmed tones, "You're not looking at your radar scope!"

Fam Trips and the Airlines

As mentioned earlier, qualified air traffic controllers were eligible to participate in the SF-160 program that governed cockpit familiarization flights for ATC specialists. The purpose of "fam" trips was to permit direct observation of in-flight procedures aboard the airplanes of participating air carriers. Most of the U.S. carriers did participate, but not those operated by foreign nations, which in any case were not covered under SF-160 provisions.

In my early days, the program was pretty restrictive—one trip per employee per airline per year, not to exceed a maximum of four such trips. So if you had already taken a fam flight with Eastern, you could not take another with Eastern in that same calendar year, and were limited to only three more, each with a different airline, until the next year. There was a typically bureaucratic and laborious process involved in applying for a fam trip, consisting of an initial application specifying flight numbers, times, and dates that was submitted to the particular carrier. The airline would respond, generally with an approval, and the facility would issue documents that would permit access to the cockpit. It would normally take at least two weeks for these steps to be completed, and if there was any "hitch" in the process, such as a change in the flight schedule or flight numbering, you had to start all over again.

On the day of the flight you had to check in at the operations desk of the carrier where a determination was made as to whether the jump seat was available—controllers were third in line behind air carrier inspectors and company personnel, so you could still be denied boarding. If that happened, most of the carriers would try to accommodate us on a different flight, although sometimes an agent would be unwilling to do so for fear of FAA retribution because the number of the new flight did not match what was on the documentation. The fact was that the airlines would have much preferred a process like the one they used for their own people, where there was no lead time or documentation involved, but a simple two-step method where you produced a valid ID and they waved you through (or not) based on jump-seat availability.

There were many benefits to the fam trip program, not the least of which was the ability to travel free, four times a year, to any city served by the airline selected. You could also count the days on which the trips were flown as duty days, and take approved annual leave at the outbound destination. These provisions drew a certain amount of negative scrutiny from other agencies, and even other divisions within the FAA, because, they claimed, the SF-160 program was not for training purposes but was in fact a perk that government employees should have been prohibited from receiving. Nevertheless, because anyone with the employment designation of GS-2152 (air traffic controller), including senior management officials who hadn't worked traffic in years, was eligible, the program survived and was actually expanded over the years prior to the 2001 terrorist attacks.

But I found my own experience in the program to be extremely valuable in several ways that had nothing to do with free transportation. If I was riding with an engaged and communicative crew, they would point out features and limitations relating to airplane (and flight crew) performance. They made the case that pilot's discretion (PD) clearances greatly improved both fuel efficiency and passenger comfort. If a controller simply issued "American 521 descend and maintain one zero thousand," the pilot was expected to begin descent immediately and maintain a constant rate of descent until reaching the newly assigned altitude. If the clearance was issued as "American 521 descend at pilot's discretion to maintain one zero thousand," the pilot could remain at his present altitude before beginning the descent at a time of his own choosing. In this way time at lower altitudes, where turbulence was more likely to occur, and where fuel consumption increased, could be minimized.

And I observed, without being told by the crews, that controllers who spoke too fast and included too many instructions in a single transmission were more likely to get "say agains" or errors in readbacks. This became an important element in my own methods at a control position, and something that I emphasized strongly to my trainees. Put simply, the principle was: You can never talk fast enough to transmit a clearance twice in less time than it takes to transmit it once at a slower rate.

Another important dimension to the fam trip program was what might be termed "the ambassadorial angle." It was a given that a certain amount of friction was bound to occur during the radio exchanges on a control frequency. When a controller walked into a cockpit, he became an individual, hopefully exhibiting tact, deference, and professionalism. Often the pilots would describe something they had recently experienced under ATC control and ask me to explain why the controller had done something or acted in a certain way. Without knowing both sides of the occurrence, I would do my best to explain in theoretical terms what I believed could have precipitated the circumstances of the event, sometimes being forced to acknowledge that there could have been a different method of handling it.

Unfortunately, some of our guys carried the adversarial attitude right into the cockpit, causing us more moderate types to wince in discomfort. To be sure, some of the flight crews exhibited the same attitude, but I believed we were guests of the airline, and that it was our duty to be polite and non-confrontational no matter what the captain or crew might do. I only experienced a negative reception once in all the years that I rode the jump seat, over a hundred trips in all. It occurred in 1975 aboard a TWA 707 en route from San Francisco to Saint Louis, designated by the airline as something like "Deluxe Service," meaning basically gourmet meals. It went like this:

When I knocked on the (open) cockpit door, the captain turned around in his seat to look at me, not saying anything. I hesitated a moment, then stepped in carrying a small Gladstone grip. The captain immediately said, "You can't bring that in here." I found this surprising since the 707 cockpit had a large bin containing the crew's luggage, with plenty of room for my small bag. But I said, "Oh, all right, what should I do with it?" The captain turned away, and either the flight engineer or first officer volunteered, "Just ask the flight attendant to stow it for you." I strapped into the jump seat, and for the entire flight none of the crew said two words to me. The conversation was dominated by the captain, who spent the whole two hours bad mouthing TWA for their rotten management, poor benefits, and especially their "unacceptable" crew scheduling practices. He said that on one occasion he had been between trips at home when crew scheduling telephoned him to discuss some aspect of his assignments for the month. "I told them to get off the phone, that they had broken my rest period, and that they would have to start my rest period all over again. I said if they didn't do that I would file a grievance with the union, and that I damn sure would not show up for work until I got a full rest period." The two other men said little, appearing to me to be less than comfortable with all of this.

About midway through the flight one of the flight attendants entered the cockpit and said there were enough first-class meals for each of us to have one. She asked if I would like to come back to the passenger cabin where I could occupy an empty seat with a tray table instead of balancing the meal tray on my lap. This was permissible under SF-160 rules, which stated that "brief absences from the cockpit are authorized for purposes of physiological needs." Although this provision was primarily to allow restroom breaks, having a meal could also be considered as meeting a physiological need. I did not answer right away, and in a moment I knew I had decided wisely. The captain turned around and said, "He can eat up here."

For the remaining time, the captain continued his screed against his employer. Upon reaching the gate, probably in violation of TWA's rules, the captain immediately unstrapped from his seat and left the airplane, saying to the first officer and flight engineer, "You guys complete the after parking checklist." The moment he was gone both of them fell all over themselves apologizing to me for the captain's rudeness and general behavior. They assured me that most of TWA's flight personnel thought controllers did a great job. "So we're really sorry," they said, "but we've got our two per cent just like any large organization."

More Fam Trips

In stark contrast, all my other trips were characterized by treatment ranging from "low-key friendly," to some shared laughs about the foibles of the system. There was also an incident where I may have saved the day, another where I was told to handle the in-flight ATC communications, and two instances where I was allowed to take the controls. The crews often told me to keep an eye out for traffic, or for anything that didn't seem right, and to let them know immediately if I observed something that might be important. In general, I believed that my role was to observe, and not to intrude in any way into matters that were exclusively within the pilots' purview. But twice I overstepped that boundary, once because the opportunity for a smart remark was too good to pass up, and a second time because I believed it was a matter of safety.

In the first case I was riding with Delta aboard a 727 en route from Boston to Bangor, Maine. The conversations in the cockpit had been uniformly engaging and informal, and so I did not hesitate when the following circumstances occurred:

We were being worked by Boston Center (ZBV) at an assigned altitude of FL 230. As we approached Bangor, the captain requested descent clearance, eliciting this exchange:

ZBV: "Delta 294, unable at this time, traffic is a company 727 eleven o'clock two-zero miles southwest bound, flight level 220."

Within a very short time, because we were northeast bound and the two flights were approaching each other at a combined speed of over 900 miles per hour, the captain transmitted:

"Center, Delta 294, we've got that traffic in sight, okay if we maintain visual separation and start our descent?"

ZBV: "Delta 294, sorry, I can't approve visual separation, only approach control can do that."

Before the captain could answer, I said, "Tell him you have an approach controller in the cockpit and he said it was all right." All three crew members laughed heartily, but they did not act on this facetious suggestion. In later years the rules were changed to allow visual separation in the en route regime, and I would not have had this golden opportunity for a smart-ass remark.

The second time I intervened, unbidden, was immediately after departure aboard a Pan Am 747 from MIA to New York. On that day there had been delays, so that the usual progression from Clearance Delivery to Ground Control to Local Control had been lengthened by the added step of Gate Hold. Gate Hold, as the name implies, was a position that a flight crew contacted, after copying their IFR clearance, for the purpose of receiving delay information and an estimated departure time. As controllers, we considered Gate Hold the most undesirable, irritating assignment in the facility. For one thing, we were constantly "chipped at" by pilots wanting updates on delays, or needing to leave the gate to make room for an arrival. When a flight was released, it was not uncommon for one or two other pilots to complain that they had called earlier than the one released, and it took repeated explanations to the effect that delay times were mostly based on conditions at the destination airport, not on the order of call-up at Gate Hold.

Most airliners were equipped with two, or sometimes three, VHF radios, and it was common practice to "tee up" in advance the expected frequencies, so that, for example, when CD instructed the pilot to call Ground Control, he would simply switch to a second radio, with GC already dialed in, then enter the next expected frequency on the radio just switched off. Normally, this would be tower frequency. After being instructed to contact the tower, the pilot would enter the departure control frequency into the previous radio. But on this day, because the frequency of Gate Hold had been added into the mix, that radio had never been re-tuned. And so a series of omissions and oversights ensued, resulting in an incident that unfolded like this:

We were holding in position on Runway 27 Left awaiting takeoff clearance as a twin Cessna departed 27 Right. Standard procedure called for the Cessna to be assigned a heading of 320 and our aircraft to be assigned 290, thereby establishing 30 degrees of divergence, legal separation even if we had lifted off side by side. Unaccountably, the local controller issued,

"Twin Cessna 45 Foxtrot turn right heading 290, runway 27 Right cleared for takeoff." Well, I thought, perhaps there had been a slower airplane off 27 Right earlier assigned 320, and Local was planning on issuing our flight a 270 heading, non-standard but still permissible and legal for all concerned. Not 20 seconds later we received takeoff clearance: "Clipper 414 heavy, runway 27 Left turn right heading 290, cleared for takeoff." My pulse rate went up a couple of notches, but of course we in the cockpit were not privy to possible coordination calls between Local and Departure Control. Maybe Local was calling the departure controller and telling him to turn the Cessna northbound.

As we rolled out of our turn to 290, Local transmitted, "Clipper 414 heavy, contact departure control." The pilot acknowledged, switching to the previous radio, triggering these exchanges, beginning with a major clue before the pilot even called:

Controller: "Continental 319, negative sir, your estimated departure time is 2015Z, time now 1935. Hold at the gate and monitor the frequency, I will keep you advised."

Pilot: "Miami departure control Clipper 414 heavy with you, out of a thousand." (No response on the frequency).

A few seconds went by as I strained against my straps in the jump seat, located on the left side of the cockpit, trying to see out the right window where the Cessna should be.

Controller: "American 450, revised departure time is now 1945Z, time now 1935. Start engines and contact ground control 127.5 for taxi."

Pilot: "Miami departure control Clipper 414 heavy with you, leaving 1800."

A few more seconds went by.

Controller: "Clipper calling, you are on gate hold frequency."

The two pilots looked at each other questioningly. I couldn't stay quiet any longer, and I said with some urgency, "I think he wants you on 119.45." The two pilots looked down at the radio console and entered the correct departure frequency. As the last digit clicked into place, we heard the stressed out voice of the departure controller, talking a mile a minute, saying "Clipper 414 heavy, if you read Miami departure control turn left immediately heading 270, traffic is a twin Cessna one o'clock one mile out of 2,000 climbing."

The pilot turned the airplane and responded, unruffled, "Roger, turning to 270, looking for traffic." Neither I nor any of the flight crew saw the Cessna, but it was pretty clear to me that we had passed it with separation nowhere near the required three miles or 1,000 feet.

The rest of the trip was uneventful, and the pilots did not comment upon or ask for any clarification of the incident. For my part, when I returned to the facility a few days later, I picked a time of slack traffic and asked the others in the TRACON if any of them had been working the afternoon of my jump seat ride with Pan Am. One of them said that he had been there, and I asked if he saw or remembered anything about a twin Cessna and a Pan Am 747. He thought for a minute, then, eyes widening, said, "Oh, the twin and Clipper? Christ yes, Local launched them on the same heading and Clipper never called. The departure controller was going ape, with the supervisor jumping up and down behind him telling him to turn the guy. It was pretty close."

On another trip aboard a DC-9, an airplane with a two-man crew, the reception as I entered the cockpit was cordial, but I observed that the captain was pretty senior and definitely steely-eyed. I put on my best "ambassador from ATC" face as the captain and first officer went through the pre-taxi checklist. Once airborne, the captain handed me his microphone, saying, "Here, you talk to them, you know the lingo better than we do, and I hate talking to these guys." For the rest of the trip I handled all the air traffic communications.

Taking the Controls

Three other fam flights stand out in my memory because they were unique, never to be repeated experiences. The first two occurred in the early 1970s, a time when some of the senior airline captains were guys who had begun their careers as barnstormers or crop dusters. They learned to fly at a time when there was little if any regulation, and their attitude in many cases was tantamount to "hang the rules, I'm the pilot in command, and nobody tells me what to do with my airplane." There was a famous case where one such pilot, towards the end of his career with Eastern, was discovered never to have received any pilot certificates. He had flown professionally and competently all through the years, passing every recurrent flight check without a problem, but had to be let go with what the airline described as "great regret" when the truth about his background was discovered. Often during my jump seat rides the conversation would turn to flying, and I was sometimes asked if I were a pilot myself. I of course replied modestly, citing my six or seven hundred hours of single-engine Cessna time. One day during a flight aboard a Northeast Airlines 727, the conversation led to the following exchange:

Captain: "So, have you ever flown a jet?"

Me: "No, the biggest airplane I ever got stick time in was the T-28."

Captain: "Would you like to try your hand at a 727?" I couldn't believe my ears, wondering in a rush of thoughts whether I could get in any trouble, then quickly deciding this was not an opportunity to pass up, so I said, "Sure!"

Captain: "OK, come on up here and take my seat."

I unstrapped from the jump seat and slid into place, after which the captain said, "Now you're on autopilot, so put your hands on the yoke and I will disengage it. Be careful with your pitch, she's very tender at cruise speeds." I heard a click, then felt a small bounce, and suddenly I was flying the airplane. The first thing I noticed was that we were climbing at about 500 feet per minute and were already two or three hundred feet above our assigned altitude. Gently I pushed forward on the yoke, instantly creating a 500 foot per minute descent. Try as I would, I simply could not hold altitude, although I did get the excursions down to plus or minus 200 feet or so. After about ten minutes the captain motioned me out of his seat, first re-engaging the autopilot, and the oscillations of the last 70 or 80 miles immediately smoothed out with the altimeter locked on FL 330. I shook my head, saying something like, "Boy, that pitch control is tough." Perhaps out of politeness, or perhaps truthfully, the captain said, "Don't worry about it. We can't do any better. We never hand fly these birds at altitude. We always let 'George' (the autopilot) do it."

Later, on a trip with Eastern, pretty much the same thing happened, and my experience at the controls was much the same. This time I was permitted to turn the airplane as we reached Wilmington (NC) to intercept the next airway northbound, and in a minor victory, managed to accomplish the turn without over banking or incurring any altitude changes greater than the ones I induced in level flight.

The third unique fam flight occurred much later in my career. It was Thanksgiving weekend in 1993 or 1994, and the flight attendants of American Airlines staged a three-day strike over a contract dispute. It began on the day I was to ride with American from MIA to DCA (Reagan

Airport in Washington). Officials at American apparently believed that the strike would be of short duration, and made the decision to keep the airplanes moving. The flights were prohibited from carrying passengers without cabin attendants. They would therefor operate empty, generating no revenue, but would keep to the regular schedule, the reasoning being that if the airplanes were grounded, it would take many days and cost much more to get the system back to normal. As I made my way to the operations desk, I wondered what these circumstances might mean for my proposed trip. Even the agent wasn't sure, saying he would approve my request, but that it was totally up to the captain to decide whether I would be allowed on board. As I entered the cockpit I asked the captain directly whether the jump seat was available, given the absence of a cabin crew. He said that American considered jump seat riders as crew, not passengers, and so there was no reason to deny me access. And so we departed, the two-man MD-80 crew and I in the cockpit. At one point I went back to the rest room and saw a completely empty cabin—a one of a kind experience, for sure.

'Flash and Dash'

After de-regulation in the late 1970s, and with a number of start-up ("upstart" as they were termed by the established carriers) airlines, competition became fierce as the new entries to the business tried to undercut the fares of the "big boys." The competition extended to the fam trip program, as many pilots believed they would get priority handling by ATC if they were carrying a controller. It wasn't true, but we did not try too hard to disabuse them of this notion. The new players were much more willing to play fast and loose with the FAA requirements governing the SF-160 program, and it became known that certain ones among them needed only to see your controller ID to allow you cockpit access. There were potential penalties for controllers who did not follow the prescribed application process, ranging from quote "recission of jump seat privileges for a minimum of two years" to outright dismissal from the agency in cases where it was determined that there had been "abuses of the program."

This meant that anyone who used the "flash and dash" method (that is, "flashed" an ID card and "dashed" aboard the aircraft) was taking a chance on some serious repercussions. I only resorted to this method twice, and I took extreme care not to misrepresent myself in any way. In both cases I started at the operations desk, saying something like, "My name is John Potter and I am an air traffic controller. Do you all participate in the SF-160 program?" If the answer was yes, I would continue, "I don't have any of the usual documentation, but I am trying to get back to Miami and wonder if I could ride the jump seat on flight 123 this afternoon. If you have any problem with this please say so, and I will understand completely." In both cases the agents checked my ID, then said that, as usual, the final determination was up to the captain. As I boarded the aircraft, I restated my case, again assuring the captains each time that if they had any concerns at all, they should not hesitate to deny me boarding.

The closest I ever came to getting into real trouble was in the aftermath of a trip that I knew was ill-advised from the get-go. At the time I was dating an Eastern flight attendant who talked me into accompanying her on a flight she was working to New York. The hotel would be free, i.e., paid for by Eastern, and she would smuggle me onto the plane in the guise of a paying passenger. This was outright fraud, and I was unwilling to take the chance, so I said if I could ride the jump seat, I would go. Eastern was one of the old carriers, more bound by the official rules of jump seat travel, but my girlfriend persuaded the flight crew to allow me aboard. I did get some strange vibes, probably because I had not had the opportunity to make my usual case, allowing them to turn me down because I hadn't established my bona fides. On the return trip, I did sit in the passenger cabin, illegally, sweating out every moment until I finally disembarked at MIA. I thought I was home free, but the next day at work I was approached by Jack Kindler, who clearly was ready for a serious conversation. It went like this:

"Did you take a jump seat ride with Eastern last Thursday?"

"Yes I did. I didn't have the paperwork, but the crew let me aboard."

"Well, I answered a phone call from Eastern yesterday questioning the fact that you had requested cockpit access without the proper documentation. They first asked for a supervisor, but I convinced them that I could handle it. They demanded to know what action we would take against you for this abuse of the program. I assured them that we took instances like this very seriously, and that you would be dealt with appropriately."

My heart sank as I asked, "Jack, did this go any farther than you?"

"No, it didn't, and you can consider yourself damn lucky that I was the one who took the call."

Jack was clearly angry that he had been put in the position of covering for my misdeeds, and I couldn't blame him. But nothing further happened in connection with the incident, and I owed him big time.

Tail-End Charlie

We who used the SF-160 program consistently had a perpetual low-level concern that somebody would do something that would cause the airlines to restrict or completely rescind their participation in the program. One of our guys took a ride with Mackey, an air taxi outfit that served the Bahamas. The carrier had allowed his family to travel for free along with him, but on the return trip their luggage was misplaced. It took several days for the bags to be located, and in the interim our traveler had approached a Mackey agent angrily, cussing him out and assuring him that "you guys are always going to be tail end Charlie when I'm working approach control." Somehow word of the incident got back to PATCO, and the union rep immediately got in touch with the right people to lay the matter to rest without any repercussions.

Another incident could have had serious consequences for one of our flight data aides. These were people hired in the aftermath of the controller strike of 1981, whose sole function was to work the flight data positions in the tower and TRACON. They never communicated directly with pilots or performed control functions of any kind, and they were not classified as air traffic controllers. Later these positions were eliminated, but in the several years following the strike they were needed because of the critical shortage of qualified ATC specialists, none of whom could be spared for flight data duties. Flight data aides were of course ineligible for the SF-160 program, but one of them ended up in the jump seat aboard People's Express, one of the post de-regulation new carriers, on a trip to Newark. People's Express was an unabashed subscriber to the "flash and dash" method of jump seat access, and after the flight to EWR, we heard competing accounts of how the wrong guy ended up in the wrong place at the wrong time.

In his version of the incident "Yogi," so nicknamed for his squat, overweight appearance, approached a ticket agent for "People's" and asked to buy a ticket to EWR. As he opened his wallet to produce a credit card, he said, the agent "happened" to see his FAA ID card, which triggered the following exchange:

Agent: "Hey man, you work for FAA? You don't need a ticket, you can ride the jump seat."

Yogi: "No, man I'm not a controller, I can't ride the jump seat."

Agent: "Sure you can—FAA? No problem. Here, let me fill out this boarding pass. Just take it down to the gate and show it to the captain."

So Yogi, not wanting to make a scene or argue, "reluctantly" took the boarding pass, and was admitted to the cockpit, the flight crew apparently assuming that he had been properly vetted in order to get the pass.

The other version of the event came in the form of a phone call from the captain of the flight, who recounted in some detail the events in the cockpit between MIA and EWR. By this time we had standard instrument departure (SID) procedures that were a part of every IFR clearance we issued. The Miami-5 (or -6 or -7, SIDs were renumbered as FLIP (Flight Information Publication) charts were updated) specified an initial climb to 5,000. But the High Departure airspace included altitudes up to 7,000, and in the vast majority of cases the controller would issue climb clearance to 7,000 on initial contact. People's Express always filed for the "inland route" with the standard first leg being direct Orlando, but our letter of agreement with the center specified that traffic using that DTA (now called ALUTO) would be placed on the Biscayne VOR 348 radial. After the airplane entered center airspace, it would be cleared direct Orlando, but in a narrowly technical sense, because the clearance had been "as filed," and the BSY 348 radial did not go direct to Orlando, there was a mismatch between the information issued on the ground and the handling by departure control.

According to the "People's" captain, who was clearly the engaging type, the conversation in the first few minutes after departure went like this:

Miami departure control: "People's 125, Miami departure, radar contact, climb and maintain 7,000, say altitude leaving."

PPX 125: "People's 125, we're out of 1500, now cleared to seven."

Captain, to Yogi: "Can you explain something to me? The Miami 5 restricts us to 5,000, but we always get cleared to 7,000. Why don't they make 7,000 the altitude on the SID?"

Yogi: "Shoot, I don't know." (The restriction was to protect flights transiting the departure airspace at 6,000 by building in separation from departures that came off without prior notice).

Miami departure control: "People's 125, turn left heading 330 to intercept the Biscayne 348 radial."

PPX 125: "OK, left to 330, join the Biscayne 348, People's 125."

Captain, to Yogi: "That's another thing I've wondered about. We file direct Orlando, get cleared as filed on the ground, but then we always get put on this radial. It's only two or three degrees different than going direct, any reason why you guys always put us on the radial?"

Yogi: "Shoot, I don't know." (The reason was to keep the aircraft centered in the DTA. There was opposite direction inbound traffic on both sides of ALUTO, and while we in the terminal could clear an airplane direct ORL with three miles separation from the inbounds, as soon as the flight entered center airspace, the standard went to five miles).

Apparently no more was said during the flight, but as soon as the crew entered operations at Newark, the captain asked to use the telephone, saying, "I'm calling Miami Tower to find out about this guy that rode up here with us. Whoever he is, he is no air traffic controller."

10. Becoming an Instructor

Going back again in time, in 1978 I was presented with a pivotal decision point in my career. Lester McNeil, now the facility training manager, approached me with an offer to accept a year's detail in the training department. The training program had advanced light years since I entered it a decade earlier. It now consisted of standardized binders of information for each control position and a full set of radar simulation exercises. Simulation could never duplicate conditions in the real world, but it was pretty realistic, as we saw amusingly demonstrated in one particular instance.

A trainee in the early stages of OJT on the Fort Lauderdale Departure position was being trained by Joe, who was an experienced controller, but not the most patient of individuals. One of the scopes had been put into enhanced target generator (ETG) status, and a number of simulated airplanes activated. As the volume of "aircraft" increased, the trainee was getting farther and farther behind, with Joe becoming increasingly agitated and red-faced. Finally, just as he might have done if they were working live traffic, Joe leaned over the trainee and gruffly announced, "Okay, I've got it," then proceeded to start issuing control instructions. The targets were controlled by entries made on the ARTS keyboard, and the training specialist performing this function at first tried to continue, but then threw up his hands amid peals of laughter saying, "All right Joe! Don't let those pretend airplanes have any pretend collisions!"

At first I told Lester I did not want the training assignment as an Evaluation and Proficiency Development Specialist (EPDS). Every controller knew that proficiency could deteriorate quickly if you did not work pretty much every day. As the great piano virtuoso Vladimir Horowitz explained, "If I miss a day of practice, I can tell the difference. If I miss two days of practice, you can tell the difference." And I had vivid memories of what it had taken to certify in the first place.

While I could still work the positions from time to time, as long as I stayed "current" ("currency" consisted of logging a minimum of 16 hours per month, combined tower and radar position time), there was no guarantee that my primary responsibilities would afford me that opportunity, and the idea of having to re-certify at the end of the year gave me considerable pause.

Moreover, there was a significant financial penalty in going to a daytime Monday through Friday work schedule. There would be no evening shift differential (10 per cent more 6:00 pm to 6:00 am), no Sunday pay (25 per cent more), no holiday pay (double time), and no overtime pay (time and a half). Over a full year, this could add up to losing the equivalent of a full pay period's worth of income or more. But Lester was very good at getting things to go his way. He revised his offer to make it a temporary detail lasting 120 days, and, although I still had some reservations, I decided to accept. The timing of this assignment, and the work itself, proved in different ways to be of enormous benefit to my career in ATC. As it turned out, I seemed to have the "gift of the gab" when it came to classroom presentations, and enough of the ham in me to be able to play the part of the pilot voices in the simulation exercises in a way that kept the trainees engaged and entertained while they were learning.

One aspect of this new job involved the orientation of "co-ops." These were college students pursuing aviation studies who became temporary employees, hired under a cooperative agreement with several local colleges, for periods lasting up to four months. There was no formal syllabus for the co-op program, which meant that their activities depended on the willingness of facility personnel to devote time and attention to them. They could be stuck in a corner somewhere and told to study the 7110.65 manual, dry reading at best, and mostly incomprehensible without the context of some operational understanding. Or they could be asked to answer telephone calls when a secretary or administrative assistant took a break.

These activities did not seem to be appropriate learning situations, so I took it upon myself to provide the students with as much interactive experience as possible. If I had a class of controller trainees, I had the students sit in on the class. While much of it would be over their heads, they were certain to pick up at least bits and pieces of worthwhile information. In the radar simulation exercises the students would act as keyboard operators, responding to controller instructions, and not incidentally observing how radar targets actually behaved. If I had no controller trainees, I would invent classroom exercises such as having the students play the part of Clearance Delivery while I voiced typical pilot call-ups, including the appropriate accents for our Spanish, German, French, Portuguese, or Italian air crews. Or I would take them up to the tower and plug in to either ground or local control and allow them to monitor me or another controller.

In one amusing incident one of the co-ops had been monitoring Clearance Delivery on a day when I was not in the facility, and reported to me later as follows: "Yesterday I was listening to Clearance Delivery, and those pilots sounded just like you!" In at least one case, my efforts seemed to have paid off. At the end of each work session the students were asked to fill out a form evaluating and critiquing their experience at the facility. Most of these contained minimal uncritical comments: "Great experience," or, "Learned a lot." But one serious and intelligent young woman took the time to go much further, writing that "time spent studying manuals without supervision or answering the telephone did not constitute meaningful experience in learning about air traffic control procedures. If it had not been for the time that Rust Potter spent instructing us and ensuring the opportunity to monitor control positions, the time at Miami Tower would not have had much value."

Of course, the two primary purposes of my new job were to prepare newly reporting personnel for on-the-job training and to keep training materials updated. Every time there was an internal procedural change or a modification of our letter of agreement with the center, four or five thick binders had to be reviewed and amended. It was not lost upon me that I became the de facto "face of the facility" to new employees, and that the first few days of interaction could set the tone for their entire time at MIA. At that time our new people all had prior experience at other facilities, including in many cases big-time approach controls like Atlanta, Chicago, or Dallas, meaning that they had all experienced training programs in their earlier careers.

For most of them, the prospect of another round of training was about as welcome as a dose of castor oil, and it didn't take me long to understand why. It seemed that many facilities devoted few resources to training, especially for people with prior experience. One sharp young man transferring from the New York TRACON sat through the first day of class exhibiting an attitude of boredom and total disengagement. I learned later that he thought his time in class was a purely pro forma exercise, after which he would be sent to the floor in short order. On the next day, when I began asking review questions about the prior day's material, he looked nonplused and could not answer a single one of them. I took him aside and asked him how much time he had spent studying, to which he replied, without embarrassment, that he had not studied at all. At New York, he said, they had told him to study the charts and local procedures, and that it was up to him to tell the training department when he was ready for OJT. In his words, "I didn't know a damn thing when I went to the floor in New York."

I explained that at MIA the determination of a trainee's readiness for the next phase depended on his passing a battery of written tests and a series of radar simulation exercises. He did not greet this as welcome news, but I told him that if he made the most of his classroom and simulation time his OJT would be a breeze. In this case and a number of others, at the conclusion of the classroom/ simulation phase, the employees expressed their approval of our program, saying it was the best syllabus they had ever been through.

Learning While Teaching

Everyone has heard some version of the old saw that you never really learn something until you teach it. I found this to be true in spades during my time as an instructor. From day one, both in the classroom and the simulation lab I found myself saying, "Gee, I never knew that," whether it was a minor point of phraseology or some element of radar control. And as I got smarter, I was able to fine tune my classroom content and the laboratory control problems. I tried as much as possible in the simulation exercises to throw in situations that I had actually experienced in the real world. Truth is stranger than fiction, in ATC no less than anywhere else, and when a trainee complained that "that would never happen" during the course of a problem I was usually able to say truthfully that indeed it had happened.

One of the first actions I took with respect to the training materials was to toughen up the written tests. They seemed to me to be far too easy, many of them containing multiple choice questions to which the correct answers were laughably obvious. I discarded a fair number of these, substituting questions that required a narrative answer. For example:

The original question might have been something like: "To which sector would a north departure aircraft routed over Vero Beach at 7,000 be handed off?

A. Palm Beach. B. Cuter. C. Marathon. D. Reefe.

Since B, C, and D were all south departure DTAs, it was an easy guess even if the trainee had no idea where Vero Beach was.

I would revise the question to something like this:

"Describe the handling of a north departure aircraft departing Tamiami routed over Vero Beach at 7,000."

There were actually several different ways the aircraft could be handled, none of which were incorrect, but one of which was optimum, either from the standpoint of service to the user or in terms of minimizing the number of internal control positions that would have to work it.

Possible answers were:

"First worked by W (South Departure), kept at 2,000, handed off to Z (North Low), climbed to 4,000, handed off to L (Fort Lauderdale departure), climbed to 7,000, handed off to Palm Beach Approach."

"First worked by W, kept at 2,000, handed off to Z, handed off to G, climbed to 3,000, handed off to L, or coordinated for climb to 7,000, handed off to Palm Beach Approach."

There were several others as well, and typically in a class of three or four trainees, there would be different answers. This created the opportunity to discuss which answer was best, which were less good, and which were flat out wrong. It also demanded a more comprehensive understanding of our airspace and procedures than simply knowing that a low altitude northbound prop would be handed off to Palm Beach. Often there were lively discussions as to why one answer was preferable to another, and I believed this was the way to make classroom information stick in a trainee's mind.

Another method I used was to present a basic traffic situation, then list a series of true/ false statements under varying circumstances. For example:

"The separation required between two aircraft on instrument flight plans, one on final for 9 Left and another on final for 9 Right is:

A. Three miles in all cases. (False. It is two miles if both are on ILS, none specified if one is on a visual approach)

B. Five miles if the lead aircraft is a heavy jet. (False. Five miles is the standard if the runways are less than 2,500 feet apart, our parallels were 5,100 feet apart)

C. Two miles if the ceiling is reported below 1,000 feet. (True. They would have to be on a published instrument approach, as the ceiling is too low to authorize a visual approach).

D. None specified if either pilot or the tower controller provides visual separation. (True)

These choices required a trainee to understand how separation requirements change according to weather, aircraft types, type of approach issued, and other circumstances, rather than simply memorizing a single number to answer a one-dimensional question. This seemed to me far more reflective of real world conditions than the exercise of rote memorization.

In the laboratory, for each radar control position there were eight scenarios, four for an east operation and four for a west operation. These were graduated in volume and complexity. In the early runs, a trainee would be given the slowest problems so that he could concentrate primarily on keeping the traffic in his airspace and only secondarily on separating the targets. Once he demonstrated mastery of the airspace, he would move up to the busier exercises. There were only two indicators available in ETG, one for the student and the other for the pseudo pilot. In a class of two or three trainees, the one(s) who were not in the "hot seat" would perform the keyboard entries or simply observe the problem as it was being run. I believed this to be a valuable component of the laboratory experience, even though there was a clear benefit to being second or third in line to run the problem. I made sure that the "opportunity" to go first was equally shared, so that no one student had an unfair advantage over the others.

About Simulation Training

There were definitely pros and cons to the simulation training. On the plus side, it was an opportunity to reinforce understanding of the TRACON airspace divisions and to practice required/ correct phraseology, all without any risk in the case of separation loss or "collisions." And it was realistic enough to provide some insight on the instructor's part as to how well a trainee handled pressure when the action heated up. There was also the opportunity to introduce emergencies or unusual situations that a trainee might never encounter in the course of OJT. The negatives were:

- Climb rates, turn rates and speed reductions or increases were uniform for a given class of aircraft. In the approach control problems, this eliminated one of the biggest uncertainties of the real world operation where no two pilots performed a speed reduction at the same rate or progressed uniformly after being assigned the same speed.
- Communications were unrealistically clean, with no poor radios or smeared transmissions.
- There could be keyboard entry errors by the pseudo pilots which, if they occurred at a critical time, could totally screw up a scenario that had been going well.

When trainees were acting as pseudo pilots for each other, there was a tendency for them to make uncommanded entries that would help out the man taking the problem. They could, for example, increase the rate of climb for an "aircraft" that was clearly not going to make an altitude restriction on departure, or make speed control entries for approach traffic when they saw that the trainee should have made them earlier. I got pretty good at detecting these unauthorized assists by listening to the click of fingers on the keyboard when no control instruction had been issued, and negating the action by instantly restoring a speed or a climb rate by a "fast" entry that instantly put the target back at the previous speed, altitude, or rate of climb.

In more than one case, when the pilot function was being performed by co-op students, I saw actions more attributable to their lack of understanding as to the purpose of simulation than deliberate cheating to benefit the trainee. After observing enough problems, the co-ops knew where each "aircraft" was supposed to go, and could easily see when a trainee missed a critical turn for one of them. They could then make the entry for the turn that should have been issued. The first time it happened, I thought that perhaps I had missed a legitimately transmitted control instruction. For the next target on the same route, I watched and listened carefully, immediately realizing that the pilot had typed in an uncommanded turn. I stopped the scenario via the "freeze" function, and asked both the trainee and the young co-op if the turn had been issued, to which they both replied that it had not. When asked why he had made an entry when the controller had issued no instruction, the pilot replied, without embarrassment that he "knew the airplane was going that way." I explained that sometimes a controller could be late issuing an instruction, or a pilot could fail to receive it, and that it was an important part of a controller's job to recognize these errors and correct them.

From the instructional perspective, simulation provided a golden opportunity to stop the problem at any point for the purpose of discussing an error or pointing out an oversight. It was important to use this feature judiciously for the obvious reason that there was no "stop" button in the real world. Every controller had to master the necessary skills both to stay out of trouble and to get out of trouble, and there was as much training value in recovering from problematic circumstances as there was in avoiding them in the first place.

Generally when a radar position was becoming more chaotic and out of control, it happened by degrees. It was not too difficult to recognize when the situation had deteriorated beyond the point of recovery, and when that occurred it was time to "stop the problem." There was now an opportunity to review the actions of the trainee for the past several minutes, identifying moments when a better ordering of priorities or a missed control instruction might have made all the difference. I found that with capable, experienced people it was almost never necessary to freeze the problem. Those who were less capable or experienced were more likely to get into situations where they couldn't complete an exercise without some pauses and explanation.

In the early stages, this was not necessarily a bad thing. But at some point every aspirant had to be able to grab the bull by the horns and show that he or she had the right stuff to be a controller at a Level V facility. One of the most insidious indicators of likely difficulties down the road was the tendency of some controllers to rely on what I called "formulaic" control. These people wanted to issue the same climb clearance, the same altitude assignment, the same heading, the same speed reduction, etc. at exactly the same points to every airplane in the problem. This could work, to a limited degree, in a slow problem where almost all the traffic was on prescribed routes. But in the hectic low-altitude sectors, or under busy conditions anywhere, it was a sure recipe for disaster.

One of the most challenging trainees I ever worked with relied heavily on the formulaic approach, and ultimately paid the price for it. She was a young woman who had come to MIA from a VFR tower, having had no prior radar experience, and, from what we later came to understand, had struggled in training at that facility. She did all right in the early problems, satisfactorily learning the airspace, and keeping things under control during the low volume exercises, but later in the program seemed unable to progress. She did not seem able to re-shuffle priorities as the traffic situation developed, and relied excessively on traffic point-outs such as a slow climber headed for an altitude "shelf" in her airspace that required a rate of climb beyond the aircraft's capability. I had emphasized both in class and in the lab that point-outs should be kept to a minimum, and that the preferred method in these cases was to vector the aircraft until the altitude restriction could be met. In other cases, there would be four or five "airplanes" that needed immediate action and weren't getting it. Time after time I would stop the problem and talk through the situations:

Me: "Okay now, you have six airplanes on your frequency. Are all of them in your airspace?"

Trainee: "I think so."

Me: "Well take a look." Mostly she would be correct, because I did my best to stop the problem before any airspace or procedural errors could occur.

Me: "There are at least four airplanes that you need to do something with. So when we start the problem again, what are you are going to do, starting with the most important thing?"

Trainee: "Well, I need to hand off Delta 916 to the center."

Me: "Yes you do, but he is still 20 miles from the boundary. Do you think that's critical at this point?"

Trainee: "No, I guess not."

Me: "What about N6787Y?" (The target was about to enter another controller's airspace without a handoff or point out).

Trainee: "I need to coordinate with Z."

Me: "Don't you have time to vector him to keep him in your airspace till he can make the altitude restriction? How about American 540? He's already handed off to L, and he's getting close to the boundary. And that Lear off Fort Lauderdale going out Marathon is on your frequency, still eastbound. You need to figure out how you are going to run him."

At this point she would look at me blankly, and I would say, "Okay, now look. Here are the priorities as I see them: Either vector 87Y or point him out, switch American 540 to L, turn the Lear back to the west and climb him in your airspace, then hand off Delta 916."

We would resume the problem and she would perform these actions, temporarily getting things under control, but before long there would be another situation requiring another freeze and a similar discussion. I would write these up on the training report, and more than once she responded tearfully, "Why did you write those things up? I did what you told me to do." These events occurred well into the syllabus at a time when she should have been much further along, and in each case I gave her some version of the following answer: "Yes, you did. But I have some bad news for you. Traffic will not stop in the real world, and I will not be in the TRACON to tell you what to do when you go to the floor." I was hoping that she would recognize that she was likely in over her head at MIA and ask to return to her prior facility. At one point she confessed that she felt enormous pressure working the low-altitude sectors and the busier problems, and I used this opportunity to suggest to her that she consider what it would take to get through OJT on multiple radar positions. In the end, after several months of struggle, she ended up washing out of training.

Lighter Moments

With experienced controllers, ETG had its lighter moments. One of my favorites occurred during a simulation exercise on Miami South Departure, including military arrivals at Homestead Air Force Base. In the TRACON we still had the old drum clocks mounted above each position. It was easier and quicker to get the time from these than from the ARTS clock, which was embedded in the system area, grouped with other information and displayed in small characters. In the ETG room there was no drum clock, but there was a digital panel showing the altimeter setting of 3002 located just above the trainee's radar display.

The scenario included a flight of four F-4s that broke up after handoff from the center, all requesting the high TACAN approach to runway 5. This necessitated clearing three of them to hold, with altitude separation, at the final approach fix, including issuing an expected approach clearance time. All of this created a few fast-paced minutes, during which the trainee was talking rapidly, and dividing his time between control instructions and coordination with Homestead GCA. So here's how it went, with two other trainees acting as keyboard operator pilots and me as the voices on the frequency:

Gourd 41: "Miami approach Gourd 41 flight request break up and clearance for individual high TACAN approach."

Trainee: "Gourd 41 Miami approach, proceed direct RAKKE, descend and maintain one-six thousand, cleared high TACAN penetration and approach runway 5."

Gourd 41: "Gourd 41 cleared to 16,000, cleared for the high TACAN."

Trainee: "Gourd 42 maintain one seven thousand, report level."

Gourd 42: "Gourd 42 leaving flight level 210, will report level 17,000."

Trainee: "Gourd 43, maintain flight level 180, report reaching."

Gourd 43: "Ok down to flight level 180, will report reaching, Gourd 43."

Trainee: "Gourd 44 maintain flight level 190, report reaching."

Gourd 44: "Gourd 44 now cleared to flight level 190, will call reaching."

Gourd 42: "Gourd 42 level 17,000."

Trainee: "Gourd 42 roger." (On landline): "HST GCA, Miami, inbounds."

GCA: "Go ahead, Miami."

Trainee: "Gourd 41, 42, 43, and 44, F-4s, will be on individual TACAN penetration and approaches to runway 5, JA."

GCA: "AF."

Gourd 43: "Gourd 43 reaching flight level 180."

Trainee: "Gourd 43 roger. Break break, Gourd 42 proceed direct RAKKE, maintain 17,000, expect approach clearance at…"

The controller stopped, looking for the non-existent drum clock, never thinking about the ARTS clock, but seizing upon the digital altimeter readout, and continuing in rapid fire fashion, "expect approach clearance at 3015, time now 3002." The other two trainees and I could not contain ourselves, bursting into laughter at the fact that the controller had issued numbers that did not exist within the 24-hour clock system and were clearly altimeter setting values.

A QWIG-y

The four-month detail to the training department passed quickly, and I resumed my controller duties, adjusting once again to the schedule of rotating shifts and oddball midweek days off. A couple of weeks after my return to the floor, as I was walking past Lester's office he called out to me in his unique and inimitable fashion: "Potter, get your damn ass in here!" I knew Lester's style well enough by this point not to be concerned about the manner of this summons, suspecting, indeed, that it might augur something good. Lester handed me a sheaf of papers. On top was an FAA Memorandum titled "Letter of Appreciation" addressed to "ATCS John R. Potter" from "SATCS (Supervisory Air Traffic Control Specialist) Lester T. McNeil." The body of the memo read, in part, "I have had the opportunity to evaluate your work as instructor in both the classroom and the simulation laboratory. Your performance during your detail to the training department was uniformly excellent. A number of your trainees have expressed to me that you did a great job." There was some additional language of the boilerplate variety, saying that the job I did reflected "great credit" upon myself, the facility, the FAA, etc. The signature at the bottom was "L.T. McNeil, EPDO (Evaluation and Proficiency Development Officer), Miami ATC Tower." In terms of my prospects at Miami Tower, this amounted to money in the bank. If Lester was on your side, you had nothing to worry about.

A letter of appreciation was nice, but the documents underneath it were even nicer. Together they constituted a personnel action titled "Quality Within Grade," or a "QWIG-y" as we informally called these actions. The GS pay scale, which covered all Civil Service employees except Senior Executive Service (SES) personnel, consisted of 15 grades, within each of which there were 10 "steps" through which one progressed based on time in grade and satisfactory performance, with salary increases at each successive point. The time intervals required to move from a lower to a higher step were: one year at the previous step to advance to steps 2, 3, and 4, two years to advance to 5, 6, and 7, three years to advance to 8, 9, and 10. So it would take 18 years to progress from step 1 to step 10 under normal circumstances. But a "QWIG-y" basically waived the time requirement for advancement within the grade, and if it came immediately after a normal step increase, you would be ahead of the game, in terms of pay, by one, two, or three years for the rest of your career. In my case, I was at the point in the GS-14 grade where the waiting period was two years, and had just reached step 6. With a wave of the administrative wand, I was now at step 7.

Storm Clouds on the Horizon

By this time (mid-1978) the first rumblings of a controller strike were beginning to be heard. At all levels of the air traffic control service there was a palpable increase in tension as PATCO ramped up organizational militancy and ever more strident demands for change. Much has been written about the strike and its causes, so that there is an abundance of resources for people who wish to learn more, and I will not attempt to distill or synthesize this huge amount of historical data. My observations will be based on my individual experience.

At MIA, a new element in the increasingly confrontational posture of the union was the creation of a local newsletter. Other facilities had been promulgating such publications for some time, and Bob Mercer felt that it was high time for the Miami chapter of PATCO to get on board. Bob was the local union rep, and performed his duties with intelligence and pragmatism. He believed that "you always have to let management know you are there," and also understood the importance of showing the union membership that its representatives were active in pursuing the best interests of the controller work force. A local "rag" could keep the issues that PATCO deemed important at the forefront, while at the same time stand as a symbol of continuing union engagement.

I was definitely taken aback when Bob approached me about being the editor of The Banner, as the newsletter was to be called. He knew that I disagreed with many of the initiatives undertaken at the local level, and that although I understood the importance of a collective voice, I did not subscribe to rabble-rousing militancy for its own sake. In addition, with a degree of insight keener than mine, he recognized that the letter of appreciation and the QWIG-y I had received after my detail to the training department might influence me to bid on a staff or management job. If I were to be selected for one of these positions I could no longer be a member of PATCO and could potentially become an opponent in the event of a strike.

I told Bob I would think about his request. In reading the newsletters of other facilities, I was basically appalled at the tone and content of many of them. One such publication ran a column entitled "Asshole of the Month." The editors would single out the chief, a supervisor, or a staff member, then proceed to list the "outrageous" actions of the individual. The "outrageous" actions were things like washing someone out of training, calling a controller on the carpet for improper or unprofessional phraseology, or a letter of warning to a controller who had improperly filled out (i.e., lied on) his time and attendance record. My first instinct was not to touch this "opportunity" with a 10-foot pole. Then it occurred to me that as editor, I might be in a position to prevent some of the worst excesses in the publications of our sister facilities.

I eventually told Bob I would take the job. In the first issue, I included some principles by which the newsletter would be governed, and led off with an editorial of my own. Any PATCO member could submit material to be included. Such material would be accepted or rejected at the sole discretion of the editor, but anything that was accepted would not be changed in any way except for the correction of spelling errors. The person offering a submission would be identified as its author.

A box showing several lines of fine print contained the following statements: "Responsibility for the contents of individual articles rests solely with the writers. The opinions expressed do not necessarily reflect the posture or the views of PATCO locally or nationally. All rights reserved (I didn't actually know if we had any rights, but if there were any it seemed prudent to reserve them)."

In my editorial, I exhorted union members to stick to things that were factually true, as opposed to firebrand perceptions of inequity or injustice. Strong statements were fine, as long as they could be backed up by evidence. For example: "On two different occasions the control frequencies at the Fort Lauderdale radar positions failed. These occurred on March 27 and March 29. The outages lasted for several minutes, resulting in at least two aircraft leaving their designated airspace. These spontaneous failures have been going on for some time, and are UNACCEPTABLE! Management must take immediate and definitive action to correct this problem once and for all!"

By contrast: "Supervisor [X] has had it in for me since the first day I reported to MIA. He never approves my leave requests, and I am always the last person to be relieved at the end of my shift. Someone needs to straighten this guy out, because the way he treats me is totally unfair." This is the type submission I would reject, on the grounds that the assertions were almost certainly untrue ("since day one?" "never approves?" "always the last?") and in any event could not be substantiated one way or the other. My final line in this first issue was, "We will not let The Banner become a forum for irresponsible union breast beating; but when a responsible voice needs to be heard, let it be ours."

Like anyone presenting himself as the visible face of something new, I was a little nervous about how the newsletter would be received by the PATCO membership. As it turned out, the reception was pretty positive, in part for a fairly unlikely reason. More than one guy came up to me with a big smile on his face, saying "All right Rusty!" then going into a pantomime of chest beating that would have done King Kong justice.

Strike Talk

As 1978 segued into 1979, talk of a general strike by PATCO escalated to the point that 1981 came to be identified as the target year for the walkout. We rarely heard the word "strike," by definition an illegal action under federal law, instead hearing references to the increasingly likely event as "PATCO '81."

Some of the submissions to The Banner contained comments like, "The continued refusal of management to address these unacceptable conditions is the reason that I believe PATCO '81 is the only way to compel the reforms we need." As editor, I was somewhat worried about these statements, wondering if I could be seen as abetting the momentum towards a strike, and whether the disclaimer that the opinions of individual writers did not necessarily reflect the views of the union at large offered any real protection.

But in yet another instance of the incredible good fortune I had experienced at critical points in my career, Lester informed me that a permanent staff position in the training department would soon come open. He said that I had better bid on that job, otherwise it was likely to go to another individual whom he saw as totally unsuited to the role of instructor. The upsides were that I knew I liked being an EPDS, and that if I were in a staff position if a strike occurred I would not be a union member and therefore would not participate. The downsides were several—I would lose the extra income available in shift work; the time as a staff member would not count towards the early retirement available to employees who spent their entire careers "on the boards." I would no longer have union protection if I ever had a "deal" (a loss of separation or an accident); and the big one for me: I would be in the position of trying to defeat the strike, dashing the hopes and aspirations of long-time friends and colleagues.

The vacancy would not be officially advertised for several weeks, giving me time to mull over the choice I would eventually make. It was during this period that Bob Mercer again approached me, saying I had done a great job with the newsletter, and making a strong pitch that I should run for one of the officer positions of the local PATCO chapter. We talked at length, again airing our differences about union activities at the facility level, then getting into the weightier matter of the potential strike and its implications. I told Bob that the militancy and open advocacy of a strike on the part of many PATCO members did not sit well with me, and that I frankly hoped the membership would vote against a strike if things progressed that far. The conversation went something like this:

Bob: "See, that's the reason we need guys like you in leadership positions. You have a good head on your shoulders, and you could do a lot to show the hotheads the reality they are facing."

Me: "I don't know about you, but it seems to me nobody is going to have much luck talking to them. They think they are going to go out for a day or two and come back in to a 100 percent salary increase, a 30-hour work week and a 15 year retirement package."

Bob: "I know what you mean. They've all got strike fever, but when you talk to them, they've got no sick leave, no annual leave, and no money in the bank. How do they think they are going to get by if a strike lasts a couple of months?"

Me: "I'll tell you the truth Bob, it looks like there is a staff position coming open, and I think I am going to bid on it."

At that Bob's demeanor changed markedly, and he said, "I really hope you won't do that. We need you, and I thought you were with us."

This exchange pretty much iced it for me. In the union's view, I was either for them or against them. There was going to be no middle road. If I took the staff job I was against them. If I didn't, I supported the strike.

And so it was that I bid on and was selected to fill the training department vacancy. In the early stages, I experienced the work in much the same way as I had while on detail. Many of the new employees thanked me for helping them get started, and there was renewed satisfaction for me in seeing them progress to full qualification after the classroom and simulation phases.

A Serious Incident

But in April 1980, there occurred an incident that had a major impact on Miami Tower and approach control, causing a schism between union and non-union personnel that grew increasingly pronounced until the strike in 1981 totally reshuffled the cards.

Like most of the airlines, Braniff International participated in the SF-160 program, allowing controllers to occupy the jump seat in the cockpit to observe air traffic control procedures from the pilot perspective. Earlier in the year Braniff had begun hiring a substantial number of new pilots who were required to undergo familiarization trips before they could act as flight crew members. The airline management issued a letter to all FAA facilities stating that Braniff's participation in the SF-160 program would be temporarily suspended until their own training requirements could be completed. The letter was signed by a Mr. Brown, vice-president of flight operations, and was displayed on the facility bulletin board to alert controllers not to apply to Braniff for jump seat privileges.

One day when there were no controller trainees nor any co-op students in the facility, Lester approached me saying that he had just received a call from the watch supervisor at Miami Center. According to the caller, a Braniff pilot had telephoned the center complaining about the handling he had received, saying that the controller had deliberately vectored his flight into an area of thunderstorms. A playback of the recorded control frequencies had revealed no irregularities, and the center supervisor suggested that perhaps the incident had occurred after the flight had been handed off to approach control. Lester handed me a note containing the flight number, an approximate time frame and identifying WESTO, located northwest of MIA, as the inbound fix over which the flight had arrived. He said, "Play back the tape of south approach control during this time period and see if there is anything to this." I removed the large multi-track spool from the recording station and placed it on another machine used for playbacks, soon locating the exchanges between the south approach controller and Braniff 343. I began to fear the worst as I recognized the voice of Roger Pomeroy, a major union activist and one of the most vocal advocates of the potential strike. It went like this:

BI 343: "Miami Approach Braniff 343 with you, leveling at 16,000 with Bravo."

Pomeroy: "Braniff 343 Miami Approach, expect landing to the west."

BI 343: "OK, landing west today."

Pomeroy: "So how are we treating you today?"

BI 343: "Say again approach?"

Pomeroy: "Braniff 343, how are we treating you? Are you getting good service?"

BI 343: "Yeah, sure, I guess so."

Pomeroy: "Let Vice President Brown know when you get back home."

BI 343: "Say that again, approach?"

Pomeroy: "Let Vice President Brown know that you got good service from Miami Approach."

BI 343: "Approach, I don't know what you mean."

On the day in question, the weather had been up and down, with a number of thunderstorm cells in the area. The normal heading from WESTO to follow a route north of the airport and later to be sequenced for the approach to Runway 27 Right was about 100, which at the time of BI 343's arrival, happened to be clear of any significant weather. But to the right of that track there were some significant buildups. The flight had been on the normal route up to this point. The exchange continued:

Pomeroy: "Braniff 343 turn right heading 170 vector for spacing, expect 27 Right at Miami."

BI 343: "Oh great, that's right in the stuff, 170."

Pomeroy: "Well I want to make sure you get this information back to your vice president Brown, you know what I mean."

BI 343: "No, I sure don't."

Pomeroy: "Well, most of the pilots don't. You taking anybody in your jump seat today?"

BI 343: "Nah, sure not."

Pomeroy: "Now you understand what I mean?"

There were a few more transmissions from both the controller and the Braniff pilot, and in the event the airplane landed without incident. I took a deep breath, seeing pretty quickly how all of this was likely to turn out. I liked Pomeroy, even though I didn't subscribe to his brand of union activism, and I couldn't understand how any controller could have put on tape the kind of statements issued to Braniff 343. I knew, too, that Lester would use the incident to bring the hammer down hard, likely costing Pomeroy his job. Well, there was no help for it at this point. I called Lester to the playback room where we listened to the tape together, after which he said, with considerable venom, "I've got you, you son of a bitch!" Then he said, "Back the tape up to when Pomeroy first takes the position and play it till he gets relieved."

During the earlier portion of the playback there had been two or three other Braniff flights on the frequency, all receiving basically the same transmissions as those issued to flight 343. In those cases the pilots did not question Pomeroy's queries as to whether they were getting good service, and simply replied "Roger," or "Sure will" in response to the instruction to "Let vice president Brown know when you get back home." The pilots were not taken off the normal routing from WESTO and did not make any complaint either on the frequency or after landing. Still, at the very least Pomeroy was guilty of using the control frequency to push Braniff into resuming the jump seat program, and the handling of BI 343 could be interpreted as a warning that if the airline wanted safe handling, they had better start letting controllers into the cockpit again.

Within short order Pomeroy received a letter of proposed removal from government service, as was the standard first step in firing a civil service employee. It gave the respondent 30 days to provide a response showing why the proposed action should not be taken. The letter ignited a furor of protest throughout the facility as Pomeroy, with the backing of PATCO at all levels, fanned the flames by making impassioned public statements about the injustice of it all, emphasizing that none of it had to do with safety or misuse of his position as an air traffic controller. Rather, he said, it was a move by FAA management to rid themselves of a dedicated union advocate who had been a constant thorn in their side. At the end of the 30 days Pomeroy was fired, and PATCO swung into action.

An Ongoing Dispute

Locally, there was some pretty extreme fallout as union members donned black armbands and later began a "code of silence." They would not speak to anyone outside the union except when necessary for strictly operational reasons. At the end of one midnight shift a black stripe, representing the armbands, appeared around the base of the tower. One up-and-coming young controller, currently on a temporary detail to a supervisor position and clearly being groomed for a permanent promotion, walked into the chief's office, took off his necktie and laid it on the desk saying, "I do not support the action against Pomeroy, so take this job and shove it."

But the larger consequences occurred over a period lasting nearly a year as PATCO financed the cost of attorneys and other experts in a bid to win back Pomeroy's job and sent him around the country to address the union membership at individual facilities. It was a huge PR coup, tailor made for the union's purposes, as the theme "if it can happen to me it can happen to you" was hammered home at ever-increasing volume.

At length there was a hearing to determine whether Pomeroy should be reinstated. Both the union and the agency had an enormous amount of credibility on the line both because of the facts in the case and because of the publicity surrounding it. If PATCO won, the message would be that the managers of the air traffic service had no control over their employees, even in cases where safety was at stake. If the FAA won, the message would be that the union did not have the power to protect its members.

In most hearings involving adverse actions against employees, there was a board of FAA officials, the respondent, a union representative, an attorney and one or two witnesses. The hearings were open, but generally attracted no interest beyond that of the principals. In this case there were more than 200 attendees ranging from top agency personnel to airline representatives to rank-and-file PATCO members. Although I was unable to attend myself, I did get plenty of information after the fact as to how the proceedings had gone. The agency had attempted to persuade Braniff to allow the pilots of flight 343 to testify that they had in fact been issued a vector heading into dangerous weather, but the airline had refused, on the grounds that their flights would forever be penalized by controllers throughout the system in retaliation. There was a legalistic angle as well, in that the charge against Pomeroy had apparently contained the phrase that his actions "may have endangered" the aircraft.

It was a simple matter for the PATCO attorneys to argue that the FAA had not even asserted that there had been in danger, much less proved it. They made the point that the flight crew had not requested vectors around the weather, that the aircraft had never actually entered the storms, and that the flight had ultimately been completed safely. As an indicator of the lengths to which the union was prepared to go, they had hired a linguistics expert to define the etymology of the word "stuff." This was the word the flight crew had used in objecting to the 170 heading issued by Pomeroy. The point of this gambit was to show that there had never been any direct reference to weather or thunderstorms, and that the word "stuff" was too generic to be interpreted as referring to weather.

The FAA in its turn argued several points: That the weather cells were clearly shown on the approach control radar display; that regardless of the particulars in the communications exchanges, Pomeroy could easily see the weather conditions to the south of the aircraft's track; and that there had been no operational reason to vector BI 343 60 degrees off course, leaving only the conclusion that Pomeroy had issued the vector for the sole purpose of pressuring the airline into resuming the SF-160 program, and thereby abused his mandate to ensure the safety of an aircraft under his control.

Pomeroy testified on his own behalf, conducting himself, according to the account relayed to me, as the consummate professional. What the assembled witnesses observed was a competent, conservative air traffic controller, with none of the fiery union activist on display. He pointed out that vectors off course were a standard technique in orchestrating spacing for a lineup of arrival aircraft, and that he had informed the flight crew that the vector was for the purpose of spacing, as confirmed on the voice recording. He also stated, with a straight face, that he had heard the flight crew's transmission of "Oh great, that's right in the stuff" as "That's right ON the stuff" meaning that the pilots considered the new heading correct and satisfactory.

At no time, he said, had it been his intention to threaten or otherwise pressure the flight crew, and explained away his remarks about vice president Brown as a "friendly reminder" that controllers would like to resume riding the jump seat with Braniff as soon as possible. He did acknowledge that these non-operational comments were not formally authorized, but pointed out that such communications were generally accepted by pilots and the FAA alike, as long as they did not detract from the "safe, orderly, and expeditious" handling that was the air traffic control mandate. The long and short of it was that Pomeroy was reinstated, handing PATCO a huge win. This and other lesser events that turned out in the union's favor fueled the perception that they couldn't lose, no doubt contributing to the eventual decision to stage a strike.

In the aftermath of the Braniff incident, the atmosphere of tension and distrust in the facility abated somewhat, but talk of a strike did not. PATCO directly approached a number of staff people and supervisors about joining the walk-out, saying that any of us who worked traffic had as great a stake in forcing the FAA to improve working conditions as they did. They assured us that even though we were not union members, we would receive their full support if we joined the job action. We all demurred, or at least temporized, and in the event no non-union personnel participated.

Pomeroy was once again in fine fettle, riding high after his stunning comeback. My last direct interaction with him before the strike occurred when I had a class of controller trainees in the ETG room. We had just finished a round of exercises and were taking a break for lunch when Pomeroy appeared with an Air Florida pilot in tow. I had twice ridden the jump seat on flights where "Joe" was the captain, and knew him to be the best kind of pilot to work with from a controller's point of view. He had been an Air Force F-4 pilot in Vietnam, and unlike most combat veterans, was more than willing to talk about his experiences. I remembered those flights as two of the most interesting I ever took, also seeing by degrees how well Joe understood the ATC system and the demands on the controllers who made it work.

A Pilot at the Scope

Pomeroy had invited him to visit the facility, and asked him if he would like to try his hand at radar control in the simulation lab. Joe agreed, and he had time before his scheduled flight, which would depart later in the day. He took off his uniform jacket and "bellied up" to the scope we would use for the exercise. We decided on the slowest problem for North Approach Control on an east operation, as most of Air Florida's flights arrived from the north and were normally handled in much the same way as the simulated targets in the scenario we had selected.

There were only eight "aircraft" in the problem, evenly divided between LONNI and WESTO, the two arrival fixes for which north approach was responsible, with start times about two minutes apart for each pair at each of the fixes. LONNI was located about 40 miles northeast of the airport, meaning that those arrivals would be vectored to a left downwind, while the ones from WESTO would be vectored to a modified straight-in approach to runway 9 Left. We told Joe not to worry about prescribed phraseology or airspace allocations, which he could not be expected to know, but to concentrate exclusively on heading assignments and speed control. Throughout the exercise we coached him, advising him when to issue a descent clearance or suggesting speed reductions when they were needed. So it went something like this:

EA 419: "Miami Approach Eastern 419 coming up on WESTO, out of 12 for 10 with Bravo."

Joe: "Eastern 419 roger, expect runway 9 Left."

EA 419: "OK, 9 Left Eastern 419."

DL 641 (over LONNI): "Miami Approach Delta 641 with you, 16,000 with Bravo."

Joe (speaking hurriedly): "Delta 641 roger, reduce speed to 170, you are number two for 9 Left."

We were not in any way out to embarrass Joe, who was being a major good sport by agreeing to try on the unfamiliar role of controller in the first place. But he was working only two airplanes, presently about 60 miles apart, and this maximum speed reduction issued to Delta 641 was overkill in the extreme. I said, in as low key a manner as I could muster, "Okay, you are right that Delta is definitely going to follow Eastern, but you have over 60 miles of airspace to work with, so you don't really need to slow him down yet. Also, we usually try to keep the first few airplanes in a sequence moving along so that we don't have to start slowing the later arrivals quite as soon." Joe nodded, and the problem continued. As it progressed to the point where there was traffic both on the downwind and on final, we began suggesting where there was a gap that could be filled or where one could be closed up because there was no airplane in a position to fill it. As expected, Joe was late on some of his turns, with a few of the targets overshooting the final, and overall a pretty ragged looking sequence. But he never had a "collision" or a loss of separation, and the problem ended after about 25 minutes. We all applauded, saying that Joe had done a great job for someone who had never vectored a radar target in his life.

Joe stood up, shaking his head and smiling a rueful smile, saying, "You guys can have this job. I wouldn't do it for all the money in the world." As he stepped out of the darkened ETG room into the brighter light of the TRACON, we saw that his uniform shirt had pronounced sweat stains under both sleeves.

Pilot Familiarization?

Pomeroy and I both felt that the exercise with Joe represented an opportunity to pursue an initiative that could be helpful in defusing some of the contention between controllers and pilots. I approached my new boss, who had replaced Lester as the EPDO, describing the experience, saying that I believed having pilots take a turn in the controller's chair could have real value as a kind of corollary to the jump seat program for ATC types. I was expecting a pat on the back for the action of having reached out to a pilot and contributed to his understanding of air traffic control operations, but instead got a reaction that bordered on hostility.

Randy Lewis, now in charge of the training department, took the position that I had exceeded my authority by devoting facility resources to an activity that was nowhere formally authorized. I pointed out that it had occurred during a break period in the controller training syllabus, and had lasted only a short time. Randy was adamant, ordering me never to offer a similar opportunity to other pilots without first clearing it through him. I bit back my irritation, and suggested as calmly as I could, that the facility contact the major air carriers on the field and say that we would soon undertake a trial program whereby pilots could participate in simulated air traffic control exercises. Randy told me he would "get back" to me, and the matter was dropped for the time being. Some time later he called me into his office to inform me that no formal program of pilot familiarization in the sim lab would be undertaken, and that no informal version, as had happened with Joe, would be permitted. I was royally pissed at this point, and said so, pointing out the regularly occurring extended periods when we had no trainees during which the lab remained idle, a perfect time to accommodate pilot familiarization. He said that there was no way we could handle the large number of requests we were likely to get, and that if we limited participation there were sure to be complaints from pilot groups that were excluded. You had to love bureaucracy.

'Work-to-Rule' Actions

In the years before the strike, there were other strategies orchestrated by the union to put pressure on the FAA. PATCO called them "work-to-rule" actions, or, as the FAA saw them, "slow downs." Especially during busy periods, it was relatively easy to "stretch out" the length of the sequence on final approach, or allow a string of airplanes taxiing for departure to get longer and longer, in both cases disrupting flight schedules, causing increased fuel burns, and incurring complaints from the users. All it took at approach control was vectoring a critical three or four airplanes at the beginning of a "push" for standard instrument approach separation (three, four, or five miles on the same runway, two miles between aircraft on the parallels) instead of the more usual procedure of issuing visual approach clearances that did not require these minimums. Once the final was 15 or so miles long, it was not going to shorten up until the volume of arrivals decreased significantly. At Local Control, three or four missed "gaps" in which to launch the departures had much the same effect. If questioned, a controller could say that the pilot had not acknowledged an instruction, or one or two strategically issued go-arounds would delay the departure sequence and add another airplane to the approach control workload.

Noise abatement requirements also figured in the mix. When Miami's Wilcox Field was built in the 1930s, it was way out in the "boonies," far from any residential or commercially developed area. As the city grew, the airport became increasingly hemmed in on all sides. In my early years, we would get one or two phone calls a week from citizens lodging complaints that varied from "those airplanes keep my baby awake" to "my china is being shattered on the cupboard shelves." For the most part, a little sympathetic or diplomatic talk about these concerns, seasoned with some high-minded comments about our awesome responsibility for aircraft safety, assuaged the callers. But as the years passed, citizen groups banded together, filing lawsuits and putting political pressure on members of the Dade County Commission.

Restrictions on our operation proliferated, ranging from taking away some of the "fan" headings we used for initial separation on takeoff, to mandating or prohibiting the use of certain runways depending on the time of day. Most of us chafed under these growing limitations, especially when they followed a new housing development that was built right under our noses. Didn't people realize, we wondered, that if you bought a house right next to a busy airport you were going to hear aircraft noise? Although politics generally prevailed, there were at least two instances where Dade County and the FAA chalked up wins in the noise abatement disputes. In one case the Air Force had promulgated a public notice that supersonic flight operations would be conducted on a certain date. On the day following, like clockwork, there were a number of complaints alleging that the loud "booms" generated during supersonic flight had caused property damage, livestock loss, psychological trauma, etc., etc. The polite response to each caller was that the supersonic operations had never taken place, having been canceled due to weather. In another case, the citizens of a residential complex located directly off the end of one of the runways had gone to court, claiming, among other things, that their property values had dropped precipitously because of aircraft noise. The lawyers defending the action had researched the sales of homes in the complex going back a number of years, and were able to show that in fact real estate values had uniformly increased, rather than decreased, during the period covered by the suit.

We were certainly not above cutting a corner on noise abatement once in a while, especially when it could be justified in the name of safety or efficiency. But consistently observing these provisions was also pretty good cover when a slowdown was being conducted. One of the requirements at Fort Lauderdale was that jet aircraft, even those cleared for a visual approach, had to turn base west of the outer marker for runway 9 Left. The outer marker was a little over six miles from the runway threshold, resulting in a longer final than would be the case for a visual approach without the noise abatement restriction. One day when "work to rule" had been called for by the union, the man working approach control at Fort Lauderdale was definitely not getting with the program, instead allowing many of the jet arrivals to turn in early. Bob Mercer, the union rep who knew there was more than one way of accomplishing a union objective, did not confront the individual directly. Instead, during a break period, he picked up a pay phone in the passenger area of the terminal and dialed the Miami Tower number. When the supervisor answered, Bob assumed the truculent manner of a resident living in the area that the noise abatement regulation was designed to protect. Without identifying himself, he launched into the following screed:

"This is Herbie Schwartz, councilman on the Fort Lauderdale city commission. I live west of the airport, and your airplanes keep flying over my house. Now, I am familiar with your noise abatement procedures, and you are violating them. If one more airplane flies over my property, my next call will be to my attorney, instructing him to sue your asses! Good-bye!"

The supervisor immediately went to the Fort Lauderdale Approach position and instructed the controller to abide by the noise abatement procedures, having been made an unwitting accomplice in the slowdown action.

Eventually the noise problem became so acute that the FAA went to the Dade County Aviation Department (DCAD), basically saying, "Look, it is your airport, and you set the noise abatement standards, so we are going to refer noise complaints to you." The county ended up establishing a dedicated office to handle the complaints. From time to time county officials would approach Miami Tower, proposing additional restrictions in terms of hours of operation, runway use, or initial headings after takeoff. In most cases we were able to make the case that if a suggested change went into effect, delays would balloon, and the airlines would not stand for it. Even later, the county set up noise sensors around the field supposedly set to detect decibel levels proving that an aircraft was not following the mandated noise abatement routing.

As might be expected, the most stringent restrictions applied between 11:00 pm and 6:00 am, a period when traffic was generally light and the resulting delays would be minimal. We developed specific noise abatement Standard Instrument Departures (SIDs) for the midnight period that would confine departure routings to the least noise sensitive areas. (NOTE: This happened late in my career, and I had had a hand in developing the SIDs. As a result, some strings were pulled, and one of the SIDs was named for me. As of this writing, the "POTTR 6 Departure" still exists, and contains the fix "POTTR" located in the middle of Biscayne Bay, just south of the Julia Tuttle Causeway).

Avoiding Delays

One of the common misconceptions among pilots is that controllers delay airplanes unnecessarily. Nothing could be further from the truth. Delays compound every element of difficulty in the air traffic controller's job, from lengthening busy periods to increasing the number of coordination calls to more smeared transmissions as pilots attempt to talk over each other or "chip" at the controller looking for more information on the delays. To a man, we hated to hit the override button to Local Control to stop departures or tell the center to start putting arrivals in a holding pattern, and we did our best to avoid being assigned Gate Hold where, even though the airplanes were not moving, it was a never-ending wrestling match on the frequency. The truth is that we at times overextended ourselves in order to "keep 'em moving."

Nevertheless, delays were part of the game, and were an important metric by which both the airlines and the air traffic system were rated. At MIA, where the weather was good most of the time, we seldom encountered conditions where we had to limit traffic. It could happen if we had an unexpected runway closure or if one of our main runways was shut down for construction, but the more usual case involved severe weather at the northern airports. When capacity at those facilities was reduced, the delays fed back through each center sector to each approach control and ultimately to the ground operation that set the flights in motion.

Each ATC facility was required to log and report delays exceeding 30 minutes with an explanation of the cause. In some instances, all flights could be subject to the delay, as in the case of a closed runway or local restrictions based on severe weather. In others, such as weather conditions in center airspace affecting a particular departure route, or an in-trail restriction for a certain airport, only the flights on that route or with that destination would be affected.

For the airlines, which were periodically ranked according to their delay history, any time a flight did not make its scheduled departure or arrival time, the minutes behind schedule were assigned to one or another of the various departments within the company—dispatch, maintenance, catering, crew scheduling, or ground crew, to name a few. Of course, none of these entities wanted to be the one to "eat" the delay, and one of the favorite dodges was to categorize a failure to meet schedule as an "ATC delay." This could certainly be a valid claim in the case of major flow restrictions or bad weather, but there were also times when it could go like this:

Pilot (of a flight already late): "Ground Northwest 119 ready for pushback at Golf 19."

Ground Control: "Northwest 119, hold for a Boeing 727 passing right to left behind you. When he is clear, pushback approved."

Pilot: "OK, hold for the 727, then push, Northwest 119."

Although it would take only a few seconds till the conflicting traffic was no longer a factor, the airline could ascribe the 10 or 15 minutes by which they had failed to make schedule to air traffic control.

Sometimes Miami Center would require us to check for release on individual flights with certain destinations. The process began with a call from either Flight Data or Gate Hold to the center. The release request would be passed to the command center, or Central Flow as it was originally known, and finally to the center that had originated the restriction. Then the communication exchange would occur in reverse, and we would release the airplane. Billy Pierce, my longtime friend and sometime supervisor, created a tongue-in-cheek document, spoofing the whole flow control process, entitled "Who's to Blame?" This is how I remember it:

"When New York Center doesn't get their requested 20 miles in trail between two airplanes, they blame Washington Center.

Washington Center blames Jacksonville Center.

Jacksonville Center blames Miami Center

Miami Center blames Departure Control for handing them off too close together.

Departure Control blames Local Control for launching them too close together.

Local Control blames Ground Control for taxiing them nose to tail.

Ground Control blames Gate Hold for releasing them.

Gate Hold blames Miami Center for granting the release.

Miami Center blames Central Flow for saying they could go.

Central flow blames New York Center for saying they could take them.

So it appears that if there is a flow control problem in New York Center's airspace, it is their own damn fault!"

Miscues Over the Years

One of the more whimsical characterizations of the air traffic controller's job describes it as "the timely correction of previously made errors." Like any cynical/ humorous observation, this one does contain a kernel of truth, and goes right to the heart of the monitoring element of controller tasking. Some cases do, in fact, involve outright errors, as for example when a controller uses an incorrect flight number or says "turn right" when he meant to say "turn left." Others are not truly errors, but occur because of the dynamic, ever-evolving "picture" that the controller is creating and constantly evaluating. One such instance in which I was personally involved went like this:

I had recently checked out on Miami South Departure Control, the position also responsible for the radar operation at Homestead Air Force Base. I was assigned the position on a nasty weather day. We did not yet have the ARTS automation system, meaning that the transponder returns for all the aircraft appeared as identical double slashes. My handoff man was Evan Gianetti, a veteran controller who had worked at Newark before reporting to Miami. A flight of four F-4s returned from a training exercise, and as commonly occurred, requested to break up into individual elements. While in formation, only the flight leader activated his transponder, but after the break up each pilot was supposed to "squawk" the appropriate code. Unfortunately, the transponder on one of the fighters was inoperative, and as a primary target the aircraft generated only a pinpoint image on the radar display. The heaviest weather returns appeared directly over Homestead, and stretched away to the southwest, the very area where the pilots would fly the approach to Runway 5.

The first three aircraft were successfully handed off to GCA, but the primary target of the fourth was totally obscured by the weather as the pilot continued on the last assigned heading of 230, taking him further and further from the airport on downwind.

This was the exchange between me, the pilot of Angel 44, and Evan:

Me: "Angel 44, radar contact lost, say your position."

Angel 44: "I'm 20 DME southwest of Homestead, and getting further. How about a turn back to the field."

Me: "Angel 44, unable to issue radar vectors, stand by one." (To Evan: "Hey, see if GCA has radar contact with Angel 44, I've lost him." Evan shook his head in the negative.)

Angel 44: "Approach, Angel 44 cancelling IFR, we are turning inbound."

Me: "Angel 44, roger."

After landing, the pilot telephoned the facility to inquire about the handling of his flight, and so it was necessary to play back the tapes of both the radar position (me) and the handoff position (Evan). Because the event concluded without mishap, we were able to laugh at what we heard as we compared my transmissions with Evan's on the landline.

Me (1821:57): "Angel 44 radar contact lost, say your position."

Angel 44 (1822:00) "I'm 20 southwest of Homestead and getting further."

Evan on landline (1821:59): "GCA Miami, do you have radar on Angel 44?"

GCA (1822:00): "Negative Miami, where is he?"

Evan (1822:03): "He's right over Homestead."

So within three seconds the pilot reported 20 miles from the airport as Evan reported him right over the airport.

A Flying Tiger

Another incident was remarkable for the extreme improbability of its ever having occurred. Like many other cases, this one involved an unlikely combination of circumstances, the absence of any one of which would have prevented the error. The cargo carrier Airlift International originally used the call sign "Tiger" because the company had been founded by ex-military pilots who, during World War II, were known as the "Flying Tigers." They operated from the southwest ramp, adjacent to Runway 9 Right, and normally used that runway for both departure and arrival. One evening a Tiger DC-8, Tiger 644, taxied for departure at Miami and later called for takeoff clearance. For reasons that never became clear, the pilot was transmitting on the local control frequency of Opa-locka airport.

Grumman Aircraft had a line of single engine GA aircraft that were designated with the names of large felines, Cheetah and Tiger being examples, and it so happened that a Grumman Tiger had taxied to 9 Right at Opa-locka a few minutes earlier. The local controller at OPF (Opa-locka) received a call triggering the following exchange:

Tiger 644: "Tower Tiger 644 ready go 9 Right."

OPF Local Controller, believing that the call had come from the small Grumman aircraft: "Tiger 644 runway 9 Right cleared for takeoff."

The Miami Tower controller observed the DC-8 taxi onto the runway, and began calling the flight crew without receiving a response, eventually aiming the red light of the light gun at the cockpit windows to stop the aircraft. About that time, OPF received another request for takeoff:

(Grumman) Tiger 764: "Tower, Tiger 764 ready at 9 Right."

There followed a confused question and answer period, and eventually the snafu was unscrambled, fortunately without any problems.

A different kind of "non-standard" event was relayed to me by Rob Halliburton, a controller who had worked at Opa-locka for several years before reporting to Miami. During at least one year during this period, OPF ran a traffic count higher than Chicago O'Hare's, consisting largely of student training operations conducted by the several flight schools on the field. OPF was a 16-hour facility, meaning that the tower opened at 7:00 am and closed at 11:00 pm. The problem was that the training operations began at first light, sometimes as much as an hour before the tower was manned, so that by the time the tower opened, both the north side and south side traffic patterns were full of touch and go traffic. It was standard procedure, at seven o'clock, for the first transmission at Local Control to be, "Attention all aircraft, the tower is now open. All pilots make a full stop landing and contact ground control for taxi." In this way the controller could build the sequence from scratch instead of having to face the impossible task of identifying all the visually identical Cessnas in two busy traffic patterns.

Rob was a pilot who owned his own airplane, based at nearby North Perry airport (HWO). He also lived in close proximity to the field. Although HWO was only about four miles from OPF, the trip by car between six and seven o'clock, in the middle of rush hour, could take 45 or 50 minutes. By airplane, it took only five or six minutes, and Rob began using his tail dragger Cessna 170 for the commute. One morning Rob was waiting anxiously at the flight line for a colleague who would accompany him on the flight as the minutes before 7:00 am ticked down. The other man was late, eventually arriving at about 6:55. They boarded the Cessna and took off immediately, but as they approached OPF, the clock struck seven, and the tower frequency erupted in a cacophony of calls from pilots in the touch and go patterns, all asking, basically, "Hey tower, are you there?"

This was very bad news, in several ways. Rob and the other guy could be in big trouble for failing to open the tower on schedule. If there were an accident involving traffic in the pattern even one minute after the tower was supposed to open, there would be hell to pay. Rob keyed up the airplane radio and transmitted, "All pilots make a full stop landing and contact ground control for taxi," then headed straight for the runway. Another pilot transmitted, "Tower I just had a tail-dragger Cessna cut me out on final!" Rob replied, "Okay, we'll take care of him."

Rob taxied to the base of the tower, shut down the engine but left the battery on, and told his colleague to start working ground control. The other man stretched the microphone cord out the airplane window and began issuing taxi instructions to pilots as they cleared the runway, while Rob double-timed up the tower stairs to open the tower. Apparently none of the pilots ever realized that the tower had not opened on schedule, and the event passed into history.

Landing at the Wrong Airport

There was a whole category of miscues under the heading "landed (or almost landed) wrong airport." One such case involved a flight from Palm Beach with a planned destination of Miami that instead ended up at Fort Lauderdale. Once again a series of omissions by both the controller and the flight crew contributed to the outcome. Arrivals handed off from Miami Center were assigned different altitudes depending on the destination. This provided an immediate indicator to the approach controller, apart from the ARTS tag that showed any destination other than Miami. By contrast, tower en route aircraft were assigned a single altitude regardless of the airport of intended landing, again displaying the destination information for a satellite airport, but presenting a blank destination field for Miami traffic. As Delta 729 came across the Palm Beach boundary, the following exchange began:

DL 729: "Miami approach Delta 729 with you, level six thousand, with information Hotel."

(Hotel was the ATIS code for Miami. The ARTS tag contained no destination information).

Controller: "Delta 729 Miami approach, expect visual approach runway 9 Left."

(Both Miami and Fort Lauderdale had a main runway designated as 9 Left).

Controller: "Delta 729, turn right heading 270, vector to downwind."

(With Fort Lauderdale located some 20 miles north of Miami, the flight crew should have realized that the turn to downwind was much too early, but did not question it).

Controller: "Delta 729 descend and maintain three thousand, report the airport in sight."

DL 729: "OK, down to three, and we've got the field, Delta 729."

Controller: "Delta 729, keep your base leg west of the outer marker. Cleared visual approach runway 9 Left, contact the tower 119.3."

(The controller did not say "Fort Lauderdale tower," and the flight crew did not recognize that 119.3 was the FLL frequency, not Miami's).

At some point the flight crew had to have recognized that they were on approach to Fort Lauderdale, but never alerted either the approach controller or the FLL tower controller that they were headed for the wrong airport. Soon after landing, the crew did advise FLL that they were bound for Miami, and in due course took off again for the short hop to MIA.

Although it initially seemed that this was a case of "all's well that ends well," a couple of days later the airline called the tower demanding an explanation as to why their flight had been vectored to the wrong airport. The controller was duly chastised for his part in the matter, but the flight crew was also disciplined—not, apparently, for never advising the controllers of their destination, but for taking off from FLL without a proper dispatch! Go figure.

There were a number of "almosts" involving aircraft being vectored to the wrong airport, eventually resulting in a sufficient number of such incidents that the ARTS system was re-programmed to display MIA in the destination field. This change reduced the number of controller errors, but did nothing to assist flight crews who mistook a nearby airport (or in several cases a highway) for their intended destination.

Mistaken Runways

Two incidents involving air carrier landings at the wrong airport occurred under very similar circumstances. To begin with, all the South Florida airports had at least one and sometimes two east/west main runways, designated 9 or 9 Left and 9 Right, plus an additional runway oriented southeast/northwest, designated as Runway 12 or 13. Both landings occurred at night, and both flight crews had been cleared for a visual approach. In the first instance, a Northwest 727 was being vectored from the northwest to runway 9 Left at Fort Lauderdale. The controller had instructed the crew to expect a visual approach, and as the aircraft approached the airport transmitted, "Northwest 474, report Fort Lauderdale in sight, now at ten o'clock and twelve miles." The pilot responded, "Field in sight," and received approach clearance. The track of the 727 would take it past Fort Lauderdale Executive Airport, located six miles north of FLL, and in hindsight it was apparent that the crew mistook the lighted east/ west runway at FXE for 9 Left at FLL. Whether they failed to make contact with the FLL controller, or did make contact and received a routine landing clearance, they did not recognize their error until after they landed.

It was very fortunate that there was no damage to the aircraft nor any injury to personnel, as the runway at FXE, at that time, was something under 5,000 feet long, less than half the length of 9 Left at FLL. The flight crew had barely managed to bring the aircraft to a stop before running off the end. Additionally, FXE was not yet a 24-hour facility so that the tower was unmanned. Because the aircraft could not legally use the short runway, the passengers were bused to FLL, while it took several days for fuel, seats, galley equipment, and other items to be removed from the aircraft to make it light enough for takeoff.

In another case, a United 727 was being vectored to 9 Left at Miami, from the northwest, with an initial exchange and eventual approach clearance issued under circumstances nearly identical to those involving the Northwest flight. The similarities in the two incidents did not end there, as Opa-locka airport, located about six miles north of MIA, with its Runway 9 Left lighted, could easily be mistaken for Miami, in the same way that FXE had been mistaken for FLL. Although a replay of the approach control tapes revealed that the flight crew had acknowledged the approach clearance and the instruction to contact Miami Tower, no call to the tower occurred. When the local controller did not receive a call, then observed the radar target on the tower BRITE display tracking towards OPF, the following exchanges occurred:

Miami Local Control: "United 312 Miami Tower, are you with me? (No response) "United 312, how do you hear me? (No response) "United 312, if you hear Miami Tower squawk ident" (No response either via radio or ident).

Local Control (on override to the approach controller): "Are you still working United 312?"

Approach Controller: "Negative. Why?"

Local Control: "Well call him, for Christ's sake, he's headed for Opa-locka."

The approach controller made several attempts to establish communication with no response.

Local Control (on override to OPF): "Opa-locka, Miami."

OPF: "Opa-locka."

Local Control: "Opa-locka, you've got a United 727 headed for your airport, supposed to be landing Miami, and we're not talking to him. Try calling him, his call sign is United 312."

The Opa-locka controller tried several times to reach the flight crew, without success. In a last ditch effort to prevent the landing, he flipped the switch controlling the runway lights off and on about a dozen times. After the flight landed, the crew contacted Miami Ground Control:

UA 312: "Miami ground, United 312 with you."

MIA Ground: "United 312, contact Opa-locka ground control 121.7."

This was a major black eye for the airline, as it was clear in the aftermath that personnel at both Miami and Opa-locka had done everything possible to prevent the incident. We later learned that the 727 had been carrying a Miami Center controller in the jump seat who at one point apparently said to the flight crew, "I think that's Opa-locka." Allegedly, the crew responded, "No, no, it's Miami, look, your buddies in the tower are flashing the runway lights to welcome us."

Regardless of the particular circumstances in any given instance, when an aircraft landed at the wrong airport, ATC was inevitably cited as being at least partially responsible. Eventually the agency added required phraseology to the handbook covering situations where a controller issued a visual approach to an airport with another in close proximity, alerting the pilot to the location of the other field.

At MIA we had perhaps half a dozen instances where a pilot mistook State Road 836, a major east-west expressway, for Runway 9 Right. The expressway was located less than a quarter mile south of 9 Right, oriented east and west, as was the runway. The lights were not typical of highway lighting, being mounted on tall poles and casting subdued illumination on the roadway. The effect was similar enough to the runway lights themselves that a number of "low approaches" occurred.

Although any error misidentifying an airport, even if no landing occurred, was cause for concern, there was one incident, as replayed on the tapes, that left us laughing. A Southwest 737 was on a wide left downwind for 9 Left at Fort Lauderdale, far enough north that both FLL and FXE were to its left. The approach controller issued a turn to base leg, after which the following exchanges occurred:

FLL Approach: "Southwest 1261, the airport is at 10 o'clock ten miles, report it in sight."

SWA 1261: "Field in sight, Southwest 1261."

FLL Approach: "Southwest 1261 cleared visual approach runway 9 Left, contact Fort Lauderdale tower 119.3."

The communications resumed:

SWA 1261: "Fort Lauderdale tower, Southwest 1261 with you for 9 Left."

FLL Tower: "Southwest 1261 Fort Lauderdale tower cleared to land Runway 9 Left."

The approach controller had not issued the advisory alerting the flight crew to the location of FXE, apparently believing that step to be unnecessary since the aircraft had already crossed the final approach course to FXE's main runway. But in hindsight it may have been a critical omission. Despite having reported FLL sight at 10 o'clock, requiring a turn of only 30 to 40 degrees, the crew made a hard turn of more than 90 degrees and lined up for runway 8 at FXE. In the process, the 737 instantly created a looming conflict with a slow-moving single engine Cessna only two or three miles ahead. The local controller at FXE saw what was happening and quickly called Fort Lauderdale on the override line:

FXE: "Lauderdale, Exec, are you working that 737? If you are, send him around, he is about to run over a Cessna."

FLL (without responding to FXE): "Southwest 1261, go around, I say again, go around, you are on final at Fort Lauderdale Executive airport and you have Cessna traffic at 12 o'clock and a mile."

The pilot executed the go around, and in due course was instructed to re-contact Miami Approach Control. The approach control position was now being worked by Ralph, a New Yorker who had earned his stripes in the New York TRACON, responsible for Kennedy, La Guardia, and Newark airports. He had the recognizable deadpan imperturbability, and definitely the accent, associated with his origins, making the replay of the ensuing exchange all the more amusing. The Southwest flight crew had not yet recognized their error, and the tone of their communications was initially nothing short of peremptory:

SWA 1261: "Miami approach, Southwest 1261 back with you. Just what was the problem? The tower sent us around and said something about traffic at Executive. What did that have to do with us?"

Ralph (slowly and laconically): "Southwest 1261 YOU were the traffic at Executive."

At this the transmissions instantly changed character as the crew apologized for the mistake, and in the replay room, those of us listening practically fell out of our chairs.

Early in my career there was an "almost" that occurred, again involving Miami and Opa-locka, but that more significantly, from my point of view, demonstrated the subtle ways in which both controllers and pilots could keep the tapes "clean" while correcting a mistake. An Eastern DC-8 was on right downwind for Runway 27 Right after being cleared for a visual approach. This put the aircraft equidistant between MIA to its right and OPF to its left. As the aircraft began its turn to base leg, which should have been to the right, the approach controller observed the radar target swinging left. Two short transmissions instantly corrected the error:

MIA Approach: "Eastern 111, you own some property up there by Opa-locka?"

EA 111: "No, sure don't."

The next radar sweep showed the aircraft in a right turn back towards MIA.

11. PATCO Takes Action

No one in the air traffic control profession or flying as a commercial pilot in the early 1980s will ever forget August 3, 1981, and the months (and years) that followed. PATCO had tried to keep its intentions about a possible strike secret, but with something approaching 16,000 members nationwide, the word always managed to get out. One strike deadline came and went with barely a ripple, but toward the end of July the writing on the wall seemed ominously clear. Air traffic controllers across the country would walk off the job at 7:00 am Sunday morning.

Miami Tower management had published two work schedules, one reflecting the normal team alignments and sequence of shift rotations, the other a contingency plan in case the strike occurred. In my capacity as a permanent staff member, I would normally report to the tower at 8:00 am for the prescribed eight and a half hour administrative work day. But if the strike did occur, the contingency plan showed me assigned to the 3:00 to 11:00 shift in the TRACON.

So, at 6:45 that morning, I tuned in one of the local news channels and watched as seven o'clock approached. At 6:59 there was a commercial break, then the newscaster reappeared, opening the next segment of the broadcast, and beginning with the words, "As of this hour the nation's air traffic controllers are on strike." I felt a distinct sinking sensation as I tried to imagine what the ramifications of this momentous event might be, but at least I would have the morning and early afternoon to follow the TV coverage that would certainly occur, and to gauge just how extensive the job action was. I was not disappointed. Throughout the day, every channel presented coverage of all the major terminals and the en route centers. Every one of them had large numbers of controllers wearing "PATCO on strike" signs and marching back in forth in front of the entrances to the facilities.

MIA was not excluded. I saw friends and long-time colleagues doing their part, with the "Wilcox Field" sign on the terminal building plainly visible. Occasionally the camera would zoom in on one of the station's reporters with a microphone in his hand, asking one of the strikers for comments on the strike. Most of the comments were various versions of: "The FAA is putting the flying public at risk by allowing the airlines to fly without the professionals at the control positions." Then the scene would cut to an FAA spokesman who would be asked whether safety was being compromised. Those replies generally went like this: "System and airport capacity have been significantly reduced and separation standards increased so that safety can be assured during this illegal job action by the controllers' union."

There were a couple of short clips showing exchanges that were substantially more "direct" than these generic pronouncements. One of them occurred when Drew Lewis, the secretary of transportation in the Reagan administration, was accosted by an army of reporters all clamoring for a quote. One of them thrust a microphone into Lewis's face and aggressively demanded, "Mr. Secretary, PATCO claims that it is only a matter of time before a disastrous mid-air collision occurs. What is your response?"

Without breaking stride or in any way pushing back, Lewis calmly replied, "My response is that every mid-air collision we have ever had occurred when those guys were working." Another short take occurred outside the gates of Washington Center after a shift change, as a line of cars slowly made its way through the exit to a stop light at the main highway. One driver had his side window open, and a reporter lost no time leaning in with his microphone, urgently demanding, "Sir, PATCO claims that there is utter chaos in Washington Center because of short staffing and high traffic loads. Please give us a statement as to the conditions in the facility today." With studied cool, from behind a pair of aviator sun glasses, the man replied, "F… you Jack, it's Miller time." Although it was "bleeped" out, there could be no doubt as to the sentiment conveyed.

As 3:00 approached, I drove into the employees' parking lot and boarded the bus to the terminal. I was wondering what kind of a reception I would get as I walked through the phalanx of strikers at the terminal doors. As it turned out, most of them greeted me in a normal manner, understanding that I could not be part of the strike and would probably be summarily fired if I didn't show up for work for any reason. A few scowled or muttered unintelligibly, but none challenged me directly.

Predictably, that first day was somewhat chaotic as all air traffic control facilities tried to assess their capabilities and institute appropriate restrictions to match those capabilities. But in the TRACON, aside from long periods between breaks, traffic volume was actually low, making for a surprisingly easy work day. Likewise, in the tower the local controller was having an easy time of it. But ground control was a different story. With differing restrictions at different destinations and on different routes of flight, it was a major struggle to line up the affected groups on taxiways in a way that would not hamper normal movements to and from the parking gates and yet allow the departure restrictions to be met efficiently. Over all, with adrenaline running high, our small group of supervisors and staffers running the operation experienced a considerable degree of satisfaction in the job we did.

President Reagan addressed the nation, calling on the controllers to report for work within 24 hours or face dismissal from federal service. Later, the deadline was extended to the first shift for which an individual was scheduled after the initial deadline. Initially, PATCO hailed this as a concession that the strike was succeeding, and urged its members to hold fast. But the real effect was to divide the ranks of the strikers, thereby eroding the solidarity upon which the union was counting. Depending on scheduled days off, an individual might have as little as 24 hours, or, in other cases, as much as two and half days to return to work.

At MIA a few men did beat the deadline and were able to protect their jobs, but for the first few days they had to run the gauntlet as they entered the terminal, enduring a torrent of abuse from the die-hards still on the picket line. There were some threats, and a few cars were vandalized, prompting the facility to make an agreement with the airport authority allowing us to park at the mid-field fire station. Each day we would line up behind a radio equipped fire truck and follow it to the parking area, then ride a bus to the back of the terminal building, in this way securing the cars and avoiding any potential confrontations.

The PATCO members who had crossed the picket line were understandably worried. The concern was that if the strike succeeded and the strikers returned to work, the "scabs," as the union considered them, would forever be blackballed by their colleagues and never be accepted as co-equals. But as the days went by, the numbers demonstrating in front of the terminal thinned out, and the FAA began issuing letters of proposed removal from federal service. Each recipient of such a letter had 30 days to provide a response as to why the removal should not be carried out. Some produced letters from medical professionals purporting to show that an illness or other condition had made them unfit for duty. Others alleged that they had been "off the grid," hiking in the wilderness, or on a small boat at sea without communications and did not know of the strike or the president's deadline. Still others claimed extreme peer pressure backed up by threats, intimidation, or direct physical harassment. A few chose not to respond at all, preferring to wait for the final administrative step of a Merit System Protection Board (MSPB) hearing where a determination would be made to either terminate or retain the employee.

There were a couple of memorable cases at MIA. Roger Pomeroy, ever the showman, appeared at the facility to contest his proposed removal dressed in a tuxedo, wearing a ten-gallon hat, and smoking a large stogie. Another man, known as "the Fonz," thought he had outfoxed the agency by having an unlisted number, enabling him to claim that he did not know about the strike. But in a stroke of bad luck (for him) the facility received a call from a hospital, apparently inquiring about some aspect of the Fonz's federal health insurance. The deputy chief who took the call told the hospital he would contact the Fonz if their medical records could provide a valid phone number. The long and short of it was that contact was made, and any potential claim about ignorance of the strike would not hold up.

Although our esprit de corps was strong, as it apparently was at other facilities operating with basic skeleton crews, it was obvious that the system could not keep operating long-term without some additional personnel. For us at Miami, and many other places hard hit by the walkout, the solution was the temporary assignment of military air traffic controllers. These people were experienced in both radar and tower control and required minimal training to achieve certification. Soldiers, sailors, airmen and marines, representing all the services, by degrees increased our staffing. There is no doubt that they were a critical factor in keeping the Miami operation, and many others, safe and effective. (There are other views, depending on the facility, as to the relative importance of the military, those who chose not to strike, or those who returned before the deadline, in maintaining the system. A book entitled "Spinning at the Boundary," by David Larsen, is an excellent complement to this writing. Dave was a controller at Toledo when the strike occurred and later became a friend and colleague at MIA. At Toledo, he and others who did not go on strike made the critical difference).

The Aftermath

In the immediate aftermath of the PATCO strike, we were scheduled for mandatory six-day work weeks, resulting in a paycheck representing 13 workdays per two-week pay period, instead of the normal ten. We welcomed the extra income, but week after week the schedule became pretty grueling.

As the influx of military personnel and new hires began to augment our numbers, we old hands were more and more in the position of OJT instructors. As described earlier, training on a control position imposed a considerable additional demand on the instructor, with the compounding disadvantage that our own proficiency suffered through a lack of individual "stick time." But there were compensations, one of which was an attitude of cooperation on the part of the pilots, who were well aware of the effort to restore the system to some semblance of normality. Three examples from my own experience during the post-strike operation:

I was working the North High Departure position with several aircraft on the frequency. An Eastern pilot, unlike the majority of others during this period, was "chipping" at me over seemingly inconsequential things, when another pilot stepped in:

Me: "Eastern 739, turn left heading 360."

EA 739: "How about 340?"

Me: "Negative, fly heading 360, I will have a turn to the northwest for you in five miles."

EA 739: "Well you know, every mile you take us out of our way costs us money."

Me: "Eastern 739, roger."

EA 739: "How about higher?"

Me: "Eastern 739 maintain 7,000, expect higher in eight miles."

EA 739: "Well you know, every mile at low altitude costs us additional fuel."

Me: "Eastern 739, roger."

EA 739: "Ok, so we don't get the heading we want, or the altitude we want. This is pretty poor service."

Anonymous Pilot: "Eastern, why don't you just shut up and let that man do his job!"

In another case, I was working the Miami North Approach position on an east operation. Two aircraft were inbound from WESTO, the arrival fix some 32 miles northwest of MIA. The lead aircraft was a Northwest 727, followed by a Southern Airways DC-9, both of which would park at gates on the south side of the airport, and would be vectored for a straight-in approach to Runway 12. The arrival altitude at WESTO was 10,000 feet, so that a timely descent was necessary in order to reach 3,000 feet at approximately ten miles from the runway threshold. It went like this:

NW 441: "Miami approach Northwest 441 with you at 10,000 with Bravo."

Me: "Northwest 441 Miami approach roger, expect a visual approach Runway 12. Fly heading 130, descend and maintain 3,000, report the airport in sight."

NW 441: "OK, 130, down to three, for Runway 12, Northwest 441."

SO 311: "Miami, Southern 311 with you, leveling at ten with Bravo."

Me: "Southern 311 Miami approach roger, expect a visual approach Runway 12, descend and maintain 3,000, report the airport in sight."

SO 311: "Southern 311, cleared to 3,000, expecting Runway 12."

The calls from the Northwest and Southern pilots had come about three minutes apart, with about 10 miles between the two aircraft. Shortly after my instructions to SO 311, I observed the altitude field on the aircraft's identification tag unwinding from 10,000, but the Northwest flight was still at 10,000 and was approaching a point 20 miles from the field. Although a jet aircraft could descend very steeply when necessary, a normal descent would have put Northwest 441 at about 6,000 feet at this point in his approach. I nudged the Northwest pilot:

Me: "Northwest 441, you are two zero miles from the airport, and I show you still at 10,000. Have you started your descent yet?"

NW 441: "Negative Miami, but we'll start down now."

A couple of minutes later, as the aircraft reached the 10-mile mark with the altitude indicating 6,000 feet, twice as high as it should have been, the following exchanges occurred:

NW 441: "Northwest 441, we have the field in sight, but we're way too high. This is a piss-poor approach."

Me: "Well, can you make it down from there, or do you need a 360 to lose some altitude?"

NW 441: "Oh, we'll shoehorn it in okay, but this whole procedure is just very poor."

Me (biting my tongue to refrain from telling the pilot that if he hadn't stayed at 10,000 for 12 miles, he would have been right where he should have been): "Northwest 441, cleared visual approach Runway 12, contact Miami Tower 118.3."

As soon as Northwest acknowledged the frequency change, the pilot of Southern 311, who was just crossing the 20-mile range mark at 6,000 transmitted:

"Approach, don't listen to that guy. There is nothing wrong with this approach. He just screwed up and didn't take his descent clearance when you gave it to him. You are doing a great job, and we appreciate it."

A Close Call

Sometime in mid-October, with staffing still pretty short, the airport was on a west operation during a very busy period. My assignment was the South Approach Control Feeder position, meaning that I would take handoffs from the center, line the aircraft up on downwind for Runway 30, and then hand them off to the Final controller who would sequence them on the final approach course. The Final controller was Rick, a supervisor known for his exacting expectations of anyone and everyone working any control position. Knowing that Rick would be quick to criticize any actions on my part that he considered less than ideal, I was very strictly minding my p's and q's.

We were both "bellied up" and focused on our traffic as I handed off a Delta L-1011, heading 120 on a left downwind to maintain a five-mile offset from the Runway 30 final. Rick took the handoff, and I issued a frequency change. There was a weather cell angling in from the west, and after a couple of minutes I heard Rick transmit in an urgent voice, "Delta 46 heavy, am I talking to you?" To be certain (and praying) that the L-1011 had changed to Rick's frequency, I issued it again, receiving no response. I also observed that because of the weather cell, DL 46 had deviated to the left, putting the aircraft very close to the opposite direction traffic already inbound on the final. Rick immediately began issuing vectors to the pilot to resolve the impending conflict, and in the event, the aircraft made the approach and landing without incident. But the fact remained that separation had been lost between the Delta flight and an Air Jamaica 727 as they passed abeam one another.

Rick and I were both relieved from our positions and taken to the maintenance space where recordings of both our positions were played back. Rick was looking daggers at me, apparently sure that I had done something wrong and that he had saved the day, but the tapes showed otherwise. It went like this:

Me: "Delta 46 heavy, contact the Miami final controller on 125.0."

DL 46: "Going to 125.0, Delta 46 heavy, so long."

The moment of truth was approaching, as the playback of Rick's position began. Did the Delta pilot take the frequency change and establish contact immediately? I felt a wave of relief as the time track showed that in fact, only a few seconds after I had issued the new frequency, the following exchanges occurred:

DL 46: "Miami final, Delta 46 heavy with you, out of five for four [thousand feet]."

Rick did not acknowledge the call, and about two minutes elapsed before he apparently noticed that the aircraft had deviated left of course and issued the urgent, "Delta 46 heavy, am I talking to you?" Although it was clear that my actions had been correct, I was doing my best to maintain a neutral expression. Nobody wants to see another controller get into a bind. Rick's expression did not change. He stormed out of the room without saying a word to me.

But it was not the last word on the incident. About six weeks later I scheduled a fam trip with Delta from Fort Lauderdale to Philadelphia. My return flight would land at Miami, so I was hoping to get a ride to

FLL after a day shift, leaving my car in the employee parking lot at MIA. As it happened, Rick, who lived near the airport in Fort Lauderdale, was assigned the same shift, and agreed to give me a ride. The incident with the L-1011 was not mentioned, and we spent a friendly 45 minutes or so in the car discussing in general terms the strike and its aftermath.

As I entered the cockpit of the aircraft, I introduced myself in the usual way and received a cordial welcome from the flight crew. The airplane was an L-1011, and the crew was a communicative group, asking how things were going at Miami and elsewhere, and expressing various statements of support for the controllers who were holding the ATC system together. As we leveled off at cruise altitude, Captain Fisher turned in his seat, saying to me, "You know, we had a situation a few weeks ago at Miami that I'd like to ask you about." I gave him my full attention, expecting to hear only partial details, based on which I would try to give at least a theoretical answer to his questions. He continued, "We were being vectored for an approach to Runway 30 by one controller, then he gave us a frequency change to another guy. We called, but didn't get an answer, then a couple of minutes later, the controller became very excited, calling traffic to our left on final. I mean, it was no problem, we had the traffic in sight, but I just wondered what happened."

For a second or two, I considered feigning total ignorance, and giving a plain vanilla answer based on workload, frequency congestion, etc. Then I reconsidered. This was the only time I had ever been questioned by a flight crew about something in which I had had a direct hand, and I decided to respond fully and honestly. I began, "Captain, it was our error. I was the controller working your flight on downwind, and it was because of the traffic volume that we had the approach control function divided between my position, called the feeder, and the other man's, called the final. When a controller gets busy, it is all about priorities. When we played back the tape, your call was loud and clear. The other man undoubtedly heard it, and was planning to answer you after a couple of other more critical transmissions, but the time got longer than he realized, especially with that weather cell moving in. The same thing has happened to me and every controller on occasion. We are all aware of it, and do our best not to leave "hangers," actions that are deferred but must be taken later, but sometimes it is unavoidable." At this, the captain nodded, saying, "Yeah, we have stuff like that happen, too."

When I returned to the facility, I immediately told Rick about my jump seat ride and my conversation. He just shook his head, saying "Small world." The final postscript occurred just before Christmas, when Delta sent a whole Christmas dinner to the facility as a thank you for keeping the ATC system going. One of the signatures on the accompanying card was Captain Fisher's.

After the Orange Bowl

Although we were still running on the adrenaline and can-do spirit that had sustained us since August, the next year began with probably the most unmanageable tower operation I had ever experienced. I reported for the midnight shift at 11:00 pm on the evening of January 1, 1982, about the time that the Orange Bowl contest for that year was concluding. Clemson had just defeated Nebraska by a score of 22 to 15, and many of the fans on both sides had flown their private aircraft into Miami for the game.

Procedures at that time required all pilots, whether on IFR flight plans or operating VFR, to contact Clearance Delivery to copy either an en route clearance or departure instructions out of the terminal control area (TCA) where positive separation was afforded to all aircraft. Owing to an excess of celebration, an epidemic of get-home-itis, a lack of familiarity with TCA procedures, or a combination of all of these, the frequencies of both Ground Control and CD by degrees became a mishmash of smeared transmissions and "say agains." To make matters worse, there were only two of us in the tower, and the two frequencies were combined at a single position. Many pilots, presumably after many attempts at communication, simply taxied without clearance, soon filling the main taxiway to 27 Right and the run-up pad with aircraft whose identification and intentions we had no way of knowing.

At the Local Control position, I was occasionally able to make out an individual call sign and issue take-off clearance. But some of the pilots were at intersections, rather than using the full length of the runway, and even with the binoculars it was difficult, in the sea of lights permeating the darkness, to make out which aircraft had actually been cleared. There were even a few pilot—initiated departures without clearance, compounding the confusion and creating a major safety hazard.

All of this was bad enough, but the situation deteriorated even further when an Eastern L-1011 landed on Runway 30 and rolled to the end. The departure ends of Runway 30 and 27 Right were close enough that when a large aircraft was in the process of exiting either one at the end, it temporarily crossed the hold short line of the other runway. Normally it only took a few seconds to clear that area, but on this night the L-1011 blew a tire just as it was making the turn. In a heartbeat, two runways were closed, with 50 or 60 aircraft awaiting departure on 27 Right.

The entire group now had to be taxied to 27 Left, over a mile away, and with far less taxiway and run up area available. All arrivals were also directed to 27 Left as the only open runway. Delays mounted, with increasing frequency congestion resulting from requests for takeoff and complaints about the delays. Despite repeated instructions to await takeoff clearance, some pilots were still simply looking for a gap in the inbound flow and initiating their own departures. There was no way of knowing how many illegal operations occurred that night, but fortunately there were no accidents.

As mentioned earlier, PATCO continued to sound the alarm about the inevitability of a catastrophic crash because its members were not at the control positions. The FAA as an agency, and every individual controller, understood that if such an event ever occurred, no matter who was working the position, the agency and the individuals would come under intense scrutiny. In the present post-strike climate, it was certain that the union would capitalize on any such occurrence if there was even a whiff of ATC error either by commission or omission.

On January 9, the "inevitable" happened when an Air Florida Boeing 737 crashed on takeoff from Washington National Airport. It was the first air carrier accident in the post-strike period, and until all the facts were known there could be speculation that air traffic control had either done, or failed to do, something that could have contributed to or prevented the tragedy. But as the recordings of the cockpit voice recorder and the radio transmissions between the tower and flight crew were replayed, it became apparent that, from the ATC perspective, the handling of the flight had been completely routine.

The actions of the flight crew, however, were another matter. Despite the fact that icing conditions were present, the crew had not elected to be de-iced, and had failed to activate one of the critical anti-ice systems installed on the aircraft. The result was seriously reduced performance of both the airfoils (wings) and engines. The aircraft struck the 14th Street bridge, killing four motorists in automobiles, and crashing into the Potomac River. Six of the aircraft's occupants survived.

Another air carrier accident occurred seven months later when a Pan American Boeing 727 crashed shortly after takeoff from New Orleans. Once again, there was collective consternation as to any possible involvement on the part of the controllers handling the flight. Analysis of the crash by the NTSB determined that the primary cause was the effect of wind shear generated by a downburst from local thunderstorm activity encountered in the first few moments after the aircraft became airborne. Whenever weather conditions figure in an incident or accident, investigators focus in great detail on what (and when) weather information was provided to the flight crew, as they did in this case. With the limited detection and sensing equipment in use at the time, the finding was that tower personnel had adequately advised the flight crew of all relevant information available.

As the months went by, staffing remained short, despite the influx of military personnel and new hires. One of the problems was that even as our numbers of new people increased, many fully qualified people were bidding out to other facilities. Finally the agency instituted a policy establishing minimum staffing, meaning that no one would be released until the minimum count was reached or exceeded.

Some of the people on the watch were supervisors or staff who had not worked traffic for a considerable period, and had to re-qualify on the positions. Some of these individuals stepped up and did very well, but in other cases the long time away from the "boards" manifested itself in unmistakable ways. Sometimes it was only a wisecrack from a controller who had remained qualified; in other instances, it was an incident that could have led to dire consequences. An example of each:

Les Topps had been in a staff position for a couple of years when the strike occurred. But he was re-trained and checked out within what some regarded as a pretty minimal period. One day he walked into the TRACON carrying his headset and was greeted by Cecil, who did not know that Les had re-certified:

Cecil: "Hey Les, I didn't expect to see you walking in here with a headset."

Les: "Oh sure, there are still got some good vectors left in it."

Cecil: "There ought to be, there ain't never been any good ones come out of it."

The Noon Balloon

In a more serious vein, Will McCutcheon, a supervisor who had been a controller at O'Hare, and still considered himself sufficiently sharp and capable to work traffic, was at the Miami South Arrival position during the busy mid-day period that we referred to as "the noon balloon." Traffic during the noon balloon flowed primarily from the north arrival fixes, located northeast and northwest of the airport, and it was common practice for the North Arrival controller to offload some of his aircraft to the South controller if they were destined to parking gates on the south side of the airport. The procedure on an east operation was to keep the arrivals from the northeast at 8,000 feet and route them east of the airport, where departures were climbing to 7,000, then turn them westbound for right traffic to Runway 9 Right. On the day in question, Will had taken handoffs on two airplanes that would be handled in this way, with about ten miles between them. When the first one cleared the departure flow to the south, the following exchanges occurred:

Will: "Delta 725, turn right heading 260."

DL 725: "Coming right to 260, Delta 725."

A minute or two later, Will realized that he would have to "widen out" DL 725 to the south to reach a proper offset for the downwind leg.

Will: "Delta 725, turn right heading 250." (The pilot was already steering 260, and the instruction should have been to turn ten degrees left to 250, but Will apparently didn't remember the previous vector). The exchange resumed:

DL 725: "You mean left to 250, don't you?"

Will: "Sir, I don't have time to debate with you. I told you to turn right and I want you to turn right immediately to a heading of 250!"

DL 725: "OK, you asked for it, turning RIGHT to 250." The pilot then began to make a turn of 350 degrees, "the long way around" to the new heading. The following airplane was now in a position for a close call or something worse with the Delta flight. Will became very agitated and began to berate the pilot of Delta 725.

Will: "Delta 725, where are you going? I gave you a heading of 250, not a 360-degree turn. I want you to call the tower after you land!"

DL 725: "You bet we will. We were on a heading of 260, you gave us a right turn to 250, which we questioned, and you restated the right turn."

As previously pointed out, errors at approach control are there for all to see, and no one in the TRACON missed any part of this one. There was considerable eye-rolling among the troops when Will, as the TRACON supervisor, took the call from the Delta captain and began saying things like, "Yes sir, the controller will be called to account for his mistake," and "No sir, there is no excuse for something like that."

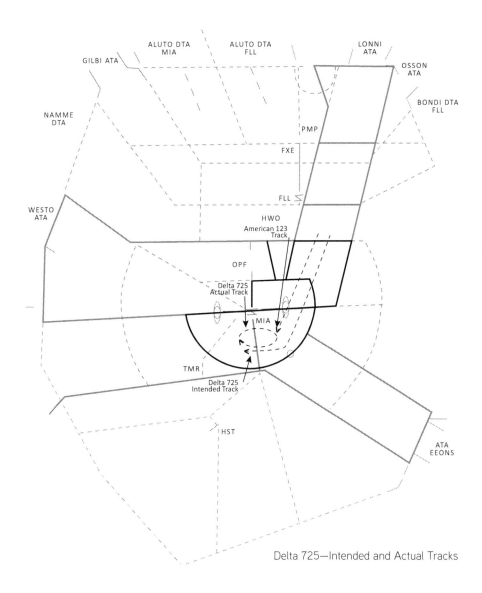

Delta 725—Intended and Actual Tracks

I had a close call of my own one day working the low-altitude satellite position. The "G" position, as it was known, was responsible for arrivals and departures from Pompano, Fort Lauderdale Executive, and Boca Raton airports. Because of short staffing, FXE tower was operating fewer hours than normal, opening at 9:00 am. On the morning in question, sometime in February, there was heavy fog covering the entire area for which the Miami TRACON was responsible. Under such conditions, the procedure for a pilot requesting an IFR clearance from an airport without an operating tower was to call the facility by telephone to receive the clearance. In addition to routing and altitude instructions, the pilot would be assigned a departure runway, an initial heading, and, most importantly, a time "window" within which to take off. This was expressed as "VIFNO," meaning the clearance was "void if not off" by a designated time.

At approximately 8:15 the TRACON supervisor brought me a flight progress strip showing a Learjet with a proposed departure time of 1330Z (8:30 am local time) departing Runway 8 at Fort Lauderdale Executive, destination Miami, assigned heading 080, initial altitude 2,000, and VIFNO 1335Z. The pilot had a 20-minute period within which he could legally take off. Shortly thereafter I received a handoff from Palm Beach on a Cessna 182 bound for Fort Lauderdale Executive. In addition to protecting 2,000 feet on the departure side of the airport until the Lear got airborne, I would have to delay approach clearance for the Cessna until either the Lear took off or the VIFNO time had passed.

As the situation developed it became apparent that the Cessna would be at the outer marker, the final approach fix for the ILS approach to Runway 8, at exactly 1335Z. On initial contact I had advised the Cessna pilot that no weather information was available at FXE, but that at both Miami and Fort Lauderdale the weather sequences were showing ceiling indefinite, sky obscured, visibility ¾ of a mile in ground fog. The following exchanges occurred:

Me: "Skylane 8654 Charlie, make one turn in the holding pattern at PRAIZ, there is traffic released at Executive that is not yet airborne."

N8654C: "Approach, 54 Charlie, I'm a little low on fuel."

Me: "Skylane 54 Charlie, can you make one 360 in lieu of flying the holding pattern?"

N8654C: "OK, making a 360, 54 Charlie."

As the Cessna completed the 360-degree turn and again approached the final approach fix, the ARTS clock showed 1337 and a few seconds, a least a full minute and possibly as much as two minutes past the Learjet's departure window. The exchanges resumed:

Me: "Skylane 54 Charlie, three miles from PRAIZ, cleared ILS Runway 8 approach, change to advisory frequency app—disregard, stand by one."

Before I could complete the word "approved," meaning that the Cessna pilot would no longer be in communication with me, the symbology of an unidentified aircraft appeared at the west boundary of FXE, on a collision course with the inbound Skylane.

Me: "Skylane 54 Charlie, cancel approach clearance, turn left immediately heading 360."

Before the pilot could acknowledge, another transmission occurred:

N334EF: "Miami departure Lear 334 Echo Foxtrot off Exec climbing to 2,000."

Me: "Lear 334 Echo Foxtrot turn left immediately heading 180, traffic is a Cessna 12 o'clock four miles eastbound descending out of 2,000."

N334EF: "Left to 180, no joy on the traffic, we're in the soup."

It was obvious to me that the Learjet had taken off on Runway 26, and I was mightily tempted to get into it with him about just what the hell he thought he was doing. But I couldn't be sure exactly what had been said during the phone call granting him the release. By sheer luck, a potentially huge problem had been avoided, and I decided the best course was simply to provide normal handling to Miami. I called the supervisor over to my position and gave him the highlights of what had just occurred, asking if he had specifically instructed the pilot to take off on Runway 8. He replied affirmatively, and told me to have the pilot call the facility after landing.

In due course, the supervisor told me he had spoken to the pilot, who acknowledged that he had been assigned Runway 8 for departure, but that, quote, "We were way down at the east end of the airport and it was "getting close" to our void time, so we took off on 26." In fact, the pilot had taken off at least two minutes after his void time in the apparent belief that it was "close enough" to the void time and understanding that the additional minutes to taxi the mile and a half plus to Runway 8 would have required him to shut down the engines, leave the aircraft, and call the facility to receive a new VIFNO time. It was neither the first nor the last time a pilot made a decision without understanding all the factors on which his ATC instructions were based.

Canceling a Flight Plan

When the Learjet pilot took off on the wrong runway, and later than his void time, the consequences could have been very bad. But there were other occurrences where pilots did, or failed to do, things required of them that varied in seriousness between annoying/troublesome and downright laughable.

Pilots on VFR flight plans were the most regular offenders, probably because, collectively, they were less experienced than users of the IFR system. A VFR flight plan consisted of information filed with a Flight Service station including the aircraft ID and type, airport of departure, planned routing and altitude, time en route, and destination airport. Its purpose was to facilitate search and rescue operations in the event that the aircraft did not arrive at its destination.

Typically, a VFR pilot would "activate" his flight plan shortly after taking off by contacting Flight Service, thereby starting the clock on the time en route for which he had filed. Once airborne, the pilot was under no obligation to make any further reports, or to advise Flight Service that he was deviating from the filed routing. Of course, good operating practice dictated that he update his progress, stating times past certain points on the route so that the area to be searched could be narrowed in the event that a search and rescue operation had to be mounted. The one hard requirement was that a pilot cancel his flight plan.

This could be done by radio at any time, but the more usual procedure was to contact Flight Service by telephone after landing to report arrival at the destination. And it was this final step that was most overlooked at the conclusion of a VFR flight. In these cases, Flight Service personnel would begin by contacting the control tower at the destination or fixed base operators at uncontrolled fields to ascertain whether the aircraft had arrived safely. If the arrival could not be verified, search and rescue could be initiated, with the pilot potentially liable for the expenses of the operation.

In the case of an IFR flight plan, if the flight terminated at a controlled field, no action by the pilot was necessary. But at an uncontrolled field, the flight plan had to be closed out. When the weather permitted, most pilots on instrument flight plans would wait till they had the airport in sight, then cancel with the approach controller. The alternative was to contact the facility providing approach control services by telephone after landing to report the approach complete. One night an incident occurred during the midnight shift that rated perhaps midway between "annoying/troublesome" and "downright laughable." Opa-locka tower was closed, and the weather was VFR, meaning that the pilot of N775XY, a Cessna 402, likely would be able to cancel his IFR flight plan before leaving the approach control frequency.

After clearance for the ILS 9L approach was issued and acknowledged, the following exchanges occurred:

Controller: "Twin Cessna 75 Xray Yankee, I will need you to cancel IFR with me before you land, or telephone the Miami TRACON after landing to report your approach complete."

N775XY: "OK, I'll cancel with you in just a minute, Xray Yankee."

But as the radar target disappeared about a half mile from the airport, there had been no further communications from the pilot. The controller tried to establish contact:

Controller: "Twin Cessna 75 Xray Yankee Miami Approach, are you still with me?" (No response).

Controller: "Twin Cessna 75 Xray Yankee, if you read, acknowledge." (No response).

Then, turning to the supervisor, "Hey Ed, I just had a twin Cessna inbound to Opa-locka IFR. He said he was going to cancel with me but he never did." This was distinctly in the "annoying" category.

The supervisor replied, "Well, did it look like he made it to the airport?" The radar coverage to the point at which the target disappeared, indicated that in all probability a normal approach and landing had been made. Nevertheless, the loop was still open, and there had been more than one instance where the FAA ended up with major egg on its face when an airplane had crashed short of the runway and the accident had not been discovered till many hours later. The supervisor said, "Let's give him a few minutes and see if he calls us on the phone."

As the minutes passed, it eventually became clear that no phone call was coming. There were no Dade County airport personnel on the field at that hour, so the supervisor contacted the sheriff's department and asked if a patrol car could be sent to Opa-locka to look for the aircraft. Within a short time the sheriff reported that they had been unable to locate the airplane. This was definitely "troublesome," but not definitive, as there were literally hundreds of aircraft parked at multiple locations on the vast ramp area, and law enforcement did not have the time or resources for an exhaustive search.

Apart from the safety of N775XY, with its flight plan still open, Opa-locka airport would be closed to further traffic for a prescribed period. It was imperative that MIA, as the controlling IFR facility, reach a final determination as to how the flight had terminated. The supervisor contacted the 24-hour facility in Oklahoma City responsible for aircraft ownership and registration records, learning the name, address and telephone number of the pilot. The residence was in Pompano, about 40 miles north of Miami. And so at 1:30 or 2:00 am, the supervisor initiated a call, answered by the pilot's mother that went something like this:

Supervisor: "Good morning ma'm, I am the air traffic control supervisor at Miami Airport. I apologize for the late hour, but I am trying to reach John Jones, the pilot of a twin Cessna registered in his name. Is he there?"

Mrs. Jones: "Oh my god, he has crashed and been killed, I just know it, I told him not to fly that airplane at night!" Then, bursting into tears, "Where do I have to go to claim his body?"

Supervisor: "No, ma'am, nothing like that has happened. We are sure he landed safely at Opa-locka airport about 20 minutes ago, but we just need to verify it. If you hear from him, would you please ask him to call Miami Tower?"

Mrs. Jones (totally losing it): "He's dead! He's dead! I just know it. Oh, god!"

The phone went dead, and the supervisor shook his head in exasperation saying, "Damn! Why couldn't the jerk have just canceled, like he was supposed to."

About 20 minutes later, the TRACON telephone rang. The supervisor picked up, and received a "lively" greeting:

"This is John Jones, the pilot of N775XY. What the hell do mean calling my mother in the middle of the night and scaring the shit out of her! I am calling my attorney in the morning, and we are going to sue your asses!" Before the supervisor could answer, the phone went dead, and he walked away from the desk, expressing a creative variety of profane and vulgar sentiments. Then he stopped and burst out laughing.

More Flight Plans

There were a couple of other incidents exemplifying the ways in which flight plans and actual flight tracks diverged significantly, both with potentially lethal consequences. In one case the pilot of a single-engine Piper Cherokee had filed a flight plan from somewhere in South Carolina or Georgia with the intended destination of Opa-locka. Flight Service was already looking for the aircraft, as it was substantially overdue, and neither Opa-locka tower nor the Miami TRACON had had any communication with the pilot. At about 10:30 pm the Miami approach controller received the first in a series of radio exchanges:

N8696G: "Miami approach, Cherokee 8696 Golf, lost, low on fuel, request help getting to Opa-locka."

MIA Approach: "Cherokee 8696 Golf Miami approach, say your position or estimated position."

N8696G: "Miami I have no idea of my position."

MIA Approach: "Cherokee 86 Golf, what was the time and location of your last known position?"

N8696G: "We were over Jacksonville about three hours ago."

MIA Approach: "Cherokee 86 Golf roger, how much fuel do you have remaining?"

N8696G: "I estimate about 30 minutes."

MIA Approach: "Cherokee 86 Golf squawk one two zero zero and ident."

The pilot advised that he had complied, but no ident was observed on radar. The exchange resumed:

MIA Approach: "Cherokee 86 Golf, what do you see below you?"

N8696G: "I see a lot of water and a few lights."

MIA Approach: "Cherokee 86 Golf roger, are you following the shoreline?"

This was a frequent query when trying to orient a pilot, as most of the civilization and airports in Florida were close to the shore.

N8696G: "That's affirmative Miami."

MIA Approach: "Cherokee 86 Golf, OK, continue along the shoreline and advise me if you see an airport. You may be beyond my radar coverage."

N8696G: "Roger Miami."

After a few minutes, with no likely radar targets appearing in the expected area, the controller made an inquiry that, in retrospect, may have saved the day.

MIA Approach: "Cherokee 86 Golf, say your heading."

N8696G: "Heading 060, coming around to 360."

MIA Approach: "Cherokee 86 Golf, if you are following the shoreline, you should be on a steady heading of about 165 or 170. Why are you turning northbound?"

N8696G: "Well I am following the shoreline, but it just keeps leading me in circles."

The controller was an experienced man, and this transmission caused a major light bulb to come on. He "cranked out" the radar display to its maximum limit of 60 nautical miles and again instructed the pilot to squawk ident. At this range the ASR radar system in use at that time could just cover Bimini, about 40 miles east of Miami Beach. The ident appeared over Bimini, a small island whose shoreline would, indeed, cause a pilot who followed it to fly in circles. Knowing that Bimini had an airport, the controller asked the pilot if he had it in sight. The pilot replied in the negative, apparently because the field either did not have runway lights or they were simply not turned on.

So the airplane had been located, but this event was not over by a long shot. With less than 30 minutes of available fuel, and a minimum of 42 miles to the nearest airport, it would be nip and tuck as to whether the pilot could make it back to Florida. The controller lost no time in issuing a vector to Miami International, starting the clock on a tense 25 minutes or so. Unbelievably, as the aircraft approached the shoreline, and the controller began asking the pilot if he had Miami airport in sight, the pilot replied by insisting that his destination was Opa-locka! With a successful conclusion to the whole event tantalizingly close, the controller was not about to brook any nonsense. Any pilot who could get so far off course as to end up 40 miles out to sea was clearly in need of some firm guidance. The controller informed the pilot in no uncertain terms that he would be landing straight in on Runway 27 Left at Miami. The aircraft landed, cleared the runway, and ran out of fuel on the taxiway.

In another case, a Piper twin Comanche was inbound to Miami during the wee hours of the midnight shift. After handoff from Miami Center, the initial exchange between the pilot and the approach controller was completely routine:

N6121C: "Miami approach, twin Comanche 6121 Charlie with you level 6,000, with information Hotel."

MIA Approach: "Twin Comanche 6121 Charlie Miami Approach, expect a visual approach runway 9 Left, report the airport in sight."

N6121C: "OK, 9 Left, I'll call the field, 21 Charlie."

Several minutes later the controller issued descent clearance to 3,000 without receiving an acknowledgement. Repeated calls elicited no response as the aircraft continued on a southeasterly heading from the arrival fix. Mode C altitude reporting showed that the aircraft remained at 6,000. For more than 30 minutes neither the heading nor the altitude changed, with the aircraft eventually overflying the airport, then the coastline, then heading out to sea. The controller tried every strategy available in cases like this, from transmitting on "guard," the emergency frequency which all pilots were advised (but not required) to monitor while in flight, to asking the pilot to "ident" via transponder if he was receiving the transmissions, to asking other pilots to relay instructions in the hope that their position in the air would provide a clearer or stronger signal.

Suddenly the twin Comanche pilot was back on the air:

N6121C: "Miami, how about a descent clearance for 21 Charlie?"

MIA Approach: "Twin Comanche 21 Charlie negative, maintain 6,000, make a 180-degree turn to heading 310, vector back to Miami."

N6121C: "21 Charlie, this heading should take us right to the airport."

MIA Approach: "Negative sir, you are 30 miles southeast of the airport, and I have been trying to contact you for the last half hour."

There was a long pause, followed by a distinct change of tone on the pilot's part as he realized what had happened. Although it was never explicitly acknowledged, it was pretty certain that the pilot had fallen asleep between the time of initial contact with approach control and his request for descent clearance. Fortunately the airplane had been under the control of the autopilot, and in the event the pilot was able to return to Miami and land safely.

An MSPB Hearing

In September 1982 there was a series of hearings in Miami conducted by the Merit Systems Protection Board (MSPB) to review the decisions to remove employees who had participated in the strike 13 months earlier. An MSPB hearing was an administrative procedure in which the agency could present evidence justifying a dismissal while the individual had an opportunity to refute the evidence or present facts and testimony as to mitigating circumstances.

The hearings were open, meaning that anyone could attend and observe the proceedings, and I decided to attend one of them in order to understand how they were conducted. I had friends who would be called in later weeks, including a woman I was dating, and I hoped to glean some information that might help them make their cases. Unfortunately, I picked an especially inopportune day, as the respondent whose case was being heard was a controller newly arrived at MIA who had been in my training class during the two weeks leading up to the strike date.

The agency basically had the individual dead to rights, as he had participated in the demonstrations outside the terminal building and had been captured on video. But while he was on the stand, he noticed me among the observers, and began an impassioned harangue to the effect that as his "supervisor" I had encouraged him to join the strike, and pointing me out to the administrative law judge in charge of the hearing. I fully expected the judge to say something about the need to provide proof of this allegation beyond a simple verbal assertion, but to my consternation he summoned me to the stand. I had never been in a witness chair before, and I had had no opportunity to prepare for this experience. The deputy chief of MIA, also present as a witness for the agency, and fearing that I might undermine the case, was looking daggers at me as "Bob" (the controller) began questioning me. It went something like this:

Bob: "Were you not my supervisor during the time I was in your class before August 3, 1981?"

Me: "I was not your supervisor. As a staff specialist I have no supervisory duties."

Bob: "Well you were the guy we saw every day. If you weren't our supervisor, who was?"

Me: "Your supervisor was the Evaluation and Proficiency Development Officer, designated as a supervisory air traffic control specialist."

Bob: "Well, you encouraged us to go on strike, because you said we would be under threat from the union if we didn't."

Me: "What I said was that the union would probably pressure all its members to strike, but that each individual had to weigh that against the fact that on the face of it the strike would be illegal. I said at some point a line was going to be drawn, and when it was, you should be sure you are on the side of it that you want to be."

There were a few more questions basically repeating the same points, and before long the judge said, "Thank you, Mr. Potter, you may step down."

When the hearing ended, the deputy chief lost no time in confronting me, asking what the hell I was doing there. I did not tell him I was trying to get some information that would assist people in getting their jobs back, saying only that I was curious as to how the MSPB conducted its proceedings. In the event, Bob's dismissal was upheld, as were those of the people I had intended to help.

Standard Phraseology (or Not)

Whenever an accident or incident occurred, the recorded radio exchanges surrounding the event were reviewed. The primary purpose of the review was to determine if anything had been communicated, or omitted, that could have caused or prevented the outcome. I was involved in one such instance that unfolded as follows:

I returned from two weeks of annual leave to be greeted by my supervisor, who by way of welcome said the words no controller wants to hear: "Come with me, I have a tape I want you to listen to." Having no idea what this could be about, I was furiously combing through my memories of my last few position assignments prior to my leave period. I knew my phraseology wasn't perfect, but I had never been called on the carpet for phraseology errors, and I couldn't think of anything that might have triggered a review of the tapes. As the playback of the Miami South Departure radar position began, I heard myself issuing vectors to the pilot of a Cherokee inbound to Tamiami (TMB), the exchanges to all appearances being completely routine. Because there was nothing unusual in these communications, I could not immediately recall the particulars of the situation. But as the aircraft approached the airport, the pilot requested a visual approach. At that point a new voice was heard as another controller relieved me from the position. I now remembered all the circumstances surrounding the incident—fortunately for me, as it turned out.

As the tape continued, the pilot reported the airport in sight, and the new controller issued a visual approach clearance to Runway 9 Right:

MIA Approach: "Cherokee 667 Yankee Whiskey, cleared visual approach Runway 9 Right, maintain visual separation from the TV antennas southwest of the airport."

The pilot acknowledged the clearance and received a frequency change to Tamiami Tower.

At that point my supervisor stopped the tape, then looked at me questioningly, saying, "Well, do you see what's wrong here?" I replied, "Well, I don't think you can instruct a pilot to maintain visual separation from an obstruction [the 2,000-foot TV antennas], but other than that I don't see a problem. How did all of this come to light in the first place?"

I learned that the newly and temporarily appointed quality assurance specialist (QATS) responsible for monitoring and correcting phraseology and procedural errors, had initiated the tape review at the behest of the Cherokee pilot who was a member of the Atlanta regional office, the entity that held authority over all field facilities in the Southern Region. Flights like that of N667YW were conducted periodically, and without prior notification, to evaluate air traffic control service. The pilot questioned only the instruction to maintain visual separation from the TV antennas, but the QATS, eager to make a name for himself, added the following "gig" to his record of the tape review: "No coordination for a visual approach nor aircraft ID furnished to Tamiami Tower." These were requirements contained in the letter of agreement between Tamiami and MIA, but I was prepared for this based on my memory of the operation. I said, "Did anybody check the handoff position at South Departure?" After I was relieved, I had picked up the handset plugged in at handoff and given the information that the QATS review had said was missing. The supervisor was not sure, but said he would check. I also asked whether TMB personnel had been asked about the coordination information. As it turned out, neither of these steps had been taken, and the QATS report ended up having to be revised, eventually clearing me of any wrongdoing.

Too Much Talking

One of my colleagues, in fact a man I had trained in the aftermath of the strike, had the unfortunate tendency to talk too much. Time on the control frequency was precious, and while most controllers would throw in an occasional transmission that had nothing to do with the operation (think "Merry Christmas," or "Have a nice day" just before a frequency change), Billy Walterston never knew when to shut up. Even on the override circuits, he would constantly call other controllers just to make conversation, often when the other guy could ill afford the distraction from his duties.

One night Billy and I were assigned to the control tower for the midnight shift, a time when traffic was slow and radio communications were sometimes spaced minutes apart. Billy had recently had a "deal" or loss of separation between two aircraft inbound to Miami from Palm Beach (PBI). The tapes showed that he was engaged in a long conversation with one of the pilots when the pilot of the second aircraft, a DC-3, contacted him, reporting level at 4,000, and overtaking the single-engine Cessna ahead at 3,000. The letter of agreement between PBI and MIA called for propeller-driven aircraft (which both of these were) to be assigned 3,000, but because of the overtake, the PBI controller had put the faster, following airplane at 4,000. The exchanges went something like this:

N295EB: "Miami approach Douglas 295 Echo Bravo with you at 4,000, we have information Juliet."

Billy: "Douglas 295 Echo Bravo Miami approach, and a good evening to you sir. Are you having a good flight?"

N295EB: "Yeah, sure, no problems."

Billy: "Well I'm really glad to hear that sir, maintain 3,000, expect vectors for Runway 9 Left at Miami."

N295EB: "Ok, down to three, Echo Bravo."

Billy apparently did not notice that the DC-3 was at 4,000, nor did he pick up on the read back when the pilot said "down to," meaning that the aircraft was changing altitude and putting it in potential conflict with the Cessna. Billy immediately went back to his "interrupted" conversation with the Cessna pilot:

Billy: "So, Cessna 44 Charlie, is this a business trip, or are you on vacation?"

N6444C: "Oh, it's strictly vacation this time."

Billy: "Well, you picked a great time for your trip, our weather has been absolutely fantastic for the past week, with no change in sight. So are you staying on the beach, or do you have family here?"

N6444C: "No, no family, we have a reservation at the Eden Roc."

Billy: "Oh you will have a ball, and I'd like to personally welcome you to South Florida."

There were a few more exchanges in this vein, then came the kind of transmission you never want to hear:

N295EB: "Approach, are you talking to this little guy right here, we had to make a hard turn to avoid him."

Billy fell all over himself apologizing, but there was no way out of this one. The playback of the radio transmissions and the automation tracks showed that the radar targets had almost touched, and that there would likely have been a midair collision but for the alertness of the DC-3 pilot. Lester McNeil had a serious "one on one" with Billy, the thrust of which was, as Lester put it in his usual unedited way, "You need to knock off all that bullshit on the frequency. If you have another incident like this, you will be on the street for at least two weeks."

Billy relayed most of this to me as we manned the tower that night, saying, "I'll tell you what, Lester plumb scared the pee-waddle out of me. From now on I am sticking strictly to book phraseology." I said it was a good decision, and you couldn't go wrong sticking to the book.

A few minutes later there came a call on Clearance Delivery from a Pan American pilot requesting clearance to a South American destination. It was on speaker, so even though Billy was working the position, I could hear the entire exchange:

PA890: "Miami clearance delivery, Clipper 890 instruments to Caracas, request clearance."

Billy: "Clipper 890 Miami clearance delivery, cleared to the Caracas airport via the Miami Five departure, CUTER transition, as filed. Maintain 5,000, expect flight level 230 ten minutes after departure. Departure frequency will be 125.0, squawk 4615."

The pilot read back the clearance verbatim, Billy advised him that the readback was correct, and issued ground control frequency for taxi. The pilot acknowledged the instruction, and that should have been the end of the exchange. But it was not to be, as Billy reverted to type:

Billy: "Clipper 890, can I ask you something?"

PA890: "Yeah sure, go ahead."

Billy: "Did you used to fly for National Airlines?" (Pan Am and National had merged a few years earlier).

PA890: "Yes sir, sure did."

Billy: "You know what, I can always tell a National pilot on the frequency. You all have a way about you that you can't miss. How are things going after the merger?"

PA890: "Thanks for saying so. We're still having some discussions about integrating the seniority lists, so it's not quite settled yet."

The conversation went on for several more minutes, and I was left thinking, so much for sticking to the book.

Creative Phraseology

Another controller was frequently guilty of using creative phraseology, usually when he was unhappy about how things were going in his sector. He salted in occasional doses of profanity, for which he was more than once pulled off the position and "counseled" about what he was putting out over the air. But two instances involving this individual caused the entire TRACON to erupt into gales of laughter. In one case, a VFR pilot called on the approach control frequency for flight following during the busy mid-day arrival rush. John, the controller, identified the aircraft as it flew through the final approach courses of runways 9 Left and 9 Right, and immediately transmitted, "Cessna 45 Hotel, what are you doing there? Don't you realize you almost got run over by the noon balloon?" Of course, "the noon balloon" was our term for the rush period, and would have no meaning to a pilot. For a good while afterward, any time a pilot was found in approach control airspace around noon time, the controller would call out to the other controllers, without keying his mike, "Oh boy, here's another zoomer pilot trying to get run over by the noon balloon."

The other incident involving John also occurred during the "noon balloon" when the frequency was busy, and there had been, as there always were, a number of instances of "smeared" transmissions, where either two pilots or a pilot and the controller both keyed their mikes at the same time. Like any other two-way radio system, and unlike a telephone, the VHF radios used in air traffic control did not permit any station to transmit and receive at the same time. John was becoming increasingly frustrated, and in what he supposed to be an effort to impose some discipline on the frequency, transmitted, "Damn it! Every time I key my mike, some idiot talks!" The joke was that when he keyed his mike, the only "idiot" who could talk was John himself.

A couple of outliers in the category of non-standard transmissions, one having the ring of truth, the other more than likely apocryphal. First a little background:

Runway separation involving two large, air carrier aircraft is defined as follows:

A departure may not begin takeoff roll until a preceding arrival has cleared the runway; an arrival may not cross the runway threshold behind a preceding departure until the preceding departure has crossed the runway end or turned to avoid any conflict; or if suitable visual landmarks are available, until the preceding departure is airborne and at least 6,000 feet from threshold.

So the situation was that an air carrier had landed, and another had been put in position on the runway awaiting takeoff clearance, while a third was on final only a couple of miles out—the very definition of a squeeze play. The arrival was taking its time exiting the runway, and it was becoming obvious that the airplane on final would have to go around—that is, until the controller issued this creative instruction to the pilot holding in position:

"Global 193, start a rapid taxi down the runway, and stand by for takeoff clearance." Technically, since the pilot had been told to taxi, he had not "begun takeoff roll" even though he was "taxiing rapidly down the runway" before the previous landing had turned off and cleared the hold bars.

Another instance allegedly occurred before my time at MIA, when a local controller was talking faster than his brain could function. He was attempting to alert the pilot of a 727 that had just taken off to traffic east of the airport, which happened to be the Goodyear blimp, orbiting the Flagler dog racing track. The transmission came out this way:

"National 106, traffic is the Bloodyear glimp over the Dogler Flag Trap."

Two Forced Landings

In 1983 I celebrated 15 years at Miami Tower, and during that entire time I had never had an honest to goodness, do-or-die emergency. Like most controllers, I had had a few "getting a little low on fuel" or "request expeditious handling to the extent feasible" requests from pilots, but never had I heard the actual words, "We are declaring an emergency." All of that changed, twice within a 30-minute period, one day when I was assigned to the TRACON during the day shift.

In the first case, I was working the Fort Lauderdale departure control position with traffic departing to the east. There were always a number of VFR flights inbound from the Bahamas, some landing at Fort

Lauderdale, while others were simply transitioning the airspace to other destinations. These aircraft could potentially conflict with the departure flow from FLL, and their pilots routinely requested VFR advisories to assist them in identifying traffic that could be a factor. I had been on position for a while, meaning that I would be relieved before too long, when the following exchange began:

N135AB: "Miami approach, twin Cessna 135 Alfa Bravo with you, VFR, 25 east of Fort Lauderdale, level at 6,500, looking for flight following into Lauderdale."

I entered the aircraft identification into the ARTS system and issued the discrete transponder code associated with the aircraft ID.

Me: "Twin Cessna 135 Alfa Bravo Miami Approach, squawk 3614 and ident."

Within a few seconds the radar target acquired its identification tag.

Me: "Twin Cessna 135 Alfa Bravo radar contact 25 miles east of Fort Lauderdale. Expect an east landing, begin a VFR descent to 2,500."

N135AB: "Miami, Alfa Bravo, I'd like to stay up here for a while, I'm a little low on fuel."

Me: "Twin Cessna 135 Alfa Bravo roger, advise me prior to making any altitude changes. Do you require priority handling?"

N135AB: "Negative, I'll be okay, just keep an eye on me."

At a point about 20 miles from the shoreline, the pilot transmitted, "Miami from AB, I just lost number one engine."

Me: "Twin Cessna 135 Alfa Bravo, can you make it to the airport on one engine?" Most twin-engine aircraft were perfectly capable of operating on one engine when necessary.

N135AB: "No problem as long as the fuel holds out."

But the fuel did not hold out. Less than two minutes later the pilot transmitted, "Mayday, mayday, 135 AB lost number two engine."

This definitely got my attention, as I observed the mode C altitude rapidly unwinding from 6,500, at a rate that would put the aircraft in the water about 10 miles east of the beach. I called to the supervisor, alerting him and the whole radar room as to what was happening. In a stroke of amazing luck, the controller working the position next to mine had the Coast Guard rescue helicopter on his frequency, and immediately asked me where the emergency aircraft was. By now I could see that the helicopter was about five miles northeast of FLL. I forced the display of

N135AB's tag to the other controller, and said, "Give the Coast Guard a heading of 110."

There were no further communications from the twin Cessna pilot, but I transmitted, "Twin Cessna 135 AB, the Coast Guard helicopter is en route to your location."

The helicopter crew had the twin Cessna in sight as it hit the water. The ditching went smoothly, with the pilot the only occupant. He was soon standing on the wing, and as later reported by the Coast Guard, "barely got his feet wet as we lowered the sling and winched him in." It was a fortunate outcome to an incident that easily could have ended differently.

I was relieved from the position and, as was standard procedure, asked to write a brief narrative describing the event. After a short break, I returned to the TRACON and was assigned the Miami South Departure control position. At this time of day activity at South Departure was usually pretty slow. There were a couple of South American flights off MIA, and then about ten minutes later I got a call from a helicopter off Homestead Air Force Base:

A61288: "Miami approach Air Force helicopter 61288, just off Homestead, we'd like flight following clear of your TCA up to Opa-locka." Even with a slow-moving helicopter the flight should not take more than 15 minutes. I replied:

Me: "Air Force 61288. Squawk 2213 and ident." I found the aircraft about six miles northwest of Homestead, tracking pretty much northbound.

Me: "Air Force 61288 radar contact six northwest of Homestead, verify altitude."

A61288: "We're VFR at 1500." This was going to be an easy one. At that altitude the helicopter would remain clear of the TCA for the whole flight. Then, less than a half hour after the twin Cessna had ditched:

A61288: "Approach, 61288 we have a chip warning light, we will have to set down on this highway." Apparently in that model helicopter, a "chip" in the gearbox of the main rotor could cause the entire assembly to seize up, preventing even the possibility of an auto rotation to a safe landing. For the second time I summoned the supervisor, who immediately got on the phone to advise law enforcement of the incident. The landing on the highway was successful, with no damage or injury to the aircraft, crew, vehicles, or their drivers. Still, even though they had both turned out well, two forced landings within the same hour left me feeling a little snake bit.

Shortly after my "two-in-one-day" experience, Eastern 855, a Lockheed 1011, almost came to grief. The flight departed at 9:00 am with a planned arrival in Nassau about 35 minutes later. As they approached Nassau, the crew experienced an oil pressure warning light on the number two engine, requiring a shutdown to avoid damaging the engine. They elected to return to Miami, but shortly thereafter, the same warning light on the number one engine appeared, followed a few minutes later by the same indication on the number three engine. The crew initially believed that the sensors were malfunctioning, as the likelihood of zero oil pressure in all three engines at once was almost nil. But with about 18 minutes to go to make it back to MIA, the number three engine flamed out, followed by the number one engine five minutes later. The aircraft was now descending without power from 16,000 feet as the crew attempted to re-start the number two engine, finally succeeding and leveling off at just 4,000 feet and still some 50 miles from the airport.

The Miami Center controllers handling the flight apprised our watch supervisor of the circumstances, including the fact that the crew had said they did not expect to reach MIA, but would likely have to ditch at sea. Soon Miami Approach was working the flight, with minimal terse exchanges, both flight crew and controllers knowing that in all probability the tapes of this event would end up in an NTSB hearing and a court of law. As it happened, a Navy C-130 had just taken off from Homestead Air Force base, and was on the same frequency as the communications relating to Eastern 855. The Navy crew contacted the approach controller:

Navy 88182: "Miami approach, Navy 88182, C-130, just off Homestead, can we provide any assistance?"

MIA Approach: "Navy 88182 Miami Approach, what capabilities do you have?"

Navy 88132: "Approach we have 50 SEAL team members on board for a training mission, with full parachute and SCUBA gear."

MIA Approach: "Navy 88182 roger, turn right immediately heading 080, vector to the emergency aircraft."

The C-130 was soon flying in a loose formation with the L-1011. As it approached the shoreline, cleared for a straight in approach to Runway

27 Left, every man not assigned to a position was either in the tower or out on the catwalk. I was among them, and to our immense relief, we saw the airplane cross the runway threshold, black smoke streaming from the number two engine mounted in the tail. The aircraft came to a stop, and the crew shut down the engine to reduce the possibility of a fire. The runway was closed for many minutes while a tug was summoned to tow the L-1011 to the hangar.

The news media, which routinely monitored law enforcement and air traffic control frequencies in the hope of getting a jump on a lead story, was all over this one. For Eastern Airlines, it was a public relations black eye of the worst sort, and it became many times worse when the facts of the incident came to light. The aircraft had been serviced the night before by an apprentice mechanic who was supposedly being monitored by a senior experienced man. After oil servicing, procedures required that the technician close the access point using O-rings, or gaskets, to seal the system correctly. This step had been omitted, allowing the oil to escape once the system was pressurized. Eastern was experiencing ongoing disputes with its unionized employees, and there was dark speculation that the maintenance oversight had not been entirely accidental. It did not help that no heads rolled in the aftermath of it all.

12. A Change in My Status

In 1984 I marked my 16th year at Miami Tower, first as a trainee, then as a full-performance-level controller working Level 5 traffic. Certain professions, air traffic control among them, offered early retirement to individuals who had worked enough years to qualify. The formula was pretty simple: if you had 20 years of time "on the boards" you could retire at age 50, or with 25 years, you could retire at any age. Other civil service employees had to put in 30 years, and could not retire until age 55.

Since day one of the strike three years earlier, I had worked continuously as a controller, but my "position of record" was EPDS, staff specialist for training. This meant that these last three years, tough ones at that, did not count as "good time" for purposes of meeting the 20-year requirement. I was aware of all this, but the fact was that the facility was still operationally understaffed, and I knew I was making a more important contribution in the operating quarters than I could have in the training department.

Then one day the facility chief called me into his office for a conversation that he began like this:

"This facility, and the whole agency, are indebted to you, and guys like you, for the incredible job you have done in maintaining the ATC system.

But as you know, your years since the strike normally wouldn't count towards controller retirement. However, the agency has decided to grant a one-time opportunity to people like you to retroactively change your status so that those years would count. It's your choice. You can either continue as you are, and we will bring you back to your staff position when we get our controller numbers back up, or you can give up the staff position and have all the years count as controller time."

I did some rapid mental calculation as I considered these options. I was 43 years old, and if I accepted the retroactive change of status, I would need only four more years of "good time" to reach the "magic 20" mark. But it would take me seven years to reach age 50. Could I hold out that long? Truth to tell, the combination of rotating shifts, constant training of "new boys (and, increasingly girls)" and always working short-handed was beginning to wear on all of us. Other considerations: if I remained in my staff job, I might still have to work most or even all of those years in the controller chair. Did I really want to retire at age 50? (Yes, if I was still on the boards; probably not, if I were back in the training department). The ideal outcome would be to get my 20 years, then go back to my staff position, meaning that I could take early retirement or continue working, at my option, once I reached age 50. Under these circumstances, I would have what was informally termed "the go to hell card" in my pocket.

I decided I did not want to give up the credit for the post-strike years, and told the chief I would accept the retroactive change of status. He then said something in which, as later events proved, I put far too much faith:

"Well all right. And if you ever decide you want your staff job back, all you have to do is ask."

A New Civil Service System

This was also the year that the federal government did away with the Civil Service Retirement System (CSRS), replacing it with the Federal Employee Retirement System (FERS). Anyone hired after January 1, 1984 would be placed under FERS, while those under CSRS could retain their status or convert to the new system at their option. CSRS was a "defined benefit" program, where an employee could calculate exactly the amount of his retirement annuity based on years of creditable service and the "high three" years of salary paid.

Although FERS did retain a provision for some guaranteed benefits, the main responsibility in providing for retirement would now fall to the employee through contributions to the Thrift Savings Plan (TSP), and Social Security. The TSP contained different investment options allowing the employee to shift his retirement funds, and imposed restrictions on maximum contributions and early withdrawals similar to those governing 401(k) plans. The contributions were tax deferred, with up to the first five per cent matched by Uncle Sam. CSRS employees could also establish an account with the TSP, but their contributions would not be matched by the government.

In the lead up to the implementation of FERS and for some time afterward, the FAA, and no doubt other agencies as well, launched a major propaganda blitz touting the "advantages" of the new program. The pitch was basically that there was "no limit" to the amount of money an employee might amass for retirement. The stock market always rose, and Social Security, pegged to the inflation rate, generally tended upward as well. At Miami Tower, only one individual covered under CSRS elected to make the change to FERS, while the rest of us made the calculation that our employer was a little too enthusiastic about the new program to be credible. As we saw it, the downsides included a limit on contributions to the TSP, with a prohibition against contributions after retirement; no annual cost of living adjustment to TSP holdings as against adjustments to the full amount of the annuity under CSRS; and the possibility of a downturn in the markets close to one's retirement date, without sufficient time to make up the difference. The man that made the change to FERS at MIA took a major hit, retiring just a couple of years after the major economic downturn of 2009.

Welcome to the West 40

Beginning about a year after the strike, construction of a whole new facility for Miami Tower and approach control was begun. The location was at the west field boundary, adjacent to the cargo hangars and loading docks. For years Dade County had wanted to reclaim the spaces occupied by the TRACON and the tower's administrative offices, and in fact these accommodations had become increasingly cramped, with no possibility of further expansion. Day by day we watched the base building taking shape and the new tower rising against the western horizon, and eventually the new building reached a stage of completion allowing the administrative personnel to make the move. This left the tower and TRACON functions in the old quarters pending installation of all the electronics necessary to make a seamless transition when the time came to move.

After construction of the shell of the tower had progressed far enough, we were encouraged to visit the tower cab as a first step in orienting ourselves to the entirely new perspective we would have as ground controllers and local controllers. There were several events during this period that had us shaking our heads (or containing our laughter) in disbelief. In a classic case of the left hand not knowing what the right hand was doing, the radio, altimeter, wind indicators and other sensitive equipment had been installed in the tower consoles before the roof was sealed. When the inevitable Florida rain showers occurred, water poured through the roof and caused enough damage that most of that equipment had to be replaced. Then, with the roof still not completed, replacements for the items damaged were put in place and a loosely fitting plastic sheet stretched over the entire console.

Another visitor reported that he had found an empty wine bottle and a blanket on the tower floor. Apparently a different kind of "orientation" had been sought out and experienced by a couple who had explored the new tower together. We had our suspicions about who the culprits might have been, but nothing was ever proven.

The biggest laugh occurred at a training day when we were shown a video taken from the new tower. It was several minutes long, showing the entrance to the facility, the elevator to the cab, and panning around the airport to provide a sense of traffic movements on the taxiways and runways. The cameraman was supplying a running narration of what was being shown. At one point he directed the camera to the approach end of 9 Right, saying, "Now you can see that the local controller has a DC-10 in position on 9 Right, and is waiting for spacing on a previous departure off 9 Left." The next sound on the recording was the roar of full power being applied to four engines of a DC-8 that was going around, followed by an upward tilt of the camera lens to capture the aircraft overflying the one holding in position. Of course we did not know the circumstances leading up to the go around since the whole operation was being worked from the old tower across the field, but that did not diminish the ensuing peals of laughter and hoots of derision.

Eventually the day came for last phase of the move. During the midnight shift, the crew was split between the old facility and the new. Several of the radar indicators were trucked across the field, put in place, and tested, after which the first transmissions were made from the new TRACON and tower. Before the day shift arrived, the move was complete. When I reported for my first shift in the new facility, it had been several months since my previous visit, when construction was still going on. I had to admit that the new quarters were impressive, including a bronze plaque at the entrance bearing the names of President Reagan, the Secretary of Transportation, and the FAA administrator. Just inside there was a brass plaque on the wall to the left, with the date of the switchover, August 25, 1985, and showing the names of all Air Traffic and Airway Facilities personnel assigned to MIA. The floors gleamed, and the office spaces were, at least by comparison to the old digs, nothing short of sumptuous. Smoking had been prohibited in the operating quarters even before the move, so that the TRACON and tower would no longer bear the pervasive reek of stale tobacco.

By most measures, the move was all to the good. But I couldn't help feeling a certain letdown over some quality of life elements that had been lost. No longer would we be riding a bus from the employee parking lot with other people who worked in the terminal building. Instead, after negotiating "kamikaze alley" (that is, the road where the cargo trucks would park and pull out without warning) we would drive in through a gated entrance activated by a security code, park in our own lot, and walk to the front door. No longer could we grab a snack or order a full meal in one of the terminal restaurants. Instead, we were relegated to "brown-bagging" our meals, buying junk food from machines, or hoping that someone would make a "chow run" for everyone during the course of a shift. In short, we were cut off from the vibrant life of the terminal that had been so much a part of the Miami Tower experience.

On that first day, I was happy to see that I was assigned to radar, the functions of which, apart from a slightly different layout in the positioning of individual scopes, were unchanged. I made it a point at the first opportunity to visit the tower in order to get an idea of the pros and cons of what was essentially a brand new operation. It was a typical day at MIA—good weather, a light east wind, and an east operation, landing and departing Runways 9 Left, 9 Right, and 12. So from the perspective of the local controller, there were some real advantages as compared with working the operation from the terminal side. Instead of being over a mile and a half away, the run up pad shared by 9 Left and 12, and the approach ends of both runways, were now basically right at your feet. And the traffic on final could be sighted, and the spacing judged, that much sooner. Additionally, the line of aircraft taxiing for takeoff was now coming toward you, providing an earlier opportunity to plan the departure sequence and optimum runway use.

A New Challenge

Ground control, however, was now a huge challenge (or more colloquially, "a royal pain in the butt"). From the old tower, we were looking almost straight down into the alleyways between the "fingers" of the concourses extending out from the terminal like spokes of a wheel. These were congested spaces, and even though they were considered non-control areas, we had been able to "suggest" strategies to pilots and ground crews to facilitate the outbound traffic flow. Equally important, we had been able to keep inbound traffic away from the exit points until the way was clear to their assigned gates. From the new tower, even with good daytime visibility, we could not see into most of the alleyways, and it seemed that at least every other flight crew, after being cleared to taxi to the ramp, would pull up short and advise that they could not get to their gate because they were blocked by an aircraft awaiting taxi clearance to the runway for departure. There was some talk of splitting the ground control functions between the old tower and the new, with the areas of responsibility divided east and west rather than north and south. (This kind of operation was not unprecedented—Dallas Fort Worth airport had dual towers, and had experienced no problems). But the idea never came to fruition, for a couple of reasons. Dade County wanted to use the old tower for ramp control, and Miami Tower management foresaw problems with having the tower staff operating with reduced numbers on both sides of the airport.

And so life at MIA went on, soon acquainting us with the difficulties of night operations and a west operation. The approach end of 27 Right was a full two miles away. The ends of 27 Left and 30 were nearly as distant, making it very hard to manage the run-up pads when it came to orchestrating the most efficient departure sequence. To compound these problems, Runway 12 during this period was relocated, moving several hundred feet to the southwest to accommodate the soon to be constructed parallel taxiways leading from the terminal to the run-up area shared with 9 Left. The process involved digging up the entire 9,300 feet of runway surface and stacking it in a huge pile just north of 9 Right so that the asphalt could be melted down and used again when the re-location was complete.

Losing one of the three runways was always a major headache, in this case made even worse by the fact that traffic taxiing to or from 9 Right had to cross two construction areas (the new runway being prepared, and the old runway being plowed under). There was a complex web of barrels, sawhorses, and temporary lights put in place blocking most of the former crossing points that were no long available, and designating the single point to be used. Pilots frequently asked for assistance in navigating this maze, especially at night when it was doubly challenging for us to provide it.

Because both the parallel and diagonal taxiways to 9 Left were basically unaffected, we initially assigned 9 Left to any pilot who called for taxi. But inevitably there were always a few heavily loaded long-range flights that required runway 9 Right, now the longest at 13,000 feet. Not surprisingly, many of these were foreign carriers with destinations in South America, the pilots of which were generally heavily accented and in need of progressive taxi instructions. One night the pilot of a Varig 747, IFR to Rio de Janeiro, called for taxi, beginning the following exchange in a Portuguese accent:

RG 842: "Miami ground, Varig 842, request taxi."

GC: "Varig 842 heavy Miami ground, taxi to runway 9 Left."

RG 842: "Varig 842, we must use runway 9 Right."

GC: "Varig 842 heavy, roger, taxi to runway 9 Right."

The aircraft moved about two airplane lengths, then stopped.

RG 842: "Ground control, Varig 842, where I am supposed to go?"

GC: "Varig 842 heavy, continue southbound, I will point out the route to Runway 9 Right."

The pilot resumed his taxi, and about one minute later there came an urgent transmission from Ramp 20, the county vehicle responsible for monitoring surface operations on the airport:

Ramp 20: "Ground control, if you're working that Varig 747, tell him to stop! His right main landing gear is fouled in the lighting cables and he is towing a whole line of barrels and sawhorses with him!"

From the old tower, this would have been immediately observable, but because of the distance from the new tower to the terminal it was impossible to discern. It took the better part of an hour to untangle the mess.

The Air Traffic AERA Concepts Team

About a year before the move to the new facility, Lester McNeil, in his inimitable fashion, had called me into his office ("Potter, get your sorry ass in here!") Although the words suggested that something dire was afoot, I had learned that when Lester, who always talked that way, had a smile on his face there was nothing to worry about. Such was the case in this instance. He told me to close the office door, then began, saying, "How would you like to be part of a group working with an FAA contractor to modernize the whole ATC system?" Well, this sounded interesting for sure, but I wanted more detail. At that time Lester couldn't tell me much beyond his understanding that the group would be composed of controllers from both terminals and from en route control centers. It would be sponsored by FAA headquarters, which had set forth the following requirement for candidates to be selected for the group: a minimum of ten years as a journeyman controller in a Level 5 terminal or center.

I recognized that opportunities like this were few and far between, if they ever came, and so I did not hesitate to say yes. At first I felt a perhaps understandable swell of pride that I had been chosen. But upon reflection, I realized that at this point in time, three years after the strike, the number of Level 5 journeymen with ten years' experience was pretty small, and my puffed up ego deflated a bit. Still, there had to be at least a few controllers still working who had more experience or better credentials than I did. I questioned Lester about this, and he gave the following pithy answer:

"Listen, half these guys can't even write a coherent sentence, or they've got a chip on their shoulder about working with the center pukes. We need somebody with brains who will go in there, contribute to the effort, and not piss everybody off. Besides, we need you to look out for our facility so the center people don't create something that will screw us." This last point was an important one: no matter how efficient the en route procedures became, the ultimate limiting factor in system capacity would remain airport acceptance rates.

I joined the team and the first meeting between our group and the contractors was in Washington, D.C., in January 1984. The MITRE Corporation did a lot of contract work for the government, much of it for the Department of Defense in developing hardware and software for the military. The company also had several contracts with FAA, now including this new project designated Automated En Route Air traffic control (AERA). There were ten of us on the team, four from terminals (Miami, Houston, Des Moines, Philadelphia) and six from centers (Boston, Atlanta, Fort Worth, Albuquerque, Minneapolis, Salt Lake City). The man from Atlanta Center also had terminal experience, making him especially valuable to the team. The MITRE people were a diverse group with expertise in many areas: human factors, software development, mathematics, and pilot experience, to name a few.

The premise of the AERA project was that the ATC system was coming up against its limits in terms of what could be accomplished by the manual and mental efforts of human beings. Aircraft were confined to rigidly determined routes and procedures whose purpose was chiefly to allow controllers to keep track of individual flights and manage the flow, with the unfortunate corollaries of delay and inefficiency to the users. Computer technology was maturing in the mid-1980s, increasingly used in both the public and the private sector. Could automation perform at least some routine controller tasks more consistently and safely than a man or woman with a headset and a radio? IBM thought so, and had accepted the challenge of developing practical applications of the concepts that we and the MITRE professionals would formulate.

From the outset it was clear that MITRE had done a considerable amount of advance homework. Many of the individuals on the team understood the application of relevant portions of FAA Order 7110.65, the document that defined separation standards, procedures and the like. They also understood what every experienced air traffic controller knew—that within a certain (fairly short) time frame, it was possible to identify and implement proactive strategies that would ensure safety and increase efficiency—but that beyond that time frame, although you could develop a long range "Plan A" that might be useful, you would almost certainly have to modify it as circumstances changed. AERA might be the key to defining air traffic control as something other than "the timely correction of previously made errors."

In this first meeting, MITRE gave us an overview of what AERA might look like. A central computer, to be developed by IBM, would be able to monitor the trajectories, or planned flight paths, of all aircraft in the IFR system. It would have the capacity to accurately project aircraft positions out to about two hours, providing constant updates to assure that no two trajectories were in conflict. Or, if a conflict were identified, to generate an alert to the controller(s) responsible for the flights. There would also be a "trial planning" function that a controller could invoke in the event a pilot wished to make changes to his flight plan. For example, if a pilot requested an altitude change from flight level 310 to 350, the requested change could be entered into the computer as a trial plan. The automation would calculate either that the change would result in one or more conflicts, or that it could be implemented without causing later problems within the two-hour window.

These capabilities would certainly be useful in the ATC world, but we in the controller group pretty quickly came up with some questions. If a conflict were detected that would not occur for two hours, more than likely in the airspace of another sector or even another center, what action should the controller receiving the alert take? Was it reasonable to deny two hours of flight at a pilot's preferred altitude to solve a problem that far in the future? If a controller ignored the alert and granted the pilot's request, what implications did that have in terms of ATC responsibility as the time of the conflict drew near? What about an alert not generated by a trial plan but based on two established trajectories? Which airplane should be taken off its route? Or would an altitude change be better than a route change? These were questions that experienced controllers had to answer every day in the present system, and they generally did a fine job of making the right decisions, given the relatively short time horizon within which those decisions were made. But with lead times of an hour or more, it would be difficult if not impossible to make good calls. Could computer algorithms be made smart enough to do it?

It didn't take us long to see that there would be great value in having the automation not only detect the conflicts, but also generate resolutions to them. Could computer algorithms be made smart enough? The

MITRE engineers definitely wanted to learn about our decision-making process, much of which was simple common sense. Examples:
- If possible, do not resolve a conflict by creating another.
- Do not take an aircraft off its trajectory to accommodate another pilot's request for a trajectory change.
- If a conflict is to be resolved by an altitude change, descend the aircraft nearer its destination (less time at the less efficient lower altitude).
- If a conflict is to be resolved by an off-course vector, issue it to the aircraft required to make the smallest deviation from its course.
- The jerk-around factor: If a flight has already received several changes of route or altitude, resolve the conflict by moving a different aircraft.

MITRE had performed simulation studies designed to determine how many actual conflicts would occur if all aircraft were on random routes rather than being confined to specific airways. Rather astonishingly, these simulations indicated that the number was fairly small—in other words, it would not take an unrealistically large amount of computer power to generate the necessary resolutions, assuming you could teach a computer common sense.

Finding Solutions

Our first attempts in collaboration with MITRE to define the logic for conflict resolution showed that it was one thing to identify conflicts, and quite another to resolve them. We all got good laugh when the first "run" of computer-generated resolutions to a single conflict resulted in a stack of paper many pages thick containing literally hundreds of lines of data. We in the controller group had said that we wanted to see a list of "all" possible solutions to a given problem, and the computer algorithms obliged, providing a list that looked something like this:
- Delta 265 turn right 10 degrees
- Delta 265 turn left 10 degrees
- Delta 265 turn right 20 degrees
- Delta 265 turn left 20 degrees
- Delta 265 turn right 30 degrees
- Delta 265 turn left 30 degrees
- Delta 265 climb to FL 290
- Delta 265 climb to FL 330
- Delta 265 climb to FL 370

- Delta 265 descend to FL 270
- Delta 265 descend to FL 250
- Delta 265 increase speed 30 knots
- Delta 265 increase speed 40 nots
- Delta 265 reduce speed 20 knots
- Delta 265 reduce speed 30 knots
- Delta 265 reduce speed 40 knots
- Delta 265 enter holding for four minutes
- Delta 265 enter holding for eight minutes

A similar list was generated for the other airplane, basically trial planning every heading, altitude, speed change, and even holding delay that would resolve the conflict. Clearly it made no sense to show a 20-degree course change when a 10-degree change would do, or an altitude change of two flight levels when one would do, or a large speed change when a small one would do. Holding would only be used to meter traffic flows, not to resolve a single conflict.

Our Air Traffic AERA Concepts Team (ATACT) had to go back to the drawing boards on this, and eventually came up with the notion that there were only six things an airplane in flight could do: turn right, turn left, climb, descend, speed up, or slow down. What would happen if we asked for one resolution in each category of maneuver, always selecting the minimum, and only the minimum, change necessary? This approach turned out to be a pretty good one, limiting a controller's choices to a maximum of six, and usually fewer than that given the altitude limitations and the narrow speed envelope within which commercial flights operated at cruise. An experienced controller could easily identify the best resolution, quickly discarding the others. As Andrew Haines, the brilliant lead engineer on the AERA project put it, "The computer will rank a maximum of six resolutions to a problem, and nobody said the lower ranked ones would be worth a damn."

The ATACT team met with MITRE two or three times a year, giving the engineers an opportunity between meetings to incorporate our input into the next iteration of development. The conflict resolution function became more nuanced as we recognized that at times a single maneuver did not come out "clean"—that is, a secondary or tertiary conflict could result from the action taken to resolve the primary problem. We created our own list of definitions characterizing the solutions produced by the automation, called "machine plans," as distinct from the controller-invoked trial planning function. Machine plans could be single maneuver (turn right 20 degrees), multiple maneuver (reduce speed 30 knots, then descend and maintain 16,000), or composite maneuver (turn left 20 degrees, descend and maintain FL 230). The collaboration between controllers and engineers produced a growing volume of documentation capturing, combining, and refining the elements of operational need versus automation capability.

At a certain point both the controller and the engineer groups saw the need for at an initial representation of what an AERA display and a computer-human interface (CHI) system might look like. The CHI experts at MITRE crafted a scripted traffic scenario to be displayed on three screens that allowed "conflicts" to be generated, identified, and then resolved by one of several resolutions presented. The AERA "suite" as it was termed was impressive, incorporating color-coding for the different types of information shown, and providing a simple, intuitive interface for controller use. Often when new technology had been introduced to the field there had been major problems in the early stages, and we were determined that AERA, in whatever final form it took, be easy to use and work as advertised.

There was an additional benefit to the AERA suite beyond contributing to the development of the system. By showing the "demo," as we called it, to industry stakeholders (think pilots, airline executives, FAA management types, working controllers) we hoped to solidify support for the project, knowing that funding for big ticket R and D efforts could sometimes be fickle. Over the ten years that AERA was under development, the demo was presented probably dozens of times, either at MITRE or "on the road" at events like the annual FAA technological symposium where vendors could hawk their wares. A few individuals from the controller team were designated to give these presentations, and I was fortunate enough to be one of them.

Membership in the ATACT team was one of my most satisfying professional experiences, creating opportunities (described in later chapters) for me that would never otherwise have occurred.

Back to a Staff Job (Not)

In 1986, the demands of working "on the boards" really began catching up with me. We were still short staffed in the operating quarters. Training new people continued unabated, and the facility management had agreed to a new schedule of shift rotation. Previously, each team had worked a week of day shifts, then a week of evening shifts, then back to days, then one week of "11 to 7s" to beef up our numbers during the busiest daytime hours, followed by three weeks alternating between days and evenings. The eighth week was five days of "mids," midnight shifts from 11:00 pm to 7:00 am. The effects of shift work in all industries that required it were well known—disruption of circadian rhythms, family problems, and even a higher incidence of personal afflictions like ulcers and depression. But at least we had our days off to recalibrate and get ready for the change coming the following week. The new schedule was known as a modified 2-2-1, meaning that the workweek would begin with two evening shifts, followed by two day shifts (or an 11 to 7 followed by another day shift) and concluding with a single "mid." The "advantage" of this schedule was that the break period between weeks was a little longer, lasting from 7:00 am on the last day till 3:00 pm on the first day back. But it meant that you had two minimum 8-hour double backs switching from evenings to days and days to midnights. It played hell with sleep patterns, and for "old guys" like me, eight hours was simply not enough time to recharge the mental batteries before the next go-around.

Although I still had another two years to go before I would reach 20 years of eligible controller time for early retirement, I decided to try to cash in the chip promised me two years earlier, and return to my staff position. Unfortunately, a new chief and deputy were now in place, and as I made my pitch, describing my conversation with their predecessors, I could see that my request was going nowhere. They knew nothing about any commitment by the former manager, and besides there were no staff vacancies available. Well, there was nothing to do at this point but to soldier on, and hope for consideration if and when a staff opening did occur.

Within a few weeks the deputy chief, a hard-nosed, humorless individual, called me into his office, saying, without preamble, that the annual staff study would be due in about a month. The people responsible for the study—the Plans and Procedures officer and a specialist—were on leave, and we could not afford to wait for them to return. Since I was "so interested" in staff work, I would be taken off the operational roster and temporarily assigned a desk to complete this important job.

This was definitely a good news/bad news situation. The staff study was a complicated undertaking, especially in those days before electronic records, requiring the collation of a year's worth of data showing how often each radar and tower position had been staffed. There were stacks of handwritten sign-on logs, and daily typewritten logs from both the tower and the TRACON that had to be analyzed. The purpose of the study was to justify the numbers required to run the facility. But most controllers spent only about four and a half hours of each 8-hour day actually working a position. So a certain amount of "creativity" was needed or else the completed document would indicate that our staffing numbers should be substantially reduced.

I had no experience to prepare me for this task, and I realized that there was a real opportunity here to fall flat on my face. The FAA order covering the staff study seemed to me, at least, a minefield of traps for the uninitiated. For instance, the previous year (the basis for the study), was defined as "the current year" while "the previous year" actually referred to the period two years earlier. For these and other reasons, I had many questions, and the only person available to me to answer them was the deputy who had assigned me the project. After several attempts to get some guidance, I began to suspect that he didn't know much more than I did about a staff study. Our conversations normally went something like this:

Me: "George, I'm not quite clear on what the order means when it says "current year." This is August, so we don't have complete data for this year."

George would look at what I had on paper so far, and then answer something like, "I'll tell you what, if I was reviewing this in the regional office, it would take me about two minutes to kick it back for a re-do. You need to start over." He never gave me any useful information, leaving me to figure things out as best I could.

As the deadline for submission approached, the Plans and Procedures officer returned from leave, and called me into his office to discuss my progress on the study. I told him there were a number of points in the document where I wasn't sure I had done the right thing, to which he replied that he was, "happy as hell about how far along it is." At the weekly staff meeting a few days later, I wasn't sure what to expect. My draft of the staff study had been reviewed, and there were still a few more days before the final version would have to be sent to the Southern Region. Had the managers approved it? Did it need some minor fixes? A wholesale revision? As chair of the meeting, George addressed the subject first thing. Remembering his uncompromising criticism at every step along the way, I about fell out of my chair when he said, "At the end of the week we will submit our annual staff study to the region. Let's hear a round of applause for Rust Potter, who did an outstanding job of putting it together for us." Go figure.

So I had not fallen flat on my face. Did this augur well for returning to a staff position? Not in the short term, as it turned out. The following week I was back in the operating quarters working the unfriendly 2-2-1 rotation.

A couple of months later, a new group of trainees was scheduled to report to the facility. The decision had been made to advertise a new staff position in the training department to provide classroom and radar simulation training to these individuals and the many more who would follow. With my pre-strike experience in this position, it seemed that I should have a pretty good shot at being selected. A few days after the bid period closed, Will McCutcheon, the manager responsible for training, called me into his office, telling me to close the door. As he began speaking, I could see that he was not smiling, and in fact appeared to be less than comfortable. He said, "I have to tell you that a selection has been made for the training position. We will be bringing Joe Ambrister back from Tamiami, and I wanted you to hear it from me first, before the general announcement is made. Nobody has better qualifications for the job than you, but we just can't spare you from the watch right now. Please keep this confidential until the selection is made public."

I was more than disappointed, to say the least. But Joe was well qualified, having served as a training instructor before being sent to Tamiami in the aftermath of the strike. I did my best to react with equanimity, saying that Joe had been a valuable asset to the facility, and that I appreciated Will's candor in leveling with me.

I returned to the TRACON and plugged in at Miami South Departure Control, the position that handled traffic in and out of Tamiami. Within the first few minutes there came a call from TMB initiated by a controller whom I knew. It went like this:

TMB: "Miami, Tamiami, release request."
Me: "Miami."
TMB: "Need a release on N7281 Quebec, Cessna 177, off 9 Left."
Me: "Cessna 7281 Quebec, turn left heading 290, released, RP."
TMB: "OK, thanks—hey, is that you Rusty?"
Me: "Yeah."
TMB: "Hey, what do you think about old Joe Ambrister coming back to Miami?"
Me: "Oh, is he? Well, that's great."

So much for keeping the big secret about the training position.

Another Option Denied

Sometime in October or November, I was approached by Dave, the Data Systems Officer. He was in charge of managing the ARTS automation system that provided individual alphanumeric tags, altitude, and speed information for each radar identified aircraft within our airspace. There were three staff specialists assigned to the Data Systems function, called Data Systems Specialists (DSSs). This specialty was a little different than training or plans and procedures in that the DSSs were required to maintain controller currency in order to be eligible for promotion to a supervisory position. They all had controller experience, but the most capable individuals relied primarily on their technical savvy about computers and software. Dave was aware that I wanted to get back to a staff position, and asked if I would be interested in working for him. The conversation went something like this:

Dave: "Would you be interested in being a DSS?"
Me: "I don't know Dave, that computer stuff is really not my forte."
Dave: "Don't worry about that. We can teach you automation, but what we really need is somebody with Miami Tower smarts to help us figure out what we want the automation to do."

We talked for several more minutes, and I decided I had better grab this opportunity, which was basically being offered to me on a silver platter. Dave said the advertisement for the position would be coming out shortly, and that I should submit my bid promptly when it did. Within a couple of weeks the vacancy was announced, and my bid was in Dave's hands. My candidacy seemed to be a "lock," given that the man making the selection had approached me up front, but a few days later Dave called me into his office, shaking his head and looking mightily pissed off. He said, "Well, we have a new DSS, and it's not you. They pulled HS (the operating initials of the man in question) off the boards and assigned him to me because he was getting so many pilot complaints. Apparently he had a couple of deals (loss of separation) and was using profanity on the frequency. I'm really sorry, I wasn't given any choice."

Time for Plan B

So I was basically 0 for 3 on attempts to regain my staff position. The last one was particularly galling, as I felt that my history and qualifications would rank me well above "HS" in any selection process. It did not seem right that actions that should have led to disciplinary measures instead landed the individual in a position that not only freed him from the pressures of the operation, but added a valuable credential to his resume.

But I was determined to keep a positive outlook. I had more than once observed that people who objected to an unfavorable outcome, endlessly arguing their cases, filing grievances or pursuing other avenues of redress were basically shooting themselves in the foot. At the very least, I intended to be the candidate against whom there were no objections. This posture had served me well a few years earlier when I was elected to the Facility Air Traffic Technical Advisory Committee (FATTAC) team. This was a group of controllers elected by their co-workers to vet suggestions made by the workforce aimed at improving the MIA operation. The group could also originate recommendations of its own to be submitted for review by management.

PATCO definitely influenced the election process by trying to get a majority of its members to agree on a slate of FATTAC nominees to the union's liking. As it was relayed to me by the local PATCO rep, the four union officers had settled on their preferred candidates for two of the three committee positions, and but could not agree on the last person. Someone brought up my name, and there was a pause, before all four of the officers agreed that I would be an effective committee member.

And so it was that when Tamiami Tower advertised a vacancy for operations supervisor, I decided to give it a shot. I really didn't want to leave MIA, but after more than 18 years in the rush and crush of high-density traffic, I needed a change. My record was clean, and I had some additional qualifications that other applicants might not have. I had bid on the same job a few years earlier, but my heart wasn't in it. The chief of TMB at the time had been there for many years, never having worked in a big facility, and he came across as a self-important jerk during the interview process. It was almost a relief when I was not selected.

This time the chief was Earl Peavey, a guy who had trained me in my early days at MIA, whom I knew and liked. In addition, the other supervisor was Mark James, who had worked at Miami for a time. Although we were not close friends, he knew me, and I felt that he would probably support my selection as a known quantity in preference to someone who was a complete unknown. Earl interviewed me by telephone from Panama City in northern Florida where he was currently the tower manager, informing me that his reporting date to TMB would be only a week or two before the supervisor bid closed. It was a cordial exchange, leaving me with the impression that I would probably be selected. Sure enough, about two weeks later I received word that the job was mine.

Although I was convinced that Miami Tower management had not done all it could to put me back on staff, they came through for me in an important way relating to my impending move. The rules relating to pay and promotion at that time permitted an individual who took a job categorized as "career progression" to save pay. They put me at the top of the GS-14 pay scale, and my annual salary increased by thousands of dollars.

My last workday at MIA was an evening shift on January 24, 1987. The weather was poor, with low ceilings, reduced visibility, and off and on rain showers. I was working Local Control on a west operation, with traffic on final and at the run-up pads for 27 Right and 27 Left almost obscured by the precipitation. For the first and only time in my life, I requested to be relieved from the position. My fellow controllers obliged, understanding that I did not want to risk having an accident or incident this late in the game.

13. Entering a New World

Three days later I drove into the parking lot at the base of the Tamiami control tower. It was an easy four-mile commute from where I lived, happily contrasting with the daily 14-mile trek to MIA in the perpetual crush of weekday traffic. It was just a dozen steps to the facility entrance rather than waiting in the rain for a bus ride to the airline terminal at Miami that might be long minutes in coming. So, I could already see some quality of life improvements.

The tower itself was a humble, bare bones structure rising perhaps 70 or 80 feet with corrugated sheet-metal siding. The interior was unabashedly utilitarian—scuffed linoleum flooring with metal steps leading to each of the four floors above ground level. There was a small elevator that had seen its better days, creaking and groaning with every ascent and descent. Half of the tower shaft housed the staircase and the elevator, while the other half provided a single room off the landing at each floor. Just opposite the entrance on the first floor was an equipment room used by Airway Facilities personnel. The second-floor space was designated a training room where manuals and study materials were kept and where briefings or self-study took place. The third floor was the office space, occupied by the facility chief and a secretary, when we were lucky enough to have one. The fourth floor was the break room, furnished with a table, chairs, refrigerator, sink, microwave and soft drink machines. A small restroom was located opposite the break room. A narrow staircase of steep steps led to the tower cab from the fourth floor landing. The cab itself appeared at first glance to be uncomfortably small and cramped, but I had to remind myself that I was used to the relatively wide open spaces at MIA.

After an enjoyable reunion with Earl, whom I had not seen for quite a few years since he had left Miami, Mark escorted me to the tower and introduced me to the staff—three individuals plus himself. It was about 9:00 am on a sunny Monday morning, and the pace seemed very moderate. Each of the controllers had plenty of time to greet me between transmissions, and I was, at least at this point, modestly reassured about the new position.

One thing I had learned at Miami, both as a trainee and as an instructor, was that attentive observation of a control position could provide an invaluable boost in preparedness when it came to actual on the job training. (Yes, I would again be a trainee—first-level supervisors were required to maintain the same operational currency and proficiency as the controllers they supervised). I always said, based on my own experience, that everyone was an expert standing in the back of the cab watching someone else work, but that expertise rapidly declined as soon as you put on the headset yourself. Accordingly, I decided on that first day to spend some time watching and listening, and asking a few questions at opportune moments.

At that time, Tamiami was the second busiest airport in Florida, at least in terms of its traffic count: 350,000 operations per year and climbing. The runway configuration was almost identical to Miami's—9 Left/ 27 Right, 9 Right/ 27 Left, and 13/31, only ten degrees different from 12/30 at MIA, but scaled down by about 50 percent (the east west parallels were each 5,000 feet long, the diagonal 4,000 feet). That day, it was an east operation, chiefly utilizing 9 Left and 9 Right, with an occasional landing on 13 for arrivals from the north parking on the south side of the airport. There were two local control positions and a single ground control/flight data/clearance delivery position.

At first I wondered how one person could handle the three functions combined at GC, but I soon realized that the number of flights requiring processing by Flight Data and Clearance Delivery was very limited, the vast majority of operations being local VFR training hops. Even Ground Control was completely manageable, since there was no parking gate capacity to worry about and the fact that the total airport surface was so small.

As I watched on the first day, the tempo picked up substantially. Soon there were four or five Cessna trainers awaiting departure at both 9 Right and 9 Left, and an equal number in the touch and go patterns on both sides of the field. Automation tracking was very limited, with ARTS tags placed only on itinerant arrivals being worked by Miami Approach Control. Most of the touch and go traffic was high-wing two-place Cessna 150 trainers, identical in profile, many with the same paint job, and small registration numbers that could not be read from any distance. Because of the scale of the BRITE radar presentation, these targets could not be assigned identification tags. Even using the smallest font the tags obliterated the entire airport and overlapped with each other to the extent that they were unreadable.

Each local controller had a sequence of flight progress strips, hand written with the aircraft identifications, to help keep track of traffic in the pattern. The strips were stacked in a bay, or rack, and the one at the bottom represented the next airplane to land. In the case of a touch and go, as soon as the pilot lifted off, the strip was placed at the top of the stack and moved down with each successive landing. This method was workable, but far from foolproof, for a variety of reasons:

- Under busy conditions, a controller might be late in re-ordering the strips.
- A pilot on downwind instructed to follow the second aircraft on final might instead see only the airplane in the number one position and turn base early; or, conversely, might fail to see the traffic to follow and continue on downwind and miss his slot.
- A pilot might not hear or recognize his call sign (or worse, use the wrong call sign) and then fail to make the required maneuver.

All of these things happened with some regularity, the problems being compounded by the fact that most of the pilots were inexperienced students in training and that many had only a limited command of English. It was immediately apparent to me that the controllers were having to spend an inordinate amount of time repeating instructions, second-guessing questionable position reports, and generally leading these "Billy Beginners" by the hand.

The Miami International Flight Service Station was also located at Tamiami. This was a 24-hour facility whose function was to process flight plans, issue NOTAMS, take local weather observations, and provide weather briefings to pilots flying cross country. The flight service people also provided airport advisory service during the hours that the tower was closed. In 1987 the hours of tower operation were from 8:00 am to 9:00 pm, a 13-hour day that had some definite advantages in terms of staffing coverage. Since controller shifts were eight hours long, there was a three-hour "overlap" between the day shift, which ended at 4:00 pm, and the evening shift that began at 1:00 pm.

If you were working days, and wanted to leave a few hours early, it was usually no problem once the one o'clock group arrived; similarly, if you were working evenings, you could often take the first three hours off. The "overlap" also provided a nice window within which to conduct briefings or classroom training, as well as an opportunity to spend some time in the office completing administrative tasks.

The opening and closing of the tower followed a set routine. At exactly 8:00 am, both the local controller and the ground controller would transmit, "Attention all aircraft, Tamiami Tower is now open." From this point on, all pilots were expected to contact ground control for taxi and local control for takeoff clearance (departures) or landing instructions (arrivals). At exactly 9:00 pm, both controllers would transmit, "Attention all aircraft, Tamiami Tower is now closed. Contact Miami Radio (the flight service station) for airport advisory service."

The morning transition to tower control generally did not cause problems. Traffic was usually light enough that aircraft identifications and positions were quickly established. When the tower closed, however, it could be a different story, especially on Thursday nights when the flight schools conducted night flying instruction. In an instant a busy touch-and-go pattern being refereed by local control became more or less a free-for-all in which the pilots were expected to keep their traffic in sight, maintaining a proper interval, and not landing until the runway was clear, all in the dark. The airport advisory service was of limited value under these conditions, being intended only to relay general information, such as "traffic is two Cessnas inbound from the northwest," or "numerous aircraft in the touch and go pattern on Runway 9 Right."

Again, because of inexperience, many of the pilots did not readily comprehend the difference between tower control and these general advisories provided by Flight Service. On a number of occasions, we observed hair-raising situations in the moments after the tower closed. A student pilot would lose sight of his traffic and ask the flight service specialist, who was sitting in a windowless room with no radar coverage or direct visibility of the airport, to point the traffic out. The specialist would advise the pilot that he could not provide that information, and the student would turn base in front of the airplane he was supposed to follow. The result would be two aircraft landing on the same runway with spacing that under tower control would be totally illegal, not to mention dangerous. Or on a west operation, students would fly the ILS approach to 9 Right directly into the face of opposite direction departures off 27 Left.

A Lesson in Humility

The first order of business was to review local orders and procedures. I was familiar with the letter of agreement between TMB and Miami Approach Control, but there were other provisions that were unique to the Tamiami operation. One of the most important was the procedure for crossing Runway 13 with traffic taxiing to 9 Right. Runway 13 intersected both 9 Right and its parallel taxiway, and normally ground control would coordinate with local control for each crossing. But because 13 was seldom used, this standard method was reversed, allowing ground traffic to cross without coordination until the local controller decided to use the runway for either a takeoff or a landing. In these cases, he would state, "13 is hot." After an affirmative acknowledgement from the ground controller, the coordination was complete.

Another local procedure was the use of a helicopter training area designated Area Alfa. Area Alfa was a section of unprepared grass within the airport boundary located south of Runway 9 Right and extending the length of the runway. The maximum altitude permitted in the area was 300 feet to ensure separation of the helicopters from fixed-wing traffic on downwind at 800 feet. No more than two helicopters could use the area at the same time, and there was no direct control by the tower other than ensuring a safe transition to and from their parking locations.

Like Miami's training syllabus, Tamiami's called for initial OJT on ground control. Besides issuing taxi clearances, the position was also responsible for flight data and clearance delivery, which functions mainly centered on pre-takeoff coordination with Miami for pilots on VFR cross-country flight plans desiring flight following. Unless the weather was down, we usually had no more than half a dozen IFR flights a day. All of this was completely familiar to me, having spent 18 years receiving these coordination calls at MIA. A typical exchange would go like this:

N6176R: "Tamiami ground, Bonanza 6176 Romeo filed VFR to Sarasota, Victor 97 at 6,500, request flight following."

TMB Ground: "Bonanza 6176 Romeo Tamiami ground, roger, standby."

TMB Ground (on coordination line): "Miami, Tamiami."

MIA: "Miami's on."

TMB: "OK Miami, need a VFR code for Bonanza 6176 Romeo, VFR to Sarasota, Victor 97 at 6,500."

After entering the aircraft ID into the ARTS system, the Miami departure controller would reply: "Bonanza 76 Romeo squawk 4315, LN."

TMB: "RP."

TMB (on ground control frequency): "Bonanza 76 Romeo, squawk 4315, departure frequency will be 125.5. Advise ready to taxi."

N6176R: "76 Romeo roger, 4315 on the transponder, 125.5 for departure control, and we're ready to taxi from Jet Center with information Delta."

This example is reflects that the pilot was knowledgeable about the ATC system, understood exactly what to request, and knew what information air traffic control needed in order to provide the requested service. In other instances it could be an uphill struggle, almost always because low-experience pilots did not have a good understanding of ATC capabilities and VFR radar service. There tended to be a "monkey-see (or hear)-monkey do" dynamic at work when one pilot would overhear an exchange like the one in the example above. There would follow a round and round series of transmissions between controller and pilot that would go something like this:

N517GH: "Tamiami ground, Cessna 517 Golf Hotel, can I get one of those transponder codes?"

TMB Ground: "Cessna 517GH Tamiami ground, say your intentions."

N517GH: "Well, I just want a transponder code."

TMB: "Cessna 7GH, are you planning a cross-country flight?"

N517GH: "That's affirmative, Tamiami."

TMB: "Cessna 7GH, say your destination, route of flight, filed altitude, and proposed departure time."

N517GH: "I don't really have a destination, I just want to cruise up and down the beach and do a little sightseeing, but I want you to watch me on radar."

TMB: "Cessna 7GH, we do not provide radar service, you will need to contact Miami Departure control with your request."

N517GH: "Ok, I will call Miami. Should I do that now?"

TMB: "Cessna 7GH, negative, either advise them on initial contact of the service you want, or if you would like me to forward your request to Miami, I can do that now."

N517GH: "Oh thanks, Tamiami, I would appreciate it if you would do that."

TMB: "Cessna 7GH, state your request."

N517GH: "Just let them know I will be calling them."

TMB (on coordination line): "Miami, Tamiami."

MIA: "Miami."

TMB: "Need a VFR code for Cessna 517GH, Cessna 150, says he wants to sightsee along the beach."

MIA: "Cessna 517GH squawk 4307, EE."

TMB: "OK, 4307, and keep a close watch on this guy, he doesn't seem to know much about flight following or traffic advisories."

MIA: "Will do, thanks Tamiami."

TMB (on GC frequency): "Cessna 517GH, squawk 4307, departure frequency will be 125.5, advise ready to taxi."

N517GH: "Roger, squawk 4307, and say again the departure frequency?"

TMB: "Cessna 7GH departure frequency will be 125.5."

N517GH: "125.5, got it, and I won't be going till later on this afternoon, I'll call you then. Good day."

TMB: "Cessna 7GH, are you still with me?" (No response, after repeated calls).

TMB (on coordination line): "Miami, Tamiami, disregard Cessna 7GH. He said he wouldn't be going till later today, then left the frequency before I could cancel his transponder code. We will try to catch him and cancel the code when he does call for taxi."

MIA: "OK, I'll keep the code for a while in case he does go."

Besides taking up a considerable amount of time, exchanges like this exhibited a number of red flags. First and foremost, it was clear that the pilot was not familiar with the terms "flight following" or "VFR advisories." Most controllers are taught not to ask a pilot if he wants a particular service because of the likelihood that the answer will be in the affirmative even if the pilot has no idea what the term means. Far better, we all knew, to make the pilot request the service specifically. In the example above, there is a major "hanger" (something that can't be dealt with now but must be remembered and dealt with later) in the form of the discrete transponder code issued to the Cessna pilot.

The total number of transponder codes available in the ARTS system was 4096, with the majority being assigned by Miami Center to aircraft on instrument flight plans. A small subset was reserved for so called "in-house" use in tagging VFR aircraft. These codes were frequently recycled. Each time a VFR pilot either landed or left Miami Approach Control's airspace, the code for that flight would again be available for another aircraft. So if 7GH's ID was removed from the system and the code assigned to another aircraft, the pilot of 7GH, using the code assigned hours earlier, might result in the Cessna being tagged with an incorrect identification.

Despite the fact that most of the Tamiami pilots were either students or relatively inexperienced private ticket holders, it did not take me long to get a handle on the ground control/ flight data/ clearance delivery functions. I could now take the position to provide relief breaks for the controllers, as well as to work toward my required 16 hours per month of operational position time. Local control, however was a brand new ballgame. All my years in the high-density environment of Miami Tower did not remotely prepare me for the busier periods on local. The combination of heavy accents, poor radios (and poor radio discipline), incorrect position reports, visually similar airplanes, and very little automation support made working the position under high workload conditions a real challenge. Time and again, in the early stages of my training, my instructor, a young man or woman half my age, would have to take the frequency to keep things under control.

The worst instance of failing to keep the picture occurred one evening shift, probably on a Thursday with night flying in progress. There were several touch-and-go aircraft in the 9 Right traffic pattern with several others at the run-up pad awaiting departure. The pilot of a Cessna 150, barely understandable because of his accent, requested takeoff clearance to remain in the pattern. I put him in position on the runway, and then, due to distraction, failed to issue the magic words "cleared for takeoff." The result was that three or four of the active touch-and-go airplanes passed over the Cessna in position, making their "bounce," and continuing their circuit. Unaccountably, neither the pilot of the airplane in position nor any of those in the air transmitted anything about this hazardous operation.

My instructor finally recognized what was happening and instructed the Cessna pilot to taxi clear of the runway. I was properly chagrined at this inexcusable mistake, and by rights should have documented the event as a series of operational errors. The fact that my instructor had only caught on belatedly was no consolation. Beyond that, because I was in training, she would have borne the blame for the incident. Despite the fact that it was my clear duty to provide a full accounting of these events, I was not about to stick a good competent controller with the stigma of an "OE" (operational error) that was clearly my fault.

Other lessons in working general aviation traffic also occurred, both during my training and even after I checked out. Here are a couple of examples, the first illustrating the problems of incorrect position reporting and the tendency of GA pilots always to answer in the affirmative when a controller asked a question:

N76852: "Tamiami tower Cherokee 76852 inbound for landing."

Me: "Cherokee 76852 Tamiami tower, say position and advise you have received (ATIS) information Juliet."

N76852: "852, I'm not exactly sure of my position, but I'm homing in on the Miami VOR."

The Miami VOR was about 15 miles north of TMB, so I transmitted, "Cherokee 852, are you north of the airport?"

N76852: "852, affirmative."

Me: "Cherokee 852 roger, enter left traffic for runway 9 Left, report three miles north."

N78852: "852, roger."

From time to time I checked the BRITE radar display, looking for a likely target that might be the Cherokee, but never saw one that fit the bill. By the time this event occurred, I was smart (or paranoid) enough to have suspicions about the Cherokee pilot's position, and I observed a target seemingly headed directly for Tamiami—about eight miles south. I transmitted, "Cherokee 852, confirm you are north of Tamiami."

N76852: "Affirmative, Tamiami."

Me: "Cherokee 852, I observe traffic eight miles to the south that appears headed our way. Are you south of the airport?"

N76852: "Affirmative, Tamiami."

Me: "Cherokee 852, you originally reported that you were to the north, did you fly past the airport?"

N76852: "Negative Tamiami, but my compass is showing an "N", so I thought I was to the north."

I quickly revised my landing instructions to the pilot, instructing him to make right traffic for 9 Right, and it all came out all right. But, I wondered, how could a pilot certified for cross-country flying not understand that if you were navigating to an airport and the compass showed that you were heading north, it could only mean that your location was to the south.

The Closing Hour

In another case there were three of us on duty in the final 20 or 30 minutes before the 9:00 pm closing hour. Fortunately, it was not a night flying Thursday, and there was no active traffic. On the BRITE display we observed a primary target (no transponder) tracking towards Tamiami from the north. As the aircraft approached the airport it appeared that the pilot was setting up for a base leg to runway 9 Left, but there was no mode C altitude information available, no visible navigation lights, nor any apparent attempt by the pilot to make radio contact. Even with binoculars we could not see the aircraft, which was now unmistakably lined up on the 9 Left final. The local controller made several calls "in the blind" (transmissions when there is no two-way radio contact) without receiving any response.

All three of us were intently focused on the runway threshold, never observing the airplane until it reached mid-field where there was enough light from the adjacent ramp areas for us to see that it was a single-engine Piper Cherokee with no lights. The pilot taxied to the nearest FBO (fixed base operator) and shut down. As he walked toward office of the FBO, we called the attendant on duty, asking him to have the pilot contact us by telephone. Soon I was having a conversation with the Cherokee pilot that went like this:

Me: "Sir, did you realize that you were landing at Tamiami?" (This lead question was to determine whether pilot had misidentified the airport, thinking he was at an uncontrolled field).

Pilot: "Oh yeah, I fly out of here all the time."

Me: "Well, did you realize that the tower was still open?" (Maybe he thought we had closed because it was getting near to nine o'clock).

Pilot: "Yeah, I know you close at nine."

Me: "We did not receive any call from you requesting permission to enter the airport traffic area or landing clearance, nor did we observe any of the required lights for night operation."

Pilot: "Yeah, sorry about that. When I started up at Pahokee, the whole electrical system went out—radio, lights, instrument panel, everything."

Me: "Well I'm sure you are aware that operating at night without navigation lights and landing at a controlled airport without radio contact are both violations of FARs. Did you make any attempt to get the electrical problems fixed before you took off?"

Pilot: "No, I didn't. There are no facilities at Pahokee, and I knew there was no tower, so I thought the best bet was just to get back here to home base."

Me: "Sir, in the future, unless the failure occurs in the air, you should telephone ahead so that we can prepare for a no radio landing."

After a few more exchanges in a similar vein, the call was concluded. We could have written up a report of the incident to be forwarded to Flight Standards, the office that investigated and ruled on pilot infractions. But as I had learned at Miami, unless there was a true compromise of safety, the better course in dealing with events like this was usually a heart to heart with the pilot rather than official action.

All in all, it was a disconcerting several months before I finally checked out, and I was forced to recognize (per Clint Eastwood) that "a man has to know his own limitations." Once I was on my own, I was able to operate by the principle that had kept me clean at Miami, and that I tried to instill in every controller I trained - namely, "No one is going to thank you for taking more airplanes than you can handle."

There were options readily available in the VFR tower environment that you could rely on to keep the workload manageable, such as.:

- Limit touch-and-go traffic. If the pattern was full, you could instruct one or two pilots to either make a full stop landing or depart the pattern.
- For arrivals, limit access to the airport traffic area, the (then) five mile circle up to 2,000 feet surrounding the airport.
- For practice approaches, controlled by Miami Approach Control, advise the Miami controller that no more practice approaches would be approved until further notice.

I did not hesitate to use these strategies when I believed it was necessary, and as I settled into my supervisory role, counseled the controllers to follow suit.

The Joys of Supervision

After my selection for the supervisor position at Tamiami, I gave considerable thought to how I would handle the job. In my 18 years at MIA I had worked for a number of supervisors, some good, some bad, and most somewhere in the middle. It was common knowledge that first-level supervision was the toughest job in the agency, since management was usually pushing one way while the controllers, and especially the union, were almost always pushing in the opposite direction. In the lead up to the strike the supervisors were browbeaten within an inch of their lives as tensions between management and the workforce rose.

Now, in 1987, PATCO had been decertified as the controllers' bargaining unit, and the organization that would replace it, NATCA, had not yet come into being. In theory, because most of the post-strike controllers either had not participated in the job action or were new hires who had not been indoctrinated in the confrontational strategies that had precipitated the strike, the frictions between management and employees should have been greatly reduced.

So, I was reasonably confident that I was ready to be a supervisor. I would do my best to live by the following principles:
- No matter how angry or upset an employee might be, I would never respond in kind (I looked at this as "killing them with kindness").
- No matter how ridiculous or unimportant an employee's concern might seem to be, I would never be dismissive, but would always respond in a way that would make the individual feel that he or she had been heard.
- In general, I would do my best to "keep it light." My longtime friend

and eventually my supervisor at MIA, Billy Pierce, was a master at this. More than once I saw him defuse a situation with a quick dash of humor and a disarming smile. After the fact, I can report that I lived faithfully by these principles. I can also report that doing so did not in the least diminish the complaints, nor in any way reduce the number of issues that I had seen my supervisors deal with. Live and learn.

Things started out well enough as the controllers and I took measure of one another. As I came to know the individuals better, I began to see that there were two or three relationships among the troops that definitely reflected bad chemistry. None of the individuals seemed to me to be malcontents, and I couldn't understand how anyone could be unhappy about anything at Tamiami, which I basically considered a garden spot. But the process of refereeing these conflicts, no matter how evenhanded I tried to be, inevitably put me in the position of being "for" one person and "against" another.

My first real challenge occurred about a year after I got to the facility. During my absence at a meeting of the AERA Concepts Team, a new employee named Leroy reported to Tamiami. For about a week or ten days he underwent classroom training and then began OJT on ground control/ clearance delivery flight data. When I returned from the meeting, Leroy introduced himself, initiating a conversation that went like this:

Leroy: "Hi Rusty, I've been looking forward to meeting you."

Me: "Same here Leroy, welcome aboard. Are you pretty well settled in both on the home front and here at work?"

Leroy: "Oh sure, and I'm ready for checkout on ground control."

Me: "Really, that fast? How many hours do you have on ground?"

Leroy: "I don't know, four or five hours I guess, but I could work the position with my eyes closed. It's a piece of cake."

Me: "Well, I grant you that the position is not that difficult. But have you worked it on a west operation?"

Leroy (with a distinctly truculent tone): "We haven't BEEN west since I got here!"

Me: "OK, has the weather been IFR at any time since you started training?"

Leroy: "No it hasn't, and what difference does that make?"

Me: "There is quite a difference when the weather is down, not being able to see the whole airport, and lots of coordination with Miami for aircraft on instrument flight plans, coordinating between our two local controllers to protect for missed approaches reference airplanes waiting for release."

Leroy: "I know how to do all that stuff, it's easy."

Me: "All right, two things: number one, I want you to get some time on a west operation, and—

Leroy: "I told you, we haven't had a west operation yet!"

Me: "Yes, you did say that, and that's my point. But the second thing is that my signature will be on the form certifying you on ground, and if you have a problem with only four or five hours of training, it will come back to me."

Leroy: "This is bullshit! I've worked at three facilities, and I don't need any more training on a Mickey Mouse ground position."

Me: "Leroy, our training order establishes a minimum number of hours training prior to check out for each position. Since I haven't worked with you, I have had no opportunity to see how you're doing. We will plug into ground every day, and it will not take long to reach that minimum, at which time I will make a decision about certifying you."

At this point Leroy was hyperventilating and turning red in the face, finally making an abrupt about face and leaving the room. Something was going on with this guy that had nothing to do with ground control training, and I soon learned some background information that bore directly on the issue. He had begun his career at Fort Lauderdale Executive airport, had checked out there, then bid on a radar facility, where he had washed out. He returned to FXE and bid on another radar facility, where he again washed out. In cases where an employee did not successfully certify, agency policy was to return him to a facility of the same type at which he had last been certified. Usually, it was the facility he had last worked at, but in this case there was no vacancy at FXE. Leroy was assigned to Tamiami, apparently over his vehement objections to being back in a VFR tower and having to move to South Florida. From the FAA's point of view, there was no room for negotiation. He either accepted assignment at TMB, or he didn't have a job. The end result was that we had a perpetually angry and resentful individual on our hands for the entire time he was with us.

And it extended beyond the facility. Shortly after his arrival at TMB, Leroy's wife gave birth to a son with serious heart defects. In the several months leading up to corrective surgery, the parents had a number of discussions with the surgeon about possible risks and probable outcomes, which Leroy recounted in detail in his own terms: "I told that doctor I would hold him strictly accountable for any problems." Or, "I let him know that his years of experience and list of credentials didn't impress me in the least." Or, "I told him I didn't appreciate his adding to our stress by giving us all the worst case scenarios about the surgery."

During this period Leroy was frequently absent from work, and in many cases, sometimes with little or no notice, requested shift swaps with other controllers in order to make appointments at the hospital. Despite the fact that he had pretty much alienated every one of his co-workers, no one ever turned down these requests, knowing the seriousness of the medical issues. Sometime after the surgery was (successfully) completed, one of the individuals who had covered shifts for Leroy asked him for a shift swap. The conversation went like this:

Bruce: "Hey Leroy, can you take my one to nine shift tomorrow and let me have your eight to four?"

Leroy: "What do you need the day shift for?"

Bruce: "Our softball team has a game tomorrow afternoon."

Leroy: "NO! I am not giving up my day shift for a goddamn ball game!"

Leroy checked out on the positions without any (operational) problems, but his attitude was unimproved. About a year later he came to me with a bid sheet in hand, partially completed, offering himself as a candidate for the position of tower chief at Gainesville Tower in northern Florida. Gainesville was a Level 1 facility, the type tower that had the minimum annual traffic count to qualify as a controlled field. The chief's position was classified at the GS-11 level, one grade above the GS-10 controller classification. There were no supervisors or staff, meaning that the chief would be responsible for all administrative functions and would, in addition, have to check out and remain operationally current as a first-level supervisor. As he was explaining his intention to bid on the job, Leroy was all smiles, knowing that he needed a positive endorsement from me to complete the application. The conversation started out well enough, but deteriorated rapidly as I made it clear that such an endorsement was not in the cards:

Me: "So, looking to move up in the world of ATC? Good for you."

Leroy: "Are you being sarcastic?"

Me: "No, I'm not. I can't fault anyone for wanting to advance in a career. But I must tell you, I don't think this is the job for you."

Leroy (instantly combatative): "Why not!!?"

Me: "There are several reasons. You will have to negotiate letters of agreement with the facility providing approach control service, probably Jacksonville Center, and you have no experience in radar. You have never served in a staff position, and you have never supervised or managed employees."

Leroy: "I have radar experience in two facilities, and Gainesville is the perfect place to learn administration and supervision."

Me: "You did not complete training in either of the radar facilities you were at, and there is no one to mentor you in the other functions."

Leroy: "Well, you can't stop me from bidding on the job."

Me: "No, I can't. But see this box right here? It asks whether you foster harmony and efficiency with the people you work with. I am going to mark this item in the negative, and once I do that, it stands for a year for any future bids you might make. They don't ask this question for controller positions. You need to bid on a radar facility and check out there, then the way is clear for future moves."

At this Leroy abruptly stood up and leaned across the table, breathing hard, with flecks of foam in the corners of his mouth. Involuntarily, I pushed back from the table, genuinely feeling threatened, as Leroy proclaimed, "You have been against me since day one, and I am not going to put up with it anymore!" I stood up too, and replied, "No one is against you. You need to take a step back, take a look at how you do things, and answer this question: Is everything going the way you want it to? If you can honestly say yes, then keep doing what you are doing. If not, maybe you should consider a different approach." No matter the soundness of this advice, it is pretty much axiomatic that those who most need to hear it are the ones least able to hear it. Leroy stormed out of the room, saying "I am going to request a change of supervisors."

Fine with me, I thought.

A New Problem

True to his word, Leroy did request that he be assigned to Mark James, my opposite number. Mark was well aware of Leroy's personality and attitude, and I wondered how he would feel about taking on an employee with so many issues. Mark and I had a private discussion at some length, resulting in an agreement that we would carry out a swap placing Leroy under Mark's supervision and assigning one of Mark's people to me.

The man I got was Bruce Faraday, an older guy who had been in the FAA almost as long as I had. On the surface, he was the complete opposite of Leroy—outgoing, friendly, easy to be around. But he too had a troubled past. He had worked at a number of VFR towers, most recently at Ponce airport in Puerto Rico, and had left each of them under a cloud. Although I never learned all the details, his departure from Ponce apparently involved some "irregularities" in time and attendance records wherein entries were made for employees who were not even present in the facility on certain days. He had reported to Tamiami about a year before my arrival, and had immediately created a controversy involving his temporary quarters allowance. When an employee changed duty stations, the FAA authorized additional funds, above the normal salary level, so that the individual could find short-term accommodations while searching for a permanent residence.

Bruce had chosen a cheap rundown motel in an area where criminal activity was known to flourish, at a cost well below the daily allowance for temporary quarters. In this way he was hoping to realize a financial windfall by pocketing the difference. Shortly after moving into the motel Bruce filed a claim against the FAA for many thousands of dollars, asserting that his room had been broken into and that thieves had stolen expensive camera equipment and other belongings. He maintained that since the government was paying for these lodgings any damages or loss occurring there should made good by Uncle Sam. The FAA, of course, took the position that he had chosen the location, and that in any event there was no record or proof that he had even owned the items he reported as missing. Bruce's claim went nowhere, and he cast himself as justifiably aggrieved over the financial loss.

It was a posture that frequently carried over into the work environment. For reasons I could never fathom, Bruce, who actually had good controller skills, seemed to use those skills deliberately to bait and antagonize pilots. For example, when a pilot would contact the tower for landing, normally five to eight miles before entering the airport traffic area, Bruce would ignore the call and several subsequent attempts by the pilot to establish two-way radio communication. In most cases the position of the aircraft was easily determined by reference to the BRITE radar display, and required the simple application of the time-honored formula utilized by local controllers everywhere: Clear the airplane to land. If you can't issue landing clearance, issue traffic to follow. If you can't issue traffic to follow, give the pilot a place to report.

But Bruce would wait until the aircraft had entered the airport traffic, then go into a long harangue against the pilot, advising him that he had failed to comply with the two-way communication rule, that he was in violation of FARs, that he was compromising safety, etc. The time it took to transmit these chastisements, plus the fact that the aircraft was now only four miles or so from the airport, degraded the service to other pilots and in most cases caused the "offending" pilot to lose a comfortably efficient landing sequence had the flight been handled normally.

Mark and I both recognized that if one of us was present in the tower, and basically breathing down Bruce's neck, this kind of thing was not likely to happen. Unfortunately, it seemed to happen with depressing regularity when we were not present. In many cases, students or low-time private pilots would take the abuse without comment, sometimes even apologizing on the frequency. But in other cases, pilots with more experience would call the tower after landing and complain about Bruce's actions. I spent many hours reviewing tapes of Bruce working local control, followed by "counseling" sessions that always followed the same pattern. We would listen to the tape, during which time Bruce would exhibit an increasingly put-upon expression, as though he was being wronged in the worst way. Then we would have an exchange that went something like this:

Me: "Well?"

BF: "Well what?"

Me: "Well, do you think you handled this guy the right way?"

BF: "He came into the airport traffic area without calling me, and was right on top of the airport when he did."

Me: "Did you just listen to the same tape I did? He called three or four times, and you never answered him UNTIL he was right on top of the airport."

BF: "Well, I was busy, and I couldn't get to him."

Me: "Let's listen again. I counted only two other transmissions by you in the three minutes or so between the time he first called and when you finally answered him. You were not busy. Or if you were, you should have told him to remain clear of the airport traffic area and given him an expected delay time."

BF: "All I did was advise him that he was supposed to establish two-way radio contact outside the traffic area."

Me: "No, you were unnecessarily derisive and accusatory, and took up frequency time you could have used to better advantage. Now, we have had these discussions before, and I will tell you again, if you think a pilot has screwed up, do not get into it with him on the frequency. You tell Mark or me, have the pilot call the tower after landing, and one of us will talk to him."

Bruce would usually stop arguing at this point, and he would depart with a hurt look on his face.

There were a couple of other incidents that demonstrated a lack of discipline and professionalism on Bruce's part. One day I came in to work and discovered a scrap of paper stuck into the vents of the locker door where I kept my headset. On it, in small block letters, was the message, "BF GC 1410Z." There was no way to identify the purveyor of the note, as every controller in the facility was down on Bruce for his manner on the control frequency, but the message was clear: at 1410 Zulu, or 10:10 am EDT, Bruce had had an exchange on ground control that bore looking into. At one level, I was tempted to ignore the whole thing, being that the anonymous writer was unlikely to follow up or question my lack of action in any way. But curiosity got the better of me, and I found an opportunity to play back the tape of ground control that included transmissions made around 1410Z. This is what I heard:

BF: "Ramp 60, ground." (Bruce was summoning the Dade County vehicle that patrolled the airport).

Ramp 60: "Roger ground, Ramp 60 is with you."

BF: "Ramp 60, there is a grey station wagon headed over here to the tower, and I need to talk to him. Could you catch up to him and tell him to call me?"

Ramp 60 (dubiously, as this was a highly non-standard request): "Uh, okay ground, I'll try and catch him."

The ramp car was at the opposite end of the field, and accelerated quickly, catching up to the station wagon as it pulled into the parking area at the base of the tower. Bruce had recognized the grey vehicle as belonging to Leo, a fellow controller whose shift was scheduled to begin at 1:00 pm. The county man talked to Leo, then transmitted, "Okay, ground, he says he will call you after he goes flying." Leo belonged to the same flying club that I did, and was planning a hop before his scheduled shift. The exchange resumed:

BF (urgently): "No no! I need to talk to him now. Put him on your car radio."

This was the height of irregularity, but soon Leo had the mic cord of Ramp 60's radio stretched out the window.

Leo: "What do you want?"

BF: "Hey Leo, this is Bruce. I need to take sick leave. Can you come up and relieve me?"

Leo: "Well, I have an airplane scheduled and I'm supposed to come in at one. But I'll cut the hop short and come up as soon as I am back."

BF: "Can't you come now? I am really hurting."

Leo: "The flying club will charge me for an hour of flight time if I cancel this late. I will take the hop and then come in."

BF: "Are you sure you can't come now? I am sick as a dog."

Anonymous pilot: "Take two aspirin and call me in the morning!"

Alone in the tape room, I burst out laughing. But I would need to get past the humor of the incident and have another heart to heart with Bruce.

The next day I "invited" Bruce to accompany me to the training room where I had a portable tape player and a cassette recording I had made from the master tape the day before. As always, he was giving me his usual, "Why-is-everybody-always-picking-on-me" look, clearly having no idea what this was about. I started the tape, and as it progressed Bruce by degrees traded his put upon expression for one of satisfaction and relief. When I switched off the machine, he was all smiles, and I gave him a moment to comment. When he didn't, we began a dialogue:

Me: "Well?"

BF: "Well what?"

Me: "Anything you'd like to say about this recording?"

BF: "It sounded okay to me, I didn't argue with any pilots or make any kind of negative comments on the frequency, so what's the problem?"

Me (shaking my head in disbelief): "How about, ground control is not your personal telephone line. You took up Ramp 60's time with personal business that in no way related to his duties, and put out several minutes of totally superfluous transmissions on a control frequency intended for other purposes. With all your years of experience, you can't tell me you don't understand exactly what I'm talking about. The next time we have one of these discussions, there is going to be some official paperwork and possible disciplinary action. Now I'm not looking for a fight with anybody, but you need to get your act together. Seriously."

The smiles disappeared, and Bruce shuffled out of the room sporting his usual "shafted again" expression.

Another Miscue

In another case. Leo, Bruce, and I were manning the tower in the last hours of the 1 to 9 shift with Bruce plugged into local control and working the frequency on speaker. We were on an east operation (landing 9 Left, 9 Right and 13). The activity level was very low. There came a call from an aircraft whose call sign we recognized as being that of a DC-3 that operated from Tamiami, initiating the following exchange:

N31D: "Tamiami tower Douglas 31 Delta 8 northwest with Bravo, parking at Jet Center."

BF: "Douglas 31D Tamiami tower make straight in approach to runway 31, report a three-mile final."

This made no sense, as the instruction would have meant a final approach from the southeast, to land opposite direction on 13-31, and could not have been made as a straight in from the northwest.

N31D: "Ok, I guess you mean straight in to 13, confirm."

BF: "Affirmative sir, straight in to 31."

The pilot made no further comment until his report at the three-mile point.

N31D: "Douglas 31D three miles out for 13.

BF: "Douglas 31D cleared to land runway 31."

N31D: "Tower, you keep saying runway 31. Verify that we are cleared to land on 13."

BF: "Oh, sorry sir, I keep clearing you to land on your call sign."

This was one of the most nonsensical, off the wall transmission I had ever heard. Leo and I doubled over with laughter, while Bruce favored us with a completely mystified look.

One of the problem dynamics of supervision was that the role often required wearing the black hat. It was much more usual, if you were a controller, to receive "input" from a supervisor when there was some question or criticism relating to your performance. Although there could be an occasional "attaboy," these were basically few and far between, the idea being that since you were expected to do a perfect job 100 per cent of the time, there was no need for acknowledgement. In Bruce's case, he had been called on the carpet a number of times for performance issues great and small, and even though we always had him dead to rights, he was feeling picked on. So it was with some relief and, frankly, great surprise, that we one day pulled a recording of Bruce that in all respects reflected service orientation, courtesy, and professionalism.

Lanny Williams, now the manager at Tamiami, and I agreed that while we needed to stay on top of Bruce for his misdeeds, it was important to recognize good performance as well. So it was time for another "tape talk" as these sessions were known. Summoning our most serious, solemn expressions, we ushered Bruce into the office. Lanny greeted him saying, "Have a seat, Bruce, I want you to listen to a tape." Being double-teamed by the manager and a supervisor generally augured something very serious, and Bruce's evident nervousness was unmistakable. The tape lasted about six or eight minutes covering a period during which a helicopter crew was having some control problems. Bruce offered all appropriate assistance, and the session ended with a transmission from the pilot saying, "Thanks for the help tower, we appreciate it." Bruce replied, "No problem, sir, have a good day."

Lanny and I had not altered our serious expressions during the playback. As the tape ended, we remained silent for a long moment as Bruce fidgeted in his chair. Then Lanny said, "Well?" Bruce shrugged his shoulders and threw up his hands, at a loss for words. Lanny continued, still serious as a heart attack, "Bruce, that was excellent handling of that helicopter, and we can all be proud of that kind of performance." Bruce sagged in place as relief washed over him. Lanny and I traded our frowns for smiles, reiterating our praise for the good job and exhorting him to keep up the good work.

Bureaucracy Strikes Again

Some months before Lanny replaced Earl Peavey as the Tamiami Tower manager, a change occurred that made facility life for me, Earl, and Mark James decidedly more difficult. It came about in an almost offhand way, demonstrating that power and influence could have profound consequences. One day, seemingly out of the blue, we were informed that Tamiami would expand its operating hours to open at 7:00 am instead of 8:00 am. The extra hour, from an operational perspective, was not terribly consequential. The day shift would run from 7 to 3, and the overlap with the 1 to 9 shift would now be only two hours instead of three.

Of far greater significance was the fact that all pay levels would be reduced by one grade because of the formula used to calculate whether a tower was a Level 1, 2, 3, 4, or 5. The formula relied on a determination of traffic density, derived by dividing the total traffic count during the busiest 16 hours of a facility's daily operation by 16, or the count from all the hours of operation for a facility like TMB that was open 16 hours or fewer, by the number of its operating hours.

So with the stroke of a pen, Tamiami was downgraded from Level 3 to Level 2. Our GS-12 controllers became GS-11s, and the supervisor grade changed from GS-13 to GS-12. It is no surprise that when you limit people's future earnings there is going to be some pretty strong resentment. It was especially galling because the character of the workday was basically unchanged. There was almost zero activity between 7 and 8 am, and the other hours remained as busy as ever. Morale took a major nosedive, and definitely did not improve when it became clear how the downgrade had come about.

What apparently had happened was that a company operating a Learjet out of TMB had contacted Southern Region officials complaining about the time it took to receive an IFR clearance and get a release from the Miami TRACON when Tamiami Tower was closed. The procedure required that the flight crew work through the flight service station, operating 24 hours per day, whose personnel would relay requests for the IFR clearance and then the release from TMB to MIA. Although these steps required only a few minutes, it was not as efficient for the pilot as simply calling the TMB ground controller, who in most cases would already have the clearance, copying it, and immediately being released. The Learjet operator scheduled early flights only once a week, meaning that on six days out of seven the tower was staffed needlessly for that first hour, and on the seventh day essentially to provide service to just one aircraft.

From the FAA's point of view, the reclassification of TMB was a clear win. An operator request had been granted, no increase in ATC staffing had been necessary, and the cost of running Tamiami Tower had decreased. As facility manager, Earl received a lot of heat from the controllers for agreeing to the extra hour of operation, but insisted that with the airport traffic count trending ever upward we would soon be a Level 3 again. Simple arithmetic, however, made it clear that unless airport activity between 7 and 8 am, and indeed in all the other hours increased substantially, dilution of the traffic density number would keep the facility at Level 2 forever.

We in the field facilities were often left shaking our heads over the way operational priorities seemed to be limited by budgetary constraints while obvious instances of wasted resources were ignored. An example of one such instance, that we tried to correct, related to periodic updates to the "controller's Bible," FAA Order 7110.65, received by every air traffic control facility. These "change" documents, as they were called, came out two or three times a year and were generally 60 to 80 pages long, containing one section explaining the changes, another specifying which pages in the existing order were to be removed, and a third providing the replacement pages to be inserted in their place. The agency saw fit to provide a copy of the order and all subsequent change documents to every employee with the ATCS designation.

At TMB, with our 16 controllers, two supervisors, and one manager, we should have received 19 copies each time an amendment to the order was promulgated, but the number was always three to four times greater. Why were we getting so many more of these mailings than the number of employees in the facility? Fighting his way through multiple layers of bureaucracy, Earl Peavey finally reached the office responsible for the updates and asked the obvious question, eliciting this response: It is too difficult to track the exact number of ATCSs at each individual facility. It is easier and more efficient (!) to establish four size categories, with a set employee count for each of them. If the number of ATCS's exceeds that count, the facility moves into the next larger category. So apparently we were one or two people above the "small" classification and therefore received the number of updates needed in a facility with 50 or 60 controllers. Go figure.

Noise Abatement

At MIA, noise issues were always at the forefront, especially when a change to operational procedures was contemplated. The impetus for increased noise abatement measures almost always originated with citizen groups who objected to airplanes overflying their neighborhoods, even though these property owners had chosen to live in an area with a major airport nearby. Still, it was true that in the first (and last) ten miles of flights departing from or arriving at MIA, large turbine-powered aircraft at low altitude and operating at high power settings made quite an impact.

Tamiami, as a general aviation airport, had only a few turbojet operations per day, the majority of its traffic being single-engine trainer aircraft. But that did not mean that we were free from dealing with noise complaints. There were some "regulars" who telephoned us constantly, alleging various problems or disturbances. Most of these complaints were frankly laughable, the callers themselves coming across as disgruntled kooks. They never gave their names or stated specifically where they lived, and, despite our best attempts to respond to their queries, never accepted our explanations. Some examples:

One frequent caller was a gentleman who lived "near" the airport. In addition to the "constant racket" of aircraft in the traffic pattern, he said, his citrus trees were wilting and dying because of "the exhaust fumes falling in my yard." Also, according to him, the lake bordering his property was becoming polluted by aircraft engine oil. When we tried to point out that there was no credible basis for these claims, he asserted that he had consulted with "experts" who agreed with him, and who would appear as witnesses in the lawsuit he was preparing. This individual had also done some research, naming an official in the Southern Region office, who, he claimed, would soon be directing Tamiami Tower to address his complaints. Earl called the named official, who stated that he had never had any communication with anyone about noise concerns at TMB.

Another caller stated that we should restrict traffic on Sunday morning, a time when he expected peace and quiet, and also the day when he mowed his lawn. He considered the mowing operation a time of quiet meditation, and did not appreciate the intrusion of airplane noise during this period. On the face of it, this claim was nothing short of preposterous. The decibels generated by a 100-horsepower engine (the power plant of the ubiquitous Cessna 150 trainer), operating at reduced power, 800 feet above ground level, amounted to a barely discernible whisper, certainly far quieter than a lawnmower three feet in front of the operator.

Although we did our best to remain good humored about these calls, there were different degrees of forbearance among our numbers, especially in the controller corps. During periods when neither Mark nor I was present in the tower, there would be one person designated as controller in charge. That person would usually be working a position, and so would have to deal with phone calls while keeping track of traffic, answering coordination lines, etc. Understandably, baseless (and repetitive) noise complaints were a serious nuisance. However, controller personalities being what they were, the worst thing you could do was to show that something was getting under your skin, because someone was definitely going to use that to provoke a reaction.

One of our young guys was a known hothead, becoming, as most of us thought, unduly worked up over seemingly minor matters. We had observed that he was especially impatient with the nuisance callers, and the stage was set for a major chain-yanking. A man who was off duty listened to ground control frequency on a portable VHF receiver and realized that his intended victim would probably be the one to answer phone calls to the tower on the outside line. The prankster dialed the tower number and was soon doing his best impersonation of the citizen whose citrus trees were being damaged by aircraft exhaust fumes. He spun out the exchange for many minutes, resulting finally in a string of epithets from the man in the tower, recorded as all communications to the tower were, and an abrupt end to the exchange as the telephone was slammed into the console. The perpetrator later reported for work, and quietly let the other controllers in on the gag, occasioning many ill-suppressed smiles and giggles over its success.

Extra-Curricular Activities

Even the busiest facilities had their slack moments, and when these occurred, controllers, being restless and action-oriented types, never failed to fill these periods with "extra-curricular" activities (remember the toilet paper web in the tower at Miami?) At TMB, traffic always died down after dark, and when the weather was below VFR minimums we might have only 15 or 20 landings and takeoffs over the course of the entire 14 hours we were open. So the "time-filler" undertakings during these low activity periods ranged from basic practical jokes to more thoughtful and cooperative efforts. Examples of each:

The tower was equipped with a hand-held fire extinguisher which, when activated, emitted a tremendous whoosh and roar. More than once a hapless victim jumped out of his skin when an unexpected blast from behind was surreptitiously directed at him. In another case, Leo was waiting at the top of the stairs for the return of his friend Brian. The staircase was steep, almost a ladder, with a wall to the right that ended at the top step. Leo was hunkered down behind the wall with the fire extinguisher at floor level, intending to surprise Brian by firing a discharge across his path about two feet in front of him. Unfortunately, the trigger mechanism stuck for a brief moment, then clicked into place as Brian's head passed the top step, releasing a freezing spray of fire suppressant at the right side of his face. After a few seconds, it was clear that Brian had not been hurt in any way, and the initial consternation gave way to peals of laughter as Brian was observed to be sporting icicles in his hair and sideburns.

These sophomoric shenanigans always took place when neither I nor Mark was present in the tower. But there were other initiatives in which I was a willing participant. These had to do with airborne vehicle design, led by Jim, one of our controllers who was an active flight instructor. He was always puzzling out what sort of shapes constructed out of simple materials would produce the best speed, range, or airborne duration time, and of course the tower catwalk was an ideal launching platform. We tried various models constructed of paper, wood or plastic, experimenting with slight modifications of wing configuration, center of gravity adjustments, and the like. In addition to being fun and interesting, these collaborative efforts had the salutary effect of reducing tensions between worker and supervisor.

One category of flight in these design exercises always seemed to elude our best efforts. Time and again we attempted to construct a viable, miniature hot-air balloon using a thin plastic bag with small birthday candles mounted on crossed popsicle sticks attached to the open end of the bag. Each time one, or a combination of all, of the following failures would occur: the bag would collapse; the bag would catch fire; the wind would blow out the candles; the wind would blow the fragile structure against the tower and it would come apart.

Finally one evening the conditions seemed ideal for another attempt. There did not seem to be a breath of air stirring, and Jim had found some slightly different components from which to fashion the assembly. Two pairs of hands held the bag open as Jim carefully lit the six candles fastened to the popsicle sticks. The holders stretched their arms out over the catwalk rail, gently releasing the bag. For a moment it hung suspended, not climbing, descending, or moving laterally. Then, under the influence of a breeze so mild we could not even feel it, began to move off to the north.

Our self-congratulatory whoops soon gave way to a more serious concern. We had expected no more than a minute or two of sustained flight, but the ghostly image of the translucent bag, lit from within, persisted as the balloon continued on a course that would take it across an active runway. What if the wind changed? Would the balloon hover over runway 9 Left, and for how long? Or if it kept moving, would it crash in the residential area just beyond the northern airport boundary? By good fortune there was no active traffic, and our worries were soon allayed when the candles suddenly winked out and the balloon returned to earth.

Exceeding My Authority (Twice)

One of the things I learned, and did my best to convey to trainees and even to checked-out controllers, was that it was always a losing proposition to get into an argument with a pilot. There were various ways to avoid wasting valuable frequency time in adversarial exchanges, and it didn't really matter who was "right" and who was "wrong." If a pilot refused an instruction, there were usually several alternatives that would accomplish the same, and always the primary, goal of separating traffic.

"Safe, orderly, and expeditious" were the ranked priorities at any control position. If you had formulated and executed your traffic management strategies successfully, you already had an operation in place that was "safe" and "orderly," meaning that you could now devote some brain power to "expeditious." As mentioned earlier, getting pilots on course or to their destinations as quickly and efficiently as possible was not only good service to the user, but helped keep the controller workload manageable as well.

In most cases, pilots understood that you were doing your best to accommodate them, and if there were a delay or a less than optimal routing or altitude assigned it was for a good reason. But occasionally, especially at a general aviation airport like Tamiami, a corporate or other professional pilot would decide that "these young kids" who worked in "toy towers" needed the benefit of his superior intelligence and experience.

There were three telling instances that I experienced myself, all of them at the ground control/ flight data/ clearance delivery position.

In the first case the pilot of a Learjet called for taxi from Jet Center, a fixed base operator located on the south side of the airport at about midfield. Runway 9 Right was quite busy, with several in the pattern and four or five Cessnas at the run-up pad awaiting departure. 9 Left had no aircraft in the pattern, and only one or two waiting for takeoff clearance. The exchange went like this:

N667GW: "Tamiami ground Lear 667 Golf Whiskey IFR to Atlanta ready to taxi from Jet Center with Echo."

Me: "Lear 667 GW Tamiami ground, taxi to runway 9 Left."

N667GW: "How about 9 Right? We're parked right next to it."

Me (thinking to myself, gee, I've been at TMB for three years, and I "never knew" Jet Center was right next to 9 Right): "Lear 67 GW, 9 Left will expedite your departure."

N667GW: "Oh give me a break, it's twice as long a taxi to 9 Left."

Me: "Lear 67 GW, understand you are requesting 9 Right for departure."

N667GW (tone of exasperation): "Of course we are."

Me: "Lear 667 GW, taxi to 9 Right, follow the red and white Cessna passing left to right on the parallel taxiway."

The pilot complied, and instead of taking about 30 seconds longer to taxi the additional 1,300 feet to 9 Left and waiting one or two minutes for takeoff, took at least a six or seven minute delay at 9 Right because of the traffic ahead of him. People who are smarter than me get what they want.

In another case the pilot of a light twin intended to make the short hop over to MIA. He was certain he understood the ATC system better than some rookie in a VFR tower, initiating an exchange that began in peremptory, impatient tones and did not improve as the transmissions went on:

N738HY: "Tamiami ground twin Comanche 738 Hotel Yankee parked at Kendall, I've got Juliet, request a tower en route clearance over to Miami."

Me: "Twin Comanche 738 HY Tamiami ground, taxi to 27 Right. Tower en route clearance is only available between two adjacent approach control facilities, how about a VFR code for clearance into the TCA?"

N738HY: "I say again, I am requesting a tower en route clearance to Miami."

Me: "Twin Comanche 38 HY tower en route is not available. I can try to work you up a regular IFR clearance if you don't want a TCA clearance."

N738HY: "Forget it, ground. We'll just go VFR."

Me: "Twin Comanche 38 HY roger, remain clear of the Miami TCA after departure, contact TMB tower 118.9 when ready."

Both MIA and TMB were on a west operation, and if the pilot had accepted the discrete transponder code and a release from the Miami TRACON, he most likely would have received instructions to make a 180-degree turn back to the east, putting him about 8 miles southeast of MIA, a perfect position for a simple base leg entry to runway 30. The whole flight would have taken a maximum of seven or eight minutes. As it was, watching the BRITE radar display, I observed the airplane flying westbound for at least 10 or 12 miles before being radar identified, then being vectored back about 20 miles to be sequenced for landing on MIA's runway 30. The pilot flew for almost 20 minutes because he was smarter than me.

The third instance occurred one year on Thanksgiving eve. The pilot of a Cessna Citation jet had filed an instrument flight plan to Philadelphia. The entire northeast portion of the country was blanketed in severe storms, and major flow control constraints had been placed on all traffic bound to the big city terminals. The Citation had an expect departure clearance time (EDCT) some two hours later than his original proposed departure time, which had already passed. During the exchanges between me and the pilot it became clear that he was in the unenviable position of any corporate flight crew member. Once a company had shelled out the big bucks for its own airplane, no CEO or other officer wanted to hear about delays, no matter what the reason. It was pretty much a case of, "If you won't go, we will get somebody who will." Corporate flying jobs had some pretty nice perks, and could be a stepping stone to employment with the airlines, so there was no shortage of candidates in the "somebody who will" category. The communications went like this:

N265CC: "Tamiami ground Citation 265 Charlie Charlie ready to copy IFR to Philadelphia."

Me: "Citation 265 CC Tamiami ground, cleared to the Philadelphia airport via the Miami 5 departure Bondi transition to maintain 2000. Expect flight level 330 ten minutes after departure. Departure frequency will be 125.5 squawk 4514."

The pilot read back the clearance correctly.

Me: "Citation 65 CC read back correct, be advised you have an expected departure clearance time of 0300 Zulu, time now 0045."

N265CC: "65CC, understand it will be a two-hour delay? We can't accept that."

I had visions of an apoplectic boss about to show up, or perhaps already there, making his displeasure known in no uncertain terms.

Me: "Citation 65 CC, there are flow control restrictions all over the system due to severe weather in the Northeast. Stand by on the frequency or check in with me from time to time and I will keep you advised of any change."

N265CC: "We can't do that, ground, we will just have to re-file our flight plan."

Me: "Sir, an EDCT time is based on your proposed departure time, which was almost an hour ago. You can't file for a time earlier than the present time, so if you do re-file, your departure will be pushed back even later."

N265CC: "Well it's unacceptable. We are going to file a new flight plan.

Me: "Citation 265 CC, let me make a suggestion. File to an intermediate destination that is not under the flow control constraints, like Norfolk. That will at least get you under way, and give you almost two hours during which the situation at Philadelphia could change. If it does, you can change your destination with ATC en route. If there is no change, and you land at Norfolk, at least you will be that much closer to Philadelphia when the restrictions are lifted."

N265CC: "No, we're not playing that game. We're going to refile."

Soon we received a new flight plan for the Citation with an EDCT time two hours later than the one reflected on the earlier clearance. Too bad you are smarter than me.

In these three cases I had done my service-oriented best to minimize delay based on information that I knew but which was not readily available to the pilots. They made their own decisions, as is every pilot's prerogative, so both parties had acted appropriately within the scope of their responsibilities.

In the News

Other cases were not so clear cut. In dealing with the public, and especially the media, field facilities like TMB had to be careful about the information they released. Officials in the regional office or at Washington headquarters definitely did not want to learn about an accident or other newsworthy event from CNN. Local news organizations monitored air traffic control frequencies, and if they heard anything even slightly out of the ordinary, the facility would immediately receive a phone call asking for information. The appropriate response was to refer the caller to the public information office in Atlanta, which would issue statements as factual data became available.

One day when I was on duty a brief but severe squall swept over the airport. For about ten minutes the wind howled and the rain poured in torrents. Then, as quickly as it had come, the storm passed. Once visibility was restored, we saw evidence of the devastating effects all over the field. Many airplanes had either broken their tie-down lines or pulled the anchoring blocks out of the ground, then flipped over. Several parked cars had broken windows, no doubt caused by flying debris. I reported the situation to MIA, which, as the so-called "hub" facility for the smaller surrounding satellite airports, would forward the information to the region. And true to form, a caller from The Miami Herald was soon, and insistently, asking me to comment on the event:

"Were any airplanes damaged?"

"Yes."

"How many, and what is the dollar cost of the damage?"

"I don't have that information. You would have to check with the Dade County airport authority."

"Were there any injuries either to pilots or people on the ground?"

"Again, you would have to contact the airport authority."

"It must have been a hell of a wind, how strong was it anyway?"

Here is where I made my mistake, replying, "Well we don't record wind information, but the indicator registers up to 50 knots, and at one point I saw the needle pegged."

Next day in the Herald the article covering the storm damage contained the statement, "FAA spokesman Rust Potter stated that wind speeds exceeded 50 knots." The only legitimate "FAA spokesmen" were those in the public information office, and so I had basically made an unauthorized statement.

At the end of the shift I decided to walk over to one of the ramp areas for a closer look at what had happened. I was displaying my FAA badge, thinking it might facilitate access not granted to the public at large. But when I got there, a substantial crowd of curious gawkers was already getting in the way of county officials who were starting the laborious process of righting airplanes, cleaning up debris, and most tellingly, mopping up fuel spills. The air was ripe with the fragrance of raw gasoline, and I was surprised that there had apparently been no attempt at crowd control.

At one point I saw an unkempt looking young man with a cigarette in his hand standing right next to an overturned Cessna leaking gas from its wing tanks. I approached him without hesitation, saying, "You need to put that cigarette out. There is gas all over the place on this ramp." He looked at me uncomprehendingly, then changing his expression to one of surly defiance. But he slowly backed off, and (wait for it) threw the still lighted butt into a puddle of rainwater clearly containing an over layer of spilled fuel. Inasmuch as I am able to report this event, you would be justified in concluding that there was no instant conflagration. As I was about to leave the scene, there the guy was again, right next to the airplane, a new cigarette in hand.

I could perhaps have been forgiven for my statement to the Herald since it was the journalist who characterized me as an "FAA spokesman." The following incident, which played out over two days, was a more blatant extension of my "authority" into matters clearly beyond my purview as a supervisory air traffic control specialist, but was also one with only a small likelihood of any negative blowback. It began with a phone call from a citizen who lived a few miles southwest of TMB. In a total departure from the usual tenor of such calls, this one began with the gentleman politely giving his name and address, initiating the following exchange:

Caller: "I'm not sure I am addressing this to the right place, but I thought I would start with you. For the last several minutes there has been an airplane circling over our neighborhood at a very low altitude. I am not a pilot, but he can't be more than a couple of hundred feet above our houses. Is this safe or even legal?"

Me: "Generally an operation like that would be in violation of federal air regulations, but there are exceptions for certain law enforcement activities. Can you describe the airplane?"

Caller: "Well, it has a high wing and one propeller, and a blue and white paint job."

Me: "OK, and could you read any of the registration number on the side of the fuselage?"

Caller: "No, I couldn't see the number, but he is still out there. Let me go out and see if I can get the number." A minute or two later the caller was back on the line, saying, "I couldn't get the number, but now he has started to fly away."

Me: "Can you tell which way he was going?"

Caller: "It looks like he was headed back your way."

Me: "All right, we will be looking for an aircraft matching your description, and if we get any further information I will call you back."

Caller: "Thank you sir, I would appreciate it."

A few minutes later the local controller received a call from a Cessna 172 southwest of the airport requesting landing instructions. The call sign identified it as one of the aircraft belonging to the Pan Air flying club, of which I myself was a member. All the Pan Air Cessnas were painted blue and white. I told the local controller to ask the pilot to call the tower after landing. I watched the airplane through the binoculars as it taxied to the Pan Air tie down area, then saw a young man emerge from the cabin and walk to the club office. A few minutes later the phone rang:

Pilot: "Uh, I was flying Cessna 5030 Romeo, and the tower asked me to call."

Me: "Yes sir, thank you for calling. We just received a phone call from a citizen who lives southwest of the airport saying an airplane matching the description of yours was flying at low altitude over his house. Was that you?"

There was a long pause, then the conversation continued something like this:

Pilot: "Ah, well, er, um.. see I was.. it was.."

I cut him off, saying, "Look, it is pretty clear that it was you. Now fortunately the gentleman did not get your side number, so no official action can or will be taken. But use your head. Don't operate in a way that is dangerous and illegal and could cause you to lose your pilot's license. How about we chalk this up to a lesson learned, and that will be an end to the whole matter. Let's have a firm handshake that there won't be any repeat of something like this, okay?

Pilot, in tones of obvious relief: "Yes sir, thank you, sir!"

After we hung up, I immediately called the concerned citizen, telling him that I had talked to the likely offender, who did not admit he had been flying too low or "flat-hatting." I said there was no way to pursue the matter further, without positive identification of the aircraft, but that I was pretty sure the young pilot had gotten the message.

The next day, at about the same time as the call a day earlier, the same caller, again identifying himself and remaining polite and low key, rang the tower and began the conversation saying, "I know you are not going to believe this, but that same airplane is here again, buzzing the neighborhood." We had a short conversation during which I said I would address the situation, including, if necessary, forwarding all information available to Flight Standards, the arm of the FAA charged with enforcement actions, and concluding when the caller advised me that the pilot was leaving the area.

This time it was not going to be a phone call. I had given the pilot a break, and received what I thought was an assurance from him that he had learned his lesson. To put it bluntly, I was seriously frosted that he had gone right out and committed the same offense again. As the aircraft entered the final about three miles out, I appointed one of the controllers as controller in charge, then left the tower, clipping on my FAA badge and cinching up my necktie. I had timed it so that I was standing on the Pan Air ramp when N5030 Romeo taxied in.

The pilot exited the aircraft and began walking across the ramp. I began a brisk stride in his direction, intercepting him a few feet from the office door. I was not smiling. Without introducing myself, I began:

Me: "I am the Tamiami Tower supervisor. I need to talk to you for a minute."

The kid was about 19 years old, and reacted as though the police were approaching him with guns drawn. Good. I wanted this to make an impression.

Me: "Yesterday I had a conversation with you about low altitude flying over a residential neighborhood. That was you, was it not?"

Pilot: "Well, ah… it… yes."

Me: "And today, about ten minutes before you landed, this same aircraft was seen doing the same thing. That was you again, right?"

Pilot: "Uh, ah.."

Me, softening the tone slightly: "Look, I'm a pilot too, and I got my license when I was about the age you are now. I did a few things that I shouldn't have, and that is probably true of most pilots. I'm guessing that your girlfriend lives in that neighborhood, is that right?"

He looked at me as though he couldn't imagine how I could have known this, but nodded his head.

Me: "Well, find another way to impress her. I have enough information right now to forward to Flight Standards, and if I do that they will come calling. I told the gentleman that complained about you to let me know if it ever happened again, and if it does, you won't be talking to me on the ramp, you will be in a hearing explaining why you shouldn't pay a big fine and lose your license. Do you understand?"

He nodded his head and I did an abrupt about face, calling over my shoulder as I walked away, "Remember, it's a minimum of 1,000 feet above populated areas."

Other Misdeeds and Oversights

Deliberate flight violations, like the one just described, were pretty rare. Others were inadvertent, generally the result of poor training or low experience on the part of the pilot. A classic example occurred one day when the 9 Left traffic pattern was busy with four or five aircraft making repeated touch-and-go practice landings. One of the airplanes blew a tire and came to a stop on the runway, unable to taxi clear. The pilot reported the situation to the local controller, who took prompt action, rescinding a previous touch and go clearance issued to the next aircraft on final:

Local Controller: "Cessna 54 Golf, go around, disabled aircraft on the runway."

N54G: "54 Golf roger."

The aircraft continued its approach, landed, slowed to taxi speed, then pulled over to the extreme right side of the runway to pass the Cessna with the blown tire, and took off again. The exchange resumed:

Local Controller: "Cessna 54 Golf, did you not understand your instructions to go around?"

N54G: "Yes sir, I did. You cleared me for a touch-and-go, so I landed, went around the disabled aircraft on the runway, and took off again."

We also experienced a number of potential violations, and a few that were clear cut, relating to the provisions for special VFR flight. Special

VFR rules relaxed the normal VFR weather minimums, which required that pilots have three miles of visibility and remain 500 feet below, 1,000 feet above, and 2,000 feet laterally from any clouds. Pilots granted a special VFR clearance could operate with one-mile visibility and needed only to remain clear of clouds. Because special VFR requests often were made under deteriorating weather conditions, they could be a trap for the unwary or inexperienced. The FAA, in a unique display of common sense required that a pilot specifically request special VFR instead of being "assumed" to want it. This meant that as controllers we could not suggest or offer it to a pilot, but some of our more creative people stretched the concept to its breaking point:

N785CD: "Tamiami tower Cessna 785 Charlie Delta 8 miles northwest for landing."

Local Controller: "Cessna 785 CD Tamiami tower, remain clear of the airport traffic area, weather is below VFR minimums, visibility two miles in haze."

N785CD: "Tower, 85 CD, I need to get the airplane back to the FBO, isn't there some way I can get in?"

Local Controller: "85 CD, are you requesting something "special?"

If the light bulb came on and the pilot asked for a special VFR clearance, he would be granted one. If the hint went right over his head, he was out of luck until the weather improved.

One day when the weather was down, a pilot inbound from Opa-locka for landing at TMB received the information that the ceiling was too low for VFR operations. There was some back and forth between local control and the pilot, concluding with a recommendation from Local that the pilot get a good weather briefing when the weather was "marginal," and that he return to OPF till the weather improved or until he discussed the situation with his flight instructor. About 30 minutes later, with the ceiling still reported at 800 feet, the pilot was back on the air with this request:

Pilot: "Tamiami tower, Cherokee 661 Papa Bravo back with you, request a marginal VFR clearance."

We in the tower believed that many of the mistakes made by students were in part due to insufficient emphasis by flight instructors on certain aspects of preparation, particularly as regards pre-flight activities. Every aircraft had its own operating manual specifying in detail how pre-flight inspection and testing were to be carried out. Fuel was to be drained to eliminate any water accumulation caused by condensation in the tanks, oil level, tire pressure, weight and balance, movement of control surfaces, and a host of other items were to be checked. There occurred three incidents demonstrating that, published information notwithstanding, there was no substitute for an additional layer of basic common sense.

In one case immediately after takeoff the student keyed his mic and began shouting over the noise of rapid banging that he was having an emergency and needed to land ASAP. When he got back on the ground, he called for taxi clearance with no trace of the racket in the background. Later examination revealed that the right hand door had been closed with the seatbelt hanging outside, allowing the metal buckle to beat a rapid tattoo on the fuselage.

In another case the ground controller may have saved the day. He observed a Cessna 150 taxiing in a way that did not look normal, weaving from side to side, at times almost leaving the taxiway into the grass area. Grabbing the binoculars, he was able to see that a tow bar was still attached to the nose wheel, being pushed along the ground, snagging on irregularities in the concrete, and forcing the nose wheel right and left. He told the pilot to stop, then summoned Ramp 60 to remove the tow bar.

A third incident occurred right under our noses. The International Flight Center ramp was immediately adjacent to the tower, so we had a bird's eye view of an embarrassing moment for a pilot intending to do a little night flying in a Piper Cherokee. We saw the man walking around the aircraft, casting off the wing tie downs, checking the oil, draining the fuel, and presumably accomplishing all the steps called for in the aircraft manual. Soon we heard the soft purr of the engine starting, followed by this amusing sequence of transmissions and events:

N4418T: "Tamiami ground Cherokee 4418 Tango ready to taxi from IFC with Delta."

Ground Controller: "Cherokee 4418 Tango Tamiami ground taxi to runway 9 Left."

The pilot acknowledged the instruction, and we heard the sound of increasing RPMs as he advanced the throttle. The airplane did not move. Soon the sound of the engine was a full-throated roar, as the airplane stayed firmly in place. The pilot tried three or four times to break free of whatever was holding him back, concluding the last attempt with a likely inadvertent transmission, saying "Ay, caramba!" A few moments later we heard the engine shut down, then saw the pilot briskly exit the cabin and hunker down under the elevators to cast off the tail tie down.

You had to love those student pilots.

These incidents were more or less par for the course at any general aviation airport where flight training made up the bulk of the traffic. There were other events, some involving language difficulties, some because of equipment problems, and others assuming non-existent pilot prerogatives.

Limited Language Skills

English is the official language of aviation and air traffic control. In theory, no applicant could earn a pilot rating in the United States without a good command of English, but because of regulatory restrictions and associated costs in their home countries, many foreign students with very poor proficiency in English came to the U.S. for training. There were also cultural differences that further detracted from full and clear communication. Two examples involving Japanese student pilots highlighted these difficulties.

The proper way to make contact with air traffic control is first to establish two-way communication, then, in the second transmission, to lay out clearly and concisely the following elements: Who you are, where you are, and what you want to do. So it would go like this:

N7715X: "Tamiami tower Cessna 7715 Xray."

TMB: "Cessna 7715 Xray Tamiami tower."

N7715X: "Cessna 15 X is 10 miles southwest with information Yankee, request a couple of touch-and-goes on 9 Right then a full stop, parking at International Flight Center."

The controller would then issue landing instructions or request that the pilot provide another position report closer in to the airport. Many beginner pilots, certainly not limited to Japanese students, did not have a firm grasp on this simple formula, often giving only their call sign, or call sign and position, and most frequently omitting what they wanted to do. In these cases the controller would have to query the pilot, saying, "Cessna 24 Uniform, say your intentions." This might or might not elicit the desired information, as in the following instance that had us enjoying a good laugh:

Japanese student pilot: "Tamiami Tower, Cessna 6747 Juliet."
TMB: "Cessna 6747 Juliet Tamiami tower."
N6747J: "Roger, Cessna 6747 Juliet."
TMB: "Cessna 47 Juliet say your intentions."
N6747J: "My intentions are become airline pirot."

Another case highlighted the strong Japanese cultural imperative of always behaving with extreme courtesy. An aircraft had reported inbound from the southwest, and the Brite radar showed that were two radar returns fairly close together. The local controller tried several times to get the student to squawk ident, but apparently that was beyond his novice understanding. The two radar targets displayed different altitude values, and so the controller went to "plan B" in an attempt to identify N47 Juliet:

TMB: "Cessna 47 Juliet, say your altitude."
N6747J: (Unintelligible)
TMB: "Cessna 47 Juliet, say….. your….. altitude."
N6747J: (Unintelligible)

The standard phraseology for asking a pilot to report his altitude was not working. So the controller continued:

TMB: "Cessna 47 Juliet, how… high… are… you?"
N6747J: "Cessna 47 Juliet, I am fine, how are you?"

Sometimes it was an aircraft equipment problem that bedeviled us, one of the most common being a stuck mic. When this happened it was impossible to communicate with the pilot of the aircraft with the problem. Even communicating with other airplanes was difficult, as when two stations keyed up at the same time there was a loud squeal on the frequency that pretty much obliterated the verbal information. More than once we in the tower were treated to "flying lessons" when a stuck mic occurred on a flight carrying both a student and a flight instructor. It would go like this:

N72???: "Tami (squeal, squeal)..wer Cess (squeal squeal) 72 (loud squeal)."
TMB: "Attention all aircraft, check your mic, someone has a stuck mic."

This generally did no good, but you had to try.

Unknown Aircraft: "Okay now, start pulling back the power and raising the nose. No, no, not so fast. Wings level, that's it. Feel the bump?

That's the stall, now nose down and add power. Whoa, not that much nose down, you're flying again, so level out...."

And on and on until the mic became unstuck long enough for the controller to get out a quick transmission such as: "Aircraft practicing stalls this is Tamiami tower, check your mic, you have had a stuck mic."

There was another category of problem committed by a small minority of pilots who should have known better. These were people who had enough public recognition to make them feel entitled to priority handling, even though "first come first served" was the principle by which the ATC system was supposed to function. One particular offender was a county commissioner who owned his own Piper Twin Comanche. He was usually right on top of the airport when he made his first call for landing instructions, and if the local controller said anything but "cleared to land," he would take issue with the response:

N2484W: "Tamiami tower Twin Comanche 2484 Whiskey 5 east for landing." (No call to establish two-way communications, true position of the aircraft almost at the east field boundary).

Local Controller: "Twin Comanche 2484 Whiskey Tamiami tower enter left downwind for 9 Left, follow a single-engine Cessna on a midfield downwind."

N2484W: "I can't follow him, I'm twice as fast as he is."

Local Controller: "Well sir, if you would call us a little bit sooner you wouldn't have that problem."

N2484W: "Tower, I don't have time for this. I am county commissioner Jorge Lopez."

Local Controller: "Understand sir. Your sequence is behind the Cessna ahead on downwind."

N2484W: "84 Whiskey, I want a phone number to call the tower."

Local Controller: "Yes, sir, please do give us a call."

When the commissioner would call, we would explain that there was no priority based on political standing unless you were the president, vice president, or an immediate family member of either.

One day after a testy exchange he got his comeuppance through no doing of air traffic control. After landing he exited the runway at a high speed, well in excess of the published taxi speed for the airport, not slowing even slightly as he charged across the ramp between the rows of parked airplanes towards his tie down spot. Later in the day a ramp attendant discovered a Cessna 150 with a slice in its rudder and a telltale paint smear. In a phone call from the FBO asking if we could shed any light on this incident we advised him to check the left wing of the Twin Comanche. The height of the damage to the rudder and the color of the paint corresponded to a scrape on the wing of Lopez's aircraft.

The Saga of the Swift

There was one pilot and aircraft combination that caused us problems throughout my time at Tamiami and beyond. The pilot was a man in his 80s, a former captain for Delta Airlines, who owned a Swift. The Swift was a type originally manufactured in the 1940s that had been out of production for years, a two-place tail-dragger that may or may not have been certified for acrobatic flight.

There were easily a dozen instances of some probable, and many unmistakeable, FAR violations and unsafe operating practices committed by this individual. It was pretty clear that he had grown up in the barnstorming days of the 1930s, a period when there was no air traffic control of any kind and no formal body of regulations governing pilot certification and aircraft maintenance standards. We were convinced that he was of the old school that believed a pilot was responsible for his airplane and his own methods of flying, and no bureaucrat was going tell him what to do or how to do it. We often saw a beat-up cargo van backed up to the Swift's tie down spot with a canvas laid out behind it covered with tools and equipment.

Through the binoculars we could see access panels hanging from various parts of the fuselage or the engine cowling open and the man leaning in doing God knows what. Unless he was a certified airframe and powerplant mechanic, which we seriously doubted, everything he was doing was not only illegal but dangerous in the extreme. Once during these questionable maintenance activities a fire broke out, potentially endangering not only the Swift and the pilot, but also the other aircraft in the tie down area. Ground control dispatched Ramp 60 to the scene and the flames were fortunately extinguished before any damage occurred.

From the ATC perspective, there were a number of occasions on which the pilot exhibited a blatant disregard for procedure and required communications. Several times we observed the Swift on the taxiway, obviously heading for the active runway, without having requested or received taxi clearance from ground control. Sometimes we would initiate a call, using the side number with which we were all too familiar, only to receive no response from the pilot. At other times he would respond saying he thought he had called for taxi, or that he "had tried several times and did not get an answer," or even, "You guys were busy and I didn't want to bother you, so I just went ahead on my own."

Creating a far more serious hazard, he would sometimes taxi onto the runway and take off without any communication or clearance from the local controller, again stating, if he responded at all, that he had requested takeoff clearance several times, that he thought he had been cleared, or that "it was taking too long, so I just picked my own spot to go." Likewise, when returning to the airport, the Swift would sometimes simply appear on short final, then land and taxi to the ramp, all without having contacted either local control or ground control.

The most serious infraction occurred one day when the pilot actually did receive proper clearance from both ground and local control. He had stated his intention to proceed to the west after taking off on 9 Left, and the local controller had approved a left downwind departure. This instruction meant that the pilot was to make a left turn of 180 degrees and fly straight westbound until clear of the airport traffic area. About three minutes after the Swift took off, the following exchange took place between local control and a Beechcraft Bonanza on the ILS approach to 9 Right:

N6757E: "Tower Bonanza 57 Echo, did you see that? A silver airplane just went over me, inverted, couldn't have been more than ten feet above my canopy."

Local Controller: "Bonanza 57 Echo, negative, we didn't see it. Did you get a side number or any part of it?"

N6757E: "57 E, negative, it was just a flash. Do you know who the aircraft was?"

Local Controller: "Bonanza 57 E, not for sure but I think we have a pretty good idea who it was."

N6757E: "Well who was it? I want to talk to that guy."

Local Controller: "Sir, we will make some inquiries and determine the identity of the aircraft as best we can. Please let us handle it."

There was no further communication with the Bonanza pilot, but when the Swift returned to its parking space we observed a man standing on the ramp nearby who rapidly approached the Swift pilot as he exited the aircraft. Even from a distance it was apparent that a heated altercation was taking place. We later learned that the pilot of the Bonanza was a Florida Highway Patrol officer. He rightly accused the other man of operating in a reckless, dangerous, and illegal manner. Flying inverted was considered an acrobatic maneuver, explicitly forbidden within the airport traffic area. Moreover, the Swift had not followed tower instructions to proceed westbound, but had turned to the south, crossing the final approach course to 9 Right about two miles from the airport. The police officer had apparently brandished his law enforcement credentials, threatening to arrest the other man, while the Swift pilot claimed that the police had no authority in the matter, it being strictly within the purview of the FAA.

By the time of the near miss with the Bonanza there had been enough incidents, followed by phone calls in which we attempted to get better cooperation from the Swift pilot, to convince us that attempts at collaboration were getting us nowhere. We began making detailed entries in the daily log each time a violation or an unsafe operating practice occurred. These included two or three instances of the aircraft running off the runway into the grass area, and two off-airport landings due to engine failure. In the second of these the Swift was badly damaged. We saw the crumpled airframe being driven off the airport on the back of a flatbed truck and assumed that the saga of the Swift had come to an end. But more than a year later the airplane was back in its old parking spot, with far worse yet to come.

We had also begun reporting each instance involving the Swift to Flight Standards, the certification and enforcement arm of the agency. Surely, we believed, the accumulated documentation would result in some positive action to curtail the worst of the violations and unsafe operating practices, yet they continued to happen. It seemed to us that Flight Standards was ignoring these serious and repeated occurrences, while focusing their attention, and often ours, on relatively minor matters.

One of the flight school operators routinely monitored the local control frequency when her students were in the touch-and-go pattern or inbound from the practice area for landing. If she believed that a student pilot had landed without clearance, she reported it to Flight Standards personnel who would then contact us to verify the information. For us it meant laboriously combing through hours of tape to find the time, date, and aircraft identification of the alleged offender. Usually the claim was correct, meaning that a local controller had inadvertently omitted a landing clearance, but in no way indicating that runway separation had not been maintained or that safety had been compromised. These instances were few and far between, and reflected more on us than on the students, who, although technically guilty of a violation, had committed no misdeeds remotely approaching those of the Swift pilot.

The final chapter in the saga of the Swift was written in exactly the way we had always feared. Felix, a young man who had replaced me after I left TMB had accepted an invitation to take a flight. Several controllers tried to talk him out of it, recounting all the dangerous stunts the pilot had pulled over the years. Felix himself was a pilot and said that he would grab the controls if the old guy did anything he didn't like. The airplane crashed, killing both men, apparently from structural failure occasioned by a high-g acrobatic maneuver. Felix's widow would have had a strong case in a lawsuit against FAA based on the years of documentation detailing the pilot's flight violations and unsafe operating practices, but instead accepted an informal settlement.

Another fatal accident occurred after I left Tamiami that for a time defied explanation. A Cessna 172 carrying a pilot and passenger departed to the west on a VFR flight plan. At some point after it was reported overdue at its destination, a search and rescue operation discovered the wreckage of the aircraft about 25 miles from the airport. Initial investigation revealed damage that was not consistent with ground impact, indicating that something had occurred during flight that brought the airplane down. One of the wings had failed upward, possibly the result of severe turbulence or an abrupt and extreme movement of the controls by the pilot. Based on weather conditions on the day in question, turbulence was basically eliminated as a factor, and only if the aircraft was operating outside of its published speed limitations could control inputs have caused the failure.

As is standard in post-accident analysis, the recoverable parts of the airplane were removed to the controlled environment of a hangar where a more detailed inspection of its components could be carried out. There a black smudge was discovered on the top surface of the wing that had failed. Through various chemical and other techniques the smudge was enhanced to the point that it could be identified as the imprint of a tire. But all three tires of the 172 were still affixed to the struts and could not have impacted the top of the wing. After further investigation officials determined that the tire causing the smudge was likely of a type routinely used on fixed-gear Cessna aircraft. It was beginning to look as though a midair collision had occurred and investigators lost no time in requesting transcripts of ATC tapes and recordings of radar tracks.

Recordings of the Tamiami ground and local control positions revealed that a few minutes before the 172 took off a solo student pilot in a Cessna 150 requested and received departure clearance to the west. Although neither aircraft was radar identified, two tracks appeared that corresponded to the takeoff times and showed convergence at the approximate location of the crash site. The tire tread on the 150 was an exact match to the imprint on the wing of the 172, and so the next step was an interview with the student. By this time the FBI was involved, as it appeared that a pilot involved in a mid-air collision resulting in two fatalities had failed to report the event. From what we understood, the young man was grilled over a number of days, but steadfastly maintained that he had seen no other airplane nor experienced anything out of the ordinary, eventually convincing his interrogators that he was telling the truth.

What had apparently happened was that the 172 had approached the 150 from below and behind, eventually catching up to the smaller airplane without ever seeing it, then started a climb. Various simulations showed that under certain conditions, with the high wing of the 172 blocking the view of the traffic above, the geometry of the encounter would have prevented both pilots from seeing the other aircraft. And although the student did not specifically recall any kind of bump or unexplained movement of the 150, investigators concluded that the collision could have been gentle enough not to cause alarm, but hard enough to cause the wing failure, after which the 172 would have fallen away below and behind the 150.

A Supervisory Program

The air traffic division of FAA was constantly under scrutiny by the aviation industry, by Congress, and by the general public. The airlines and pilot groups lobbied for reduced delays and more service; Congress was focused on reducing budgetary outlays; and the public at large never failed to be negatively captivated by lurid accounts in the press of accidents or claims by the controllers' union that passenger safety was at serious risk. In the dual hope of improving public perceptions and, perhaps, actually mitigating the causes of these concerns and criticisms, the agency implemented a number of different programs. Each of these debuted with some fanfare, a catchy title, and often a poster style logo.

In the early 1970s it was System Error Elimination (SEE), advertised as an initiative to curtail separation errors. The logo was a large eyeball with two small airplanes, nose to nose, superimposed over the iris. Later there was total quality management (TQM), aimed at applying elements of the business world to the conduct of ATC operations. For those of us with many years as controllers, these and others each looked like a "program du jour," here today, gone tomorrow, without ever achieving any substantive change.

One such initiative that affected me directly in my role as supervisor at Tamiami was the Supervisory Identification Program (SIDP). The concept was a good one, the purpose being to vet applicants for supervisory positions through peer evaluations and workshops intended to expose these candidates to real-world personnel problems and issues. Many selections for promotion, supposedly governed by the Merit Promotion Program (MPP), were cynically looked on by the workforce as MPP by another name, or Man Previously Picked. It often seemed as though management had made up their minds before a vacancy was even advertised that a certain person would get the job. Equally often, in the perception of the rank and file journeymen, it seemed that the selectee had made a blatant effort to curry favor with the selecting official, or that his sole desire for the position was based on his inability to take the heat in the kitchen—in other words, a wish to get "off the boards." Those perceived as not up to their present job didn't have a lot of credibility if they became supervisors, and one of the prime difficulties in labor management relations was the friction between workers and the first line of supervision.

The process under SIDP began after a bid closed and all the applicants were identified. A questionnaire was then distributed to the other controllers in the facility that asked a number of questions and allowed personal observations on the fitness of the individuals under consideration for the position to be filled. Not surprisingly, many of the responses contained scathingly negative comments, but these peer evaluations alone did not lead either to automatic disqualification or guaranteed selection. Many hard-core union members considered any fellow worker wishing to move into management as a traitor to the cause of improved controller benefits, while others believed fervently that the best controllers would never be, or even want to be, a member of management. These absolutist views had to be held in perspective, as many excellent controllers did in fact become supervisors and performed capably in their new positions.

The next step in the process was the structured workshop where senior FAA managers played the roles of controller, fellow supervisor, facility manager and the like. This was the "make or break" phase for a candidate. A poor showing in the workshop exercise meant being dropped from further consideration, or in the case of people like me and Mark James who were already supervisors, being assigned some form of additional training. We heard of a few cases where this happened to current supervisors, but Mark and I made it through without being tripped up.

Not that it was easy. Even with a few years of direct experience under my belt, I could see how easily someone could make a bad mistake. Some examples:

A manager play-acting a controller who may have come to work drunk staggers a bit, slurs his words, and then asks which control position he should take. Do you accuse him outright and send him for a medical evaluation? Do you simply not assign a position and duck the issue? Do you ask him if he has been drinking and do you believe his answer? If you do accuse him, will he file a grievance? Do you have enough evidence to justify your action? If you duck the issue are you fulfilling your supervisory responsibilities?

Or, in my case, a female "employee" came to me asking for a private conversation. She began detailing intimate details of her home life, saying she was unhappy to the point that it was affecting her ability to do her job, then hitting me with the question, "Do you think I'm attractive?" Talk about stepping on a land mine! What I said next would be the equivalent of setting of an explosion or carefully defusing the device. The one advantage I had was that since it was all make believe, I could tailor my answer to a reality of my own making.

I said something like, "Doris (always use the employee's name), it is not my job to judge you by that kind of criteria. I care about how well you do your job, and to be honest, despite what you have been telling me, I see no indication that your performance has deteriorated. But of course, it is important for each of us to be at our best when we put on that headset and key the mic. So what I would say to you is this: you have three choices. You can enroll in the Employee Assistance Program and receive counseling to help you work through the issues you have described, while continuing to work, or you can apply for sick leave based on a stated inability to do the job. In that case you will undergo a full psychological evaluation, which could result in permanent medical disqualification. The third option is to try to deal with the situation on your own."

"Doris" replied, "No, I don't want to do counseling or go to a shrink. I'll just handle it myself."

I said, "Okay, Doris, but now that you have shared this information with me, I will be watching you more closely, and if I see any indication that your work is not up to snuff I may have to order you to be evaluated. Let's meet again in a couple of weeks, or sooner if you like, and see how things are going then."

That was basically the end of that particular scenario. It was followed by interactions with a "peer supervisor," an angry "pilot" and a "manager" who wanted to assign me more duties than was reasonable. At the end there was an informal debrief where the play actor officials asked questions, made suggestions, and even offered a few compliments: "Do you think you should have offered her the option to continue working instead of insisting on one of the other choices?" "You might have suggested she take annual leave to give herself a chance to re-assess." "Good job on scheduling a follow-up conversation. Shows you are engaged and remaining attentive to her problems."

I thought I had heard the last of SIDP as it pertained to me in any way, but that was not quite the case. Because Mark and I had gone through the process, the controllers had written evaluations on both of us of the kind that were done for supervisor candidates. Since the write ups were supposed to be anonymous, they were returned to the facility after the candidate to whom they applied was either promoted or dropped from the list of eligibles. The idea was that the information could be used constructively to improve the interface between employee and supervisor. The problem was that the documents were Xerox copies in the original handwriting of the author, with only the name blanked out. Particularly in a small facility like TMB, it was immediately obvious who had written what.

Most of the evaluations were either generic, without citing any particulars, or were based on an individual interaction with either me or Mark. Examples: "Shows favoritism." Or, "did not relieve me from a control position within the two-hour limit." But one was a screed that basically accused me of dereliction of duty. It said, among other things that I "was never in the tower, but spent all [my] time in the chief's office writing songs." At first I was at a loss as to the basis for this claim, but I later remembered something from at least two years earlier. I had, indeed, composed a "song" in the chief's office. It was late in the evening shift after traffic had died down to nothing, and took me all of about 15 minutes. I titled it "The Tamiami Rap," and it was to be "performed" in spoken tones with a rap cadence. It went like this:

> Hi wings, low wings, all in line,
> The operation's going just fine.
> Full stops, options, touch and goes
> And only south side local knows
> Who's on final, who's on base,
> And who's in someone else's place!
> Hotel Yankee seems to hate us,
> Never does report the ATIS.
> Chief's on local, doing fine, Used 27, but we're on 9!

It was a lighthearted take on daily life in the tower, referring to a specific airplane that all of us had worked at one time or another, and ragging the chief for working local control without ever having had any OJT or being certified on the position. Proud of my work, I had read it to the controllers on duty on the day that I composed it, and got responses ranging from polite chuckles to full throated laughter.

Based on this recollection, I was surprised at the vehemence with which the writer had characterized this single event. I considered confronting the individual, but since the comments were supposed to be anonymous, I decided not to. For a few weeks afterwards he took pains to avoid me, realizing that I knew full well who he was.

Like all other "programs du jour," SIDP came to an end, after a run of only about a year and a half. The seeds of this untimely demise had been planted at the time of the program's debut. The demands on the Southern Region staff, at times having to process peer evaluations if there were even a single bidder from a center or large terminal were huge, and caused long delays in moving the candidate forward. Worse than that, the officials that staged the workshops had to be "second level" or higher in the agency—in other words, first-line supervisors were excluded from this function. At Tamiami, our manager was the second-level above Mark and me, and was constantly being called away, often to remote locations, to officiate at SIDP events. The agency soon realized that in addition to the costs of travel, hotels, and per diem, there was a penalty in terms of lost oversight in the field facilities from which these second level supervisors were so often absent.

A Trainee Smarter Than Me

Besides Leroy and Bruce Faraday, there was one other individual that caused me, and others, varying degrees of heartburn. Mac was a new hire, straight out of the FAA academy, assigned to TMB as his first facility. Typically, a new hire came on the job full of energy, excitement, and a positive go-getter attitude, then over time, with the daily grind of training and the worry about successfully checking out, became less enthusiastic, sometimes to the point of outright negativity over the whole experience. For Mac, the initial phase seemed to be totally missing. He gave every appearance of being fed up and disillusioned from day one. Predictably, this posture made it harder for him to tackle the effort of OJT, and harder for his instructors to offer the positive encouragement that every trainee needed.

I acted as Mac's instructor more often than I had with any other person in training, both to spare the controllers the burden of working with him, and because it looked to me as though he might never check out. In general, I liked the instructor role. But in Mac's case, it was an uphill struggle. Any time I corrected him on something, or made a suggestion that would help him out, he pushed back, saying he had not made a mistake, or completely ignoring the suggestion. He was basically going nowhere fast, and he did not help himself by some of the sentiments he expressed in the tower. Despite his mediocre performance, he more than once denigrated the job of air traffic control, saying in so many words that anyone with any intelligence would not be a controller, but would be doing something more worthy. He seemed to have no sense of humor, and always reacted the wrong way when he was the target of the typical jibes that controllers exchanged. One example:

Mac: "I don't know why everybody makes such a big deal out of this. There's nothing to this job, hell, a monkey could do this job."

Beth: "Mac, you're living proof!"

Everyone present burst into gales of laughter, while Mac just scowled, muttering, "Don't laugh at me."

One day when I was training Mac on ground control, a pilot requested to reposition a Cessna 150 from the north side of the airport to another FBO on the south side. The pilot was unfamiliar with the airport and asked for progressive instructions. The route required three turns: a left turn from the ramp to enter the 27 Right parallel taxiway westbound, another left at a diagonal connector taxiway, and a final left onto the 13 parallel taxiway southeastbound. As the pilot turned onto the diagonal, the following exchange began:

Pilot: "Ground, 31 Yankee, am I going the right way here?"

Mac: "31 Yankee affirmative, continue straight ahead."

I waited for Mac to add the instruction to turn left at the next intersection, where the diagonal met the 13 parallel, but he did not do so. This was critical, because the diagonal led directly to an entry point to runway 13 on the far side of the parallel.

Me (to Mac): "Mac, tell 31 Yankee to turn left at the next taxiway."

Mac: "I did."

Me: "No, you didn't. You told him to go straight ahead and he could get on the active runway."

Mac: "I told him to turn."

At this point I could have taken the frequency and issued the instruction myself, but I thought there might be a teachable moment here, so I checked with the local controller to verify that there was no traffic for runway 13. Sure enough, the 150 continued "straight ahead" as instructed and ended up on the runway.

Me (to Mac): "Well?"

Unbelievably, Mac keyed the mic and began excoriating the pilot:

Mac: "31 Yankee, I told you to turn on the parallel taxiway, and you have entered an active runway without clearance."

This was not an early phase of Mac's training. He should by this time have easily handled this event, and certainly should not have chided the pilot when it was obvious that Mac himself was at fault.

I had by now been at Tamiami for more than four years, and this was one of a number of events that had increasingly eroded my satisfaction with the job. My pilot and controller experience was being little utilized. Instead, I was mostly refereeing silly disputes and complaints entailing interactions that were usually confrontational. A short list:

- At rating time, every controller who was not rated outstanding wanted a detailed one-on-one explanation as to why he or she was rated only excellent or satisfactory.
- One of our people saw a dog tied to a pickup truck parked on one of the ramps and called the SPCA. The SPCA agent found the owner and let him know that someone in the control tower had lodged the complaint, whereupon the owner came to the tower and basically threatened all of us.
- There was a plumbing failure that happened after hours, causing a major flood on all the floors below the tower cab. When I came in all the carpeted areas were soaked, with water running down the staircase. I went to a nearby grocery store to rent a wet vacuum and spent the entire shift mopping up, pausing only to listen to gripes about unsafe working conditions and the intention to file grievances.

A Facility Evaluation

Then there was the facility evaluation. All field facilities were evaluated periodically for compliance with agency directives as well as their own directives. Our evaluation was scheduled for early January 1991. Early in December I received a call from Johnny Miles, now the manager at MIA, who also wore the hat of hub manager, responsible for smaller facilities in the surrounding region. I had been used to the easy give and take first with Earl Peavey and later with Lanny Williams, so I got off to a shaky start when Johnny called. We knew that in addition to Tamiami, Fort Lauderdale tower would be evaluated at or around the same time, so when the call came it went like this:

Johnny: "Next week, Lanny Williams will be leaving Tamiami to be the manager at Fort Lauderdale. That means we need someone to replace Lanny. How would you like a temporary promotion to the manager position?"

This sounded like a set up for a major fall, so I made what I thought was a reasonable response:

Me: "Johnny, you know both TMB and FLL have facility evaluations coming up in about six weeks. Don't you think it would make sense to defer those changes until after the evals?"

There was a pregnant pause, after which Johnny said, in distinctly emphatic tones, "I am offering you an opportunity. Do you want it or not?" I replied, "Well, when you put it like that I will do the best I can."

The countdown clock was now ticking, and I began looking through the 60-page evaluation checklist with a sinking heart. As a controller at Miami I barely knew when the evaluators were in the facility, and there had not been an evaluation during my time on staff. Most of the operational stuff was familiar to me, but a substantial percentage of the checklist was devoted to administrative matters—records to be kept, periodic reviews of certain things to be made and documented, etc. Many of the Tamiami local orders were a decade or more old and were in need of updating. The visibility chart was way out of date, referring to landmarks that no longer existed or were no longer visible because new construction around the airport had blocked them from view. We had no secretary during this period, and because my workdays were entirely devoted to eval preparation, Mark was needed full time to oversee the daily operation. So it was clear from the outset that I was on my own, and would bear full responsibility for the findings of the evaluation team.

In the six weeks between the time I was "anointed" temporary facility manager and the date of the evaluation, with the exception of Christmas Day, I was at the facility seven days a week, working 12 to 14 hours on each of them. In many instances I had to "wag" an action, and a justification for it, in attempting to meet a checklist requirement. About two weeks before the eval date, with an alarmingly high number of pages in the checklist still to go, I realized that even working 24 hours a day I would never cover all the remaining items needing to be checked or reviewed. So now it was a question of parsing the list and sorting it into categories of "more important" and "less important" matters, hoping to score well on those tagged "more important" and taking a lesser hit on the others.

Both the mental strain and the long hours were beginning to wear on me. Because I had chosen to make this effort, there was not, nor would there be, any acknowledgement of or any form of increased compensation for it. At one point Johnny Miles sent one of the Miami Tower staff to check up on me, having told Lanny Williams, who passed it on to me, that he was "concerned" that preparations at Tamiami were not going well. I thought to myself, "Well, when you put a rookie into a big league role, you get what you get. Remember my suggestion that we wait till after the evaluations before shuffling personnel?"

Finally the day came when the evaluators walked through the front door, and at that point it was actually a relief. For better or for worse, my seven-day work weeks and 12-hour days were at an end. I had heard that some evaluation teams made it their business to be hard-nosed and confrontational, but it was immediately apparent that this one had a different outlook. They took a more collegial and friendly approach, asking a lot of questions about why or how I had done certain things, sometimes offering suggestions and giving me a chance to change something before scoring it.

There were two amusing things that happened in the three days that the evaluators were present. One occurred during a period when they were monitoring the tower operation, while the other took place as they were concluding their report. In the first instance, they were watching a young guy working ground control. He had struggled mightily to get certified, and was at that point well on his way to washing out on local control. One of the things I had stressed to the controllers who would be working the operation during the evaluation was this: Do not try to change the way you work to please the evaluators. If you do, you will get incredibly screwed up and make a far worse impression. Work as you always do, and take your lumps, if any, when all is said and done.

But in Richard's case, the advice went unheeded, as glaringly reflected during the several minutes he was working a Cessna taxiing out for departure. Richard twice issued instructions to the pilot to pull off the taxiway to allow opposite direction traffic to pass. Twice the pilot failed to comply, ending up nose to nose with the inbound aircraft, whose pilot then had to briefly enter the active runway to resolve the conflict. About the time the outbound Cessna reached the run-up pad and was changed to tower frequency, one of the evaluators shook her head and said, "Boy that guy is definitely a hazard to aviation." It was a throwaway line that we often used when a pilot didn't follow instructions, usually signifying, as in this case, nothing more than minor annoyance. But hey, this was an evaluator talking! Richard, serious as could be, turned to the local controller and said, "Leo, change that Cessna back to my frequency. He is a hazard to aviation, and I am taking him back to Jet Center." There was an electric moment of stunned disbelief on the part of the other controllers and the evaluators alike, but no reaction other than a certain amount of eye rolling. Mark discreetly took the lady who made the comment aside and told her Richard would not be with us much longer as he was almost out of training hours on local with zero chance of being certified.

The other "smiler" happened after the eval report was finished. There would still be a full de-brief, with Johnny Miles present, but for now the evaluator said, with a twinkle in his eye, "What kind of lights do you have on those trees you use as night-time visibility markers?" He had caught me fair and square on a clear oversight related to the visibility chart. Many of the markers could be used for both daytime and nighttime visibility determinations, as, for example, "Radio tower ¾ miles southwest" or "Chevron sign ½ mile east", being that these objects were lighted at night. But I had inadvertently included the trees, suitable only for daytime visibility measurements, in the nighttime column.

The formal de-brief lasted a couple of hours, with the evaluators going through each item on the checklist. Most they rated as satisfactory, even offering a compliment here and there when it appeared that I had done more than required on a particular item. The error on the visibility chart and one other relatively minor finding were the only "Unsats" recorded on the final report, leading to a final score of 98 percent. I couldn't believe it, considering how unqualified I had been to mastermind a full facility evaluation. My relief was palpable, and I thought surely Johnny would be pleased as well. But after the evaluators left, his only comment was, "Well, you made it through. Don't let up now."

14. Out of Tamiami

During these years at Tamiami I had continued as a member of the AERA Concepts Team, meeting with the mixed group of center and terminal controllers along with the engineers and human factors people from MITRE two or three times annually. At first, when I returned from one of these trips I would write up a one-page synopsis of our progress in developing the AERA system for inclusion in the daily read file. I thought these reports would be of interest to anyone in the ATC field since presumably AERA would figure importantly in the job once it was deployed to the field. But what I found instead was that when one of them was posted in the daily read file there would soon be anonymous comments scribbled across the text, expressing such sentiments as "Bullshit!" or "Total waste of time" or "Nice vacation while we are here busting our ass." Needless to say, after a couple of go-arounds, I discontinued my reports.

There was one more staff opening at MIA that I bid on for which I was definitely qualified. But the job went to a young man half my age, a representative, in the view of Johnny Miles, of "the future of FAA." Johnny believed that an important element of his mandate as a manager was to groom the next generation of controllers to take over staff and management functions after us "old" guys (I was now age 50) retired. This did not always work out so well, as in the case of this particular selection, the individual was eventually forced out after it was discovered that he was using drugs.

All of these events in 1991 left me with a major sour taste, and it was clear to me that within the Miami hub, my prospects were severely limited. I made up my mind to look for opportunities elsewhere, starting with the connections I had made through the AERA team. The chairman of the team was Jim Buckles, assigned to the Requirements Branch at FAA headquarters. Jim did a great job in his role, relating easily and informally to us as controllers, while at the same time deftly handling the bureaucratic overhead of his position. I knew he was someone I could talk to candidly. At the next team meeting I met with him privately for a conversation that went like this:

Me: "Jim, I am looking for a move out of Tamiami Tower. I am fed up with telling people when to eat lunch, when to go to the bathroom, not to argue with pilots or each other, and generally getting pushback on every little thing. I want something with a technical or programmatic focus."

Jim: "I can relate to that. What did you have in mind?"

Me: "Well, my seven years on AERA suggests that there might be a role relating to that apart from being one of the controller members."

Jim: "I'll tell you something in confidence that you can't repeat until it is announced publicly. Management of the AERA project is about to be handed off to the FAA Technical Center in Atlantic City. They do a lot of research and development stuff that will in the future include AERA. I would wait till they take over and then make your move."

I thanked Jim for the heads up, and sure enough, by the time of the next meeting there was a new team chairman from the Tech Center. Stan Psczsolkowski (Stan, if you're reading this, I apologize for my spelling!) was not a controller but had an engineering background, and, like Jim, was both knowledgeable and approachable. I made a slightly edited version of the same pitch I had made to Jim, asking about job opportunities at the Tech Center. He referred me to the manager of the office that handled air traffic control simulations. That office, designated as ACD-340, was run by Bob Ulanch, another manager whom I found to be professional without being overly formal. He thanked me for my interest, saying there were no openings at the present time but that he would let me know if any occurred. Well, I thought, too bad, but all you can do is put irons in the fire and stay tuned for future developments.

A couple of months passed, and then one day in August a telephone call for me came to the tower. I picked up the line, and a new career path immediately opened up when the caller said, "Hi Rust, Bob Ulanch. Are you still interested in coming up here?" Much would be determined in the next few seconds as I considered my answer. I really did not want to leave Florida, for both professional and personal reasons. The Miami hub was where I was known, and despite Johnny Miles' focus on younger people, there was still a chance that an opportunity might develop somewhere within the Hub. My dad's health was by degrees declining, and there was no other family member living nearby, giving me further pause about moving away. But the Tech Center would be something totally different, perhaps even leading to some kind of contract work post-retirement. I was now eligible to retire, having met the combined requirements of reaching age 50 and chalking up 20 years' experience as a controller and first line supervisor. With the so-called "go to hell" card in my pocket, I could work as many, or as few, years as I chose and then make an exit at my discretion. And so I took a deep breath and said, "Yes, Bob, absolutely."

The last couple of months at Tamiami, before my departure in early November, were basically a breeze, given the new horizons that had opened up for me. Even the controllers seemed happy for me, some expressing regrets that I would be leaving, others simply turning down the volume on their concerns and complaints. Despite the fact that it had been entirely my choice, I had decidedly mixed feelings as I pulled out of the parking lot on my last day. I had always thought that I would live out a full career in south Florida, and the reality of moving a thousand miles away hit me hard. But the die was cast. I could only hope to make the best of this opportunity, the likes of which would be offered to very few ATCSs.

A Different World

My first day in my new job was November 20, 1991. In a curious small-world coincidence it was also the day that my brother Hop began his new job in the Air Carrier Training Branch of Flight Standards at FAA headquarters in Washington. Eastern Airlines had shut down six months earlier, adding several thousand more pilots to the ranks of the unemployed. Through a combination of fortunate circumstances, he had leapfrogged over the many individuals who had been "on the street" for much longer, and landed one of the very few positions for which an airline pilot was qualified. We frequently compared notes on our mutual good fortune.

It didn't take me long to understand what a hugely different world the Tech Center was compared to the two field facilities where I had worked. At Miami and Tamiami, we operated under a perpetual budget crunch. You could hardly find the dollars for an extra roll of toilet paper, and the larger expenditures, such as a paid move to a new job, were essentially a thing of the past. Not so at the Tech Center. It did not belong to one of the several administrative regions that governed the towers and centers, but received its own independent funding. Moreover, because much of its work involved long-range testing and development projects, these funds were generally not subject to sudden draconian cuts.

Another factor that differentiated the Tech Center from a field facility was the small (to me surprisingly small) number of air traffic controllers among the total facility complement of some 2,000 employees. There were four of us assigned to ACD-340, the simulations branch, and perhaps another half dozen scattered throughout other departments. We were basically looked at as a valuable asset, frequently consulted by engineers and human factors specialists working on projects related to airports or air traffic control.

Toward the end of my first week an individual approached our group saying, "Hey, any of you guys want to go to New Orleans? We are going to be looking at a camera system that is supposed to measure whether an airport is in compliance with TERPS criteria." (TERPS was the set of standards that spelled out required obstruction clearance minimums on the arrival path to a runway). Mark and Jeff, two of my new colleagues, immediately said yes. The man then turned to me and said, "What about you?" I said, "Well I only reported four days ago and I have no background or other information on this project, so I don't think I could add much to whatever determinations are going to be made about the system." He looked at me quizzically and said, "Hey, don't you want to go to New Orleans? We've got the money." I looked at Jeff, the lead in our group. He nodded his head with a smile and said, "Sure, why don't you go with us." In the event, the trip was fun and interesting, and I contributed almost nothing to the report of our findings. None of this could ever have happened if I were in a field facility.

Several other things soon became apparent as well. My new position was back at the GS-14 level, meaning that my base salary would grow by the amount I had lost at Tamiami via the policy of awarding only 50 per cent of the cost of living increases each year. But my opportunity to savor the extra dollars was short lived. Unlike Florida, New Jersey levied a state income tax, the collection of which essentially took those dollars back. It was also clear that there was no set of ongoing duties assigned to our group, nor any direct hands on supervision by management. When there was a simulation exercise under development, or when an exercise was actually in progress, we were busy but these activities occurred only two or three times a year. The rest of the time we were on our own, with a kind of freedom to come and go not remotely imaginable in any tower or center.

As it happened, I had arrived about two weeks before we would host a group of controllers and supervisors from both Denver Center and Denver Tower. The new Denver airport, then under construction, would require a wholesale revision of airspace delegation and arrival routes to fully utilize the planned four-runway parallel approach operation. The Tech Center had full mock-ups of both an en route control room and a terminal TRACON, with the capability of handling an integrated simulation. Although much of the development work was complete, we were still in a last-minute scramble to make sure that the new procedures would in all respects function as advertised. We spent many long hours in the two labs checking that there were no software hiccups that could compromise the various traffic flows being simulated.

Because the same laboratory resources were exclusively used in the daytime to test and troubleshoot equipment either proposed for deployment to the field or already deployed but exhibiting problems, simulation work was always scheduled in the evening. My three colleagues, all married, disliked this scheduling, but I had always preferred the evening shift, where it was just us and the technicians, not to mention the 10 per cent pay differential paid for any hours worked after 6:00 pm.

When the Denver personnel arrived I was again struck by the realization that the world of air traffic control was indeed a small one. The man heading up the terminal group was a former colleague from MIA, now the Plans and Procedures officer at Denver tower. Since I was primarily in a learning mode on this first exercise, there was a real advantage in connecting with someone whom I knew and with whom I could talk candidly. We had several conversations that added considerably to my understanding of what the simulation was about from the perspective of the end users.

Over the two weeks that the simulation ran there were a few stops and starts, but at the conclusion the controllers from both DEN (the tower) and ZDV (the center) agreed that the overall results confirmed the viability of the proposed procedures. Bill Cassada, the lead for DEN, later wrote a nice letter of appreciation commending Jeff, Mark, Rick, and me for our efforts in making the exercise a success. This seemed to me a good start to my new job. And there would be much more to follow when the Denver airport was nearing completion.

Closely Spaced Parallel Approaches

Most of the simulation work during my time at the Tech Center related to closely spaced parallel approach operations. Simultaneous parallel approaches referred to operations conducted under instrument weather conditions where aircraft were permitted to fly literally wing to wing on instrument approaches to parallel runways. These procedures were already in use at airports where the spacing between runway centerlines was sufficient. The standard at the time was a minimum of 4,300 feet.

At MIA the centerlines between 9 Right and 9 Left were separated by 5,100 feet, allowing us to run "simos" when the weather was down. But there were a number of other airports whose runways did not meet the 4,300-foot minimum separation standard, and therefore required that a "staggered" interval be established and maintained between aircraft on the two final approach courses. For approach controllers, this type of operation involved "shooting the gap." One controller would establish an interval between pairs of aircraft on his final, while the other would vector each of his aircraft to intercept the adjacent final with appropriate diagonal separation between one of the pairs. This meant prolonged periods of high intensity precision vectoring, always aiming for, but not falling below, the minimum gap permitted.

With parallel approaches, the two finals could be run essentially independent of one another. Our simulations were designed to explore the feasibility of conducting parallel approaches on runways separated by less than the then 4,300-foot minimum, thereby permitting the operation at additional airports and reducing system delays.

In order to run the "parallels" there were a number of specific requirements, in terms of staffing, equipment, and procedures. Each runway required both a feeder and a final controller, plus a third controller designated as the monitor. The job of the monitor positions was to detect any deviations from the assigned localizer and take immediate action to correct either the errant pilot or to break out the aircraft on the adjacent final. Sometimes both actions were needed.

It took six individual radar displays (five if the monitors shared a scope) and six separate radio frequencies, including those assigned to the two required local control positions, to support the operation. The video map had to display a no-transgression zone at least 2,000 feet wide between the finals, and each runway had to have a fully functional ILS system. Procedurally, aircraft in the two arrival streams came together at a point about 15 miles from the runway thresholds, each intercepting its respective localizer with a minimum of 1,000 feet altitude separation from the other. There had to be at least two miles of straight and level flight before the higher aircraft joined the glide slope and began a descent, at which point altitude separation was lost and the monitor function came into play. The monitor controllers transmitted and received on the local control frequency associated with their runway, overriding the local control positions when necessary.

Even with all of this in place, there were several factors that limited the effectiveness of the parallel operation. One was the 15-sweep-per-minute antenna rotation rate of the approach surveillance radar (ASR) systems in use at terminal radar facilities. This translated into four seconds between each radar "hit," an interval during which an aircraft with a groundspeed of 180 knots would travel about 1,200 feet. In the case of an extreme off-course deviation, by the time of the second hit, the aircraft could be well into the no transgression zone. With multiple aircraft on the final, it usually took at least two antenna rotations for a controller to detect and react to the deviation of a particular flight. For the controller monitoring the adjacent approach course, there was a further delay for the pilot to receive instructions and establish the turn necessary to comply. In addition, the localizer signal, or beam, was subject to a certain amount of "spread" as the distance from the transmitter increased. This meant that two pilots in aircraft side by side could each receive an on-centerline indication in the cockpit while the actual distance between aircraft was reduced below the nominal separation between runways.

In addition to these factors, the radar presentation itself could be problematic. It was possible to attenuate or reduce the aircraft targets so that the returns became smaller "blips," making it easier to determine whether they were exactly on centerline. But the video mapping at the time was not digitized. Rather, the maps were created by a process of etching lines into an opaque coating on a transparent plate. When magnified to create more detail within the critical 15 miles where the approaches needed to be monitored, the lines became "fuzzy." This could result, for example, in the boundary of the no transgression zone, or the localizers themselves, appearing to be hundreds of feet wide.

If the radar update rate could be increased and the video map display could provide clearer definition, it should be possible to observe trends and take action more promptly. In the world of simulation, software adjustments could produce any radar scan rate that might be desired. But a better mapping display for monitoring purposes was only now being developed and at this stage was unavailable. Moreover, if the simulation exercises were to produce any useful information, the real-world limitations, both fiscal and technical, had to be taken into account.

There were two ways using existing technology to achieve an increased radar update rate. One method was to install two ASR antennae back to back. Although the 15 rotations per minute would not change, there would now be two "hits" per antenna revolution, meaning that a new position for each aircraft being monitored would be generated every two seconds. This was a marked improvement over the four-second interval, but an airplane traveling at 180 knots would still cover more than 600 feet between sweeps.

The other method utilized an array of dipoles in a 360-degree circle around a central receiving point. The advantage of this system was that in contrast with the rotating antenna, there were no moving parts. Each dipole received its signal in sequence, relaying it to the central receiver. In theory, there was no practical limit to the speed with which these signals could be collected, but in reality the ability to process the data into a meaningful visual display was limited. In addition, the dipoles were extremely sensitive to moisture. Even an early morning patina of dew could seriously compromise their function.

There was an additional innovation incorporated into some of the parallel approach exercises, the so-called one-degree offset operation. If one of the localizers was offset from direct alignment with the runway by one degree, the separation of the final approach courses increased by about 100 feet per mile from the runway thresholds out to the localizer intercept points 15 miles from the airport. This small variation from a straight-in approach was essentially transparent to a pilot reaching minimums, but had a couple of advantages from the perspective of the monitor controllers.

Consider the example of parallel ILS-equipped runways with centerlines separated by 3,000 feet. Let's call them 18 Right and 18 Left. Without the offset, the two finals would be separated by 3,000 feet, both on a bearing of 180, to their respective the runways. If the localizer for 18 Left were offset by one degree, the bearing to the threshold would be 181, with the intercept points now about 4,500 feet apart. So instead of handling pairs of aircraft with only 3,000 feet separation for the entire 15 miles, monitor controllers had some extra separation to work with as the distance between localizers gradually decreased, reaching 3,000 feet only at the runway thresholds. Another plus for the controllers was the fact that target definition and position display accuracy improved incrementally with increased proximity to the radar antenna.

Running the "Sims"

In the real world, simultaneous parallel approaches were not run every day. At MIA, where the weather was above VFR minimums over 95 per cent of the time, the operation was conducted only occasionally. At other airports the operation was more common, but probably was utilized less than half the time. When "simos" were in use, even for a full eight-hour shift, off-course deviations requiring intervention by the monitor controllers were exceedingly rare. In other words, real-world data about the number and severity of "blunders," as these events were termed, was sparse to the point of being useless from a statistical point of view.

So what should the simulations look like? How many blunders, and what kind of information should be collected in order to provide a credible basis for evaluating the safety and effectiveness of the closely spaced parallel approach operation? Contractor personnel trained in statistical analysis helped us air traffic types to understand the "how many" part of the question. It was clear that "x" number of blunders had to occur and that within that number some percentage would be successfully resolved. This would establish with a high degree of probability the rate of successful intervention by the monitor controllers. The question was, what was the value of "x?"

According to our experts, if 200 blunders took place, and only five, or 2.5 per cent, were not successfully resolved, we would be able to assert with 95 per cent confidence that the true percentage of failed interventions within a larger group would fall between 0.8 per cent and 5.7 per cent. The difference between these values was known as the confidence interval. Clearly, a larger number of blunders, assuming that the rate of failed interventions remained similarly small, would result in a narrower "spread" between the upper and lower limits of the confidence interval. But each simulation run lasted only about an hour, and the number of blunder opportunities within each usually amounted to a dozen or fewer. It took a full two weeks to reach even the 200 number. The time, expense, and number of personnel involved combined to impose a practical limitation on what could be accomplished.

On the air traffic side, the basic question was how to define a successful intervention. The IFR standard of 1,000 feet or three miles obviously did not apply, as the aircraft were operating less than a mile apart on parallel localizers at the same altitude. I do not now remember the exact standards agreed upon, but the specified minimum miss distances were pretty minimal—something like 300 feet vertically or 500 feet horizontally, with each of those numbers reduced in the case where both vertical and horizontal separation existed.

The starting point for a simulation was a computer-generated list of aircraft, taking into account the representation of each type in the fleet of air carriers and the general aviation class. Typical performance characteristics, speeds on final, and even small variations within these general categories were programmed. Using a table of target start times for aircraft on the two localizers, Jeff, Mark, Rick and I picked out likely pairs as candidates for deliberately introduced blunders. For example, if two 737s began their respective approaches within a few seconds of each other, they would be side by side, or nearly so. We could then direct the remote pilot operators controlling the targets to turn one towards the other and later evaluate the response time of the monitor controllers and the distance between targets at the point of closest proximity. With different aircraft types, we could estimate that a faster aircraft with a later start time would eventually pull alongside an earlier starting slower aircraft on the adjacent final, creating another blunder opportunity.

Typically these exercises took place over a two-week period. They involved a large number of Tech Center personnel, from programmers, to radar technicians, to remote pilot operators, to our controller group. Groups of radar-qualified controllers from terminal field facilities were brought in to perform the monitor function. The FAA had also contracted with several companies throughout the country that provided airliner simulator training to participate. Through the magic of electronics and software, these simulators, "flown" by qualified type-rated pilots, were integrated into the exercises and became additional targets mixed in with those generated by computer.

In addition, the parallel approach program was subject to a fair amount of high-level interest and scrutiny. The higher-ups in the FAA were concerned with the big bucks being consumed. ALPA, the airline pilots' union, was focused on safety. Airline managers were interested in how delays could be mitigated and costs reduced. Representatives from each of these groups were often present, acting as observers over the course of the simulation period.

While the technical sophistication of the exercises was undeniable, the process of creating and introducing blunders was by comparison somewhat primitive. I frequently performed that function while the others in our group stationed themselves in the mock TRACON or the remote pilot lab. We communicated with one another by hand held UHF radios. On a scope duplicating the display that the controllers were using, I would watch the "blunder" pairs earlier selected. Taking into account relative speeds and positioning, I would set up a blunder like this:

Me (on UHF radio to a coordinator in the pilot lab): "Hey Rosie, set up USAIR 650 for a 30-degree off course deviation to the left in about 45 seconds. I will call the turn."

Rosie would acknowledge, then go to the pilot station controlling the target representing USAIR 650. Many of our "sims" were run on parallel runways 18 Left and 18 Right, so if USAIR 650 was on the approach to 18 Right, tracking 180, the operator would enter 150 on the heading control, then wait for my command to execute the turn. When I estimated that the turn would put the target on a direct intercept course to traffic on the 18 Left final, often one of the flight simulators, hopefully adding increased realism relating to pilot response time, I would announce "GO." The operator would punch the "execute" key and the target would begin to turn left, off course, heading directly for a simulated collision. The monitor controllers would issue commands, and eventually the two targets would separate. They would not disappear as would be the case if a real-world collision were to occur.

The raw data from each run was usually available within a few minutes of its completion. As expected, the number of unsuccessful interventions by the monitor controllers was very low. Many of the individual exercises concluded without a single instance where separation fell below the specified minimums. This was good news in relation to the ultimate goal of increasing the number of airports where simultaneous parallel approaches could be conducted, but there were a couple of things I wondered about. One was the human factor. In the real world, as a monitor controller, you would spend hours and hours waiting for an off-course deviation that never came. Even the most disciplined among us would find our focus relaxing a little as those hours went by. In the "sims" the monitor controllers knew that the next blunder was at most only a few minutes away and therefore maintained a uniformly high degree of vigilance. I believed that this subtle difference could be critical in initiating action to resolve a blunder, possibly skewing the results derived in the post-run analysis.

The other factor was technical, relating to target display and the determination of target positions during an off-course deviation. The radar return of an individual target was not a pinpoint, but represented an area perhaps a hundred or two hundred feet across. Separation was defined as the distance between target centers. The miss distance in a blunder could only be measured between the target positions displayed with each radar sweep. There was no way to interpolate information between these discrete "hits." So with a radar update rate of once every four seconds and a target moving at over 300 feet per second, the two points of closest proximity between "aircraft" before and after flight paths crossed could be 700 feet and 500 feet. These values met or exceeded the established minimum miss distance, but did not account for the strong likelihood that somewhere along the 1,200 feet of travel by the deviating aircraft between radar sweeps the separation from traffic on the adjacent localizer was considerably less. It seemed to me that, taken together, these uncertainties could call into question the validity of the conclusions drawn from the simulations. But those determinations were the job of people who were smarter than me (but who probably couldn't run blunders as well as I could).

These simulations confirmed that the rate of unsuccessful intervention by monitor controllers varied in relation to exactly the factors that common sense might suggest—a slow radar update rate, more closely spaced runways, and poor definition of the video map at the monitor position all correlated with a higher incidence of decreased miss distances during a blunder. Another factor that emerged in the post-run analyses that had not been specifically targeted for investigation, was that the chance of a successful resolution when a fast aircraft blundered into a slower one was markedly lower than in cases where the targets were of similar speeds. As the "Blundermeister," I looked for these opportunities as representing the worst-case scenario for the parallel approach operation.

Briefing the Brass

During the periods between simulations, our group was sometimes called upon for assistance in briefing the upper echelons of FAA and airline management on studies or projects that related to air traffic. Several of the supervisors over us were former Flight Service Station employees and managers who had no direct experience in tower, TRACON, or en route control. Although they were classified as air traffic controllers, there was a world of difference between the work in Flight Service (basically assembling information and disseminating it to pilots) and the hands-on, real-time separation of aircraft done by center and terminal personnel. The Tech Center was one of the few places where an employee from Flight Service could be promoted above the GS-13 or GS-14 level, but they were sometimes at a loss when it came to a question about simulation results or something in the real world like flow control. To be fair, some of the people being briefed and asking questions were themselves not well informed about the realities of aircraft performance and the attendant limitations on control strategies.

I remember an instance during a briefing on the results of one of the parallel runway simulations where the questioner asked, "Why can't you just assign different altitudes to the aircraft involved in a blunder?" The question was based on the observation that monitor controllers almost always issued vectors to one or both of the targets, often not including altitude assignments. The manager chairing the meeting was caught somewhat flat-footed, clearly stuck for a reasonable answer.

Our direct supervisor, seated with us towards the back of the room, urgently whispered, "Can you help him?" One of us (not me) spoke up, giving the following explanation: "You have to realize that both aircraft are in the landing configuration with landing gear, flaps, and slats all extended. They are operating with high drag and high power settings. Once they pass the final approach fix they are below the minimum vectoring altitude, descending on a 3-degree glide slope at 600 or 700 feet per minute, depending on airspeed. In many cases the deviating aircraft is in the lead, and therefore at a lower altitude than traffic on the adjacent final. You can't issue a descent, and for a pilot to comply with a climb instruction he must reverse the descent and overcome drag imposed by the aircraft configuration. In the time it takes to establish altitude separation the targets have long since passed. In cases where the deviating aircraft cannot be returned to its proper track, the most effective blunder resolutions depend on identifying which target will be in the lead at the projected point where flight paths cross, then issuing vectors to increase the separation at that point."

In another case, the questioner, in trying to respond to the airlines' concern that faster aircraft were being assigned slower airspeeds to maintain a gap behind slower traffic headed for the same airport, asked, "Why can't the faster airplane just pass the slower one?" The answer to that was something like this: "There are limited circumstances where that can be done, and most controllers will take those opportunities when traffic conditions will permit. If the flow is light or moderate, or the distance to the airport is great enough, there can be time to vector the faster traffic off course, pass up the slower one, then rejoin the routing or the airway. As traffic volume increases and the distance to the airport gets shorter, there are two constraints that usually rule out this strategy. One is the proximity of arrival and departure routes, with traffic travelling in opposite directions, around a terminal hub. The other is that often the approach control facility will call for a certain in-trail interval between successive arrivals, such as ten miles. Once those gaps are established, even if a faster aircraft could pass a slower one, there is no place to put it and still maintain the required ten miles."

Worthy Projects?

In other cases our controller group was called upon to offer advice on projects being worked on "in house" in other departments of the Tech Center. I was involved in two of these, both, I privately concluded, representing a large investment of time and money for a questionable benefit. Both projects had been under way for a number of years, and I wondered why some form of controller input had not been solicited long before now. Still, I was being asked for my help and I resolved to provide it as best I could.

The first of these was the "heads-up" display of certain control tower information that was usually provided by dials or individual screens recessed into the console placed just below the level of the windows. Information such as wind speed and direction, altimeter setting, and temperature were available at a glance. Someone had decided that the necessity of looking downward to these indicators distracted a controller from looking out at his traffic. Maybe controller awareness could be improved by projecting the information directly onto the window glass so that the individual could see it without looking down.

I immediately saw some potential problems with this approach. The images displayed by the prototypes they showed me were either too faint to be read easily, or too bold, possibly obscuring the view of traffic. In addition to that, there would have to be at least two, and possibly three, different projection systems in order to assure equal access to the information by multiple control positions around the tower cab. The glass in tower windows was of a specialized type, designed to prevent fogging up and to shed precipitation. No doubt the type of glass needed for the heads-up projections was also specialized. Were these requirements compatible, and at what expense?

In the end, I limited my comments to my own experience, which was that it was not necessary to have a constant display of routine information. I said that every tower controller had to learn to scan his instruments in a way that did not detract from the task of managing traffic, and left it at that.

Another project about which I was asked to offer advice was an even bigger stretch in terms of its potential utility. The engineers had crafted a laboratory mock-up of a tower with an array of speakers mounted around the interior circumference of the cab. Based on the knowledge that our human binaural hearing enabled us determine the direction from which a sound source emanated, the concept was that a receiver would route pilot transmissions to a speaker corresponding to the direction of the aircraft from the airport. In theory this would assist a controller in locating the airplane and issuing appropriate landing instructions, especially at general aviation airports with a lot of student flying and the attendant incorrect position reports.

But for me, this was frankly in the "YGBSM" category of impractical ideas, for several reasons. Except during periods of very low activity, controllers wore headsets for the very good reason that a speaker broadcasts throughout the tower. With multiple positions manned, each specialist needed to monitor his frequency discretely. The constant barrage of verbiage from a speaker would be an annoyance and a distraction to all. And there was a far simpler method of determining the position of an inbound airplane available, one that eliminated the need for a speaker array and the related disadvantages. Flight Service stations had an instrument for issuing direction finding (DF) steers consisting of a simple dial with a needle that pointed in the direction from which a radio transmission was coming. In this case I told the project manager that there had never been a need established for the capability they were trying to develop, and that I believed R&D resources could be better utilized elsewhere.

The ATCA Convention

As Tech Center employees, our controller group was permitted and encouraged to attend the annual Air Traffic Control Association (ATCA) conference and exposition, which included air traffic personnel who were not eligible for membership in NATCA, meaning supervisors, staff, and Flight Service specialists. Each year the organization sponsored a convention event, basically a trade show where vendors could hawk their wares, demonstrating and exhibiting new technologies in the hope of landing a lucrative contract with FAA.

I was privileged one year to be the presenter of the AERA Demo, the scripted sequence of computer screens illustrating the capabilities being designed into the system. From a traditional point of view, AERA represented a radical departure from the established way in which the ATC system was being run. The idea that algorithms were going to separate airplanes simply did not "compute" in the minds of some. Old hands in the business reacted with considerable skepticism, sometimes expressing their reservations in the bluntest of terms, as in the case of a veteran controller from New York Center. He watched the demonstration impassively, and said nothing when it was over. We had a short exchange that went like this:

Me: "So, what did you think?"

ZNY Controller: "That will never work in my sector."

Other convention attendees were more polite, but noncommittal. There was a German delegation of five or six people led by one individual who approached me saying,

"What is this?"

I replied, "This a demonstration of AERA, short for automated en route air traffic control. The system will greatly expand the look-ahead time based on aircraft trajectories, identifying potential conflicts up to two hours in the future and generating resolutions to those conflicts. Would you like to see the demo?"

I got a simple reply: "Ja."

At the conclusion I said I would be happy to answer any questions they might have. The leader of the group nodded slightly, saying "Thank you," and the delegation moved on to the next display.

Later a group of Japanese approached me, assembling themselves around the three screens used in the demo. They were all smiling politely, but no one spoke. I broke the silence by saying, "This is a demonstration of AERA. That stands for automated en route air traffic control. Would you like to see it?" They were all nodding and smiling as I spoke, and continued to do so when I finished, but still did not say anything. As I ran through the demo, they all crowded around more closely, smiling more broadly and nodding more vigorously as I covered each successive point in the briefing. When it was over I asked if there were any questions, eliciting another round of nods and smiles and concluding with bows from each of them as they backed away. To this day I don't know if they understood a word I said.

There were also addresses by individual presenters covering subjects of interest to the aviation community, as well as symposiums led by people with experience and supposed expertise in their field. I attended one of the latter, seeing once again that the world of air traffic control was indeed a small one. The panel was composed of supervisors and managers from each of the ATC options, that is, Flight Service, terminals and centers.

One of the Flight Service representatives looked familiar to me. She was a woman named Jean, with a different last name than when I had first known her 14 or 15 years earlier. Back then she had been a cooperative education student, a "co-op" from the local community college in Miami. She came to Miami Tower after graduating, for the purpose of receiving some basic instruction in non-radar procedures. During this time, pre-1980, all controller candidates were required to attend a four-month course at the FAA Academy, a tough test designed to weed out the marginal and identify those with the right stuff. Most of the students who failed Academy training did so because they did not pass the non-radar phase. In an effort to reduce the failure rate, the agency had decided to give these young people a leg up by sending them to field facilities in advance of their Academy date to get some basic orientation to the mysteries of non-radar control.

Jean and four other co-ops with pending Academy reporting dates were assigned to Miami Tower for non-radar indoctrination. This was in 1978 or 1979, the period prior to the PATCO strike, when I was a training specialist. I would have the group for one week. They were all well aware of the Academy washout rate, and at least on the first day paid rapt attention to what I had to say. But on the second day Jean approached me, beginning a conversation that went like this:

Jean: "Could I be excused from class for the rest of the week? I am getting married on Saturday, and I have a million things to do."

Me: "Well, a couple of things. First, you will have to ask my boss, the training manager, for permission to be excused. But please consider this: This is your opportunity to learn some stuff that could be the difference between passing and failing in Oklahoma City. There won't be another chance to make it up. Frankly, if it were me, with a career on the line, I would stay in class and let others plan the wedding. But you should make the decision, bearing in mind the possible consequences."

Jean did not appear in class for the remainder of the week, and as they left at the conclusion the other students thanked me, saying that they felt better prepared for the challenge of non-radar.

Jean's disappearance was not a big surprise to me. About three years later, while I was still at MIA, the training manager approached me saying, "Hey, do you remember a co-op student named Jean who was in that group that you gave the non-radar class to a couple or three years ago?" I said that I did. He continued, "Well, she has filed a grievance saying that she was not given an opportunity to attend the class, that she washed out of the Academy, and wants another chance based on disparate treatment compared to the others in that group who all passed.

I said, with considerable emphasis, "Oh no, that's not what happened. She asked to be excused from the class because of her wedding and I advised her strongly not to give up the opportunity. Next thing I knew she was gone." The EPDO replied, "It gets better. The agency has decided to allow her to complete the class that you gave, then, based on a determination that she has demonstrated acceptable competence, to recycle her through the Academy program. And she wants you to be her instructor." Although at that point I still had my EPDS (training specialist) designation, I was working six-day weeks on the boards, and the last thing I needed was to get caught in the middle of a labor-management dispute.

As it turned out, Jean did not get her wish to have me as her instructor. She was given some version of the class she had missed with me, taught by none other than the guy who had washed her out of non-radar at the Academy. He had been an instructor there during Jean's first attempt and transferred to MIA after the strike. Apparently Jean had objected mightily and filed another grievance based on continuing unfair treatment. The long and short of it was that after two failures, she ended up in a Flight Service station. And low and behold, was now a member of a panel of experts at a major business convention. Go figure.

A Stint at FAA Headquarters

During my time at the Tech Center, I continued to serve on the ATACT team, attending meetings two or three times a year on the AERA project. The agency had decided to do something different in designating the team chairmen, all of whom had been supervisors or managers assigned to the position as a short-term detail. Either because it was felt that this was not the way to utilize these resources, or that each successive team chair had to start from scratch in getting up to speed on the project, the chairmanship was now being rotated among us, the team members. There were pros and cons to this approach. On the one hand, the position was now being filled by someone with up-to-the-minute knowledge of our progress to date. But the downside was that most of the members had not had supervisory or management experience and were not well equipped to navigate the bureaucratic intricacies of keeping a big-budget undertaking like AERA on course.

My turn came up in the fall of 1993 when the Tech Center allowed me to accept a 120-day detail in the Requirements Branch at FAA headquarters. In talking to my fellow team members who had held the position of team chairman before me, I learned that duty at headquarters was no walk in the park. They all advised me to expect long days and short deadlines in dealing with everything that would cross my desk. So it was with some trepidation that I reported to Charlie, the head of the branch, on that first day. I immediately saw that he was no stuffed-shirt bureaucrat, but exhibited the typical can-do attitude shared by most controllers. It was also clear that he was busier than anyone, and expected me to hit the ground running. Even before I had fully settled in Charlie approached me urgently saying, "I need you to put together a week-long briefing on AERA for a bunch of Eurocontrol representatives. They will be hosted by MITRE, and you will have MITRE's help in putting the presentation together. They will be here next week. So get your ass out to MITRE and get to work. Keep me informed of your progress."

Wow! One week to prepare for 40 hours of presentation and discussion on AERA? I couldn't imagine how I was going to fill up that much time. I hoped that MITRE would have a generous amount of amplifying technical material to complement the operational aspects that I would be addressing. And so I spent most of my first week not at headquarters but at the MITRE offices in McLean, Virginia. I was not surprised to find that the MITRE people who had been meeting with our team were totally on board with and in full support of the Eurocontrol briefing. But the warnings I had received about long days in my new position turned out to be spot on, and I was in major scramble mode for the whole week.

As it turned out, the Europeans were on the whole a rather courtly bunch. They listened attentively, only occasionally interrupting me to ask a question. I realized pretty quickly that they had done their homework on AERA, at times making comments that indicated an understanding at least equal to my own about how the system was designed to work. Their real purpose seemed to be to compare/ contrast the AERA capabilities with a system of their own, known by the acronym ODID, or Operational Display and Input Development. They had brought a floppy disk (remember, this was 1993) showing a sequence of slides illustrating ODID's capabilities. It took only a few minutes to run through the series, and at the end I was struck by the clean simplicity of what I had just seen. Every controller knows that for every potential traffic conflict there is one "good call" and one or more "bad calls" available to resolve it. Good calls minimized controller workload and delays to aircraft. Bad calls would ensure separation, but required more work and imposed greater penalties on the users.

To identify the "good call" solution to a traffic conflict, you had to first determine what would happen if you took no action. In a crossing situation, that meant projecting which airplane would pass behind the other, no matter by how small a margin, then issuing a small course correction to that pilot to ensure legal separation. The "bad call" would have been to reverse the geometry of the encounter, causing the aircraft that was already behind, to cross in front of the one in the lead. The core of ODID was to magnify the area where flight paths crossed, with ample lead time, instantly revealing the best solution to a conflict, and relieving the controller of a difficult judgment call. I felt some momentary discomfort as I contrasted this simple and elegant innovation with the technical complexities of AERA, with its trial planning, computer generated resolutions, and the cost and time investment in its development.

As instructed, I wrote up a daily synopsis of the briefing for Charlie. He never acknowledged these communications, which I chalked up to the principle that no news is good news. In fact, I rarely saw Charlie. The pace of activity in the office was pretty much full-on frantic, with Charlie constantly being summoned away to meet with this committee or that committee on Capitol Hill, or to brief congressmen or airline representatives on any number of issues. In due course the agency received a letter from Eurocontrol expressing appreciation for the AERA briefing, a copy of which eventually found its way to my desk.

Like everyone else in the branch, I had my share of short-notice demands come my way. Sometimes it was a congressional staffer or even a congressman himself who showed up wanting a quick and dirty update on AERA, or even unrelated FAA issues or programs. At other times it might be someone from the command center seeking information on how AERA would work in conjunction with flow control, or a call from MITRE to come out and look at something they had developed in preparation for the next team meeting. The most memorable event, from my perspective, involved a delegation of our old friends, the Japanese. It was obvious from the outset that they were all management types from the Japanese FAA equivalent. Only one of their number spoke, asking questions in heavily accented English, and revealing almost no understanding of the realities of ATC operations. I made it a point to speak slowly, in short sentences, and to pause frequently as I ran through the presentation of AERA capabilities.

At the end, their spokesman thanked me profusely as the group exited the briefing room, proffering the obligatory round of smiles and bows. I wrote yet another unacknowledged summary of the briefing and went on to further chapters of the high speed juggling act that characterized life at headquarters. About a month later I received a small package covered in international postage and vertical lines of Japanese ideograms. It contained a beautifully crafted jewelry box with ivory and jade inlays along with the business card of (I assumed) the leader of the delegation I had briefed. The two words "Thank You," written in stilted letters, appeared at the bottom of the card.

The End of an AERA

My 120-day detail would end on or about January 1, 1994, and sometime in December Charlie asked me if I would be interested in another 120 days as AERA team chairman. At one level I read this as some kind of acknowledgement that I was doing a decent job, and so I of course accepted. But in the light of later events, it seemed possible that this reappointment may have had little relation to any supposed merit of mine in my role to date.

The first major item of the new year was a team meeting, scheduled for late January. It was the first, and as it turned out, the only one for which I would be team chairman. Preparations for the meeting required many long days of coordination and cajoling, getting the field facilities to release team members and persuading the proper authorities to sign off on the funding to finance the trip. In addition to that there was major planning with MITRE for their part in the effort. Fortunately it all came together in time for the team to meet, as planned, in Newport Beach, California.

The meeting did not go well. Instead of the expected headway in producing more gee-whiz ideas and straw man presentations that we had come to expect from MITRE, we were seeing basically a rehash of things already covered and documented. Joe, the only MITRE representative in attendance, began taking pointed potshots from some of the team members who were dissatisfied with the apparent lack of progress. This was entirely uncalled for, and I, as well as some of the team, understood that Joe could only follow the marching orders he was given by his bosses who themselves were responding to what the FAA wanted (or didn't want) done. I finally called a time out and asked Joe to leave the room. There followed a heated discussion where opinions ranging from "we ought to all just resign from the team" to "let's write a letter to Congress and explain our concerns" were offered.

I said I thought there was more going on than we were currently aware of, and that I thought a mass resignation or taking our concerns outside the requirements branch might spell the death knell of AERA. I suggested that we brainstorm together, identifying questions to which we wanted answers. I would then compose a draft letter to Charlie and give the branch a chance to respond, after which we could consider further action. We more or less came to agreement on this approach, some more reluctantly than others.

By the end of the meeting we had agreed on a final draft of the letter, which I submitted to Charlie upon returning to Washington. A couple of days later he called me into his office and made it clear that he was, to say the least, not pleased. The substance of the discussion was that it was up to me to rein in the more radical elements of the team and ride out what might be only a temporary halt in the process of developing AERA. Although he did not give me detailed information, I learned enough to understand that the costs of the program were already seriously overrunning initial estimates with no end point in sight. The FAA was under fire for an effort that had lasted ten years without producing anything of practical value for the ATC system.

From that point on, I was basically treading water, with a much-reduced volume of work relating to AERA. Towards the end of my detail, which would expire in May, David Hinson, the FAA administrator, called a meeting of everyone involved in the project. He said that Congress had called a halt to our funding and that no further development was contemplated "at this time." He went on to offer expressions of appreciation to all who had contributed, saying that none of us was to blame for this outcome. Despite these assurances, I wondered if anything in our letter to Charlie had any bearing on the FAA's decision or Hinson's remarks. It seemed probable that the ATACT team would soon be receiving an official communication saying we were disbanded.

Time would tell. In August, the expected letter arrived. Shortly thereafter one of the team members sent a message to all of us expressing the satisfaction and personal fulfillment he had experienced working with what he termed "the finest group of fellow professionals" he had ever known. I received a letter of appreciation from Charlie at the conclusion of my detail. It was a positive letter, filled with all the buzz words about my "dedication," my "hard work," and my willingness to accept an assignment involving "long periods away from [my] home." What it didn't include was acknowledgement of any concrete achievement. It appeared that there was no future at headquarters.

Which was actually fine with me. I returned to the more measured pace at the Tech Center for what would be a final ten months there.

The New Denver Airport

I arrived back in New Jersey in time to see the endless news coverage of O.J. Simpson in his Ford Bronco being pursued by a fleet of law enforcement vehicles. We had a couple of short parallel runway simulations during which I discovered that some enhancements had been made to the display from which the "Blundermeister" worked. A small window had been added that basically provided a separation countdown meter of the probable miss distance, with a 30-degree off course turn, of one of the targets. This was helpful, but not a perfect indicator of the precise moment to initiate a blunder, for the same reason that there was uncertainty in calculating the minimum separation after the fact. The system could only compare positions of the two "aircraft" involved based on discrete radar hits, with no information provided between those contacts. You had to figure out the likely moment when the number on the countdown meter would go no lower and the next update would show the number rising. If you guessed right, you had done your best to create a worst-case encounter between the two targets. If you waited for the first update showing the projected miss distance increasing, you were already late.

In December the same players from Denver TRACON and Denver Center who had been present for the revised airspace exercise conducted three years earlier returned for an important simulation prior to the scheduled airport opening. There were two sets of parallel runways labeled 17R-35L, 17L-35R, 16R-34L, and 16L-34R. Eventually, it was hoped, Denver would be able to run simultaneous parallel approaches to all four runways, but for now we would simulate the operation using only three of the four. The 17s were on the west side of the field with the 16s on the east side. Separation between the centerlines of 17 Left and 16 Right was more than adequate, exceeding the 4,300-foot minimum by a comfortable margin. But between 17 Right and 17 left, the distance was slightly under 3,000 feet. Not only did we have to establish that safety between traffic on the 17s could be maintained, but that monitor controllers could successfully resolve off-course deviations potentially involving three airplanes. The simulation would be conducted based on standard terminal radar equipment—an ASR antenna providing position updates every four seconds and TRACON displays at the monitor stations identical to those used at other control positions.

Not surprisingly, high-ranking officials from all the stakeholder organizations were present in abundance on the day the exercise began. FAA, ALPA, airline management, and the Denver airport authority all had people looking over our shoulders during every run. Mark, Rick and I shared the duties at the "Blundermeister" position, and after a couple of days the post-sim analyses showed that there was an unacceptably high incidence of miss distances lower than the minimum prescribed. This was exceedingly bad news on all fronts.

United and Continental airlines had spent millions moving their resources from Stapleton airport based on assurances that some of these costs would be recouped by the efficiencies and reduced delays that would result from the new airport design. FAA had signed off on the design during the planning stages. ALPA's position was that their pilots would not accept "simos" based on these preliminary simulation results. The Denver airport authority, already under fire for major cost overruns, was looking at the possibility that the capacity of the new airport would provide little or no improvement over that of the old one. We were about to prove that the $4.8 billion installation would not function as advertised. And so with the clock ticking, the FAA called a halt to the simulation, idling the entire host of technicians, controllers, pilots and others while the costs of the exercise continued unabated.

No doubt there was some feverish scrambling at the highest levels of the agency to find a way of salvaging the promise of the new airport. Technology came to the rescue in the form of a new display designated as the precision runway monitor (PRM). There was already a deployment "waterfall," or prioritized schedule for installation in field facilities, of the new equipment based on determinations of critical need. Denver was not at or even near the top of the list, but within three days several PRM displays were delivered to the Tech Center for use at the monitor positions, and the simulation resumed.

Within the first few runs it became apparent that the capabilities of the PRM represented a giant leap forward. As noted earlier, the operation being simulated was triple parallel approaches to runways 17 Right, 17 Left, and 16 Right, basically a north to south arrival flow. This meant that any off-course deviations would be towards either the east or the west. The PRM could be programmed to "stretch" the scale of the east-west axis to be eight or ten times larger for a given distance than on the north-south axis. The monitor controllers would see the targets on the individual finals separated by an inch or two representing the required three-mile longitudinal, or in-trail, interval. But when a deviation occurred even the smallest heading change was greatly exaggerated, making a turn of three degrees look more like 30 or 40 degrees. Because of the stretched scale, the target also appeared to accelerate rapidly. These unmistakable indications occurred at the first radar hit after the deviation began, enabling an instant response by the monitor controllers.

To the satisfaction, not to say great relief, of all concerned, results from the simulation using the PRM equipment validated that the triple parallel approach operation could be conducted safely, and with the stroke of a pen the FAA administrator advanced Denver to the top of the deployment waterfall. The airport finally opened in February 1995, a day on which a heavy snowstorm occurred. The opening had been delayed some 16 months while officials had dealt with, and continued to deal with, myriad problems. Because of its location east of the city, the airport experienced heavier snowfalls than those at Stapleton. The baggage system did not work, the de-icing stations were so far from the runways that aircraft would often accumulate unsafe amounts of ice in the time it took to taxi to the run-up pads, and the only access to the passenger terminal was a two-lane state road. But from the ATC perspective, everything worked like a charm. I guess we were the only ones smiling on opening day.

15. Returning to Miami

Miami Tower was for me a kind of alma mater, the place where I had learned the business of air traffic control. When I transferred to Tamiami, I still had hopes of making it back to the facility someday. The move to the Tech Center did not diminish that hope, and after the detail in Washington I began to put out feelers for possible openings at MIA. There was a process called "VolAp," yet another FAA acronym, short for voluntary application. If you were interested in a particular job or a particular location you could submit a form basically stating that if a position of a certain type came open, you wished to be considered for it. The normal advertising and bidding process would still take place, but your name would be in the hat. I submitted a VolAp requesting consideration for any staff position at Miami Tower.

Several months went by without any response from the Southern Region. It was apparent that my voluntary application was pretty much an extreme long shot. Johnny Miles was still the manager at Miami, and now at the age of 53 I probably did not rank high on his list of potential candidates. There were other factors as well that militated against my prospects, such as no "return rights" from the Tech Center. In some cases, such as an assignment at the FAA Academy, you had the right to return to the region where you had previously been stationed. Because there were no return rights, I would not be eligible for an agency-paid move, and would have to pay the costs myself. Finally, my experience at the Tech Center was not likely to be viewed as substantially improving my qualifications for field facility work. The one "plus" on my resume was the detail at headquarters. I knew that Johnny Miles valued diversity of experience and a (presumed) enhanced understanding of the agency's greater mission.

By December, about six months after I submitted the VolAp, with no nibbles of any kind, I decided to play the last card available in the effort to get back to MIA. Hardship transfers were sometimes granted, strictly at agency discretion, when an employee could make the case for a compelling need for the relocation. I was not entirely comfortable even considering this approach, as most of the hardship transfers with which I was familiar smacked of an end run around the normal competitive bidding process. Nevertheless, I did have one point of justification in my favor. My dad has just turned 81 years old, had been hospitalized twice during my time in New Jersey, and was under constant care from his doctor. His health was clearly failing. I believed his circumstances would support a claim at least as genuine as many others for a hardship transfer. I had a lengthy meeting with my father's physician who filled me in on the medical realities and the none-too-encouraging outlook for the future. He agreed to write a letter summarizing it all, and concluding with a strong recommendation that a family member should be nearby to monitor the situation.

I now had an objective and documented basis for my hardship claim. And in yet another instance of the good fortune I had enjoyed throughout my career, two men who had been fellow controllers during my early days at MIA were now in positions of responsibility in the Southern Region. Appending the doctor's letter, I wrote to each them, doing my best to phrase my request for their support in terms that would not seem a presumption on past friendships. I did not receive a reply from either of them, although there was a later postscript during which I learned that one of them had spoken to Johnny Miles in my favor.

Sometime in late January, I received notification that I had been selected for a traffic management position at Miami Tower. I would be going back to the place that I considered home, and for a day or two I was all smiles. But (and it seemed there was always a "but") there were a couple of potentially sticky issues attendant upon this new job. Traffic management specialists did not routinely work traffic, but they were required to maintain currency, meaning spending a minimum of 16 hours per month assigned to a control position. I would have to re-qualify as a controller and regain my second-class medical certificate, which I had allowed to lapse while I was at the Tech Center.

Apart from my age, the hearing problem that had occurred at the end of my Navy tour had become progressively worse, to the point that I was now wearing a hearing aid. Would that constitute grounds for denying my medical clearance? Even if it didn't, I wasn't sure how wearing a headset with an earpiece in one ear and listening for other critical information with the other would play out in practical terms. There were no immediate answers to those questions, so I would have to see what happened and consider my options when they were eventually resolved.

Before reporting to MIA, I would be required to attend a two-week course in traffic management at the FAA Academy in Oklahoma City. I would be accompanied on the two-day drive from New Jersey by a woman I had begun dating several years earlier. She was one of the engineers at MITRE who had been a regular at our team meetings, and had also worked on a project relating to (wait for it) traffic management. She was smart, beautiful, charming, and a consummate professional. It was not lost upon me that my transfer to Florida would sooner or later spell the end of a relationship I had come to value, so it was time to fish or cut bait. Before we hit the road, I cast a line in the form of an engagement ring, and was rewarded with a gratifying "strike." We set a date for October, some seven months hence, during which time I would get resettled and she would wind up her career at MITRE, then move to Miami. I said good-bye to the Tech Center for the last time on March 25, 1995.

Home Again

On April 17, I walked through the door of Miami Tower for what would be a final nine years in the FAA. There were lots of new faces, but still a good number of people from my earlier years. Lanny Williams, now the manager for training, Pat Grillo, the assistant facility manager, Billy Pierce, now an operations supervisor, and even Johnny Miles all welcomed me warmly. It was one of the happiest days of my entire career.

Not long after the feel-good, hail-fellow-well-met rituals concluded, the realities of field facility work asserted themselves in no uncertain terms. There was a deadline only a few days away for a quarterly report mandated by the Southern Region to be submitted by every facility. Miami was now considered a "hub," meaning a central clearing house for a number of nearby smaller facilities. We were responsible for collecting and collating reports from each of these and rolling them up into a master submission. Apparently I had arrived just in time for the second of these exercises, known by the acronym QPR or quarterly performance review. According to Pat Grillo, the first QPR report had been "a disaster," and a substantial improvement was expected this time around. At the morning meeting Johnny went around the room briefly explaining what work each staff member was assigned. He pointed to Ricky, saying, "You've got QPR," then pointed at me and said, "You help him. Go!"

Ricky and I left the room and went to the "bullpen," an area containing six or eight desks for staff use. I asked Ricky what QPR was all about. He rolled his eyes and shook his head saying, "It's a huge pain in the ass that we shouldn't even be doing. The region already has all this information, but is forcing us to do the work of sorting it out and putting it an organized form." Looking at the thick binder containing the information from QPR number one, I had to agree with Ricky's assessment. The following is a partial list of the kinds of information required:

- Total staffing at each facility (available in regional personnel records)
- Number of controllers fully certified since last report (the region processed a promotion to the full performance pay level with each certification)
- Number of controllers in training (easily calculated from the items above)
- Number of grievances filed by the union since last report (these were reported as they occurred)
- Number of operational errors since last report (individually reported as they occurred)
- Percentages of women and minorities at each facility (available in regional personnel records)

Unfortunately, we were basically starting from scratch, with only four or five days until the due date of the report. The satellite facilities never submitted their information until we asked for it, and there were at least half a dozen of these for which we were responsible. Ricky would contact the satellites and I would begin rounding up the information for Miami Tower. It meant badgering the perennially overworked administrative assistant and the equally busy Quality Assurance specialist, both of whom had to dig through three months of records to account for the reporting period being covered. It was slow work. It seemed to me that we were going to have to ask for an extension on the deadline. But apparently every facility in the Southern Region had requested an extension the first time around, and the head of the air traffic division had put out the word that no extensions would be granted this time. We worked until eight or nine o'clock at night on the last two days. Lanny Williams came out to help us on the final evening, and with a final push we managed to complete the report on time.

My third day in the facility, Wednesday, April 19, was the day the federal building in Oklahoma City was bombed. I had driven past the building 12 days earlier on my way back to Florida from the FAA academy. It was a sober reminder of the times we lived in and presaged the events of September 11, 2001 six years later.

Back to the Floor (Briefly)

With QPR behind us, it was time to address my new designation as a traffic management specialist. I had learned from Lanny Williams some things I would otherwise never have known about how I had come to be selected for the position. One of my contacts in the Southern Region had spoken with Johnny Miles about my petition for a hardship transfer, asking if I would be an asset to Miami Tower. Johnny was in no way obligated to honor this request, but had solicited input from people who knew me and who had worked with me before. The first question he asked of Lanny and Billy was whether they thought I could check out through the control positions again. They said they thought I could, but that my real value as a facility member was likely to be in the area of training.

Billy also told Johnny that I could "write a hell of a letter," referring to an incident back in 1978 when Billy was my supervisor. I and two others had left the facility early and had received letters of warning for this violation of agency regulations. The deputy chief at the time also issued a similar letter to Billy for "authorizing" the early go. Of course he had done no such thing, and had been briefly absent from the control room when we left. I wrote a letter to the chief and the deputy, with a copy to PATCO, stating in part: "Mr. Pierce did not authorize our early departure, and in fact had briefed us at the previous training day that all shift assignments were "eight for eight," [meaning that all controllers were to remain in the facility until the defined end of the shift]. Issuing a disciplinary letter to Mr. Pierce does nothing to ensure compliance with agency regulations and only creates a difficult situation been employee and supervisor. The letter of warning to Mr. Pierce should be immediately rescinded."

Lanny had reviewed my performance as a supervisor at Tamiami when he was the manager, highlighting my dealings with our "problem children" and reminding Johnny of my work on the facility evaluation of 1991. The long and short of it was that Johnny was convinced that my record showed I was, in his words, "a company man," and he accepted the hardship transfer.

Johnny took an early opportunity to tell me what he expected in terms of requalifying as a controller. I would have six months to check out through the tower and a year to check out in the TRACON. I had fortunately squeaked through the audiology portion of the physical exam, and so I would begin retraining immediately. Airspace and procedures had changed very little in the time I had been gone, but some of my "old" techniques and methods were no longer used. In my 19 years at MIA I had always had a pad and pen handy to scribble down call signs or other temporary information. But on the first day in the TRACON, as soon as I began writing my instructor abruptly informed me that "you don't have time to make notes. Just enter it on the keyboard." This did not suit me. I believed there were times when you "didn't have time" to divert your attention to the keyboard, but needed a quick and dirty way to record information you would use a little later. It looked like it was going to be another long struggle in training.

Then the gods of good fortune, who had smiled upon me unfailingly at critical points in my career, once again stepped in. There had been a vacancy in the training department shortly before my return to MIA that had been filled by a controller who had transferred from Miami Center. She was sharp and capable, but had no experience in terminal operations. What she did have was an understanding of traffic management from the center perspective. So what was wrong with this picture? The controller with no terminal experience was going to train new employees while the guy with years of experience in the training department was going to have to learn the new discipline of traffic management? With the stroke of a pen I became a training specialist and Teri was assigned to the traffic management unit. We were scheduled to receive a fairly steady stream of new controllers, meaning that the training effort would be pretty much continuous for the foreseeable future. I was back in my element, and the issue of recertifying "on the boards" fell by the wayside. I never worked live traffic again.

ATC Instructor Redux

My first class of trainees were "A-Siders," that is controllers who had certified through the tower and would now prepare for OJT in the TRACON. A class like this one had a very different flavor from other groups who were new to the facility. These guys knew each other well, and there was a considerable amount of ragging on one another both in the classroom and the ETG radar lab. I could tell I had a little rust on my gears after eight years away from the facility, occasionally pausing a lesson in order to refresh myself on some particular point of information. I believed I was serving the class well by trying to be thorough and accurate, but one of the trainees went to Lanny Williams and complained that the class was "dragging." Okay, I would pick up the pace. Then when we reached the next written test in the classroom portion, one of them told me there was no way he was ready for the exam, that there had not been enough time to study for it. Welcome to the push-pull of life in a field facility.

In the simulation portion of the class things went better. I played my usual roles of pilot and controllers at other positions and facilities, throwing in just enough pilot wisecracks to make the exercises fun. The guys were engaged, happy to be "doing something" instead of passively listening in a classroom. And they were much tougher on each other than I was on any of them. We were all plugged into the same communications circuit, and just like in the real world if two microphones were keyed at the same time there was a prominent "zzzt" heard by all of us. If the controller running the problem made a mistake, the other two at the pseudo-pilot positions would immediately key their mics to create the sound. It could go like this:

Controller (to an "airplane" in an area where the top of his area of jurisdiction was 5,000): "Delta 611, climb and maintain 7,000"

"Zzzt".

Or issuing an incorrect frequency: "American 412, contact Miami Center on 123.3"

"Zzzt."

It lightened things up considerably, and there were no further complaints (at least none that got back to me).

On the last day of the class there was a lengthy final exam, asking questions on all the A-side radar positions (all except Miami approach control and Miami South Departure). One of the individuals in the class had done fine in the simulation phase, but had always exhibited what appeared to be a lackadaisical attitude in the classroom. I wondered if he was truly prepared for the exam. Besides the factual questions, each trainee had to draw from memory separate diagrams of the airspace assigned each of the 14 control positions. This was no mean feat, as the geographical boundaries were irregular, and even in the same sector the altitude strata could differ from one location to the next. It usually took an hour or more to complete the test, but Mike spent about 25 minutes writing and drawing as fast as he could, and turned in a paper with zero mistakes. Controllers are a strange breed.

Other classes followed, each helping me get my feet back on the ground with respect to the Miami operation. Typically in a class of three, two would do fine and one would struggle. Often the one who struggled would push back against my attempts to suggest ways to improve, but none went to management with a complaint after the first class. In some cases I would be training people I had worked with before, as when Leo, formerly a co-op student and later a Tamiami controller, appeared for A-side radar training. Also in the class were Chris, who had come from North Perry, and a third guy from Fort Lauderdale. Leo and Chris did fine, with Chris demonstrating his sketching skills as each radar position was studied. As noted earlier, each position had a single letter identifier that would be superimposed over a radar target at the bottom of the ARTS tag leader line. In this way the controller working the position could identify his traffic at a glance, while other controllers could see who was working any target in our airspace. Chris drew cartoon caricatures incorporating the appropriate letter into the sketch, via an L-shaped necktie, a W-shaped shirt collar, or an H-shaped pair of glasses. These were clever and amusing, so I made each sketch the first page of the training manual section dedicated to the relevant radar position.

Morris, the Fort Lauderdale controller, struggled both in the classroom and the lab, and was very touchy about any criticism. For example, a quiz on the Fort Lauderdale approach control position was labeled, "R Position, Fort Lauderdale North Feeder." There were four or five factual questions, then a final instruction stating, "Draw the airspace." Morris drew the departure control airspace. When I marked it wrong, he bristled, saying that the question had not specified what airspace was to be drawn. I pointed out, in as low key a way as possible, that the title of the exam and the earlier questions should have left no doubt as to what was being asked. He was not mollified, insisting that he was being treated unfairly, and saying he was going to complain. I wasn't worried. Lanny would back me up on this one.

Another class of A-siders transitioning to radar training consisted of two controllers I had worked with at Tamiami plus a third who had come from Opa-locka. Both Brian and Robert were sharp young men with commendable records. Brian had served in CIC aboard a Navy aircraft carrier. He controlled the fighters that launched the raid on Libya in the late 1980s. Robert had excelled at the FAA Academy, graduating at the top of his class and earning recognition as an honor student. Uma was a woman whose background consisted solely of VFR tower experience. She had qualified in the tower at MIA, but according to the unofficial rumor mill was barely competent to handle the busier periods. I sensed that this particular class would present some challenges, and later events proved my intuitions correct. Robert and Brian sailed through the syllabus, written exams and simulation problems. Uma struggled, largely because she was searching for a "formula" that would always work in the radar environment. Every control session, even in the simulation lab, was a little different. You had to be able to identify those subtleties and vary your strategies accordingly. Some of the debriefs with Uma included crying jags and extra classroom time for her alone as I attempted build her confidence. In the end, it was all for naught. She ended up washing out at MIA and transferring.

Many of the A-side controllers had had no prior radar experience. In addition to that, they were subject to being called out of class to staff the tower. These factors combined to disrupt the training schedule, a disadvantage to both the student learning curve and the next group of trainees who were waiting in the wings. By contrast, B-siders, those who would train on all the TRACON positions and none in the tower, usually had an easier time of it. During this period, all controllers selected for radar training alone had prior experience, meaning that most of those classes consisted of learning airspace, frequencies, and letter of agreement provisions. I did not have to spend a lot of time teaching basic radar separation methods, instead allowing the trainees to demonstrate that they knew how to stay in their own areas of jurisdiction.

A Mixed Bag

Predictably, in both A-side and B-side classes there were individuals representing the previously described controller types: hot shots, professional perfectionists, not flashy but safe and competent, and strugglers. The strugglers presented the biggest challenge, but in many cases these people would surprise you. Just when you thought there was no hope, the light bulb would come on and literally between one simulation exercise and the next he would go from screwing up right and left to being fully in command of the problem. As an instructor, you lived for these moments.

But it was equally rewarding when things went without a hiccup, or when an unlikely star emerged. The best B-side class I ever had consisted of Troy, Phil, and Paul, all of whom had come from Level 4 or Level 5 radar facilities. There was no bickering or complaining, no ragging on one another, and never a question about their successful completion of the training syllabus. They were dedicated, always asking good questions, and always returned early from breaks, seemingly eager to tackle the next exercise. These guys were good, and checked out in record time when they hit the floor. The most memorable (and unlikely) star was an A-sider whose sole prior experience was at North Perry, strictly a general aviation airport with a VFR tower. He had qualified in our tower, and would now undertake the classroom and simulation syllabus for the TRACON. He was a young man, small in stature, but fit and muscular, with long hair that hung well below his shoulders.

Because he was an A-sider awaiting radar training, who worked only in the tower, and because of his long hair, he earned the improbable sobriquet "Tower Chick." On the very first session in the lab, he made no mistakes. Of course, it was a slow exercise, and maybe he had just been lucky. But as we progressed through the busier problems, nothing changed. He was in complete control, making good calls in every traffic situation, and never exhibited any indication that he was being pushed beyond his comfort level. He was a consummate "natural" who, with no prior radar experience, demonstrated an extraordinary level of competence from start to finish. I ultimately referred to "Tower Chick" as the complete "Zen" controller.

An Attack from Cuba

At some point the staff designations of Plans and Procedures Officer/ Specialist and EPDO/ EPDS (training officer and training specialist) had been eliminated and replaced by new designations. There would be one supervisor, now called the Support Manager, for both functions. He would oversee a cadre of subordinates known as support specialists. In theory, individuals in this group would no longer have areas of specialization but could be called upon for any function relating to operation of the facility. In practice, for the most part, we staff members continued as before, working in the areas to which we were accustomed. But there were exceptions, especially when an unusual event occurred.

One such event was an attack by Cuban fighters on two aircraft operated by Hermanos al Rescate, or Brothers to the Rescue. The group was composed of Cuban exiles who believed it was their duty to carry messages of hope and freedom to the people of Fidel Castro's Cuba. On February 24, 1996, Brothers to the Rescue flew two Cessna 337 Skymasters near the boundary of territorial waters surrounding Cuba. The Brothers had been operating similar flights for several years, at times even flying over the island to drop leaflets bearing their message. They often communicated with Castro's air traffic controllers, broadcasting a mix of information: identification, intention, and always a generous amount of polemic decrying the repression and deprivation imposed by the long time dictatorship. The Cuban government had lodged a number of protests against these operations, but the United States had taken no firm action to curtail them.

This time would be different. Despite the fact that the two Cessnas were over international waters, a flight of Russian-supplied MIGs suddenly appeared and shot them down, killing four men. While the political ramifications were ominous, there developed an immediate practical concern when the exile community in South Florida announced that they would launch a flotilla of boats to proceed to the site for the purpose of honoring the "patriots" who had given their lives in the name of freedom. Johnny Miles became the point man in coordinating among the various agencies involved in protecting the flotilla, and more importantly, in preventing another international incident.

Air traffic control, the Coast Guard, and other elements of the military would ensure that the boats remained in international waters and be ready to respond to any potential threats from Cuba. Both the local and national press were all over the event, and it fell to us staff members to make sure that Southern Region officials were kept up to speed on developments as they occurred. Fortunately it all came off without a hitch, leading to a commendation for Johnny and indirectly reflecting credit upon Miami Tower.

The ValueJet Crash

Aircraft accidents, especially those involving an air carrier, always provided a great amount of fodder for the media. At times the coverage was incomplete, inaccurate, or downright sensationalistic. If the aircraft was being controlled within the ATC system, there were pointed questions about what the controller knew, what he did or did not do, and in many cases multiple rounds of second guessing by laymen and experts alike.

When ValueJet 592 crashed in the Everglades just minutes after takeoff on May 11, 1996, the aftermath followed a familiar pattern. At least one media source demanded to know why air traffic control had not "ordered the pilot to return to the airport before the crash occurred." Opinion pieces like this were highly irresponsible, reflecting zero understanding of the role of ATC in any emergency, and not recognizing some clear and basic facts. ATC does not "order" a pilot to do anything in an emergency situation. The role of a controller in these cases is to prioritize handling of the emergency, and clear the way for the pilot in command to take the actions he considers necessary.

The total time between the ValueJet flight crew's initial report of the need to return to the airport and ground impact was a little over three minutes. At a distance of some 20 miles from the airport and an altitude of 10,000 feet, it would have taken at least three times that long to reverse course, descend, and land. Anyone could see that there was nothing either the pilot or the controller could have done to avert the crash.

The accident remained in the news for several weeks, but as investigators progressed in their fact-finding efforts, both the focus of the investigation and media attention shifted away from air traffic control. ValueJet had had a history of safety infractions, and it now appeared that there had been a serious oversight with respect to certain items of cargo carried in the baggage hold. Canisters of compressed oxygen had ruptured and ignited, causing an intense fire that burned its way into the passenger cabin and destroyed the aircraft's control cables and electronics. The final report by the NTSB cited both the company and SabreTech, a contractor responsible for aircraft loading, as bearing primary responsibility for the accident.

Another accident occurred on August 7, 1997. A Douglas DC-8 operated by the cargo carrier FineAir crashed immediately after takeoff, killing three crew members, a passenger, and one other person. Since the only communication with air traffic control had been while the aircraft was on the ground, there was no media or investigatory attention on ATC. An article in The Miami Herald noted that the aircraft had hit the ground in "one of the few vacant lots in Dade County," and it was indeed fortunate that the takeoff had been on runway 27 Right. There was an open area just beyond the approach lights for 9 Left where the initial impact occurred. The airplane's momentum carried it across the heavily traveled artery of Milam Dairy Road, luckily encountering no automobile traffic, and into a small shopping center where it struck the person on the ground.

The tower controllers and other observers had noted that the airplane pitched up sharply as soon as it left the ground. Investigators zeroed in on the loading and weight and balance information calculated for the flight, determining that the numbers for these items were within acceptable parameters. But because the heavier pallets were placed too far aft, the center of gravity was no longer within acceptable limits for the DC-8. The immediate nose high attitude precipitated a stall, and the low altitude and low airspeed made it impossible for the flight crew to recover.

Even in cases where ATC handling is completely routine and air traffic controllers are not found to have been a contributing cause, the facility controlling the accident aircraft still must supply recordings, written transcripts, and controller statements to the NTSB and other investigating authorities. We support specialists assembled and collated all of this information.

As noted earlier, ATC is often called upon to cooperate with law enforcement in investigating crimes involving aircraft. Sometimes it is a matter of surveillance from the air of activities on the ground. In other instances the issue could be a stolen aircraft or, most frequently, an airplane used to transport drugs. Most of the time there is a considerable amount of up-front coordination to set the stage for an apprehension that will stand up legally and result in a conviction in court. But in one case at MIA the evidence, one might say, "fell right into our lap." Late one day on the evening shift Charlie was working a Piper Aztec inbound from the Bahamas. As the pilot approached a right downwind entry to 9 Left, he requested a 360-degree turn. There was no other traffic in the picture, and there was no obvious reason for this delaying maneuver, but there was no reason to deny it either. The pilot made the turn, reported the airport in sight, was cleared for a visual approach, and switched to tower frequency.

About that time a citizen who lived south of the airport telephoned the tower to report that she had heard a loud thump in her back yard, and had discovered a heavy canvas bag that she believed had been dropped from or fallen off an aircraft. The supervisor immediately notified the Dade County sheriff's department. One unit was dispatched to the lady's house while other units converged on the GAC general aviation ramp. By the time the aircraft landed and taxied in, the canvas bag had been recovered and found to contain illegal drugs. The officers at GAC were alerted, and when the pilot stepped out of the aircraft he was greeted by a couple of deputies and a pair of handcuffs. Months later there was a ceremony recognizing the benefits of inter-agency cooperation, with Charlie receiving a certificate of appreciation for his part in the arrest.

Training Videos and Other Duties

Each day of the week, including weekends and holidays, there was a scheduled briefing period. These generally occurred during the first hour of the day shift and were given to a single controller team by a staff member. Since staff members were present in the facility only during the week, it was necessary to create a video recording to be shown on those days when no staff member was available. Most of the items briefed were dry and boring. Even when the session was conducted live the controller attendees were restless and inattentive, and the "canned" video presentations were still less engaging. One of our staff, Dave, was a consummate showman. Live or on tape, he ad-libbed freely, at least keeping the attention of his audience if not openly entertaining them. On one tape he went a little too far while briefing some significant changes to the Miami operation, eliciting hearty rounds of laughter from the controllers, but a quite different reaction from Johnny Miles.

One of the items on the agenda that week was the relocation and re-naming of the Miami VOR. The navaid was being moved from its position about six nautical miles northwest of Opa-locka to a point almost exactly on the final approach course to 9 Left at Miami. The new designation was Dolphin, whose three-letter identifier would become DHP. Dave introduced this subject saying, "OK, now I want to tell you about the Diptheria VOR." At some point he mentioned that the actual designator was Dolphin, but for the most part continued to use "Diptheria." At another point, teeing up an introduction to a new subject, he said, "Now listen up. Here is something that will REALLY touch your G-spot." According to Lanny Williams, when Johnny saw the tape he was not amused. He said that training days were not a forum for Dave's comedy routine, and that henceforth Dave would not give briefings either in person or on tape.

I made my share of briefing videos, and for the most part played it straight. Occasionally, when an item was clearly in the YGBSM category, I would pause and make a facial expression that I hoped would convey my agreement that the item was beyond ridiculous. But in one case something made it on to one of my tapes that I had no intention of putting there. Another staff member, Ron, was manning the video camera while I sat at a table with the briefing binder in front of me. He would give me the "go" signal and I would start talking, but after a sentence or two Ron would recognize that the sound was not being recorded. This happened three or four times to our increasing frustration. The last time it happened, Ron interrupted, saying, "Cut, cut, we're still not getting sound." I gave the camera a middle finger salute, and we re-wound to try it again. This time the sound function operated properly, and I completed the agenda items. We packed up the gear and called it a day.

Fast forward to about a week later. One of the supervisors approached me with a serious look on his face, saying, "You know, you should review your tapes before you send them up to the training room. Giving the finger to the training class was not a great idea." Instantly I understood what had happened. We had not rewound far enough on that last shoot and my gesture of annoyance was captured for all to see. Remembering Dave's experience, I hoped it would not come to Johnny's attention. The one bright spot was that despite the supervisor's take, the controllers present for the briefing favored me with comments like, "Hey, great job, best briefing tape ever."

Some Dubious Ideas

Sometimes field facilities were called upon to comment on changes being considered or proposed for implementation. These could originate from headquarters, the regional office, or stakeholder groups such as the FAA Managers Association (FMA). I was often asked to make a first draft response to these solicitations, either because someone thought I would do a good job or, equally likely, because no one else wanted to do it. I welcomed the opportunity, especially in cases where I did not believe the idea had merit. In one case we were asked to evaluate a proposal to change the method of designating taxiways, the specifics of which struck me as particularly ill advised. Instead of the simple single or double-letter designators currently in use, the plan was to identify taxiways by color. There were no advantages to be gained that I could see, and a number of disadvantages summarized as follows:

- At large airports there were more taxiways than letters of the alphabet, and many more than there were individual colors.
- Taxiway charts were not likely to be published in color, nor was concrete likely to be painted.
- Color names would have to be written out on taxiway signage, requiring larger signs at greater cost and increasing obstruction to visibility of the airport surface.
- Color names would not be easily understood by foreign pilots compared to the universally used international terminology for letter designators.

It would be like pulling teeth with these guys, unacceptably increasing the number and length of individual transmissions to get the instruction across.

Another case involved a series of recommendations for changes to required phraseology. The package was composed by a controller work group with the goal of reducing phraseology in order to reduce frequency congestion. Some of the suggestions were in the no-brainer, should have been done long ago category, as for example when a controller issues an instruction to a pilot to maintain visual separation from other traffic. Existing phraseology required a controller to instruct a pilot who had reported another aircraft in sight to "maintain visual separation from that traffic." The work group proposed eliminating the words "from that traffic." The phraseology was changed.

There were several other recommendations that I disagreed with, and apparently my thoughts mostly represented the opinions of a majority of other comments. The following is a summary:

The work group suggested that when a pilot who has been vectored for landing sequence by approach control contacts the tower for landing clearance, the tower not be required to state its identification. My comment: What about the possibility that the tower identification is garbled or not used by the pilot? Controllers will tend to assume that any transmission addressed to "tower" is meant for them. Or the possibility that the pilot has dialed in an incorrect frequency? It happens often between Miami and Fort Lauderdale, which have similar frequencies (118.3/ 119.3).

Another suggestion involved eliminating the manufacturer's name in issuing traffic, e.g.:

"Traffic 12 o'clock six miles, six thousand, 737" vs. "Boeing 737."

My comment: How about, "Traffic 12 o'clock six miles, six thousand, 300" vs. "A-300?"

The work group recommended eliminating the requirement to specify the type aircraft on final approach when putting departure traffic in position to await takeoff clearance. I strongly disagreed. My comment: It is the pilot's prerogative to accept or refuse any instruction. The type aircraft in conjunction with the distance from the runway provide important information based on which a pilot will decide whether to go into position or hold short.

The group recommended substituting the word "stop" for "hold" in hold short situations, e.g.:

"United 121 stop short of runway 12" vs. "Hold short of runway 12." Or "Taxi into position and stop." vs. "Taxi into position and hold."

My comment: Use of "stop" with "stop short" is okay, although with time it will become as commonplace as "hold short" with no reduction in verbiage. "Taxi into position and stop" used routinely will dilute the imperative connotation when "stop" is used emphatically in critical situations. For example, an aircraft is instructed to hold short of a runway and the controller sees that the pilot will not comply. The controller must be brief and emphatic. "Cessna 15 Xray, STOP!"

A Major Shake-up at MIA

In March 1998 I returned from a week's annual leave and received a phone message to contact Lanny Williams ASAP. In the week I had been gone both Johnny Miles and Pat Grillo had been relieved of their positions as manager and assistant manager at Miami Tower. Indirectly these actions resulted from a media blitz investigating illegal drug use by air traffic controllers. A controller from the New York area who had been fired for drug offenses had made some very public statements about how widespread drug abuse was among the controller corps, and of course this was an irresistible story line for the various news agencies. But the direct cause leading to the reassignment of Johnny and Pat was an event that occurred late one afternoon within the facility. Johnny himself had discovered a controller unconscious in a bathroom stall with a needle stuck in his arm. The on-airport EMTs were summoned and arrived within minutes, possibly saving the victim's life.

FAA policy prohibits illegal substance use both on and off duty. Even the use of certain legal drugs, properly prescribed, require the individual to inform management about the medication and impose a duty on supervisors not to assign an active control position until the course of treatment is complete. There is also a policy provision, applicable under certain circumstances, whereby management can elect to place an off-duty drug offender in a program of counseling and rehabilitation after which he can be returned to duty. This is a one-time only opportunity.

From this point on the sequence of events gets a bit hazy. On-duty drug abuse, as happened in this instance, is a different matter altogether. If the case is proven, the individual will be removed from his position in accordance with federal law. There was no doubt that the man was on duty, and toxicology reports confirmed the presence of heroin in his system. But Johnny did not, as he was required to do, report the incident to his superiors in the Southern Region. There was a rumor that the daily sign-on sheet had been changed to show that the individual was on leave. Apparently both Pat and Lanny Williams had tried to convince Johnny to inform the region, but Johnny had elected to go the route of counseling and rehab, treating the matter as an off-duty offense. All of this might have passed into history without further attention or controversy but for two things that happened after the fact. Someone called the FAA administrator's hot line, basically an avenue for whistle blowers to report questionable activities. More damning was the EMT's report, which found its way into the hands of the press, and launched a torrent of investigative probes. Together these events put the agency in a position where it had to take action.

So what now for Miami Tower? Most of us felt that we had been pushed hard under Johnny's leadership. But we had also experienced pride and satisfaction because the facility had received a number of commendations for such things as high scores on evaluations, low numbers of operational errors, and minimum grievances by the union. Clearly a new regime would be installed, and while that could mean good news, we old hands were well aware of the principle stated as "better the devil that you know than the devil that you don't."

As it turned out, the interim appointees to the manager and assistant manager positions were people I would have chosen myself given the opportunity. Ron Liszt and Cecil Hall were guys I had worked with as fellow controllers during the pre-strike years. Both had gone on to management and supervisory positions. Ron had been in the air traffic division of the Southern Region and, as I later learned, had spoken on my behalf while my voluntary application to return to Miami was pending. I hoped these temporary assignments might become permanent, but it was not to be. Ron had been involved in the determination to remove Johnny from the manager's chair, and it would not have looked good politically for him to then fill the vacancy.

Within a few months the permanent "new regime" was put in place. The manager was Bob Carville, reporting from Chicago O'Hare. The assistant manager was Jorge Fernandez whose background included San Juan CERAP and San Antonio tower. Bob was, like me, an old hand, having originally entered on duty in 1970 after military service. Bob was definitely "old school," having lived through the turbulent years leading up to the strike of 1981. There was a telling incident not long after he arrived when he was presented with a birthday cake. It was a common practice among the staff and managers to recognize an individual in this way, but Bob appeared completely nonplussed. In an attempt to lighten an awkward moment I said, "Wow, Bob, I guess it's been at least a year since you got a cake on your last birthday at Chicago, right?" He shook his head and rolled his eyes, signaling unmistakably that things were not done this way at O'Hare. Jorge was younger by at least 20 years, clearly representing the new generation that would run the agency in the future, and less molded by the confrontations of the past. He was all for birthday cakes and other celebrations that acknowledged an individual or a group.

By degrees I came to see that I would have no problem getting along with these new managers. In fact, life as a staff member proved to be somewhat easier than it had been under Johnny Miles and Pat Grillo. Johnny and Pat focused on the details of every staff member's work. Bob and Jorge had more the outlook that "if it ain't broke, don't fix it." For me this meant having pretty much a free hand in my role as classroom and simulation instructor. They never monitored a classroom lesson or a lab exercise, apparently assuming that if there were no complaints from either the trainees or the operational supervisors in the tower and TRACON, I must be doing something right. I learned via the grapevine that Jorge had told someone he had received "a lot of good comments" from my trainees, and had described me as "the hardest working guy in the bullpen."

It also didn't hurt that MIA was selected as the 1999 Southern Region facility of the year, based on a self-nomination document of which I was the principal author. Bob was not the effusive type, but when we won the competition against the other Southern Region facilities, he was all smiles. It was a major feather in his cap, and he did convey a nice acknowledgement.

A New Administrator

In 1997 President Clinton appointed a new FAA administrator to succeed David Hinson. Jane Garvey was the first female to become agency director, a position acknowledged to be one of the toughest in government service. Since its founding, NATCA been pushing for a new pay scale for air traffic controllers, and in Jane Garvey had apparently found a sympathetic ear. As we in the field understood it, there had been many rounds of negotiations without any discernible progress. At some point, we heard, Jane dismissed the labor management people advising her. These expert negotiators had understandably taken a position of yielding very little at the bargaining table, pointing out that air traffic controllers were already among the most highly paid of all government workers. The word was that the union and the new administrator reached an agreement expanding the number of pay levels within the ATC facility classification system, with large salary increases for workers in the busiest facilities. This augured well for us at Miami Tower since we were already at the top compensation level under the GS system.

But there were still some fairly large hurdles to clear. Congress put the agency on notice that there would not be additional appropriations made to fund the substantially increased costs of the new pay system. The agency would have to find the money within its existing budget. This meant that the other divisions of FAA, notably Flight Standards, Airway Facilities, and Security, would all fall upon lean times. There was definite resentment of "those prima donnas" in air traffic control who received this generous windfall. There was also a question of implementation. No doubt driven by the need to spread out the financial impact, the agency decided to phase in the new pay levels over a three-year period. Not surprisingly, the result was a considerable amount of confusion and controversy.

My own case typified the similar experiences of others. There were target dates established in each of the three years when the increases would become effective. Following each of these I received a form called a personnel action showing the effective date of the increase, but for several pay periods thereafter, my paycheck continued to reflect the old rate. Compounding the problem, annual cost of living raises had to be included in the calculations. Were these to be based on the old rate, the new rate, or on some combination of these based on the portion of the year that the new rate was supposed to be in effect but in fact was not being paid?

We all wanted to believe that eventually it would all be sorted out and we would get what we were due, but in actuality the whole process dragged out for such an extended period that there was no way of knowing for sure. I was luckier than most because I had an inside track with our administrative assistant. I put together a package containing the personnel actions and the subsequent time and attendance reports to show the number of pay periods for which I had not been compensated in full. Lisa, who was a fireball of activity and initiative in her capacity as administrative assistant, shepherded the information through the appropriate channels in the regional office, and the amount shown on my next T and A report was gratifyingly large. I could not tell if it was accurate in terms of dollars and cents, but I decided to call it square with the agency. Over the course of the three years, my salary increased by roughly 30 per cent, and was now more than 20 times higher than my entry-level pay in 1968.

There were other wrinkles ironed out over the course of the three-year implementation period that proved, once again, how fortunate I had been at critical points in my career. The initial agreement between FAA and NATCA had applied only to union members. In other words, managers and staff would not benefit from the new system and would end up with smaller paychecks than the controllers. This issue generated enough heat that the agency ultimately included all field facility personnel in the new program, but excluded people in such positions as Academy instructors or Tech Center employees. My move had been timed just right. In addition, the formula used to move an employee from the old GS system into the new structure worked to my considerable advantage. Everyone received a nice bump up, but only two of us were at the top of the GS-14 scale, and therefore received the highest possible increase available to former GS-14s. Jeff and I were both staff members, and this outcome did not sit too well with NATCA members, whose base salaries were now lower than ours.

There was one final chapter to the whole business of the pay reclassification. NATCA took the position that the union had "gotten you guys (meaning staff members) a big pay raise." This was disingenuous in the extreme, as they had tried to limit the raise to union members only, reasoning that if larger numbers were included it would be a tougher sell to the powers that be. Nevertheless, after the agency expanded the re-class to include us, NATCA decided to open union membership—sort of—to any non-management personnel with the GS-2152 (air traffic controller) designation. The pitch to recruit us potential new members was two-fold: that we would not be enjoying our higher salaries had it not been for the union; and that more members meant more clout in future labor management negotiations with "better benefits for everybody."

The problem was that we would not be covered by the same contract that applied to working controllers. There were differences relating to duty time allowance for union business and, most tellingly, in the right to accumulate credits for time off not charged to annual leave. If a controller wanted a day off when staffing was too short to allow it, he could ask an equally qualified off-duty colleague to take the shift for him. The man taking the shift would "bank" a day that he could later use for time off without depleting his accrued leave. Also, the maximum amount of regular annual leave an employee could accrue in a year was 208 hours. Anything over that amount fell into the category of "use or lose," meaning that if the excess were carried into the new leave year the employee would lose it. Under the voluntary substitution program, there was no limit. There were guys who had more than 2,000 hours in the bank, and would never have to use annual leave for time off again, but we on staff would not be allowed to accumulate time off credits in this way.

Despite what to me were glaring inequalities in the contract provisions applicable to staff as compared with those in the controller contract, all staff members but one elected to become NATCA members. I was the lone holdout. I could not see giving up a fixed percentage of my salary for union dues in exchange for benefits that were at best ephemeral and at worst nonexistent. There were other considerations as well. Unlike the rest of the staff, I could retire at any time. But the gist of my rationale rested on two points, reiterated in several pointed discussions with NATCA members who lobbied me to make Miami "100 per cent NATCA." With minor variations, those discussions went like this:

NATCA: "You know, you are the only staff guy that hasn't joined the union. Why?"

Me: "Well, for a couple of reasons. In my role as training instructor I sometimes have to recommend that a trainee be washed out. The union generally represents the employee in these cases, and as a union member I would be in an untenable position."

NATCA: "Oh come on, we understand that you would have to do your job, and nobody would hold it against you."

Me: "Okay, let me ask you this. You guys can accumulate an unlimited amount of credit time, but that is not available to staff members. Our dues will go to support your priorities, so are you willing to have the dollars represented by your dues used to fight for the same right for us?"

NATCA: "You guys are under a different contract than we are."
Me: "My point exactly."
Within two years every staff member who had joined the union resigned their membership. Why? In a nutshell because, quote, "They haven't done a damn thing for me."

The New, New Tower

There were big changes underway at MIA in the 1990s. American Airlines undertook a wholesale construction project, building a new concourse, while Miami-Dade County was fashioning its own improvements to the terminal building. As these facilities expanded, more and more of the tower view of the ramp area, and even the approach end of 27 Right, was obstructed. Through the use of sophisticated software and computer imaging, architectural engineers determined that if the height of the tower were increased from its present level of 200 feet to 300 feet, the view of the critical areas would be restored. It was not feasible to build on top of the existing tower structure, and so the "new new" tower at length came into being—not, however, without one major setback, or fiasco, depending on one's point of view.

The issue centered on a dispute between NATCA, the controllers' bargaining unit, and FAA management over what the union called an unacceptable flaw in the tower design. The tower windows were installed as separate panes, affording a 360-degree view of the airport and the immediately surrounding airspace, with framing members, called "mullions," placed between each pair. The mullions were about six inches wide, and because of the orientation of the tower cab, one of them precisely obstructed the line of sight from the local control position to the run up pad and threshold of 9 Left.

NATCA called it a safety issue, while management officials countered that controllers had participated in the planning stage, including the opportunity to stand in a full-scale mock-up of the tower cab, and approved the proposed design. The union took its case to the media, and after some protracted wrangling, the entire cab was removed and replaced, at a cost of some $5 million, and a delay of more than a year.

In the waning months of 1999 there was a growing concern about "Y2K," what would happen in the cyber world with the new millennium. Would the Internet and computers everywhere function as usual at 12:01

am on January 1, 2000? The question was particularly germane as it applied to the air traffic automation system. There had always been automation failures from time to time in individual facilities, but the prospect of every center and terminal crashing at once was more than daunting. The one hopeful factor was that if there were problems, they would occur at midnight, a time when traffic activity was low, and that they could either be remedied or contingency measures could be put in place before the full crush of daytime traffic was felt. Our automation people were assigned the midnight shift to deal with the worst-case scenario should it occur, but the transition to the year 2000 occurred without a hitch.

Grounding All Aircraft on 9-11

On September 9, 2001, I returned to Miami on a jump seat ride from Bangor, Maine, with a change in Boston, where ominous events would unfold two days later. It would be the last time I would ever enjoy the privilege of the SF-160 program. On the morning of Tuesday, September 11, I was in the radar simulation lab with two guys new to Miami Tower when someone stuck his head in and said, "Hey, did you hear that an airplane just crashed into the World Trade Center?" Our initial reaction was that it was probably some yo-yo in a Cherokee hot-dogging it for thrills. A little later, we learned that it was an air carrier, and we started wondering how a flight crew could have been so far off course on a beautiful VFR day. After the second collision, it was clear that these were not accidents, and that all the rules regarding safety and security, for the airlines, for ATC, and for the country at large would need to change.

For the first time in history, the FAA ordered all airborne aircraft to land at the nearest airport and imposed an indefinite and total ground stop on all departures. These measures were too late to prevent the attack on the Pentagon, but a fourth hijacked flight, later determined to be bound for the capitol building in Washington, was prevented from reaching its objective through the heroism of a group of passengers. Analyzing cellphone contacts between passengers and family members, as well as cockpit voice recordings, investigators determined that these individuals had stormed the cockpit and overpowered the hijackers. Although the aircraft crashed, the heroic actions of these men will always be remembered as representing America's resolve in standing up to terrorism.

In the aftermath of the attacks there were a number of hearings to determine what had been done right or wrong in responding to the events of 9-11-2001. One of the most open criticisms of the agency concerned the coordination between it and the military. Fighters scrambled to join up on suspected hijacked flights never reached their rendezvous. In this as in all high-profile cases, there was a certain amount of grandstanding by public figures wishing to make a name for themselves as warriors against international terror. The fact that three of the four aircraft reached their targets prompted some sharp questioning, most of it done by people without the technical background to understand the reality of the situation. For those in the know, it rankled that the incredible achievement of getting more than 4,000 airplanes safely on the ground in something under three hours received scant acknowledgement.

At MIA, the immediate impact of the airspace shutdown was fairly minimal. Because we were way down "at the end of the world" on the tip of the Florida peninsula, only a few flights were directed to land at our airport. It was the facilities more in the middle of the country—places like Atlanta, Chicago, and Dallas—that bore the brunt of the traffic. In the longer term, we experienced the same upheavals as the other major terminals. Police officers searched our cars each time we entered the facility parking lot, military personnel patrolled the terminal carrying automatic rifles, and the fam trip program was cancelled.

Before long, a change to hijack procedures was promulgated, with some laughably transparent new phraseology to be used by controllers in the case of a suspected hijacking. I wish I could quote it here, but it was supposed to be kept from the general public. Suffice it to say, I doubt that any hijacker would have been fooled by the stilted and improbable language controllers were now required to use.

STARS Will Come Out

In July 2002 we received word that the Miami TRACON would undergo a wholesale modification via the installation of STARS displays. The acronym stood for Standard Terminal Automation Replacement System and was scheduled to be fully operational by July 8, 2003. The consoles would replace the older generation Digital Entry Display Subsystem (DEDS) equipment that had been in use for years in conjunction with the various iterations of ARTS technology. There were many advantages to the new system in terms of capacity, reliability, and innovations not previously available. The old consoles were large and cumbersome, weighing many hundreds of pounds, and had to be wheeled about on casters when one of them had to be replaced. When a DEDS unit failed, technicians had to remove it, replace it, and examine both internal and external components to isolate the problem. By contrast, the new scopes were smaller, lighter, and more easily transportable. Moreover, they were self-contained. Each carried its own box of electronics, dubbed "the pizza box" because of its size and shape, easily removed and replaced when necessary, and eliminating the need for a protracted period of maintenance analysis.

From the controller perspective, STARS technology was a huge leap forward. The video mapping and the alphanumerics were pin-sharp. There was color-coding for such things as low altitude and conflict alerts, radio failure or hijack. The display of weather returns was upgraded significantly, with the capability of selecting four separate severity levels differentiated via the combination of a unique color for each cell and contrasting stippling within each cell. There was even a trend function whereby a controller could fast forward the appearance of display updates to get an idea of a storm's development and movement.

In contrast to the old system, a controller could temporarily suppress a weather return without attenuating the radar returns of his aircraft targets. Coordination with the satellite towers would be reduced via a new capability enabling those towers to generate a list at the departure control position of aircraft awaiting release. The departure controller could pick his time to grant the release, simply clicking on the aircraft ID and generating a message in the tower. Voice calls over the speaker and the need to respond at inopportune times would be mostly eliminated.

There were other features of STARS that for us old hands, trained in pre-automation days, represented major BRS (Buck Rogers Stuff). When an aircraft dropped its alphanumeric tag because of transponder failure, the system would continue to track the primary target with a flashing indication that secondary (transponder) tracking had failed. If the primary target disappeared, the identification tag would remain at the point of last contact and flash. Under the old system, a dropped tag coasted for a few seconds, then dropped to the coast suspend list for a few minutes, then disappeared entirely. All of us had been caught at one time or another with a flight progress strip in front of us, representing an active flight, but no target or tag on the scope, and no response to attempts at radio contact. There was no way to tell when or where radar contact had been lost if you did not catch the short coast period, and the airplane could have crashed or flown out of our airspace with no transfer of control.

Another "cool" feature of STARS was the ability to place the identification tag of an aircraft released for departure from a satellite airport directly off the end of the runway. With STARS the tag would remain in place until the aircraft appeared and the tag acquired, whereas under the old system you could not do this—the tag would drop within a few seconds. Again, more than once it had happened that an aircraft on an IFR flight plan released from one of the satellites had not "tagged up" as expected, and had never called departure control.

I experienced one of these events myself in the days before STARS after releasing a Cessna 150 on an IFR training flight from Tamiami. Fortunately I was not super busy, and I noticed that the flight progress strip representing the aircraft had been sitting in front of me for a suspiciously long time. I called Tamiami to inquire about the status of the flight, initiating a series of interphone and radio exchanges that went like this:

Me: "Tamiami Miami, what's happening with Cessna 7525 Echo? Is he still going to go?"

TMB: "Aren't you working him? He took off at least ten minutes ago."

Me: "No I'm not working him. I'll give him a call. Why don't you call him too."

I punched off the coordination line and tried twice to contact the pilot without a response. A minute or two later TMB called me back saying that the pilot was still on tower frequency and that they had instructed him to contact me. Apparently the pilot had not heard the tower instruction to call departure control issued immediately after takeoff, and the ARTS identification was still in the departure tabular list. Radio communications were finally established:

N7525E: "Miami departure, Cessna 7525 Echo with you level 2,000."

Me: "Cessna 7525 Echo Miami departure, squawk ident and say your position."

At this point another voice came on the frequency, obviously that of the instructor. I recognized her as the long-time owner of one of the flight schools.

N25E: "Miami, we are not getting a light on the transponder, I don't believe it's working. We are about 15 northwest of Tamiami still heading 290."

I was able to identify a faint primary return that matched the reported position and heading, and at this point I became seriously frosted, to the point of breaking with my own self-imposed rule of never getting into it with a pilot on the frequency. This woman was an experienced pilot who should have known better, and I let her know it:

Me: "Cessna 25 Echo, radar contact one eight miles northwest of Tamiami, turn right heading 360 to intercept Victor 97. Why did you not contact me immediately after takeoff?"

N25E: "The tower never told us to change to departure control."

Me: "Even if that is so, you should have asked the tower for a frequency change. Any instrument rated pilot knows you don't fly 20 miles on an instrument flight plan under tower control."

Perhaps the most significant innovation provided by STARS was the ability to accept inputs from up to 16 radar facilities. At MIA we had the potential to utilize any of four systems (MIA, Fort Lauderdale, Fort Myers, Miami Center) with a fifth display option available via a mosaic function, whereby a combination of radar inputs could be selected. Each console could select its radar source independently of the others, a capability formerly unavailable. If a DEDS display lost its radar connection, no alternate source could be accessed. It was immediately out of service, requiring the controller to move to another scope and hopefully pick up the traffic picture again. If an antennae malfunctioned or a cable was cut, there was no longer a need to wait the agonizing few minutes until an alternate radar was selected at a central panel. With one click of the trackball, every position in the house was up and running on the next radar sweep of the new source.

Preparing for STARS

With a firm implementation date one year hence, the facility was mandated to create what was termed a STARS training plan. Jorge Fernandez asked me to take on the task, whose parameters were not at all clear. Wouldn't I have to have a pretty good understanding of STARS in order to craft something credible? As it turned out, Raytheon personnel would train a designated group of facility members as STARS cadre instructors. This meant that the present task would be only to identify the time frames and resources needed to accomplish everything by the start date of July 8, 2003. I didn't think this would be too difficult, until I saw the schedule for delivery of the equipment and the number of training hours that would be required.

According to the master plan created by the FAA Program Office, the equipment would arrive at the facility on April 7. Training time would be an estimated 80 hours per controller, with a minimum of 30 days allotted to Airway Facilities for maintenance training and system checks. There would be only two months in which to train over 120 operational personnel. The simulation lab would have only three STARS consoles, and only a limited number of people could be spared from watch coverage for each training session. Clearly the time line was grossly unrealistic. I would do my best to lay this out in terms that anyone could understand. The following are excerpts from the training plan:

"A number of variables or unknown factors will impact upon the execution of this plan, thus creating the possibility that the training might take longer than expected or (more remotely) that it might be completed early. Chief among these factors are:
- Number of days per week training can be conducted.
- Number of hours per day training can be conducted.
- Number of CPCs [certified professional controllers] trained per lab session.
- Adherence to training schedules by bargaining unit members and cadre instructors.
- Availability of sufficient personnel to meet backfill overtime to support proposed training schedules.

"In order to meet the July 8, 2003 implementation date…with 120 operational personnel to be trained, laboratory/proficiency/refresher training must begin no later than January 14 based on:
- Three STARS consoles in the 220-square-foot lab available, 3 CPCs trained per session.
- 16 hours training conducted per day.
- Training conducted 7 days per week.
- 70 hours combined laboratory/proficiency/ refresher time per employee.

"While the STARS training plan contemplates 80 hours per employee, we believe that an allowance of 70 hours will be more than adequate…"

"The January 14 start date is derived as follows:
- 120 employees X 70 hours = 8400 required training hours
- 3 platforms X 16 hours per day = 48 hours available per day
- 8400 divided by 48 = 175 days to complete training"

The document was submitted to the Program Office without modification, but I expected some form of the usual response when a field facility tried to make a case for its requirements. Generally, we would hear something like, "owing to budgetary constraints and fixed manufacturing and installation contracts, no modification can be made to the STARS deployment and implementation schedule. All training on and testing of the system must be accomplished in the time period between the dates of delivery and formal commissioning of the equipment." No acknowledgement of the disconnect between required training and resources needed.

A Break in Scheduling

This time, however, we were in for a pleasant surprise. The Program Office agreed to lend us the STARS equipment slated for installation later in the waterfall at Charlotte, North Carolina. If we could find a suitable location, an entire mock TRACON would be set up prior to our proposed training start date of January 14. This would permit the deliveries to both MIA and CLT to be made on schedule, with the full three months between April and July available to Airway Facilities to train on our equipment. In another stroke of good fortune Miami-Dade County owned a building practically adjacent to the tower with spaces sufficient to our needs. We would have access, without cost, for as long as necessary.

In October, the facility sent me to the rechristened William J. Hughes Technical Center in Atlantic City to observe a STARS shakedown being conducted by the Philadelphia TRACON. Information from the on airport ASR antenna was being duplicated on STARS consoles while the traffic was being worked on the old equipment at the facility. It was an opportunity to observe first-hand how the displays functioned, and to renew contact with my former Tech Center colleagues.

In November, I was part of a group selected for a week of training at the Raytheon facility in Marlboro, Massachusetts. The class would familiarize us with AT Coach, a software package used to script and run simulated targets, and prepare us for development of the exercises we would need for STARS training. Although it was designed to be user friendly, the system required a certain facility with computer and software functions, skills that frankly were not my forte. Fortunately we worked in teams of two, and I grabbed Jeff, a young guy with pretty fair computer smarts, to be my teammate. By the end of the week, I had some understanding of AT Coach and its capabilities, but was left hoping I would have a teammate back at the facility when it came to crafting training scenarios.

In December the first class for cadre instructors took place at the FAA Academy in Oklahoma City. Twelve of us from the Miami hub attended. The Raytheon instructors for the course were all former air traffic controllers, now retired, who had landed a nice contracting gig. I made it a point to get to know them and collect business cards, with an eye to possible future opportunities for myself. The class lasted three weeks, consisting of a combination of lectures with slides, hands on practice, and periodic tests of exactly the right kind.

Armed with a checklist of more than 400 (!) items reflecting the myriad capabilities of the system, the instructors would sit with us one-on-one at a display and enunciate a series of functions. We would respond by carrying out each function as it was called for. I wasn't sure about my classmates, but I didn't think I was getting a solid enough grip on this huge volume of information. On the weekend before the final week of the class, I stayed in my hotel room on both days reviewing, reviewing, and reviewing. It was basically a brute-force left-brain memorization exercise, but it served me well when it came to the "final exam." I only missed a few of the 400 functions.

Back at MIA

Back at the facility, after more than a year of controversy, the new 300-foot tower was in operation, having been commissioned while we were at the cadre instructor class. The Christmas holidays were upon us with about three weeks to go until the STARS classes would begin. The spaces in the building lent to us by the county were empty, but had no facilities of any kind—no chairs or desks, no minimal kitchen equipment, and no accommodations for break periods. All of this would need to be handled before the consoles were delivered. I was busy trying to develop a syllabus that would fit the two-week period allotted for each group

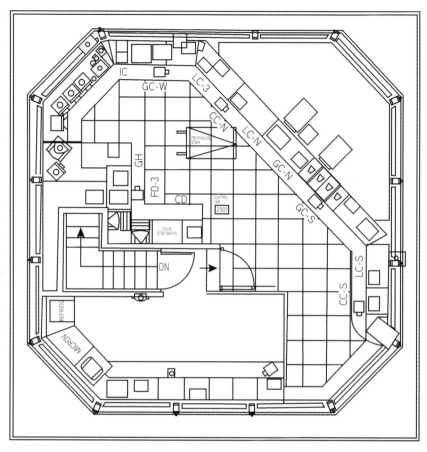

CAB POSITION IDENTIFIERS		
FD3	–	FLIGHT DATA
CD	–	CLEARANCE DELIVERY
GH	–	GATE HOLD
GCN	–	GROUND CONTROL NORTH
GCS	–	GROUND CONTROL SOUTH
GCW	–	GROUND CONTROL WEST
CC	–	CAB COORDINATOR
LCN	–	LOCAL CONTROL NORTH
LCS	–	LOCAL CONTROL SOUTH
IC	–	CAB SUPERVISOR / CIC

CONTROL TOWER POSITIONS 2006

The 1968 tower located on top of the terminal had fewer positions, i.e., only one CC, no designated supervisor position, no third local control group (LCS-3), no west ground control (GW-W). All the other positions did exist, configured somewhat differently. The move to the first new tower in 1985 basically preserved the 1968 configuration.

of trainees, finally realizing that the best way to do it was to adapt the same material we had been given in Oklahoma City rather than trying to reinvent the wheel. This entailed paring down the PowerPoint and lecture portions in order to maximize the hands on time.

In the middle of all this Jorge informed me that I would have to spend three days conducting operational development plan (ODP) training. ODP was a euphemism for "remedial," the agency having adopted the acronym to lessen the stigma attached to the former term. The "candidate" would be Nat Braden. Everybody liked Nat. He was a big guy, rumored to have tried out for the Miami Dolphins. But he kept getting himself in trouble in the operating quarters, and here we were once again with an operational error that he had either caused or failed to prevent. I was often the guy who applied whatever corrective training management determined that an individual needed, and generally did so gladly. I believed that in most cases operational errors occurred not because the controller was negligent or did not understand the rules, but rather resulted from a combination of circumstances that might have tripped up anyone. Part of my job, as I saw it, was to offer encouragement and hopefully to restore the individual's confidence when he went back to the floor.

The problem was that we were in major scramble mode trying to get the off-site rooms and the syllabus ready. I rarely pushed back on anything I was asked to do, but in this case I let Jorge know that I considered preparation of the STARS lab the first priority, pointing out the time crunch, and asking if Nat's ODP class could be handled by someone else. He said that Nat really needed somebody whose heart was in it, and he wanted me to do it. I was ready to drop it at that point, but just then Carl, one of the supervisors, with whom I had been working closely since our return from Oklahoma City, walked in. He had apparently picked up on the tail end of my conversation with Jorge, and jumped in with his own take, that went like this:

Carl: "What's going on here?"

Jorge: "I am assigning Rust to do Nat Braden's ODP training."

Carl: "What? You've got to be kidding me. F.... Nat Braden. We need Rusty over at the lab."

My sentiments exactly, expressed by none other than the supervisor who had criticized me for giving the camera the finger on the training video. But it did no good. I ended up in the classroom with Nat, and our efforts at preparation for STARS became even more compressed.

After I finished with Nat, I saw that Carl had made good, even miraculous, progress on getting the mock lab ready. Chairs with attached writing platforms were in place, a sink, microwave and refrigerator had been installed, and an area with a couch and a TV had been placed away from the classroom area. Charlotte's system had been installed by Raytheon people, who would be present for the first few classes to assist us in getting started. Although no one besides me had looked at the syllabus, I was happy with it. So all in all it seemed to me we were ready to go.

STARS Training

Although I was not privy to the details, there had apparently been some protracted negotiations between NATCA and the agency about how the STARS training was to be accomplished. The union seized upon the 80-hour figure initially estimated as the minimum necessary to ensure that controllers were adequately prepared for the new system, also persuading management to allow overtime pay on Sunday, which was generally not permitted. The facility had crafted a master schedule for the entire 25-week period during which the training would take place, reflecting successive controller groups and three to four cadre instructors assigned to each of the two daily shifts (0700-1500, 1500-2300). Half of the instructors were staff or supervisors, the other half of the group being bargaining unit members.

In theory, instructional duties would be shared equitably throughout the shift, but in fact most of the NATCA guys had no wish to stand up in front of the class in the role of "salesman" for the new program. The supervisors, too, preferred not to take on the instructor role. On most of the shifts to which I was assigned, I was the instructor the majority of the time. I always made it clear that if someone else wanted to take a turn at it they were welcome to do so, but that I was more than happy to do it any time or all the time. All of this came into sharp focus one day when I was a few minutes late getting to the lab. One of the union members was just beginning the day's lesson when I walked in. He stopped in mid-sentence saying, "Thank God you're here," and walking away from the dais where the briefing binder lay open. This particular guy, Chris, was sharp, professional, computer savvy, and not the militant type. He was probably smarter than me on the overall STARS system, and it was a mystery to me why he was so averse to acting as instructor.

Most controllers did not like training of any kind. For many of them it was too passive an exercise, in addition to which many routine briefing items fell into the category of "who cares." Over the years the FAA had taken some hits during accident investigations and especially in the course of subsequent lawsuits because investigators or plaintiffs' lawyers were able to prove that a controller had never been "trained" in a particular area. For example, if an accident or incident involved severe weather and an individual's training jacket did not include an entry titled "How Thunderstorms Develop" or something similar, it tended to imply some responsibility on the agency's part for the actions or omissions of its employee.

So it was no surprise that my "audiences" displayed varying degrees of boredom, inattention and restlessness. There was also the fact that being away from the facility allowed a certain "relaxed" attitude, no less for the instructors and supervisors than the controllers themselves. Some brought their children or their dogs to the training days, while others busied themselves with personal projects in the considerable amount of slack time during each shift.

It was clear early on that the 80 hours allotted for each class was over generous in the extreme. The interface with STARS was largely modeled on the ARTS system in use since the early 1970s, meaning that with a few tweaks here and there a controller familiar with ARTS would have a good handle on STARS. Despite the 400-item checklist covering the system's many capabilities, it was apparent that only a very small subset of these would be used in routine day-to-day operations. The long and short of it was that a week per class would have been more than sufficient, and that the costs of the longer period were buying the agency very little.

At the end of each class, the "students" were asked to fill out an evaluation of the training experience. The form asked a number of obvious questions: organization of the material, quality of training aids, adequacy of break periods (would anyone have the temerity to assert that there were not enough breaks?), finally concluding with a couple of queries about how well we the instructors performed. Despite the previously described attitude of disengagement, most of the controllers rated the training positively, saying they felt prepared for the new system, and a few even naming me and (no surprise) Chris as having done a good job.

The last few classes were for staff and managers, and were considerably easier than the sessions with controller groups. For me the finish line was in sight, as I had already planned to take a long period of time off in conjunction with some scheduled surgery once the cutover to STARS was made. I had one last task to perform at the behest of management, that being to draft a letter to the chief pilots of the airlines that served MIA. The letter would alert them to the implementation of STARS and advise them of the measures being taken to ensure safety. Below are excerpts from the letter:

"Effective 1201 am on June 29, 2003, the Miami ATCT and approach control facility will begin operations utilizing the Standard Terminal Automation Replacement System (STARS). This state-of-the-art technology replaces the previous generation equipment, which dates back more than two decades. Air traffic controllers will have an array of new capabilities available with which to enhance both safety and service.

The transition is expected to go smoothly, and to be transparent from the perspective of ATC system users. To ensure that present safety levels are maintained or exceeded during the transition, several initiatives are planned for the early stages of STARS operation."

Later paragraphs went on to communicate temporarily reduced arrival rates at both Miami and Fort Lauderdale, and the caution that in the event of severe weather additional constraints might be imposed.

On June 29 Miami Tower and TRACON began using STARS. A couple of the old DEDS displays were still in the radar room, operating in what was termed "shadow mode," so that if there were a major malfunction of the new system the controllers would have a backup. For the first few days there were also cadre instructors from the controller corps assigned to each shift to assist and trouble shoot any problems that might arise. There had been some discussion of placing me in that role, but I prevailed upon the managers to assign only those instructors who were operationally current and qualified. Although there were some minor glitches, none was serious enough to require reverting to the backup mode. It looked as though STARS was here to stay.

16. Winding Up My Air Traffic Career

My surgery took place the day after the STARS cutover. Following that, I took my longest period of leave in the entire 35 years I had been with FAA, finally returning to the facility in September. Although I had not looked into it in great detail, I had begun to understand some things about retirement that were worth knowing. For example, cost-of-living increases for retirees were based on the consumer price index calculated for the previous year. In order to receive the full increase, you had to have been retired for the full 12 months of that year, with a reduction of one twelfth of that increase for each month or partial month not in retirement status. It looked like December 31, 2003 would be a sensible retirement date.

But we had one new controller that fall, known as "Joe Dirt" because his facial hair made him a dead ringer for the character in the movie of that same name. Working with "Joe" I realized that compared to the selection of exercises we had in the old ARTS ETG lab, those in the STARS library were pretty skimpy. To a certain degree I had to "fake it" with Joe, often starting only a few targets manually to acquaint him with the various flows and airspace divisions. Fortunately he was a sharp controller and had no problem checking out on the floor despite the paucity of opportunity in the lab.

In November, I made a decision to put off retirement for one year, based on two considerations. One was that if any meaningful upgrade to the STARS simulation exercises was going to be made, it would not happen in the six weeks or so before the end of December. The extra year would give me ample time, and not incidentally, would provide me with an additional two per cent in the multiplication factor used to calculate my retirement annuity.

The other consideration was an unexpected change affecting the training department that occurred when Lanny Williams was replaced as support manager. There had been no warning that this was coming, and so I was at a total loss when I walked in one morning and saw that his office was completely empty with the plaque bearing his name removed. Had he retired? I could not believe he would do it in this way, and before long the circumstances began to emerge.

The new support manager would be Sarah Colgate, who had come to MIA as a support specialist. She had been the facility manager at two centers and one tower, so this step down on the career progression ladder was a little puzzling. But she volunteered her reasons for doing so, saying that she was fed up with the unending headaches attendant upon her previous positions, and looked forward to doing the "real work" of the air traffic division. This was completely understandable to me, having observed and in a small way lived the experiences she talked about. At first we got along well as colleagues and even friends, twice socializing outside of work hours.

But about a year after her arrival, Sarah was back in a supervisory role having been selected as an operations manager. She had no direct experience as a terminal controller, but was now in a position where she had to make informed strategic decisions—weather reroutes, airport acceptance rates, and actions to be taken in case of equipment problems to name a few. According to some of the ops supervisors who reported to her, she always asked one of them to make these decisions, leaving them in the position of wondering, "Who do I go to when I have a question?"

After a relatively short period in the ops manager's chair, Sarah was back in an administrative role. She had convinced Bob Carville that the training department was "a mess" and laid the alleged problems squarely at the feet of Lanny Williams. I had worked for years with Lanny as a controller, as a fellow training specialist, and under his supervision. No one brought more attention and commitment to the training function than Lanny, so I could not imagine how she had made this case. But by the end of November Lanny was reassigned as an ops manager, filling the job vacated by Sarah.

On the same day that I discovered the gutted office, I opened my email to find a final communication from Lanny, dated the last day of his term as support manager. It was a letter of commendation acknowledging my contributions to the implementation of STARS. Letters like this were generally replete with superlatives, which had to be taken with a grain of salt. But the last few lines were a source of major satisfaction, stating:

"Your dedication and initiative throughout the last year have been clearly evident to all, and you continue to demonstrate those attributes in training new personnel on STARS, and in refining our training scenarios. On behalf of all facility personnel please accept this well-deserved expression of commendation for all you have done to make STARS successful at Miami Tower."

A New Management Style

Sarah jumped into her role as support manager with a no-nonsense, even humorless approach that basically did not serve her well. She called a staff meeting early on, saying that these would be scheduled weekly, and beginning with a minutes-long diatribe about how fouled up the training department was. Normally I would have just let this go, knowing that a public argument over the facts was not likely to produce any good result. But I had the perfect fact-based rebuttal that went like this:

"Sarah, I am surprised that you think training is in such bad shape. Earlier this week Jose, the NATCA rep, came to me unbidden and thanked me for the good job we were doing in simulation training. He said the trainees had spoken positively of their experience in the lab, and their performance on the floor bore out their preparation."

This pretty much ended any continuing friendly relationship between Sarah and me. She was caught short for a moment, then with an angry expression said, "Well I'm not talking about what you do." The furtive smiles around the table from the other staffers let me know that I had scored a bullseye on this one.

Things did not get better for Sarah as the meeting progressed. The FAA Internet firewall had been partially breached, allowing many commercial solicitations to appear in our in boxes. The agency had set up an address to which these unwelcome communications could be forwarded and presumably dealt with, and Sarah asked us all whether we were still getting these spam offerings, triggering a rapid fire exchange that went like this:

Sarah: "Are you all still getting a lot of spam?"

Jeff: "Oh yeah, I get that one about penis enlargement a couple of times a day."

Sarah (clearly not pleased): "Well, just forward it to that designated address."

Russ: "NO! NO! Send it to me, send it to me!"

There was a gratifying roar of laughter from around the table, doing nothing to improve Sarah's outlook but greatly lightening up the mood for the rest of us.

There were a couple of other events during Sarah's tenure as support manager that seemed to cast her past career and assignment to Miami Tower in a different light. Someone overheard her making a phone call to a higher-up official at headquarters in which she described Bob Carville as an ineffective and incompetent manager. The other instance involved me directly on a day when I was busy in the sim lab creating new training scenarios. Via the paging system installed throughout the facility I was summoned to the bullpen where Sarah was waiting for me, unmistakably loaded for bear. The following conversation ensued:

Sarah: "What is this bs about cartoons being used in the training syllabus?"

I was initially at a loss, knowing full well that we did not use cartoons in any phase of our classroom presentations. I said as much, to which Sarah replied, "Don't give me that! I know that there are cartoons in the training materials!" It took me a few moments to realize that she was talking about the caricature sketches, done by one of my trainees years earlier, showing the letter identifier of each radar position. These I had placed in the training binders as the first page of each relevant section. I selected one of the manuals and opened it to the first of the sketches, saying, "You mean these?" With her expression set in a deep frown and without saying a word, Sarah began ripping out the pictures, then tearing them into shreds. After the last one was destroyed, there was a long silence, following which the "conversation" resumed:

Me (in as neutral a tone as I could muster): "What is the problem with the sketches?"

Sarah: "They are offensive!"

Me: "How are they offensive?"

Sarah: "I am offended by them. How long have they been in the binders?"

Me: "More than eight years, and there has never been a complaint about them."

Sarah: "Well get rid of them."

With that she walked away, leaving me shaking my head in disbelief.

That should have been the end of it, but the more I thought about how it had all gone down, the madder I got. What had triggered this? Why hadn't she first approached me, explained how the whole business had come to her attention, and asked me if there was any reason why the "offending" pictures couldn't be removed? I decided to give her a day or two to cool down, then try to have a more reasoned discussion. Good plan, but the "discussion" we ended up having was anything but reasoned, as reflected in the following exchange:

Me: "Sarah, I'd like to ask you how the sketches in the training binders came to your attention and who objected to them."

Sarah: "No, I am absolutely not going to discuss that."

Me: "You can count on me to hold anything you tell me in complete confidence."

Sarah: "No! I am not going to discuss it."

Me: "You know, word of what happened a couple of days ago will get around, and unless you explain the facts of the matter, everyone will develop his own, and most likely inaccurate, theory of what transpired."

Sarah: "I don't care. I will not discuss it."

From this point on the temperature in the room rose considerably, leading to the most heated exchange I had ever had with anyone in all my years with FAA.

Me: "All right, I will give you an example of what I mean by telling you my theory. I think you had a meeting with the NATCA rep that had nothing to do with training but in which the head-butting got pretty severe. Seeing that the issue at hand was going nowhere, the rep threw out the business of the sketches as an unrelated curve ball, and you took the bait. How am I doing so far, hitting pretty close to home?"

Sarah, voice raised: "I don't want to hear your theory, and I am not going to explain myself!"

Me: "Okay, but I am only one of potentially a hundred or so people who will develop their own versions of what happened. We'd all be better off if you would give a clear and simple explanation of the actual facts."

Looking back, and with an assist from the rumor mill, it seemed that Sarah's selection as a support specialist at MIA may not have been entirely at her option. Her time in each of the facility manager positions had been pretty short. The periods that she held the staff position, the ops manager position, and finally the support manager position were also short. It wasn't a stretch to infer that in each case an event or a series of events had resulted in her "moving on." I breathed a little more freely when she retired in the spring, after about six months in her final job with FAA.

Creating New Scenarios

In the early months of 2004 we had no new trainees, affording me the opportunity to work without interruption on creating the new simulation scenarios. Although I had to teach myself some new skills, it was pretty much a straightforward exercise of making data entries on the AT Coach computer. By degrees I got better at using the system, eventually reaching the point where I was able to complete three or four problems in a day instead of one or two problems a week. For each radar position there would be eight scenarios, divided equally between an east and a west operation, and increasing in intensity and volume as the trainee progressed through the sequence. I completed the effort with a total of more than 60 simulations on file. The task was complete—or so I thought until I realized that it might be possible to add an important element.

Before STARS and AT Coach, it had not been possible to script background traffic bearing the correct position symbol (the letter of the responsible radar position). The exercises were "sterile," meaning that the controller was working in a vacuum, basically dodging empty airspace delegated to other positions with his traffic. AT Coach could generate the proper position symbol for each target in the simulation, so it did not make sense to limit ourselves to the old sterile format. It would be much more true to life if the areas adjacent to, underlying and overlying the airspace being trained on had some targets identified with the responsible function.

As an example, the North High Departure ("D") controller had to ensure that his traffic topped a "shelf" to the north at 3,000 feet or above to protect the lower surface-to-2000 foot stratum assigned to the Fort Lauderdale South Departure ("Z") controller. It would greatly reinforce the understanding of our airspace divisions if some "Z" targets could be placed in that area at 2,000 feet. It was all too easy to fudge on making a climb restriction by a few hundred feet if there was no traffic, but no controller was going to fudge on actual separation.

By now I understood that the AT Coach software permitted cut and paste actions, meaning that I could include one of the "Z" scenarios in each of the "D" exercises. The hard part was that the "Z" scenario traffic was all unscripted with the exception of initial start time and point, heading, altitude and speed. After that someone training on "Z" had to issue a series of control instructions to each target. I now had to modify the entire scenario by determining what commands to enter into the automation to get them to the proper place at the proper time.

It took at least half a dozen reruns of the problem containing the add-in traffic to make the presentation of the background targets effective. I had a list of handwritten notes that grew longer with each repetition, containing notations such as "Start American 621 two minutes earlier." Reduce speed of N85JP to 200K at 1340Z." "Assign 64Y a 200 degree heading initially." And because "D" abutted virtually every other position in the house, the process had to be repeated multiple times. All in all, it took longer to accomplish this secondary task than it had to create the original problems themselves. But we now had two ways for a trainee to learn the flows of each radar position: a "clean" version, without the clutter of background traffic, and the version more representing real world conditions.

A College ATC Program

There was another effort underway during this period, actually the continuation of something that had begun two years earlier. Miami-Dade Community College (MDCC) was one of the institutions designated by FAA to teach courses in the College Training Initiative (CTI) program. At the time, these courses were a pre-requisite for anyone wishing to apply for the job of air traffic controller and covered the basics of center and terminal operations, non-radar control, and weather. Miami Tower and the college had entered into an agreement whereby a limited number of students enrolled in the CTI program could spend time in the facility as unpaid interns. These sessions were similar in purpose to the cooperative education program conducted 30 years earlier, with the exception that the "co-ops" were actually salaried employees of the agency working 40 hours per week for a full semester. The goal was to afford these prospective employees the opportunity to observe first-hand the real-world application of what they were learning in the classroom.

From the outset there had been problems with the interns. The first group reported only a few months after the terrorist attacks of 9-11-2001, and NATCA expressed concerns that the students selected were not being properly vetted. Security throughout the agency had been tightened considerably, including a new requirement that foreign nationals had to be cleared through the U.S. State Department in order to be granted access to an ATC facility. Not all of the students were U.S. citizens, and it was not certain that the process of selecting intern candidates was rigorous enough. The program continued, but in all five of the sessions conducted since the start there emerged a similar pattern—great enthusiasm on the part of the students, decreasing over time to the point that a number of them simply stopped attending at all. I had worked closely with the co-ops in the 1970s and later received formal recognition for it, so I believed that we owed the current crop of aspirants the same level of attention and commitment.

After the fifth group had come and gone, I wrote a letter to the managers describing what I felt were the shortcomings of the program and recommending some changes. Excerpts appear below:

"The Miami Tower student intern program is not functioning effectively and should be improved by the allocation of sufficient resources to support it. If those resources are not available, the program should be terminated."

"The most negative interpretation is that the agency is not delivering what it promises ... compounding factors are: too many students scheduled per session; too many hours scheduled per student; no defined instructional/ orientation program; no designated individual to oversee and coordinate intern activities."

"MDCC and at least some of the students who have participated in the program would no doubt affirm its value. While the "anything is better than nothing" attitude is understandable it is not justification for an inferior level of support by the facility and the agency. If Miami Tower is going to continue sponsorship of the program, we must commit ourselves, at a minimum, to the following;

- Establishment of a designated intern coordinator, available to the students when they are in the facility.
- Creation of defined orientation modules, including a minimum of 20 per cent of the students' hours devoted to face-to-face briefing/orientation.
- Reduction in the number of interns per session to a maximum of three.
- Reduction in the number of attendance hours per week to eight (four hours on two days).
- Establishment of those hours in advance, with advance notice to the college, so that they can select candidates who are all able to participate at the designated times.

I received a polite acknowledgement of my "concerns," but the program continued until the summer. In the fall, it was not renewed.

I took another long summer leave, returning in late August. Upon my return to the facility, I learned that Lanny Williams and Billy Pierce also intended to retire at the end of the year. We members of the "old guard" had hung in there during the difficult years of the strike and its aftermath and now looked forward to handing over the reins to a new generation of staff and supervisors.

Post-Retirement Possibilities

As my remaining time with FAA dwindled down to months, then weeks, I began to look at post-retirement possibilities. For years the en route centers and some of the larger metroplex TRACONs had used contract instructors to perform the role that I had filled. Staff positions had been reduced agency-wide below the numbers authorized in earlier years, and when a class was in session I was basically unavailable for any other staff duties.

It seemed to me that it would make sense to hire one or two contractors, thus freeing up the diminished staff for other work. I had several discussions with Jorge Fernandez during which he agreed with me in principle, but pointed out that there would have to be a strong case made for the use of contractors. He suggested that I draft a letter of justification, an invitation I was more than happy to accept. In it I pointed out that the cost of a contract employee was far below that of a staff member, certainly in terms of salary, but more importantly in terms of retirement benefits, leave allowances, health care costs, and, most of all, the fact that a contractor would work only part time, that is when a class was scheduled.

I had no great hope that a contract opportunity would magically appear at the perfect time, that being before my retirement date, but not so early that another applicant might beat me to the punch. It only made sense to develop a "plan B," and I thought I had the makings of one in my pocket. In the course of developing the agreement with MDCC covering the intern program I had met several times with Marjan, the lady who headed up the CTI initiative. I knew that air traffic controllers, both retired and active, had been hired by the college to teach the CTI courses, so I believed I would be a viable candidate for such a position.

In fact, the college was having trouble recruiting qualified people for the job, meaning that my potential interest was received pretty positively. As Marjan and I discussed which courses I might be interested in teaching, I said I wouldn't want to take on more than two in one semester, while she expressed the hope that I would consider a third and even a fourth class. I held my ground, committing to teach classes in tower control and non-radar, each of these to be held twice weekly for two-hour periods beginning at 8:00 pm. With a final handshake we concluded with an agreement that I would teach the two classes beginning in the winter semester after the first of the year. I left Marjan's office with a binder about four inches thick describing what the FAA required in each of the courses mandated in the CTI program.

Late in November the last two controllers I would ever train as an FAA employee reported for classroom and simulation training on radar. These guys constituted the perfect class from my perspective—just two of them, meaning minimal time between runs for each of them, and both qualified controllers but without terminal radar experience. Sid came from Fort Lauderdale Executive airport, acknowledged as having the toughest local control position throughout the Miami hub, while Darren had been a controller at Miami Center. They both obviously had good controller smarts, but would need my best efforts in familiarizing them with our TRACON operation. They were attentive, studied hard, asked good questions, and caught on with no trouble in the lab exercises. In later years they both went on to supervisory positions. As it worked out, their last day in the classroom, and mine, fell on Friday, December 31, 2004.

I walked out the door at the end of the day shift with no lack of mixed feelings. I loved my job, so why was I retiring (a little late to be asking that question)? I had extended my career by a year, and during that period had thought long and hard about my decision. It had finally come down to a few salient points that convinced me I was doing the right thing. I was the oldest man in the facility (64) with 36 years in the FAA plus four years of military service. I was within two percentage points of being "maxed out" in terms of the multiplier used to calculate my retirement annuity, and had completed a full three years at the higher salary level of the new pay scale.

These were practical, objective facts. But there was a subjective consideration that influenced me at least equally. I had first become an instructor in 1978 at the age of 37 with ten years' experience at MIA. My trainees in that period were no more than ten or twelve years younger than me, and could easily picture themselves a decade hence as an established veteran. I was current and qualified in both the tower and the TRACON and could plug into a live position with them to provide a look into the real world. In 2004, no young man or woman could see themselves in the "old guy" that I had become, and I was not operationally certified. The advancing years had undeniably reduced or eliminated a couple of important motivational factors.

Off to School

On January 5, 2005, I reported to the Homestead campus of Miami Dade College (re-christened by dropping the word "community" from its name) for my first class. My "retirement" had lasted a whole four days, abruptly ending with the onset of a four-month period that I remember as one of busiest, and most frustrating, times of my life.

I had armed myself with my own course outlines, setting forth what I considered the most important concepts for both the tower and non-radar classes. I included information about what a student's grade would be based on (quizzes, final exam, attendance) and my contact information (college email address) for any questions or concerns that might arise outside of class hours. As I walked into the classroom, I entered upon a scene of near pandemonium. There were 35 students, many of whom knew each other. It was a new semester and a new course in an unfamiliar subject. I surmised that this beginning was basically par for the course. But this was a seriously large bunch. The course was advertised as including time in a tower simulator, for which the students paid extra. Simulation exercises were conducted one individual at a time, and I could not imagine how this many people were going to get any meaningful simulator experience in the number of hours allotted.

After establishing some semblance of order, I began talking about the course outline, a copy of which had been distributed to each member of the class. There appeared to be a typical level of inattention as I began, but when I began speaking about the grading the questions (and wheedling) went into high gear:

- What if I miss a quiz? Well you will get a zero for that day.
- Oh, that's not fair, what if it was unavoidable? Well, if you make arrangements in advance for a legitimate absence that is approved, you may get a chance for a make-up.
- Can I get extra credit by doing a special project? No.
- What if I drop out? Your class results will be governed by the college policy on dropouts.
- Will there be homework? There is no homework per se, but you will be expected to study the materials before class, and there will be at least a verbal review if not a quiz on the previous day's material.
- But I don't have time to study! Well then, I guess you just take your chances.

It would have gone on like this for the entire class period. I wrapped it up by saying that I would be available during breaks and after each class if anyone had questions or anything else on their mind. I had learned long ago that students were happy to eat up the allotted time with endless questioning before the class began, but I found that their curiosity became seriously diminished when they were on their own time after class.

The first order of business was basic phraseology—the format for initiating and responding to pilot and interphone coordination calls. I began this by asking how many in the class had pilot experience. Eight or ten hands went up. How many had controller experience? No hands went up.

How many had a relative or friend who was an air traffic controller? Four or five hands went up. So, for the next class, study the Tamiami airport diagram, be familiar with the communication protocols, and know the international verbiage for letters of the alphabet (alpha, bravo, etc.)

As I had done in my instructor role at MIA, I structured the tower course to follow the same progression that pilots follow when operating at a towered airfield: ground control, local control (departures), local control (arrivals). This was the basic VFR tower operation, representing the type facility to which new hires for the terminal option were likely to be assigned. Later, I would add on flight data and clearance delivery when it came time to discuss instrument flight plans.

Throughout the two-hour period, there had been a low hum of conversation that clearly had nothing to do with the material being presented, ending in a crescendo of babble that, as far as I could tell, was equally unrelated to anything to do with tower control. This was going to be a long haul, and I had not yet had my first day instructing the non-radar course.

Two days later in the next class, I wrote a call sign on the white board along with the type aircraft and the location on the field (N7565M, Cherokee, parked at Jet Center). I picked out one of the students and initiated an exchange that went like this:

Me: "Ok, this guy is calling for taxi for takeoff and the active runway is 9 Left. As the ground controller at Tamiami Airport, how would you respond?"

Student (eyes down, shifting uncomfortably in his seat, remaining silent for a long period, then speaking in a barely audible voice): "EN 7565 EM Cherokee parked at Jet Center taxi."

Me: "Now remember, letters are spoken using the international naming conventions. What are those terms for EN and EM?"

Student: "I don't know."

Me (turning away from this guy): "Anybody. How do we refer to these letters in ATC communications?"

A few hands went up, and I called on an individual who looked as though he had some smarts.

Student: "November and Mike."

Me: "Right. So, same question. How would you respond to a request for taxi?"

Student: "November 7565 Mike taxi to runway 9 Left."

Me: "That's the right idea. Remember to include your identification on initial contact to confirm that the pilot is on the right frequency.

For the rest of the class I wrote different call signs on the board and went to a different student each time to repeat the exercise. Despite the information from the first go-around, only about one out of five came anywhere near close to getting it right.

This pattern continued throughout the class. No matter how many times we reviewed material and repeated exams, a majority of the class did not catch on. But there was one "star" who pretty much aced every test with 100s or high 90s. I began to realize that he was as incredulous as I was over the poor performance of his classmates. When (for the eighth or tenth time) I would ask a basic question and get an incorrect response, he would shake his head, slam the desktop and mutter under his breath. A few weeks into the course I approached this individual, as I couldn't remember how he had responded to my questions on opening day about pilot and controller experience. The exchange went like this:

Me: "You seem to be catching on to this stuff very well. You have gotten 100s and high 90s on every quiz and test. Do you have pilot or controller experience?"

Him: "No, I don't know anything about flying."

Me: "Well you are head and shoulders above everyone else in this class. How do you do it?"

Him: "Because I study my ass off every night!"

Oh, for a dozen like him!

17. Teaching the Next Generation

In the real world of ATC, non-radar was something of a dying discipline. With the expansion of radar coverage and the advent of GPS navigation, fewer and fewer facilities had a need for non-radar procedures. Nevertheless, the powers that be saw fit to continue the requirement for non-radar training at the FAA Academy, and it continued to be one of the most difficult hurdles in the entire controller curriculum. It seemed to me that if I could give my CTI students a leg up in mastering the intricacies of non-radar control they would be to a certain extent ahead of the game when they reached the academy.

In comparison with tower training, non-radar is pretty abstract. It is one thing to lay out an airport diagram, with its runways and taxiways labeled, perhaps placing small airplane models on the overlay and discussing separation standards and the various "magic words" for keeping the flow safe and orderly. It is quite another to look at a stack of flight progress strips with time notations, fix abbreviations, and a column of altitude figures, using this information to determine where separation exists, where it is decreasing, what can be done, what must be done, and when another airplane can be added to the mix. Time, altitude, comparative speeds, and course divergence all had to be taken into account in determining control actions.

I spent a considerable amount of time crafting a map of make-believe non-radar airspace with an airport at the center and with airways radiating out from the field. I created a "what clears what" table and placed fixes at strategic points that would (and would NOT) permit or require a control action once an aircraft reported fix passage. These pages were distributed to each student and would serve as a basis for discussion and exercises.

I announced that each day we would spend the first 20 minutes or so of the class period doing a strip marking exercise. Each student would have four or five flight progress strips representing aircraft in the problem. There would be a digital clock projected on a large screen at the front of the room for reference in recording time notations. I had prepared a list of five or six pilot reports for each aircraft that I would call out at the appropriate times. These exercises would not be graded or counted in any way toward a final grade, but each student would be expected to participate and turn in their strips at the conclusion of the exercise.

Predictably, there was considerable moaning and groaning each time the flight progress strips were handed out and, equally predictably, 10 or 12 students did pretty well, another 10 or 12 did pretty poorly, and the rest appeared to be beyond redemption. On the first day as I was collecting the strips, there was one student who had not made a single entry on any of his. I told him he was expected to participate in the exercises, but he casually informed me that since they didn't count he wasn't going to bother. I didn't argue. But I would make sure to include strip marking questions on every quiz and the final exam. Can you say, "What goes around comes around?"

About midway through the semester I got a call from Marjan, the manager of the CTI program, summoning me to her office. When I got there she informed me that a student had made a complaint. The student was a young woman whose name I recognized from the tower class. She fell into the middle category academically, hardly a brilliant performer, but certainly not among the poorest. I was initially apprehensive, unable to imagine what the nature of the complaint could be, but Marjan soon put my mind at ease as she recounted her meeting with the student and the aftermath. It had gone like this:

Student: "I have a complaint on behalf of myself and several other students in the tower class."

Marjan: "I don't want to hear about any other students in the class. If they have a problem, they need to see me individually. Now, what is your problem?"

Student: "Well our instructor is making the course too difficult. He is treating us like experienced controllers and we are just students with a heavy class workload."

Marjan: "How do you mean?"

Student: "He is quizzing us on all this stuff about phraseology and how many feet of separation you need between two airplanes landing and taking off, with different answers for all kinds of airplanes. It's too hard and it's not fair."

Marjan: "All right, I will look into it."

Marjan went on to tell me that before she even called me in she spoke to another instructor, asking him if it was expecting too much of the students to learn phraseology and runway separation standards. Fortunately for me that instructor had said that on the contrary, that was exactly what the students needed to learn and what the course was designed to teach. The meeting concluded with Marjan thanking me for doing a good job, and encouraging me to keep on doing it.

Throughout the non-radar course the distribution of student performance was similar to that of the tower class, the overall results being somewhat poorer. But my "star" continued to excel despite the greater difficulty of the course content. There was a core set of non-radar rules that served as the basis for every quiz and class discussion. The class was being asked in every instance to answer questions that had been asked over and over again—questions such as:

- What is the required time separation when releasing a following airplane behind a leading airplane with a filed airspeed 44 knots faster?
- N12345 was airborne at 1315Z on a routing that will diverge in less than two minutes by 45 degrees from the routing of N54321 awaiting takeoff clearance. What is the earliest time that N54321 can be released?
- Airways V325 and V289 diverge from the same navaid by 23 degrees. With traffic on both airways, what is the minimum DME mileage that one of the aircraft must have passed to achieve separation?

When it came time for the final exams in both classes, I informed the students candidly that the questions would all be on information they had studied and been quizzed on before. Disappointingly, but perhaps not surprisingly, the results on the final exam differed little from those of the interim quizzes.

For the first time in my experience as an instructor, I walked out of the classroom on the last day with a profound sense of relief. I did not feel as though the long hours of preparation and my best efforts at communicating the essentials of the two courses had produced a result that could be called satisfactory. There had been failures in both classes and, with a few exceptions, poor performance overall. There had been unmistakable hostility on the part of a few individuals who apparently had been expecting an easy slide through a gut course. I decided then and there that I would not teach CTI classes again.

Greetings Warm and Cold

The spring and summer of 2005 represented the first period of "unlimited horizons" since high school summer vacations. I was not working. I was not looking for a job. My FAA retirement had kicked in, and I was financially comfortable. Life was sweet—sort of. I still missed being an instructor in a discipline I knew well, but for the moment I was more than happy to just "cruise."

There was a surprising postscript to the CTI classes. In July I received emails from two of my former students. I had never provided my personal email address to anyone in either class, so I am not sure how they came to have it. Perhaps they had asked the college personnel office or hacked their way into the college's records. In any event, the messages arrived about a week apart, seemingly without contact or collaboration between the two senders. Both communications expressed appreciation and support, one of them reading, "I know the course was rough on you, but you did a great job, and I hope you will return in the fall." Was this for real? Was it a hoax perpetrated by a student whose sentiments were entirely the opposite of those expressed? I did not respond to the messages, and so never found out for sure.

The year segued into September, the time of year traditionally devoted to finishing up summer activities and gearing up for "serious" things, like work or school. I didn't want to "cruise" forever, so what avenues were worth exploring? In yet another instance of the supreme good fortune I seemed to have enjoyed at important junctures in life, a prime opportunity materialized. Jorge Fernandez began his telephone call to me with the words, "Are you still interested in contract work here at the facility?"

As we talked, I learned that I would first be interviewed and then hopefully hired by the Washington Consulting Group, the organization that provided contract instructors at Miami Center and many other facilities as well. But first there would be some bureaucratic hoops to jump through. Despite the fact of my long career with, and recent retirement from, the FAA, I would have to undergo an FBI background check and furnish fingerprints. The first set of prints taken were lost in the system, requiring another go around, and the background check proceeded at what I can only describe as a leisurely pace. The long and short of it was that my first day back at MIA in my new status did not take place until the first week of December.

That first day represented a true homecoming for me. I received many warm greetings from my former co-workers, and even from some new arrivals who recognized that they could quite possibly become my students in the classroom or simulators. Jorge had written an information memo for the daily read file alerting the troops to my return and including a few words describing my background in training, saying I would be a great asset to the facility. As I basked in the glow of all this, I had no inkling that my good fortune was about to hit a serious speed bump.

There had been some substantial procedural changes in the year I had been gone. The most significant of these was an expansion of the northeast arrival corridor to accommodate parallel, side-by-side arrivals. Apparently the facility had fought this, and with good reason. Widening the corridor necessarily narrowed the adjacent departure airspace and caused the east departure flows from both Miami and Fort Lauderdale to remain at low altitude for longer periods. Besides that, overloading one quadrant of the traditional "bow-tie" configuration that most approach controls used for inbound traffic was bound to cause problems during an arrival rush, especially when MIA was on a west operation. It was a scant 32 miles from the Miami Center boundary to the finals for 26 Left, 26 Right, and 27. The aircraft came in high (10,000 and 11,000 feet) and fast, needing to slow to 250 knots before they could descend, and essentially already established on a long base leg. The result for the approach controller was often a sequence of airplanes that were too high and too fast to be smoothly integrated into an otherwise safe and sane line up of traffic on final and downwind. But the powers that be had mandated the new procedure in order to relieve pressure on the centers working ever-larger volumes from the major airports in the Northeast.

I knew I would have to bone up on the re-configured airspace, and decided to look at the controller training manuals that contained maps of each radar position's area of responsibility. I didn't find them. They were apparently now stored in a place different from where they used to be, so I started poking around the bullpen, the group of cubicles where staff members (and contractors?) worked. One of the cubicles belonged to a guy who I knew had responsibilities in training. He was absent that day, so I went in, looked at the open shelves above his desk, and moved a few papers around, still not finding the manuals. Well, I would have to leave this for another time. I settled into my old cubicle, unoccupied during my absence, and began checking my computer for emails and access to training files.

The next day the guy in whose cubicle I had looked came in. I approached him with a smile, extending my hand for a handshake. He stopped in his tracks, fixed me with a cold stare, and without preamble stated in icy tones, "Who gave you permission to go through my desk?" I was floored. It took me a few seconds to react, but I finally managed to say, "I didn't go through your desk. I looked for the training manuals on your shelves and desktop, but didn't find them." He replied, "You stay the hell out of my cubicle!" and stalked off. I followed him and ventured an appeal to our former working relationship, trying to downplay the tension in the exchange we had just had. I said, "Come on, we worked together before, and we'll be working to together again, let's shake hands and forget it." With great vehemence he replied, "We are not working together. You are on your own." At this point I gave up, thinking, "Suits me just fine."

That should have been the end of it, but two of the other specialists in the bullpen who had overheard the exchange went to Jorge, expressing their concern over the unwarranted hostility of which I had been the recipient. Jorge called me and the other guy into his office for a private meeting, urging us to "go have a beer together" and to work things out since we would (uh-oh) "be working together." I waited for some sign of acceptance by the aggrieved staffer, but none was forthcoming, so I held my peace.

By bits and pieces I learned some factual background that seemed to bear upon the incident. Ron had taken over the functions I normally performed after my retirement. He had let it be known that he considered the training materials to be entirely inadequate, seriously hampering his ability to teach the classes effectively, and faulted me for the insufficiency of the lesson plans and other materials. Of course, he had had a year to improve them or create new ones and had not done so. There had also apparently been an incident involving a new employee in the tower class who complained to management that he was not getting meaningful instruction. He had kept a log of the hours and minutes that Ron had been present in (and absent from) the classroom. This record showed that with the exception of a few short periods during each session, the employee had been largely left on his own.

All of this, combined with Jorge's letter in the read file about my return and the value I would bring to simulation training in the soon to arrive new tower simulator, seemed to contribute to Ron's resentments against me.

The Show Must Go On

By degrees this inauspicious beginning faded into irrelevance as all of us with training responsibilities geared up for what promised to be a substantial challenge. 2006 marked 25 years since the strike of 1981, also the number of years a controller needed to retire "at any age" if all his or her years had been in controller or first line supervisor positions. Over half of the workforce would be eligible for retirement over the next couple of years. Additional personnel losses would come as both pre-strike veterans and post-1981 hires reached the mandatory retirement age of 56. As had happened during the late 1960s, the agency was once again faced with the need to hire and train thousands of new controllers. In recognition of this fact, the FAA renewed the policy under which I had been hired at MIA, namely, that all facilities would be required to accept zero experience candidates. In 1968, I had been the only one taken by Miami Tower. In 1981, only one of our new hires was without prior controller experience. This time there would be classes of six or eight people, all needing detailed basics and expanded OJT hours when they reached the floor.

The first order of business was to revamp our lesson plans. The existing materials had been geared to newly selected employees with at least VFR tower experience, necessarily positing a certain level of core knowledge.

Our revisions would have to provide that knowledge to the fullest extent possible in classroom and simulator instruction. There was considerable discussion of how best to balance the need for adequate training of these "newbies" with some reasonable determination of curriculum length. Clearly we needed to get these people qualified. But if the agency was going to put them into a high-density terminal as their first facility, it would have to accept that training was going to take longer—possibly a lot longer.

The other big effort was integrating the new tower simulator into the training program. Technically it was a masterpiece of sophistication. The graphics were high quality and the detail represented in the airport layout was spot on. With a few keystrokes different weather conditions and visibility could be called up at any point in a training scenario. An aircraft could be caused to burst into flames with the ability to summon fire rescue equipment from the midfield fire station. The big problem was the voice activated aircraft movements. Simple commands given one time only tended to produce correct responses from the targets. But if there was any complexity in a trainee's transmission, or even if a correct command were repeated, the system didn't know what to do with it.

A prime example: a taxiing aircraft would be instructed to hold short of a runway. The instruction would be acknowledged, but as the aircraft approached the holding point it maintained its taxi speed right up to the hold line then abruptly stopped. To a controller exercising the monitor function, ensuring that his instructions were being carried out, it appeared for all the world as though the "pilot" did not intend to stop. The controller would repeat the hold short command, and the system would respond, "unable." There were other less serious features of the system's responses that degraded the realism of an exercise. Many times one taxiing aircraft would be instructed to follow another only three or four airplane lengths ahead. The system would respond, "not in sight." But if an aircraft at the run-up pad were issued a command such as, "hold short, traffic on a three-mile final," the system would respond "in sight" even when the target had not yet appeared on the display.

Over time, many of these problems were eliminated by programming macro commands of standard instructions into the computer. For example, "Taxi to runway 8 Right via taxiway November" was a standard clearance for the American flights parked at Concourse D. These fixes improved the exercises greatly, but did require a pseudo pilot to enter the appropriate macro. We who administered tower simulator training became familiar with the quirks in the system and were able to offer helpful hints to our trainees. There was no value in seeing a controller tripped up by an inappropriate system response.

There had been some ugly talk among both the staff and the controller group after learning that Miami Tower would be getting its share of new employees with no prior experience. The gist of it was, "We need to wash every one of them out till the FAA gets the message that you can't send these people here as their first facility." I was of a different view. I had made it here, and without any of the classroom and simulator capabilities for training that now existed. If we were lucky enough to get some sharp candidates early on, we could establish a precedent that would give those following the first wave a fair chance at checking out.

It seemed to me that we owed them every consideration, because the policy was if you didn't check out at your first facility you were out of a job. I pictured a young man or woman who had waited a substantial amount of time on a list of eligibles, quit a job, spent four months at the academy, traveled to Miami on his or her own dime, finally entering on duty at a facility they did not choose, with a high probability of washing out. Life definitely threw curve balls, and it was up to us to provide the best coaching possible.

The early days of my first training assignment as a contract instructor initially made me reconsider this hopeful view. Although I never understood all the details, a young woman who had been through the academy twice reported to MIA for duty. She had apparently not passed the academy course the first time, but owing to circumstances unknown to me had been "recycled" through the program and graduated successfully. With this history I would not have expected her to be assigned to a facility like ours. But here she was, several weeks ahead of the date that a tower training class, including her, would be convened. In what I considered a major good call, Jorge Fernandez explained the basics of her circumstances and said I should spend these weeks with Mei Lin prepping her for the class.

In some ways this assignment was exactly my cup of tea—one on one with someone who needed the all help I could give, and presumably was heavily invested in soaking up every bit of it. We started out with flight data and clearance delivery, the first two positions on which she would train in the tower, and where her performance and aptitude would first be assessed by her instructors and supervisors. The first few days were not encouraging. Either the academy was not teaching even the simple fundamentals of an instrument flight plan clearance, or Mei Lin had forgotten everything she was supposed to have learned. It was back to square one: clearance limit, routing, altitude, frequency, transponder code. I prepared flight progress strips matching the format used in the tower, and we practiced over and over again. Then we went on to special cases: check for release, ground stop, EDCT time, gate hold, expired flight plan, weather re-routes. It was tough going on each of these at first, but with repetition she caught on, and as she did so her confidence and "go-getter" attitude increased in proportion. She never got discouraged or became resentful in any way. I was convinced that, although it would be a long haul, she would hang in there and reach full certification.

It worked out that I would teach the tower class in which she and three other new employees would participate. The new people seemed to be as clueless as Mei Lin had been at the beginning. One of them appeared very negative about the material and the classroom work, seemingly unwilling to dive in and engage with the practice sessions. Maybe I was going too fast. At one point I gave them an hour of self-study so that they could practice on their own without being, so to speak "under the gun." As I was heading back to the training room I overheard some lively discussion among the students. I stopped and listened for a minute or two, soon realizing that Mei Lin was explaining things and encouraging the others in much the same manner as I would have done. She won my ongoing support for good that day.

New Training Supervisor

Soon after my arrival as a contract instructor there was a major change to the whole training program. Recognizing that we would have multiple classes going on at once, and believing that some form of standardized curriculum would be necessary, facility management created the position of training officer. This was basically a return to the structure that existed before the positions of Plans and Procedures officer and EPDO (Evaluation and Proficiency Development) officer were combined under the title support manager. It was the right call at the right time, and the individual chosen for the new position was the right guy. Dan had come to Miami as a controller from Boston Tower, with background in military air traffic control before that. I had trained him as "B-sider" (radar only) prior to my retirement, and he had been sharp, sailing through the classroom work and simulation, then checking out without any problem. He went on to become a supervisor at Palm Beach before returning to MIA.

By this time a couple of other contract instructors had been hired, both former MIA controllers. We now had a mix of FAA support staff and our own cadre of Washington Consulting Group employees sharing responsibility for classroom and simulation training. Dan hit the ground running, assigning each of us a piece of the radar curriculum for review and revision. He called me into his office privately, saying that what he most remembered from his own experience in the training program was the overview I had presented on the first day of class. He said that at Boston and at other facilities where he had worked the approach had been to teach each radar position in sequence. This method basically required trainees to learn blocks of airspace by rote memorization instead of the more intuitive process of discovering how altitude and boundary limits were defined by adjoining sectors.

When Dan had been my trainee there had been no formal overview portion of the radar course. I simply talked "off the cuff," using an overall map of our airspace, tracing the route of a departure or arrival aircraft, and explaining how they had to make good a climb rate to top a "shelf" or to be altitude restricted because of overlying/ underlying airspace. Dan asked that I create a lesson plan formalizing all of this while the other support specialists and contract instructors reworked the syllabus for each individual radar position.

As I began work on this assignment it immediately became clear that this was a new day in the training department. I had been used to doing things as I saw fit, working with my classes on an open-ended schedule, without ever being questioned or supervised in any way. Management professed themselves to be "very happy" with my performance, never monitoring a classroom or simulator session or exhibiting any concern over the time it took to complete a class. I determined how long a break the students could take and how many simulation exercises an individual needed to be ready for OJT.

With Dan in charge, each of us had to report our progress on our assignments regularly. Once classes began, we were expected to stick strictly to the timeline of the lesson plans. Lunch breaks were 30 minutes, class breaks 10 minutes out of each hour, no exceptions. If there were students in the hallway two minutes after the hour, Dan was immediately on them, telling them to get back to class. In the simulation phase, six problems were scheduled each day. A problem would run for 50 minutes, and no exercise was to be terminated early. If you did the math, this meant that there were 15 minutes per problem to debrief the student, write up a detailed training report, and re-load AT Coach for the next exercise. In practical effect the only break we the instructors got was 30 minutes for lunch, the 10 minutes between simulation runs being taken up with debriefing, training report documentation, and preparation for the next run.

For each radar position there was a set of problems representing both an east and a west operation, increasing in complexity as a student progressed through them. The final step per position was an evaluation problem during which there were to be no comments or helpful hints from the instructor. Instead we were to document the trainee's performance in as much detail as possible. A separation error meant immediate failure of the evaluation with one retake permitted. A failure on the retake meant an end to a career at MIA and possibly an end to employment as an air traffic controller.

Much of this was at odds with my perspective on training. There was a mighty big difference between simulation and the real world, and I frankly believed that a trainee should have the right to a make or break effort in handling live traffic. The value of simulation, as I saw it, was to improve the odds of successful facility certification, as we had done in the past. In the realm of OJT, there were provisions for allotting extra hours if a student continued to show progress. A similar approach in simulation training would be a reasonable and more productive policy, it seemed to me. Although I understood the agency's position with respect to the need for standardization and equal treatment of trainees, we would not be permitted to give extra help to those who needed it, nor was there any recognition of the fact that some people were "naturals" while others could be slow starters.

My own experience as a trainee was a case in point. I absolutely would not have succeeded in this new program if it had existed when I was in training all those years ago. I came within an inch of washing out on approach control and only managed to get certified because my supervisor and instructors were willing to hang in there with me until I got the picture.

Over the years it was demonstrated time and again that a slow starter could become a good controller given the necessary support and resources. What we were really measuring today with zero experience students was two different elements that did not confirm or invalidate an individual's potential for success in the air traffic business. One was the ability to catch on quickly. While this was a definite plus for trainee and instructor alike, it also had the potential for creating a "hot shot" type, willing to push the limits beyond the norms. The other element was luck. Each student worked the exact same set of problems in the exact same sequence. Whether in the real world or the simulation lab, if you made some good decisions early, the entire complexion of a busy traffic scenario could be favorably influenced in the direction of less delay, greater efficiency, and fewer separation problems needing to be resolved.

A trainee with no radar experience might guess right and make those good calls; equally, he or she might guess wrong early on and then spend the rest of the exercise in a reactive mode, "putting out fires" instead of proactively orchestrating a nice orderly flow. Based on these two probabilities we who saw the same scenarios day after day could tell within the first two or three minutes how a particular student was likely to fare as the simulation progressed.

Every new student was thoroughly briefed on the structure of the training program and most simply dived in and took their chances. I routinely exceeded my authority by telling them that if they felt they needed extra help they should make a formal request to management, in writing, and request a written reply. That way, if they failed training, they would have grounds for appeal based on a denial of the additional instruction requested. To my knowledge, no trainee ever followed this course. But several who were struggling approached me quietly asking if there was any way I could help them out. Although I was risking my own job, in a couple of cases I provided extra simulation runs off the books. There wasn't much that Dan didn't know about what went on in the training department, so I was never sure whether I had gotten away with these policy breaches or whether Dan elected to give me a pass either because of my history in the facility or because he understood my motivations.

My First Tower Class

We all remember "firsts" in our lives. Over the six years of my time as a contract instructor I taught probably six or eight radar classes (interspersed with a like number of tower classes), and my specific memories of those later groups are less differentiated. But I recall the first ones in some detail.

The first tower class consisted of five individuals, Miles, Ryan, Natalie, Tom, and Mike. Four of whom were fresh out of the academy and a fifth who had prior military experience. They seemed so young! But apparently they had all done well in Oklahoma City, and it didn't take me long to see that this group was exactly what we needed to establish that zero experience trainees could make it at Miami Tower. They were sharp, asked good questions, and most gratifyingly, were enthusiastically engaged.

I told them up front that when I called on one of them it wasn't for the purpose of "catching them out" on some point of understanding—or, as I put it, you had to be willing to be stupid on the way to getting smart. I said that a wrong answer was just as valuable as a right answer. If you made a mistake you tended to remember it and were unlikely to make it again. I did have a concern about one of the group because, although he was doing just as well as the others, he seemed to lack confidence in his own knowledge and understanding. This would not serve him well in the heat of busy operations.

As the class progressed it became apparent that Ryan and Miles were the stars of the class. It was a joy to be the instructor for these guys. They soon caught on to my mannerisms and gestures, such as blowing a gentle raspberry when there was an incorrect answer, or pulling down the corner of one eye as a reaction to "YGBSM" type information. At the conclusion of the class we posed for pictures demonstrating each of these for the camera. Mike, the individual whose confidence I questioned, could make fun of his own misgivings. He sat with his back to a wall where a pull-down map was mounted, and when asked a question he would pull the map down over his face and upper body.

When it came time to report to the tower, each of the group, Miles, Ryan, Natalie, Tom, and Mike, were assigned to a team. I took a few days off after the class and when I returned Mike was gone. I asked Jorge Fernandez what had happened. After one day of OJT in the tower Mike had come to Jorge and resigned from the agency, saying that the job was not for him. Jorge and the chief spoke with him at length, offering a possible transfer to a lower activity facility, and asking if he had in any way been treated unfairly or discouraged from continuing training. Mike assured them that he had been treated well and had no complaints against the agency or any individual. I was personally relieved to hear that, but it was always something of a downer when someone I had instructed did not complete the program.

Tom and Natalie did well in tower training, but both transferred out before going on to radar. Miles and Ryan checked out faster than some trainees with prior experience. As I had hoped, this pretty well put an end to the idea that a person with no air traffic background could not make it at MIA. Jorge Fernandez put an exclamation point on their success one day when Ryan's parents visited the facility, referring to their son as "our rookie of the year."

Radar Training Class

The first radar class opened with, no surprise, my overview lesson. There were eight trainees, seven of whom were without prior experience. The eighth had come from LaGuardia Tower, but had not worked radar before. Not unexpectedly it was soon apparent that this group fairly represented the breakdown of the air traffic controller body at large—one or two hotshots, three or four middle of the roaders, a couple of strugglers, and one or two who looked as though they didn't have a prayer.

My co-instructor was Lori, a woman who began her career at North Perry tower shortly after the strike of 1981. She had been at MIA for about 20 years, and was by this time a seasoned veteran. She maintained her operational currency and was very sharp on procedures and regulations. I frequently consulted Lori myself in cases where I wanted to be sure my understanding of something in a lesson plan was correct. In the course of her career Lori had conducted plenty of OJT, but had never taught in the classroom or simulation lab. The idea was that she would learn by observing my methods, but knowing her as I did I had no doubt that she would soon chart her own course in the training department.

Lori was like the "good conscience" of the facility. If a co-worker was not following procedures, she let the individual know; if an instructor said something inaccurate, she jumped in with a correction; if a management policy was unrealistic, she did not hesitate to say so. And so on this first day she led off with some emphatic admonitions: don't exceed your break period; no texting in class; no talking while the instructor is speaking; remain in the classroom during self-study periods; study on your own to supplement classroom work. She even caught me on a few things, in most cases justifiably, but there were a couple of instances when we disagreed. Lori could irritate me, but there was mutual respect, too. She told me I was the only instructor other than herself that she trusted to do the job right, and I recognized her smarts and dedication.

The overview lesson was scheduled to take 24 days, all in the classroom, and the information would be coming thick and fast. As I had done in the days when "overview" was informal, I started out by saying that the students were not expected to remember every single item in the lesson plan, but should mainly just listen and begin to form a framework for the individual position lessons that would follow. The introduction went something like this:

"The key to understanding the MIA operation is how the two major airports, Fort Lauderdale and Miami, work individually and in relation to each other. Both airports are oriented east and west with arrival routings from the northeast, northwest, southeast, and southwest. On the departure side of the airport, for example the east side on an east operation, the arrivals stay high until they pass the airport on downwind. On the arrival side, the west side in this case, the inbounds begin descent as soon as they enter our airspace. Departing aircraft tunnel under the arrivals from the northeast and southeast and "top" the inbounds from the northwest and southwest. The same principal applies when the airports are operating west.

There are low altitude sectors north of each airport that handle the satellite fields, but no low altitude sector south of Miami—only a designated area delegated to Homestead tower."

I could already see dawning expressions of "What the hell is he talking about?" so I immediately projected a radar map of our airspace on the whiteboard and drew lines of different colors annotated with the appropriate altitudes showing how the arrival and departure routes crossed. A picture is worth a thousand words, as the saying goes.

'Name That Airspace'

The rest of the course consisted of presenting the highlights for each operating position—standard departure headings, letters of agreement with the towers and Miami Center, and most importantly, the airspace configuration for each. I made the point repeatedly that they should master all the airspace before tackling the classroom and sim lab work for the individual control functions. It was not a matter of learning it today and forgetting it tomorrow, I said. It would take constant practice drawing and re-drawing every sector in the house until the entire area was as familiar as the streets in your own neighborhood.

The acid test for mastery of the airspace was an exercise I called "Name That Airspace." It was conducted near the end of the course, like this: I would put the laser pointer on a random area of the video map and say, "OK, starting at the surface account for the allocation of every altitude up to 16,000, position by position." The answer, using the ARTS letter designations for the TRACON positions, would go like this: "Surface to 3 is G, 4 to 8 is R, 9 is L, 10 to 16 is N."

I had always known that peer pressure was a tremendous motivator, and so one student would be selected to perform the exercise with the others watching. They were pretty merciless with each other, making "buzzer" sounds or booing and hissing when their comrade made a mistake. But overall the class developed a gratifying sense of solidarity. They were soon drawing airspace on the whiteboard during breaks, and had even crafted a "dunce cap" made from a plastic coffee cup and rubber bands. If someone didn't know an answer or made a mistake, either he would put the dunce cap on himself or a classmate would do the honors for him, all in a spirit of good comraderie.

I had made the point early on that they should help each other because, fairly or not, they would be judged unofficially, via the facility grapevine, as a group. I had seen more than once how a group, or even a pair of trainees could get a bad rap if even one was either legitimately struggling or exhibiting a bad attitude.

In early January 2009 the class was well into the classroom and simulation portions of the individual radar positions. We lost one member during an evaluation problem, mainly, I believed because his command of English was not the best. I hated to have anyone I had trained fail the program, and in this case it was especially disappointing because Tex had been a whiz in the early airspace exercises. I had predicted that he would do well, but he just had not been able to get the words out in the heat of a busy traffic problem.

There was an "almost" failure who pulled out of the dive at the last minute and eventually went on to full certification. Time after time Tommy had seemed clueless in the sim lab. All the instructors who had worked with him shared the same impression that he was on his way out. Then one day as we administered the next to last problem before the final evaluation, he turned the corner. Every controller, as a trainee or an instructor, has experienced or observed the golden moment when the light bulb came on. But Tommy's case was the most extreme about face I had ever seen. In the prior problem he had made mistakes left and right, speaking hesitantly, giving every indication of being down the tubes. This time he began rattling off instructions quickly and confidently, and never slowed down till the exercise was over. We couldn't believe this was the same guy that had struggled so hard.

Towards the end of the class, someone opened the door to the sim lab saying, "On your next break go watch TV. A Cactus (USAIR) A-320 lost both engines after a bird strike and landed in the Hudson. Everybody got out." It was January 15, the day Captain "Sully" Sullenberger executed the Miracle on the Hudson. Besides being an example of superior airmanship and professional cool, it was a between-your-eyes demonstration for these new guys that this air traffic control and flying business was serious stuff.

ATSAT Administrator

I had begun a secondary contracting job in 2006 as an administrator for the ATSAT test. The acronym stood for Air Traffic Selection and Training, and had been developed to replace the old Civil Service exam that the FAA had used for years. In yet another instance of good luck at the right time, the opportunity came about because Lanny Williams had been one of the first hired for the administrator job. Soon afterwards he contacted me, and we became the ATSAT administrators for the Miami area.

A great deal of research and validation had gone into the development of ATSAT, with the goal of identifying and measuring the kinds of knowledge and skills needed to become an air traffic controller. The test was 100 per cent computer based, consisting of seven distinct parts:

- Air Traffic Scenarios Test

- Analogies Test
- Angles Test
- Applied Mathematics Test
- Dials Test
- Letter Factory Test
- Scan Test

At one point I took the test myself just to see what the applicants were up against. It was not easy. With all my years of experience I barely reached the level of "best qualified" (a score of 85 percent or better). By their titles alone six of the sections looked as though they were reasonably relevant to controlling airplanes. But "Letter Factory?" This was the section on which I believed I had performed the most poorly, and which seemed to me the least likely to bear significantly on an applicant's future success. On the computer screen there were three conveyor belts bearing boxes of different colors. With the mouse you had to pick off each box and place it in the appropriately colored bin. You also had to keep track of how full each bin was. Any attempt to place a box in a bin that was full generated an error. Finally, the exercise would stop at random points and ask how many green boxes, or orange boxes had been placed in the bins. How was this important? The last thing you needed to do during a busy period of ATC operations was look back at actions that had already been taken and closed out.

The job itself was mostly straightforward and routine. The testing took place in a hotel conference area where we set up a dozen laptops or more. The next day the "aspirants" would report and be checked in against a list prepared in advance. We would spend about 20 minutes on pre-test briefing including, saliently, the need to read carefully and follow exactly the instructions that appeared at the beginning of each section. Each part would be individually timed, with no opportunity to return to a section once time had expired. We could answer no questions during the test but could assist if there were an equipment or software problem. Once the test began, we kept a log recording the times each student exited and re-entered the room, which they were permitted to do freely at their own discretion. At the end of the day, we downloaded the results from each laptop to a thumb drive and sent the data to FAA. We then erased the entire test from the laptops in order to ensure security and locked up the room till the next day.

The data collected from each student was in two parts: raw scores from each section to be combined into a final grade; and a far deeper dive into the particulars of how a particular individual had handled every element of every section—number of keystrokes, time taken between answers, number and length of break periods, etc. The intention was to follow the progress of each person through his or her career and zero in on test factors that correlated with successful facility qualification.

All of this was a quantum leap forward from the old pencil-and-paper multiple-choice examinations of the past. But the heavy hand of bureaucracy was still to be felt. The FAA had established early the policy that ATSAT testing would be offered no more than a certain number of miles from the CTI college attended by the applicants. This meant that in many cases the agency bore the cost of hotel space, travel and lodging for administrators, and shipping of equipment to and from the location. The most extreme example in my own experience occurred when Lanny and I went to San Juan, Puerto Rico, to test six applicants. At a cost of more than $15,000, covering airfare, hotel charges, and air freighting of equipment to and from the site, final preparation for the testing was complete. The next day we waited, with six laptops fired up and ready to go, for the six individuals to appear. The first guy appeared on time, followed by….. no others. For a few hundred dollars the agency could have bought this man an airline ticket to Miami and included him in one of the many groups we tested locally. And worse was yet to come.

About three years after its inception the ATSAT testing contract was re-bid, with Robinson Aviation losing out to another contractor. The new company elected not to rehire any of the RVA (Robinson Aviation) employees, thus ending that chapter except for several pleasant postscripts: at least three of the individuals in groups I had tested later became my classroom and simulation trainees at MIA.

A New CTI School

Once again luck was on my side when Broward Community College, a two-year institution in Fort Lauderdale, approached the facility for assistance in qualifying to teach CTI courses. All such institutions were required to develop in-depth syllabi covering the subjects mandated for CTI classes. Officials from BCC wanted any and all help we could give them in furnishing and developing materials for the courses. Whether this effort was technically within my job description I was never sure, but facility management allowed me to participate. My first question was whether any of our training materials were proprietary and should not be shared with the college. I was assured that I had carte blanche to in effect hand over all our materials. I did just that with our tower training binder, adding a few explanatory tweaks that I thought would be helpful.

After several meetings at the facility the college personnel expressed great appreciation for our help, saying they were more than happy with the materials and our advice. One of them approached me about their next objective, which was to identify and hire qualified instructors. Would I be interested in a position with BCC? I told her that in principle I would be very interested, but that given my current contracting responsibilities I could not consider such an offer at the present time. Well, could I suggest any others who might be interested? I knew that Ron had made some noises about retirement, and so, qualifying my answer carefully, I said that while I could not speak for Ron, I thought it might be worth their while to sound him out. The lady thanked me, we exchanged contact information, and as far as I knew that would be the last of any interactions between BCC and me.

But it was not the last. Several months later I got a call from one of the college officials during which he explained that they had completed all course development for the CTI program. The FAA would be sending a couple of emissaries to evaluate and hopefully to approve the syllabi, leading to certification of BCC to offer the courses. Would I be willing to be present during that process? My experience as an ATC instructor and as someone who could validate the course materials would be extremely helpful, they said.

On the appointed day I met with the college officials and the FAA evaluators. The FAA guys were of my generation—a good sign, I believed. One was a retired academy instructor. The other was still working, and clearly had field experience similar to my own. From the outset it was clear that these gentlemen and I were very much on the same page about what it took to craft and implement a successful curriculum at the college level. They were impressed that the college had reached out to Miami Tower and that the materials to be used in the courses were virtually the same as those we used at the facility. I was able to explain exactly why MIA's training was structured the way it was, even giving examples of my own techniques in both the classroom and the simulators. They ate it up, never asking directly whether I would be teaching at BCC, but giving every indication that they were pleased with what they were hearing and seeing. At the end of the day I was pretty confident that BCC would have no trouble being accredited as a CTI school. Sure enough, within a short time I learned that the college had received FAA approval and would soon begin offering the courses that controller candidates were required to take.

Later that year, while I was away on summer leave, I received an email from Ron. He asked if I would be willing to act as a reference for him in applying for an instructor position at Broward Community College. I agreed, taking this as a final indicator that our unfortunate beginning three years earlier was now firmly in the past. When I returned to the facility in August, I learned that Ron had retired and had been hired by the college.

Not long afterwards Ron called me, saying that he had been tasked with building a series of radar simulation scenarios. What did I think would be appropriate for college students trying to learn the basics, he asked. I told him that if I were doing it I would use the airspace and procedures that MIA used for Fort Lauderdale. This would make it a relatively simple single airport operation with only three radar positions to contend with—departure control, approach control, and the low altitude sector to the north. Well, how should the students be prepared in classroom training for the simulation exercises? Just as we do at Miami, I said. Have them draw the airspace until they know it cold, show examples on the white board of traffic flows, provide at least the basics of phraseology, separation standards, letter of agreement provisions, etc. The long and short of our exchange was that I would provide the sections of the radar training binder covering the Fort Lauderdale positions and that Ron would develop the traffic scenarios.

A year later, the BCC CTI program was fully up and running. An entire complex, funded by a wealthy donor, had been created, with both tower and radar simulation capabilities better than we had at Miami. The college scheduled a day of dedication during which the wealthy donor and others who had contributed to the effort would be honored. There was a substantial crowd present, numbering at least several hundred by my estimation. As I walked into the venue where the event would be held, I saw a distinguished looking gentleman in a dark suit approaching, realizing almost immediately that it was Ron. He greeted me warmly. I responded by saying he looked like the CEO of Broward Community College, Incorporated. We exchanged a few further pleasantries and then the ceremony began.

One of the college deans acted as master of ceremonies, touting the sophistication of the new complex and expressing on behalf of the community a large measure of gratitude for the generosity of the man who had made it possible. He went on to name a number of other individuals, each of whom was asked to stand and be recognized. Although I was not sure it would happen, he eventually called my name. I stood, and received a light smattering of applause plus some vigorous fist pumps from former and present colleagues at MIA.

Some Changes, Good and Otherwise

In my last two years as an advisor and instructor, a number of things changed:

Good: The MITRE Corporation was engaged to help craft some computer-based training software for the facility. They came to town a number of times, reuniting me with some of the engineers who had worked with us on the AERA program, and with Dennis and Dusty, two of my former colleagues on the ATACT team, now retired and working as consultants to MITRE. This effort resulted in the creation of some exercises that supplemented classroom instruction, notably, airspace drill. The various sections of airspace were displayed randomly and not connected, showing only the borders. There was a list of altitudes, such as SFC-2, 30-50, etc. in a separate list. A trainee would have to "grab" each piece of airspace, place it correctly on a video map, then pick the appropriate altitude range and place it within each section.

Otherwise: The training contract held by Washington Consulting Group was rebid, with WCG losing out to Raytheon. We in the field found that Raytheon's requirements were distinctly more onerous than those we had lived under previously. At the end of each workweek we had to log on to the company website and record our hours for that week. The problem was that the workweek for most employees ended on Friday. The site was ill equipped to handle the crush of thousands of contractors trying to access the site in the same few hours, and the company was none too understanding if your hours didn't get posted.

During this period I underwent knee replacement surgery, requiring several weeks of absence from the job. I spent endless hours collecting medical reports, prognostications and the like justifying the absence while receiving firm admonitions that failure to produce the required documentation could result in my being deemed to have forfeited my position.

Good and Otherwise: The radar lab underwent a major reconfiguration, the purpose of which was to reduce the crowding and noise level within the confined space. Up to this time we had routinely been training three controllers at a time at the three displays that side by side took up the entire length of the small room. At each one there were three people—instructor, trainee, and pseudo-pilot, sitting cheek by jowl and all talking at once. It was distracting and uncomfortable, no doubt about it, but the fix had some distinct downsides. The pseudo-pilots would be located to a separate room one floor below and would communicate via headsets over a closed circuit telephone line. The biggest problem was that the pilots were no longer looking at the same display as the trainee and instructor. The interface was a small 12-inch screen showing all targets, not just those being worked in the exercise.

In a busy scenario it was impossible to pick out the target of a particular control instruction, meaning that the pilots had to respond strictly to the voice commands. If the controller misstated an aircraft ID, there was no way for the pilot to readily ask for a correction. Worse than that, the commands had to be entered by clicking on a drop down list, finding the aircraft number, highlighting it, identifying the type maneuver (altitude, speed, heading) and typing it in. In a busy problem it was hard to keep up, resulting in delayed responses, many "say agains" and ultimately degrading a student's perceived performance.

On top of that, it meant that the pseudo-pilots had to handle all verbal communications as well as the command entries. This eliminated, for me, one of the most useful elements of simulation training—the ability for me, the instructor, to act as the voices of the aircraft crews and those on coordination lines. The pseudo-pilots could not approximate the kind of real-life exchanges that I knew, and their inability to follow easily what a controller trainee was doing reduced the value of their own experience.

Good: The number of radar exercises per day was reduced from 6 to 5. Lori, the good conscience of the facility, prevailed upon Dan to make the change, saying that both students and instructors were pretty much burned out for the last exercise when we were running six. So now we had a little breathing room, and it made a huge difference.

Otherwise: Dan was pulled out of the facility for a year's detail at headquarters to assist in evaluating and planning field training objectives. I hated to see him go, and my concerns were not baseless. Things became slack. Trainees had to be "rounded up" at the end of break periods. We were also getting more contract instructors, which was good news on the one hand, but at least for me produced an unexpected fallout. They were all recently retired controllers from MIA, meaning that they brought recency of experience to the job, but they also tended to be more hard line in their approach to training. I believed that instilling confidence in these "newbies" was a big part of making them successful in the program, and never came down hard on anyone unless it was obvious that they were not making an effort. There were complaints from some trainees, which tended to give all of us a black eye. The days when controller training had been "my show" were long past.

My Last Class

I began what would be my last tower class around Christmas time in 2011, continuing into the new year. My co-instructor was Ellen, a young woman who had come to us from Homestead tower where she had been a controller employed by the Department of Defense. She had been at the facility for about 14 years and was now detailed to the training department. I had trained her in 2002, and regularly chided her for having been a worrywart in class. She had often asked if some point of information would be on the test. Of course I never answered that question directly, but in one instance asked her, "True or False? You should never study anything that is not on the test." She took this ragging in good humor, and I felt that our different styles complemented each other effectively

One of our students, a young man who had come from San Juan, named Fernando, struggled some during the ground control phase. He eventually caught on, but we were concerned about how he would do on local control. I thought a bit of lightening up might be helpful, and composed a couple of verses based on the lyrics and melody of the rock group ABBA's hit song "Fernando." It went like this:

Have you studied hard Fernando,
Are Ellen's words and Rusty's ringing in your ears?
Are you ready for your training?
Will you get certified within a couple years?
Don't ever be distracted put aside all doubts and fears.
There'll be LAHSO ties for you to fix
Use all your tricks, Fernando,
Don't confuse line up and wait
Don't hesitate, Fernando.
Just move your traffic the right way,
Survive another day,
And pretty soon you'll be
A CPC, Fernando.

Second verse:
Now I'm old and grey Fernando,
Since many years I haven't held a headset in my hand.
Have the things I've told you helped you,
And do you think that now you better understand
The magic words it takes to tell an airplane cleared to land?
There is traffic in the skies at night
Their lights are bright, Fernando.
You will get them on the ground,
Or send them around, Fernando.
Your mic switch is the key
To safety and efficiency,
And soon they'll safely be
Parked at Concourse D, Fernando.

Upon hearing a rendition of this composition, Fernando was all smiles, saying he was going to adopt the words as his theme song for completing training on local control.

Saying Goodbye

In April I was in the midst of another radar class when I began making plans for another extended absence during May, June, and July. These had been granted routinely in all the previous years of my contract gig, and I had no reason to anticipate anything different this time around.

But the Raytheon lead at the facility told me that there was budgetary pressure to reduce the number of contract instructors and my request would have to be denied.

And so it was time for a major decision. I had been a contract instructor for six and a half years, having had at least a hand in the training of 80 controllers or more. I was 71 years old, long in the tooth by any standards for the position I held. The age gap between me and the next oldest man in the facility was now closer to 20 years than 10. One of the trainees in my radar class was two years older than my grandson. Was this the time to pull the plug? I talked it over with Jorge Fernandez, who had additional information about Raytheon and the future outlook for contract instructing. He basically told me that if I decided to resign my position I was probably doing it "at just the right time." I took a few days to mull it all over, finally reaching the decision that I would step down.

Which didn't mean it was an easy decision. I still loved the job. I was concerned about "abandoning" the trainees I was currently with. And I couldn't imagine not being connected in some way to the ever-fascinating world of ATC. Nevertheless, I set a date in the middle of May as my last day. During the last week I made an effort to say good-bye individually to as many of former students as possible, also composing a farewell message to be posted in the read file, after I left, for the ones I had missed. I wrote:

"Friday, May 11 [2012] marked my final day as an ATC instructor at MIA tower. This chapter was the third in a series of assignments to the facility, which together totaled some 35 years. And in many ways it has been the most satisfying, as it allowed me to concentrate on the area that has always been near and dear to me, training new people.

Counting noses on the picture board, there are at least 80 of you who have been with me for some phase of your training. Many of you are now fully certified; others are well on their way, and some are just getting started. All of you should know that I consider it a privilege to have been your instructor. If you ever serve in a similar role, you will come to understand the great satisfaction of seeing someone catch on to and ultimately master the elements of this challenging job.

I regret that I did not have the opportunity to say good-bye to each of you individually, but I wish you all the best in a long and fulfilling career. I also expect an invitation to your check out party if you are yet fully certified!

Keep 'em separated,
Rusty"

The last day was devoted to hum drum administrative stuff—cleaning out my desk and cubicle, turning in my headset, signing some final papers for Raytheon. My last act I performed with a distinct lump in my throat. I had detached the key ring affixed to my facility key and turned the key in. On the spur of the moment I asked Ellen, whose cubicle was adjacent to mine if she would do something of symbolic importance to me. Would she for the next week carry my key chain into and out of the facility, finally hanging it in my cubicle at least until the next occupant took it over? She agreed with, I thought, a damp eye. At that we shook hands for the last time and I walked out the door.

Well, what now, I thought? Maybe I'll write a book about all this.

A Warm Celebration

In May 2016 the facility celebrated 75 years of continuous operation. I had missed the 25th anniversary by two years when I was hired in 1968. The 50th occurred in 1991 while I was at Tamiami, 10 years after the strike of 1981. Many of the MIA "alumni" attended, fired strikers and retirees alike, giving the event the distinct flavor of a reunion. We all signed a sheet that was later recreated on a brass plaque and displayed in the facility trophy case.

By 2016 the number of old hands attending was markedly reduced. But it was gratifying to see that the new generation, including many of my former trainees, had spearheaded the effort of making the event happen. County officials reviewed some interesting history, including the fact that there had been five different towers over the course of the 75 years. The first had been a temporary installation located on the north ramp adjacent to Northwest 36th Street. When the new terminal opened in 1957 that tower was physically moved and placed atop the new building. It was the only time in history that a tower (carried on a flatbed truck) had been issued a clearance to cross an active runway. That was the tower I had trained in and worked in for 17 of my first 18 years at MIA. Then in 1985 the facility moved to a new TRACON and tower on the west side of the field. Finally in 2003 the "new" new tower had been commissioned and remains in operation today.

In the evening there was a dinner and a fun round of shared "war stories" and reminiscences. The master of ceremony addressed the assemblage, numbering 150 people or so, asking a series of questions and asking for hand raising in response. It went like this:

- How many here worked at Miami Tower during the 2000s? About a third of the hands were raised.
- How many worked at MIA during the 1990s? About 20 hands went up.
- How many worked at MIA during the 1980s? 8 or 10 hands were raised.
- How about the 1970s? There was a show of 4 or five hands.
- How about the 1960s? No response—until I raised my hand, as the only "alum" with a history that reached back that far.

Final Reflections

There comes a time (or perhaps a number of times) in every life when a particular chapter comes to a definitive end. It is natural at such times to reflect on the road travelled and perhaps on the one, or several, not taken. What might I have been instead of an air traffic controller? I had learned to be verbally agile, able to come up quickly with the "right words" to address a real-time situation. Could I have been a lawyer, using that same skill in the courtroom? How about an ad man, formulating exactly the key words to "sell" a product?

During my pre-hire interview at Miami Center I had been questioned as to why, given my educational background, I would choose the air traffic control profession. Even my mother seemed to believe that somehow I could have had a "better" career. By contrast, most people seemed impressed by my chosen field, usually offering comments along the lines of, "Wow, that's a high pressure job with a lot of responsibility." My dad was very proud to introduce me to someone new as "my son, he's an air traffic controller at Miami International."

When I ask myself about possible other choices I might have made, I have no regrets, and feel a large measure of satisfaction. I ended up with a job that was mostly about specific achievements and immediately visible results. Even my time on staff and at headquarters connected to the real world of airplanes and pilots. I saw probably several hundred individuals in whose training I had had a hand progress to full certification and successful careers. I saw the technical side of the business progress by light years, while the human skills needed to make the system work remained pretty constant.

Most of all, I lived through a career experience shared by only a small number of others. I was one of an elite fraternity, not one of the millions of people in "regular" jobs. At one of our class reunions each member was asked to write a short biography covering his life since graduation. I concluded mine with these words: "At times I have been asked whether I ever wished I had chosen a different career path. I usually reply by saying that there were definitely times when I did. Those days with a sky full of airplanes and thunderstorms all over the place come to mind. But overall I would not trade my experience in air traffic control for anything else I can imagine."

A Few Postscripts

A. What Happened to AERA?

All of us on the ATACT team wondered if our ten years of work on AERA had resulted in anything tangible for the ATC system. As it turned out, some of the basic elements survived in a new capability dubbed URET, or User Request Evaluation Tool. URET would not provide solutions to detected conflicts between aircraft but would be a passive capability. A controller could enter a trial plan, that is, a proposed change to an aircraft trajectory, and the system would identify any conflicts within a parameter future time. URET also monitored trajectory conformance, which depended on an aircraft adhering within certain limits to its proposed flight plan. If the flight exceeded those limits the automation would calculate a new trajectory, then display a notification of the new trajectory and check it for conflicts.

The work on AERA produced personal benefits for two team members. Dusty and I each married one of the smart and beautiful MITRE engineers.

B. What happened to ATSAT?

What happened to ATSAT, the Air Traffic Selection and Training test into which huge amounts of money, research, and development had been poured, was yet another example of a soundly based worthwhile initiative being discarded in response to wrong-headed bureaucratic priorities. Certain groups complained that ATSAT was discriminatory in that the pool of candidates that successfully passed the test was insufficiently diverse. Without knowing why at the time, Lanny Williams had been summoned to FAA headquarters to administer the test to no less an official than the agency administrator, who apparently did not exactly ace the exam.

In 2014 ATSAT was replaced by a new test referred to as BA, or Biographical Assessment. There was nothing in the BA reasonably related to controller skills. Instead it asked a series of questions about an individual's history and life experience, then weighted the answers to arrive at a final score. This change might have taken place "under the radar" except for the fact that some 2,500 prior candidates (that "insufficiently diverse" group), all of whom had passed CTI training and ATSAT, were now deemed ineligible for selection to a controller position pending successful completion of the BA. At least one individual did not pass the BA and asked to be told the basis for his failure, given that he had qualified under the old criteria.

This triggered a back and forth period of negotiations and ultimately a lawsuit under FOIA, the Freedom of Information Act, to force the agency to reveal exactly what standards a candidate had to meet. Determined digging by investigative reporters unearthed the information and more. There was an email from an FAA official acknowledging that BA had no relevant bearing on controller aptitude. It was discovered that test answers had been leaked and given to certain applicants ahead of time. When these revelations became public, it was something of a bombshell. Questions on the BA included the following, and were assigned point values:

In what subject did you do the most poorly in high school? The answer "science" earned a score of 10.

Have you been unemployed for the last 3 years? A "yes" answer earned the applicant 10 points.

Do you have pilot experience? A "yes" rated 2 points.

Do you have air traffic control experience? A "yes" was worth 5 points.

By what rationale was poor performance in science worth five times more than pilot experience? And how was being unemployed for three years an indicator of controller aptitude twice as strong as direct air traffic experience? These questions were never satisfactorily answered. The attorney representing the individual who brought the FOIA lawsuit termed the BA "social engineering at its finest."

In the wake of these revelations, the FAA added a second examination to the application process that purportedly touched on some of the same indicators contained in ATSAT.

C. What Happened to Fernando?

Fernando checked out in the tower and eventually through the A-side radar positions. He had "moved his traffic the right way" and become a CPC.

Glossary

ARTS (Automated Radar Tracking System): Software system introduced in 1972 allowing radar targets to be tagged with individual aircraft identifications and providing continuous ground speed and altitude information

ATIS (Automatic Terminal Information Service): A continuous recording of routine information relating to the approach types and runways in use, navigation aid outages, weather advisories in effect, taxiway closures, notices to airmen and other relevant data. Pilots must report receipt of the current ATIS or be advised of all the items therein contained.

Class B Airspace: An area of positive control established at high density terminals). Certain pilot qualifications and aircraft equipment are mandatory, and specific ATC authorization is required for an aircraft to operate within the area (originally designated as TCA, or terminal control area).

Class C Airspace: An area established at medium density airports within which service to VFR aircraft is provided. Two way radio communications required before an aircraft may enter the area (originally designated as Stage 3, later as TRSA or terminal radar service area).

DF (direction finder) Steer: A service normally provided by a Flight Service Station to assist pilot navigation. When a pilot transmits on the appropriate frequency the specialist receives an indication of the bearing to the aircraft. If the pilot is instructed to fly the reciprocal of that bearing, the aircraft will home in on the DF receiver (normally co-located with the Flight Service Station).

EPR (engine pressure ratio): A comparison of the pressure of air entering a jet engine with the pressure of the exhaust gas. It is an indicator of power output and cannot be allowed to be too high or too low.

Federal Air Regulations (FAR's): The body of rules relating to pilot certification, maintenance standards, airport equipment and the like.

ICAO (International Civil Aviation Organization): Rule making body whose standards are used by most countries in governing the aviation and air traffic control industries. Most of its provisions are not applicable in the U.S. which has established its own set of Federal Air Regulations.

IDENT: An ATC instruction to the pilot of a transponder equipped aircraft. The pilot response produces a "bloom" of the radar target or a flashing "ID" in the data block of an aircraft tracked by automation.

Instrument Flight Rules (IFR): Defined in Part 91 of Federal Air Regulations. Pilots must meet minimum experience requirements and hold an instrument rating. Must file an IFR flight plan and comply with all air traffic control instructions relating to altitude, speed, and navigation. May operate in clouds with reference to instruments only.

ILS (Instrument Landing System): Ground based navigational equipment consisting of a localizer providing both azimuth (left/right) information and a glide slope providing vertical guidance to an aircraft on the approach to a runway. Also refers to the cockpit equipment used to select and display the information from the ground.

LAHSO: Acronym for land and hold short, used when two aircraft land simultaneously on intersecting runways and one is instructed to hold short of the intersection.

Line Up and Wait: ICAO phraseology replacing "taxi into position and hold", used to put an aircraft in takeoff position on a runway to await takeoff clearance.

STARS (Standard Terminal Automation Replacement System): Automation replacing ARTS in the early 2000's. STARS retained all capabilities of ARTS and added many more.

Substantial Damage: Damage or failure which adversely affects the structural strength, performance, or flight characteristics of the aircraft and which would normally require major repair or replacement of the affected component.

Visual Flight Rules (VFR): Defined in Part 91 of Federal Air Regulations. Minimum weather requirements are 3 miles visibility and ceiling 1000 feet above ground level. Pilots are responsible for seeing and avoiding other traffic and remaining a safe distance from obstacles and persons or structures on the ground. No flight plan is required.

Made in the USA
Columbia, SC
30 September 2020